Part of JIST's Top Careers™ Series

Top 100 Computer and Technical CAREERS™

Your Complete Guidebook to Major Jobs in Many Fields at All Training Levels

FOURTH EDITION

Michael Farr

Top 100 Computer and Technical Careers, Fourth Edition

Your Complete Guidebook to Major Jobs in Many Fields at All Training Levels

Published by JIST Works, an imprint of JIST Publishing
7321 Shadeland Station, Suite 200
Indianapolis, IN 46256-3923
Phone: 800-648-JIST Fax: 877-454-7839
E-mail: info@jist.com Web site: www.jist.com

Some books by Michael Farr:
Best Jobs for the 21st Century
Overnight Career Choice
Same-Day Resume
Next-Day Job Interview
The Quick Resume & Cover Letter Book
The Very Quick Job Search

JIST's Top Careers™ Series:
Top 300 Careers
Top 100 Health-Care Careers
100 Fastest-Growing Jobs
Top 100 Careers Without a Four-Year Degree
Top 100 Careers for College Graduates
Top 100 Computer and Technical Careers

Visit www.jist.com for free job search information, table of contents, sample pages, and ordering information on our many products.

Quantity discounts are available for JIST products. Have future editions of JIST books automatically delivered to you on publication through our convenient standing order program. Please call 800-648-JIST or visit www.jist.com for a free catalog and more information.

Acquisitions Editor: Susan Pines
Development Editor: Stephanie Koutek
Database Work: Laurence Shatkin
Cover Layout: Alan Evans
Interior Design and Layout: Marie Kristine Parial-Leonardo
Proofreaders: Paula Lowell, Jeanne Clark

Printed in the United States of America

10 09 08 9 8 7 6 5 4 3 2 1

Library of Congress Cataloging-in-Publication data is on file with the Library of Congress.

ISBN: 978-1-59357-602-8

Relax. You Don't Have to Read This Whole Book!

You don't need to read this entire book. I've organized it into easy-to-use sections so you can get just the information you want. You will find everything you need to

- ★ Learn about the 100 top computer and technical careers, including their daily tasks, pay, outlook, and required education and skills.
- ★ Match your personal skills to the careers.
- ★ Take seven steps to land a good job in less time.

To get started, simply scan the table of contents to learn more about these sections and to see a list of the jobs described in this book. Really, this book is easy to use, and I hope it helps you.

Who Should Use This Book?

This is more than a book of job descriptions. I've spent quite a bit of time thinking about how to make its contents useful for a variety of situations, including

- ★ **Exploring career options.** The job descriptions in Part II give a wealth of information on many of the most desirable jobs in the labor market. The assessment in Part I can help you focus your career options.
- ★ **Considering more education or training.** The information helps you avoid costly mistakes in choosing a career or deciding on additional training or education—and it increases your chances of planning a bright future.
- ★ **Job seeking.** This book helps you identify new job targets, prepare for interviews, and write targeted resumes. The advice in Part III has been proven to cut job search time in half.
- ★ **Career planning.** The job descriptions help you explore your options, and Parts III and IV provide career planning advice and other useful information.

Source of Information

The job descriptions come from the good people at the U.S. Department of Labor, as published in the most recent edition of the *Occupational Outlook Handbook.* The *OOH* is the best source of career information available, and the descriptions include the most current, accurate data on jobs. Thank you to all the people at the Department of Labor who gather, compile, analyze, and make sense of this information. It's good stuff, and I hope you can make good use of it.

Mike Farr

Mike Farr

Contents

Summary of Major Sections

Introduction. Provides an explanation of the job descriptions, how best to use the book, and other details. *Begins on page 1.*

Part I: Using the Job-Match Grid to Choose a Career. Match your skills and preferences to the jobs in this book. *Begins on page 13.*

Part II: Descriptions of the Top 100 Computer and Technical Careers. Presents thorough descriptions of the top 100 computer and technical jobs. Education and training requirements for these jobs vary from on-the-job training to a four-year college degree or more. Each description gives information on the nature of the work, work environment, employment, training, other qualifications, advancement, job outlook, earnings, related occupations, and sources of additional information. The jobs are presented in alphabetical order. The page numbers where specific descriptions begin are listed in the detailed contents. *Begins on page 31.*

Part III: Quick Job Search—Seven Steps to Getting a Good Job in Less Time. This relatively brief but important section offers results-oriented career planning and job search techniques. It includes tips on identifying your key skills, defining your ideal job, using effective job search methods, writing resumes, organizing your time, improving your interviewing skills, and following up on leads. The last part of this section features professionally written and designed resumes for some of the top computer and technical jobs. *Begins on page 301.*

Part IV: Important Trends in Jobs and Industries. This section includes three well-written articles on labor market trends. The articles are worth your time. Titles of the articles are "Tomorrow's Jobs," "Employment Trends in Major Industries," and "STEM Occupations: High-Tech Jobs for a High-Tech Economy." *Begins on page 361.*

Index: Lists all jobs mentioned in this book in alphabetical order. *Begins on page 393.*

Detailed Contents

Introduction

This book is about improving your life, not just about selecting a job. The career you choose will have an enormous impact on how you live your life.

A huge amount of information is available on occupations, but most people don't know where to find accurate, reliable facts to help them make good career decisions—or they don't take the time to look. Important choices such as what to do with your career and whether to get additional training or education deserve your time.

If you are considering more training or education—whether additional course work, a college degree, or an advanced degree—this book will help with solid information. Training or education beyond high school is now typically required to get better jobs, but many good jobs can be learned through on-the-job experience, informal training, and technical training or education lasting from several months to two years. The education and training needed for the jobs described in *Top 100 Computer and Technical Careers* vary enormously. This book provides descriptions for major jobs requiring computer and technical skills and gives you the facts you need for exploring your options.

A certain type of work or workplace may interest you as much as a certain type of job. If your interests and values lead you to work in healthcare, for example, you can do this in a variety of work environments, in a variety of industries, and in a variety of jobs. For this reason, I suggest you begin exploring alternatives by following your interests and finding a career path that allows you to use your talents doing something you enjoy.

Also, remember that money is not everything. The time you spend in career planning can pay off in higher earnings, but being satisfied with your work—and your life—is often more important than how much you earn. This book can help you find the work that suits you best.

Keep in Mind That Your Situation Is Not "Average"

Projected employment growth and earnings trends are quite positive for many occupations and industries. Keep in mind, however, that the averages in this book will not be true for many individuals. Within any field, many people earn more and many earn less than the average.

My point is that your situation is probably not average. Some people do better than others, and some are willing to accept less pay for a more desirable work environment. Earnings vary enormously in different parts of the country, in different occupations, and in different industries. But this book's solid information is a great place to start. Good information will give you a strong foundation for good decisions.

Four Important Labor Market Trends That Will Affect Your Career

Our economy has changed in dramatic ways over the past 10 years, with profound effects on how we work and live. Part IV of this book provides more information on labor market trends, but in case you don't read it, here are four trends that you simply *must* consider.

1. Education Pays

I'm sure you won't be surprised to learn that people with higher levels of education and training have higher average earnings. The data that follows comes from the U.S. Department of Labor. I've selected data to show you the median earnings for people with various levels of education. (The median is the point where half earn more and half earn less.) Based on this information, I computed the earnings advantage of people at various education levels over those who did not graduate from high school. I've also included information showing the average percentage of people at that educational level who are unemployed.

Earnings for Year-Round, Full-Time Workers Age 25 and Over, by Educational Attainment

Level of Education	Median Annual Earnings	Premium Over High School Dropouts	Unemployment Rate
Professional degree	$76,648	$54,860	1.1%
Doctoral degree	$74,932	$53,144	1.4%
Master's degree	$59,280	$37,492	1.7%
Bachelor's degree	$50,024	$28,236	2.3%
Associate degree	$37,492	$15,704	3.0%
Some college, no degree	$35,048	$13,260	3.9%
High school graduate	$30,940	$9,152	4.3%
High school dropout	$21,788	—	6.8%

Source: Bureau of Labor Statistics

As you can see in the table, the more education and training you have, the more you are likely to earn—and the less likely you are to be unemployed. These two factors can make an enormous difference in long-term earnings. For example, the earnings gap between a four-year college graduate and someone with a high school education is now $19,000 a year. That's enough to buy a nice car, make a down payment on a house, or even take a month's vacation for two to Europe. As you see, over a lifetime, these additional earnings can make an enormous difference in the college graduate's lifestyle.

And there's more. Jobs that require education and training beyond high school are projected to grow significantly faster than jobs that do not. Research shows that people with higher educational levels are less likely to be unemployed and that they remain unemployed for shorter periods of time. Overall, the data on earnings and other criteria indicate that people with more education and training do better than those with less. There are exceptions, of course, but for most people, more education and training results in higher earnings and lower rates of unemployment.

Many jobs can be obtained without a college degree, but most better-paying jobs now require either training beyond high school or substantial work experience.

2. Knowledge of Computer and Other Technologies Is Increasingly Important

Jobs requiring computer and technical skills are projected to be among the fastest-growing jobs in America. As you look over the list of jobs in the table of contents for *Top 100 Computer and Technical Careers,* you will notice the enormous variety of technical jobs. The education and training requirements for these jobs range from on-the-job experience to a four-year college degree and more. But even jobs that do not appear to be technical often call for computer literacy or technical skills. Managers, for example, are often expected to understand and use spreadsheet, word-processing, and database software.

In all fields, people without job-related technical and computer skills will have a more difficult time finding good opportunities than people who have these skills. Employers tend to hire people with the skills they need, and people without these abilities won't get the best jobs. So consider upgrading your job-related computer and technology skills if you need to—and plan to stay up to date on your current and future jobs.

3. Ongoing Education and Training Are Essential

School and work once were separate activities, and most people did not go back to school after they began working. But with rapid changes in technology, most people are now required to learn throughout their work lives. Jobs are constantly upgraded, and today's jobs often cannot be handled by people who have only the knowledge and skills that were adequate for workers a few years ago. To remain competitive, people without technical or computer skills must get them. Those who do not will face increasingly limited job options.

What this means is that you should upgrade your job skills throughout your working life. This may include taking formal courses, reading work-related Web sites and magazines, signing up for on-the-job training, or participating in other forms of education. Upgrading your work-related skills on an ongoing basis is no longer optional for most jobs, and you ignore doing so at your peril.

4. Good Career Planning Has Increased in Importance

Most people spend more time watching TV in a week than they spend on career planning during an entire year. Yet most people will change their jobs many times and make major career changes five to seven times.

While you probably picked up this book for its information on jobs, it also provides a great deal of information on career planning. For example, Part III gives good career and job search advice, and Part IV has useful information on labor market trends. I urge you to read these and related materials because career-planning and job-seeking skills are the keys to survival in this new economy.

Tips on Using This Book

This book is based on information from a variety of government sources and includes the most up-to-date and accurate data available. The entries are well written and pack a lot of information into short descriptions. *Top 100 Computer and Technical Careers* can be used in many ways, and I've provided tips for these four major uses:

- ★ For people exploring career, education, or training alternatives
- ★ For job seekers
- ★ For employers and business people
- ★ For counselors, instructors, and other career specialists

Tips for People Exploring Career, Education, or Training Alternatives

Top 100 Computer and Technical Careers is an excellent resource for anyone exploring career, education, or training alternatives. Many people do not have a good idea of what they want to do in their careers. They may be considering additional training or education but may not know what sort they should get. If you are one of these people, *Top 100 Computer and Technical Careers* can help in several ways. Here are a few pointers.

Review the list of jobs. Trust yourself. Research studies indicate that most people have a good sense of their interests. Your interests can be used to guide you to career options you should consider in more detail.

Begin by looking over the occupations listed in the table of contents. Look at all the jobs, because you may identify previously overlooked possibilities. If other people will be using this book, please don't mark in it. Instead, on a separate sheet of paper, list the jobs that interest you. Or make a photocopy of the table of contents and mark the jobs that interest you.

Next, carefully read the descriptions of the jobs that most interest you. A quick review will often eliminate one or more of these jobs based on pay, working conditions, education required, or other considerations. After you have identified the three or four jobs that seem most interesting, research each one more thoroughly before making any important decisions.

Study the jobs and their training and education requirements. Too many people decide to obtain additional training or education without knowing much about the jobs the training will lead to. Reviewing the descriptions in this book is one way to learn more about an occupation before you enroll in an education or training program. If you are currently a student, the job descriptions in this book can also help you decide on a major course of study or learn more about the jobs for which your studies are preparing you.

Do not be too quick to eliminate a job that interests you. If a job requires more education or training than you currently have, you can obtain this training in many ways.

Don't abandon your past experience and education too quickly. If you have significant work experience, training, or education, these should not be abandoned too quickly. Many skills you have learned and used in previous jobs or other settings can apply to related jobs. Many times, after people carefully consider what they want to do, they change careers and find that the skills they have can still be used.

Top 100 Computer and Technical Careers can help you explore career options in several ways. First, carefully review descriptions for jobs you have held in the past. On a separate sheet of paper, list the skills needed in those jobs. Then do the same for jobs that interest you now. By comparing the lists, you will be able to identify skills you used in previous jobs that you could also use in jobs that interest you for the future. These "transferable" skills form the basis for moving to a new career.

You can also identify skills you have developed or used in nonwork activities, such as hobbies, family responsibilities, volunteer work, school, military, and extracurricular interests. The descriptions can be used even if you want to stay with the same employer. For example, you may identify jobs within your organization that offer more rewarding work, higher pay, or other advantages over your present job. Read the descriptions related to these jobs, as you may be able to transfer into another job rather than leave the organization.

Tips for Job Seekers

You can use the descriptions in this book to give you an edge in finding job openings and in getting job offers—even when you are competing with people who have better credentials. Here are some ways *Top 100 Computer and Technical Careers* can help you in the job search.

Identify related job targets. You may be limiting your job search to a small number of jobs for which you feel qualified, but by doing so you eliminate many jobs you could do and enjoy. Your search for a new job should be broadened to include more possibilities.

Go through the entire list of jobs in the table of contents and check any that require skills similar to those you have. Look at all the jobs, as doing so sometimes helps you identify targets you would otherwise overlook.

Many people are not aware of the many specialized jobs related to their training or experience. The descriptions in *Top 100 Computer and Technical Careers* are for major job titles, but a variety of more-specialized jobs may require similar skills. The "Other Major Career Information Sources" section later in this introduction lists sources you can use to find out about more-specialized jobs.

The descriptions can also point out jobs that interest you but have higher responsibility or compensation levels. Although you may not consider yourself qualified for such jobs now, you should think about seeking jobs that are above your previous levels but within your ability to handle.

Prepare for interviews. This book's job descriptions are an essential source of information to help you prepare for interviews. If you carefully review the description of a job before an interview, you will be much better prepared to emphasize your key skills. You should also review descriptions for past jobs and identify skills needed in the new job.

Negotiate pay. The job descriptions in this book will help you know what pay range to expect. Note that local pay and other details can differ substantially from the national averages in the descriptions.

Tips for Employers and Business People

Employers, human resource professionals, and other business users can use this book's information to write job descriptions, study pay ranges, and set criteria for new employees. The information can also help you conduct more-effective interviews by providing a list of key skills needed by new hires.

Tips for Counselors, Instructors, and Other Career Specialists

Counselors, instructors, and other career specialists will find this book helpful for their clients or students exploring career options or job targets. My best suggestion to professionals is to get this book off the shelf and into the hands of the people who need it. Leave it on a table or desk and show people how the information can help them. Wear this book out—its real value is as a tool used often and well.

Additional Information About the Projections

For more information about employment change, job openings, earnings, unemployment rates, and training requirements by occupation, consult *Occupational Projections and Training Data,* published by the Bureau of Labor Statistics. For occupational information from an industry perspective, including some occupations and career paths that *Top 100 Computer and Technical Careers* does not cover, consult another BLS publication, *Career Guide to Industries.* This book is also available from JIST with enhanced content under the title *40 Best Fields for Your Career.*

Information on the Major Parts of This Book

This book was designed to be easy to use. The table of contents provides brief comments on each part, and that may be all you need. If not, here are some additional details you may find useful in getting the most out of this book.

Part I: Using the Job-Match Grid to Choose a Career

Part I features an assessment with checklists and questions to match your skills and preferences to the jobs in this book. The seven skills covered in the assessment are artistic, communication, interpersonal, managerial, mathematics, mechanical, and science. The five job characteristics covered in the assessment are economically sensitive, geographically concentrated, hazardous conditions, outdoor work, and physically demanding.

Part II: Descriptions of the Top 100 Computer and Technical Careers

Part II is the main part of this book and is probably the reason you picked it up. It contains brief, well-written descriptions for 100 major jobs that require computer and other technical skills. The content for these job descriptions comes from the U.S. Department of Labor and is considered by many people to be the most accurate and up-to-date data available. The jobs are presented in alphabetical order. The table of contents provides a page number that shows where each description begins.

Together, the jobs in Part II provide enormous variety at all levels of earnings, training, and education. One way to explore career options is to go through the table of contents and identify those jobs that seem interesting. If you are interested in medical jobs, for example, you can quickly spot those you want to learn more about. You may also see other jobs that look interesting, and you should consider those as well. Another way to pinpoint interesting jobs is to do the assessment in Part I.

Next, read the descriptions for the jobs that interest you and, based on what you learn, identify those that *most* interest you. These are the jobs you should consider.

(STEM) As you review the job descriptions, you'll notice a graphic bearing the word STEM. This graphic flags occupations that focus on science, technology, engineering, and mathematics. STEM careers have become increasingly central to economic competitiveness and growth. The U.S. Department of Education and the U.S. Department of Labor encourage people to take advantage of opportunities in STEM careers. For more information, read the article in Part IV called "STEM Occupations: High-Tech Jobs for a High-Tech Economy."

How the 100 Jobs Were Selected

The jobs included in this book are selected from the 270 jobs covered in detail by the *Occupational Outlook Handbook,* published by the U.S. Department of Labor. They are jobs that require considerable use of computers, science, or technology. In recent years, technology has not only created many new jobs; it is playing an increasing role in many formerly low-tech jobs. For example, urban and regional planners starting out nowadays are expected to be proficient in the use of geographic information system (GIS) technology. Drafters sometimes spend the whole day manipulating data at a computer terminal rather than holding a pencil at an old-fashioned drafting table.

The size of the workforce for these jobs varies from a high of 2.5 million (registered nurses) to a low of 3,000 (mathematicians). Half of the jobs have a workforce over 100,000 and therefore account for a lot of job openings. Even if overall employment in such a job is shrinking, the large workforce guarantees many job opportunities because of retirements and turnover, so such jobs are worth your consideration for that reason alone. Jobs in this book that have a small workforce generally have high entry requirements (for example, mathematicians need at least a master's degree), so there is usually less competition for the limited number of openings.

Details on Each Section of the Job Descriptions

Each occupational description in this book follows a standard format, making it easier for you to compare jobs. The following overview describes the kinds of information found in each part of a description and offers tips on how to interpret the information.

Job Title

This is the title used for the job in the *Occupational Outlook Handbook.* For occupations that focus on science, technology, engineering, and math, you'll see a "STEM" graphic. These jobs offer particularly good opportunities in today's economy.

*O*NET Codes*

The numbers that appear just below the title of every job description are from the Occupational Information Network (O*NET), a major occupational information system created by the U.S. Department of Labor and used by state employment service offices to classify applicants and job openings and by some career information centers and libraries to file occupational information.

Through the O*NET at www.online.onetcenter.org, you can search for occupations that match your skills, or you may search by keyword or O*NET code. For each occupation, O*NET reports information about tasks performed, knowledge, skills, abilities, and work activities. It also lists interests; work styles, such as independence; and work values, such as achievement, that are well suited to the occupation. The O*NET is also available as a book titled the *O*NET Dictionary of Occupational Titles* (JIST).

Significant Points

The bullet points in this part of a description highlight key characteristics for each job, such as recent trends or education and training requirements.

Nature of the Work

What workers do on the job, what tools and equipment they use, and how closely they are supervised is discussed in this section. Some descriptions mention alterative job titles or occupational specialties.

Work environment. This subsection discuses the workplace, physical activities, and typical hours of workers in the occupation. It describes opportunities for part-time work, the extent of travel required, special equipment that is used, and the risk of injury that workers may face.

Information on various worker characteristics, such as the average number of hours worked per week, is obtained from the Current Population Survey (CPS), a survey of households conducted by the U.S. Census Bureau for the Bureau of Labor Statistics (BLS). Other sources include articles as well as the Web sites of professional associations, unions, and trade groups. Information found on the Internet or in periodicals is verified through interviews with workers; professional associations; unions; and others with occupational knowledge, such as university professors and career counselors.

Training, Other Qualifications, and Advancement

After gathering your initial impressions of what a job is all about, it is important to understand how to prepare for it. The Training, Other Qualifications, and Advancement section explains the steps necessary to enter and advance in an occupation.

Education and training. This subsection describes the most significant sources of education and training, the type of education or training preferred by employers, and the typical length of training.

Licensure. The kinds of mandatory licenses or certifications associated with an occupation are described in this subsection. To be certified or licensed, a worker usually is required to complete one or more training courses and pass one or more examinations. Most occupations do not have mandatory licensure or certification requirements. Some occupations have professional credentials granted by different organizations, in which case the most widely recognized organizations are listed.

Other qualifications. Additional qualifications that are not included in the previous subsections, such as the desirable skills, aptitudes, and personal characteristics that employers look for, are discussed in this section.

Advancement. This subsection details advancement opportunities after gaining experience in an occupation. Advancement can come in several forms, including advancement within the occupation, such as promotion to a management position; advancement into other occupations; and advancement to self-employment. Certain types of certification can serve as a form of advancement. Voluntary certification often demonstrates a level of competency to employers and can result in more responsibility, higher pay, or a new job.

Information in the Training, Other Qualifications, and Advancement section comes from interviews with workers; Web sites; training materials; and interviews with the organizations that grant degrees, certifications, or licenses or are otherwise associated with the occupation.

Employment

This section reports the number of jobs the occupation recently provided, the key industries where these jobs are found, and the number or proportion of self-employed workers in the occupation, if significant. Information in this section comes from various surveys by the BLS.

Job Outlook

In planning for the future, you need to consider potential job opportunities. This section describes the factors that will result in employment growth or decline.

Employment change. This subsection reflects the occupational projections in the National Employment Matrix. Each occupation is assigned a descriptive phrase based on its projected percent change in employment over the 2006–2016 period. This phrase describes the occupation's projected employment change relative to the projected average employment change for all occupations combined.

Many factors are examined in projecting the employment change for each occupation. One such factor is changes in technology. New technology can either create new job opportunities or eliminate jobs by making workers obsolete. Another factor that influences employment trends is demographic change. By affecting the services demanded, demographic change can influence occupational growth or decline.

Another factor affecting job growth or decline is changes in business practices, such as restructuring businesses or outsourcing (contracting out) work. Corporate restructuring has made many organizations "flatter," resulting in fewer middle management positions. Also, in the past few years, jobs in some occupations have been "off-shored"—moved to low-wage foreign countries. The substitution of one product or service for another can also affect employment projections. Competition from foreign trade usually has a negative effect on employment. Often, foreign manufacturers can produce goods more cheaply than they can be produced in the United States, and the cost savings can be passed on in the form of lower prices with which U.S. manufacturers cannot compete. Another factor is job growth or decline in key industries. If an occupation is concentrated in an industry that is growing rapidly, it is likely that that occupation will grow rapidly as well.

Job prospects. In some cases, this book mentions that an occupation is likely to provide numerous or relatively few job openings. This information reflects the projected change in employment, as well as replacement needs. Large occupations in which workers frequently enter and leave generally provide the most job openings—reflecting the need to replace workers who transfer to other occupations or who stop working.

Key Phrases Used in the Job Descriptions

This table explains how to interpret the key phrases that describe projected changes in employment. It also explains the terms for the relationship between the number of job openings and the number of job seekers.

Changing Employment Between 2006 and 2016

If the statement reads	Employment is projected to
Grow much faster than average	Increase 21 percent or more
Grow faster than average	Increase 14 to 20 percent
Grow about as fast as average	Increase 7 to 13 percent
Grow more slowly than average	Increase 3 to 6 percent
Little or no change	Decrease 2 percent to increase 2 percent
Decline slowly or moderately	Decrease 3 to 9 percent
Decline rapidly	Decrease 10 percent or more

Opportunities and Competition for Jobs

If the statement reads	Job openings compared to job seekers may be
Very good to excellent opportunities	More numerous
Good or favorable opportunities	In rough balance
May face or can expect keen competition	Fewer

Projections Data

The employment projections table lists employment statistics from the National Employment Matrix. It includes 2006 employment, projected 2016 employment, and the 2006–2016 change in employment in both numerical and percentage terms. Numbers below 10,000 are rounded to the nearest hundred, numbers above 10,000 are rounded to the nearest thousand, and percentages are rounded to the nearest whole number. Numerical and percentage changes are calculated using non-rounded 2006 and 2016 employment figures and then are rounded for presentation in the employment projections table.

Earnings

This section discusses typical earnings and how workers are compensated—by means of annual salaries, hourly wages, commissions, piece rates, tips, or bonuses. Within every occupation, earnings vary by experience, responsibility, performance, tenure, and geographic area. Information on earnings in the major industries in which the occupation is employed may be given. Some statements contain additional earnings data from non-BLS sources. Starting and average salaries of federal workers are based on 2007 data from the U.S. Office of Personnel Management. The National Association of Colleges and Employers supplies information on average salary offers in 2007 for students graduating with a bachelor's, master's, or Ph.D. degree in certain fields. A few statements contain additional earnings information from other sources, such as unions, professional associations, and private companies. These data sources are cited in the text.

Benefits account for a significant portion of total compensation costs to employers. Benefits such as paid vacation, health insurance, and sick leave may not be mentioned because they are so widespread. Although not as common as traditional benefits, flexible hours and profit-sharing plans may be offered to attract and retain highly qualified workers. Less common benefits also include childcare, tuition for dependents, housing assistance, summers off, and free or discounted merchandise or services.

Related Occupations

Occupations involving similar duties, skills, interests, education, and training are listed here. This allows you to look up these jobs if they also interest you.

Sources of Additional Information

No single publication can describe all aspects of an occupation. Thus, this section lists the mailing addresses of associations, government agencies, unions, and other organizations that can provide occupational information. In some cases, toll-free telephone numbers and Internet addresses also are listed. Free or relatively inexpensive publications offering more information may be mentioned; some of these publications also may be available in libraries, in school career centers, in guidance offices, or on the Internet.

Part III: Quick Job Search—Seven Steps to Getting a Good Job in Less Time

For more than 25 years, I've been helping people find better jobs in less time. If you have ever experienced unemployment, you know it is not pleasant. Unemployment is something most people want to get over quickly—in fact, the quicker the better. Part III will give you some techniques to help.

I know that most of you who read this book want to improve yourselves. You want to consider career and training options that lead to a better job and life in whatever way you define this—better pay, more flexibility, more-enjoyable or more-meaningful work, proving to your mom that you really can do anything you set your mind to, and other reasons. That is why I include advice on career planning and job search in Part III. It's a short part, but it includes the basics that are most important in planning your career and in reducing the time it takes to get a job. I hope it will make you think about what is important to you in the long run.

The second section of Part III showcases professionally written resumes for some of America's top computer and technical jobs. Use these as examples when creating your own resume. I know you will resist completing the activities in Part III, but consider this: It is often not the best person who gets the job, but the best job seeker. People who do their career planning and job search homework often get jobs over those with better credentials because they have these distinct advantages:

1. **They get more interviews,** including many for jobs that will never be advertised.
2. **They do better in interviews.**

People who understand what they want and what they have to offer employers present their skills more convincingly and are much better at answering problem questions. And, because they have learned more about job search techniques, they are likely to get more interviews with employers who need the skills they have.

Doing better in interviews often makes the difference between getting a job offer and sitting at home. And spending time planning your career can make an enormous difference to your happiness and lifestyle over time. So please consider reading Part III and completing its activities. I suggest you schedule a time right now to at least read Part III. An hour or so spent there can help you do just enough better in your career planning, job seeking, and interviewing to make the difference.

Part IV: Important Trends in Jobs and Industries

This section is made up of three very good articles on labor market trends. These articles come directly from U.S. Department of Labor sources and are interesting, well written, and short. One is on overall trends, with an emphasis on occupational groups; another is on trends in major industry groups; and the third is on in-demand careers in science, technology, engineering, and math (STEM). I know they sound boring, but the articles are quick reads and will give you a good idea of factors that will impact your career in the years to come.

The first article is titled "Tomorrow's Jobs." It highlights many important trends in employment and includes information on the fastest-growing jobs, jobs with high pay at various levels of education, and other details.

The second article is titled "Employment Trends in Major Industries." I included this information because you may find that you can use your skills or training in industries you have not considered. The article provides a good review of major trends with an emphasis on helping you make good employment decisions. This information can help you seek jobs in industries that offer higher pay or that are more likely to interest you. Many people overlook one important fact—the industry you work in is as important as the occupation you choose.

The third article, "STEM Occupations," describes today's high-tech jobs.

Some Additional Jobs to Consider

This book includes only 100 jobs, but many other occupations have aspects that can be considered computer-oriented or technical in nature. You can look up the jobs that interest you in one of the references mentioned in the following section, "Other Major Career Information Sources."

★ Accountants and Auditors

★ Actors, Producers, and Directors

★ Air Traffic Controllers

★ Archivists, Curators, and Museum Technicians

★ Boilermakers

★ Bookbinders and Bindery Workers

★ Budget Analysts

★ Coin, Vending, and Amusement Machine Servicers and Repairers

★ Commercial and Industrial Designers

★ Computer Operators

★ Cost Estimators

★ Electricians

★ Financial Analysts and Personal Financial Advisors

★ Financial Managers

★ Graphic Designers

★ Health Educators

★ Home Appliance Repairers

★ Industrial Production Managers

★ Jewelers and Precious Stone and Metal Workers

★ Landscape Architects

★ Librarians

★ Market and Survey Researchers

★ Private Detectives and Investigators

★ Sales Representatives, Wholesale and Manufacturing

Other Major Career Information Sources

The information in this book will be very useful, but you may want or need additional information. Keep in mind that the job descriptions here cover major jobs and not the many more-specialized jobs that are often related to them. Each job description in this book provides some sources of information related to that job, but here are additional resources to consider.

The *Occupational Outlook Handbook* (or the *OOH*): Updated every two years by the U.S. Department of Labor, this book provides descriptions for 270 major jobs covering more than 85 percent of the workforce. The *OOH* is the source of the job descriptions used in this book.

The *Enhanced Occupational Outlook Handbook:* Includes all descriptions in the *OOH* plus descriptions of nearly 6,000 more-specialized jobs related to them.

The *O*NET Dictionary of Occupational Titles:* The only printed source of the more than 900 jobs described in the U.S. Department of Labor's Occupational Information Network database.

The *New Guide for Occupational Exploration:* An important career reference that allows you to explore all major O*NET jobs based on your interests.

Best Jobs for the 21st Century: Includes descriptions for the 500 jobs (out of more than 900) with the best combination of earnings, growth, and number of openings. Useful lists make jobs easy to explore (examples: highest-paying jobs by level of education or training; best jobs overall; and best jobs for different ages, personality types, interests, and many more). It is the lead book in JIST's popular *Best Jobs* series.

Part

I

Using the Job-Match Grid to Choose a Career

By the Editors at JIST

This book describes so many occupations—how can you choose the best job for you? This section is your answer! It can help you to identify the jobs where your abilities will be valued, and you can rule out jobs that have certain characteristics you'd rather avoid. You will respond to a series of statements and use the Job-Match Grid to match your skills and preferences to the most appropriate jobs in this book.

So grab a pencil and get ready to mark up the following sections.

Thinking About Your Skills

Everybody knows that skills are important for getting and keeping a job. Employers expect you to list relevant skills on your resume. They ask about your skills in interviews. And they expect you to develop skills on the job so that you will remain productive as new technologies and new work situations emerge.

But maybe you haven't thought about how closely skills are related to job satisfaction. For example, let's say you have enough communication skills to hold a certain job where these skills are used heavily, but you wouldn't really *enjoy* using them. In that case, this job probably would be a bad choice for you. You need to identify a job that will use the skills that you *do* enjoy using.

That's why you need to take a few minutes to think about your skills: the ones you're good at and the ones you like using. The checklists that follow can help you do this. On each of the seven skills checklists that follow, use numbers to indicate how much you agree with each statement:

3 = I strongly agree

2 = I agree

1 = There's some truth to this

0 = This doesn't apply to me

Artistic Skills

_________ I am an amateur artist.

_________ I have musical talent.

(continued)

(continued)

_________ I enjoy planning home makeovers.
_________ I am good at performing onstage.
_________ I enjoy taking photos or shooting videos.
_________ I am good at writing stories, poems, articles, or essays.
_________ I have enjoyed taking ballet or other dance lessons.
_________ I like to cook and plan meals.
_________ I can sketch a good likeness of something or somebody.
_________ Playing music or singing is a hobby of mine.
_________ I have a good sense of visual style.
_________ I have participated in amateur theater.
_________ I like to express myself through writing.
_________ I can prepare tasty meals better than most people.
_________ I have a flair for creating attractive designs.
_________ I learn new dance steps or routines easily.
_________ **Total for Artistic Skills**

A note for those determined to work in the arts: Before you move on to the next skill, take a moment to decide whether working in some form of art is essential to you. Some people have exceptional talent and interest in a certain art form and are unhappy unless they are working in that art form—or until they have given their best shot at trying to break into it. If you are that kind of person, the total score shown above doesn't really matter. In fact, you may have given a 3 to just *one* of the statements above, but if you care passionately about your art form, you should toss out ordinary arithmetic and change the total to 100.

Communication Skills

_________ I am good at explaining complicated things to people.
_________ I like to take notes and write up minutes for meetings.
_________ I have a flair for public speaking.
_________ I am good at writing directions for using a computer or machine.
_________ I enjoy investigating facts and showing other people what they indicate.
_________ People consider me a good listener.
_________ I like to write letters to newspaper editors or political representatives.
_________ I have been an effective debater.
_________ I like developing publicity fliers for a school or community event.
_________ I am good at making diagrams that break down complex processes.
_________ I like teaching people how to drive a car or play a sport.
_________ I have been successful as the secretary of a club.

________ I enjoy speaking at group meetings or worship services.
________ I have a knack for choosing the most effective word.
________ I enjoy tutoring young people.
________ Technical manuals are not hard for me to understand.
________ **Total for Communication Skills**

Interpersonal Skills

________ I am able to make people feel that I understand their point of view.
________ I enjoy working collaboratively.
________ I often can make suggestions to people without sounding critical of them.
________ I enjoy soliciting clothes, food, and other supplies for needy people.
________ I am good at "reading" people to tell what's on their minds.
________ I have a lot of patience with people who are doing something for the first time.
________ People consider me outgoing.
________ I enjoy taking care of sick relatives, friends, or neighbors.
________ I am good at working out conflicts between friends or family members.
________ I enjoy serving as a host or hostess for houseguests.
________ People consider me a team player.
________ I enjoy meeting new people and finding common interests.
________ I am good at fundraising for school groups, teams, or community organizations.
________ I like to train or care for animals.
________ I often know what to say to defuse a tense situation.
________ I have enjoyed being an officer or advisor for a youth group.
________ **Total for Interpersonal Skills**

Managerial Skills

________ I am good at inspiring people to work together toward a goal.
________ I tend to use time wisely and not procrastinate.
________ I usually know when I have enough information to make a decision.
________ I enjoy planning and arranging programs for school or a community organization.
________ I am not reluctant to take responsibility when things turn out wrong.
________ I have enjoyed being a leader of a scout troop or other such group.
________ I often can figure out what motivates somebody.
________ People trust me to speak on their behalf and represent them fairly.
________ I like to help organize things at home, such as shopping lists and budgets.

(continued)

(continued)

________ I have been successful at recruiting members for a club or other organization.

________ I have enjoyed helping run a school or community fair or carnival.

________ People find me persuasive.

________ I enjoy buying large quantities of food or other products for an organization.

________ I have a knack for identifying abilities in other people.

________ I am able to get past details and look at the big picture.

________ I am good at delegating authority rather than trying to do everything myself.

________ **Total for Managerial Skills**

Mathematics Skills

________ I have always done well in math classes.

________ I enjoy balancing checkbooks for family members.

________ I can make mental calculations quickly.

________ I enjoy calculating sports statistics or keeping score.

________ Preparing family income tax returns is not hard for me.

________ I like to tutor young people in math.

________ I have taken or plan to take courses in statistics or calculus.

________ I enjoy budgeting the family expenditures.

________ **Subtotal for Mathematics Skills**

x 2 **Multiply by 2**

________ **Total for Mathematics Skills**

Mechanical Skills

________ I have a good sense of how mechanical devices work.

________ I like to tinker with my car or motorcycle.

________ I can understand diagrams of machinery or electrical wiring.

________ I enjoy installing and repairing home stereo or computer equipment.

________ I like looking at the merchandise in a building-supply warehouse store.

________ I can sometimes fix household appliances when they break down.

________ I have enjoyed building model airplanes, automobiles, or boats.

________ I can do minor plumbing and electrical installations in the home.

________ **Subtotal for Mechanical Skills**

x 2 **Multiply by 2**

________ **Total for Mechanical Skills**

Science Skills

_________ Some of my best grades have been in science classes.

_________ I enjoy tweaking my computer's settings to make it run better.

_________ I have a good understanding of the systems and organs of the human body.

_________ I have enjoyed performing experiments for a science fair.

_________ I have taken or plan to take college-level courses in science.

_________ I like to read about new breakthroughs in science and technology.

_________ I know how to write programs in a computer language.

_________ I enjoy reading medical or scientific magazines.

_________ **Subtotal for Science Skills**

x 2 **Multiply by 2**

_________ **Total for Science Skills**

Finding Your Skills on the Job-Match Grid

Okay, you've made a lot of progress so far. Now it's time to review what you've said about skills so you can use these insights to sort through the jobs listed on the Job-Match Grid.

Look at your totals for the seven skills listed previously. Enter your totals in the left column on this scorecard:

Total	Skill	Rank
_________	Artistic	_________
_________	Communication	_________
_________	Interpersonal	_________
_________	Managerial	_________
_________	Mathematics	_________
_________	Mechanical	_________
_________	Science	_________

Next, enter the rank of each skill in the right column—that is, the highest-scored skill gets ranked #1, the next-highest #2, and so forth. **Important:** Keep in mind that *the numbers in the Total column are only a rough guideline.* If you feel that a skill should be ranked higher or lower than its numerical total would suggest, *go by your impressions rather than just by the numbers.*

Now turn to the Job-Match Grid and find the columns for your #1-ranked and #2-ranked skills. Move down through the grid, going from page to page, and notice what symbols appear in those columns. If a row of the grid has a black circle (●) in *both* columns, circle the occupation name—or, if someone else will be using this book, jot down the name on a piece of paper. These occupations use a high level of both skills, or the skills are essential to these jobs.

Go through the Job-Match Grid a second time, looking at the column for your #3-ranked skill. If a *job you have already circled* has a black circle (●) or a bull's-eye (◉) in the column for your #3-ranked skill, put a check mark next to the occupation name. If none of your selected jobs has a black circle or a bull's-eye in this column, look for a white circle (○) and mark these jobs with check marks.

A second note for those determined to work in the arts: If a *particular* art form is essential for you to work in, you almost certainly know which occupations involve that art form and which don't. So not every job that has a black circle (●) in the "Artistic" column is going to interest you. Circle only the jobs that have a black circle in this column that *are* related to your art form (if you're not sure, look at the description of the occupation in this book) and that also have a symbol of some kind (●, **o**, or ○) in the column for your #2-ranked skill. As you circle each job, also give it a check mark, because there will be so few of them that you won't need to go through the Job-Match Grid a second time. If you have a more general interest in the arts, follow the general instructions.

Your Hot List of Possible Career Matches

Now that you have made a first and second cut of the jobs on the Job-Match Grid, you can focus on the occupations that look most promising at this point. Write the names of the occupations that are both *circled* and *checked:*

______________________	______________________
______________________	______________________
______________________	______________________
______________________	______________________
______________________	______________________
______________________	______________________
______________________	______________________

This is your Hot List of occupations that you are going to explore in detail *if* they are not eliminated by certain important job-related factors that you'll consider next.

Thinking About Other Job-Related Factors

Next, you need to consider four other job-related factors:

- ★ Economic sensitivity
- ★ Outdoor work
- ★ Physically demanding work
- ★ Hazardous conditions

Economic Sensitivity

You've read about how our nation's economy has gone up and down over the years. When the economy is on an upswing, there are more job openings, but when it veers downward toward recession, jobs are harder to find.

Are you aware that these trends affect some occupations more than others? For example, during an economic upswing, people do more vacation traveling and businesses send more workers on business trips. This keeps travel agencies very busy, so they need to hire more travel agents. When the economy is going down, people cut back on their vacation travel, businesses tell their workers to use teleconferencing instead of business trips, and travel agents are not in demand. Some may be laid off, and people who want to enter this field may find very few openings. By contrast, most jobs in the health-care field are not sensitive to the economy, and automotive mechanics are just as busy as ever during economic slowdowns because people want to keep their old cars running.

So this issue of economic sensitivity (and its opposite, job security) is one that may affect which occupation you choose. Some people want to avoid economically sensitive occupations because they don't want to risk losing their job (or having difficulty finding a job) during times of recession. Other people are willing to risk being in an economically sensitive occupation because they want to profit from the periods when both the economy and the occupation are booming.

How important is it to you to be in an occupation that *doesn't* go through periods of boom and bust along with the nation's economy? Check one:

_________ It doesn't matter to me.

_________ It's not important, but I'd consider it.

_________ It's somewhat important to me.

_________ It's very important to me.

If you answered "It doesn't matter to me," skip to the next section, "Outdoor Work." Otherwise, turn back to the Job-Match Grid and find the column for "Economically Sensitive."

If you answered "It's not important, but I'd consider it," see whether any of the jobs on your Hot List have a black circle (●) in this column. If so, cross them off and write an "E" next to them.

If you answered "It's somewhat important to me," see whether any of the jobs on your Hot List have a black circle (●) or a bull's-eye (◉) in this column. If so, cross them off and write an "E" next to them.

If you answered "It's very important to me," see whether any of the jobs on your Hot List have *any* symbol (●, ◉, or ○) in this column. If so, cross them off and write an "E" next to them.

Outdoor Work

Some people prefer to work indoors in a climate-controlled setting, such as an office, a classroom, a factory floor, a laboratory, or a hospital room. Other people would rather work primarily in an outdoor setting, such as a forest, an athletic field, or a city street. And some would enjoy a job that alternates between indoor and outdoor activities.

What is *your* preference for working indoors or outdoors? Check one:

_________ It's very important to me to work **indoors.**

_________ I'd prefer to work mostly **indoors.**

_________ Either indoors or outdoors is okay with me.

_________ I'd prefer to work mostly **outdoors.**

_________ It's very important to me to work **outdoors.**

If you answered "Either indoors or outdoors is okay with me," skip to the next section, "Physically Demanding Work." Otherwise, turn to the Job-Match Grid and find the column for "Outdoor Work."

If you answered "It's very important to me to work **indoors,**" see whether any of the jobs on your Hot List have *any* symbol (●, ◉, or ○) in this column. If so, cross them off and write an "O" next to them.

If you answered "I'd prefer to work mostly **indoors,**" see whether any of the jobs on your Hot List have a black circle (●) in this column. If so, cross them off and write an "O" next to them.

If you answered "I'd prefer to work mostly **outdoors,**" see whether any of the jobs on your Hot List have *no* symbol—just a blank—in this column. If so, cross them off and write an "O" next to them. All the jobs remaining on your Hot List should have some kind of symbol (●, ◉, or ○) in this column.

If you answered "It's very important to me to work **outdoors,**" see whether any of the jobs on your Hot List have either *no* symbol or just a white circle (○) in this column. If so, cross them off and write an "O" next to them. All the jobs remaining on your Hot List should have either a black circle (●) or a bull's-eye (◉) in this column.

Physically Demanding Work

Jobs vary by how much muscle power they require you to use. Some jobs require a lot of lifting heavy loads, standing for long times, climbing, or stooping. On other jobs, the heaviest thing you lift is a notebook or telephone handset, and most of the time you are sitting. Still other jobs require only a moderate amount of physical exertion.

What is *your* preference for the physical demands of work? Check one:

_________ I don't care whether my work requires heavy or light physical exertion.

_________ I want my work to require only light physical exertion.

_________ I want my work to require no more than occasional moderate physical exertion.

_________ I want my work to require moderate physical exertion, with occasional heavy exertion.

_________ I want my work to require a lot of heavy physical exertion.

If you answered "I don't care whether my work requires heavy or light physical exertion," skip to the next section, "Hazardous Conditions." Otherwise, turn to the Job-Match Grid and find the column for "Physically Demanding Work."

If you answered "I want my work to require only light physical exertion," see whether any of the jobs on your Hot List have *any* symbol (●, ◉, or ○) in this column. If so, cross them off and write a "P" next to them.

If you answered "I want my work to require no more than occasional moderate physical exertion," see whether any of the jobs on your Hot List have either a black circle (●) or a bull's-eye (◉) in this column. If so, cross them off and write a "P" next to them.

If you answered "I want my work to require moderate physical exertion, with occasional heavy exertion," see whether any of the jobs on your Hot List have either a black circle (●), a white circle (○), or *no* symbol in this column. If so, cross them off and write a "P" next to them. All the jobs remaining on your Hot List should have a bull's-eye (◉) in this column.

If you answered "I want my work to require a lot of heavy physical exertion," see whether any of the jobs on your Hot List have either *no* symbol or just a white circle (○) or a bull's-eye (◉) in this column. If so, cross them off and write a "P" next to them. All the jobs remaining on your Hot List should have a black circle (●) in this column.

Hazardous Conditions

Every day about 9,000 Americans sustain a disabling injury on the job. Many workers have jobs that require them to deal with hazardous conditions, such as heat, noise, radiation, germs, toxins, or dangerous machinery. These workers need to wear protective clothing or follow safety procedures to avoid injury.

What is *your* preference regarding hazardous conditions on the job? Check one:

_________ I want hazardous workplace conditions to be very unlikely.

_________ I want hazardous conditions to be unlikely or minor.

_________ I am willing to accept some major workplace hazards.

If you answered "I am willing to accept some major workplace hazards," skip to the section "Geographically Concentrated Jobs." Otherwise, turn to the Job-Match Grid and find the column for "Hazardous Conditions."

If you answered "I want hazardous workplace conditions to be very unlikely," see whether any of the jobs on your Hot List have *any* symbol (●, ◉, or ○) in this column. If so, cross them off and write an "H" next to them.

If you answered "I want hazardous conditions to be unlikely or minor," see whether any of the jobs on your Hot List have a black circle (●) in this column. If so, cross them off and write an "H" next to them.

If Every Job on Your Hot List Is Now Crossed Off

It's possible that you have crossed off *all* the occupations on your Hot List. If so, consider these two options:

★ You may want to relax some of your requirements. Maybe you were too hasty in crossing off some of the jobs. Take another look at the four job-related factors and decide whether you could accept work that doesn't meet the requirements you set previously—for example, work that is not as much indoors or outdoors as you specified. If you change your mind now, you can tell by the letters in the margin which jobs you crossed off for which reasons.

★ You may want to add to your Hot List by considering additional skills. So far you have considered only occupations that involve your top three skills. You may want to add jobs that have a black circle (●) or a bull's-eye (◉) in the column for your #4-ranked skill and possibly for your #5-ranked skill. If you do add any jobs, be sure to repeat your review of the four job-related factors.

Evaluating Occupations Described in This Book

You are now ready to make the jump from the checklists to the detailed information about jobs in this book. The first detailed issue you need to consider is whether you will be able to find work in your area or have to relocate.

Geographically Concentrated Jobs

Turn to the Job-Match Grid one more time and find the column for "Geographically Concentrated." Look at all the occupations on your Hot List that haven't been crossed off. If there is a symbol in this column, especially a bull's-eye (◉) or a black circle (●), it means that employment for this occupation tends to be concentrated in certain geographic areas. For example, most acting jobs are found in big cities because that's where you'll find most theaters, TV studios, and movie studios. Most water transportation jobs are found on the coasts and beside major lakes and rivers.

If a symbol shows that a Hot List occupation *is* geographically concentrated, the location of the jobs may be obvious, as in the examples of acting and water transportation. If it's not clear to you where the jobs may be found, find the occupation in "The Job Descriptions" section and look for the facts under the heading "Employment" in the description. Once you understand where most of the jobs are, you have to make some decisions:

★ **Are most of the job openings in a geographic location where I am now or would enjoy living?** If you answered "yes" to this question, repeat this exercise for all the other occupations still on your Hot List. Then jump to the next heading, "Nature of the Work." If you answered "no," proceed to the next bulleted question.

★ **If most of the job openings are in a distant place where I don't want to relocate, am I willing to take a chance and hope to be one of the few workers who get hired in an *uncommon* location?** If you answered "yes," take a good look at the Job Outlook information in the job description. If the outlook for the occupation is very good and if you expect to have some of the advantages mentioned there (such as the right degree, in some cases), taking a chance on being hired in an unusual location may be a reasonable decision. On the other hand, if the outlook is only so-so or not good and if you have no special qualifications, you probably are setting yourself up for disappointment. You should seriously consider changing your mind about this decision. At least speak to people in your area who are knowledgeable about the occupation to determine whether you have any chance of success. If you answered "no"—you are not willing to take a chance—cross off this occupation and write a "G" next to it. (If you now have no jobs left on your Hot List, see the previous section titled "If Every Job on Your Hot List Is Now Crossed Off.")

Nature of the Work

When you read the job description for an occupation on your Hot List, you will see that the "Nature of the Work" section discusses what workers do on the job, what tools and equipment they use, and how closely they are supervised. Keep in mind that this is an overview of a diverse collection of workers, and in fact few workers perform the full set of tasks itemized here. In fact, in many cases the workforce covered by the job description is so diverse that it actually divides into several occupational specialties, which are italicized.

Here are some things to think about as you read this section:

★ Note the kinds of problems, materials, and tools you will encounter on the job. Are these a good match for your interests?

★ Also note the work activities mentioned here. Do you think they will be rewarding? Are there many that stand out as unpleasant or boring?

The work environment subsection identifies the typical hours worked, the physical and psychological environment, physical activities and susceptibility to injury, special equipment, and the extent of travel required. If conditions vary between the occupational specialties, that is mentioned here. Here are some things to look for in the work environment subsection:

★ If you have a disability, note the physical requirements that are mentioned here and consider whether you can meet these requirements with or without suitable accommodations.

★ If you're bothered by conditions such as heights, stress, or a cramped workspace, see whether this section mentions any conditions that would discourage you.

★ Note what this section says about the work schedule and the need for travel, if any. This information may be good to know if you have pressing family responsibilities or, on the other hand, a desire for unusual hours or travel.

★ If you find a working condition that bothers you, be sure to check the wording to see whether it *always* applies to the occupation or whether it only *may* apply. Even if it seems to be a condition that you cannot avoid, find out for sure by talking to people in the occupation or educators who teach related courses. Maybe you can carve out a niche that avoids the unappealing working condition.

Training, Other Qualifications, and Advancement

In the "Training, Other Qualifications, and Advancement" section, you can see how to prepare for the occupation and how to advance in it. It identifies the significant entry routes—those that are most popular and that are preferred by employers. It mentions any licensure or certification that may be necessary for entry or advancement. It also identifies the particular skills, aptitudes, and work habits that employers value. Look for these topics in this section:

★ Compare the entry requirements to your background and to the educational and training opportunities that are available to you. Be sure to consider nontraditional and informal entry routes, if any are possible, as well as the formal routes. Ask yourself, Am I willing to get the additional education or training that will be necessary? Do I have the time, money, ability, interest, and commitment?

★ Maybe you're already partway down the road to job entry. In general, you should try to use your previous education, training, and work experience rather than abandon it. Look for specifics that are already on your resume—educational accomplishments, skills, work habits—that will meet employers' expectations. If you have some of these qualifications already, this occupation may be a better career choice than some others.

★ If you are ready to apply for a job in a certain occupation, pay attention to what the "other qualifications" subsection says about relevant skills and personal attributes. This information can help you decide what to emphasize in your resume and in interviews so that you'll be a stronger job candidate.

Employment

The "Employment" section in the job description reports how many jobs the occupation currently provides, the industries that provide the most jobs, and the number or proportion of self-employed or part-time workers in the occupation, if significant. In this section, you'll want to pay attention to these facts:

★ Note the industries that provide most of the employment for the occupation. This knowledge can help you identify contacts who can tell you more about the work, and later it can help in your job hunting.

★ If you're interested in self-employment or part-time work, see whether these work arrangements are mentioned here.

Job Outlook

The "Job Outlook" section describes the economic forces that will affect future employment in the occupation. Here are some things to look for in this section:

★ The information here can help you identify occupations with a good job outlook so that you will have a better-than-average chance of finding work. Be alert for any mention of an advantage that you may have over other job seekers (for example, a college degree or geographic location) or any other factor that might make your chances better or worse.

★ If you are highly motivated and highly qualified for a particular occupation, don't be discouraged by a bad employment outlook. Job openings occur even in shrinking or overcrowded occupations, and with exceptional talent or good personal connections, you may go on to great success.

★ These projections are the most definitive ones available, but they are not foolproof and apply only to a 10-year time span. No matter what occupation you choose, you will need to adapt to changes.

Projections Data

This section consists of a table of numerical data. It shows how many people were employed in the occupation in 2006, how many are projected to be employed in 2016, and the difference between these two figures in both numerical and percentage terms. These figures form the basis of some information in the "Job Outlook" section, but they add to the previous information in several ways that you may find useful:

★ The figures indicate whether the occupation has a large or small workforce. A large occupation can provide many job openings—even if it is shrinking in size—because of job turnover. Conversely, a small occupation may provide few job openings even though it is growing rapidly.

- ★ Often the table consists of more than one row because the occupation covers several specializations. In such cases, you can see which specializations have the largest workforces and which have the most promising projections for employment growth.

Earnings

The "Earnings" section discusses the wages for the occupation. Here are some things to keep in mind:

- ★ The wage figures are national averages. Actual wages in your geographic region may be considerably higher or lower. Also, a median figure means that half of the workers earn more and half earn less, and the actual salary any one worker earns can vary greatly from that number.
- ★ Note the date of the wage figures and keep in mind that, although most of the figures are comparable with one another, they may lag behind current wage levels. However, wage inflation is currently at a low rate, so the figures remain generally relevant for several years.
- ★ Remember to consider *all* the pluses and minuses of the job. Not every day of the work week is payday, so make your choice based on the whole occupation, not just the paycheck.

Related Occupations

The "Related Occupations" section identifies occupations that are similar to the one featured in the job description in terms of tasks, interests, skills, education, or training. You may find this section interesting for these reasons:

- ★ If you're interested in an occupation but not strongly committed to pursuing it, this section may suggest another occupation with similar rewards that may turn out to be a better fit. Try to research these related occupations, but keep in mind that they may not all be included in this book.
- ★ You may want to choose one of these occupations as your Plan B goal if your original goal should not work out. In that case, it helps to identify an occupation that involves similar kinds of problems and work settings but requires *less* education or training.

Sources of Additional Information

This section in each job description lists several sources and resources you can turn to for more information about the occupation. Try to consult at least some of these sources. This book should be only the beginning of your career decision-making process. You need more detailed information from several viewpoints to make an informed decision.

If licensure or certification is mentioned as a requirement in the "Training, Other Qualifications, and Advancement" section, one of the sources listed here should have detailed information about the procedures that apply where you live. Be sure to investigate these matters so you will understand the hurdles that stand between you and job entry and can plan a course of action.

Don't rely entirely on the Web sites listed here. You especially need to talk to and observe individual workers to learn what their workdays are like, what the workers enjoy and dislike about the job, how they got hired, and what effects the job has had on other aspects of their lives. Maybe you can make contact with local workers through the local chapter of an organization listed here.

Narrowing Down Your Choices

The information in the job descriptions should help you cross more jobs off your Hot List. And what you learn by turning to other resources should help you narrow down your Hot List jobs to a few promising choices and maybe one best bet. Here are some final considerations: Have I talked to people who are actually doing this work? Am I fully aware of the pluses and minuses of this job? If there are aspects of the job that I don't like, how do I expect to avoid them or overcome them? If the odds of finding a job opening are not good, why do I expect to beat the odds? What is my Plan B goal if I lose interest in my original goal or don't succeed at it?

The Job-Match Grid

The grid on the following pages provides information about the personal skills and job characteristics for occupations covered in this book. Use the directions and questions that start at the beginning of this section to help you get the most from this grid.

Below is what the symbols on the grid represent. If a job has no symbol in a column, it means that the skill or job characteristic is not important or relevant to the job.

Personal Skills

- ● Essential or high-skill level
- ◉ Somewhat essential or moderate-skill level
- ○ Basic-skill level

Job Characteristics

- ● Highly likely
- ◉ Somewhat likely
- ○ A little likely

Job-Match Grid

	Personal Skills							Job Characteristics				
	Artistic	Communication	Interpersonal	Managerial	Mathematics	Mechanical	Science	Economically Sensitive	Outdoor Work	Physically Demanding Work	Hazardous Conditions	Geographically Concentrated
Actuaries		○	○	○	●		◉					
Agricultural and food scientists		◉	○	◉	●	●	●		◉	○	○	
Aircraft and avionics equipment mechanics and service technicians		○	○		◉	●	◉	◉	●	◉	○	◉
Aircraft pilots and flight engineers		●	●	●	●	◉	●	●	○	◉	●	○
Architects, except landscape and naval	●	◉	◉	◉	●	●	◉	◉	◉	○		
Armed forces		◉	◉	◉	○	○	○		◉	◉	●	◉
Atmospheric scientists		◉	○	◉	●	●	●	○	◉			
Audiologists		●	◉	●	◉	○	●					
Automotive body and related repairers	○	○	○		○	●	○		○	◉	○	
Automotive service technicians and mechanics		○	○		○	●	◉		○	◉	○	
Biological scientists		◉	○	◉	●	●	●	○	◉	○	○	
Broadcast and sound engineering technicians and radio operators		○	◉		◉	●	◉		○			○
Cardiovascular technologists and technicians		◉	○	○	●	●	●			○		
Chemists and materials scientists	○	◉	○	◉	●	●	●	◉			○	
Chiropractors		●	◉	●	◉	○	●			○		
Clinical laboratory technologists and technicians		◉	○	○	●	●	●			○	○	
Computer and information systems managers		●	●	●	●	●	●	◉				
Computer control programmers and operators		○			◉	◉	○	○				
Computer programmers		◉	○	○	●	◉	●	○				
Computer scientists and database administrators		◉	○	○	●		●	○				
Computer software engineers		◉	◉	◉	●	●	●	○				
Computer support specialists and systems administrators		◉	◉	○	◉	●	◉	○				
Computer systems analysts		◉	○	○	●		●	○				
Computer, automated teller, and office machine repairers		○	○		○	●	○		○	○		
Conservation scientists and foresters		◉	○	◉	●	●	●	○	●	◉	○	●
Dental assistants		◉	◉	○	○	●	◉			◉	◉	
Dental hygienists		◉	◉	○	◉	●	◉			○	◉	
Dentists	○	●	●	●	◉	●	●			○	◉	
Desktop publishers	●	○	○		○	◉	○	○				
Diagnostic medical sonographers		◉	○	○	●	●	●					
Diesel service technicians and mechanics		○	○		○	●	◉	○	○	◉	○	

Personal Skills: ●—Essential or high skill level; ◉—Somewhat essential or moderate skill level; ○—Basic skill level
Job Characteristics: ●—Highly likely; ◉—Somewhat likely; ○—A little likely

	Personal Skills							Job Characteristics				
	Artistic	Communication	Interpersonal	Managerial	Mathematics	Mechanical	Science	Economically Sensitive	Outdoor Work	Physically Demanding Work	Hazardous Conditions	Geographically Concentrated
Dietitians and nutritionists		●	●	○	◉	○	●					
Drafters	●	◉	○		◉	●	○	◉				
Economists		◉	○	◉	●							
Electrical and electronics installers and repairers		○	○		◉	●	○			○	◉	
Electronic home entertainment equipment installers and repairers	◉	○	○		◉	●	○	●		◉		
Elevator installers and repairers		○	○		○	●	○	●	○	●	●	
Emergency medical technicians and paramedics		●	●	●	○	●	●		●	●	●	
Engineering and natural sciences managers		●	●	●	●	●	●	◉				
Engineering technicians	○	◉	○		●	●	●	○	○	○	○	
Engineers	◉	◉	○	◉	●	●	●	◉	○	○	○	◉
Environmental scientists and hydrologists	○	◉	○	◉	●	●	●	○	●	○		
Geoscientists	○	◉	○	◉	●	●	●	○	●	○		
Heating, air-conditioning, and refrigeration mechanics and installers		○	○		○	●	○	◉	○	◉	○	
Heavy vehicle and mobile equipment service technicians and mechanics		○	○		○	●	◉	●	○	◉	○	
Industrial machinery mechanics and maintenance workers		○			○	●	○	○		◉	◉	○
Licensed practical and licensed vocational nurses		◉	●	○	○	●	●			◉	◉	
Machinists	◉	○			●	●	◉	○		◉	◉	
Mathematicians		○	○	○	●		◉					
Medical and health services managers		●	●	●	◉	◉	◉					
Medical records and health information technicians		◉	○	○	◉		◉					
Medical scientists		◉	○	◉	●	●	●	○			○	
Medical transcriptionists		●	○	○	○	○	●					
Medical, dental, and ophthalmic laboratory technicians	◉	○	◉		○	●	◉			○		
Millwrights		○	○		◉	●	○	●	○	◉	◉	◉
Nuclear medicine technologists		◉	○	○	●	●	●				◉	
Occupational health and safety specialists and technicians		◉	○	◉	◉	◉	◉		○	◉	◉	
Occupational therapist assistants and aides		◉	●	○	○	●	◉			◉	◉	
Occupational therapists		●	●	◉	◉	◉	◉			○	◉	
Operations research analysts		○	○	○	●		◉	○				
Opticians, dispensing	◉	◉	◉	○	◉	◉	○	○		○		
Optometrists	○	●	◉	●	◉	◉	●				◉	
Pharmacists		●	◉	◉	●	○	●			○		

(continued)

Personal Skills: ●—Essential or high skill level; ◉—Somewhat essential or moderate skill level; ○—Basic skill level
Job Characteristics: ●—Highly likely; ◉—Somewhat likely; ○—A little likely

(continued)

	Personal Skills							Job Characteristics				
	Artistic	Communication	Interpersonal	Managerial	Mathematics	Mechanical	Science	Economically Sensitive	Outdoor Work	Physically Demanding Work	Hazardous Conditions	Geographically Concentrated
Pharmacy aides		◉	◉	○	○		○			○		
Pharmacy technicians		◉	◉	○	◉	◉	◉			○		
Photographers	●	○	○	○	○	●	○	◉	◉	◉		
Photographic process workers and processing machine operators	○	○			○	●	○	○		○	◉	
Physical therapist assistants and aides		◉	◉	○	○	◉	◉			●	◉	
Physical therapists		●	●	○	◉	○	●			●	◉	
Physician assistants		●	●	○	●	◉	●			◉	◉	
Physicians and surgeons	◉	●	●	●	◉	●	●			◉	◉	
Physicists and astronomers	○	◉	○	○	●	●	●	○	○			○
Podiatrists	○	●	●	●	◉	◉	●					
Power plant operators, distributors, and dispatchers		○	◉	○	●	○	●				◉	
Precision instrument and equipment repairers	○	○			◉	●	○			◉		
Prepress technicians and workers	◉	◉	○		◉	◉	○	○		○		
Printing machine operators		○			○	●	○	○		●	◉	
Psychologists		●	●	○	◉		◉					
Radiation therapists		●	◉	●	◉	◉	●			●		
Radio and telecommunications equipment installers and repairers		○	○		◉	●	◉	○	●	◉		◉
Radiologic technologists and technicians		◉	◉	○	●	●	◉			◉	◉	
Registered nurses		●	●	◉	●	●	●			◉	◉	
Respiratory therapists		●	●	○	●	●	●			○	◉	
Sales engineers	○	●	●		◉	○	◉	●				
Science technicians	○	◉	○		●	●	●	◉	○	○	○	
Semiconductor processors		○			●	◉	●	◉		○		●
Small engine mechanics		○	○		○	●	◉	◉	○	◉	○	
Social scientists, other		◉	◉	○	◉	○	○					
Speech-language pathologists	○	●	●	○	●	○	●					
Stationary engineers and boiler operators		○	○	○	○	●	○				◉	
Statisticians		○	○	○	●		◉					
Surgical technologists		◉	◉	○	●	●	●			◉	◉	
Surveyors, cartographers, photogrammetrists, and surveying and mapping technicians	◉	◉	◉	○	◉	◉	◉	◉	◉	◉		
Teachers—postsecondary	◉	●	●	●	●		◉					
Television, video, and motion picture camera operators and editors	●	○	○	○	○	●	○		◉	◉		●
Tool and die makers	○	○			●	●	◉	○		◉	◉	
Urban and regional planners	◉	◉	◉	◉	●	○	○	○	○			

Personal Skills: ●—Essential or high skill level; ◉—Somewhat essential or moderate skill level; ○—Basic skill level
Job Characteristics: ●—Highly likely; ◉—Somewhat likely; ○—A little likely

	Personal Skills							Job Characteristics				
	Artistic	Communication	Interpersonal	Managerial	Mathematics	Mechanical	Science	Economically Sensitive	Outdoor Work	Physically Demanding Work	Hazardous Conditions	Geographically Concentrated
Veterinarians	○	●	●	●	●	●	●		○	●	●	
Veterinary technologists and technicians		◉	◉	◉	◉	●	◉	○	○	●	●	
Water and liquid waste treatment plant and system operators		○	○	○	◉	●	◉		◉	◉	●	

Personal Skills: ●—Essential or high skill level; ◉—Somewhat essential or moderate skill level; ○—Basic skill level
Job Characteristics: ●—Highly likely; ◉—Somewhat likely; ○—A little likely

Part II

Descriptions of the Top 100 Computer and Technical Careers

This is the book's major section. It contains descriptions for 100 major occupations that require computer and technical skills. The jobs are arranged in alphabetical order, and STEM jobs are identified by an icon next to their titles. Refer to the table of contents for a list of the jobs and the page numbers where their descriptions begin.

Review the table of contents to discover occupations that interest you, and then find where their descriptions begin. If you are interested in medical jobs, for example, you can go through the list and quickly pinpoint those you want to learn more about. Or use the assessment in Part I to identify several possible career matches.

While the descriptions in this section are easy to understand, the introduction to this book provides additional information for interpreting them. Keep in mind that the descriptions present information that is average for the country. Conditions in your area and with specific employers may be quite different.

Also, you may come across jobs that sound interesting but require more education and training than you have or are considering. Don't eliminate them too soon. There are many ways to obtain education and training, and most people change jobs and careers many times. You probably have more skills than you realize that can transfer to new jobs, so consider taking some chances. You often have more opportunities than barriers, but you have to go out and find the opportunities. Use the descriptions to learn more about possible jobs and look into the suggested resources to help you take the next step.

STEM Actuaries

(O*NET 15-2011.00)

Significant Points

- A strong background in mathematics is essential; actuaries must pass a series of examinations to gain full professional status.
- About 6 out of 10 actuaries are employed in the insurance industry.
- Employment opportunities should remain good for those who qualify, because the stringent qualifying examination system restricts the number of candidates.

Nature of the Work

Through their knowledge of statistics, finance, and business, actuaries assess the risk of events occurring and help create policies that minimize risk and its financial impact on companies and clients. One of the main functions of actuaries is to help businesses assess the risk of certain events occurring and formulate policies that minimize the cost of that risk. For this reason, actuaries are essential to the insurance industry.

Actuaries assemble and analyze data to estimate the probability and likely cost of an event such as death, sickness, injury, disability, or loss of property. Actuaries also address financial questions, including those involving the level of pension contributions required to produce a certain retirement income level and the way in which a company should invest resources to maximize return on investments in light of potential risk. Using their broad knowledge of statistics, finance, and business, actuaries help design insurance policies, pension plans, and other financial strategies in a manner which will help ensure that the plans are maintained on a sound financial basis.

Most actuaries are employed in the insurance industry, specializing in either life and health insurance or property and casualty insurance. They produce probability tables or use more sophisticated dynamic modeling techniques that determine the likelihood that a potential event will generate a claim. From these tables, they estimate the amount a company can expect to pay in claims. For example, property and casualty actuaries calculate the expected number of claims resulting from automobile accidents, which varies depending on the insured person's age, sex, driving history, type of car, and other factors. Actuaries ensure that the price, or premium, charged for such insurance will enable the company to cover claims and other expenses. This premium must be profitable, yet competitive with other insurance companies. Within the life and health insurance fields, actuaries help to develop long-term-care insurance and annuity policies, the latter a growing investment tool for many individuals.

Actuaries in other financial service industries manage credit and help price corporate security offerings. They also devise new investment tools to help their firms compete with other financial service companies. Pension actuaries work under the provisions of the Employee Retirement Income Security Act (ERISA) of 1974 to evaluate pension plans covered by that Act and report on the plans' financial soundness to participants, sponsors, and federal regulators. Actuaries working for the government help manage social programs such as Social Security and Medicare.

Actuaries may help determine company policy and may need to explain complex technical matters to company executives, government officials, shareholders, policyholders, or the public in general. They may testify before public agencies on proposed legislation that affects their businesses or explain changes in contract provisions to customers. They also may help companies develop plans to enter new lines of business or new geographic markets by forecasting demand in competitive settings.

Consulting actuaries provide advice to clients on a contract basis. The duties of most consulting actuaries are similar to those of other actuaries. For example, some may evaluate company pension plans by calculating the future value of employee and employer contributions and determining whether the amounts are sufficient to meet the future needs of retirees. Others help companies reduce their insurance costs by lowering the level of risk the companies take on. For example, they may provide advice on how to lessen the risk of injury on the job. Consulting actuaries sometimes testify in court regarding the value of potential lifetime earnings of a person who is disabled or killed in an accident, the current value of future pension benefits (in divorce cases), or other values arrived at by complex calculations. Some actuaries work in reinsurance, a field in which one insurance company arranges to share a large prospective liability policy with another insurance company in exchange for a percentage of the premium.

Work environment. Actuaries have desk jobs, and their offices usually are comfortable and pleasant. They often work at least 40 hours a week. Some actuaries—particularly consulting actuaries—may travel to meet with clients. Consulting actuaries also may experience more erratic employment and be expected to work more than 40 hours per week.

Training, Other Qualifications, and Advancement

Actuaries need a strong foundation in mathematics, statistics, and general business. They generally have a bachelor's degree and are required to pass a series of exams in order to become certified.

Education and training. Actuaries need a strong background in mathematics and general business. Usually, actuaries earn an undergraduate degree in mathematics, statistics or actuarial science, or a business-related field such as finance, economics or business. While in college, students should complete coursework in economics, applied statistics and corporate finance, which is a requirement for professional certification. Furthermore, many students obtain internships to gain experience in the profession prior to graduation. About 100 colleges and universities offer an actuarial science program, and most offer a degree in mathematics, statistics, economics, or finance.

Some companies hire applicants without specifying a major, provided that the applicant has a working knowledge of mathematics—including calculus, probability, and statistics—and has demonstrated this knowledge by passing one or two actuarial exams required for professional designation. Companies increasingly prefer well-rounded individuals who, in addition to having acquired a strong technical background, have some training in business and liberal arts and possess strong communication skills.

Beginning actuaries often rotate among different jobs in an organization, such as marketing, underwriting, financial reporting and product development, to learn various actuarial operations and phases of insurance work. At first, they prepare data for actuarial projects or perform other simple tasks. As they gain experience, actuaries may supervise clerks, prepare correspondence, draft reports, and conduct research. They may move from one company to another early in their careers as they advance to higher positions.

Licensure. Two professional societies sponsor programs leading to full professional status in their specialty: the Society of Actuaries (SOA) and the Casualty Actuarial Society (CAS). The SOA certifies actuaries in the fields of life insurance, health benefits systems, retirement systems, and finance and investment. The CAS gives a series of examinations in the property and casualty field, which includes car, homeowners, medical malpractice, workers compensation, and personal injury liability.

Three of the first four exams in the SOA and CAS examination series are jointly sponsored by the two societies and cover the same material. For this reason, students do not need to commit themselves to a specialty until they have taken the initial examinations, which test an individual's competence in probability, statistics, and other branches of mathematics and finance. The first few examinations help students evaluate their potential as actuaries. Many prospective actuaries begin taking the exams in college with the help of self-study guides and courses. Those who pass one or more examinations have better opportunities for employment at higher starting salaries than those who do not.

Many candidates find work as an actuary immediately after graduation and work through the certification process while gaining some experience in the field. In fact, many employers pay the examination fees and provide their employees time to study. As actuaries pass exams, they are often rewarded with a pay increase. Despite the fact that employers are supportive during the exam process, home study is necessary and many actuaries study for months to prepare for each exam.

The process for gaining certification in the Casualty Actuarial Society is predominantly exam based. To reach the first level of certification, the Associate or ACAS level, a candidate must complete seven exams, attend one course on professionalism and complete the coursework in applied statistics, corporate finance, and economics required by both the SOA and CAS. This process generally takes from four to six years. The next level, the Fellowship or FCAS level, requires passing two additional exams in advanced topics, including investment and assets and dynamic financial analysis and the valuation of insurance. Most actuaries reach the fellowship level two to three years after attaining Associate status.

The certification process of the Society of Actuaries blends exams with computer learning modules and coursework. After taking the initial exams, candidates must choose a specialty: group and health benefits, individual life and annuities, retirement benefits, pensions, investments or finance/enterprise risk management. To reach the Associate or ASA level, a candidate must complete the initial four exams, the coursework in applied statistics, corporate finance and economics required by the SOA and CAS, eight computer modules with two corresponding assessments and a course in professionalism. This process generally takes from four to six years. To attain the Fellowship or FSA level, a candidate must pass two additional exams within a chosen specialty and must complete three computer modules and a professionalism course. Attaining Fellowship status usually takes an additional two to three years after becoming an Associate.

Specific requirements apply to pension actuaries, who verify the financial status of defined benefit pension plans for the federal government. These actuaries must be enrolled by the Joint Board of the U.S. Treasury Department and the U.S. Department of Labor for the Enrollment of Actuaries. To qualify for enrollment, applicants must meet certain experience and examination requirements, as stipulated by the Board.

Other qualifications. In addition to knowledge of mathematics, computer skills are becoming increasingly important. Actuaries should be able to develop and use spreadsheets and databases, as well as standard statistical analysis software. Knowledge of computer programming languages, such as Visual Basic for Applications, SAS, or SQL, is also useful.

To perform their duties effectively, actuaries must keep up with current economic and social trends and legislation, as well as with developments in health, business, and finance that could affect insurance or investment practices. Good communication and interpersonal skills also are important, particularly for prospective consulting actuaries.

Advancement. Advancement depends largely on job performance and the number of actuarial examinations passed. Actuaries with a broad knowledge of the insurance, pension, investment, or employee benefits fields can rise to administrative and executive positions in their companies. Actuaries with supervisory ability may advance to management positions in other areas, such as underwriting, accounting, data processing, marketing, and advertising. Increasingly, actuaries with knowledge of business are beginning to rise to high-level positions within their companies, such as Chief Risk Officer, Chief Financial Officer, or other executive level positions. These generally require that actuaries use their abilities for assessing risk and apply it to the entire company as a whole. Furthermore, some experienced actuaries move into consulting, often by opening their own consulting firm. Some actuaries transfer to college and university faculty positions. (See the section on teachers—postsecondary elsewhere in this book.)

Employment

Actuaries held about 18,000 jobs in 2006. Over half of all actuaries were employed by insurance carriers. Approximately 21 percent work for professional, scientific and technical consulting services. Others worked for insurance agents and brokers and in the management of companies and enterprises industry. A relatively small number of actuaries are employed by government agencies.

Job Outlook

Employment of actuaries is expected to grow rapidly through 2016. Job opportunities should remain good for those who qualify, because the stringent qualifying examination system restricts the number of candidates.

Employment change. Employment of actuaries is expected to increase by about 24 percent over the 2006–2016 period, which is much faster than the average for all other occupations. Employment growth in the insurance industry—the largest employer of actuaries—is expected to continue at a stable pace, while more significant job growth is likely in other industries, such as health care and consulting firms.

Projections data from the National Employment Matrix

Occupational Title	SOC Code	Employment, 2006	Projected employment, 2016	Change, 2006-2016 Number	Change, 2006-2016 Percent
Actuaries	15-2011	18,000	22,000	4,300	24

NOTE: Data in this table are rounded.

Steady demand by the insurance industry should ensure that actuarial jobs in this key industry will remain stable during the projection period. Although relatively few new jobs will be created, actuaries will continue to be needed to develop, price, and evaluate a variety of insurance products and calculate the costs of new risks. The demand for actuaries in life insurance has been growing rapidly as a result of the rise in popularity of annuities, a financial product offered primarily by life insurance companies. In addition, the risk of terrorism and natural disasters has created a large demand for actuaries in property insurance.

Some new employment opportunities for actuaries should also become available in the health-care field as health-care issues and Medicare reform continue to receive attention. Increased regulation of managed health-care companies and the desire to contain health-care costs will continue to provide job opportunities for actuaries, who will also be needed to evaluate the risks associated with new medical issues, such as genetic testing and the impact of new diseases. Others in this field are involved in drafting health-care legislation.

A significant proportion of new actuaries will find employment with consulting firms. Companies that may not find it cost effective to employ their own actuaries are increasingly hiring consulting actuaries to analyze various risks. Other areas with notable growth prospects are information services and accounting services. Also, because actuarial skills are increasingly seen as useful to other industries that deal with risk, such as the airline and the banking industries, additional job openings may be created in these industries.

Despite the increase in employment overall, there has been some decline in the demand for pension actuaries. This is due in large part to the decline of defined benefit plans, which required review by an actuary, in favor of investment based retirement funds, such as 401ks.

Job prospects. Opportunities for actuaries should be good, particularly for those who have passed at least one or two of the initial exams. In addition, a small number of jobs will open up each year to replace actuaries who leave the occupation to retire or transfer new jobs. Candidates with additional knowledge or experience, such as computer programming skills, will be particularly attractive to employers. Most jobs in this occupation are located in urban areas, but opportunities vary by geographic location.

Earnings

Median annual earnings of actuaries were $82,800 in May 2006. The middle 50 percent earned between $58,710 and $114,570. The lowest 10 percent had earnings of less than $46,470, while the top 10 percent earned more than $145,600.

According to the National Association of Colleges and Employers, annual starting salaries for graduates with a bachelor's degree in actuarial science averaged $53,754 in 2007.

Insurance companies and consulting firms give merit increases to actuaries as they gain experience and pass examinations. Some companies also offer cash bonuses for each professional designation achieved. A 2007 survey by Life Office Management Association, Inc. of the largest U.S. insurance and financial services companies indicated that the average base salary for an entry-level actuary was $53,111. Associate actuaries, who direct and provide leadership in the design, pricing, and implementation of insurance products, received an average salary of $109,167. Actuaries at the highest technical level without managerial responsibilities reportedly were paid an average of $125,946.

Related Occupations

Actuaries need a strong background in mathematics, statistics, and related fields. Other workers whose jobs involve such skills include accountants and auditors, budget analysts, economists, market and survey researchers, financial analysts and personal financial advisors, insurance underwriters, mathematicians, and statisticians.

Sources of Additional Information

Career information on actuaries specializing in pensions is available from

- American Society of Pension Actuaries, 4245 N. Fairfax Dr., Suite 750, Arlington, VA 22203. Internet: http://www.aspa.org

For information about actuarial careers in life and health insurance, employee benefits and pensions, and finance and investments, contact

- Society of Actuaries (SOA), 475 N. Martingale Rd., Suite 600, Schaumburg, IL 60173-2226. Internet: http://www.soa.org

For information about actuarial careers in property and casualty insurance, contact

- Casualty Actuarial Society (CAS), 4350 N. Fairfaix Dr., Suite 250 Arlington, VA 22203. Internet: http://www.casact.org
- The SOA and CAS jointly sponsor a Web site for those interested in pursuing an actuarial career. Internet: http://www.BeAnActuary.org

For general information on a career as an actuary, contact

- American Academy of Actuaries, 1100 17th St. NW, 7th Floor, Washington, DC 20036. Internet: http://www.actuary.org

STEM Agricultural and Food Scientists

(O*NET 19-1011.00, 19-1012.00, and 19-1013.00)

Significant Points

- About 14 percent of agricultural and food scientists work for federal, state, or local governments.
- A bachelor's degree in agricultural science is sufficient for some jobs in product development; a master's or Ph.D. degree is required for research or teaching.

- Opportunities for agricultural and food scientists are expected to be good over the next decade, particularly for those holding a master's or Ph.D. degree.

Nature of the Work

The work of agricultural and food scientists plays an important part in maintaining the nation's food supply by ensuring agricultural productivity and food safety. Agricultural scientists study farm crops and animals and develop ways of improving their quantity and quality. They look for ways to improve crop yield with less labor, control pests and weeds more safely and effectively, and conserve soil and water. They research methods of converting raw agricultural commodities into attractive and healthy food products for consumers. Some agricultural scientists look for ways to use agricultural products for fuels.

In the past two decades, rapid advances in the study of genetics have spurred the growth of biotechnology. Some agricultural and food scientists use biotechnology to manipulate the genetic material of plants and crops, attempting to make these organisms more productive or resistant to disease. Advances in biotechnology have opened up research opportunities in many areas of agricultural and food science, including commercial applications in agriculture, environmental remediation, and the food industry. Interest in the production of biofuels, or fuels manufactured from agricultural derivatives, has also increased. Some agricultural scientists work with biologists and chemists to develop processes for turning crops into energy sources, such as ethanol produced from corn.

Another emerging technology expected to affect agriculture is nanotechnology—a molecular manufacturing technology which promises to revolutionize methods of testing agricultural and food products for contamination or spoilage. Some food scientists are using nanotechnology to develop sensors that can quickly and accurately detect contaminant molecules in food.

Many agricultural scientists work in basic or applied research and development. Basic research seeks to understand the biological and chemical processes by which crops and livestock grow, such as determining the role of a particular gene in plant growth. Applied research uses this knowledge to discover mechanisms to improve the quality, quantity, or safety of agricultural products. Other agricultural scientists manage or administer research and development programs, or manage marketing or production operations in companies that produce food products or agricultural chemicals, supplies, and machinery. Some agricultural scientists are consultants to business firms, private clients, or government.

Depending on the agricultural or food scientist's area of specialization, the nature of the work performed varies.

Food scientists and technologists usually work in the food processing industry, universities, or the federal government to create and improve food products. They use their knowledge of chemistry, physics, engineering, microbiology, biotechnology, and other sciences to develop new or better ways of preserving, processing, packaging, storing, and delivering foods. Some food scientists engage in basic research, discovering new food sources; analyzing food content to determine levels of vitamins, fat, sugar, or protein; or searching for substitutes for harmful or undesirable additives, such as nitrites. Others engage in applied research, finding ways to improve the content of food or to remove harmful additives. They also develop ways to process, preserve, package, or store food according to industry and government regulations. Traditional food processing research into baking, blanching, canning, drying, evaporation, and pasteurization also continues. Other food scientists enforce government regulations, inspecting food processing areas and ensuring that sanitation, safety, quality, and waste management standards are met.

Food technologists generally work in product development, applying the findings from food science research to improve the selection, preservation, processing, packaging, and distribution of food.

Plant scientists study plants, helping producers of food, feed, and fiber crops to feed a growing population and conserve natural resources. *Agronomists* and *crop scientists* not only help increase productivity, but also study ways to improve the nutritional value of crops and the quality of seed, often through biotechnology. Some crop scientists study the breeding, physiology, and management of crops and use genetic engineering to develop crops resistant to pests and drought. Some plant scientists develop new technologies to control or eliminate pests and prevent their spread in ways appropriate to the specific environment. They also conduct research or oversee activities to halt the spread of insect-borne disease.

Soil scientists study the chemical, physical, biological, and mineralogical composition of soils as it relates to plant growth. They also study the responses of various soil types to fertilizers, tillage practices, and crop rotation. Many soil scientists who work for the federal government conduct soil surveys, classifying and mapping soils. They provide information and recommendations to farmers and other landowners regarding the best use of land and plants to avoid or correct problems, such as erosion. They may also consult with engineers and other technical personnel working on construction projects about the effects of, and solutions to, soil problems. Because soil science is closely related to environmental science, persons trained in soil science also work to ensure environmental quality and effective land use.

Animal scientists work to develop better, more efficient ways of producing and processing meat, poultry, eggs, and milk. Dairy scientists, poultry scientists, animal breeders, and other scientists in related fields study the genetics, nutrition, reproduction, and growth of domestic farm animals. Some animal scientists inspect and grade livestock food products, purchase livestock, or work in technical sales or marketing. As extension agents or consultants, animal scientists advise agricultural producers on how to upgrade animal housing facilities properly, lower mortality rates, handle waste matter, or increase production of animal products, such as milk or eggs.

Work environment. Agricultural scientists involved in management or basic research tend to work regular hours in offices and laboratories. The work environment for those engaged in applied research or product development varies, depending on specialty and on type of employer. For example, food scientists in private industry may work in test kitchens while investigating new processing techniques. Animal scientists working for federal, state, or university research stations may spend part of their time at dairies, farrowing houses, feedlots, farm animal facilities, or outdoors conducting research. Soil and crop scientists also spend time outdoors conducting research on farms and agricultural research stations.

Training, Other Qualifications, and Advancement

Most agricultural and food scientists need at least a master's degree to work in basic or applied research, whereas a bachelor's degree is sufficient for some jobs in applied research or product development, or jobs in other occupations related to agricultural science.

Education and training. Training requirements for agricultural scientists depend on the type of work they perform. A bachelor's degree in agricultural science is sufficient for some jobs in product development or assisting in applied research, but a master's or doctoral degree is generally required for basic research or for jobs directing applied research. A Ph.D. in agricultural science usually is needed for college teaching and for advancement to senior research positions. Degrees in related sciences such as biology, chemistry, or physics or in related engineering specialties also may qualify people for many agricultural science jobs.

All states have a land-grant college that offers agricultural science degrees. Many other colleges and universities also offer agricultural science degrees or agricultural science courses. However, not every school offers all specialties. A typical undergraduate agricultural science curriculum includes communications, mathematics, economics, business, and physical and life sciences courses, in addition to a wide variety of technical agricultural science courses. For prospective animal scientists, these technical agricultural science courses might include animal breeding, reproductive physiology, nutrition, and meats and muscle biology. Graduate students usually specialize in a subfield of agricultural science, such as animal breeding and genetics, crop science, or horticulture science, depending on their interests. For example, those interested in doing genetic and biotechnological research in the food industry need a strong background in life and physical sciences, such as cell and molecular biology, microbiology, and inorganic and organic chemistry. Undergraduate students, however, need not specialize. In fact, undergraduates who are broadly trained often have greater career flexibility.

Students preparing to be food scientists take courses such as food chemistry, food analysis, food microbiology, food engineering, and food processing operations. Those preparing as soil and plant scientists take courses in plant pathology, soil chemistry, entomology, plant physiology, and biochemistry, among others. Advanced degree programs include classroom and fieldwork, laboratory research, and a thesis or dissertation based on independent research.

Other qualifications. Agricultural and food scientists should be able to work independently or as part of a team and be able to communicate clearly and concisely, both orally and in writing. Most of these scientists also need an understanding of basic business principles, the ability to apply statistical techniques, and the ability to use computers to analyze data and to control biological and chemical processing.

Certification and advancement. Agricultural scientists who have advanced degrees usually begin in research or teaching. With experience, they may advance to jobs as supervisors of research programs or managers of other agriculture-related activities.

The American Society of Agronomy certifies agronomists and crop advisors, and the Soil Science Society of America certifies soil scientists and soil classifiers. To become certified in soil science or soil classification, applicants must have a bachelor's degree in soil science and five years of experience or a graduate degree and three years experience. Certification in agronomy requires a bachelor's degree in agronomy or a related field and five years experience or a graduate degree and three years. Crop advising certification requires either four years of experience or a bachelor's degree in agriculture and two years of experience. To receive any of these certifications, applicants must also pass designated examinations and agree to adhere to a code of ethics. Each certification is maintained through continuing education.

Employment

Agricultural and food scientists held about 33,000 jobs in 2006. In addition, many people trained in these sciences held faculty positions in colleges and universities. (See the statement on postsecondary teachers elsewhere in this book.)

About 14 percent of agricultural and food scientists work for federal, state, or local governments. State and local governments employed about 5 percent, while the federal government employed another 9 percent in 2006, mostly in the U.S. Department of Agriculture. Educational services accounted for another 18 percent of jobs. Other agricultural and food scientists worked for agricultural service companies, commercial research and development laboratories, seed companies, wholesale distributors, and food products companies. About 5,500 agricultural scientists were self-employed in 2006, mainly as consultants.

Job Outlook

Job growth among agricultural and food scientists should be about as fast as the average for all occupations. Opportunities are expected to be good over the next decade, particularly for those holding a master's or Ph.D. degree.

Employment change. Employment of agricultural and food scientists is expected to grow 9 percent between 2006 and 2016, about as fast as the average for all occupations. Past agricultural research has created higher yielding crops, crops with better resistance to pests and plant pathogens, and more effective fertilizers and pesticides. Research is still necessary, however, particularly as insects and diseases continue to adapt to pesticides and as soil fertility and water quality continue to need improvement. This creates more jobs for agricultural scientists.

Emerging biotechnologies will play an ever larger role in agricultural research. Scientists will be needed to apply these technologies to the creation of new food products and other advances. Moreover, increasing demand is expected for biofuels and other agricultural products used in industrial processes. Agricultural scientists will be needed to find ways to increase the output of crops used in these products.

Agricultural scientists will also be needed to balance increased agricultural output with protection and preservation of soil, water, and ecosystems. They increasingly encourage the practice of sustainable agriculture by developing and implementing plans to manage pests, crops, soil fertility and erosion, and animal waste in ways that reduce the use of harmful chemicals and do little damage to farms and the natural environment.

Job growth for food scientists and technologists will be driven by the demand for new food products and food safety measures. Food research is expected to increase because of heightened public awareness of diet, health, food safety, and biosecurity—preventing the introduction of infectious agents into herds of animals. Advances in biotechnology and nanotechnology should also spur demand, as

Projections data from the National Employment Matrix

Occupational Title	SOC Code	Employment, 2006	Projected employment, 2016	Change, 2006-2016	
				Number	Percent
Agricultural and food scientists	19-1010	33,000	36,000	3,100	9
Animal scientists	19-1011	5,400	5,900	500	10
Food scientists and technologists	19-1012	12,000	13,000	1,200	10
Soil and plant Scientists	19-1013	16,000	17,000	1,300	8

NOTE: Data in this table are rounded.

food scientists and technologists apply these technologies to testing and monitoring food safety.

Fewer new jobs for agricultural and food scientists are expected in the federal government, mostly because of budgetary constraints at the U.S. Department of Agriculture.

Job prospects. Opportunities should be good for agricultural and food scientists with a master's degree, particularly those seeking applied research positions in a laboratory. Master's degree candidates also can seek to become certified crop advisors, helping farmers better manage their crops. Those with a Ph.D. in agricultural and food science will experience the best opportunities, especially in basic research and teaching positions at colleges and universities.

Graduates with a bachelor's degree in agricultural or food science can sometimes work in applied research and product development positions under the guidance of a Ph.D. scientist, but usually only in certain subfields, such as food science and technology. The federal government also hires bachelor's degree holders to work as soil scientists.

Most people with bachelor's degrees find work in positions related to agricultural or food science rather than in jobs as agricultural or food scientists. A bachelor's degree in agricultural science is useful for managerial jobs in farm-related or ranch-related businesses, such as farm credit institutions or companies that manufacture or sell feed, fertilizer, seed, and farm equipment. In some cases, people with a bachelor's degree can provide consulting services or work in sales and marketing—promoting high-demand products such as organic foods. Bachelor's degrees also may help people become farmers, ranchers, and agricultural managers; agricultural inspectors; or purchasing agents for agricultural commodity or farm supply companies.

Employment of agricultural and food scientists is relatively stable during periods of economic recession. Layoffs are less likely among agricultural and food scientists than in some other occupations because food is a staple item and its demand fluctuates very little with economic activity.

Earnings

Median annual earnings of food scientists and technologists were $53,810 in May 2006. The middle 50 percent earned between $37,740 and $76,960. The lowest 10 percent earned less than $29,620, and the highest 10 percent earned more than $97,350. Median annual earnings of soil and plant scientists were $56,080 in May 2006. The middle 50 percent earned between $42,410 and $72,020. The lowest 10 percent earned less than $33,650, and the highest 10 percent earned more than $93,460. In May 2006, median annual earnings of animal scientists were $47,800.

The average federal salary in 2007 was $91,491 in animal science and $79,051 in agronomy.

According to the National Association of Colleges and Employers, beginning salary offers in 2007 for graduates with a bachelor's degree in animal sciences averaged $35,035 a year; plant sciences, $31,291 a year; and in other agricultural sciences, $37,908 a year.

Related Occupations

The work of agricultural scientists is closely related to that of other scientists, including biological scientists, chemists, and conservation scientists and foresters. It also is related to the work of managers of agricultural production, such as farmers, ranchers, and agricultural managers. Certain specialties of agricultural science also are related to other occupations. For example, the work of animal scientists is related to the work of veterinarians.

Sources of Additional Information

Information on careers in agricultural science is available from

- American Society of Agronomy, Crop Science Society of America, Soil Science Society of America, 677 S. Segoe Rd., Madison, WI 53711-1086. Internet: http://www.agronomy.org
- Living Science, Purdue University, 1140 Agricultural Administration Bldg., West Lafayette, IN 47907-1140. Internet: http://www.agriculture.purdue.edu/USDA/careers

Information on careers in food science and technology is available from

- Institute of Food Technologists, 525 W. Van Buren, Suite 1000, Chicago, IL 60607. Internet: http://www.ift.org

Information on getting a job as an agricultural scientist with the federal government is available from the Office of Personnel Management through USAJOBS, the federal government's official employment information system. This resource for locating and applying for job opportunities can be accessed through the Internet at http://www.usajobs.opm.gov or through an interactive voice response telephone system at (703) 724-1850 or TDD (978) 461-8404. These numbers are not toll free, and charges may result.

Aircraft and Avionics Equipment Mechanics and Service Technicians

(O*NET 49-2091.00 and 49-3011.00)

Significant Points

- Most workers learn their jobs in 1 of about 170 schools certified by the Federal Aviation Administration (FAA).
- Job opportunities should be favorable for persons who have completed an aircraft mechanic training program, but keen

competition is likely for jobs at major airlines, which offer the best pay and benefits.

- Job opportunities are likely to continue to be best at small commuter and regional airlines, at FAA repair stations, and in general aviation.

Nature of the Work

To keep aircraft in peak operating condition, aircraft and avionics equipment mechanics and service technicians perform scheduled maintenance, make repairs, and complete inspections required by the Federal Aviation Administration (FAA).

Many aircraft mechanics, also called airframe mechanics, power plant mechanics, and avionics technicians, specialize in preventive maintenance. They inspect aircraft engines, landing gear, instruments, pressurized sections, accessories—brakes, valves, pumps, and air-conditioning systems, for example—and other parts of the aircraft, and do the necessary maintenance and replacement of parts. They also keep records related to the maintenance performed on the aircraft. Mechanics and technicians conduct inspections following a schedule based on the number of hours the aircraft has flown, calendar days since the last inspection, cycles of operation, or a combination of these factors. In large, sophisticated planes equipped with aircraft monitoring systems, mechanics can gather valuable diagnostic information from electronic boxes and consoles that monitor the aircraft's basic operations. In planes of all sorts, aircraft mechanics examine engines by working through specially designed openings while standing on ladders or scaffolds or by using hoists or lifts to remove the entire engine from the craft. After taking an engine apart, mechanics use precision instruments to measure parts for wear and use x-ray and magnetic inspection equipment to check for invisible cracks. They repair or replace worn or defective parts. Mechanics also may repair sheet metal or composite surfaces; measure the tension of control cables; and check for corrosion, distortion, and cracks in the fuselage, wings, and tail. After completing all repairs, they must test the equipment to ensure that it works properly.

Other mechanics specialize in repair work rather than inspection. They find and fix problems that pilot's describe. For example, during a preflight check, a pilot may discover that the aircraft's fuel gauge does not work. To solve the problem, mechanics may troubleshoot the electrical system, using electrical test equipment to make sure that no wires are broken or shorted out, and replace any defective electrical or electronic components. Mechanics work as fast as safety permits so that the aircraft can be put back into service quickly.

Some mechanics work on one or many different types of aircraft, such as jets, propeller-driven airplanes, and helicopters. Others specialize in one section of a particular type of aircraft, such as the engine, hydraulics, or electrical system. *Airframe mechanics* are authorized to work on any part of the aircraft except the instruments, power plants, and propellers. *Powerplant mechanics* are authorized to work on engines and do limited work on propellers. *Combination airframe-and-powerplant mechanics*—called A&P mechanics—work on all parts of the plane except the instruments. Most mechanics working on civilian aircraft today are A&P mechanics. In small, independent repair shops, mechanics usually inspect and repair many different types of aircraft.

Avionics systems—components used for aircraft navigation and radio communications, weather radar systems, and other instruments and computers that control flight, engine, and other primary functions—are now an integral part of aircraft design and have vastly increased aircraft capability. *Avionics technicians* repair and maintain these systems. Their duties may require additional licenses, such as a radiotelephone license issued by the U.S. Federal Communications Commission (FCC). Because of the increasing use of technology, more time is spent repairing electronic systems, such as computerized controls. Technicians also may be required to analyze and develop solutions to complex electronic problems.

Work environment. Mechanics usually work in hangars or in other indoor areas. When hangars are full or when repairs must be made quickly, they may work outdoors, sometimes in unpleasant weather. Mechanics often work under time pressure to maintain flight schedules or, in general aviation, to keep from inconveniencing customers. At the same time, mechanics have a tremendous responsibility to maintain safety standards, and this can cause the job to be stressful.

Frequently, mechanics must lift or pull objects weighing more than 70 pounds. They often stand, lie, or kneel in awkward positions and occasionally must work in precarious positions, such as on scaffolds or ladders. Noise and vibration are common when engines are being tested, so ear protection is necessary.

Aircraft mechanics usually work 40 hours a week on 8-hour shifts around the clock. Overtime and weekend work is frequent.

Training, Other Qualifications, and Advancement

Most workers learn their jobs in one of about 170 trade schools certified by the FAA. Most mechanics who work on civilian aircraft are certified by the FAA as an "airframe mechanic" or a "powerplant mechanic."

Education and training. Although a few people become mechanics through on-the-job training, most learn their jobs in one of about the 170 schools certified by the FAA. About one-third of these schools award two-year and four-year degrees in avionics, aviation technology, or aviation maintenance management.

FAA standards established by law require that certified mechanic schools offer students a minimum of 1,900 class hours. Coursework in schools normally lasts from 18 to 24 months and provides training with the tools and equipment used on the job. Aircraft trade schools are placing more emphasis on technologies such as turbine engines, composite materials—including graphite, fiberglass, and boron—and aviation electronics, which are increasingly being used in the construction of new aircraft.

Courses in mathematics, physics, chemistry, electronics, computer science, and mechanical drawing are helpful because they demonstrate many of the principles involved in the operation of aircraft, and knowledge of these principles is often necessary to make repairs. Recent technological advances in aircraft maintenance require mechanics to have an especially strong background in electronics to get or keep jobs in this field.

Courses that develop writing skills also are important because mechanics are often required to submit reports. Mechanics must be able to read, write, and understand English.

A few mechanics are trained on the job by experienced mechanics. They must be supervised by certified mechanics until they have FAA certificates.

Licensure. The FAA requires at least 18 months of work experience for an airframe or powerplant certificate, although completion of a program at an FAA-certified mechanic school can be substituted for the work experience requirement. Mechanics and technicians also must pass an exam for certification and take at least 16 hours of training every 24 months to keep their certificate current. Many mechanics take training courses offered by manufacturers or employers, usually through outside contractors.

The FAA also offers a combined certificate that allows for certification as both an airframe and a powerplant mechanic, the A&P certificate. For a combined A&P certificate, mechanics must acquire at least 30 months of experience working with both engines and airframes, or experience combined with the completion of an FAA-certified mechanic school program. FAA regulations also require current work experience to keep the A&P certificate valid. Applicants must have at least 1,000 hours of work experience in the previous 24 months or take a refresher course. Most airlines require that mechanics have a high school diploma and an A&P certificate. Applicants for all certificates must pass written and oral tests and demonstrate that they can do the work authorized by the certificate.

Avionics technicians need an FAA mechanics' certificate. They also must be trained and qualified and have the proper tools to work on avionics equipment. Many have avionics repair experience from the military or from working for avionics manufacturers.

Other qualifications. Applicants must be at least 18 years of age. Some aircraft mechanics in the Armed Forces acquire enough general experience to satisfy the work experience requirements for the FAA certificate. With additional study, they may pass the certifying exam. In general, however, jobs in the military services are too specialized to provide the broad experience required by the FAA. Most Armed Forces mechanics have to complete the entire FAA training program, although a few receive some credit for the material they learned in the service. In any case, military experience is a great advantage when seeking employment; employers consider applicants with formal training to be the most desirable applicants.

Aircraft mechanics must do careful and thorough work that requires a high degree of mechanical aptitude. Employers seek applicants who are self-motivated, hard working, enthusiastic, and able to diagnose and solve complex mechanical problems. Additionally, employers prefer mechanics who can perform a variety of tasks. Agility is important for the reaching and climbing necessary to do the job. Because they may work on the tops of wings and fuselages on large jet planes, aircraft mechanics must not be afraid of heights.

Advances in computer technology, aircraft systems, and the materials used to manufacture airplanes have made mechanics' jobs more highly technical. Aircraft mechanics must possess the skills necessary to troubleshoot and diagnose complex aircraft systems. They also must continually update their skills with and knowledge of new technology and advances in aircraft technology.

Advancement. As aircraft mechanics gain experience, they may advance to lead mechanic (or crew chief), inspector, lead inspector, or shop supervisor positions. Opportunities are best for those who have an aircraft inspector's authorization. To obtain an inspector's authorization, a mechanic must have held an A&P certificate for at least three years, with 24 months of hands-on experience.

In the airlines, where promotion often is determined by examination, supervisors sometimes advance to executive positions. Those with broad experience in maintenance and overhaul might become inspectors with the FAA. With additional business and management training, some open their own aircraft maintenance facilities. Mechanics with the necessary pilot licenses and flying experience may take the FAA examination for the position of flight engineer, with opportunities to become pilots.

Mechanics and technicians learn many different skills in their training that can be applied to other jobs, and some transfer to other skilled repairer occupations or electronics technician jobs. For example, some avionics technicians continue their education and become aviation engineers, electrical engineers (specializing in circuit design and testing), or communication engineers. Others become repair consultants, in-house electronics designers, or join research groups that test and develop products.

Employment

Aircraft and avionics equipment mechanics and service technicians held about 138,000 jobs in 2006; about 5 in 6 of these workers was an aircraft mechanic and service technician.

Employment of aircraft and avionics equipment mechanics and service technicians primarily is concentrated in a small number of industries. More than half of aircraft and avionics equipment mechanics and service technicians worked in air transportation and support activities for air transportation. Around 18 percent worked in aerospace product and parts manufacturing and about 16 percent worked for the federal government. Most of the rest worked for companies that operate their own planes to transport executives and cargo.

Most airline mechanics and service technicians work at major airports near large cities. Civilian mechanics employed by the U.S. Armed Forces work at military installations. Mechanics who work for aerospace manufacturing firms typically are located in California or in Washington state. Others work for the FAA, many at the facilities in Oklahoma City, Atlantic City, Wichita, or Washington, DC. Mechanics for independent repair shops work at airports in every part of the country.

Job Outlook

Job growth for these mechanics and technicians is expected to be about as fast as the average for all occupations. Job opportunities should be favorable for people who have completed an aircraft mechanic training program, but keen competition is likely for jobs at major airlines.

Employment change. Employment is expected to increase by 10 percent during the 2006–2016 period, about as fast as the average for all occupations. Passenger traffic is expected to increase as the result of an expanding economy and a growing population, and the need for aircraft mechanics and service technicians will grow accordingly.

Job prospects. Most job openings for aircraft mechanics through the year 2016 will stem from the need to replace the many mechanics expected to retire over the next decade. In addition, some mechanics will leave to work in related fields, such as automobile repair, as their skills are largely transferable to other maintenance and repair occupations.

Also contributing to favorable future job opportunities for mechanics is the long-term trend toward fewer students entering technical schools to learn skilled maintenance and repair trades. Many of the students who have the ability and aptitude to work on planes are choosing to go to college, work in computer-related fields, or go into other repair and maintenance occupations with better working conditions. If this trend continues, the supply of trained aviation mechanics may not keep up with the needs of the air transportation industry.

Job opportunities will continue to be the best at small commuter and regional airlines, at FAA repair stations, and in general aviation. Commuter and regional airlines is the fastest growing segment of the air transportation industry, but wages in these airlines tend to be lower than those in the major airlines, so they attract fewer job applicants. Also, some jobs will become available as experienced mechanics leave for higher paying jobs with the major airlines or transfer to other occupations. At the same time, general aviation aircraft are becoming increasingly sophisticated, boosting the demand for qualified mechanics. Mechanics will face more competition for jobs with large airlines because the high wages and travel benefits that these jobs offer generally attract more qualified applicants than there are openings. Also, there is an increasing trend for large airlines to outsource aircraft and avionics equipment mechanic jobs overseas; however, most airline companies prefer that aircraft maintenance be performed in the U.S. because overseas contractors may not comply with more stringent U.S. safety regulations.

In spite of these factors, job opportunities with the airlines are expected to be better than they have been in the past. But, in general, prospects will be best for applicants with experience. Mechanics who keep abreast of technological advances in electronics, composite materials, and other areas will be in greatest demand. Also, mechanics who are mobile and willing to relocate to smaller rural areas will have better job opportunities. The number of job openings for aircraft mechanics in the federal government should decline as the Government increasingly contracts out service and repair functions to private repair companies.

Avionics technicians who do not have FAA certification, but who are prepared to master the intricacies of the aircraft while working with certified A&P mechanics, should have good opportunities. However, certified technicians who are trained to work with complex aircraft systems, performing some duties normally performed by certified A&P mechanics, should have the best job prospects. Additionally, technicians with licensing that enables them to work on the airplane, either removing or reinstalling equipment, are expected to be in especially high demand.

Earnings

Median hourly earnings of aircraft mechanics and service technicians were about $22.95 in May 2006. The middle 50 percent earned between $18.96 and $28.12. The lowest 10 percent earned less than $14.94, and the highest 10 percent earned more than $34.51. Median hourly earnings in the industries employing the largest numbers of aircraft mechanics and service technicians in May 2006 were

Scheduled air transportation $27.46
Nonscheduled air transportation 23.33
Federal government 23.19
Aerospace product and parts manufacturing 21.58
Support activities for air transportation 19.57

Median hourly earnings of avionics technicians were about $22.57 in May 2006. The middle 50 percent earned between $19.02 and $26.65. The lowest 10 percent earned less than $15.65, and the highest 10 percent earned more than $30.33.

Mechanics who work on jets for the major airlines generally earn more than those working on other aircraft. Those who graduate from an aviation maintenance technician school often earn higher starting salaries than individuals who receive training in the Armed Forces or on the job. Airline mechanics and their immediate families receive reduced-fare transportation on their own and most other airlines.

About 3 in 10 aircraft and avionics equipment mechanics and service technicians are members of unions or covered by union agreements. The principal unions are the International Association of Machinists and Aerospace Workers, and the Transport Workers Union of America. Some mechanics are represented by the International Brotherhood of Teamsters.

Related Occupations

Workers in some other occupations that involve similar mechanical and electrical work are electricians, electrical and electronics installers and repairers, and elevator installers and repairers.

Sources of Additional Information

Information about jobs with a particular airline can be obtained by writing to the personnel manager of the company.

For general information about aircraft and avionics equipment mechanics and service technicians, contact

- Professional Aviation Maintenance Association, 400 Commonwealth Dr., Warrendale, PA 15096. Internet: http://www.pama.org

For information on jobs in a particular area, contact employers at local airports or local offices of the state employment service.

Information on obtaining positions as aircraft and avionics equipment mechanics and service technicians with the federal government is available from the Office of Personnel Management through USAJOBS, the federal government's official employment information system. This resource for locating and applying for job opportunities can be accessed through the Internet at http://www.usajobs.opm.gov or through an interactive voice response telephone system at (703) 724-1850 or TDD (978) 461-8404. These numbers are not toll free, and charges may result.

Projections data from the National Employment Matrix

Occupational Title	SOC Code	Employment, 2006	Projected employment, 2016	Change, 2006-16	
				Number	Percent
Aircraft and avionics equipment mechanics and service technicians	—	138,000	152,000	14,000	10
Avionics technicians	49-2091	16,000	17,000	1,300	8
Aircraft mechanics and service technicians	49-3011	122,000	135,000	13,000	11

NOTE: Data in this table are rounded.

Aircraft Pilots and Flight Engineers

(O*NET 53-2011.00 and 53-2012.00)

Significant Points

- Regional and low-cost airlines offer the best opportunities; pilots attempting to get jobs at the major airlines will face strong competition.
- Pilots usually start with smaller commuter and regional airlines to acquire the experience needed to qualify for higher paying jobs with national or major airlines.
- Many pilots have learned to fly in the military, but growing numbers have college degrees with flight training from civilian flying schools that are certified by the Federal Aviation Administration (FAA).
- Earnings of airline pilots are among the highest in the nation.

Nature of the Work

Pilots are highly trained professionals who either fly airplanes or helicopters to carry out a wide variety of tasks. Most are *airline pilots, copilots*, and *flight engineers* who transport passengers and cargo. However, 1 out of 5 pilots is a commercial pilot involved in dusting crops, spreading seed for reforestation, testing aircraft, flying passengers and cargo to areas not served by regular airlines, directing firefighting efforts, tracking criminals, monitoring traffic, and rescuing and evacuating injured persons.

Before departure, pilots plan their flights carefully. They thoroughly check their aircraft to make sure that the engines, controls, instruments, and other systems are functioning properly. They also make sure that baggage or cargo has been loaded correctly. They confer with flight dispatchers and aviation weather forecasters to find out about weather conditions en route and at their destination. Based on this information, they choose a route, altitude, and speed that will provide the safest, most economical, and smoothest flight. When flying under instrument flight rules—procedures governing the operation of the aircraft when there is poor visibility—the pilot in command, or the company dispatcher, normally files an instrument flight plan with air traffic control so that the flight can be coordinated with other air traffic.

Takeoff and landing are the most difficult parts of the flight, and require close coordination between the two pilots. For example, as the plane accelerates for takeoff, the pilot who is flying the take off concentrates on the runway while the other pilot scans the instrument panel. To calculate the speed they must attain to become airborne, pilots consider the altitude of the airport, outside temperature, weight of the plane, and speed and direction of the wind. The moment the plane reaches takeoff speed, the nonflying pilot informs the flying pilot, who then pulls back on the controls to raise the nose of the plane. Captains and first officers usually alternate flying each leg from takeoff to landing.

Unless the weather is bad, the flight itself is relatively routine. Airplane pilots, with the assistance of autopilot and the flight management computer, steer the plane along their planned route and are monitored by the air traffic control stations they pass along the way. They regularly scan the instrument panel to check their fuel supply; the condition of their engines; and the air-conditioning, hydraulic, and other systems. Pilots may request a change in altitude or route if circumstances dictate. For example, if the ride is rougher than expected, pilots may ask air traffic control if pilots flying at other altitudes have reported better conditions; if so, they may request an altitude change. This procedure also may be used to find a stronger tailwind or a weaker headwind to save fuel and increase speed. In contrast, because helicopters are used for short trips at relatively low altitude, helicopter pilots must be constantly on the lookout for trees, bridges, power lines, transmission towers, and other dangerous obstacles as well as low-flying general aviation aircraft. Regardless of the type of aircraft, all pilots must monitor warning devices designed to help detect sudden shifts in wind conditions that can cause crashes.

Pilots must rely completely on their instruments when visibility is poor. On the basis of altimeter readings, they know how high above ground they are and whether they can fly safely over mountains and other obstacles. Special navigation radios give pilots precise information that, with the help of special charts, tells them their exact position. Other very sophisticated equipment provides directions to a point just above the end of a runway and enables pilots to land completely without an outside visual reference. Once on the ground, pilots must complete records on their flight and the aircraft maintenance status for their company and the FAA.

The number of nonflying duties that pilots have depends on the employment setting. Airline pilots have the services of large support staffs and, consequently, perform few nonflying duties. However, because of the large numbers of passengers, airline pilots may be called upon to coordinate handling of disgruntled or disruptive passengers. Also, under the Federal Flight Deck Officer program airline pilots who undergo rigorous training and screening are deputized as federal law enforcement officers and are issued firearms to protect the cockpit against intruders and hijackers. Pilots employed by other organizations, such as charter operators or businesses, have many other duties. They may load the aircraft, handle all passenger luggage to ensure a balanced load, and supervise refueling; other nonflying responsibilities include keeping records, scheduling flights, arranging for major maintenance, and performing minor aircraft maintenance and repairs.

Except on small aircraft, two pilots usually make up the cockpit crew. Generally, the most experienced pilot, the *captain*, is in command and supervises all other crew members. The pilot and the copilot, often called the first officer, share flying and other duties, such as communicating with air traffic controllers and monitoring the instruments. Some large aircraft have a third crewmember, the flight engineer, who assists the pilots by monitoring and operating many of the instruments and systems, making minor in-flight repairs, and watching for other aircraft. The flight engineer also assists the pilots with the company, air traffic control, and cabin crew communications. New technology can perform many flight tasks, however, and virtually all new aircraft now fly with only two pilots, who rely more heavily on computerized controls.

Some pilots are flight instructors. They teach their students in ground-school classes, in simulators, and in dual-controlled planes and helicopters. A few specially trained pilots are examiners or check pilots. They periodically fly with other pilots or pilot's license applicants to make sure that they are proficient.

Work environment. Most pilots spend a considerable amount of time away from home because the majority of flights involve overnight layovers. When pilots are away from home, the airlines provide hotel accommodations, transportation between the hotel and airport, and an allowance for meals and other expenses.

Airline pilots, especially those on international routes, often experience jet lag—fatigue caused by many hours of flying through different time zones. To guard against pilot fatigue, which could result in unsafe flying conditions, the FAA requires airlines to allow pilots at least 8 hours of uninterrupted rest in the 24 hours before finishing their flight duty.

Commercial pilots face other types of job hazards. The work of test pilots, who check the flight performance of new and experimental planes, may be dangerous. Pilots who are crop-dusters may be exposed to toxic chemicals and seldom have the benefit of a regular landing strip. Helicopter pilots involved in rescue and police work may be subject to personal injury.

Although flying does not involve much physical effort, the mental stress of being responsible for a safe flight, regardless of the weather, can be tiring. Pilots must be alert and quick to react if something goes wrong, particularly during takeoff and landing.

FAA regulations limit flying time of airline pilots of large aircraft to a maximum of 100 hours a month or 1,000 hours a year. Most airline pilots fly an average of 65 to 75 hours a month and work at least an additional 65 to 75 hours a month performing nonflying duties. Most pilots have variable work schedules, working several days on, then several days off. Airlines operate flights at all hours of the day and night, so work schedules often are irregular. Flight assignments are based on seniority; the sooner pilots are hired, the stronger their bidding power is for preferred assignments.

Commercial pilots also may have irregular schedules, flying 30 hours one month and 90 hours the next. Because these pilots frequently have many nonflying responsibilities, they have much less free time than do airline pilots. Except for corporate flight department pilots, most commercial pilots do not remain away from home overnight. But, they may work odd hours. However, if the company owns a fleet of planes, pilots may fly a regular schedule.

Flight instructors may have irregular and seasonal work schedules, depending on their students' available time and the weather. Instructors frequently work in the evening or on weekends.

Training, Other Qualifications, and Advancement

All pilots who are paid to transport passengers or cargo must have a commercial pilot's license with an instrument rating issued by the FAA. Helicopter pilots also must hold a commercial pilot's license with a helicopter rating.

Education and training. Although some small airlines hire high school graduates, most airlines require at least two years of college and prefer to hire college graduates. In fact, most entrants to this occupation have a college degree. Because the number of college-educated applicants continues to increase, many employers are making a college degree an educational requirement. For example, test pilots often are required to have an engineering degree.

Pilots also need flight experience to qualify for a license. Completing classes at a flight school approved by the FAA can reduce the amount of flight experience required for a pilot's license. In 2006, the FAA certified about 600 civilian flying schools, including some colleges and universities that offer degree credit for pilot training. Initial training for airline pilots typically includes a week of company indoctrination; three to six weeks of ground school and simulator training; and 25 hours of initial operating experience, including a check-ride with an FAA aviation safety inspector. Once trained, pilots are required to attend recurrent training and simulator checks once or twice a year throughout their career.

Licensure. To qualify for FAA licensure, applicants must be at least 18 years old and have at least 250 hours of flight experience.

The U.S. Armed Forces have always been an important source of experienced pilots because of the extensive flying time and experience on jet aircraft and helicopters. Those without Armed Forces training may become pilots by attending flight schools or by taking lessons from FAA-certified flight instructors. Applicants also must pass a strict physical examination to make sure that they are in good health and have 20/20 vision with or without glasses, good hearing, and no physical handicaps that could impair their performance. They must pass a written test that includes questions on the principles of safe flight, navigation techniques, and FAA regulations, and must demonstrate their flying ability to FAA or designated examiners.

To fly during periods of low visibility, pilots must be rated by the FAA to fly by instruments. Pilots may qualify for this rating by having the required hours of flight experience, including 40 hours of experience in flying by instruments; they also must pass a written examination on procedures and FAA regulations covering instrument flying and demonstrate to an examiner their ability to fly by instruments. Requirements for the instrument rating vary depending on the certification level of flight school.

Airline pilots must fulfill additional requirements. Captains must have an airline transport pilot's license. Applicants for this license must be at least 23 years old and have a minimum of 1,500 hours of flying experience, including night and instrument flying, and must pass FAA written and flight examinations. Usually, they also have one or more advanced ratings depending on the requirements of their particular job. Because pilots must be able to make quick decisions and accurate judgments under pressure, many airline companies reject applicants who do not pass required psychological and aptitude tests. All licenses are valid so long as a pilot can pass the periodic physical and eye examinations and tests of flying skills required by the FAA and company regulations.

Other qualifications. Depending on the type of aircraft, new airline pilots start as first officers or flight engineers. Although some airlines favor applicants who already have a flight engineer's license, they may provide flight engineer training for those who have only the commercial license. Many pilots begin with smaller regional or commuter airlines, where they obtain experience flying passengers on scheduled flights into busy airports in all weather conditions. These jobs often lead to higher paying jobs with bigger, national or major airlines.

Companies other than airlines usually require less flying experience. However, a commercial pilot's license is a minimum requirement, and employers prefer applicants who have experience in the type of craft they will be flying. New employees usually start as first officers, or fly less sophisticated equipment.

Advancement. Advancement for pilots usually is limited to other flying jobs. Many pilots start as flight instructors, building up their flying hours while they earn money teaching. As they become more experienced, these pilots occasionally fly charter planes or perhaps get jobs with small air transportation firms, such as air-taxi companies. Some advance to flying corporate planes. A small number get flight engineer jobs with the airlines.

In the airlines, advancement usually depends on seniority provisions of union contracts. After one to five years, flight engineers advance according to seniority to first officer and, after 5 to 15 years, to captain. Seniority also determines which pilots get the more desirable routes. In a nonairline job, a first officer may advance to captain and, in large companies, to chief pilot or director of aviation in charge of aircraft scheduling, maintenance, and flight procedures.

Employment

Civilian aircraft pilots and flight engineers held about 107,000 jobs in 2006. About 79,000 worked as airline pilots, copilots, and flight engineers. The rest were commercial pilots who worked as flight instructors at local airports or for large businesses that fly company cargo and executives in their own airplanes or helicopters. Some commercial pilots flew small planes for air-taxi companies, usually to or from lightly traveled airports not served by major airlines. Others worked for a variety of businesses, performing tasks such as dusting crops, inspecting pipelines, or conducting sightseeing trips.

Pilots are located across the country, but airline pilots usually are based near major metropolitan airports or airports operating as hubs for the major airlines.

Federal, state, and local governments employed pilots. A few pilots were self-employed.

Job Outlook

Regional airlines and low-cost carriers will present the best opportunities; pilots attempting to get jobs at the major airlines will face strong competition.

Employment change. Employment of aircraft pilots and flight engineers is projected to grow 13 percent from 2006 to 2016, about as fast as the average for all occupations. Population growth and an expanding economy are expected to boost the demand for air travel, contributing to job growth. New jobs will be created as airlines expand their capacity to meet this rising demand by increasing the number of planes in operation. However, employment growth will be limited by productivity improvements as airlines switch to larger planes and adopt the low-cost carrier model that emphasizes faster turnaround times for flights, keeping more pilots in the air rather than waiting on the ground. Also, fewer flight engineers will be needed as new planes requiring only two pilots replace older planes that require flight engineers.

Job prospects. Job opportunities are expected to continue to be better with the regional airlines and low-cost carriers, which are growing faster than the major airlines. Opportunities with air cargo carriers also should arise because of increasing security requirements for shipping freight on passenger airlines, growth in electronic commerce, and increased demand for global freight. Business, corporate, and on-demand air taxi travel also should provide some new jobs for pilots.

Pilots attempting to get jobs at the major airlines will face strong competition, as those firms tend to attract many more applicants than the number of job openings. Applicants also will have to compete with laid-off pilots for any available jobs. Pilots who have logged the greatest number of flying hours using sophisticated equipment typically have the best prospects. For this reason, military pilots often have an advantage over other applicants.

In the long run, demand for air travel is expected to grow along with the population and the economy. In the short run, however, employment opportunities of pilots generally are sensitive to cyclical swings in the economy. During recessions, when a decline in the demand for air travel forces airlines to curtail the number of flights, airlines may temporarily furlough some pilots.

Earnings

Earnings of aircraft pilots and flight engineers vary greatly depending whether they work as airline or commercial pilots. Earnings of airline pilots are among the highest in the nation, and depend on factors such as the type, size, and maximum speed of the plane and the number of hours and miles flown. For example, pilots who fly jet aircraft usually earn higher salaries than pilots who fly turboprops. Airline pilots and flight engineers may earn extra pay for night and international flights. In May 2006, median annual earnings of airline pilots, copilots, and flight engineers were $141,090.

Median annual earnings of commercial pilots were $57,480 in May 2006. The middle 50 percent earned between $40,780 and $83,760. The lowest 10 percent earned less than $28,450, and the highest 10 percent earned more than $115,220.

Airline pilots usually are eligible for life and health insurance plans. They also receive retirement benefits and, if they fail the FAA physical examination at some point in their careers, they get disability payments. In addition, pilots receive an expense allowance, or "per diem," for every hour they are away from home. Some airlines also provide allowances to pilots for purchasing and cleaning their uniforms. As an additional benefit, pilots and their immediate families usually are entitled to free or reduced-fare transportation on their own and other airlines.

More than half of all aircraft pilots are members of unions. Most of the pilots who fly for the major airlines are members of the Air Line Pilots Association, International, but those employed by one major airline are members of the Allied Pilots Association.

Related Occupations

Although they are not in the cockpit, air traffic controllers and airfield operations specialists also play an important role in making

Projections data from the National Employment Matrix

Occupational Title	SOC Code	Employment, 2006	Projected employment, 2016	Change, 2006-16 Number	Change, 2006-16 Percent
Aircraft pilots and flight engineers	53-2010	107,000	121,000	14,000	13
Airline pilots, copilots, and flight engineers	53-2011	79,000	90,000	10,000	13
Commercial pilots	53-2012	28,000	31,000	3,600	13

NOTE: Data in this table are rounded.

sure flights are safe and on schedule, and participate in many of the decisions that pilots must make.

Sources of Additional Information

For information about job opportunities, salaries, and qualifications, write to the personnel manager of the particular airline.

For information on airline pilots, contact

- Air Line Pilots Association, International, 1625 Massachusetts Ave. NW, Washington, DC 20036.
- Air Transport Association of America, Inc., 1301 Pennsylvania Ave. NW, Suite 1100, Washington, DC 20004.
- Federal Aviation Administration, 800 Independence Ave. SW, Washington, DC 20591. Internet: http://www.faa.gov

For information on helicopter pilots, contact

- Helicopter Association International, 1635 Prince St., Alexandria, VA 22314.

For information about job opportunities in companies other than airlines, consult the classified section of aviation trade magazines and apply to companies that operate aircraft at local airports.

STEM Architects, Except Landscape and Naval

(O*NET 17-1011.00)

Significant Points

- About 1 in 5 architects are self-employed—more than 2 times the proportion for all occupations.
- Licensing requirements include a professional degree in architecture, at least 3 years of practical work training, and passing all divisions of the Architect Registration Examination.
- Architecture graduates may face competition, especially for jobs in the most prestigious firms.

Nature of the Work

People need places in which to live, work, play, learn, worship, meet, govern, shop, and eat. These places may be private or public; indoors or out; rooms, buildings, or complexes, and architects design them. Architects are licensed professionals trained in the art and science of building design who develop the concepts for structures and turn those concepts into images and plans.

Architects create the overall aesthetic and look of buildings and other structures, but the design of a building involves far more than its appearance. Buildings also must be functional, safe, and economical and must suit the needs of the people who use them. Architects consider all these factors when they design buildings and other structures.

Architects may be involved in all phases of a construction project, from the initial discussion with the client through the entire construction process. Their duties require specific skills—designing, engineering, managing, supervising, and communicating with clients and builders. Architects spend a great deal of time explaining their ideas to clients, construction contractors, and others. Successful architects must be able to communicate their unique vision persuasively.

The architect and client discuss the objectives, requirements, and budget of a project. In some cases, architects provide various predesign services: conducting feasibility and environmental impact studies, selecting a site, preparing cost analysis and land-use studies, or specifying the requirements the design must meet. For example, they may determine space requirements by researching the numbers and types of potential users of a building. The architect then prepares drawings and a report presenting ideas for the client to review.

After discussing and agreeing on the initial proposal, architects develop final construction plans that show the building's appearance and details for its construction. Accompanying these plans are drawings of the structural system; air-conditioning, heating, and ventilating systems; electrical systems; communications systems; plumbing; and, possibly, site and landscape plans. The plans also specify the building materials and, in some cases, the interior furnishings. In developing designs, architects follow building codes, zoning laws, fire regulations, and other ordinances, such as those requiring easy access by people who are disabled. Computer-aided design and drafting (CADD) and Building Information Modeling (BIM) technology has replaced traditional paper and pencil as the most common method for creating design and construction drawings. Continual revision of plans on the basis of client needs and budget constraints is often necessary.

Architects may also assist clients in obtaining construction bids, selecting contractors, and negotiating construction contracts. As construction proceeds, they may visit building sites to make sure that contractors follow the design, adhere to the schedule, use the specified materials, and meet work quality standards. The job is not complete until all construction is finished, required tests are conducted, and construction costs are paid. Sometimes, architects also provide postconstruction services, such as facilities management. They advise on energy efficiency measures, evaluate how well the building design adapts to the needs of occupants, and make necessary improvements.

Often working with engineers, urban planners, interior designers, landscape architects, and other professionals, architects in fact spend a great deal of their time coordinating information from, and the work of, other professionals engaged in the same project.

They design a wide variety of buildings, such as office and apartment buildings, schools, churches, factories, hospitals, houses, and airport terminals. They also design complexes such as urban centers, college campuses, industrial parks, and entire communities.

Architects sometimes specialize in one phase of work. Some specialize in the design of one type of building—for example, hospitals, schools, or housing. Others focus on planning and predesign services or construction management and do minimal design work.

Work environment. Usually working in a comfortable environment, architects spend most of their time in offices consulting with clients, developing reports and drawings, and working with other architects and engineers. However, they often visit construction sites to review the progress of projects. Although most architects work approximately 40 hours per week, they often have to work nights and weekends to meet deadlines.

Training, Other Qualifications, and Advancement

There are three main steps in becoming an architect. First is the attainment of a professional degree in architecture. Second is work experience through an internship, and third is licensure through the passing of the Architect Registration Exam.

Education and training. In most states, the professional degree in architecture must be from one of the 114 schools of architecture that have degree programs accredited by the National Architectural Accrediting Board. However, state architectural registration boards set their own standards, so graduation from a non-accredited program may meet the educational requirement for licensing in a few states.

Three types of professional degrees in architecture are available: a five-year bachelor's degree, which is most common and is intended for students with no previous architectural training; a two-year master's degree for students with an undergraduate degree in architecture or a related area; and a three- or four-year master's degree for students with a degree in another discipline.

The choice of degree depends on preference and educational background. Prospective architecture students should consider the options before committing to a program. For example, although the five-year bachelor of architecture offers the fastest route to the professional degree, courses are specialized, and if the student does not complete the program, transferring to a program in another discipline may be difficult. A typical program includes courses in architectural history and theory, building design with an emphasis on CADD, structures, technology, construction methods, professional practice, math, physical sciences, and liberal arts. Central to most architectural programs is the design studio, where students apply the skills and concepts learned in the classroom, creating drawings and three-dimensional models of their designs.

Many schools of architecture also offer postprofessional degrees for those who already have a bachelor's or master's degree in architecture or other areas. Although graduate education beyond the professional degree is not required for practicing architects, it may be required for research, teaching, and certain specialties.

All state architectural registration boards require architecture graduates to complete a training period—usually at least three years—before they may sit for the licensing exam. Every state, with the exception of Arizona, has adopted the training standards established by the Intern Development Program, a branch of the American Institute of Architects and the National Council of Architectural Registration Boards (NCARB). These standards stipulate broad training under the supervision of a licensed architect. Most new graduates complete their training period by working as interns at architectural firms. Some states allow a portion of the training to occur in the offices of related professionals, such as engineers or general contractors. Architecture students who complete internships while still in school can count some of that time toward the three-year training period.

Interns in architectural firms may assist in the design of one part of a project, help prepare architectural documents or drawings, build models, or prepare construction drawings on CADD. Interns also may research building codes and materials or write specifications for building materials, installation criteria, the quality of finishes, and other, related details.

Licensure. All states and the District of Columbia require individuals to be licensed (registered) before they may call themselves architects and contract to provide architectural services. During the time between graduation and becoming licensed, architecture school graduates generally work in the field under the supervision of a licensed architect who takes legal responsibility for all work. Licensing requirements include a professional degree in architecture, a period of practical training or internship, and a passing score on all divisions of the Architect Registration Examination. The examination is broken into nine divisions consisting of either multiple choice or graphical questions. The eligibility period for completion of all divisions of the exam varies by state.

Most states also require some form of continuing education to maintain a license, and many others are expected to adopt mandatory continuing education. Requirements vary by state but usually involve the completion of a certain number of credits annually or biennially through workshops, formal university classes, conferences, self-study courses, or other sources.

Other qualifications. Architects must be able to communicate their ideas visually to their clients. Artistic and drawing ability is helpful, but not essential, to such communication. More important are a visual orientation and the ability to understand spatial relationships. Other important qualities for anyone interested in becoming an architect are creativity and the ability to work independently and as part of a team. Computer skills are also required for writing specifications, for two- and three-dimensional drafting using CADD programs, and for financial management.

Certification and advancement. A growing number of architects voluntarily seek certification by the National Council of Architectural Registration Boards. Certification is awarded after independent verification of the candidate's educational transcripts, employment record, and professional references. Certification can make it easier to become licensed across states. In fact, it is the primary requirement for reciprocity of licensing among state Boards that are NCARB members. In 2007, approximately one-third of all licensed architects had this certification.

After becoming licensed and gaining experience, architects take on increasingly responsible duties, eventually managing entire projects. In large firms, architects may advance to supervisory or managerial positions. Some architects become partners in established firms, while others set up their own practices. Some graduates with degrees in architecture also enter related fields, such as graphic, interior, or industrial design; urban planning; real estate development; civil engineering; and construction management.

Employment

Architects held about 132,000 jobs in 2006. Approximately 7 out of 10 jobs were in the architectural, engineering, and related services industry—mostly in architectural firms with fewer than five workers. A small number worked for residential and nonresidential building construction firms and for government agencies responsible for housing, community planning, or construction of government buildings, such as the U.S. Departments of Defense and Interior, and the General Services Administration. About 1 in 5 architects are self-employed.

Job Outlook

Employment of architects is expected to grow faster than the average for all occupations through 2016. Keen competition is expected for positions at the most prestigious firms, and opportunities will be best for those architects who are able to distinguish themselves with their creativity.

Projections data from the National Employment Matrix

Occupational Title	SOC Code	Employment, 2006	Projected employment, 2016	Change, 2006-2016	
				Number	Percent
Architects, except landscape and naval	17-1011	132,000	155,000	23,000	18

NOTE: Data in this table are rounded.

Employment change. Employment of architects is expected to grow by 18 percent between 2006 and 2016, which is faster than the average for all occupations. Employment of architects is strongly tied to the activity of the construction industry. Strong growth is expected to come from nonresidential construction as demand for commercial space increases. Residential construction, buoyed by low interest rates, is also expected to grow as more people become homeowners. If interest rates rise significantly, home building may fall off, but residential construction makes up only a small part of architects' work.

Current demographic trends also support an increase in demand for architects. As the population of Sunbelt states continues to grow, the people living there will need new places to live and work. As the population continues to live longer and baby-boomers begin to retire, there will be a need for more healthcare facilities, nursing homes, and retirement communities. In education, buildings at all levels are getting older and class sizes are getting larger. This will require many school districts and universities to build new facilities and renovate existing ones.

In recent years, some architecture firms have outsourced the drafting of construction documents and basic design for large-scale commercial and residential projects to architecture firms overseas. This trend is expected to continue and may have a negative impact on employment growth for lower level architects and interns who would normally gain experience by producing these drawings.

Job prospects. Besides employment growth, additional job openings will arise from the need to replace the many architects who are nearing retirement, and others who transfer to other occupations or stop working for other reasons. Internship opportunities for new architectural students are expected to be good over the next decade, but more students are graduating with architectural degrees and some competition for entry-level jobs can be anticipated. Competition will be especially keen for jobs at the most prestigious architectural firms as prospective architects try to build their reputation. Prospective architects who have had internships while in school will have an advantage in obtaining intern positions after graduation. Opportunities will be best for those architects that are able to distinguish themselves from others with their creativity.

Prospects will also be favorable for architects with knowledge of "green" design. Green design, also known as sustainable design, emphasizes energy efficiency, renewable resources such as energy and water, waste reduction, and environmentally friendly design, specifications, and materials. Rising energy costs and increased concern about the environment has led to many new buildings being built green.

Some types of construction are sensitive to cyclical changes in the economy. Architects seeking design projects for office and retail construction will face especially strong competition for jobs or clients during recessions, and layoffs may ensue in less successful firms. Those involved in the design of institutional buildings, such as schools, hospitals, nursing homes, and correctional facilities, will be less affected by fluctuations in the economy. Residential construction makes up a small portion of work for architects, so major changes in the housing market would not be as significant as fluctuations in the nonresidential market.

Despite good overall job opportunities some architects may not fare as well as others. The profession is geographically sensitive, and some parts of the nation may have fewer new building projects. Also, many firms specialize in specific buildings, such as hospitals or office towers, and demand for these buildings may vary by region. Architects may find it increasingly necessary to gain reciprocity in order to compete for the best jobs and projects in other states.

Earnings

Median annual earnings of wage-and-salary architects were $64,150 in May 2006. The middle 50 percent earned between $49,780 and $83,450. The lowest 10 percent earned less than $39,420, and the highest 10 percent earned more than $104,970. Those just starting their internships can expect to earn considerably less.

Earnings of partners in established architectural firms may fluctuate because of changing business conditions. Some architects may have difficulty establishing their own practices and may go through a period when their expenses are greater than their income, requiring substantial financial resources.

Many firms pay tuition and fees toward continuing education requirements for their employees.

Related Occupations

Architects design buildings and related structures. Construction managers, like architects, also plan and coordinate activities concerned with the construction and maintenance of buildings and facilities. Others who engage in similar work are landscape architects, civil engineers, urban and regional planners, and designers, including interior designers, commercial and industrial designers, and graphic designers.

Sources of Additional Information

Information about education and careers in architecture can be obtained from

- The American Institute of Architects, 1735 New York Ave. NW, Washington, DC 20006. Internet: http://www.aia.org
- Intern Development Program, National Council of Architectural Registration Boards, Suite 1100K, 1801 K St. NW, Washington, D.C. 20006. Internet: http://www.ncarb.org

Armed Forces

(O*NET 55-1011.00, 55-1012.00, 55-1013.00, 55-1014.00, 55-1015.00, 55-1016.00, 55-1017.00, 55-1019.99, 55-2011.00, 55-2012.00, 55-2013.00, 55-3011.00, 55-3012.00, 55-3013.00,

55-3014.00, 55-3015.00, 55-3016.00, 55-3017.00, 55-3018.00, and 55-3019.99)

Significant Points

- Some training and duty assignments are hazardous, even in peacetime; hours and working conditions can be arduous and vary substantially, and personnel must strictly conform to military rules at all times.
- Enlisted personnel need at least a high school diploma or its equivalent while officers need a bachelor's or graduate degree.
- Opportunities should be excellent in all branches of the Armed Forces for applicants who meet designated standards.
- Military personnel are eligible for retirement after 20 years of service.

Nature of the Work

Maintaining a strong national defense requires workers who can do such diverse tasks as run a hospital, command a tank, program a computer system, operate a nuclear reactor, or repair and maintain a helicopter. The military provides training and work experience in these and many other fields for more than 2.6 million people. More than 1.4 million people serve in the active Army, Navy, Marine Corps, and Air Force, and more than 1.2 million serve in their Reserve components and the Air and Army National Guard. The Coast Guard, which is also discussed in this statement, is part of the Department of Homeland Security.

The military distinguishes between enlisted and officer careers. Enlisted personnel, who make up about 84 percent of the Armed Forces, carry out the fundamental operations of the military in combat, administration, construction, engineering, health care, human services, and other areas. Officers, who make up the remaining 16 percent of the Armed Forces, are the leaders of the military, supervising and managing activities in every occupational specialty.

The sections that follow discuss the major occupational groups for enlisted personnel and officers.

Enlisted occupational groups. *Administrative careers* include a wide variety of positions. The military must keep accurate information for planning and managing its operations. Both paper and electronic records are kept on personnel and on equipment, funds, supplies, and all other aspects of the military. Administrative personnel record information, prepare reports, maintain files, and review information to assist military officers. Personnel may work in a specialized area such as finance, accounting, legal affairs, maintenance, supply, or transportation.

Combat specialty occupations include enlisted specialties such as infantry, artillery, and Special Forces, whose members operate weapons or execute special missions during combat. People in these occupations normally specialize by type of weapon system or combat operation. These personnel maneuver against enemy forces and position and fire artillery, guns, mortars, and missiles to destroy enemy positions. They also may operate tanks and amphibious assault vehicles in combat or scouting missions. When the military has especially difficult or specialized missions to perform, they call upon Special Forces teams. These elite combat forces maintain a constant state of readiness to strike anywhere in the world on a moment's notice. Team members from the Special Forces conduct offensive raids, demolitions, intelligence, search-and-rescue missions, and other operations from aboard aircraft, helicopters, ships, or submarines.

Construction occupations in the military include personnel who build or repair buildings, airfields, bridges, foundations, dams, bunkers, and the electrical and plumbing components of these structures. Personnel in construction occupations operate bulldozers, cranes, graders, and other heavy equipment. Construction specialists also may work with engineers and other building specialists as part of military construction teams. Some personnel specialize in areas such as plumbing or electrical wiring. Plumbers and pipefitters install and repair the plumbing and pipe systems needed in buildings and on aircraft and ships. Building electricians install and repair electrical-wiring systems in offices, airplane hangars, and other buildings on military bases.

Electronic and electrical equipment repair personnel repair and maintain electronic and electrical equipment used in the military. Repairers normally specialize by type of equipment, such as avionics, computer, optical, communications, or weapons systems. For example, electronic instrument repairers install, test, maintain, and repair a wide variety of electronic systems, including navigational controls and biomedical instruments. Weapons maintenance technicians maintain and repair weapons used by combat forces; most of these weapons have electronic components and systems that assist in locating targets and in aiming and firing the weapon.

Engineering, science, and technical personnel in the military require specific knowledge to operate technical equipment, solve complex problems, or provide and interpret information. Personnel normally specialize in one area, such as space operations, information technology, environmental health and safety, or intelligence. Space operations specialists use and repair ground-control command equipment related to spacecraft, including electronic systems that track the location and operation of a craft. Information technology specialists develop software programs and operate computer systems. Environmental health and safety specialists inspect military facilities and food supplies for the presence of disease, germs, or other conditions hazardous to health and the environment. Intelligence specialists gather and study aerial photographs and various types of radar and surveillance systems to discover information needed by the military.

Health care personnel assist medical professionals in treating and providing services for men and women in the military. They may work as part of a patient-service team in close contact with doctors, dentists, nurses, and physical therapists. Some specialize in emergency medical treatment, the operation of diagnostic tools such as x-ray and ultrasound equipment, laboratory testing of tissue and blood samples, maintaining pharmacy supplies or patients' records, constructing and repairing dental equipment or eyeglasses, or some other health care task.

Human resources development specialists recruit and place qualified personnel and provide training programs. Personnel in this career area normally specialize by activity. For example, recruiting specialists provide information about military careers to young people, parents, schools, and local communities and explain the Armed Service's employment and training opportunities, pay and benefits, and service life. Personnel specialists collect and store information about the people in the military, including information on their previous and current training, job assignments, promotions, and health. Training specialists and instructors teach classes, give demonstrations, and teach military personnel how to perform their jobs.

Machine operator and production personnel operate industrial equipment, machinery, and tools to fabricate and repair parts for a variety of items and structures. They may operate engines, turbines, nuclear reactors, and water pumps. Often, they specialize by type of work performed. Welders and metalworkers, for instance, work with various types of metals to repair or form the structural parts of ships, submarines, buildings, or other equipment. Survival equipment specialists inspect, maintain, and repair survival equipment such as parachutes and aircraft life support equipment.

Media and public affairs personnel assist with the public presentation and interpretation of military information and events. They take and develop photographs; film, record, and edit audio and video programs; present news and music programs; and produce artwork, drawings, and other visual displays. Other public affairs specialists act as interpreters and translators to convert written or spoken foreign languages into English or other languages.

Protective service personnel include those who enforce military laws and regulations and provide emergency response to natural and human-made disasters. For example, military police control traffic, prevent crime, and respond to emergencies. Other law enforcement and security specialists investigate crimes committed on military property and guard inmates in military correctional facilities. Firefighters put out, control, and help prevent fires in buildings, on aircraft, and aboard ships.

Support service personnel provide subsistence services and support the morale and well-being of military personnel and their families. Food service specialists prepare all types of food in dining halls, hospitals, and ships. Counselors help military personnel and their families deal with personal issues. They work as part of a team that may include social workers, psychologists, medical officers, chaplains, personnel specialists, and commanders. Religious program specialists assist chaplains with religious services, religious education programs, and related administrative duties.

Transportation and material handling specialists ensure the safe transport of people and cargo. Most personnel within this occupational group are classified according to mode of transportation, such as aircraft, motor vehicle, or ship. Aircrew members operate equipment on aircraft. Vehicle drivers operate all types of heavy military vehicles, including fuel or water tank trucks, semi-trailers, heavy troop transports, and passenger buses. Quartermasters and boat operators navigate and pilot many types of small watercraft, including tugboats, gunboats, and barges. Cargo specialists load and unload military supplies, using equipment such as forklifts and cranes.

Vehicle and machinery mechanics conduct preventive and corrective maintenance on aircraft, automotive and heavy equipment, heating and cooling systems, marine engines, and powerhouse station equipment. These workers typically specialize by the type of equipment that they maintain. For example, aircraft mechanics inspect, service, and repair helicopters, airplanes, and drones. Automotive and heavy equipment mechanics maintain and repair vehicles such as humvees, trucks, tanks, self-propelled missile launchers, and other combat vehicles. They also repair bulldozers, power shovels, and other construction equipment. Heating and cooling mechanics install and repair air-conditioning, refrigeration, and heating equipment. Marine engine mechanics repair and maintain gasoline and diesel engines on ships, boats, and other watercraft. They also repair shipboard mechanical and electrical equipment. Powerhouse mechanics install, maintain, and repair electrical and mechanical equipment in power-generating stations.

Officer occupational groups. *Combat specialty officers* plan and direct military operations, oversee combat activities, and serve as combat leaders. This category includes officers in charge of tanks and other armored assault vehicles, artillery systems, Special Forces, and infantry. Combat specialty officers normally specialize by the type of unit that they lead. Within the unit, they may specialize by type of weapon system. Artillery and missile system officers, for example, direct personnel as they target, launch, test, and maintain various types of missiles and artillery. Special operations officers lead their units in offensive raids, demolitions, intelligence gathering, and search-and-rescue missions.

Engineering, science, and technical officers have a wide range of responsibilities based on their area of expertise. They lead or perform activities in areas such as space operations, environmental health and safety, and engineering. These officers may direct the operations of communications centers or the development of complex computer systems. Environmental health and safety officers study the air, ground, and water to identify and analyze sources of pollution and its effects. They also direct programs to control safety and health hazards in the workplace. Other personnel work as aerospace engineers to design and direct the development of military aircraft, missiles, and spacecraft.

Executive, administrative, and managerial officers oversee and direct military activities in key functional areas such as finance, accounting, health administration, international relations, and supply. Health services administrators, for instance, are responsible for the overall quality of care provided at the hospitals and clinics they operate. They must ensure that each department works together. As another example, purchasing and contracting managers negotiate and monitor contracts for the purchase of the billions of dollars worth of equipment, supplies, and services that the military buys from private industry each year.

Health care officers provide health services at military facilities, on the basis of their area of specialization. Officers who examine, diagnose, and treat patients with illness, injury, or disease include physicians, registered nurses, and dentists. Other health care officers provide therapy, rehabilitative treatment, and additional services for patients. Physical and occupational therapists plan and administer therapy to help patients adjust to disabilities, regain independence, and return to work. Speech therapists evaluate and treat patients with hearing and speech problems. Dietitians manage food service facilities and plan meals for hospital patients and for outpatients who need special diets. Pharmacists manage the purchase, storage, and dispensing of drugs and medicines. Physicians and surgeons in this occupational group provide the majority of medical services to the military and their families. dentists treat diseases, disorders, and injuries of the mouth. Optometrists treat vision problems by prescribing eyeglasses or contact lenses. Psychologists provide mental health care and also conduct research on behavior and emotions.

Human resource development officers manage recruitment, placement, and training strategies and programs in the military.

Recruiting managers direct recruiting efforts and provide information about military careers to young people, parents, schools, and local communities. Personnel managers direct military personnel functions such as job assignment, staff promotion, and career counseling. Training and education directors identify training needs and develop and manage educational programs designed to keep military personnel current in the skills they need.

Media and public affairs officers oversee the development, production, and presentation of information or events for the public. These officers may produce and direct motion pictures, videos, and television and radio broadcasts that are used for training, news, and entertainment. Some plan, develop, and direct the activities of military bands. Public information officers respond to inquiries about military activities and prepare news releases and reports to keep the public informed.

Protective service officers are responsible for the safety and protection of individuals and property on military bases and vessels. Emergency management officers plan and prepare for all types of natural and human-made disasters. They develop warning, control, and evacuation plans to be used in the event of a disaster. Law enforcement and security officers enforce all applicable laws on military bases and investigate crimes when the law has been broken.

Support services officers manage food service activities and perform services in support of the morale and well-being of military personnel and their families. Food services managers oversee the preparation and delivery of food services within dining facilities located on military installations and vessels. Social workers focus on improving conditions that cause social problems such as drug and alcohol abuse, racism, and sexism. Chaplains conduct worship services for military personnel and perform other spiritual duties according to the beliefs and practices of all religious faiths.

Transportation officers manage and perform activities related to the safe transport of military personnel and material by air and water. These officers normally specialize by mode of transportation or area of expertise because, in many cases, they must meet licensing and certification requirements. Pilots in the military fly various types of specialized airplanes and helicopters to carry troops and equipment and to execute combat missions. Navigators use radar, radio, and other navigation equipment to determine their position and plan their route of travel. Officers on ships and submarines work as a team to manage the various departments aboard their vessels. Ship engineers direct engineering departments aboard ships and submarines, including engine operations, maintenance, repair, heating, and power generation.

Work environment. Most military personnel live and work on or near military bases and facilities throughout the United States and the world. These bases and facilities usually offer comfortable housing and amenities, such as stores and recreation centers. Service members move regularly to complete their training or to meet the needs of their branch of service. Some are deployed to defend national interests. Military personnel must be physically fit, mentally stable, and ready to participate in or support combat missions that maybe difficult and dangerous and involve time away from family. Some, however, are never deployed near combat areas. Specific work environments and conditions depend on branch of service, occupational specialty, and other factors.

In many circumstances, military personnel work standard hours, but personnel must be prepared to work long hours to fulfill missions, and they must conform to strict military rules at all times. Work hours depend on occupational specialty and mission.

Training, Other Qualifications, and Advancement

To join the military, people must meet age, educational, aptitude, physical, and character requirements. These requirements vary by branch of service and vary between officers, who usually have a college degree, and enlisted personnel, who often do not. People are assigned an occupational specialty based on their aptitude, former training, and the needs of the military. All service members must sign a contract and commit to a minimum term of service. After joining the military, all receive general and occupation-specific training.

People thinking about enlisting in the military should learn as much as they can about military life before making a decision. Doing so is especially important if you are thinking about making the military a career. Speaking to friends and relatives with military experience is a good idea. Find out what the military can offer you and what it will expect in return. Then, talk to a recruiter, who can determine whether you qualify for enlistment, explain the various enlistment options, and tell you which military occupational specialties currently have openings. Bear in mind that the recruiter's job is to recruit promising applicants into his or her branch of military service, so the information that the recruiter gives you is likely to stress the positive aspects of military life in the branch in which he or she serves.

Ask the recruiter for the branch you have chosen to assess your chances of being accepted for training in the occupation of your choice, or, better still, take the aptitude exam to see how well you score. The military uses this exam as a placement exam, and test scores largely determine an individual's chances of being accepted into a particular training program. Selection for a particular type of training depends on the needs of the service, your general and technical aptitudes, and your personal preference. Because all prospective recruits are required to take the exam, those who do so before committing themselves to enlist have the advantage of knowing in advance whether they stand a good chance of being accepted for training in a particular specialty. The recruiter can schedule you for the Armed Services Vocational Aptitude Battery without any obligation. Many high schools offer the exam as an easy way for students to explore the possibility of a military career, and the test also affords an insight into career areas in which the student has demonstrated aptitudes and interests. The exam is not part of the process of joining the military as an officer.

If you decide to join the military, the next step is to pass the physical examination and sign an enlistment contract. Negotiating the contract involves choosing, qualifying for, and agreeing on a number of enlistment options, such as the length of active-duty time, which may vary according to the option. Most active-duty programs have first-term enlistments of four years, although there are some two-year, three-year, and six-year programs. The contract also will state the date of enlistment and other options—for example, bonuses and the types of training to be received. If the service is unable to fulfill any of its obligations under the contract, such as providing a certain kind of training, the contract may become null and void.

All branches of the Armed Services offer a delayed entry program (DEP) by which an individual can delay entry into active duty for up to one year after enlisting. High school students can enlist during their senior year and enter a service after graduation. Others choose this program because the job training they desire is not currently available, but will be within the coming year, or because they need time to arrange their personal affairs.

The process of joining the military as an officer is different. Officers must meet educational, physical, and character requirements, but they do not take an aptitude test, for example. The education and training section that follows includes more information.

Education and training. All branches of the Armed Forces usually require their members to be high school graduates or have equivalent credentials, such as a GED. In 2006, more than 98 percent of recruits were high school graduates. Officers usually need a bachelor's or graduate degree. Training varies for enlisted and officer personnel and varies by occupational specialty.

Enlisted personnel training. Following enlistment, new members of the Armed Forces undergo initial-entry training, better known as "basic training" or "boot camp." Through courses in military skills and protocol recruit training provides a six- to 13-week introduction to military life. Days and nights are carefully structured and include rigorous physical exercise designed to improve strength and endurance and build each unit's cohesion.

Following basic training, most recruits take additional training at technical schools that prepare them for a particular military occupational specialty. The formal training period generally lasts from 10 to 20 weeks, although training for certain occupations—nuclear power plant operator, for example—may take as long as a year. Recruits not assigned to classroom instruction receive on-the-job training at their first duty assignment.

Many service people get college credit for the technical training they receive on duty, which, combined with off-duty courses, can lead to an associate degree through programs in community colleges such as the Community College of the Air Force. In addition to on-duty training, military personnel may choose from a variety of educational programs. Most military installations have tuition assistance programs for people wishing to take courses during off-duty hours. The courses may be correspondence courses or courses in degree programs offered by local colleges or universities. Tuition assistance pays up to 100 percent of college costs up to a credit-hour and annual limit. Each branch of the service provides opportunities for full-time study to a limited number of exceptional applicants. Military personnel accepted into these highly competitive programs receive full pay, allowances, tuition, and related fees. In return, they must agree to serve an additional amount of time in the service. Other highly selective programs enable enlisted personnel to qualify as commissioned officers through additional military training.

Warrant officer training. Warrant officers are technical and tactical leaders who specialize in a specific technical area; for example, Army aviators make up one group of warrant officers. The Army Warrant Officer Corps constitutes less than 5 percent of the total Army. Although the Corps is small in size, its level of responsibility is high. Its members receive extended career opportunities, worldwide leadership assignments, and increased pay and retirement benefits. Selection to attend the Warrant Officer Candidate School is highly competitive and restricted to those who meet rank and length-of-service requirements. The only exception is the Army aviator warrant officer, which has no prior military service requirements.

Officer training. Officer training in the Armed Forces is provided through the federal service academies (Military, Naval, Air Force, and Coast Guard); the Reserve Officers Training Corps (ROTC) program offered at many colleges and universities; Officer Candidate School (OCS) or Officer Training School (OTS); the National Guard (State Officer Candidate School programs); the Uniformed Services University of Health Sciences; and other programs. All are highly selective and are good options for those wishing to make the military a career. Some are directly appointed. People interested in obtaining training through the federal service academies must be unmarried and without dependants to enter and graduate, while those seeking training through OCS, OTS, or ROTC need not be single.

Federal service academies provide a four-year college program leading to a Bachelor of Science (B.S.) degree. Midshipmen or cadets are provided free room and board, tuition, medical and dental care, and a monthly allowance. Graduates receive regular or reserve commissions and have a five-year active-duty obligation or more if they are entering flight training.

To become a candidate for appointment as a cadet or midshipman in one of the service academies, applicants are required to obtain a nomination from an authorized source, usually a member of Congress. Candidates do not need to know a member of Congress personally to request a nomination. Nominees must have an academic record of the requisite quality, college aptitude test scores above an established minimum, and recommendations from teachers or school officials; they also must pass a medical examination. Appointments are made from the list of eligible nominees. Appointments to the Coast Guard Academy, however, are based strictly on merit and do not require a nomination.

ROTC programs train students in 273 Army, 130 Navy and Marine Corps, and 144 Air Force units at participating colleges and universities. Trainees take three to five hours of military instruction a week, in addition to regular college courses. After graduation, they may serve as officers on active duty for a stipulated period. Some may serve their obligation in the Reserves or National Guard. In the last two years of an ROTC program, students typically receive a monthly allowance while attending school, as well as additional pay for summer training. ROTC scholarships for two, three, and four years are available on a competitive basis. All scholarships pay for tuition and have allowances for textbooks, supplies, and other costs.

College graduates can earn a commission in the Armed Forces through OCS or OTS programs in the Army, Navy, Air Force, Marine Corps, Coast Guard, and National Guard. These programs consist of several weeks of intensive academic, physical, and leadership training. These officers generally must serve their obligation on active duty.

Those with training in certain health professions may qualify for direct appointment as officers. In the case of people studying for the health professions, financial assistance and internship opportunities are available from the military in return for specified periods of military service. Prospective medical students can apply to the Uniformed Services University of Health Sciences, which offers a salary and free tuition in a program leading to a Doctor of Medicine (M.D.) degree. In return, graduates must serve for seven years in either the military or the Public Health Service. Direct appointments also are available for those qualified to serve in other specialty areas, such as the judge advocate general (legal) or chaplain corps. Flight training is available to commissioned officers in each branch of the

Armed Forces. In addition, the Army has a direct enlistment option to become a warrant officer aviator.

Other qualifications. In order to join the services, enlisted personnel must sign a legal agreement called an enlistment contract, which usually involves a commitment of up to eight years of service. Depending on the terms of the contract, two to six years are spent on active duty, and the balance is spent in the National Guard or Reserves. The enlistment contract obligates the service to provide the agreed-upon job, rating, pay, cash bonuses for enlistment in certain occupations, medical and other benefits, occupational training, and continuing education. In return, enlisted personnel must serve satisfactorily for the period specified.

Requirements for each service vary, but certain qualifications for enlistment are common to all branches. In order to enlist, usually one must be at least 17 years old, be a U.S. citizen or an alien holding permanent resident status, not have a felony record, and possess a birth certificate. Applicants who are 17 years old must have the consent of a parent or legal guardian before entering the service. For active service in the Army, the maximum age is 42; for the Navy and Air Force the maximum age is 35. Coast Guard enlisted personnel must enter active duty before their 28th birthday, whereas Marine Corps enlisted personnel must not be over the age of 29 when entering. Applicants must pass a written examination—the Armed Services Vocational Aptitude Battery—and meet certain minimum physical standards, such as height, weight, vision, and overall health. Officers must meet different age and physical standards depending on their branch of service.

Women are eligible to enter most military specialties; for example, they may become mechanics, missile maintenance technicians, heavy equipment operators, and fighter pilots, or they may enter into medical care, administrative support, and intelligence specialties. Generally, only occupations involving direct exposure to combat are excluded.

Advancement. Each service has different criteria for promoting personnel. Generally, the first few promotions for both enlisted and officer personnel come easily; subsequent promotions are much more competitive. Criteria for promotion may include time in service and in grade, job performance, a fitness report (supervisor's recommendation), and passing scores on written examinations. Table 1 shows the officer, warrant officer, and enlisted ranks by service.

People planning to apply the skills gained through military training to a civilian career should first determine how good the prospects are for civilian employment in jobs related to the military specialty that interests them. Second, they should know the prerequisites for the related civilian job. Because many civilian occupations require a license, certification, or minimum level of education, it is important to determine whether military training is sufficient for a person to enter the civilian equivalent occupation or, if not, what additional training will be required. Occupational descriptions in this book discuss the job outlook, training requirements, and other aspects of civilian occupations for which military training and experience are helpful. Additional information often can be obtained from school counselors.

Table 1. Military rank and employment for active duty personnel, January 2007

Grade	Rank and title **Army**	**Navy**	**Air Force**	**Marine Corps**	**Total Employment**
Commissioned officers:					
O-10	General	Admiral	General	General	40
O-9	Lieutenant General	Vice Admiral	Lieutenant General	Lieutenant General	136
O-8	Major General	Rear Admiral (U)	Major General	Major General	285
O-7	Brigadier General	Rear Admiral (L)	Brigadier General	Brigadier General	449
O-6	Colonel	Captain	Colonel	Colonel	11,345
O-5	Lieutenant Colonel	Commander	Lieutenant Colonel	Lieutenant Colonel	28,566
O-4	Major	Lieutenant Commander	Major	Major	44,908
O-3	Captain	Lieutenant	Captain	Captain	70,131
O-2	1st Lieutenant	Lieutenant (JG)	1st Lieutenant	1st Lieutenant	26,894
O-1	2nd Lieutenant	Ensign	2nd Lieutenant	2nd Lieutenant	23,331
Warrant officers:					
W-5	Chief Warrant Officer	Chief Warrant Officer	—	Chief Warrant Officer	591
W-4	Chief Warrant Officer	Chief Warrant Officer	—	Chief Warrant Officer	2,661
W-3	Chief Warrant Officer	Chief Warrant Officer	—	Chief Warrant Officer	4,676
W-2	Chief Warrant Officer	Chief Warrant Officer	—	Chief Warrant Officer	5,627
W-1	Warrant Officer	Warrant Officer	—	Warrant Officer	3,084
Enlisted personnel:					
E-9	Sergeant Major	Master Chief Petty Officer	Chief Master Sergeant	Sergeant Major/ Master Gunnery Sergeant	10,596
E-8	1st Sergeant/Master Sergeant	Senior Chief Petty Officer	Senior Master Sergeant	1st Sergeant/Master Sergeant	26,987
E-7	Sergeant First Class	Chief Petty Officer	Master Sergeant	Gunnery Sergeant	98,497
E-6	Staff Sergeant	Petty Officer 1st Class	Technical Sergeant	Staff Sergeant	169,725
E-5	Sergeant	Petty Officer 2nd Class	Staff Sergeant	Sergeant	248,226
E-4	Corporal	Petty Officer 3rd Class	Senior Airman	Corporal	257,974
E-3	Private First Class	Seaman	Airman 1st Class	Lance Corporal	186,830
E-2	Private	Seaman Apprentice	Airman	Private 1st Class	83,987
E-1	Private	Seaman Recruit	Airman Basic	Private	57,644

Source: U.S. Department of Defense, Defense Manpower Data Center

Table 2. Military enlisted personnel by broad occupational category and branch of military service, January 2007

Occupational Group - Enlisted	Army	Air Force	Coast Guard	Marine Corps	Navy	Total, all services
Administrative occupations	8,912	23,366	1,683	9,460	22,512	65,933
Combat specialty occupations	120,297	427	856	47,250	5,508	174,338
Construction occupations	16,848	4,979	—	5,597	5,927	33,351
Electronic and electrical repair occupations	35,932	37,722	4,351	14,656	51,424	144,085
Engineering, science, and technical occupations	36,451	46,304	1,110	22,915	38,853	145,633
Health care occupations	29,242	16,805	821	—	24,950	71,818
Human resource development occupations	16,464	12,741	1	6,113	6,756	42,075
Machine operator and precision work occupations	5,727	7,134	1,583	2,301	7,913	24,658
Media and public affairs occupations	6,541	7,574	136	2,340	4,726	21,317
Protective service occupations	25,455	31,483	3,050	5,872	13,122	78,982
Support services occupations	12,014	1,608	1,268	2,289	9,930	27,109
Transportation and material handling occupations	58,237	32,464	11,479	22,344	43,026	167,550
Vehicle machinery mechanic occupations	49,679	44,025	5,821	19,340	49,166	168,031
Total, by service (1)	421,855	271,009	32,477	160,484	287,118	1,172,913

Note: Occupational employment does not sum to totals because occupational information is not available for all personnel. Source: U.S. Department of Defense, Defense Manpower Data Center.

Employment

In 2007, more than 2.6 million people served in the Armed Forces. More than 1.4 million were on active duty—about 505,000 in the Army, 339,000 in the Navy, 340,000 in the Air Force, and 179,000 in the Marine Corps. In addition, more than 1.2 million people served in their Reserve components and the Air and Army National Guard, and 40,000 individuals served in the Coast Guard, which is now part of the Department of Homeland Security. Table 2 shows the occupational composition of the active-duty enlisted personnel in January 2007; table 3 presents similar information for active-duty officers, including noncommissioned warrant officers.

Military personnel are stationed throughout the United States and in many countries around the world. About half of all military jobs in the U.S. are located in California, Texas, North Carolina, Virginia, Florida, and Georgia. Approximately 250,000 service members were deployed in support of Operations Enduring Freedom and Iraqi Freedom as of April 30, 2007. An additional 363,000 individuals were stationed outside the United States, including 168,000 assigned to ships at sea. About 105,000 were stationed in Europe, mainly in Germany, and another 70,000 were assigned to East Asia and the Pacific area, mostly in Japan and the Republic of Korea.

Job Outlook

Opportunities should be excellent for qualified individuals in all branches of the Armed Forces through 2016.

Employment change. The United States spends a significant portion of its overall budget on national defense. Despite reductions in personnel due to the elimination of the threats of the Cold War, the number of active-duty personnel is expected to remain roughly constant through 2016. However, recent conflicts and the resulting strain on the military may lead to an increase in the number of active-duty personnel. The current goal of the Armed Forces is to maintain a force sufficient to fight and win two major regional conflicts at the same time. Political events, however, could lead to a significant restructuring with or without an increase in size.

Job prospects. Opportunities should be excellent for qualified individuals in all branches of the Armed Forces through 2016. Many military personnel retire with a pension after 20 years of service, while they still are young enough to start a new career. About 168,000 personnel must be recruited each year to replace those who complete their commitment or retire. Since the end of the draft in 1973, the military has met its personnel requirements with volunteers. When the economy is good and civilian employment opportunities generally are more favorable, it is more difficult for all the

Table 3. Military officer personnel by broad occupational category and branch of service, January 2007

Occupational Group - Officer	Army	Air Force	Coast Guard	Marine Corps	Navy	Total, all services
Combat specialty occupations	19,421	2,861	81	4,684	1,260	28,307
Engineering, science, and technical occupations	20,189	19,852	1,057	3,639	7,873	52,610
Executive, administrative, and managerial occupations	11,262	9,013	231	2,572	5,437	28,515
Health care occupations	9,953	8,970	5	—	7,737	26,665
Human resource development occupations	2,151	2,275	184	293	643	5,546
Media and public affairs occupations	237	408	19	170	265	1,099
Protective service occupations	2,611	1,229	96	327	275	4,538
Support services occupations	1,596	768	—	38	884	3,286
Transportation occupations	13,112	23,540	1,736	7,188	27,049	72,625
Total, by service (1)	82,884	69,284	7,853	18,998	51,558	230,577

Note: Occupational employment does not sum to totals because occupational information is not available for all personnel. Source: U.S. Department of Defense, Defense Manpower Data Center.

services to meet their recruitment quotas. It is also more difficult to meet these goals during times of war, when recruitment goals typically rise.

Educational requirements will continue to rise as military jobs become more technical and complex. High school graduates and applicants with a college background will be sought to fill the ranks of enlisted personnel, while virtually all officers will need at least a bachelor's degree and, in some cases, a graduate degree as well.

Earnings

The earnings structure for military personnel is shown in table 4. Most enlisted personnel started as recruits at Grade E-1 in 2007; however, those with special skills or above-average education started as high as Grade E-4. Most warrant officers had started at Grade W-1 or W-2, depending upon their occupational and academic qualifications and the branch of service of which they were a member, but warrant officer typically is not an entry-level occupation and, consequently, most of these individuals had previous military service. Most commissioned officers started at Grade O-1; some with advanced education started at Grade O-2, and some highly trained officers—for example, physicians and dentists—started as high as Grade O-3. Pay varies by total years of service as well as rank. Because it usually takes many years to reach the higher ranks, most personnel in higher ranks receive the higher pay rates awarded to those with many years of service.

In addition to receiving their basic pay, military personnel are provided with free room and board (or a tax-free housing and subsistence allowance), free medical and dental care, a military clothing allowance, military supermarket and department store shopping privileges, 30 days of paid vacation a year (referred to as leave), and travel opportunities. In many duty stations, military personnel may receive a housing allowance that can be used for off-base housing. This allowance can be substantial, but varies greatly by rank and duty station. For example, in fiscal year 2007, the average housing allowance for an E-4 with dependents was $1,151.24 per month; for a comparable individual without dependents, it was $910.66. The allowance for an O-4 with dependents was $1,856.97 per month; for a comparable individual without dependents, it was $1,611.69. Other allowances are paid for foreign duty, hazardous duty, submarine and flight duty, and employment as a medical officer. Athletic and other facilities—such as gymnasiums, tennis courts, golf courses, bowling centers, libraries, and movie theaters—are available on many military installations. Military personnel are eligible for retirement benefits after 20 years of service.

The Veterans Administration (VA) provides numerous benefits to those who have served at least 24 months of continuous active duty in the Armed Forces. Veterans are eligible for free care in VA hospitals for all service-related disabilities, regardless of time served; those with other medical problems are eligible for free VA care if they are unable to pay the cost of hospitalization elsewhere. Admission to a VA medical center depends on the availability of beds, however. Veterans also are eligible for certain loans, including loans to purchase a home. Veterans, regardless of health, can convert a military life insurance policy to an individual policy with any participating company upon separation from the military. In addition, job counseling, testing, and placement services are available.

Veterans who participate in the Montgomery GI Bill Program receive education benefits. Under this program, Armed Forces personnel may elect to deduct up to $100 a month from their pay during the first 12 months of active duty, putting the money toward their future education. In fiscal year 2007, veterans who served on active

Table 4. Military basic monthly pay by grade for active duty personnel, April 2007

	Years of service					
Grade	Less than 2	Over 4	Over 8	Over 12	Over 16	Over 20
O-10	—	—	—	—	—	$13,659.00
O-9	—	—	—	—	—	11,946.60
O-8	$8,453.10	$8,964.90	$9,577.20	$10,030.20	$10,447.80	11,319.00
O-7	7,023.90	7,621.20	8,052.90	8,548.80	9,577.20	10,236.00
O-6	5,206.20	6,094.50	6,380.10	6,414.60	7,423.80	8,180.10
O-5	4,339.80	5,291.10	5,628.60	6,110.10	6,776.40	7,158.00
O-4	3,744.60	4,688.40	5,244.60	5,882.40	6,187.50	6,252.30
O-3	3,292.20	4,392.00	4,833.00	5,228.40	5,355.90	5,355.90
O-2	2,844.30	3,857.40	3,936.60	3,936.60	3,936.60	3,936.60
O-1	2,469.30	3,106.50	3,106.50	3,106.50	3,106.50	3,106.50
W-5	—	—	—	—	—	5,845.80
W-4	3,402.00	3,868.50	4,222.20	4,574.10	5,035.50	5,392.20
W-3	3,106.80	3,412.80	3,711.30	4,129.20	4,515.60	4,751.40
W-2	2,732.70	3,124.50	3,443.70	3,755.10	3,973.80	4,191.00
W-1	2,413.20	2,828.40	3,193.50	3,451.20	3,622.80	3,856.20
E-9	—	—	—	4,203.90	4,459.50	4.821.60
E-8	—	—	3,364.80	3,606.00	3,835.80	4,161.30
E-7	2,339.10	2,780.70	3,055.20	3,250.20	3,511.20	3,644.10
E-6	2,023.20	2,419.80	2,744.10	2,928.30	3,043.50	3,064.50
E-5	1,854.00	2,171.40	2,454.90	2,582.10	2,582.10	2,582.10
E-4	1,699.50	1,978.50	2,062.80	2,062.80	2,062.80	2,062.80
E-3	1,534.20	1,729.20	1,729.20	1,729.20	1,729.20	1,729.20
E-2	1,458.90	1,458.90	1,458.90	1,458.90	1,458.90	1,458.90
E-1 4 months or more	1,301.40	1,301.40	1,301.40	1,301.40	1,301.40	1,301.40
E-1 Less than 4 months	1,203.90	—	—	—	—	—

Source: U.S. Department of Defense, Defense Finance and Accounting Service.

duty for 3 or more years or who spent 2 years in active duty plus 4 years in the Selected Reserve received $1,075 a month in basic benefits for 36 months of full-time institutional training. Those who enlisted and serve less than 3 years received $873 a month for 36 months for the same. In addition, each service provides its own contributions to the enlistee's future education. The sum of the amounts from all these sources becomes the service member's educational fund. Upon separation from active duty, the fund can be used to finance educational costs at any VA-approved institution. Among those institutions which are approved by the VA are many vocational, correspondence, certification, business, technical, and flight training schools; community and junior colleges; and colleges and universities.

Sources of Additional Information

Each of the military services publishes handbooks, fact sheets, and pamphlets describing entrance requirements, training and advancement opportunities, and other aspects of military careers. These publications are widely available at all recruiting stations, at most state employment service offices, and in high schools, colleges, and public libraries. Information on educational and other veterans' benefits is available from VA offices located throughout the country.

In addition, the Defense Manpower Data Center, an agency of the Department of Defense, publishes *Military Career Guide Online*, a compendium of military occupational, training, and career information designed for use by students and jobseekers. This information is available on the Internet: http://www.todaysmilitary.com.

The *Occupational Outlook Quarterly* also provides information about military careers and training in its spring 2007 article "Military training for civilian careers (Or: How to gain practical experience while serving your country)," available online at http://www.bls.gov/opub/ooq/2007/spring/art02.pdf.

STEM Atmospheric Scientists

(O*NET 19-2021.00)

Significant Points

- About 37 percent of atmospheric scientists are employed by the federal government; most of these work in the National Weather Service.
- A bachelor's degree in meteorology, or in a closely related field with courses in meteorology, is the minimum educational requirement; a master's degree is necessary for some positions, and a Ph.D. degree is required for most basic research positions.
- Atmospheric scientists should have favorable job prospects, but opportunities as weather broadcasters are rare and highly competitive.

Nature of the Work

Atmospheric science is the study of the atmosphere—the blanket of air covering the Earth. Atmospheric scientists, commonly called *meteorologists*, study the atmosphere's physical characteristics, motions, and processes, and the way in which these factors affect the rest of our environment. The best known application of this knowledge is forecasting the weather. In addition to predicting the weather, atmospheric scientists attempt to identify and interpret climate trends, understand past weather, and analyze today's weather. Weather information and meteorological research are also applied in air-pollution control, agriculture, forestry, air and sea transportation, defense, and the study of possible trends in the Earth's climate, such as global warming, droughts, and ozone depletion.

Atmospheric scientists who forecast the weather are known as *operational meteorologists*; they are the largest group of specialists. These scientists study the Earth's air pressure, temperature, humidity, and wind velocity, and they apply physical and mathematical relationships to make short-range and long-range weather forecasts. Their data come from weather satellites, radars, sensors, and stations in many parts of the world. Meteorologists use sophisticated computer models of the world's atmosphere to make long-term, short-term, and local-area forecasts. More accurate instruments for measuring and observing weather conditions, as well as high-speed computers to process and analyze weather data, have revolutionized weather forecasting. Using satellite data, climate theory, and sophisticated computer models of the world's atmosphere, meteorologists can more effectively interpret the results of these models to make local-area weather predictions. These forecasts inform not only the general public, but also those who need accurate weather information for both economic and safety reasons, such as the shipping, air transportation, agriculture, fishing, forestry, and utilities industries.

The use of weather balloons, launched a few times a day to measure wind, temperature, and humidity in the upper atmosphere, is currently supplemented by sophisticated atmospheric satellite monitoring equipment that transmits data as frequently as every few minutes. Doppler radar, for example, can detect airflow patterns in violent storm systems, allowing forecasters to better predict thunderstorms, flash floods, tornadoes, and other hazardous winds, and to monitor the direction and intensity of storms.

Some atmospheric scientists work in research. *Physical meteorologists*, for example, study the atmosphere's chemical and physical properties; the transmission of light, sound, and radio waves; and the transfer of energy in the atmosphere. They also study factors affecting the formation of clouds, rain, and snow; the dispersal of air pollutants over urban areas; and other weather phenomena, such as the mechanics of severe storms. *Synoptic meteorologists* develop new tools for weather forecasting using computers and sophisticated mathematical models of atmospheric activity. *Climatologists* study climactic variations spanning hundreds or even millions of years. They also may collect, analyze, and interpret past records of wind, rainfall, sunshine, and temperature in specific areas or regions. Their studies are used to design buildings, plan heating and cooling systems, and aid in effective land use and agricultural production. Environmental problems, such as pollution and shortages of fresh water, have widened the scope of the meteorological profession. *Environmental meteorologists* study these problems and may evaluate and report on air quality for environmental impact statements. Other research meteorologists examine the most effective ways to control or diminish air pollution.

Work environment. Weather stations are found everywhere—at airports, in or near cities, and in isolated and remote areas. Some atmospheric scientists also spend time observing weather conditions and collecting data from aircraft. Weather forecasters who work for radio or television stations broadcast their reports from station studios, and may work evenings and weekends. Meteorologists in smaller weather offices often work alone; in larger ones, they work as part of a team. Those who work for private consulting firms or for companies analyzing and monitoring emissions to improve air quality usually work with other scientists or engineers; fieldwork and travel may be common for these workers.

Most weather stations operate around the clock, 7 days a week. Jobs in such facilities usually involve night, weekend, and holiday work, often with rotating shifts. During weather emergencies, such as hurricanes, meteorologists may work overtime. Operational meteorologists also are often under pressure to meet forecast deadlines. Meteorologists who are not involved in forecasting tasks work regular hours, usually in offices.

Training, Other Qualifications, and Advancement

A bachelor's degree in meteorology or atmospheric science, or in a closely related field with courses in meteorology, usually is the minimum educational requirement for an entry-level position as an atmospheric scientist. A master's degree is necessary for some positions, and a Ph.D. degree is required for most basic research positions.

Education and training. The preferred educational requirement for entry-level meteorologists in the federal government is a bachelor's degree—not necessarily in meteorology—with at least 24 semester hours of meteorology/atmospheric science courses, including six hours in the analysis and prediction of weather systems, six hours of atmospheric dynamics and thermodynamics, three hours of physical meteorology, and two hours of remote sensing of the atmosphere or instrumentation. Other required courses include three semester hours of ordinary differential equations, six hours of college physics, and at least 9 hours of courses appropriate for a physical science major—such as statistics, chemistry, physical oceanography, physical climatology, physical hydrology, radiative transfer, aeronomy (the study of the upper atmosphere), advanced thermodynamics, advanced electricity and magnetism, light and optics, and computer science. Sometimes, a combination of education and appropriate experience may be substituted for a degree.

Although positions in operational meteorology are available for those with only a bachelor's degree, obtaining a second bachelor's degree or a master's degree enhances employment opportunities, pay, and advancement potential. A master's degree usually is necessary for conducting applied research and development, and a Ph.D. is required for most basic research positions. Students planning on a career in research and development do not necessarily need to major in atmospheric science or meteorology as an undergraduate. In fact, a bachelor's degree in mathematics, physics, or engineering provides excellent preparation for graduate study in atmospheric science.

Because atmospheric science is a small field, relatively few colleges and universities offer degrees in meteorology or atmospheric science, although many departments of physics, earth science, geography, and geophysics offer atmospheric science and related courses. In 2007, the American Meteorological Society listed approximately 100 undergraduate and graduate atmospheric science programs. Many of these programs combine the study of meteorology with another field, such as agriculture, hydrology, oceanography, engineering, or physics. For example, hydrometeorology is the blending of hydrology (the science of Earth's water) and meteorology, and is the field concerned with the effect of precipitation on the hydrologic cycle and the environment.

Prospective students should make certain that courses required by the National Weather Service and other employers are offered at the college they are considering. Computer science courses, additional meteorology courses, a strong background in mathematics and physics, and good communication skills are important to prospective employers.

Students should also take courses in subjects that are most relevant to their desired area of specialization. For example, those who wish to become broadcast meteorologists for radio or television stations should develop excellent communication skills through courses in speech, journalism, and related fields. Students interested in air quality work should take courses in chemistry and supplement their technical training with coursework in policy or government affairs. Prospective meteorologists seeking opportunities at weather consulting firms should possess knowledge of business, statistics, and economics, as an increasing emphasis is being placed on long-range seasonal forecasting to assist businesses.

Beginning atmospheric scientists often do routine data collection, computation, or analysis, and some basic forecasting. Entry-level operational meteorologists in the federal government usually are placed in intern positions for training and experience. During this period, they learn about the Weather Service's forecasting equipment and procedures, and rotate to different offices to learn about various weather systems. After completing the training period, they are assigned to a permanent duty station.

Certification and advancement. The American Meteorological Society (AMS) offers professional certification for consulting meteorologists, administered by a Board of Certified Consulting Meteorologists. Applicants must meet formal education requirements, pass an examination to demonstrate thorough meteorological knowledge, have a minimum of five years of experience or a combination of experience plus an advanced degree, and provide character references from fellow professionals. In addition, AMS also offers professional certification for broadcast meteorologists.

Experienced meteorologists may advance to supervisory or administrative jobs, or may handle more complex forecasting jobs. After several years of experience, some meteorologists establish their own weather consulting services.

Employment

Atmospheric scientists held about 8,800 jobs in 2006. Although several hundred people teach atmospheric science and related courses in college and university departments of meteorology or atmospheric science, physics, earth science, or geophysics, these individuals are classified as college or university faculty, rather than atmospheric scientists. (See the statement on postsecondary teachers elsewhere in this book.)

The federal government was the largest single employer of civilian meteorologists, accounting for about 37 percent. The National Oceanic and Atmospheric Administration (NOAA) employed most federal meteorologists in National Weather Service stations throughout the nation; the remainder of NOAA's meteorologists worked mainly in research and development or management. The U.S. Department of Defense employed several hundred civilian meteorologists. In addition to civilian meteorol-

Projections data from the National Employment Matrix

Occupational Title	SOC Code	Employment, 2006	Projected employment, 2016	Change, 2006-2016	
				Number	Percent
Atmospheric and space scientists	19-2021	8,800	9,700	900	11

NOTE: Data in this table are rounded.

ogists, hundreds of Armed Forces members are involved in forecasting and other meteorological work. (See the statement on the Armed Forces elsewhere in this book.) Others worked for professional, scientific, and technical services firms, including private weather consulting services; radio and television broadcasting; air carriers; and state government.

Job Outlook

Employment is expected to increase about as fast as the average. Atmospheric scientists should have favorable job prospects, but opportunities in broadcasting are rare and highly competitive.

Employment change. Employment of atmospheric scientists is projected to grow 11 percent over the 2006–2016 decade, about as fast as the average for all occupations. The National Weather Service has completed an extensive modernization of its weather forecasting equipment and finished all hiring of meteorologists needed to staff the upgraded stations. The Service has no plans to increase the number of weather stations or the number of meteorologists in existing stations. Employment of meteorologists in other federal agencies is expected to decline.

In private industry, on the other hand, job opportunities for atmospheric scientists are expected to be better than in the federal government. As research leads to continuing improvements in weather forecasting, demand should grow for private weather consulting firms to provide more detailed information than has formerly been available, especially to climate-sensitive industries. Farmers, commodity investors, radio and television stations, and utilities, transportation, and construction firms can greatly benefit from additional weather information more closely targeted to their needs than the general information provided by the National Weather Service. Additionally, research on seasonal and other long-range forecasting is yielding positive results, which should spur demand for more atmospheric scientists to interpret these forecasts and advise climate-sensitive industries. However, because many customers for private weather services are in industries sensitive to fluctuations in the economy, the sales and growth of private weather services depend on the health of the economy.

There will continue to be demand for atmospheric scientists to analyze and monitor the dispersion of pollutants into the air to ensure compliance with federal environmental regulations, but related employment increases are expected to be small. Efforts toward making and improving global weather observations also could have a positive impact on employment.

Job prospects. Atmospheric scientists should have favorable job prospects, as the number of graduates is expected to be in rough balance with the number of openings. Opportunities in broadcasting are rare and there will be very few job openings in this industry. Openings for academic and government positions should result primarily from replacement needs as older workers retire or leave the occupation for other reasons.

Earnings

Median annual earnings of atmospheric scientists in May 2006 were $77,150. The middle 50 percent earned between $55,530 and $96,490. The lowest 10 percent earned less than $39,090, and the highest 10 percent earned more than $119,700.

The average salary for meteorologists employed by the federal government was $84,882 in 2007. Many meteorologists in the federal government with a bachelor's degree received a starting salary of $35,752, or slightly higher in areas of the country where the prevailing local pay level is higher.

Related Occupations

Workers in other occupations concerned with the physical environment include environmental scientists and hydrologists, geoscientists, physicists and astronomers, mathematicians, and engineers.

Sources of Additional Information

Information about careers in meteorology and a listing of colleges and universities offering meteorology programs is provided by the American Meteorological Society on the Internet at: http://www.ametsoc.org

General information about meteorology and careers in atmospheric science can also be obtained from the National Oceanic and Atmospheric Administration on the Internet at: http://www.noaa.gov

Information on obtaining a position as a meteorologist with the federal government is available from the Office of Personnel Management through USAJOBS, the federal government's official employment information system. This resource for locating and applying for job opportunities can be accessed through the Internet at http://www.usajobs.opm.gov or through an interactive voice response telephone system at (703) 724-1850 or TDD (978) 461-8404. These numbers are not toll free, and charges may result.

Audiologists

(O*NET 29-1121.00)

Significant Points

- More than half worked in health care facilities; many others were employed by educational services.
- A master's degree in audiology (hearing) is the standard level of education required; however, a doctoral degree is becoming more common for new entrants.
- Few openings are expected because of the small size of the occupation.
- Job prospects will be favorable for those possessing the doctoral (Au.D.) degree.

Nature of the Work

Audiologists work with people who have hearing, balance, and related ear problems. They examine individuals of all ages and identify those with the symptoms of hearing loss and other auditory, balance, and related sensory and neural problems. They then assess the nature and extent of the problems and help the individuals manage them. Using audiometers, computers, and other testing devices, they measure the loudness at which a person begins to hear sounds, the ability to distinguish between sounds, and the impact of hearing loss on an individual's daily life. In addition, audiologists use computer equipment to evaluate and diagnose balance disorders. Audiologists interpret these results and may coordinate them with medical, educational, and psychological information to make a diagnosis and determine a course of treatment.

Hearing disorders can result from a variety of causes including trauma at birth, viral infections, genetic disorders, exposure to loud noise, certain medications, or aging. Treatment may include examining and cleaning the ear canal, fitting and dispensing hearing aids, and fitting and programming cochlear implants. Audiologic treatment also includes counseling on adjusting to hearing loss, training on the use of hearing instruments, and teaching communication strategies for use in a variety of environments. For example, they may provide instruction in listening strategies. Audiologists also may recommend, fit, and dispense personal or large area amplification systems and alerting devices.

In audiology clinics, audiologists may independently develop and carry out treatment programs. They keep records on the initial evaluation, progress, and discharge of patients. In other settings, audiologists may work with other health and education providers as part of a team in planning and implementing services for children and adults. Audiologists who diagnose and treat balance disorders often work in collaboration with physicians, and physical and occupational therapists.

Some audiologists specialize in work with the elderly, children, or hearing-impaired individuals who need special treatment programs. Others develop and implement ways to protect workers' hearing from on-the-job injuries. They measure noise levels in workplaces and conduct hearing protection programs in factories and in schools and communities.

Audiologists who work in private practice also manage the business aspects of running an office, such as developing a patient base, hiring employees, keeping records, and ordering equipment and supplies.

A few audiologists conduct research on types of, and treatment for, hearing, balance, and related disorders. Others design and develop equipment or techniques for diagnosing and treating these disorders.

Work environment. Audiologists usually work at a desk or table in clean, comfortable surroundings. The job is not physically demanding but does require attention to detail and intense concentration. The emotional needs of patients and their families may be demanding. Most full-time audiologists work about 40 hours per week, which may include weekends and evenings to meet the needs of patients. Some work part time. Those who work on a contract basis may spend a substantial amount of time traveling between facilities.

Training, Other Qualifications, and Advancement

All states require audiologists to be licensed or registered. Licensure or registration requires at least a master's degree in audiology; however, a first professional, or doctoral, degree is becoming increasingly necessary.

Education and training. Individuals must have at least a master's degree in audiology to qualify for a job. However, a first professional or doctoral degree is becoming more common. As of early 2007, eight states required a doctoral degree or its equivalent. The professional doctorate in audiology (Au.D.) requires approximately eight years of university training and supervised professional experience.

In early 2007, the Accreditation Commission of Audiology Education accredited more than 50 Au.D. programs and the Council on Academic Accreditation in Audiology and Speech-Language Pathology (CAA) accredited over 70 graduate programs in audiology. Graduation from an accredited program may be required to obtain a license in some states. Requirements for admission to programs in audiology include courses in English, mathematics, physics, chemistry, biology, psychology, and communication. Graduate coursework in audiology includes anatomy; physiology; physics; genetics; normal and abnormal communication development; auditory, balance, and neural systems assessment and treatment; diagnosis and treatment; pharmacology; and ethics.

Licensure and certification. Audiologists are regulated by licensure or registration in all 50 states. Forty-one states have continuing education requirements for licensure renewal, the number of hours required varies by state. Twenty states and the District of Columbia also require audiologists to have a Hearing Aid Dispenser license to dispense hearing aids; for the remaining 30 states, an audiologist license is all that is needed to dispense hearing aids. Third-party payers generally require practitioners to be licensed to qualify for reimbursement. States set requirements for education, mandating a master's or doctoral degree, as well as other requirements. For information on the specific requirements of your state, contact that state's licensing board.

In some states, specific certifications from professional associations satisfy some or all of the requirements for state licensure. Certification can be obtained from two certifying bodies. Audiologists can earn the Certificate of Clinical Competence in Audiology (CCC-A) offered by the American Speech-Language-Hearing Association; they may also be certified through the American Board of Audiology.

Other qualifications. Audiologists should be able to effectively communicate diagnostic test results, diagnoses, and proposed treatments in a manner easily understood by their patients. They must be able to approach problems objectively and provide support to patients and their families. Because a patient's progress may be slow, patience, compassion, and good listening skills are necessary.

It is important for audiologists to be aware of new diagnostic and treatment technologies. Most audiologists participate in continuing education courses to learn new methods and technologies.

Advancement. With experience, audiologists can advance to open their own private practice. Audiologist working in hospitals and clinics can advance to management or supervisory positions.

Projections data from the National Employment Matrix

Occupational Title	SOC Code	Employment, 2006	Projected employment, 2016	Change, 2006-2016	
				Number	Percent
Audiologists	29-1121	12,000	13,000	1,200	10

NOTE: Data in this table are rounded.

Employment

Audiologists held about 12,000 jobs in 2006. More than half of all jobs were in health care facilities—offices of physicians or other health practitioners, including audiologists; hospitals; and outpatient care centers. About 13 percent of jobs were in educational services, including elementary and secondary schools. Other jobs for audiologists were in health and personal care stores, including hearing aid stores; scientific research and development services; and state and local governments.

A small number of audiologists were self-employed in private practice. They provided hearing health care services in their own offices or worked under contract for schools, health care facilities, or other establishments.

Job Outlook

Average employment growth is projected. However, because of the small size of the occupation, few job openings are expected. Job prospects will be favorable for those possessing the Au.D. degree.

Employment change. Employment of audiologists is expected to grow 10 percent from 2006 to 2016, about as fast as the average for all occupations. Hearing loss is strongly associated with aging, so rapid growth in older population groups will cause the number of people with hearing and balance impairments to increase markedly. Medical advances also are improving the survival rate of premature infants and trauma victims, who then need assessment and sometimes treatment. Greater awareness of the importance of early identification and diagnosis of hearing disorders in infants also will increase employment. A number of states require that newborns be screened for hearing loss and receive appropriate early intervention services.

Employment in educational services will increase along with growth in elementary and secondary school enrollments, including enrollment of special education students.

Growth in employment of audiologists will be moderated by limitations on reimbursements made by third-party payers for the tests and services they provide.

Job prospects. Job prospects will be favorable for those possessing the Au.D. degree. Only a few job openings for audiologists will arise from the need to replace those who leave the occupation, because the occupation is relatively small and workers tend to stay in this occupation until they retire.

Earnings

Median annual earnings of wage-and-salary audiologists were $57,120 in May 2006. The middle 50 percent earned between $47,220 and $70,940. The lowest 10 percent earned less than $38,370, and the highest 10 percent earned more than $89,160. Some employers may pay for continuing education courses.

Related Occupations

Audiologists specialize in the prevention, diagnosis, and treatment of hearing problems. Workers in related occupations include occupational therapists, optometrists, physical therapists, psychologists, recreational therapists, rehabilitation counselors, and speech-language pathologists.

Sources of Additional Information

State licensing boards can provide information on licensure requirements. State departments of education can supply information on certification requirements for those who wish to work in public schools.

For information on the specific requirements of your state, contact that state's licensing board. Career information, a description of the CCC-A credential, and information on state licensure is available from

- American Speech-Language-Hearing Association, 10801 Rockville Pike, Rockville, MD 20852. Internet: http://www.asha.org

Information on American Board of Audiology certification is available from

- American Board of Audiology, 11730 Plaza America Dr., Suite 300, Reston, VA 20190. Internet: http://www.americanboardofaudiology.org

For information on the Au.D. degree, contact

- Audiology Foundation of America, 8 N. 3rd St., Suite 406, Lafayette, IN 47901. Internet: http://www.audfound.org

Automotive Body and Related Repairers

(O*NET 49-3021.00 and 49-3022.00)

Significant Points

- To become a fully skilled automotive body repairer, formal training followed by on-the-job instruction is recommended because fixing newer automobiles requires advanced skills.
- Excellent job opportunities are projected because of the large number of older workers who are expected to retire in the next 10 to 15 years.
- Repairers need good reading ability and basic mathematics and computer skills to use print and digital technical manuals.

Nature of the Work

Most of the damage resulting from everyday vehicle collisions can be repaired, and vehicles can be refinished to look and drive like new. *Automotive body repairers*, often called collision repair technicians, straighten bent bodies, remove dents, and replace crumpled parts that cannot be fixed. They repair all types of vehicles, and although some work on large trucks, buses, or tractor-trailers, most work on cars and small trucks. They can work alone, with only general direction from supervisors, or as specialists on a repair team. In some shops, helpers or apprentices assist experienced repairers.

Each damaged vehicle presents different challenges for repairers. Using their broad knowledge of automotive construction and repair techniques, automotive body repairers must decide how to handle each job based on what the vehicle is made of and what needs to be fixed. They must first determine the extent of the damage and order any needed parts.

If the car is heavily damaged, an automotive body repairer might start by realigning the frame of the vehicle. Repairers chain or clamp frames and sections to alignment machines that use hydraulic pressure to align damaged components. "Unibody" vehicles—designs built without frames—must be restored to precise factory specifications for the vehicle to operate correctly. For these vehicles, repairers use benchmark systems to accurately measure how much each section is out of alignment, and hydraulic machinery to return the vehicle to its original shape.

Once the frame is aligned, repairers can begin to fix or replace damaged body parts. If the vehicle or part is made of metal, body repairers will use a pneumatic metal-cutting gun or other tools to remove badly damaged sections of body panels and then weld in replacement sections. Less serious dents are pulled out with a hydraulic jack or hand prying bar or knocked out with handtools or pneumatic hammers. Small dents and creases in the metal are smoothed by holding a small anvil against one side of the damaged area while hammering the opposite side. Repairers also remove very small pits and dimples with pick hammers and punches in a process called metal finishing. Body repairers use plastic or solder to fill small dents that cannot be worked out of plastic or metal panels. On metal panels, they file or grind the hardened filler to the original shape and clean the surface with a media blaster—similar to a sand blaster—before repainting the damaged portion of the vehicle.

Body repairers also repair or replace the plastic body parts that are increasingly used on new vehicles. They remove damaged panels and identify the type and properties of the plastic used. With most types of plastic, repairers can apply heat from a hot-air welding gun or immerse the panel in hot water and press the softened section back into shape by hand. Repairers replace plastic parts that are badly damaged or very difficult to fix. A few body repairers specialize in fixing fiberglass car bodies.

Some body repairers specialize in installing and repairing glass in automobiles and other vehicles. *Automotive glass installers and repairers* remove broken, cracked, or pitted windshields and window glass. Glass installers apply a moisture-proofing compound along the edges of the glass, place the glass in the vehicle, and install rubber strips around the sides of the windshield or window to make it secure and weatherproof.

Many large shops make repairs using an assembly-line approach where vehicles are fixed by a team of repairers who each specialize in one type of repair. One worker might straighten frames while another repairs doors and fenders, for example. In most shops, automotive painters do the painting and refinishing, but in small shops, workers often do both body repairing and painting. (Automotive painters are not included in this discussion.)

Work environment. Repairers work indoors in body shops that are noisy with the clatter of hammers against metal and the whine of power tools. Most shops are well ventilated to disperse dust and paint fumes. Body repairers often work in awkward or cramped positions, and much of their work is strenuous and dirty. Hazards include cuts from sharp metal edges, burns from torches and heated metal, injuries from power tools, and fumes from paint. However, serious accidents usually are avoided when the shop is kept clean and orderly and safety practices are observed. Automotive repair and maintenance shops averaged 4 cases of work-related injuries and illnesses per 100 full-time workers in 2005, compared to 4.6 per 100 workers in all private industry.

Most automotive body repairers work a standard 40-hour week. More than 40 hours a week may be required when there is a backlog of repair work to be completed. This may include working on weekends.

Training, Other Qualifications, and Advancement

Automotive technology is rapidly becoming more sophisticated, and most employers prefer applicants who have completed a formal training program in automotive body repair or refinishing. Most new repairers complete at least part of this training on the job. Many repairers, particularly in urban areas, need a national certification to advance past entry-level work.

Education and training. A high school diploma or GED is often all that is required to enter this occupation, but more specific education and training is needed to learn how to repair newer automobiles. Collision repair programs may be offered in high school or in postsecondary vocational schools and community colleges. Courses in electronics, physics, chemistry, English, computers, and mathematics provide a good background for a career as an automotive body repairer. Most training programs combine classroom instruction and hands-on practice.

Trade and technical school programs typically award certificates to graduates after six months to a year of collision repair study. Some community colleges offer two-year programs in collision repair. Many of these schools also offer certificates for individual courses, so that students are able to take classes incrementally or as needed.

New repairers begin by assisting experienced body repairers in tasks such as removing damaged parts, sanding body panels, and installing repaired parts. Novices learn to remove small dents and make other minor repairs. They then progress to more difficult tasks, such as straightening body parts and returning them to their correct alignment. Generally, it takes three to four years of hands-on training to become skilled in all aspects of body repair, some of which may be completed as part of a formal education program. Basic automotive glass installation and repair can be learned in as little as six months, but becoming fully qualified can take several years.

Continuing education and training are needed throughout a career in automotive body repair. Automotive parts, body materials, and electronics continue to change and to become more complex. To keep up with these technological advances, repairers must continue to gain new skills by reading technical manuals and furthering their education with classes and seminars. Many companies within the automotive body repair industry send employees to advanced training programs to brush up on skills or to learn new techniques.

Other qualifications. Fully skilled automotive body repairers must have good reading ability and basic mathematics and computer skills. Restoring unibody automobiles to their original form requires repairers to follow instructions and diagrams in technical manuals and to make precise three-dimensional measurements of the position of one body section relative to another. In addition, repairers should enjoy working with their hands and be able to pay attention to detail while they work.

Certification and advancement. Certification by the National Institute for Automotive Service Excellence (ASE), although voluntary, is the pervasive industry credential for non entry-level automotive body repairers. This is especially true in large, urban areas. Repairers may take up to four ASE Master Collision Repair and Refinish Exams. Repairers who pass at least one exam and have two years of hands-on work experience earn ASE certification. The completion of a postsecondary program in automotive body repair may be substituted for one year of work experience. Those who pass all four exams become ASE Master Collision Repair and Refinish Technicians. Automotive body repairers must retake the examination at least every five years to retain their certification. Many vehicle manufacturers and paint manufacturers also have product certification programs that can advance a repairer's career.

As beginners increase their skills, learn new techniques, earn certifications, and complete work more rapidly, their pay increases. An experienced automotive body repairer with managerial ability may advance to shop supervisor, and some workers open their own body repair shops. Other repairers become automobile damage appraisers for insurance companies.

Employment

Automotive body and related repairers held about 206,000 jobs in 2006; about 13 percent specialized in automotive glass installation and repair. Fifty-eight percent of repairers worked for automotive repair and maintenance shops in 2006, while 20 percent worked for automobile dealers. Others worked for organizations, such as trucking companies, that maintain their own motor vehicles. A small number of repairers worked for wholesalers of motor vehicles, parts, and supplies. More than 15 percent of automotive body repairers were self-employed, roughly double the number for all installation, maintenance, and repair occupations.

Job Outlook

Employment of automotive body and related repairers is expected to grow about as fast as average through the year 2016, and job opportunities are projected to be excellent due to a growing number of retirements in this occupation.

Employment change. Employment of automotive body repairers is expected to grow 12 percent over the 2006–2016 decade, as compared to 10 percent for all occupations. Demand for qualified body repairers will increase as the number of vehicles on the road continues to grow. With more motor vehicles in use, more vehicles will be damaged in accidents. In addition, new automotive designs of lighter weight are prone to greater collision damage than are older, heavier designs, so more repairs are needed. Employment growth will continue to be concentrated in automotive body, paint, interior, and glass repair shops, with little or no change in automotive dealerships.

Despite the anticipated increase in the number of auto accidents, the increasing demand for automotive body repairers will be tempered by improvements in the quality of vehicles. Also, technological innovations that enhance safety will reduce the likelihood of accidents.

Demand for automotive body repair services will similarly be constrained as more vehicles are declared a total loss after accidents. In many such cases, the vehicles are not repaired because of the high cost of replacing the increasingly complex parts and electronic components and because of the extensive damage that results when airbags deploy. Also, higher insurance premiums and deductibles mean that minor damage is more often going unrepaired. Larger shops are instituting productivity enhancements, such as employing a team approach to repairs, which may limit employment growth by reducing the time it takes to make repairs.

Job prospects. Employment growth will create some opportunities, but the need to replace experienced repairers who transfer to other occupations or who retire or stop working for other reasons will account for the majority of job openings over the next 10 years. Opportunities will be excellent for people with formal training in automotive body repair and refinishing. Those without any training or experience in automotive body refinishing or collision repair—before or after high school—will face competition for these jobs.

Experienced body repairers are rarely laid off during a general slowdown in the economy as the automotive repair business is not very sensitive to changes in economic conditions. Although repair of minor dents and crumpled fenders is often put off when drivers have less money, major body damage must be repaired before a vehicle can be driven safely.

Earnings

Median hourly wage-and-salary earnings of automotive body and related repairers, including incentive pay, were $16.92 in May 2006. The middle 50 percent earned between $13.00 and $22.33 an hour. The lowest 10 percent earned less than $10.10, and the highest 10 percent earned more than $28.71 an hour. Median hourly earnings of automotive body and related repairers were $17.85 in automobile dealers and $16.66 in automotive repair and maintenance.

Median hourly wage-and-salary earnings of automotive glass installers and repairers, including incentive pay, were $14.77. The

Projections data from the National Employment Matrix

Occupational Title	SOC Code	Employment, 2006	Projected employment, 2016	Change, 2006-16	
				Number	Percent
Automotive body and related repairers	—	206,000	232,000	26,000	12
Automotive body and related repairers	49-3021	183,000	204,000	21,000	12
Automotive glass installers and repairers	49-3022	24,000	28,000	4,400	19

NOTE: Data in this table are rounded.

middle 50 percent earned between $11.44 and $18.42 an hour. The lowest 10 percent earned less than $9.19, and the highest 10 percent earned more than $22.22 an hour. Median hourly earnings in automotive repair and maintenance shops, the industry employing most automotive glass installers and repairers, were $14.80.

The majority of body repairers employed by independent repair shops and automotive dealers are paid on an incentive basis. Under this system, body repairers are paid a set amount for various tasks, and earnings depend on both the amount of work assigned and how fast it is completed. Employers frequently guarantee workers a minimum weekly salary. Body repairers who work for trucking companies, buslines, and other organizations that maintain their own vehicles usually receive an hourly wage.

Helpers and trainees typically earn between 30 percent and 60 percent of the earnings of skilled workers. They are paid by the hour until they are skilled enough to be paid on an incentive basis.

Employee benefits vary widely from business to business. However, industry sources report that benefits such as paid leave, health insurance, and retirement assistance are increasingly common in the collision repair industry. Automotive dealerships are the most likely to offer such incentives.

Related Occupations

Repairing damaged motor vehicles often involves working on mechanical components, as well as vehicle bodies. Automotive body repairers often work closely with individuals in several related occupations, including automotive service technicians and mechanics, diesel service technicians and mechanics, auto damage appraisers, and painting and coating workers, except construction and maintenance. Automotive glass installers and repairers complete tasks very similar to those of glaziers.

Sources of Additional Information

Additional details about work opportunities may be obtained from automotive body repair shops, automobile dealers, or local offices of your state employment service. state employment service offices also are a source of information about training programs.

For general information about automotive body repairer careers, contact any of the following sources:

- Automotive Careers Today, 8400 Westpark Dr., MS #2, McLean, VA 22102. Internet: http://www.autocareerstoday.org
- Automotive Service Association, P.O. Box 929, Bedford, Texas 76095. Internet: http://www.asashop.org
- Inter-Industry Conference On Auto Collision Repair Education Foundation (I-CAR), 5125 Trillium Blvd., Hoffman Estates, IL 60192. Internet: http://www.collisioncareers.org
- National Automobile Dealers Association, 8400 Westpark Dr., McLean, VA 22102. Internet: http://www.nada.org

For general information about careers in automotive glass installation and repair, contact

- National Glass Association. 8200 Greensboro Dr., Suite 302, McLean, VA 22102. Internet: http://www.glass.org

For information on how to become a certified automotive body repairer, write to

- National Institute for Automotive Service Excellence (ASE), 101 Blue Seal Dr. SE, Suite 101, Leesburg, VA 20175. Internet: http://www.asecert.org

For a directory of certified automotive body repairer programs, contact

- National Automotive Technician Education Foundation, 101 Blue Seal Dr., SE, Suite 101, Leesburg, VA 20175. Internet: http://www.natef.org

For a directory of accredited private trade and technical schools that offer training programs in automotive body repair, contact

- Accrediting Commission of Career Schools and Colleges of Technology, 2101 Wilson Blvd., Suite 302, Arlington, VA 22201. Internet: http://www.accsct.org

STEM Automotive Service Technicians and Mechanics

(O*NET 49-3023.00, 49-3023.01, and 49-3023.02)

Significant Points

- Automotive service technicians and mechanics must continually adapt to changing technology and repair techniques as vehicle components and systems become increasingly sophisticated.
- Formal automotive technician training is the best preparation for these challenging technology-based jobs.
- Opportunities should be very good for automotive service technicians and mechanics with diagnostic and problem-solving skills, knowledge of electronics and mathematics, and mechanical aptitude.

Nature of the Work

Automotive service technicians inspect, maintain, and repair automobiles and light trucks that run on gasoline, electricity, or alternative fuels such as ethanol. Automotive service technicians' and mechanics' responsibilities have evolved from simple mechanical repairs to high-level technology-related work. The increasing sophistication of automobiles requires workers who can use computerized shop equipment and work with electronic components while maintaining their skills with traditional handtools. As a result, automotive service workers are now usually called technicians rather than mechanics. (Service technicians who work on diesel-powered trucks, buses, and equipment are discussed in section on diesel service technicians and mechanics in this book. Motorcycle technicians—who repair and service motorcycles, motor scooters, mopeds, and small all-terrain vehicles—are discussed in this book's section on small engine mechanics.)

Today, integrated electronic systems and complex computers regulate vehicles and their performance while on the road. Technicians must have an increasingly broad knowledge of how vehicles' complex components work and interact. They also must be able to work with electronic diagnostic equipment and digital manuals and reference materials.

When mechanical or electrical troubles occur, technicians first get a description of the problem from the owner or, in a large shop, from the repair service estimator or service advisor who wrote the repair order. To locate the problem, technicians use a diagnostic approach. First, they test to see whether components and systems are secure and working properly. Then, they isolate the components or systems that might be the cause of the problem. For example, if an air-conditioner malfunctions, the technician might check for a simple problem, such as a low coolant level, or a more complex issue, such as a bad drive-train connection that has shorted out the air conditioner. As part of their investigation, technicians may test drive the vehicle or use a variety of testing equipment, including onboard and handheld diagnostic computers or compression gauges. These tests may indicate whether a component is salvageable or whether a new one is required.

During routine service inspections, technicians test and lubricate engines and other major components. Sometimes technicians repair or replace worn parts before they cause breakdowns or damage the vehicle. Technicians usually follow a checklist to ensure that they examine every critical part. Belts, hoses, plugs, brake and fuel systems, and other potentially troublesome items are watched closely.

Service technicians use a variety of tools in their work. They use power tools, such as pneumatic wrenches to remove bolts quickly; machine tools like lathes and grinding machines to rebuild brakes; welding and flame-cutting equipment to remove and repair exhaust systems, and jacks and hoists to lift cars and engines. They also use common handtools, such as screwdrivers, pliers, and wrenches, to work on small parts and in hard-to-reach places. Technicians usually provide their own handtools, and many experienced workers have thousands of dollars invested in them. Employers furnish expensive power tools, engine analyzers, and other diagnostic equipment.

Computers are also commonplace in modern repair shops. Service technicians compare the readouts from computerized diagnostic testing devices with benchmarked standards given by the manufacturer. Deviations outside of acceptable levels tell the technician to investigate that part of the vehicle more closely. Through the Internet or from software packages, most shops receive automatic updates to technical manuals and access to manufacturers' service information, technical service bulletins, and other databases that allow technicians to keep up with common problems and learn new procedures.

High technology tools are needed to fix the computer equipment that operates everything from the engine to the radio in many cars. In fact, today most automotive systems, such as braking, transmission, and steering systems, are controlled primarily by computers and electronic components. Additionally, luxury vehicles often have integrated global positioning systems, Internet access, and other new features with which technicians will need to become familiar. Also, as more alternate-fuel vehicles are purchased, more automotive service technicians will need to learn the science behind these automobiles and how to repair them.

Automotive service technicians in large shops often specialize in certain types of repairs. For example, *transmission technicians and rebuilders* work on gear trains, couplings, hydraulic pumps, and other parts of transmissions. Extensive knowledge of computer controls, the ability to diagnose electrical and hydraulic problems, and other specialized skills are needed to work on these complex components, which employ some of the most sophisticated technology used in vehicles. *Tune-up technicians* adjust ignition timing and valves and adjust or replace spark plugs and other parts to ensure efficient engine performance. They often use electronic testing equipment to isolate and adjust malfunctions in fuel, ignition, and emissions control systems.

Automotive air-conditioning repairers install and repair air-conditioners and service their components, such as compressors, condensers, and controls. These workers require special training in federal and state regulations governing the handling and disposal of refrigerants. *Front-end mechanics* align and balance wheels and repair steering mechanisms and suspension systems. They frequently use special alignment equipment and wheel-balancing machines. *Brake repairers* adjust brakes, replace brake linings and pads, and make other repairs on brake systems. Some technicians specialize in both brake and front-end work.

Work environment. While most automotive service technicians worked a standard 40 hour week in 2006, 30 percent worked longer hours. Some may work evenings and weekends to satisfy customer service needs. Generally, service technicians work indoors in well-ventilated and -lighted repair shops. However, some shops are drafty and noisy. Although many problems can be fixed with simple computerized adjustments, technicians frequently work with dirty and greasy parts, and in awkward positions. They often lift heavy parts and tools. Minor cuts, burns, and bruises are common, but technicians can usually avoid serious accidents if safe practices are observed.

Training, Other Qualifications, and Advancement

Automotive technology is rapidly increasing in sophistication, and most training authorities strongly recommend that people seeking work in automotive service complete a formal training program in high school or in a postsecondary vocational school or community college. However, some service technicians still learn the trade solely by assisting and learning from experienced workers. Acquiring National Institute for Automotive Service Excellence (ASE) certification is important for those seeking work in large, urban areas.

Education and training. Most employers regard the successful completion of a vocational training program in automotive service technology as the best preparation for trainee positions. High school programs, while an asset, vary greatly in scope. Graduates of these programs may need further training to become qualified. Some of the more extensive high school programs participate in Automotive Youth Education Service (AYES), a partnership between high school automotive repair programs, automotive manufacturers, and franchised automotive dealers. All AYES high school programs are certified by the National Institute for Automotive Service Excellence. Students who complete these programs are well prepared to enter entry-level technician positions or to advance their technical education. Courses in automotive repair, electronics, physics, chemistry, English, computers, and mathematics provide a good educational background for a career as a service technician.

Postsecondary automotive technician training programs usually provide intensive career preparation through a combination of classroom instruction and hands-on practice. Schools update their curriculums frequently to reflect changing technology and equipment. Some trade and technical school programs provide concentrated training for six months to a year, depending on how many hours the student attends each week, and award a certificate. Community college programs usually award a certificate or an associate degree. Some students earn repair certificates in a particular skill and leave to begin their careers. Associate degree programs, however, usually take two years to complete and include classes in English, basic mathematics, computers, and other subjects, as well as automotive repair. Recently, some programs have added classes on customer service, stress management, and other employability skills. Some formal training programs have alliances with tool manufacturers that help entry-level technicians accumulate tools during their training period.

Various automobile manufacturers and participating franchised dealers also sponsor two-year associate degree programs at postsecondary schools across the nation. Students in these programs typically spend alternate six- to 12-week periods attending classes full time and working full time in the service departments of sponsoring dealers. At these dealerships, students work with an experienced worker who provides hands-on instruction and timesaving tips.

Those new to automotive service usually start as trainee technicians, technicians' helpers, or lubrication workers, and gradually acquire and practice their skills by working with experienced mechanics and technicians. In many cases, on-the-job training may be a part of a formal education program. With a few months' experience, beginners perform many routine service tasks and make simple repairs. While some graduates of postsecondary automotive training programs are often able to earn promotion to the journey level after only a few months on the job, it typically takes two to five years of experience to become a fully qualified service technician, who is expected to quickly perform the more difficult types of routine service and repairs. An additional one to two years of experience familiarizes technicians with all types of repairs. Complex specialties, such as transmission repair, require another year or two of training and experience. In contrast, brake specialists may learn their jobs in considerably less time because they do not need complete knowledge of automotive repair.

Employers increasingly send experienced automotive service technicians to manufacturer training centers to learn to repair new models or to receive special training in the repair of components, such as electronic fuel injection or air-conditioners. Motor vehicle dealers and other automotive service providers may send promising beginners or experienced technicians to manufacturer-sponsored technician training programs to upgrade or maintain employees' skills. Factory representatives also visit many shops to conduct short training sessions.

Other qualifications. The ability to diagnose the source of a problem quickly and accurately requires good reasoning ability and a thorough knowledge of automobiles. Many technicians consider diagnosing hard-to-find troubles one of their most challenging and satisfying duties. For trainee automotive service technician jobs, employers look for people with strong communication and analytical skills. Technicians need good reading, mathematics, and computer skills to study technical manuals. They must also read to keep up with new technology and learn new service and repair procedures and specifications.

Training in electronics is vital because electrical components, or a series of related components, account for nearly all malfunctions in modern vehicles. Trainees must possess mechanical aptitude and knowledge of how automobiles work. Experience working on motor vehicles in the Armed Forces or as a hobby can be very valuable.

Certification and advancement. ASE certification has become a standard credential for automotive service technicians. While not mandatory for work in automotive service, certification is common for all non entry-level technicians in large, urban areas. Certification is available in one or more of eight different areas of automotive service, such as electrical systems, engine repair, brake systems, suspension and steering, and heating and air-conditioning. For certification in each area, technicians must have at least two years of experience and pass the examination. Completion of an automotive training program in high school, vocational or trade school, or community or junior college may be substituted for one year of experience. For ASE certification as a Master Automobile Technician, technicians must be certified in all eight areas.

By becoming skilled in multiple auto repair services, technicians can increase their value to their employer and their pay. Experienced technicians who have administrative ability sometimes advance to shop supervisor or service manager. Those with sufficient funds many times open independent automotive repair shops. Technicians who work well with customers may become automotive repair service estimators.

Employment

Automotive service technicians and mechanics held about 773,000 jobs in 2006. Automotive repair and maintenance shops and automotive dealers employed the majority of these workers—29 percent each. In addition, automotive parts, accessories, and tire stores employed 7 percent of automotive service technicians. Others worked in gasoline stations; general merchandise stores; automotive equipment rental and leasing companies; federal, state, and local governments; and other organizations. Almost 17 percent of service technicians were self-employed, more than twice the proportion for all installation, maintenance, and repair occupations.

Job Outlook

The number of jobs for automotive service technicians and mechanics is projected to grow faster than average for all occupations over the next decade. Employment growth will create many new jobs, but total job openings will be significantly larger because many skilled technicians are expected to retire and will need to be replaced.

Employment change. Employment of automotive service technicians and mechanics is expected to increase 14 percent between 2006 and 2016, compared to 10 percent for all occupations. It will add a large number of new jobs, about 110,000, over the decade. Demand for technicians will grow as the number of vehicles in operation increases, reflecting continued growth in the driving age population and in the number of multi-car families. Growth in demand will be offset somewhat by continuing improvements in the quality and durability of automobiles, which will require less frequent service.

Employment growth will continue to be concentrated in automobile dealerships and independent automotive repair shops. Many new jobs also will be created in small retail operations that offer after-warranty repairs, such as oil changes, brake repair, air-conditioner service, and other minor repairs generally taking less than 4 hours to complete. Employment of automotive service technicians and mechanics in gasoline service stations will continue to decline, as fewer stations offer repair services.

Job prospects. In addition to openings from growth, many job openings will be created by the need to replace a growing number of retiring technicians. Job opportunities in this occupation are expected to be very good for those who complete high school or postsecondary automotive training programs and who earn ASE certification. Some employers report difficulty in finding workers with the right skills. People with good diagnostic and problem-solving abilities, and training in basic electronics and computer courses are

Projections data from the National Employment Matrix

Occupational Title	SOC Code	Employment, 2006	Projected employment, 2016	Change, 2006-16 Number	Change, 2006-16 Percent
Automotive service technicians and mechanics	49-3023	773,000	883,000	110,000	14

NOTE: Data in this table are rounded.

expected to have the best opportunities. Those without formal automotive training are likely to face competition for entry-level jobs.

Most people who enter the occupation can expect steady work, even during downturns in the economy. Although car owners tend to postpone maintenance and repair on their vehicles when their budgets are strained, employers usually cut back on hiring new workers during economic downturns instead of letting experienced workers go.

Earnings

Median hourly wage-and-salary earnings of automotive service technicians and mechanics, including commission, were $16.24 in May 2006. The middle 50 percent earned between $11.96 and $21.56 per hour. The lowest 10 percent earned less than $9.17, and the highest 10 percent earned more than $27.22 per hour. Median annual earnings in the industries employing the largest numbers of service technicians were as follows:

Local government, excluding schools	$19.07
Automobile dealers	18.85
Automotive repair and maintenance	14.55
Gasoline stations	14.51
Automotive parts, accessories, and tire stores	14.38

Many experienced technicians employed by automobile dealers and independent repair shops receive a commission related to the labor cost charged to the customer. Under this system, weekly earnings depend on the amount of work completed. Employers frequently guarantee commissioned technicians a minimum weekly salary.

Automotive service technicians who are members of labor unions, such as the International Association of Machinists and Aerospace Workers; the International Union, United Automobile, Aerospace, and Agricultural Implement Workers of America; the Sheet Metal Workers' International Association; and the International Brotherhood of Teamsters, may enjoy more benefits than non-union workers do.

Related Occupations

Other workers who repair and service motor vehicles include automotive body and related repairers, diesel service technicians and mechanics, and small engine mechanics.

Sources of Additional Information

For more details about work opportunities, contact local automobile dealers and repair shops or local offices of the state employment service. The state employment service also may have information about training programs.

For general information about a career as an automotive service technician, contact

- Automotive Careers Today, 8400 Westpark Dr., MS #2, McLean, VA 22102. Internet: http://www.autocareerstoday.org
- Career Voyages, U.S. Department of Labor, 200 Constitution Ave., NW, Washington, DC 20210. Internet: http://www.careervoyages.gov/automotive-main.cfm
- National Automobile Dealers Association, 8400 Westpark Dr., McLean, VA 22102. Internet: http://www.nada.org

A list of certified automotive service technician training programs can be obtained from

- National Automotive Technicians Education Foundation, 101 Blue Seal Dr., SE, Suite 101, Leesburg, VA 20175. Internet: http://www.natef.org

For a directory of accredited private trade and technical schools that offer programs in automotive service technician training, contact

- Accrediting Commission of Career Schools and Colleges of Technology, 2101 Wilson Blvd., Suite 302, Arlington, VA 22201. Internet: http://www.accsct.org

Information on automobile manufacturer-sponsored programs in automotive service technology can be obtained from

- Automotive Youth Educational Systems (AYES), 100 W. Big Beaver, Suite 300, Troy, MI 48084. Internet: http://www.ayes.org

Information on how to become a certified automotive service technician is available from

- National Institute for Automotive Service Excellence (ASE), 101 Blue Seal Dr. SE, Suite 101, Leesburg, VA 20175. Internet: http://www.asecert.org

STEM Biological Scientists

(O*NET 19-1020.01, 19-1021.00, 19-1021.01, 19-1021.02, 19-1022.00, 19-1023.00, and 19-1029.99)

Significant Points

- Biotechnological research and development should continue to drive employment growth.
- A Ph.D. degree usually is required for independent research, but a master's degree is sufficient for some jobs in applied research or product development; temporary postdoctoral research positions are common.
- Competition for jobs is expected.

Nature of the Work

Biological scientists study living organisms and their relationship to the environment. They perform research to gain a better understanding of fundamental life processes or apply that understanding to developing new products or processes. Most specialize in one area of biology, such as zoology (the study of animals) or microbiology (the study of microscopic organisms). (Medical scientists, whose work is closely related to that of biological scientists, are discussed elsewhere in this book.)

Many biological scientists work in research and development. Some conduct basic research to advance our knowledge of living organisms, including bacteria and other infectious agents. Basic biological research enhances our understanding so that we can develop solutions to human health problems and improve the natural environment. These biological scientists mostly work in government, university, or private industry laboratories, often exploring new areas of research. Many expand on specialized research they started in graduate school.

Many research scientists must submit grant proposals to obtain funding for their projects. Colleges and universities, private industry, and federal government agencies such as the National Institutes of Health and the National Science Foundation contribute to the support of scientists whose research proposals are determined to be financially feasible and to have the potential to advance new ideas or processes.

Biological scientists who work in applied research or product development use knowledge gained by basic research to develop new drugs, treatments, and medical diagnostic tests; increase crop yields; and develop new biofuels. They usually have less freedom than basic researchers do to choose the emphasis of their research, and they spend more time working on marketable treatments to meet the business goals of their employers. Biological scientists doing applied research and product development in private industry may be required to describe their research plans or results to nonscientists who are in a position to veto or approve their ideas. These scientists must consider the business effects of their work. Scientists often work in teams, interacting with engineers, scientists of other disciplines, business managers, and technicians. Some biological scientists also work with customers or suppliers and manage budgets.

Scientists usually conduct research in laboratories using a wide variety of other equipment. Some conduct experiments involving animals or plants. This is particularly true of botanists, physiologists, and zoologists. Some biological research also takes place outside the laboratory. For example, a botanist might do field research in tropical rain forests to see which plants grow there, or an ecologist might study how a forest area recovers after a fire. Some marine biologists also work outdoors, often on research vessels from which they study fish, plankton, or other marine organisms.

Swift advances in knowledge of genetics and organic molecules spurred growth in the field of biotechnology, transforming the industries in which biological scientists work. Biological scientists can now manipulate the genetic material of animals and plants, attempting to make organisms more productive or resistant to disease. Basic and applied research on biotechnological processes, such as recombining DNA, has led to the production of important substances, including human insulin and growth hormone. Many other substances not previously available in large quantities are now produced by biotechnological means. Some of these substances are useful in treating diseases.

Today, many biological scientists are involved in biotechnology. Those working on various genome (chromosomes with their associated genes) projects isolate genes and determine their function. This work continues to lead to the discovery of genes associated with specific diseases and inherited health risks, such as sickle cell anemia. Advances in biotechnology have created research opportunities in almost all areas of biology, with commercial applications in areas such as medicine, agriculture, and environmental remediation.

Most biological scientists specialize in the study of a certain type of organism or in a specific activity, although recent advances have blurred some traditional classifications.

Aquatic biologists study micro-organisms, plants, and animals living in water. *Marine biologists* study salt water organisms, and *limnologists* study fresh water organisms. Much of the work of marine biology centers on molecular biology, the study of the biochemical processes that take place inside living cells. Marine biologists sometimes are mistakenly called oceanographers, but oceanography is the study of the physical characteristics of oceans and the ocean floor. (See the occupational profiles for environmental scientists and hydrologists and for geoscientists.)

Biochemists study the chemical composition of living things. They analyze the complex chemical combinations and reactions involved in metabolism, reproduction, and growth. Biochemists do most of their work in biotechnology, which involves understanding the complex chemistry of life.

Botanists study plants and their environments. Some study all aspects of plant life, including algae, fungi, lichens, mosses, ferns, conifers, and flowering plants; others specialize in areas such as identification and classification of plants, the structure and function of plant parts, the biochemistry of plant processes, the causes and cures of plant diseases, the interaction of plants with other organisms and the environment, and the geological record of plants.

Microbiologists investigate the growth and characteristics of microscopic organisms such as bacteria, algae, or fungi. Most microbiologists specialize in environmental, food, agricultural, or industrial microbiology; virology (the study of viruses); immunology (the study of mechanisms that fight infections); or bioinformatics (the use of computers to handle or characterize biological information, usually at the molecular level). Many microbiologists use biotechnology to advance knowledge of cell reproduction and human disease.

Physiologists study life functions of plants and animals, both in the whole organism and at the cellular or molecular level, under normal and abnormal conditions. Physiologists often specialize in functions such as growth, reproduction, photosynthesis, respiration, or movement, or in the physiology of a certain area or system of the organism.

Biophysicists study how physics, such as electrical and mechanical energy and related phenomena, relates to living cells and organisms. They perform research in fields such as neuroscience or bioinformatics.

Zoologists and wildlife biologists study animals and wildlife—their origin, behavior, diseases, and life processes. Some experiment with live animals in controlled or natural surroundings, while others dissect dead animals to study their structure. Zoologists and wildlife biologists also may collect and analyze biological data to determine the environmental effects of current and potential uses of land and water areas. Zoologists usually are identified by the animal group they study—ornithologists study birds, for example, mammalogists study mammals, herpetologists study reptiles, and ichthyologists study fish.

Ecologists investigate the relationships among organisms and between organisms and their environments, examining the effects of population size, pollutants, rainfall, temperature, and altitude. Using knowledge of various scientific disciplines, ecologists may collect, study, and report data on the quality of air, food, soil, and water.

(Agricultural and food scientists, sometimes referred to as biological scientists, are discussed elsewhere in this book, as are medical scientists, whose work is closely related to that of biological scientists.)

Work environment. Biological scientists usually are not exposed to unsafe or unhealthy conditions. Those who work with dangerous organisms or toxic substances in the laboratory must follow strict safety procedures to avoid contamination. Many biological scientists, such as botanists, ecologists, and zoologists, do field studies that involve strenuous physical activity and primitive living conditions. Biological scientists in the field may work in warm or cold climates, in all kinds of weather.

Marine biologists encounter a variety of working conditions. Some work in laboratories; others work on research ships, and those who work underwater must practice safe diving while working around sharp coral reefs and hazardous marine life. Although some marine biologists obtain their specimens from the sea, many still spend a good deal of their time in laboratories and offices, conducting tests, running experiments, recording results, and compiling data.

Many biological scientists depend on grant money to support their research. They may be under pressure to meet deadlines and to conform to rigid grant-writing specifications when preparing proposals to seek new or extended funding.

Biological scientists typically work regular hours. While the 40-hour work week is common, longer hours are not uncommon. Researchers may be required to work odd hours in laboratories or other locations (especially while in the field), depending on the nature of their research.

Training, Other Qualifications, and Advancement

Most biological scientists need a Ph.D. degree in biology or one of its subfields to work in research or development positions. A period of postdoctoral work in the laboratory of a senior researcher has become common for biological scientists who intend to conduct research or teach at the university level.

Education and training. A Ph.D. degree usually is necessary for independent research, industrial research, and college teaching, as well as for advancement to administrative positions. A master's degree is sufficient for some jobs in applied research, product development, management, or inspection; it also may qualify one to work as a research technician or a teacher. The bachelor's degree is adequate for some nonresearch jobs. For example, graduates with a bachelor's degree may start as biological scientists in testing and inspection or may work in jobs related to biological science, such as technical sales or service representatives. Some work as research assistants, laboratory technicians, or high school biology teachers. (See the statements elsewhere in this book on clinical laboratory technologists and technicians and on science technicians.) Many with a bachelor's degree in biology enter medical, dental, veterinary, or other health profession schools.

In addition to required courses in chemistry and biology, undergraduate biological science majors usually study allied disciplines such as mathematics, physics, engineering, and computer science. Computer courses are beneficial for modeling and simulating biological processes, operating some laboratory equipment, and performing research in the emerging field of bioinformatics. Those interested in studying the environment also should take courses in environmental studies and become familiar with applicable legislation and regulations. Prospective biological scientists who hope to work as marine biologists should have at least a bachelor's degree in a biological or marine science. However, students should not overspecialize in undergraduate study, as knowledge of marine biology often is acquired in graduate study.

Most colleges and universities offer bachelor's degrees in biological science, and many offer advanced degrees. Advanced degree programs often emphasize a subfield such as microbiology or botany, but not all universities offer curricula in all subfields. Larger universities frequently have separate departments specializing in different areas of biological science. For example, a program in botany might cover agronomy, horticulture, or plant pathology. Advanced degree programs typically include classroom and fieldwork, laboratory research, and a thesis or dissertation.

Biological scientists with a Ph.D. often take temporary postdoctoral research positions that provide specialized research experience. Postdoctoral positions may offer the opportunity to publish research findings. A solid record of published research is essential in obtaining a permanent position involving basic research, especially for those seeking a permanent college or university faculty position.

Other qualifications. Biological scientists should be able to work independently or as part of a team and be able to communicate clearly and concisely, both orally and in writing. Those in private industry, especially those who aspire to management or administrative positions, should possess strong business and communication skills and be familiar with regulatory issues and marketing and management techniques. Those doing field research in remote areas must have physical stamina. Biological scientists also must have patience and self-discipline to conduct long and detailed research projects.

Advancement. As they gain experience, biological scientists typically gain greater control over their research and may advance to become lead researchers directing a team of scientists and technicians. Some work as consultants to businesses or to government agencies. However, those dependent on research grants are still constrained by funding agencies, and they may spend much of their time writing grant proposals. Others choose to move into managerial positions and become natural science managers (see engineering and natural sciences managers elsewhere in this book). They may plan and administer programs for testing foods and drugs, for example, or direct activities at zoos or botanical gardens. Those who pursue management careers spend much of their time preparing budgets and schedules. Some leave biology for nontechnical managerial, administrative, or sales jobs.

Employment

Biological scientists held about 87,000 jobs in 2006. In addition, many biological scientists held biology faculty positions in colleges and universities but are not included in these numbers. Those whose primary work involves teaching and research are considered postsecondary teachers. (See the statement on teachers—postsecondary elsewhere in this book.)

About 39 percent of all biological scientists were employed by federal, state, and local governments. Federal biological scientists worked mainly for the U.S. Departments of Agriculture, Interior, and Defense and for the National Institutes of Health. Most of the rest worked in scientific research and testing laboratories, the pharmaceutical and medicine manufacturing industry, or colleges and universities.

Job Outlook

Biological scientists can expect to face competition for jobs. After a recent period of rapid expansion in research funding, moderate growth in research grants should drive average employment growth over the next decade.

Employment change. Employment of biological scientists is projected to grow 9 percent over the 2006–2016 decade, about as fast as the average for all occupations, as biotechnological research and development continues to drive job growth. The federal government funds much basic research and development, including many areas of medical research that relate to biological science. Recent budget increases at the National Institutes of Health have led to large increases in federal basic research and development expenditures, with research grants growing both in number and dollar amount. Nevertheless, the increase in expenditures has slowed substantially and is not expected to match its past growth over the 2006–2016 projection period. This may result in a highly competitive environment for winning and renewing research grants.

Biological scientists enjoyed very rapid employment gains since the 1980s—reflecting, in part, the growth of biotechnology companies. Employment growth should slow somewhat, as fewer new biotechnology firms are founded and existing firms merge or are absorbed by larger biotechnology or pharmaceutical firms. Some companies may conduct a portion of their research and development in other lower-wage countries, further limiting employment growth. However, much of the basic biological research done in recent years has resulted in new knowledge, including the isolation and identification of genes. Biological scientists will be needed to take this knowledge to the next stage, which is the understanding how certain genes function within an entire organism, so that medical treatments can be developed to treat various diseases. Even pharmaceutical and other firms not solely engaged in biotechnology use biotechnology techniques extensively, spurring employment increases for biological scientists. For example, biological scientists are continuing to help farmers increase crop yields by pinpointing genes that can help crops such as wheat grow worldwide in areas that currently are hostile to the crop. Continued work on chronic diseases should also lead to growing demand for biological scientists.

In addition, efforts to discover new and improved ways to clean up and preserve the environment will continue to add to job growth. More biological scientists will be needed to determine the environmental impact of industry and government actions and to prevent or correct environmental problems such as the negative effects of pesticide use. Some biological scientists will find opportunities in environmental regulatory agencies, while others will use their expertise to advise lawmakers on legislation to save environmentally sensitive areas. New industrial applications of biotechnology, such as new methods for making ethanol for transportation fuel, also will spur demand for biological scientists.

There will continue to be demand for biological scientists specializing in botany, zoology, and marine biology, but opportunities will be limited because of the small size of these fields. Marine biology, despite its attractiveness as a career, is a very small specialty within biological science.

Job prospects. Doctoral degree holders are expected to face competition for basic research positions. Furthermore, should the number of advanced degrees awarded continue to grow, applicants for research grants are likely to face even more competition. Currently, about 1 in 4 grant proposals are approved for long-term research projects. In addition, applied research positions in private industry may become more difficult to obtain if increasing numbers of scientists seek jobs in private industry because of the competitive job market for independent research positions in universities and for college and university faculty.

Prospective marine biology students should be aware that those who would like to enter this specialty far outnumber the very few openings that occur each year for the type of glamorous research jobs that many would like to obtain. Almost all marine biologists who do basic research have a Ph.D.

People with bachelor's and master's degrees are expected to have more opportunities in nonscientist jobs related to biology. The number of science-related jobs in sales, marketing, and research management is expected to exceed the number of independent research positions. Non-Ph.D.s also may fill positions as science or engineering technicians or as medical health technologists and technicians. Some become high school biology teachers.

Biological scientists are less likely to lose their jobs during recessions than are those in many other occupations because many are employed on long-term research projects. However, an economic downturn could influence the amount of money allocated to new research and development efforts, particularly in areas of risky or innovative research. An economic downturn also could limit the possibility of extension or renewal of existing projects.

Earnings

Median annual earnings of biochemists and biophysicists were $76,320 in 2006. The middle 50 percent earned between $53,390

Projections data from the National Employment Matrix

Occupational Title	SOC Code	Employment, 2006	Projected employment, 2016	Change, 2006-2016 Number	Change, 2006-2016 Percent
Biological scientists	19-1020	87,000	95,000	8,000	9
Biochemists and biophysicists	19-1021	20,000	23,000	3,200	16
Microbiologists	19-1022	17,000	19,000	1,900	11
Zoologists and wildlife biologists	19-1023	20,000	22,000	1,700	9
Biological scientists, all other	19-1029	29,000	30,000	1,100	4

NOTE: Data in this table are rounded.

and $100,060. The lowest 10 percent earned less than $40,820, and the highest 10 percent earned more than $129,510. Median annual earnings of biochemists and biophysicists employed in scientific research and development services were $79,990 in 2006.

Median annual earnings of microbiologists were 57,980 in 2006. The middle 50 percent earned between $43,850 and $80,550. The lowest 10 percent earned less than $35,460, and the highest 10 percent earned more than $108,270.

Median annual earnings of zoologists and wildlife biologists were $53,300 in 2006. The middle 50 percent earned between $41,400 and $67,200. The lowest 10 percent earned less than $32,800, and the highest 10 percent earned more than $84,580.

According to the National Association of Colleges and Employers, beginning salary offers in 2007 averaged $34,953 a year for bachelor's degree recipients in biological and life sciences.

In the federal government in 2007, general biological scientists earned an average salary of $72,146; microbiologists, $87,206; ecologists, $76,511; physiologists, $100,745; geneticists, $91,470; zoologists, $110,456; and botanists, $67,218.

Related Occupations

Many other occupations deal with living organisms and require a level of training similar to that of biological scientists. These include medical scientists, agricultural and food scientists, conservation scientists and foresters, and engineering and natural sciences managers, as well as health occupations such as physicians and surgeons, dentists, and veterinarians.

Sources of Additional Information

For information on careers in the biological sciences, contact

- American Institute of Biological Sciences, 1444 I St. NW, Suite 200, Washington, DC 20005. Internet: http://www.aibs.org

For information on careers in biochemistry or biological sciences, contact

- Federation of American Societies for Experimental Biology, 9650 Rockville Pike, Bethesda, MD 20814. Internet: http://www.faseb.org

For information on careers in botany, contact

- The Botanical Society of America, 4475 Castleman Ave., P.O. Box 299, St. Louis, MO 63166. Internet: http://www.botany.org

For information on careers in physiology, contact

- American Physiology Society, 9650 Rockville Pike, Bethesda, MD 20814. Internet: http://www.the-aps.org

Information on obtaining a biological scientist position with the federal government is available from the Office of Personnel Management through USAJOBS, the federal government's official employment information system. This resource for locating and applying for job opportunities can be accessed through the Internet at http://www.usajobs.opm.gov or through an interactive voice response telephone system at (703) 724-1850 or TDD (978) 461-8404. These numbers are not toll free, and charges may result.

Broadcast and Sound Engineering Technicians and Radio Operators

(O*NET 27-4011.00, 27-4012.00, 27-4013.00, and 27-4014.00)

Significant Points

- Job applicants will face keen competition for jobs in major metropolitan areas, where pay generally is higher; prospects are expected to be better in small cities and towns.
- Technical school, community college, or college training in broadcast technology, electronics, or computer networking provides the best preparation.
- About 30 percent of these workers are in broadcasting, mainly in radio and television stations, and 17 percent work in the motion picture, video, and sound recording industries.
- Evening, weekend, and holiday work is common.

Nature of the Work

Broadcast and sound engineering technicians and radio operators set up, operate, and maintain a wide variety of electrical and electronic equipment used in almost any radio or television broadcast, concert, play, musical recording, television show, or movie. With such a range of work, there are many specialized occupations within the field.

Audio and video equipment technicians set up and operate audio and video equipment, including microphones, sound speakers, video screens, projectors, video monitors, and recording equipment. They also connect wires and cables and set up and operate sound and mixing boards and related electronic equipment for concerts, sports events, meetings and conventions, presentations, and news conferences. They may set up and operate associated spotlights and other custom lighting systems.

Broadcast technicians set up, operate, and maintain equipment that regulates the signal strength, clarity, and the range of sounds and colors of radio or television broadcasts. These technicians also operate control panels to select the source of the material. Technicians may switch from one camera or studio to another, from film to live programming, or from network to local programming.

Sound engineering technicians operate machines and equipment to record, synchronize, mix, or reproduce music, voices, or sound effects in recording studios, sporting arenas, theater productions, or movie and video productions.

Radio operators mainly receive and transmit communications using a variety of tools. These workers also repair equipment, using such devices as electronic testing equipment, handtools, and power tools. One of their major duties is to help to maintain communication systems in good condition.

The transition to digital recording, editing, and broadcasting has greatly changed the work of broadcast and sound engineering technicians and radio operators. Software on desktop computers has replaced specialized electronic equipment in many recording and editing functions. Most radio and television stations have replaced videotapes and audiotapes with computer hard drives and other computer data storage systems. Computer networks linked to specialized equipment dominate modern broadcasting. This transition has forced technicians to learn computer networking and software skills. (See the statement on computer support specialists and systems administrators elsewhere in this book.)

Broadcast and sound engineering technicians and radio operators perform a variety of duties in small stations. In large stations and at the networks, technicians are more specialized, although job assignments may change from day to day. The terms "operator," "engineer," and "technician" often are used interchangeably to describe these jobs. Workers in these positions may monitor and log outgoing signals and operate transmitters; set up, adjust, service, and repair electronic broadcasting equipment; and regulate fidelity, brightness, contrast, volume, and sound quality of television broadcasts.

Technicians also work in program production. *Recording Engineers* operate and maintain video and sound recording equipment. They may operate equipment designed to produce special effects, such as the illusions of a bolt of lightning or a police siren. *Sound mixers* or *re-recording mixers* produce soundtracks for movies or television programs. After filming or recording is complete, these workers may use a process called "dubbing" to insert sounds. *Field technicians* set up and operate portable transmission equipment outside the studio. Because television news coverage requires so much electronic equipment and the technology is changing so rapidly, many stations assign technicians exclusively to news.

Chief Engineers, transmission engineers, and *broadcast field supervisors* oversee other technicians and maintain broadcasting equipment.

Work environment. Broadcast and sound engineering technicians and radio operators generally work indoors in pleasant surroundings. However, those who broadcast news and other programs from locations outside the studio may work outdoors in all types of weather or in other dangerous conditions. Technicians doing maintenance may climb poles or antenna towers, while those setting up equipment do heavy lifting.

Technicians at large stations and the networks usually work a 40-hour week under great pressure to meet broadcast deadlines, and may occasionally work overtime. Technicians at small stations routinely work more than 40 hours a week. Evening, weekend, and holiday work is usual because most stations are on the air 18 to 24 hours a day, 7 days a week. Even though a technician may not be on duty when the station is broadcasting, some technicians may be on call during nonwork hours; these workers must handle any problems that occur when they are on call.

Technicians who work on motion pictures may be on a tight schedule and may work long hours to meet contractual deadlines.

Training, Other Qualifications, and Advancement

Both broadcast and sound engineering technicians usually receive some kind of formal training prior to beginning work. Audio and video technicians usually learn the skills they need through a year or more of on-the-job training, but some have formal education after high school. Radio operators usually train for several months on the job.

Education and training. The best way to prepare for a broadcast and sound engineering technician job is to obtain technical school, community college, or college training in broadcast technology, electronics, or computer networking. For broadcast technicians, an associate degree is recommended. Sound engineering technicians usually complete vocational programs, which usually takes about a year, although there are shorter programs. Prospective technicians should take high school courses in math, physics, and electronics.

When starting out, broadcast and sound engineering technicians learn skills on the job from experienced technicians and supervisors. These beginners often start their careers in small stations and, once experienced, transfer to larger ones. Large stations usually hire only technicians with experience. Many employers pay tuition and expenses for courses or seminars to help technicians keep abreast of developments in the field.

Audio and video equipment technicians generally need a high school diploma. Many recent entrants have a community college degree or other forms of postsecondary degrees, although they are not always required. These technicians may substitute on-the-job training for formal education requirements. Many audio and video technicians learn through long-term on-the-job training, lasting from one to several years, depending on the specifics of their job. Working in a studio as an assistant is a good way of gaining experience and knowledge.

Radio operators usually are not required to complete any formal training. This is an entry-level position that generally requires on-the-job training.

In the motion picture industry, people are hired as apprentice editorial assistants and work their way up to more skilled jobs. Employers in the motion picture industry usually hire experienced freelance technicians on a picture-by-picture basis. Reputation and determination are important in getting jobs.

Continuing education to become familiar with emerging technologies is recommended for all broadcast and sound engineering technicians and radio operators.

Other qualifications. Building electronic equipment from hobby kits and operating a "ham," or amateur, radio are good ways to prepare for these careers, as is working in college radio and television stations. Information technology skills also are valuable because digital recording, editing, and broadcasting are now the norm. Broadcast and sound engineering technicians and radio operators must have manual dexterity and an aptitude for working with electrical, electronic, and mechanical systems and equipment.

Certification and advancement. Licensing is not required for broadcast technicians. However, certification by the Society of Broadcast Engineers is a mark of competence and experience. The certificate is issued to experienced technicians who pass an examination.

Experienced technicians can become supervisory technicians or chief engineers. A college degree in engineering is needed to become chief engineer at a large television station.

Employment

Broadcast and sound engineering technicians and radio operators held about 105,000 jobs in 2006. Their employment was distributed among the following detailed occupations:

Audio and video equipment technicians	50,000
Broadcast technicians	38,000
Sound engineering technicians	16,000
Radio operators	1,500

About 30 percent worked in broadcasting (except Internet) and 17 percent worked in the motion picture, video, and sound recording industries. About 13 percent were self-employed. Television stations employ, on average, many more technicians than radio stations. Some technicians are employed in other industries, producing employee communications, sales, and training programs. Technician jobs in television and radio are located in virtually all cities; jobs in radio also are found in many small towns. The highest paying and most specialized jobs are concentrated in New York City, Los Angeles, Chicago, and Washington, DC—the originating centers for most network or news programs. Motion picture production jobs are concentrated in Los Angeles and New York City.

Job Outlook

Employment is expected to grow faster than average through 2016. But people seeking entry-level jobs as technicians in broadcasting are expected to face keen competition in major metropolitan areas. Prospects are expected to be better in small cities and towns.

Employment change. Overall employment of broadcast and sound engineering technicians and radio operators is expected to grow 17 percent over the 2006–2016 decade, which is faster than the average for all occupations. Job growth in radio and television broadcasting will be limited by consolidation of ownership of radio and television stations and by labor-saving technical advances, such as computer-controlled programming and remotely controlled transmitters. Stations often are consolidated and operated from a single location, reducing employment because one or a few technicians can provide support to multiple stations. Offsetting these trends, however, is a move toward digital broadcasting that will increase employment opportunities. As of February 2009, television stations will only be allowed to broadcast digital signals and, by law, will be forced to turn off their analog signals. Technicians who can install and operate digital transmitters will be in demand as stations attempt to meet this deadline. Radio stations are beginning to broadcast digital signals as well, but there is no law that will require them to do so.

Projected job growth varies among detailed occupations in this field. Employment of audio and video equipment technicians is expected to grow 24 percent through 2016, which is much faster than the average for all occupations. Not only will these workers have to set up audio and video equipment, but they will have to maintain and repair it as well. Employment of broadcast technicians and sound engineering technicians is expected to grow 12 percent and 9 percent respectively, through 2016, about as fast as the average for all occupations. Advancements in technology will enhance the capabilities of technicians to produce higher quality radio and television programming. Employment of radio operators, on the other hand, is projected to decline rapidly by 16 percent through 2016 as more stations control programming and operate transmitters remotely.

Employment of broadcast and sound engineering technicians in the cable and pay television portion of the broadcasting industry is expected to grow as the range of products and services expands, including cable Internet access and video-on-demand. Employment of these workers in the motion picture industry is expected to grow rapidly. However, this job market is expected to remain competitive because of the large number of people who are attracted by the glamour of working in motion pictures.

Job prospects. People seeking entry-level jobs as technicians in broadcasting are expected to face keen competition in major metropolitan areas, where pay generally is higher and the number of qualified jobseekers typically exceeds the number of openings. Prospects for entry-level positions are expected to be better in small cities and towns for beginners with appropriate training.

In addition to employment growth, job openings will result from the need to replace experienced technicians who leave this field. Some of these workers leave for other jobs that require knowledge of electronics, such as computer repairer or industrial machinery repairer.

Earnings

Television stations usually pay higher salaries than radio stations; commercial broadcasting usually pays more than public broadcasting; and stations in large markets pay more than those in small markets.

Median annual earnings of audio and video equipment technicians in May 2006 were $34,840. The middle 50 percent earned between $26,090 and $46,320. The lowest 10 percent earned less than $19,980, and the highest 10 percent earned more than $62,550. Median annual earnings in motion picture and video industries, which employed the largest number of audio and video equipment technicians, were $34,530.

Median annual earnings of broadcast technicians in May 2006 were $30,690. The middle 50 percent earned between $20,880 and $45,310. The lowest 10 percent earned less than $15,680, and the highest 10 percent earned more than $64,860. Median annual earnings in radio and television broadcasting, which employed the largest number of broadcast technicians, were $27,380.

Median annual earnings of sound engineering technicians in May 2006 were $43,010. The middle 50 percent earned between $29,270 and $65,590. The lowest 10 percent earned less than $21,050, and the highest 10 percent earned more than $90,770.

Median annual earnings of radio operators in May 2006 were $37,890. The middle 50 percent earned between $28,860 and $48,280. The lowest 10 percent earned less than $20,790, and the highest 10 percent earned more than $57,920.

Projections data from the National Employment Matrix

Occupational Title	SOC Code	Employment, 2006	Projected employment, 2016	Change, 2006-2016	
				Number	Percent
Broadcast and sound engineering technicians and radio operators ..	27-4010	105,000	123,000	18,000	17
Audio and video equipment technicians	27-4011	50,000	62,000	12,000	24
Broadcast technicians	27-4012	38,000	42,000	4,600	12
Radio operators	27-4013	1,500	1,300	-300	-16
Sound engineering technicians	27-4014	16,000	18,000	1,500	9

NOTE: Data in this table are rounded.

Related Occupations

Broadcast and sound engineering technicians and radio operators need the electronics training necessary to operate technical equipment, and they generally complete specialized postsecondary programs. Occupations with similar characteristics include engineering technicians, science technicians, and electrical and electronics installers and repairers. Broadcast and sound engineering technicians also may operate computer networks, as do computer support specialists and systems administrators. Broadcast technicians on some live radio and television programs screen incoming calls; these workers have responsibilities similar to those of communications equipment operators.

Sources of Additional Information

For career information and links to employment resources, contact

- National Association of Broadcasters, 1771 N St. NW, Washington, DC 20036. Internet: http://www.nab.org

For information on certification, contact

- Society of Broadcast Engineers, 9182 North Meridian St., Suite 150, Indianapolis, IN 46260. Internet: http://www.sbe.org

For information on audio and video equipment technicians, contact

- InfoComm International, 11242 Waples Mill Rd., Suite 200, Fairfax, VA 22030. Internet: http://www.infocomm.org

Cardiovascular Technologists and Technicians

(O*NET 29-2031.00)

Significant Points

- Employment is expected to grow much faster than average; technologists and technicians trained to perform certain procedures will be in particular demand.
- About 3 out of 4 jobs are in hospitals.
- The vast majority of workers complete a two-year junior or community college program.

Nature of the Work

Cardiovascular technologists and technicians assist physicians in diagnosing and treating cardiac (heart) and peripheral vascular (blood vessel) ailments.

Cardiovascular technologists and technicians schedule appointments perform ultrasound or cardiovascular procedures, review doctors' interpretations and patient files, and monitor patients' heart rates. They also operate and care for testing equipment, explain test procedures, and compare findings to a standard to identify problems. Other day-to-day activities vary significantly between specialties.

Cardiovascular technologists may specialize in any of three areas of practice: invasive cardiology, echocardiography, or vascular technology.

Invasive cardiology. Cardiovascular technologists specializing in invasive procedures are called *cardiology technologists*. They assist physicians with cardiac catheterization procedures in which a small tube, or catheter, is threaded through a patient's artery from a spot on the patient's groin to the heart. The procedure can determine whether a blockage exists in the blood vessels that supply the heart muscle. The procedure also can help to diagnose other problems. Part of the procedure may involve balloon angioplasty, which can be used to treat blockages of blood vessels or heart valves without the need for heart surgery. Cardiology technologists assist physicians as they insert a catheter with a balloon on the end to the point of the obstruction. Another procedure using the catheter is electrophysiology test, which help locate the specific areas of heart tissue that give rise to the abnormal electrical impulses that cause arrhythmias.

Technologists prepare patients for cardiac catheterization by first positioning them on an examining table and then shaving, cleaning, and administering anesthesia to the top of their leg near the groin. During the procedures, they monitor patients' blood pressure and heart rate with EKG equipment and notify the physician if something appears to be wrong. Technologists also may prepare and monitor patients during open-heart surgery and during the insertion of pacemakers and stents that open up blockages in arteries to the heart and major blood vessels.

Noninvasive technology. Technologists who specialize in vascular technology or echocardiography perform noninvasive tests using. Tests are called "noninvasive" if they do not require the insertion of probes or other instruments into the patient's body. For example, procedures such as Doppler ultrasound transmit high-frequency sound waves into areas of the patient's body and then processes reflected echoes of the sound waves to form an image. Technologists view the ultrasound image on a screen and may record the image on videotape or photograph it for interpretation and diagnosis by a physician. As the technologist uses the instrument to perform scans and record images, technologists check the image on the screen for subtle differences between healthy and diseased areas, decide which images to include in the report to the physician, and judge whether the images are satisfactory for diagnostic purposes. They also explain the procedure to patients, record any additional medical history the patient relates, select appropriate equipment settings, and change the patient's position as necessary. (See the statement on diagnostic medical sonographers elsewhere in this book to learn more about other sonographers.)

Vascular technology. Technicians who assist physicians in the diagnosis of disorders affecting the circulation are known as *vascular technologists* or *vascular sonographers*. Vascular technologists complete patients' medical history, evaluate pulses and assess blood flow in arteries and veins by listening to the vascular flow sounds for abnormalities, and assure the appropriate vascular test has been ordered. Then they perform a noninvasive procedure using ultrasound instruments to record vascular information such as vascular blood flow, blood pressure, oxygen saturation, cerebral circulation, peripheral circulation, and abdominal circulation. Many of these tests are performed during or immediately after surgery. Vascular technologists then provide a summary of findings to the physician to aid in patient diagnosis and management.

Echocardiography. This area of practice includes giving electrocardiograms (EKGs) and sonograms of the heart. Cardiovascular technicians who specialize in EKGs, stress testing, and those who perform Holter monitor procedures are known as cardiographic or *electrocardiograph* (or *EKG*) *technicians*.

To take a basic EKG, which traces electrical impulses transmitted by the heart, technicians attach electrodes to the patient's chest, arms, and legs, and then manipulate switches on an EKG machine to

Projections data from the National Employment Matrix

Occupational Title	SOC Code	Employment, 2006	Projected employment, 2016	Change, 2006-2016	
				Number	Percent
Cardiovascular technologists and technicians	29-2031	45,000	57,000	12,000	26

NOTE: Data in this table are rounded.

obtain a reading. An EKG is printed out for interpretation by the physician. This test is done before most kinds of surgery or as part of a routine physical examination, especially on persons who have reached middle age or who have a history of cardiovascular problems.

EKG technicians with advanced training perform Holter monitor and stress testing. For Holter monitoring, technicians place electrodes on the patient's chest and attach a portable EKG monitor to the patient's belt. Following 24 or more hours of normal activity by the patient, the technician removes a tape from the monitor and places it in a scanner. After checking the quality of the recorded impulses on an electronic screen, the technician usually prints the information from the tape for analysis by a physician. Physicians use the output from the scanner to diagnose heart ailments, such as heart rhythm abnormalities or problems with pacemakers.

For a treadmill stress test, EKG technicians document the patient's medical history, explain the procedure, connect the patient to an EKG monitor, and obtain a baseline reading and resting blood pressure. Next, they monitor the heart's performance while the patient is walking on a treadmill, gradually increasing the treadmill's speed to observe the effect of increased exertion. Like vascular technologists and cardiac sonographers, cardiographic technicians who perform EKG, Holter monitor, and stress tests are known as "noninvasive" technicians.

Technologists who use ultrasound to examine the heart chambers, valves, and vessels are referred to as *cardiac sonographers*, or *echocardiographers*. They use ultrasound instrumentation to create images called echocardiograms. An echocardiogram may be performed while the patient is either resting or physically active. Technologists may administer medication to physically active patients to assess their heart function. Cardiac sonographers also may assist physicians who perform transesophageal echocardiography, which involves placing a tube in the patient's esophagus to obtain ultrasound images.

Work environment. Cardiovascular technologists and technicians spend a lot of time walking and standing. Heavy lifting may be involved to move equipment or transfer patients. These workers wear heavy protective aprons while conducting some procedures. Those who work in catheterization laboratories may face stressful working conditions because they are in close contact with patients with serious heart ailments. For example, some patients may encounter complications that have life-or-death implications.

Some cardiovascular technologists and technicians may have the potential for radiation exposure, which is kept to a minimum by strict adherence to radiation safety guidelines. In addition, those who use sonography can be at an increased risk for musculoskeletal disorders such as carpel tunnel syndrome, neck and back strain, and eye strain. However, greater use of ergonomic equipment and an increasing awareness will continue to minimize such risks.

Technologists and technicians generally work a 5-day, 40-hour week that may include weekends. Those in catheterization laboratories tend to work longer hours and may work evenings. They also may be on call during the night and on weekends.

Training, Other Qualifications, and Advancement

The most common level of education completed by cardiovascular technologists and technicians is an associate degree. Certification, although not required in all cases, is available.

Education and training. Although a few cardiovascular technologists, vascular technologists, and cardiac sonographers are currently trained on the job, most receive training in two- to four-year programs. The majority of technologists complete a two-year junior or community college program, but four-year programs are increasingly available. The first year is dedicated to core courses and is followed by a year of specialized instruction in either invasive, noninvasive cardiovascular, or noninvasive vascular technology. Those who are qualified in an allied health profession need to complete only the year of specialized instruction.

The Joint Review Committee on Education in Cardiovascular Technology reviews education programs seeking accreditation. The Commission on Accreditation of Allied Health Professionals (CAAHEP) accredits these education programs; as of 2006, there were 31 programs accredited in cardiovascular technology in the United States. Similarly, those who want to study echocardiography or vascular sonography may also attend CAAHEP accredited programs in diagnostic medical sonography. In 2006, there were 147 diagnostic medical sonography programs accredited by CAAHEP. Those who attend these accredited programs are eligible to obtain professional certification.

Unlike most other cardiovascular technologists and technicians, most EKG technicians are trained on the job by an EKG supervisor or a cardiologist. On-the-job training usually lasts about eight to 16 weeks. Most employers prefer to train people already in the health care field—nursing aides, for example. Some EKG technicians are students enrolled in two-year programs to become technologists, working part time to gain experience and make contact with employers. One-year certification programs exist for basic EKGs, Holter monitoring, and stress testing.

Licensure and certification. Some states require workers in this occupation to be licensed. For information on a particular state, contact that state's medical board. Certification is available from two organizations: Cardiovascular Credentialing International (CCI) and the American Registry of Diagnostic Medical Sonographers (ARDMS). The CCI offers four certifications—Certified Cardiographic Technician (CCT), Registered Cardiac Sonographer (RCS), Registered Vascular Specialist (RVS), and Registered Cardiovascular Invasive Specialist (RCIS). The ARDMS offers Registered Diagnostic Cardiac Sonographer (RDCS) and Registered Vascular Technologist (RVT) credentials. Some states require certification as part of licensure. In other states, certification is not required but many employers prefer it.

Other qualifications. Cardiovascular technologists and technicians must be reliable, have mechanical aptitude, and be able to follow detailed instructions. A pleasant, relaxed manner for putting patients at ease is an asset. They must be articulate as they must communicate technically with physicians and also explain procedures simply to patients.

Advancement. Technologists and technicians can advance to higher levels of the profession as many institutions structure the occupation with multiple levels, each having an increasing amount of responsibility. Technologists and technicians also can advance into supervisory or management positions. Other common possibilities include working in an educational setting or conducting laboratory work.

Employment

Cardiovascular technologists and technicians held about 45,000 jobs in 2006. About 3 out of 4 jobs were in hospitals (public and private), primarily in cardiology departments. The remaining jobs were mostly in offices of physicians, including cardiologists, or in medical and diagnostic laboratories, including diagnostic imaging centers.

Job Outlook

Employment is expected to grow much faster than average; technologists and technicians trained to perform certain procedures will be in particular demand.

Employment change. Employment of cardiovascular technologists and technicians is expected to increase by 26 percent through the year 2016, much faster than the average for all occupations. Growth will occur as the population ages, because older people have a higher incidence of heart disease and other complications of the heart and vascular system. Procedures such as ultrasound are being performed more often as a replacement for more expensive and more invasive procedures. Due to advances in medicine and greater public awareness, signs of vascular disease can be detected earlier, creating demand for cardiovascular technologists and technicians to perform various procedures.

Employment of vascular technologists and echocardiographers will grow as advances in vascular technology and sonography reduce the need for more costly and invasive procedures. Electrophysiology is also becoming a rapidly growing specialty. However, fewer EKG technicians will be needed, as hospitals train nursing aides and others to perform basic EKG procedures. Individuals trained in Holter monitoring and stress testing are expected to have more favorable job prospects than those who can perform only a basic EKG.

Medicaid has relaxed some of the rules governing reimbursement for vascular exams, which is resulting in vascular studies becoming a more routine practice. As a result of increased use of these procedures, individuals with training in vascular studies should have more favorable employment opportunities.

Job prospects. Some additional job openings for cardiovascular technologists and technicians will arise from replacement needs as individuals transfer to other jobs or leave the labor force. Although growing awareness of musculoskeletal disorders has made prevention easier, some cardiovascular technologists and technicians have been forced to leave the occupation early because of this disorder.

It is not uncommon for cardiovascular technologists and technicians to move between the specialties within the occupation by obtaining certification in more than one specialty.

Earnings

Median annual earnings of cardiovascular technologists and technicians were $42,300 in May 2006. The middle 50 percent earned between $29,900 and $55,670. The lowest 10 percent earned less than $23,670, and the highest 10 percent earned more than $67,410. Median annual earnings of cardiovascular technologists and technicians in 2006 were $41,960 in offices of physicians and $41,950 in general medical and surgical hospitals.

Related Occupations

Cardiovascular technologists and technicians operate sophisticated equipment that helps physicians and other health practitioners to diagnose and treat patients. So do diagnostic medical sonographers, nuclear medicine technologists, radiation therapists, radiologic technologists and technicians, and respiratory therapists.

Sources of Additional Information

For general information about a career in cardiovascular technology, contact

- Alliance of Cardiovascular Professionals, Thalia Landing Offices, Bldg. 2, 4356 Bonney Rd., Suite 103, Virginia Beach, VA 23452-1200. Internet: http://www.acp-online.org

For a list of accredited programs in cardiovascular technology, contact

- Committee on Accreditation for Allied Health Education Programs, 1361 Park St, Clearwater, FL 33756. Internet: http://www.caahep.org
- Society for Vascular Ultrasound, 4601 Presidents Dr., Suite 260, Lanham, MD 20706-4381. Internet: http://www.svunet.org

For information on echocardiography, contact

- American Society of Echocardiography, 1500 Sunday Dr., Suite 102, Raleigh, NC 27607. Internet: http://www.asecho.org

For information regarding registration and certification, contact

- Cardiovascular Credentialing International, 1500 Sunday Dr., Suite 102, Raleigh, NC 27607. Internet: http://www.cci-online.org
- American Registry of Diagnostic Medical Sonographers, 51 Monroe St., Plaza East One, Rockville, MD 20850-2400. Internet: http://www.ardms.org

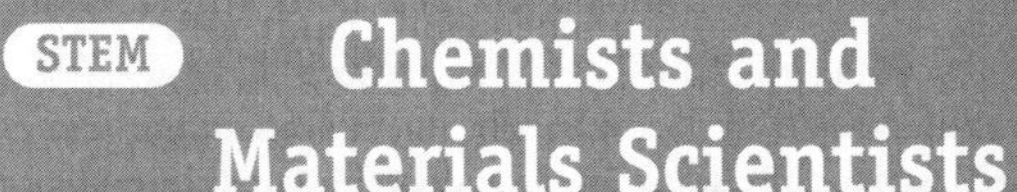

Chemists and Materials Scientists

(O*NET 19-2031.00 and 19-2032.00)

Significant Points

- A bachelor's degree in chemistry or a related discipline is the minimum educational requirement; however, many research jobs require a master's degree or, more often, a Ph.D.
- Job growth will occur in professional, scientific, and technical services firms as manufacturing companies continue to outsource their research and development and testing operations to these smaller, specialized firms.

- New chemists at all levels may experience competition for jobs, particularly in declining chemical manufacturing industries; graduates with a master's degree, and particularly those with a Ph.D., will enjoy better opportunities at larger pharmaceutical and biotechnology firms.

Nature of the Work

Everything in the environment, whether naturally occurring or of human design, is composed of chemicals. Chemists and materials scientists search for and use new knowledge about chemicals. Chemical research has led to the discovery and development of new and improved synthetic fibers, paints, adhesives, drugs, cosmetics, electronic components, lubricants, and thousands of other products. Chemists and materials scientists also develop processes such as improved oil refining and petrochemical processing that save energy and reduce pollution. Applications of materials science include studies of superconducting materials, graphite materials, integrated-circuit chips, and fuel cells. Research on the chemistry of living things spurs advances in medicine, agriculture, food processing, and other fields.

Many chemists and materials scientists work in research and development (R&D). In basic research, they investigate the properties, composition, and structure of matter and the laws that govern the combination of elements and reactions of substances to each other. In applied R&D, these scientists create new products and processes or improve existing ones, often using knowledge gained from basic research. For example, synthetic rubber and plastics resulted from research on small molecules uniting to form large ones, a process called polymerization. R&D chemists and materials scientists use computers and a wide variety of sophisticated laboratory instrumentation for modeling, simulation, and experimental analysis.

The use of computers to analyze complex data has allowed chemists and materials scientists to practice combinatorial chemistry. This technique makes and tests large quantities of chemical compounds simultaneously to find those with certain desired properties. Combinatorial chemistry has allowed chemists to produce thousands of compounds more quickly and inexpensively than was formerly possible and assisted in the sequencing of human genes. Specialty chemists, such as medicinal and organic chemists, work with life scientists to translate this knowledge into new drugs.

Developments in the field of chemistry that involve life sciences will expand, resulting in more interaction among biologists, engineers, computer specialists, and chemists. (*Biochemists*, whose work encompasses both biology and chemistry, are discussed in this book's statement on biological scientists.)

Chemists also work in production and quality control in chemical manufacturing plants. They prepare instructions for plant workers that specify ingredients, mixing times, and temperatures for each stage in the process. They also monitor automated processes to ensure proper product yield and test samples of raw materials or finished products to ensure that they meet industry and government standards, including regulations governing pollution. Chemists report and document test results and analyze those results in hopes of improving existing theories or developing new test methods.

Chemists often specialize. *Analytical chemists* determine the structure, composition, and nature of substances by examining and identifying their various elements or compounds. These chemists are absolutely crucial to the pharmaceutical industry because pharmaceutical companies need to know the identity of compounds that they hope to turn into drugs. Furthermore, analytical chemists develop analytical techniques and study the relationships and interactions among the parts of compounds. They also identify the presence and concentration of chemical pollutants in air, water, and soil.

Organic chemists study the chemistry of the vast number of carbon compounds that make up all living things. Organic chemists who synthesize elements or simple compounds to create new compounds or substances that have different properties and applications have developed many commercial products, such as drugs, plastics, and elastomers (elastic substances similar to rubber). *Inorganic chemists* study compounds consisting mainly of elements other than carbon, such as those in electronic components.

Physical and *theoretical chemists* study the physical characteristics of atoms and molecules and the theoretical properties of matter; and they investigate how chemical reactions work. Their research may result in new and better energy sources. *Macromolecular chemists* study the behavior of atoms and molecules. *Medicinal chemists* study the structural properties of compounds intended for applications to human medicine.

Materials chemists study and develop new materials to improve existing products or make new ones. In fact, virtually all chemists are involved in this quest in one way or another.

The work of materials chemists is similar to, but separate from, the work of materials scientists. Materials scientists apply physics as well as chemistry to study all aspects of materials. Chemistry, however, plays an increasingly dominant role in materials science because it provides information about the structure and composition of materials.

Materials scientists study the structures and chemical properties of various materials to develop new products or enhance existing ones. They also determine ways to strengthen or combine materials or develop new materials for use in a variety of products. Materials science encompasses the natural and synthetic materials used in a wide range of products and structures, from airplanes, cars, and bridges to clothing and household goods. Materials scientists often specialize in specific areas such as ceramics or metals.

Work environment. Chemists and materials scientists usually work regular hours in offices and laboratories. R&D chemists and materials scientists spend much time in laboratories but also work in offices when they do theoretical research or plan, record, and report on their lab research. Although some laboratories are small, others are large enough to incorporate prototype chemical manufacturing facilities as well as advanced testing equipment. In addition to working in a laboratory, materials scientists also work with engineers and processing specialists in industrial manufacturing facilities. Chemists do some of their work in a chemical plant or outdoors—gathering water samples to test for pollutants, for example. Some chemists are exposed to health or safety hazards when handling certain chemicals, but there is little risk if proper procedures are followed.

Chemists and materials scientists typically work regular hours. A 40-hour work week is usual, but longer hours are not uncommon. Researchers may be required to work odd hours in laboratories or other locations, depending on the nature of their research.

Training, Other Qualifications, and Advancement

A bachelor's degree in chemistry or a related discipline is the minimum educational requirement; however, many research jobs require a master's degree or, more often, a Ph.D.

Education and training. A bachelor's degree in chemistry or a related discipline usually is the minimum educational requirement for entry-level chemist jobs. While some materials scientists hold a degree in materials science, degrees in chemistry, physics, or electrical engineering are also common. Most research jobs in chemistry and materials science require a master's degree or, more frequently, a Ph.D.

Many colleges and universities offer degree programs in chemistry. In 2007, the American Chemical Society (ACS) had approved approximately 640 bachelors, 310 masters, and 200 doctoral degree programs. In addition to these programs, other advanced degree programs in chemistry were offered at several hundred colleges and universities. The number of colleges that offer a degree program in materials science is small but gradually increasing.

Students planning careers as chemists and materials scientists should take courses in science and mathematics, should like working with their hands building scientific apparatus and performing laboratory experiments, and should like computer modeling.

In addition to taking required courses in analytical, inorganic, organic, and physical chemistry, undergraduate chemistry majors usually study biological sciences; mathematics; physics; and increasingly, computer science. Computer courses are essential because employers prefer job applicants who are able to apply computer skills to modeling and simulation tasks and operate computerized laboratory equipment. This is increasingly important as combinatorial chemistry and advanced screening techniques are more widely applied. Courses in statistics are useful because both chemists and materials scientists need the ability to apply basic statistical techniques.

People interested in environmental specialties also should take courses in environmental studies and become familiar with current legislation and regulations. Specific courses should include atmospheric, water, and soil chemistry, and energy.

Graduate students studying chemistry commonly specialize in a subfield, such as analytical chemistry or polymer chemistry, depending on their interests and the kind of work they wish to do. For example, those interested in doing drug research in the pharmaceutical industry usually develop a strong background in medicinal or synthetic organic chemistry. However, students normally need not specialize at the undergraduate level. In fact, undergraduates who are broadly trained have more flexibility when searching for jobs than if they have narrowly defined their interests. Most employers provide new graduates additional training or education.

In government or industry, beginning chemists with a bachelor's degree work in quality control, perform analytical testing, or assist senior chemists in R&D laboratories. Many employers prefer chemists and materials scientists with a Ph.D., or at least a master's degree, to lead basic and applied research. Within materials science, a broad background in various sciences is preferred. This broad base may be obtained through degrees in physics, engineering, or chemistry. Although many companies prefer hiring Ph.D.s, some may employ materials scientists with bachelor's and master's degrees.

Other qualifications. Because R&D chemists and materials scientists are increasingly expected to work on interdisciplinary teams, some understanding of other disciplines, including business and marketing or economics, is desirable, along with leadership ability and good oral and written communication skills. Interaction among specialists in this field is increasing, especially for specialty chemists in drug development. One type of chemist often relies on the findings of another type of chemist. For example, an organic chemist must understand findings on the identity of compounds prepared by an analytical chemist.

Experience, either in academic laboratories or through internships, fellowships, or work-study programs in industry, also is useful. Some employers of research chemists, particularly in the pharmaceutical industry, prefer to hire individuals with several years of postdoctoral experience.

Perseverance, curiosity, and the ability to concentrate on detail and to work independently are essential.

Advancement. Advancement among chemists and materials scientists usually takes the form of greater independence in their work or larger budgets. Others choose to move into managerial positions and become natural sciences managers (described elsewhere in this book as Engineering and Natural Sciences Managers). Those who pursue management careers spend more time preparing budgets and schedules and setting research strategy. Chemists or materials scientists who develop new products or processes sometimes form their own companies or join new firms to develop these ideas.

Employment

Chemists and materials scientists held about 93,000 jobs in 2006. Chemists accounted for about 84,000 of these, while materials scientists accounted for about 9,700 jobs. In addition, many chemists and materials scientists held faculty positions in colleges and universities but are not included in these numbers. (See the statement on teachers—postsecondary elsewhere in this book.)

About 41 percent of all chemists and material scientists are employed in manufacturing firms—mostly in the chemical manufacturing industry; firms in this industry produce plastics and synthetic materials, drugs, soaps and cleaners, pesticides and fertilizers, paint, industrial organic chemicals, and other chemical products. About 18 percent of chemists and material scientists work in scientific research and development services; 12 percent work in architectural, engineering, and related services. Companies whose products are made of metals, ceramics, and rubber employ most materials scientists. In addition, thousands of people with a background in chemistry and materials science hold teaching positions in high schools and in colleges and universities. (See the statement on teachers—postsecondary elsewhere in this book.)

Chemists and materials scientists are employed in all parts of the country, but they are mainly concentrated in large industrial areas.

Job Outlook

Average job growth is expected. New chemists at all levels may experience competition for jobs, particularly in declining chemical manufacturing industries. Graduates with a master's degree or a Ph.D., will enjoy better opportunities, especially at larger pharmaceutical and biotechnology firms.

Employment change. Employment of chemists and materials scientists is expected to grow 9 percent over the 2006–2016 decade, about as fast as the average for all occupations. Job growth will occur in professional, scientific, and technical services firms as manufacturing companies continue to outsource their R&D and testing operations to these smaller, specialized firms.

Chemists should experience employment growth in pharmaceutical and biotechnology research, as recent advances in genetics open new avenues of treatment for diseases. Employment of chemists in the nonpharmaceutical chemical manufacturing industries is expected to decline over the projection period, along with overall declining employment in these industries.

Employment of materials scientists should continue to grow as manufacturers of diverse products seek to improve their quality by using new materials and manufacturing processes.

Within the chemical manufacturing industries, job growth for chemists is expected to be strongest in pharmaceutical and biotechnology firms. Biotechnological research, including studies of human genes, continues to offer possibilities for the development of new drugs and products to combat illnesses and diseases that have previously been unresponsive to treatments derived by traditional chemical processes. Stronger competition among drug companies and an aging population are contributing to the need for new drugs.

The remaining chemical manufacturing industries are expected to employ fewer chemists as companies divest their R&D operations. To control costs, most chemical companies, including many large pharmaceutical and biotechnology companies, will increasingly turn to scientific R&D services firms to perform specialized research and other work formerly done by in-house chemists. As a result, these firms will experience healthy growth. Also, some companies are expected to conduct an increasing amount of manufacturing and research in lower-wage countries, further limiting domestic employment growth. Quality control will continue to be an important issue in chemical manufacturing and other industries that use chemicals in their manufacturing processes.

Chemists also will be employed to develop and improve the technologies and processes used to produce chemicals for all purposes, and to monitor and measure air and water pollutants to ensure compliance with local, state, and federal environmental regulations. Environmental research will offer many new opportunities for chemists and materials scientists. To satisfy public concerns and to comply with government regulations, chemical manufacturing industries will continue to invest billions of dollars each year in technology that reduces pollution and cleans up existing waste sites. Research into traditional and alternative energy sources should also lead to employment growth among chemists.

Job prospects. New chemists at all levels may experience competition for jobs, particularly in declining chemical manufacturing industries. Graduates with a bachelor's degree in chemistry may find science-related jobs in sales, marketing, and middle management. Some become chemical technicians or technologists or high school chemistry teachers. In addition, bachelor's degree holders are increasingly finding assistant research positions at smaller research organizations.

Graduates with an advanced degree, and particularly those with a Ph.D., will enjoy better opportunities. Larger pharmaceutical and biotechnology firms will offer more openings for these workers. Furthermore, chemists with an advanced degree will continue to fill most senior research and upper management positions; however, similar to other occupations, applicants face strong competition for the limited number of upper management jobs.

In addition to jobs openings resulting from employment growth, some job openings will result from the need to replace chemists and materials scientists who retire or otherwise leave the labor force, although not all positions will be filled.

During periods of economic recession, layoffs of chemists may occur—especially in the industrial chemicals industry. Layoffs are less likely in the pharmaceutical industry, where long development cycles generally overshadow short-term economic conditions. The traditional chemical industries, however, provide many raw materials to the automotive manufacturing and construction industries, both of which are vulnerable to temporary slowdowns during recessions.

Earnings

Median annual earnings of chemists in 2006 were $59,870. The middle 50 percent earned between $44,780 and $82,610. The lowest 10 percent earned less than $35,480, and the highest 10 percent earned more than $106,310. Median annual earnings of materials scientists in 2006 were $74,610. The middle 50 percent earned between $55,170 and $96,800. The lowest 10 percent earned less than $41,810, and the highest 10 percent earned more than $118,670. Median annual earnings in the industries employing the largest numbers of chemists in 2006 are shown below:

Federal executive branch	$88,930
Scientific research and development services	68,760
Basic chemical manufacturing	62,340
Pharmaceutical and medicine manufacturing	57,210
Testing laboratories	45,730

According to the National Association of Colleges and Employers, beginning salary offers in July 2007 for graduates with bachelor's degrees in chemistry averaged $41,506 a year.

In 2007, annual earnings of chemists in nonsupervisory, supervisory, and managerial positions in the federal government averaged $89,954.

Related Occupations

The research and analysis conducted by chemists and materials scientists is closely related to work done by agricultural and food sci-

Projections data from the National Employment Matrix

Occupational Title	SOC Code	Employment, 2006	Projected employment, 2016	Change, 2006-2016	
				Number	Percent
Chemists and materials scientists	19-2030	93,000	102,000	8,500	9
Chemists	19-2031	84,000	91,000	7,600	9
Materials scientists	19-2032	9,700	11,000	800	9

NOTE: Data in this table are rounded.

entists, biological scientists, medical scientists, engineering and natural sciences managers, chemical engineers, materials engineers, physicists and astronomers, and science technicians.

Sources of Additional Information

General information on career opportunities and earnings for chemists is available from

- American Chemical Society, Education Division, 1155 16th St. NW, Washington, DC 20036. Internet: http://www.acs.org

Information on obtaining a position as a chemist with the federal government is available from the Office of Personnel Management through USAJOBS, the federal government's official employment information system. This resource for locating and applying for job opportunities can be accessed through the Internet at http://www.usajobs.opm.gov or through an interactive voice response telephone system at (703) 724-1850 or TDD (978) 461-8404. These numbers are not toll free, and charges may result.

Chiropractors

(O*NET 29-1011.00)

Significant Points

- Job prospects should be good; employment is expected to grow faster than average because of increasing consumer demand for alternative health care.
- Chiropractors must be licensed, requiring 2 to 4 years of undergraduate education, the completion of a 4-year chiropractic college course, and passing scores on national and state examinations.
- About 52 percent of chiropractors are self employed.
- Earnings are relatively low in the beginning but increase as the practice grows.

Nature of the Work

Chiropractors, also known as *doctors of chiropractic* or *chiropractic physicians*, diagnose and treat patients with health problems of the musculoskeletal system and treat the effects of those problems on the nervous system and on general health. Many chiropractic treatments deal specifically with the spine and the manipulation of the spine. Chiropractic medicine is based on the principle that spinal joint misalignments interfere with the nervous system and can result in lower resistance to disease and many different conditions of diminished health.

The chiropractic approach to health care stresses the patient's overall health. Chiropractors provide natural, drugless, nonsurgical health treatments, relying on the body's inherent recuperative abilities. They also recognize that many factors affect health, including exercise, diet, rest, environment, and heredity. Chiropractors recommend changes in lifestyle that affect those factors. In some situations, chiropractors refer patients to or consult with other health practitioners.

Like other health practitioners, chiropractors follow a standard routine to get information needed to diagnose and treat patients. They take the patient's medical history; conduct physical, neurological, and orthopedic examinations; and may order laboratory tests. X rays and other diagnostic images are important tools because of the chiropractor's emphasis on the spine and its proper function. Chiropractors also analyze the patient's posture and spine using a specialized technique. For patients whose health problems can be traced to the musculoskeletal system, chiropractors manually adjust the spinal column.

Some chiropractors use other alternative medicines in their practices, including therapies using water, light, massage, ultrasound, electric, acupuncture, and heat. They also may apply supports such as straps, tapes, and braces to manually adjust the spine. Chiropractors counsel patients about health concepts such as nutrition, exercise, changes in lifestyle, and stress management, but chiropractors do not prescribe drugs or perform surgery.

In addition to general chiropractic practice, some chiropractors specialize in sports injuries, neurology, orthopedics, pediatrics, nutrition, internal disorders, or diagnostic imaging.

Many chiropractors are solo or group practitioners who also have the administrative responsibilities of running a practice. In larger offices, chiropractors delegate these tasks to office managers and chiropractic assistants. Chiropractors in private practice are responsible for developing a patient base, hiring employees, and keeping records.

Work environment. Chiropractors work in clean, comfortable offices. Like other health practitioners, chiropractors are sometimes on their feet for long periods. Chiropractors who take x rays must employ appropriate precautions against the dangers of repeated exposure to radiation.

Chiropractors work, on average, about 40 hours per week, although longer hours are not uncommon. Solo practitioners set their own hours but may work evenings or weekends to accommodate patients. Like other health care practitioners, chiropractors in a group practice will sometimes be on call or treat patients of other chiropractors in the group.

Training, Other Qualifications, and Advancement

Chiropractors must be licensed, which requires two to four years of undergraduate education, the completion of a four-year chiropractic college course, and passing scores on national and state examinations.

Education and training. In 2007, 16 chiropractic programs and two chiropractic institutions in the United States were accredited by the Council on Chiropractic Education. Applicants must have at least 90 semester hours of undergraduate study leading toward a bachelor's degree, including courses in English, the social sciences or humanities, organic and inorganic chemistry, biology, physics, and psychology. Many applicants have a bachelor's degree, which may eventually become the minimum entry requirement. Several chiropractic colleges offer prechiropractic study, as well as a bachelor's degree program. Recognition of prechiropractic education offered by chiropractic colleges varies among the states.

Chiropractic programs require a minimum of 4,200 hours of combined classroom, laboratory, and clinical experience. During the first two years, most chiropractic programs emphasize classroom and laboratory work in sciences such as anatomy, physiology, public health, microbiology, pathology, and biochemistry. The last two years focus on courses in manipulation and spinal adjustment and provide clinical experience in physical and laboratory diagnosis, neurology, orthopedics, geriatrics, physiotherapy, and nutrition. Chiropractic programs and institutions grant the degree of Doctor of Chiropractic.

Chiropractic colleges also offer postdoctoral training in orthopedics, neurology, sports injuries, nutrition, rehabilitation, radiology, industrial consulting, family practice, pediatrics, and applied chiropractic sciences. Once such training is complete, chiropractors may take specialty exams leading to "diplomate" status in a given specialty. Exams are administered by specialty chiropractic associations.

Licensure. All states and the District of Columbia regulate the practice of chiropractic and grant licenses to chiropractors who meet the educational and examination requirements established by the state. Chiropractors can practice only in states where they are licensed. Some states have agreements permitting chiropractors licensed in one state to obtain a license in another without further examination, provided that their educational, examination, and practice credentials meet state specifications.

Most state licensing boards require at least two years of undergraduate education, but an increasing number are requiring a four-year bachelor's degree. All boards require the completion of a four-year program at an accredited chiropractic college leading to the Doctor of Chiropractic degree.

For licensure, most state boards recognize either all or part of the four-part test administered by the National Board of Chiropractic Examiners. State examinations may supplement the National Board tests, depending on state requirements. All states except New Jersey require the completion of a specified number of hours of continuing education each year in order to maintain licensure. Chiropractic associations and accredited chiropractic programs and institutions offer continuing education programs.

Other qualifications. Chiropractic requires keen observation to detect physical abnormalities. It also takes considerable manual dexterity, but not unusual strength or endurance, to perform adjustments. Chiropractors should be able to work independently and handle responsibility. As in other health-related occupations, empathy, understanding, and the desire to help others are good qualities for dealing effectively with patients.

Advancement. Newly licensed chiropractors can set up a new practice, purchase an established one, or enter into partnership with an established practitioner. They also may take a salaried position with an established chiropractor, a group practice, or a health care facility.

Employment

Chiropractors held about 53,000 jobs in 2006. Most chiropractors work in a solo practice, although some are in group practice or work for other chiropractors. A small number teach, conduct research at chiropractic institutions, or work in hospitals and clinics. Approximately 52 percent of chiropractors were self employed.

Many chiropractors are located in small communities. However, the distribution of chiropractors is not geographically uniform. This occurs primarily because new chiropractors frequently establish their practices in close proximity to one of the few chiropractic educational institutions.

Job Outlook

Employment is expected to grow faster than average because of increasing consumer demand for alternative health care. Job prospects should be good.

Employment change. Employment of chiropractors is expected to increase 14 percent between 2006 and 2016, faster than the average for all occupations. Projected job growth stems from increasing consumer demand for alternative health care. Because chiropractors emphasize the importance of healthy lifestyles and do not prescribe drugs or perform surgery, chiropractic care is appealing to many health-conscious Americans. Chiropractic treatment of the back, neck, extremities, and joints has become more accepted as a result of research and changing attitudes about alternative, noninvasive health care practices. The rapidly expanding older population, with its increased likelihood of mechanical and structural problems, also will increase demand for chiropractors.

Demand for chiropractic treatment, however, is related to the ability of patients to pay, either directly or through health insurance. Although more insurance plans now cover chiropractic services, the extent of such coverage varies among plans. Chiropractors must educate communities about the benefits of chiropractic care in order to establish a successful practice.

Job prospects. Job prospects for new chiropractors are expected to be good. In this occupation, replacement needs arise almost entirely from retirements. Chiropractors usually remain in the occupation until they retire; few transfer to other occupations. Establishing a new practice will be easiest in areas with a low concentration of chiropractors.

Earnings

Median annual earnings of salaried chiropractors were $65,220 in 2006. The middle 50 percent earned between $45,710 and $96,500 a year.

In 2005, the mean salary for chiropractors was $104,363 according to a survey conducted by *Chiropractic Economics* magazine.

In chiropractic, as in other types of independent practice, earnings are relatively low in the beginning and increase as the practice grows. Geographic location and the characteristics and qualifications of the practitioner also may influence earnings.

Salaried chiropractors typically receive heath insurance and retirement benefits from their employers, whereas self-employed chiropractors must provide for their own health insurance and retirement.

Related Occupations

Chiropractors treat patients and work to prevent bodily disorders and injuries. So do athletic trainers, massage therapists, occupa-

Projections data from the National Employment Matrix

Occupational Title	SOC Code	Employment, 2006	Projected employment, 2016	Change, 2006-2016	
				Number	Percent
Chiropractors	29-1011	53,000	60,000	7,600	14

NOTE: Data in this table are rounded.

tional therapists, physical therapists, physicians and surgeons, podiatrists, and veterinarians.

Sources of Additional Information

General information on a career as a chiropractor is available from the following organizations:

- American Chiropractic Association, 1701 Clarendon Blvd., Arlington, VA 22209. Internet: http://www.acatoday.org
- International Chiropractors Association, 1110 North Glebe Rd., Suite 650, Arlington, VA 22201. Internet: http://www.chiropractic.org
- World Chiropractic Alliance, 2950 N. Dobson Rd., Suite 3, Chandler, AZ 85224.

For a list of chiropractic programs and institutions, as well as general information on chiropractic education, contact

- Council on Chiropractic Education, 8049 North 85th Way, Scottsdale, AZ 85258-4321. Internet: http://www.cce-usa.org

For information on state education and licensure requirements, contact

- Federation of Chiropractic Licensing Boards, 5401 W. 10th St., Suite 101, Greeley, CO 80634-4400. Internet: http://www.fclb.org

For more information on the national chiropractic licensing exam, contact

- National Board of Chiropractic Examiners, 901 54th Ave., Greeley, CO 80634-4400. Internet: http://www.nbce.org

For information on admission requirements to a specific chiropractic college, as well as scholarship and loan information, contact the college's admissions office.

Clinical Laboratory Technologists and Technicians

(O*NET 29-2011.00 and 29-2012.00)

Significant Points

- Faster than average employment growth and excellent job opportunities are expected.
- Clinical laboratory technologists usually have a bachelor's degree with a major in medical technology or in one of the life sciences; clinical laboratory technicians generally need either an associate degree or a certificate.
- Most jobs will continue to be in hospitals, but employment will grow faster in other settings.

Nature of the Work

Clinical laboratory testing plays a crucial role in the detection, diagnosis, and treatment of disease. Clinical laboratory technologists—also referred to as clinical laboratory scientists or medical technologists—and clinical laboratory technicians, also known as medical technicians or medical laboratory technicians, perform most of these tests.

Clinical laboratory personnel examine and analyze body fluids, and cells. They look for bacteria, parasites, and other microorganisms; analyze the chemical content of fluids; match blood for transfusions; and test for drug levels in the blood that show how a patient is responding to treatment. Technologists also prepare specimens for examination, count cells, and look for abnormal cells in blood and body fluids. They use microscopes, cell counters, and other sophisticated laboratory equipment. They also use automated equipment and computerized instruments capable of performing a number of tests simultaneously. After testing and examining a specimen, they analyze the results and relay them to physicians.

With increasing automation and the use of computer technology, the work of technologists and technicians has become less hands-on and more analytical. The complexity of tests performed, the level of judgment needed, and the amount of responsibility workers assume depend largely on the amount of education and experience they have. Clinical laboratory technologists usually do more complex tasks than clinical laboratory technicians do.

Clinical laboratory technologists perform complex chemical, biological, hematological, immunologic, microscopic, and bacteriological tests. Technologists microscopically examine blood and other body fluids. They make cultures of body fluid and tissue samples, to determine the presence of bacteria, fungi, parasites, or other microorganisms. Technologists analyze samples for chemical content or a chemical reaction and determine concentrations of compounds such as blood glucose and cholesterol levels. They also type and cross match blood samples for transfusions.

Clinical laboratory technologists evaluate test results, develop and modify procedures, and establish and monitor programs, to ensure the accuracy of tests. Some technologists supervise clinical laboratory technicians.

Technologists in small laboratories perform many types of tests, whereas those in large laboratories generally specialize. Clinical chemistry technologists, for example, prepare specimens and analyze the chemical and hormonal contents of body fluids. Microbiology technologists examine and identify bacteria and other microorganisms. Blood bank technologists, or immunohematology technologists, collect, type, and prepare blood and its components for transfusions. Immunology technologists examine elements of the human immune system and its response to foreign bodies. Cytotechnologists prepare slides of body cells and examine these cells microscopically for abnormalities that may signal the beginning of a cancerous growth. Molecular biology technologists perform complex protein and nucleic acid testing on cell samples.

Clinical laboratory technicians perform less complex tests and laboratory procedures than technologists do. Technicians may prepare specimens and operate automated analyzers, for example, or they may perform manual tests in accordance with detailed instructions. They usually work under the supervision of medical and clinical laboratory technologists or laboratory managers. Like technologists, clinical laboratory technicians may work in several areas of the clinical laboratory or specialize in just one. Phlebotomists collect blood samples, for example, and histotechnicians cut and stain tissue specimens for microscopic examination by pathologists.

Work environment. Clinical laboratory personnel are trained to work with infectious specimens. When proper methods of infection control and sterilization are followed, few hazards exist. Protective masks, gloves, and goggles often are necessary to ensure the safety of laboratory personnel.

Working conditions vary with the size and type of employment setting. Laboratories usually are well lighted and clean; however, specimens, solutions, and reagents used in the laboratory sometimes produce fumes. Laboratory workers may spend a great deal of time on their feet.

Hours of clinical laboratory technologists and technicians vary with the size and type of employment setting. In large hospitals or in independent laboratories that operate continuously, personnel usually work the day, evening, or night shift and may work weekends and holidays. Laboratory personnel in small facilities may work on rotating shifts, rather than on a regular shift. In some facilities, laboratory personnel are on call several nights a week or on weekends, in case of an emergency.

Training, Other Qualifications, and Advancement

Clinical laboratory technologist generally require a bachelor's degree in medical technology or in one of the life sciences; clinical laboratory technicians usually need an associate degree or a certificate.

Education and training. The usual requirement for an entry-level position as a clinical laboratory technologist is a bachelor's degree with a major in medical technology or one of the life sciences; however, it is possible to qualify for some jobs with a combination of education and on-the-job and specialized training. Universities and hospitals offer medical technology programs.

Bachelor's degree programs in medical technology include courses in chemistry, biological sciences, microbiology, mathematics, and statistics, as well as specialized courses devoted to knowledge and skills used in the clinical laboratory. Many programs also offer or require courses in management, business, and computer applications. The Clinical Laboratory Improvement Act requires technologists who perform highly complex tests to have at least an associate degree.

Medical and clinical laboratory technicians generally have either an associate degree from a community or junior college or a certificate from a hospital, a vocational or technical school, or the Armed Forces. A few technicians learn their skills on the job.

The National Accrediting Agency for Clinical Laboratory Sciences (NAACLS) fully accredits about 470 programs for medical and clinical laboratory technologists, medical and clinical laboratory technicians, histotechnologists and histotechnicians, cytogenetic technologists, and diagnostic molecular scientists. NAACLS also approves about 60 programs in phlebotomy and clinical assisting. Other nationally recognized agencies that accredit specific areas for clinical laboratory workers include the Commission on Accreditation of Allied Health Education Programs and the Accrediting Bureau of Health Education Schools.

Licensure. Some states require laboratory personnel to be licensed or registered. Licensure of technologists often requires a bachelor's degree and the passing of an exam, but requirements vary by state and specialty. Information on licensure is available from state departments of health or boards of occupational licensing.

Certification and other qualifications. Many employers prefer applicants who are certified by a recognized professional association. Associations offering certification include the Board of Registry of the American Society for Clinical Pathology, the American Medical Technologists, the National Credentialing Agency for Laboratory Personnel, and the Board of Registry of the American Association of Bioanalysts. These agencies have different requirements for certification and different organizational sponsors.

In addition to certification, employers seek clinical laboratory personnel with good analytical judgment and the ability to work under pressure. Technologists in particular are expected to be good at problem solving. Close attention to detail is also essential for laboratory personnel because small differences or changes in test substances or numerical readouts can be crucial to a diagnosis. Manual dexterity and normal color vision are highly desirable, and with the widespread use of automated laboratory equipment, computer skills are important.

Advancement. Technicians can advance and become technologists through additional education and experience. Technologists may advance to supervisory positions in laboratory work or may become chief medical or clinical laboratory technologists or laboratory managers in hospitals. Manufacturers of home diagnostic testing kits and laboratory equipment and supplies also seek experienced technologists to work in product development, marketing, and sales.

Professional certification and a graduate degree in medical technology, one of the biological sciences, chemistry, management, or education usually speeds advancement. A doctorate usually is needed to become a laboratory director. Federal regulation requires directors of moderately complex laboratories to have either a master's degree or a bachelor's degree, combined with the appropriate amount of training and experience.

Employment

Clinical laboratory technologists and technicians held about 319,000 jobs in 2006. More than half of jobs were in hospitals. Most of the remaining jobs were in offices of physicians and in medical and diagnostic laboratories. A small proportion was in educational services and in all other ambulatory health care services.

Job Outlook

Rapid job growth and excellent job opportunities are expected. Most jobs will continue to be in hospitals, but employment will grow faster in other settings.

Employment change. Employment of clinical laboratory workers is expected to grow 14 percent between 2006 and 2016, faster than the average for all occupations. The volume of laboratory tests continues to increase with both population growth and the development of new types of tests.

Technological advances will continue to have opposing effects on employment. On the one hand, new, increasingly powerful diagnostic tests will encourage additional testing and spur employment. On the other, research and development efforts targeted at simplifying routine testing procedures may enhance the ability of nonlaboratory personnel—physicians and patients in particular—to perform tests now conducted in laboratories.

Although hospitals are expected to continue to be the major employer of clinical laboratory workers, employment is expected to grow faster in medical and diagnostic laboratories, offices of physicians, and all other ambulatory health care services.

Job prospects. Job opportunities are expected to be excellent because the number of job openings is expected to continue to

Projections data from the National Employment Matrix

Occupational Title	SOC Code	Employment, 2006	Projected employment, 2016	Change, 2006-2016	
				Number	Percent
Clinical laboratory technologists and technicians	29-2010	319,000	362,000	43,000	14
Medical and clinical laboratory technologists	29-2011	167,000	188,000	21,000	12
Medical and clinical laboratory technicians	29-2012	151,000	174,000	23,000	15

NOTE: Data in this table are rounded.

exceed the number of job seekers. Although significant, job growth will not be the only source of opportunities. As in most occupations, many additional openings will result from the need to replace workers who transfer to other occupations, retire, or stop working for some other reason.

Earnings

Median annual wage-and-salary earnings of medical and clinical laboratory technologists were $49,700 in May 2006. The middle 50 percent earned between $41,680 and $58,560. The lowest 10 percent earned less than $34,660, and the highest 10 percent earned more than $69,260. Median annual earnings in the industries employing the largest numbers of medical and clinical laboratory technologists were

Federal government	$57,360
Medical and diagnostic laboratories	50,740
General medical and surgical hospitals	49,930
Offices of physicians	45,420
Colleges, universities, and professional schools	45,080

Median annual wage-and-salary earnings of medical and clinical laboratory technicians were $32,840 in May 2006. The middle 50 percent earned between $26,430 and $41,020. The lowest 10 percent earned less than $21,830, and the highest 10 percent earned more than $50,250. Median annual earnings in the industries employing the largest numbers of medical and clinical laboratory technicians were

General medical and surgical hospitals	$34,200
Colleges, universities, and professional schools	33,440
Offices of physicians	31,330
Medical and diagnostic laboratories	30,240
Other ambulatory health care services	29,560

According to the American Society for Clinical Pathology, median hourly wages of staff clinical laboratory technologists and technicians in 2005 in various specialties and laboratory types were

	Hospital	Private clinic	Physician office laboratory
Cytotechnologist	$26.39	31.64	25.69
Histotechnologist	21.50	21.63	23.29
Medical technologist	21.77	20.00	20.00
Histotechnician	18.50	20.86	18.27
Medical laboratory technician	17.41	16.94	16.63
Phlebotomist	11.70	12.15	11.25

Related Occupations

Clinical laboratory technologists and technicians analyze body fluids, tissue, and other substances, using a variety of tests. Similar or related procedures are performed by chemists and materials scientists, science technicians, and veterinary technologists and technicians.

Sources of Additional Information

For a list of accredited and approved educational programs for clinical laboratory personnel, contact

- National Accrediting Agency for Clinical Laboratory Sciences, 8410 W. Bryn Mawr Ave., Suite 670, Chicago, IL 60631. Internet: http://www.naacls.org

Information on certification is available from

- American Association of Bioanalysts, Board of Registry, 906 Olive St., Suite 1200, St. Louis, MO 63101. Internet: http://www.aab.org
- American Medical Technologists, 10700 Higgins Rd., Suite 150, Rosemont, IL 60018. Internet: http://www.amt1.com
- American Society for Clinical Pathology, 33 West Monroe Street, Suite 1600, Chicago, IL 60603. Internet: http://www.ascp.org
- National Credentialing Agency for Laboratory Personnel, P.O. Box 15945, Lenexa, KS 66285. Internet: http://www.nca-info.org

Additional career information is available from

- American Association of Blood Banks, 8101 Glenbrook Rd., Bethesda, MD 20814. Internet: http://www.aabb.org
- American Society for Clinical Laboratory Science, 6701 Democracy Blvd., Suite 300, Bethesda, MD 20817. Internet: http://www.ascls.org
- American Society for Cytopathology, 400 West 9th St., Suite 201, Wilmington, DE 19801. Internet: http://www.cytopathology.org
- Clinical Laboratory Management Association, 989 Old Eagle School Rd., Suite 815, Wayne, PA 19087. Internet: http://www.clma.org

STEM Computer and Information Systems Managers

(O*NET 11-3021.00)

Significant Points

- Employment of computer and information systems managers is expected to grow faster than the average for all occupations through the year 2016.
- Many managers possess advanced technical knowledge gained from working in a computer occupation.

- Job opportunities will be best for applicants with a strong understanding of business and good communication skills.

Nature of the Work

In the modern workplace, it is imperative that technology works both effectively and reliably. Computer and information systems managers play a vital role in the implementation of technology within their organizations. They do everything from helping to construct a business plan to overseeing network security to directing Internet operations.

Computer and information systems managers plan, coordinate, and direct research and facilitate the computer-related activities of firms. They help determine both technical and business goals in consultation with top management and make detailed plans for the accomplishment of these goals. This requires a strong understanding of both technology and business practices.

Computer and information systems managers direct the work of systems analysts, computer programmers, support specialists, and other computer-related workers. They plan and coordinate activities such as installation and upgrading of hardware and software, programming and systems design, development of computer networks, and implementation of Internet and intranet sites. They are increasingly involved with the upkeep, maintenance, and security of networks. They analyze the computer and information needs of their organizations from an operational and strategic perspective and determine immediate and long-range personnel and equipment requirements. They assign and review the work of their subordinates and stay abreast of the latest technology to ensure the organization does not lag behind competitors.

The duties of computer and information systems managers vary greatly. *Chief technology officers (CTOs)*, for example, evaluate the newest and most innovative technologies and determine how these can help their organizations. The chief technology officer often reports to the organization's chief information officer, manages and plans technical standards, and tends to the daily information technology issues of the firm. Because of the rapid pace of technological change, chief technology officers must constantly be on the lookout for developments that could benefit their organizations. Once a useful tool has been identified, the CTO must determine an implementation strategy and sell that strategy to management.

Management information systems (MIS) directors or *information technology (IT) directors* manage computing resources for their organizations. They often work under the chief information officer and plan and direct the work of subordinate information technology employees. These managers ensure the availability, continuity, and security of data and information technology services in their organizations. In this capacity, they oversee a variety of user services, such as an organization's help desk, which employees can call with questions or problems. MIS directors also may make hardware and software upgrade recommendations based on their experience with an organization's technology.

Project managers develop requirements, budgets, and schedules for their firms' information technology projects. They coordinate such projects from development through implementation, working with internal and external clients, vendors, consultants, and computer specialists. These managers are increasingly involved in projects that upgrade the information security of an organization.

Work environment. Computer and information systems managers spend most of their time in offices. Most work at least 40 hours a week, and some may have to work evenings and weekends to meet deadlines or solve unexpected problems. Some computer and information systems managers may experience considerable pressure in meeting technical goals with short deadlines or tight budgets. As networks continue to expand and more work is done remotely, computer and information systems managers have to communicate with and oversee off-site employees using modems, laptops, e-mail, and the Internet.

Like other workers who spend most of their time using computers, computer and information systems managers are susceptible to eyestrain, back discomfort, and hand and wrist problems such as carpal tunnel syndrome.

Training, Other Qualifications, and Advancement

Computer and information systems managers are generally experienced workers who have both technical expertise and an understanding of business and management principles. A strong educational background and experience in a variety of technical fields are needed.

Education and training. A bachelor's degree usually is required for management positions, although employers often prefer a graduate degree, especially an MBA with technology as a core component. This degree differs from a traditional MBA in that there is a heavy emphasis on information technology in addition to the standard business curriculum. This preparation is becoming important because more computer and information systems managers are making important technology decisions as well as business decisions for their organizations.

Some universities offer degrees in management information systems. These degrees blend technical subjects with business, accounting, and communications courses. A few computer and information systems managers attain their positions with only an associate or trade school degree, but they must have sufficient experience and must have acquired additional skills on the job. To aid their professional advancement, many managers with an associate degree eventually earn a bachelor's or master's degree while working.

Certification and other qualifications. Computer and information systems managers need a broad range of skills. Employers look for managers who have experience with the specific software or technology used on the job, as well as a background in either consulting or business management. The expansion of electronic commerce has elevated the importance of business insight, and consequently, many computer and information systems managers are called on to make important business decisions. Managers need a keen understanding of people, management processes, and customers' needs.

Advanced technical knowledge is essential for computer and information systems managers, who must understand and guide the work of their subordinates yet also explain the work in nontechnical terms to senior managers and potential customers. Therefore, many computer and information systems managers have worked as a systems analyst, for example, or as a computer support specialist, programmer, or other information technology professional.

Although certification is not necessarily required for most computer and information systems manager positions, there is a wide variety of certifications available that may be helpful in getting a job. These

Projections data from the National Employment Matrix

Occupational Title	SOC Code	Employment, 2006	Projected employment, 2016	Change, 2006-16	
				Number	Percent
Computer and information systems managers	11-3021	264,000	307,000	43,000	16

NOTE: Data in this table are rounded.

certifications are often product-specific, and they are generally administered by software or hardware companies rather than independent organizations.

As computer systems become more closely connected with day-to-day operations of businesses, computer and information systems managers are also expected to be aware of business practices. They must possess strong interpersonal, communication, and leadership skills because they are required to interact not only with staff members, but also with other people inside and outside their organizations. They must possess team skills to work on group projects and other collaborative efforts. They also must have an understanding of how a business functions, how it earns revenue, and how technology relates to the core competencies of the business. As a result, many firms now prefer to give these positions to people who have spent time outside purely technical fields.

Advancement. Computer and information systems managers may advance to progressively higher leadership positions in the information technology department. A project manager might, for instance, move up to the chief technology officer position and then to chief information officer. On occasion, some may become managers in non-technical areas such as marketing, human resources, or sales because in high technology firms an understanding of technical issues is helpful in those areas.

Employment

Computer and information systems managers held about 264,000 jobs in 2006. About 1 in 4 computer managers worked in service-providing industries, mainly in computer systems design and related services. This industry provides services related to the commercial use of computers on a contract basis, including custom computer programming services; computer systems integration design services; computer facilities management services, including computer systems or data-processing facilities support services; and other computer-related services, such as disaster recovery services and software installation. Other large employers include insurance and financial firms, government agencies, and manufacturers.

Job Outlook

The increasing use of technology in the workplace is projected to lead to faster-than-average growth in this occupation. Because of employment increases and the high demand for technical workers, prospects should be excellent for qualified job candidates.

Employment change. Employment of computer and information systems managers is expected to grow 16 percent over the 2006–2016 decade, which is faster than the average for all occupations. New applications of technology in the workplace will continue to drive demand for workers, fueling the need for more managers.

Despite the downturn in the technology sector in the early part of the decade, the outlook for computer and information systems managers remains strong. To remain competitive, firms will continue to install sophisticated computer networks and set up more complex intranets and Web sites. Keeping a computer network running smoothly is essential to almost every organization.

Because so much business is carried out over computer networks, security will continue to be an important issue for businesses and other organizations. Although software developers continue to improve their products to remove vulnerabilities, attackers are becoming ever more complex in their methods. Organizations need to understand how their systems are vulnerable and how to protect their infrastructure and Internet sites from hackers, viruses, and other attacks. The emergence of security as a key concern for businesses should lead to strong growth for computer managers. Firms will increasingly hire security experts to fill key leadership roles in their information technology departments because the integrity of their computing environments is of utmost importance. As a result, there will be a high demand for managers proficient in computer security issues.

With the explosive growth of electronic commerce and the capacity of the Internet to create new relationships with customers, the role of computer and information systems managers will continue to evolve. Workers who have experience in Web applications and Internet technologies will become increasingly vital to their companies.

Opportunities for those who wish to become computer and information systems managers should be closely related to the growth of the occupations they supervise and the industries in which they are found. (See the statements on computer programmers, computer software engineers, computer support specialists and systems administrators, computer systems analysts, and computer scientists and database administrators elsewhere in this book.)

Job prospects. Prospects for qualified computer and information systems managers should be excellent. Fast-paced occupational growth and the limited supply of technical workers will lead to a wealth of opportunities for qualified individuals. While technical workers remain relatively scarce in the United States, the demand for them continues to rise. This situation was exacerbated by the economic downturn in the early 2000s, when many technical professionals lost their jobs. Since then, many workers have chosen to avoid this work since it is perceived to have poor prospects.

Workers with specialized technical knowledge and strong communications skills will have the best prospects. People with management skills and an understanding of business practices and principles will have excellent opportunities, as companies are increasingly looking to technology to drive their revenue.

Earnings

Earnings for computer and information systems managers vary by specialty and level of responsibility. Median annual earnings of these managers in May 2006 were $101,580. The middle 50 percent earned between $79,240 and $129,250. Median annual earnings in the industries employing the largest numbers of computer and information systems managers in May 2006 were as follows:

Computer systems design and related services $109,130
Management of companies and enterprises 105,980
Data processing, hosting, and related services 105,200
Insurance carriers 102,180
Colleges, universities, and professional schools 83,280

The Robert Half Technology 2007 Salary Guide lists the following annual salary ranges for various computer and information systems manager positions: Chief Technology Officer (CTO), $101,000–$157,750; Chief Security Officer, $97,500–$141,000; Vice President of Information Technology, $107,500–$157,750; Information Technology Manager, Technical Services Manager, $62,500–$88,250.

In addition, computer and information systems managers, especially those at higher levels, often receive employment-related benefits, such as expense accounts, stock option plans, and bonuses.

Related Occupations

The work of computer and information systems managers is closely related to that of computer programmers, computer software engineers, computer systems analysts, computer scientists and database administrators, and computer support specialists and systems administrators. Computer and information systems managers also have some high-level responsibilities similar to those of top executives.

Sources of Additional Information

For information about a career as a computer and information systems manager, contact

- Association of Information Technology Professionals, 401 North Michigan Ave., Suite 2400, Chicago, IL 60611. Internet: http://www.aitp.org

STEM Computer Control Programmers and Operators

(O*NET 51-4011.00 and 51-4012.00)

Significant Points

- Manufacturing industries employ almost all of these workers.
- Workers learn in apprenticeship programs, informally on the job, and in secondary, vocational, or postsecondary schools; many entrants have previously worked as machinists or machine setters, operators, and tenders.
- Despite the projected slow decline in employment, job opportunities should be excellent, as employers are expected to continue to have difficulty finding qualified workers.

Nature of the Work

Computer control programmers and operators use computer numerically controlled (CNC) machines to cut and shape precision products, such as automobile, aviation, and machine parts. CNC machines operate by reading the code included in a computer-controlled module, which drives the machine tool and performs the functions of forming and shaping a part formerly done by machine operators. CNC machines include machining tools such as lathes, multi-axis spindles, milling machines, laser cutting machines, and wire electrical discharge machines. CNC machines cut away material from a solid block of metal or plastic—known as a workpiece—to form a finished part. Computer control programmers and operators normally produce large quantities of one part, although they may produce small batches or one-of-a-kind items. They use their knowledge of the working properties of metals and their skill with CNC programming to design and carry out the operations needed to make machined products that meet precise specifications.

CNC programmers—also referred to as *numerical tool and process control programmers*—develop the programs that run the machine tools. They review three-dimensional computer aided/automated design (CAD) blueprints of the part and determine the sequence of events that will be needed to make the part. This may involve calculating where to cut or bore into the workpiece, how fast to feed the metal into the machine, and how much metal to remove.

Next, CNC programmers turn the planned machining operations into a set of instructions. These instructions are translated into a computer aided/automated manufacturing (CAM) program containing a set of commands for the machine to follow. These commands normally are a series of numbers (hence, numerical control) that describes where cuts should occur, what type of cut should be used, and the speed of the cut. After the program is developed, CNC programmers and operators check the programs to ensure that the machinery will function properly and that the output will meet specifications. Because a problem with the program could damage costly machinery and cutting tools or simply waste valuable time and materials, computer simulations may be used to check the program before a trial run. If errors are found, the program must be changed and retested until the problem is resolved. In addition, growing connectivity between CAD/CAM software and CNC machine tools is raising productivity by automatically translating designs into instructions for the computer controller on the machine tool. These new CAM technologies enable programs to be easily modified for use on other jobs with similar specifications.

After the programming work is completed, *CNC setup operators*—also referred to as computer-controlled machine tool operators, metal and plastic—set up the machine for the job. They download the program into the machine, load the proper cutting tools into the tool holder, position the workpiece (piece of metal or plastic that is being shaped) on the CNC machine tool—spindle, lathe, milling machine, or other machine—and then start the machine. During the test run of a new program, the setup operator, who may also have some programming skills, or the CNC programmer closely monitors the machine for signs of problems, such as a vibrating work piece, the breakage of cutting tools, or an out-of-specification final product. If a problem is detected, a setup operator or CNC programmer will modify the program using the control module to eliminate the problems or to improve the speed and accuracy of the program.

Once a program is completed, the operation of the CNC machine may move from the more experienced setup operator to a less-skilled machine operator. Operators load workpieces and cutting tools into a machine, press the start button, monitor the machine for problems, and measure the parts produced to check that they match specifications. If they encounter a problem that requires modification to the cutting program, they shut down the machine and wait for a more experienced CNC setup operator to fix the problem. Many CNC operators start at this basic level and gradually perform more setup tasks as they gain experience.

Regardless of skill level, all CNC operators detect some problems by listening for specific sounds—for example, a dull cutting tool that needs changing or excessive vibration. Machine tools rotate at high speeds, which can create problems with harmonic vibrations in the workpiece. Vibrations cause the machine tools to make minor cutting errors, hurting the quality of the product. Operators listen for vibrations and then adjust the cutting speed to compensate. CNC operators also ensure that the workpiece is being properly lubricated and cooled, because the machining of metal products generates a significant amount of heat.

Since CNC machines can operate with limited input from the operator, a single operator may monitor several machines simultaneously. Typically, an operator might monitor two machines cutting relatively simple parts from softer materials, while devoting most of his or her attention to a third machine cutting a much more difficult part from hard metal, such as stainless steel. Operators are often expected to carefully schedule their work so that all of the machines are always operating.

Work environment. Most machine shops are clean, well lit, and ventilated. Most modern CNC machines are partially or totally enclosed, minimizing the exposure of workers to noise, debris, and the lubricants used to cool workpieces during machining. Nevertheless, working around machine tools can be noisy and presents certain dangers, and workers must follow safety precautions. Computer-controlled machine tool operators, metal and plastic, wear protective equipment, such as safety glasses to shield against bits of flying metal and earplugs to dampen machinery noise. They also must exercise caution when handling hazardous coolants and lubricants. The job requires stamina because operators stand most of the day and, at times, may need to lift moderately heavy workpieces.

Numerical tool and process control programmers work on desktop computers in offices that typically are near, but separate from, the shop floor. These work areas usually are clean, well lit, and free of machine noise. Numerical tool and process control programmers occasionally need to enter the shop floor to monitor CNC machining operations. On the shop floor, CNC programmers encounter the same hazards and exercise the same safety precautions as do CNC operators.

Many computer control programmers and operators work a 40-hour week. CNC operators increasingly work evening and weekend shifts as companies justify investments in more expensive machinery by extending hours of operation. Overtime is common during peak production periods.

Training, Other Qualifications, and Advancement

Computer control programmers and operators train in various ways—in apprenticeship programs, informally on the job, and in secondary, vocational, or postsecondary schools. In general, the more skills needed for the job, the more education and training are needed to qualify. Many entrants have previously worked as machinists or machine setters, operators, and tenders.

Education and training. The amount and type of education and training needed depends on the type of job. Entry-level CNC machine operators may need only a couple of weeks of on-the-job training to reach proficiency. Setup operators and programmers, however, may need years of experience or formal training to write or modify programs. Programmers and operators can receive their training in various ways—in apprenticeship programs, informally on the job, and in secondary, vocational, or postsecondary schools. A growing number of computer control programmers and more skilled operators receive their formal training from community or technical colleges. For some specialized types of programming, such as that needed to produce complex parts for the aerospace or shipbuilding industries, employers may prefer individuals with a degree in engineering.

For those interested in becoming computer control programmers or operators, high school or vocational school courses in mathematics (trigonometry and algebra), blueprint reading, computer programming, metalworking, and drafting are recommended. Apprenticeship programs consist of shop training and related classroom instruction. In shop training, apprentices learn filing, handtapping, and dowel fitting, as well as the operation of various machine tools. Classroom instruction includes math, physics, programming, blueprint reading, CAD software, safety, and shop practices. Skilled computer control programmers and operators need an understanding of the machining process, including the complex physics that occur at the cutting point. Thus, most training programs teach CNC operators and programmers to perform operations on manual machines prior to operating CNC machines.

As new automation is introduced, computer control programmers and operators normally receive additional training to update their skills. This training usually is provided by a representative of the equipment manufacturer or a local technical school. Many employers offer tuition reimbursement for job-related courses.

Certification and other qualifications. Employers prefer to hire workers who have a basic knowledge of computers and electronics and experience with machine tools. In fact, many entrants to these occupations have previously worked as machinists or machine setters, operators, and tenders. Persons interested in becoming computer control programmers or operators should be mechanically inclined and able to work independently and do highly accurate work.

To boost the skill level of all metalworkers and to create a more uniform standard of competency, a number of training facilities and colleges have recently begun implementing curriculums by incorporating national skills standards developed by the National Institute of Metalworking Skills (NIMS). After completing such a curriculum and passing a performance requirement and written exam, trainees are granted an NIMS credential that provides formal recognition of competency in a metalworking field. Completion of a formal certification program provides expanded career opportunities.

Advancement. Computer control programmers and operators can advance in several ways. Experienced CNC operators may become CNC programmers, and some are promoted to supervisory or administrative positions in their firms. A few open their own shops.

Employment

Computer control programmers and operators held about 158,000 jobs in 2006. About 89 percent were computer-controlled machine tool operators, metal and plastic, and about 11 percent were numerical tool and process control programmers. Manufacturing employs

Projections data from the National Employment Matrix

Occupational Title	SOC Code	Employment, 2006	Projected employment, 2016	Change, 2006-16	
				Number	Percent
Computer control programmers and operators	51-4010	158,000	153,000	-5,700	-4
Computer-controlled machine tool operators, metal and plastic	51-4011	141,000	136,000	-4,200	-3
Numerical tool and process control programmers	51-4012	18,000	16,000	-1,500	-8

NOTE: Data in this table are rounded.

almost all of these workers. Employment was concentrated in fabricated metal products manufacturing, machinery manufacturing, plastics products manufacturing, and transportation equipment manufacturing making mostly aerospace and automobile parts. Although computer control programmers and operators work in all parts of the country, jobs are most plentiful in the areas where manufacturing is concentrated.

Job Outlook

Despite the projected slow decline in employment of computer control programmers and operators, job opportunities should be excellent, as employers are expected to continue to have difficulty finding qualified workers.

Employment change. Employment of computer control programmers and operators is expected to decline slowly by 4 percent through 2016. While CNC machine tools will be increasingly used, advances in CNC machine tools and manufacturing technology will further automate the production process, boosting CNC operator productivity and limiting employment. The demand for computer control programmers also will be negatively affected by the increasing use of software (CAD/CAM) that automatically translates part and product designs into CNC machine tool instructions.

Job prospects. Computer control programmers and operators should have excellent job opportunities despite the projected slow decline in employment. Due to the limited number of people entering training programs, employers are expected to continue to have difficulty finding workers with the necessary skills and knowledge.

Earnings

Median hourly earnings of computer-controlled machine tool operators, metal and plastic, were $15.23 in May 2006. The middle 50 percent earned between $12.10 and $18.84. The lowest 10 percent earned less than $9.91, whereas the top 10 percent earned more than $22.45. Median hourly earnings in the manufacturing industries employing the largest numbers of computer-controlled machine tool operators, metal and plastic, in May 2006 were

Metalworking machinery manufacturing $17.45
Other fabricated metal product manufacturing..........15.34
Machine shops; turned product; and screw, nut,
and bolt manufacturing 14.85
Motor vehicle parts manufacturing..........................14.12
Plastics product manufacturing 12.32

Median hourly earnings of numerical tool and process control programmers were $20.42 in May 2006. The middle 50 percent earned between $16.14 and $25.61. The lowest 10 percent earned less than $13.11, while the top 10 percent earned more than $31.85.

Many employers, especially those with formal apprenticeship programs, offer tuition assistance for training classes.

Related Occupations

Occupations most closely related to computer control programmers and operators are other metal and plastic working occupations, which include machinists; tool and die makers; machine setters, operators, and tenders—metal and plastic; and welding, soldering, and brazing workers. Numerical tool and process control programmers apply their knowledge of machining operations, metals, blueprints, and machine programming to write programs that run machine tools. Computer programmers also write detailed programs to meet precise specifications.

Sources of Additional Information

For general information about computer control programmers and operators, contact

- Precision Machine Products Association, 6700 West Snowville Rd., Brecksville, OH 44141-3292. Internet: http://www.pmpa.org/industry-careers/

For a list of training centers and apprenticeship programs, contact

- National Tooling and Metalworking Association, 9300 Livingston Rd., Fort Washington, MD 20744.

For more information on credential standards and apprenticeship, contact

- The National Institute for Metalworking Skills, 10565 Fairfax Blvd., Suite 203, Fairfax, VA 22030. Internet: http://www.nims-skills.org/home/index.htm

STEM Computer Programmers

(O*NET 15-1021.00)

Significant Points

- Almost 8 out of 10 computer programmers held an associate's degree or higher in 2006; nearly half held a bachelor's degree, and 2 out of 10 held a graduate degree.
- Employment of computer programmers is expected to decline by four percent through 2016.
- Job prospects will be best for applicants with a bachelor's degree and experience with a variety of programming languages and tools.

Nature of the Work

Computer programmers write, test, and maintain the detailed instructions, called programs, that computers follow to perform their functions. Programmers also conceive, design, and test logical structures for solving problems by computer. With the help of other computer specialists, they figure out which instructions to use to make computers do specific tasks. Many technical innovations in pro-

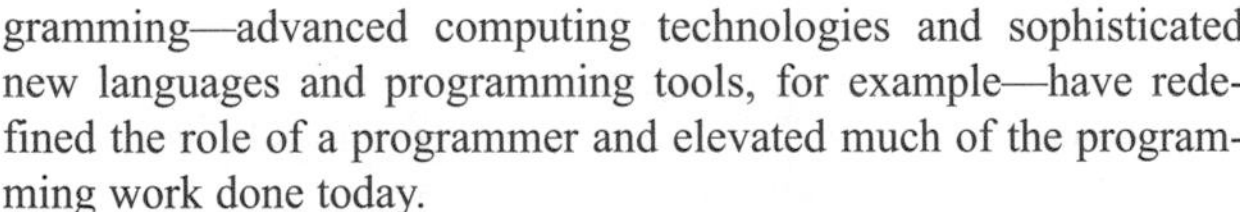

gramming—advanced computing technologies and sophisticated new languages and programming tools, for example—have redefined the role of a programmer and elevated much of the programming work done today.

Job titles and descriptions may vary, depending on the organization, but computer programmers are individuals whose main job function is programming. Programmers usually write programs according to the specifications given by computer software engineers and systems analysts. (Sections on computer software engineers and on computer systems analysts appear elsewhere in this book.) After engineers and analysts design software—describing how it will work—the programmer converts that design into a logical series of instructions that the computer can follow. The programmer codes these instructions in a conventional programming language such as COBOL; an artificial intelligence language such as Prolog; or one of the more advanced object-oriented languages, such as Java, C++, or ACTOR.

Different programming languages are used depending on the purpose of the program. Programmers generally know more than one programming language, and because many languages are similar, they often can learn new languages relatively easily. In practice, programmers often are referred to by the language they know, such as Java programmers, or by the type of function they perform or environment in which they work—for example, database programmers, mainframe programmers, or Web programmers.

Programmers also update, repair, modify, and expand existing programs. Some, especially those working on large projects that involve many programmers, use computer-assisted software engineering (CASE) tools to automate much of the coding process. These tools enable a programmer to concentrate on writing the unique parts of a program. Programmers working on smaller projects often use "programmer environments," applications that increase productivity by combining compiling, code walk through, code generation, test data generation, and debugging functions. Programmers also use libraries of basic code that can be modified or customized for a specific application. This approach yields more reliable and consistent programs and increases programmers' productivity by eliminating some routine steps.

Programs vary widely depending on the type of information they will access or generate. For example, the instructions involved in updating financial records are very different from those required to simulate flight for pilot training. Simple programs can be written in a few hours, but some programs draw data from many existing systems or use complex mathematical formulas. These programs may take more than a year to create. In most cases, several programmers work together as a team under a senior programmer's supervision.

Programmers test a program by running it to ensure that the instructions are correct and that the program produces the desired outcome. If errors do occur, the programmer must make the appropriate change and recheck the program until it produces the correct results. This process is called testing and debugging. Programmers may continue to fix problems for as long as a program is used.

Programmers working on a mainframe, a large centralized computer, may prepare instructions for a computer operator who will run the program. Programmers also may contribute to the instruction manual for a program.

Programmers in software development companies may work directly with experts from various fields to create specialized software—either programs designed for specific clients or packaged software for general use—ranging from games and educational software to programs for desktop publishing and financial planning. Programming of packaged software constitutes one of the most rapidly growing segments of the computer services industry.

Increasingly, advanced software platforms are bridging the gap between computer programmers and computer users. New platforms, such as spreadsheet, accounting, and enterprise resource planning applications, have created demand for computer specialists who have first-hand knowledge of a user-base. These workers use such platforms to develop programs that meet the specific needs of this base. Computer programmers often are responsible for creating the software platform, and then fine-tuning the final program after it has been made.

Computer programmers often are grouped into two broad types—applications programmers and systems programmers. *Applications programmers* write programs to handle a specific job, such as a program to track inventory within an organization. They also may revise existing packaged software or customize generic applications purchased from vendors. *Systems programmers*, in contrast, write programs to maintain and control computer systems software for operating systems, networked systems, and database systems. These workers make changes in the instructions that determine how the network, workstations, and central processing unit of a system handle the various jobs they have been given, and how they communicate with peripheral equipment such as terminals, printers, and disk drives. Because of their knowledge of the entire computer system, systems programmers often help applications programmers determine the source of problems that may occur with their programs.

In some organizations, workers known as *programmer-analysts* are responsible for both the systems analysis and programming. (A more detailed description of the work of programmer-analysts is presented in the section on computer systems analysts elsewhere in this book.)

Work environment. Programmers spend the majority of their time in front of a computer terminal, and work in clean, comfortable offices. Telecommuting is becoming more common, however, as technological advances allow more work to be done from remote locations.

Most computer programmers work about 40 hours per week. Long hours or weekend work may be required, however, to meet deadlines or fix unexpected technical problems. About four percent work part-time, compared with about 15 percent for all occupations.

Like other workers who spend long periods in front of a computer terminal typing at a keyboard, programmers are susceptible to eyestrain, back discomfort, and hand and wrist problems such as carpal tunnel syndrome.

Training, Other Qualifications, and Advancement

A bachelor's degree commonly is required for computer programming jobs, although a two-year degree or certificate may be adequate for some positions. Employers favor applicants who already have relevant programming skills and experience. Skilled workers who keep up to date with the latest technology usually have good opportunities for advancement.

Education and training. Most programmers have a bachelor's degree, but a two-year degree or certificate may be adequate for some jobs. Some computer programmers hold a college degree in computer science, mathematics, or information systems, whereas others have taken special courses in computer programming to supplement their degree in a field such as accounting, finance, or another area of business. In 2006, more than 68 percent of computer programmers had a bachelor's degree or higher, but as the level of education and training required by employers continues to rise, this proportion is expected to increase.

Employers who use computers for scientific or engineering applications usually prefer college graduates who have a degree in computer or information science, mathematics, engineering, or the physical sciences. Employers who use computers for business applications prefer to hire people who have had college courses in management information systems and business, and who possess strong programming skills. A graduate degree in a related field is required for some jobs.

Most systems programmers hold a four-year degree in computer science. Extensive knowledge of a variety of operating systems is essential for such workers. This includes being able to configure an operating system to work with different types of hardware and being able to adapt the operating system to best meet the needs of a particular organization. Systems programmers also must be able to work with database systems, such as DB2, Oracle, or Sybase.

In addition to educational attainment, employers highly value relevant programming skills, as well as experience. Although knowledge of traditional programming languages still is important, employers are placing an emphasis on newer, object-oriented languages and tools such as C++ and Java. Additionally, employers seek people familiar with fourth- and fifth-generation languages that involve graphic user interface and systems programming. College graduates who are interested in changing careers or developing an area of expertise may return to a two-year community college or technical school for specialized training. In the absence of a degree, substantial specialized experience or expertise may be needed.

Entry-level or junior programmers may work alone on simple assignments after some initial instruction, or they may be assigned to work on a team with more experienced programmers. Either way, beginning programmers generally must work under close supervision.

Because technology changes so rapidly, programmers must continuously update their knowledge and skills by taking courses sponsored by their employer or by software vendors, or offered through local community colleges and universities.

Certification and other qualifications. When hiring programmers, employers look for people with the necessary programming skills who can think logically and pay close attention to detail. Programming calls for patience, persistence, and the ability to perform exacting analytical work, especially under pressure. Ingenuity and creativity are particularly important when programmers design solutions and test their work for potential failures. The ability to work with abstract concepts and to do technical analysis is especially important for systems programmers because they work with the software that controls the computer's operation.

Because programmers are expected to work in teams and interact directly with users, employers want programmers who are able to communicate with non-technical personnel. Business skills are also important, especially for those wishing to advance to managerial positions.

Certification is a way to demonstrate a level of competence and may provide a jobseeker with a competitive advantage. In addition to language-specific certificates, product vendors or software firms also offer certification and may require professionals who work with their products to be certified. Voluntary certification also is available through various other organizations.

Advancement. For skilled workers who keep up to date with the latest technology, prospects for advancement are good. In large organizations, programmers may be promoted to lead programmer and be given supervisory responsibilities. Some applications programmers may move into systems programming after they gain experience and take courses in systems software. With general business experience, programmers may become programmer-analysts or systems analysts, or may be promoted to managerial positions. Programmers with specialized knowledge and experience with a language or operating system may work in research and development and may even become computer software engineers. As employers increasingly contract with outside firms to do programming jobs, more opportunities should arise for experienced programmers with expertise in a specific area to work as consultants.

Employment

Computer programmers held about 435,000 jobs in 2006. Programmers are employed in almost every industry, but the largest concentration is in computer systems design and related services. Large numbers of programmers also work for software publishers, financial institutions, insurance carriers, educational institutions, government agencies, and management of companies and enterprises. Many computer programmers work independently as consultants on a temporary or contract basis, some of whom are self-employed. About 17,000 computer programmers were self-employed in 2006.

Job Outlook

Employment of computer programmers is expected to decline slowly. Job prospects should be best for those with a bachelor's degree and experience with a variety of programming languages and tools.

Employment change. Employment of computer programmers is expected to decline slowly, decreasing by 4 percent from 2006 to 2016. The consolidation and centralization of systems and applications, developments in packaged software, advances in programming languages and tools, and the growing ability of users to design, write, and implement more of their own programs mean that more programming functions can be performed by other types of information workers, such as computer software engineers.

Another factor contributing to employment decline will be the offshore outsourcing of programming jobs. Because they can transmit their programs digitally, computer programmers can perform their job function from anywhere in the world, allowing companies to employ workers in countries that have lower prevailing wages. Computer programmers are at a much higher risk of having their jobs outsourced abroad than are workers involved in more complex and sophisticated information technology functions, such as software engineering. Much of the work of computer programmers requires little localized or specialized knowledge and can be made routine once knowledge of a particular programming language is mastered—and computer programming languages have become known internationally.

Nevertheless, employers will continue to need some local programmers, especially those who have strong technical skills and who understand an employer's business and its programming

Projections data from the National Employment Matrix

Occupational Title	SOC Code	Employment, 2006	Projected employment, 2016	Change, 2006-2016	
				Number	Percent
Computer programmers	15-1021	435,000	417,000	-18,000	-4

NOTE: Data in this table are rounded.

requirements. This means that programmers will have to keep abreast of changing programming languages and techniques. Given the importance of networking and the expansion of client/server, Web-based, and wireless environments, organizations will look for programmers who can support data communications and help implement business and intranet strategies. Demand for programmers with strong object-oriented programming capabilities and technical specialization in areas such as client/server programming, wireless applications, multimedia technology, and graphic user interface likely will stem from the expansion of intranets, extranets, and Internet applications. Programmers also will be needed to create and maintain expert systems and embed these technologies in more products. Finally, a growing emphasis on cybersecurity will lead to increased demand for programmers who are familiar with digital security issues, and are skilled in using appropriate security technology.

Job prospects. Although employment is projected to decline, numerous job openings will result from the need to replace programmers who leave the labor force or transfer to other occupations. Prospects for these openings should be best for applicants with a bachelor's degree and experience with a variety of programming languages and tools. The languages that are in demand today include C++, Java, and other object-oriented languages, as well as newer, domain-specific languages that apply to computer networking, database management, and Internet application development. As technology evolves, however, and newer, more sophisticated tools emerge, programmers will need to update their skills in order to remain competitive. Obtaining vendor-specific or language-specific certification also can provide a competitive edge.

Jobs for both systems and applications programmers should be most plentiful in computer consulting businesses. These establishments are part of the computer systems design and related services industry, which is projected to be among the fastest growing industries in the economy over the 2006 to 2016 period.

Earnings

Median annual earnings of wage-and-salary computer programmers were $65,510 in May 2006. The middle 50 percent earned between $49,580 and $85,080 a year. The lowest 10 percent earned less than $38,460, and the highest 10 percent earned more than $106,610. Median annual earnings in the industries employing the largest numbers of computer programmers in May 2006 are shown below:

Software publishers $79,270
Computer systems design and related services 67,880
Management of companies and enterprises 67,170
Insurance carriers 65,650

According to the National Association of Colleges and Employers, starting salary offers for computer programmers averaged $49,928 per year in 2007.

According to Robert Half Technology, a firm providing specialized staffing services, average annual starting salaries in 2007 ranged from $55,250 to $90,250 for applications development programmers/analysts, and from $60,250 to $94,750 for software developers. Average starting salaries for mainframe systems programmers ranged from $52,250 to $70,750.

Related Occupations

Other professional workers who deal extensively with data include computer software engineers, computer scientists and database administrators, computer systems analysts, statisticians, mathematicians, engineers, commercial and industrial designers, and operations research analysts.

Sources of Additional Information

State employment service offices can provide information about job openings for computer programmers. Municipal chambers of commerce are an additional source of information on an area's largest employers.

Further information about computer careers is available from

- Association for Computing Machinery, 2 Penn Plaza, Suite 701, New York, NY 10121-0701. Internet: http://www.acm.org
- Institute of Electrical and Electronics Engineers Computer Society, Headquarters Office, 1730 Massachusetts Ave. NW, Washington, DC 20036-1992. Internet: http://www.computer.org
- National Workforce Center for Emerging Technologies, 3000 Landerholm Circle SE, Bellevue, WA 98007. Internet: http://www.nwcet.org
- University of Washington Computer Science and Engineering Department, AC101 Paul G. Allen Center, Box 352350, 185 Stevens Way, Seattle, WA 98195-2350. Internet: http://www.cs.washington.edu/WhyCSE

STEM Computer Scientists and Database Administrators

(O*NET 15-1011.00, 15-1061.00, 15-1081.00, 15-1099.04, 15-1099.05, and 15-1099.99)

Significant Points

- Education requirements range from an associate degree to a doctoral degree.
- Employment is expected to increase much faster than the average as organizations continue to expand their use of technology.
- Workers must be able to learn new technologies quickly for these constantly evolving occupations.

Nature of the Work

The rapid and widespread use of computers and information technology has generated a need for highly trained workers proficient in various job functions. These computer specialists include computer scientists, database administrators, and network systems and data communication analysts. Job tasks and occupational titles used to describe these workers evolve rapidly and continually, reflecting new areas of specialization or changes in technology, as well as the preferences and practices of employers.

Computer scientists work as theorists, researchers, or inventors. Their jobs are distinguished by the higher level of theoretical expertise and innovation they apply to complex problems and the creation or application of new technology. The areas of computer science research range from complex theory to hardware design to programming-language design. Some researchers work on multidisciplinary projects, such as developing and advancing uses of virtual reality, extending human-computer interaction, or designing robots. They may work on design teams with electrical engineers and other specialists.

Computer science researchers employed by academic institutions (covered in the statement on teachers—postsecondary, elsewhere in this book) have job functions that are similar in many ways to those employed by other organizations. In general, researchers in academic settings have more flexibility to focus on pure theory, while those working in other organizations usually focus on projects that have the possibility of producing patents and profits. However, some researchers in non-academic settings have considerable latitude in determining the direction of their research.

With the Internet and electronic business generating large volumes of data, there is a growing need to be able to store, manage, and extract data effectively. *Database administrators* work with database management systems software and determine ways to organize and store data. They identify user needs and set up new computer databases. In many cases, database administrators must integrate data from outdated systems into a new system. They also test and coordinate modifications to the system when needed, and troubleshoot problems when they occur. An organization's database administrator ensures the performance of the system, understands the platform on which the database runs, and adds new users to the system. Because many databases are connected to the Internet, database administrators also must plan and coordinate security measures with network administrators. With the growing volume of sensitive data and the increasing interconnectedness of computer networks, data integrity, backup systems, and database security have become increasingly important aspects of the job of database administrators.

Network systems and data communications analysts, also referred to as *network architects*, design, test, and evaluate systems such as local area networks (LANs), wide area networks (WANs), the Internet, intranets, and other data communications systems. Systems are configured in many ways and can range from a connection between two offices in the same building to globally distributed networks, voice mail, and e-mail systems of a multinational organization. Network systems and data communications analysts perform network modeling, analysis, and planning, often requiring both hardware and software solutions. For example, a network may involve the installation of several pieces of hardware, such as routers and hubs, wireless adaptors, and cables, while also requiring the installation and configuration of software, such as network drivers. Analysts also may research related products and make necessary hardware and software recommendations.

Telecommunications specialists focus on the interaction between computer and communications equipment. These workers design voice and data communication systems, supervise the installation of the systems, and provide maintenance and other services to clients after the systems are installed.

The growth of the Internet and the expansion of the World Wide Web (the graphical portion of the Internet) have generated a variety of occupations related to the design, development, and maintenance of Web sites and their servers. For example, *webmasters* are responsible for all technical aspects of a Web site, including performance issues such as speed of access, and for approving the content of the site. *Internet developers* or *Web developers*, also called *Web designers*, are responsible for day-to-day site creation and design.

Work environment. Computer scientists and database administrators normally work in offices or laboratories in comfortable surroundings. They typically work about 40 hours a week, the same as many other professional or office workers. However, evening or weekend work may be necessary to meet deadlines or to solve specific problems. Telecommuting is increasingly common for many computer professionals as networks expand, allowing more work to be done from remote locations through modems, laptops, electronic mail, and the Internet. However, some work still must be done in the office for security or other reasons.

Like other workers who spend long periods in front of a computer terminal typing on a keyboard, computer scientists and database administrators are susceptible to eyestrain, back discomfort, and hand and wrist problems such as carpal tunnel syndrome or cumulative trauma disorder.

Training, Other Qualifications, and Advancement

Rapidly changing technology requires an increasing level of skill and education on the part of workers in these occupations. Employers look for professionals with an ever-broader background and range of skills, including technical knowledge and also communication and other interpersonal skills.

Education and training. While there is no universally accepted way to prepare for a job as a network systems analyst, computer scientist, or database administrator, most employers place a premium on some formal college education. A bachelor's degree is a prerequisite for many jobs; however, some jobs may require only a two-year degree. Relevant work experience also is very important. For more technically complex jobs, persons with graduate degrees are preferred. Most computer scientist positions require a Ph.D. degree, as their main job function is research. Computer scientists having only a bachelor's or master's degree are generally limited in their ability to advance.

For database administrator and network systems and data communication analyst positions, most employers seek applicants who have bachelor's degrees in computer science, information science, or management information systems (MIS). MIS programs usually are part of the business school or college and differ considerably from computer science programs, emphasizing business and management-oriented coursework and business computing courses. Employers increasingly prefer applicants with a master's degree in business administration (MBA) with a concentration in information systems, as more firms move their business to the Internet. For some network systems and data communication analysts, such as webmasters, an associate degree or certificate is sufficient, although

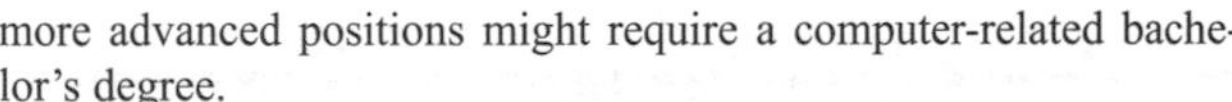

more advanced positions might require a computer-related bachelor's degree.

Most community colleges and many independent technical institutes and proprietary schools offer an associate's degree in computer science or a related information technology field. Many of these programs may be geared more toward meeting the needs of local businesses and are more occupation specific than are four-year degree programs. Some jobs may be better suited to the level of training that such programs offer. Employers usually look for people who have broad knowledge and experience related to computer systems and technologies, strong problem-solving and analytical skills, and good interpersonal skills. Courses in computer science or systems design offer good preparation for a job in these computer occupations. For jobs in a business environment, employers usually want systems analysts to have business management or closely related skills, while a background in the physical sciences, applied mathematics, or engineering is preferred for work in scientifically oriented organizations. Art or graphic design skills may be desirable for webmasters or Web developers.

Despite employers' preference for those with technical degrees, individuals with post-secondary degrees in a variety of other subjects may find employment in these occupations. Given the rapid pace of technological change, a degree generally has more value as a demonstration of an individual's ability to learn, rather than as a certification of a certain skill set. Generally speaking, coursework in computer science and an undergraduate degree are sufficient qualifications, especially if the applicant has a reasonable amount of experience.

Certification and other qualifications. Computer scientists and database administrators must be able to think logically and have good communication skills. Because they often deal with a number of tasks simultaneously, the ability to concentrate and pay close attention to detail also is important. Although computer specialists sometimes work independently, they frequently work in teams on large projects. As a result, they must be able to communicate effectively with computer personnel, such as programmers and managers, as well as with users or other staff who may have no technical computer background.

Jobseekers can enhance their employment opportunities by earning certifications, most of which are offered through private companies, with many related to specific products. Many employers regard these certifications as the industry standard. For example, one method of acquiring enough knowledge to get a job as a database administrator is to become certified in database management with a certain software package. Voluntary certification also is available through various organizations associated with computer specialists. Professional certification may afford a jobseeker a competitive advantage.

Because technology is so closely connected to the functioning of businesses, many workers in these occupations come from elsewhere in the business or industry to become computer specialists. This background can be very useful, in that it helps them to better understand how their networking and database tools are being used within the organization.

Advancement. Computer scientists may advance into managerial or project leadership positions. Many having advanced degrees choose to leave private industry for academic positions. Database administrators may advance into managerial positions, such as chief technology officer, on the basis of their experience managing data and enforcing security. Computer specialists with work experience and considerable expertise in a particular subject or a certain application may find lucrative opportunities as independent consultants or may choose to start their own computer consulting firms.

Technological advances come so rapidly in the computer field that continuous study is necessary to keep one's skills up to date. Employers, hardware and software vendors, colleges and universities, and private training institutions offer continuing education. Additional training may come from professional development seminars offered by professional computing societies.

Employment

Computer scientists and database administrators held about 542,000 jobs in May 2006, including about 58,000 who were self-employed. Employment was distributed among the detailed occupations as follows:

Network systems and data communication analysts 262,000
Computer specialists, all other...........................136,000
Database administrators 119,000
Computer and information scientists, research........25,000

Although they are increasingly employed in every sector of the economy, the greatest concentration of these workers is in the computer systems design and related services industry. Firms in this industry provide services related to the commercial use of computers on a contract basis, including custom computer programming services; computer systems integration design services; computer facilities management services, including computer systems or data processing facilities support services for clients; and other computer-related services, such as disaster recovery services and software installation. Many computer scientists and database administrators are employed by Internet service providers; Web search portals; and data processing, hosting, and related services firms. Others work for government, manufacturers of computer and electronic products, insurance companies, financial institutions, and universities.

A growing number of computer specialists, such as network and data communications analysts, are employed on a temporary or contract basis; many of these individuals are self-employed, working independently as contractors or consultants. For example, a company installing a new computer system may need the services of several network systems and data communication analysts just to get the system running. Because not all of the analysts would be needed once the system is functioning, the company might contract for such employees with a temporary help agency or consulting firm, or with the network systems analysts themselves. Such jobs may last from several months to 2 years or more. This growing practice enables companies to bring in people with the exact skills they need to complete a particular project, rather than having to spend time or money training or retraining existing workers. Often, experienced consultants then train a company's in-house staff as a project develops.

Job Outlook

Computer scientists and database administrators are projected to be one of the fastest growing occupations over the next decade. Strong employment growth combined with a limited supply of qualified

Projections data from the National Employment Matrix

Occupational Title	SOC Code	Employment, 2006	Projected employment, 2016	Change, 2006-2016	
				Number	Percent
Computer scientists and database administrators	—	542,000	742,000	200,000	37
Computer and information scientists, research	15-1011	25,000	31,000	5,400	22
Database administrators	15-1061	119,000	154,000	34,000	29
Network systems and data communications analysts	15-1081	262,000	402,000	140,000	53
Computer specialists, all other	15-1099	136,000	157,000	21,000	15

NOTE: Data in this table are rounded.

workers will result in excellent employment prospects for this occupation and a high demand for their skills.

Employment change. The computer scientists and database administrators occupation is expected to grow 37 percent from 2006 to 2016, much faster than average for all occupations. Employment of these computer specialists is expected to grow as organizations continue to adopt and integrate increasingly sophisticated technologies. Job increases will be driven by very rapid growth in computer systems design and related services, which is projected to be one of the fastest growing industries in the U.S. economy.

The demand for networking to facilitate the sharing of information, the expansion of client-server environments, and the need for computer specialists to use their knowledge and skills in a problem-solving capacity will be major factors in the rising demand for computer scientists and database administrators. Firms will continue to seek out computer specialists who are able to implement the latest technologies and are able to apply them to meet the needs of businesses as they struggle to maintain a competitive advantage.

As computers continue to become more central to business functions, more sophisticated and complex technology is being implemented across all organizations, fueling demand for computer scientists and database administrators. There is growing demand for network systems and data communication analysts to help firms maximize their efficiency with available technology. Expansion of electronic commerce—doing business on the Internet—and the continuing need to build and maintain databases that store critical information on customers, inventory, and projects are fueling demand for database administrators familiar with the latest technology. Because of the increasing reliance on the Internet among businesses, information security is an increasing concern.

The development of new technologies leads to demand for various kinds of workers. The expanding integration of Internet technologies into businesses, for example, has resulted in a growing need for specialists who can develop and support Internet and intranet applications. The growth of electronic commerce means that more establishments use the Internet to conduct their business online. It also means more security specialists are needed to protect their systems. The spread of such new technologies translates into a need for information technology professionals who can help organizations use technology to communicate with employees, clients, and consumers. Explosive growth in these areas also is expected to fuel demand for specialists who are knowledgeable about network, data, and communications security.

Job prospects. Computer scientists and database administrators should continue to enjoy excellent job prospects. As technology becomes more sophisticated and complex, however, these positions will demand a higher level of skill and expertise from their employees. Individuals with an advanced degree in computer science or computer engineering or with an MBA with a concentration in information systems should enjoy favorable employment prospects. College graduates with a bachelor's degree in computer science, computer engineering, information science, or MIS also should enjoy favorable prospects, particularly if they have supplemented their formal education with practical experience. Because employers continue to seek computer specialists who can combine strong technical skills with good business skills, individuals with a combination of experience inside and outside the IT arena will have the best job prospects.

In addition to growth, many job openings will arise from the need to replace workers who move into managerial positions or other occupations or who leave the labor force.

Earnings

Median annual earnings of computer and information scientists, research, were $93,950 in May 2006. The middle 50 percent earned between $71,930 and $118,100. The lowest 10 percent earned less than $53,590, and the highest 10 percent earned more than $144,880. Median annual earnings of computer and information scientists employed in computer systems design and related services in May 2006 were $95,340.

Median annual earnings of database administrators were $64,670 in May 2006. The middle 50 percent earned between $48,560 and $84,830. The lowest 10 percent earned less than $37,350, and the highest 10 percent earned more than $103,010. In May 2006, median annual earnings of database administrators employed in computer systems design and related services were $72,510, and for those in management of companies and enterprises, earnings were $67,680.

Median annual earnings of network systems and data communication analysts were $64,600 in May 2006. The middle 50 percent earned between $49,510 and $82,630. The lowest 10 percent earned less than $38,410, and the highest 10 percent earned more than $101,740. Median annual earnings in the industries employing the largest numbers of network systems and data communications analysts in May 2006 are shown below:

Wired telecommunications carriers	$72,480
Management of companies and enterprises	68,490
Management, scientific, and technical consulting services	67,830
Computer systems design and related services	67,080
State government	52,020

Median annual earnings of all other computer specialists were $68,570 in May 2006. Median annual earnings of all other computer specialists employed in computer systems design and related services were $67,370, and, for those in management of companies and enterprises, earnings were $63,610 in May 2006.

Robert Half International, a firm providing specialized staffing services, noted the following salary ranges for computer-related occupations in their 2007 Salary Guide:

Occupation	Low		High
Database manager	$84,750	-	$116,000
Network architect	78,000	-	112,250
Database developer	73,500	-	103,000
Senior web developer	71,000	-	102,000
Database administrator	70,250	-	102,000
Network manager	68,750	-	93,000
Web developer	54,750	-	81,500
LAN/WAN administrator	51,000	-	71,500
Web administrator	49,750	-	74,750
Web designer	47,000	-	71,500
Telecommunications specialist	47,500	-	69,500

Related Occupations

Others who work with large amounts of data are computer programmers, computer software engineers, computer and information systems managers, engineers, mathematicians, statisticians, and actuaries.

Sources of Additional Information

Further information about computer careers is available from

- Association for Computing Machinery (ACM), 1515 Broadway, New York, NY 10036. Internet: http://www.acm.org
- Institute of Electrical and Electronics Engineers Computer Society, Headquarters Office, 1730 Massachusetts Ave. NW, Washington, DC 20036-1992. Internet: http://www.computer.org
- Software & Information Industry Association, 1090 Vermont Ave. NW, 6th floor, Washington, DC 20005. Internet: http://www.siia.net

STEM Computer Software Engineers

(O*NET 15-1031.00 and 15-1032.00)

Significant Points

- Computer software engineers are one of the occupations projected to grow the fastest and add the most new jobs over the 2006–2016 decade.
- Excellent job prospects are expected for applicants with at least bachelor's degree in computer engineering or computer science and with practical work experience.
- Computer software engineers must continually strive to acquire new skills in conjunction with the rapid changes that occur in computer technology.

Nature of the Work

Computer software engineers apply the principles of computer science and mathematical analysis to the design, development, testing, and evaluation of the software and systems that make computers work. The tasks performed by these workers evolve quickly, reflecting new areas of specialization or changes in technology, as well as the preferences and practices of employers. (A separate section on computer hardware engineers appears in the engineers section of this book.)

Software engineers can be involved in the design and development of many types of software, including computer games, word processing and business applications, operating systems and network distribution, and compilers, which convert programs to machine language for execution on a computer.

Computer software engineers begin by analyzing users' needs, and then design, test, and develop software to meet those needs. During this process they create the detailed sets of instructions, called algorithms, that tell the computer what to do. They also may be responsible for converting these instructions into a computer language, a process called programming or coding, but this usually is the responsibility of *computer programmers*. (A separate section on computer programmers appears elsewhere in this book.) Computer software engineers must be experts in operating systems and middleware to ensure that the underlying systems will work properly.

Computer applications software engineers analyze users' needs and design, construct, and maintain general computer applications software or specialized utility programs. These workers use different programming languages, depending on the purpose of the program. The programming languages most often used are C, C++, and Java, with Fortran and COBOL used less commonly. Some software engineers develop both packaged systems and systems software or create customized applications.

Computer systems software engineers coordinate the construction, maintenance, and expansion of an organization's computer systems. Working with the organization, they coordinate each department's computer needs—ordering, inventory, billing, and payroll recordkeeping, for example—and make suggestions about its technical direction. They also might set up the organization's intranets—networks that link computers within the organization and ease communication among various departments.

Systems software engineers also work for companies that configure, implement, and install the computer systems of other organizations. These workers may be members of the marketing or sales staff, serving as the primary technical resource for sales workers. They also may help with sales and provide customers with technical support. Since the selling of complex computer systems often requires substantial customization to meet the needs of the purchaser, software engineers help to identify and explain needed changes. In addition, systems software engineers are responsible for ensuring security across the systems they are configuring.

Computer software engineers often work as part of a team that designs new hardware, software, and systems. A core team may comprise engineering, marketing, manufacturing, and design people, who work together to release a product.

Work environment. Computer software engineers normally work in clean, comfortable offices or in laboratories in which computer equipment is located. Software engineers who work for software vendors and consulting firms frequently travel overnight to meet with customers. Telecommuting is also becoming more common, allowing workers to do their jobs from remote locations.

Most software engineers work at least 40 hours a week, but about 17 percent work more than 50 hours a week. Software engineers also may have to work evenings or weekends to meet deadlines or solve unexpected technical problems.

Like other workers who spend long hours typing at a computer, software engineers are susceptible to eyestrain, back discomfort, and hand and wrist problems such as carpal tunnel syndrome.

Training, Other Qualifications, and Advancement

Most employers prefer applicants who have at least a bachelor's degree and experience with a variety of computer systems and technologies. In order to remain competitive, computer software engineers must continually strive to acquire the latest technical skills. Advancement opportunities are good for those with relevant experience.

Education and training. Most employers prefer applicants who have at least a bachelor's degree and broad knowledge of, and experience with, a variety of computer systems and technologies. The usual college major for applications software engineers is computer science or software engineering. Systems software engineers often study computer science or computer information systems. Graduate degrees are preferred for some of the more complex jobs. In 2006, about 80 percent of workers had a bachelor's degree or higher.

Academic programs in software engineering may offer the program as a degree option or in conjunction with computer science degrees. Because of increasing emphasis on computer security, software engineers with advanced degrees in areas such as mathematics and systems design will be sought after by software developers, government agencies, and consulting firms.

Students seeking software engineering jobs enhance their employment opportunities by participating in internships or co-ops. These experiences provide students with broad knowledge and experience, making them more attractive to employers. Inexperienced college graduates may be hired by large computer and consulting firms that train new employees in intensive, company-based programs.

Certification and other qualifications. Systems software vendors offer certification and training programs, but most training authorities say that program certification alone is not sufficient for the majority of software engineering jobs.

People interested in jobs as computer software engineers must have strong problem-solving and analytical skills. They also must be able to communicate effectively with team members, other staff, and the customers they meet. Because they often deal with a number of tasks simultaneously, they must be able to concentrate and pay close attention to detail.

As technology advances, employers will need workers with the latest skills. Computer software engineers must continually strive to acquire new skills if they wish to remain in this dynamic field. To help keep up with changing technology, workers may take continuing education and professional development seminars offered by employers, software vendors, colleges and universities, private training institutions, and professional computing societies. Computer software engineers also need skills related to the industry in which they work. Engineers working for a bank, for example, should have some expertise in finance so that they understand banks' computer needs.

Advancement. As with most occupations, advancement opportunities for computer software engineers increase with experience. Entry-level computer software engineers are likely to test designs. As they become more experienced, engineers may begin helping to design and develop software. Eventually, they may advance to become a project manager, manager of information systems, or chief information officer, especially if they have business skills and training. Some computer software engineers with several years of experience or expertise find lucrative opportunities working as systems designers or independent consultants.

Employment

Computer software engineers held about 857,000 jobs in 2006. Approximately 507,000 were computer applications software engineers, and about 350,000 were computer systems software engineers. Although they are employed in most industries, the largest concentration of computer software engineers—more than 29 percent—is in computer systems design and related services. Many computer software engineers also work for establishments in other industries, such as software publishers, government agencies, manufacturers of computers and related electronic equipment, financial institutions, insurance providers, and management of companies and enterprises.

An increasing number of computer software engineers work as independent consultants on a temporary or contract basis, many of whom are self-employed. About 17,000 computer software engineers were self-employed in 2006.

Job Outlook

Job prospects should be excellent, as computer software engineers are expected to be among the fastest-growing occupations through the year 2016.

Employment change. Employment of computer software engineers is projected to increase by 38 percent over the 2006 to 2016 period, which is much faster than the average for all occupations. This occupation will generate about 324,000 new jobs, over the projections decade, one of the largest employment increases of any occupation.

Employment growth will result as businesses and other organizations adopt and integrate new technologies and seek to maximize the efficiency of their computer systems. Competition among businesses will continue to create incentive for sophisticated technological innovations, and organizations will need more computer software engineers to implement these changes.

Demand for computer software engineers will also increase as computer networking continues to grow. For example, expanding Internet technologies have spurred demand for computer software engineers who can develop Internet, intranet, and World Wide Web applications. Likewise, electronic data-processing systems in business, telecommunications, government, and other settings continue to become more sophisticated and complex. Implementing, safeguarding, and updating computer systems and resolving problems will fuel the demand for growing numbers of systems software engineers.

New growth areas will also continue to arise from rapidly evolving technologies. The increasing uses of the Internet, the proliferation of Web sites, and mobile technology such as wireless Internet have created a demand for a wide variety of new products. As individuals and businesses rely more on hand-held computers and wireless networks, it will be necessary to integrate current computer systems with this new, more mobile technology.

In addition, information security concerns have given rise to new software needs. Concerns over "cyber security" should result in businesses and government continuing to invest heavily in software that protects their networks and vital electronic infrastructure from attack. The expansion of this technology in the next 10 years will lead to an increased need for computer engineers to design and develop the software and systems to run these new applications and integrate them into older systems.

As with other information technology jobs, outsourcing of software development to other countries may temper somewhat employment growth of computer software engineers. Firms may look to cut costs by shifting operations to foreign countries with lower prevailing wages and highly educated workers. Jobs in software engineering are less prone to being offshored than are jobs in other computer specialties, however, because software engineering requires innovation and intense research and development.

Job prospects. As a result of rapid employment growth over the 2006 to 2016 decade, job prospects for computer software engineers should be excellent. Those with practical experience and at least a bachelor's degree in computer engineering or computer science should have the best opportunities. Employers will continue to seek computer professionals with strong programming, systems analysis, interpersonal, and business skills. In addition to jobs created through employment growth, many job openings will result from the need to replace workers who move into managerial positions, transfer to other occupations, or leave the labor force. Consulting opportunities for computer software engineers also should continue to grow as businesses seek help to manage, upgrade, and customize their increasingly complicated computer systems.

Earnings

In May 2006, median annual earnings of wage-and-salary computer applications software engineers were $79,780. The middle 50 percent earned between $62,830 and $98,470. The lowest 10 percent earned less than $49,350, and the highest 10 percent earned more than $119,770. Median annual earnings in the industries employing the largest numbers of computer applications software engineers in May 2006 were as follows:

Software publishers $84,560
Computer systems design and related services 78,850
Management, scientific, and technical consulting services 78,850
Management of companies and enterprises 78,580
Insurance carriers 74,230

In May 2006, median annual earnings of wage-and-salary computer systems software engineers were $85,370. The middle 50 percent earned between $67,620 and $105,330. The lowest 10 percent earned less than $53,580, and the highest 10 percent earned more than $125,750. Median annual earnings in the industries employing the largest numbers of computer systems software engineers in May 2006 are as follows:

Research and development in the physical, engineering, and life sciences $97,220
Scientific research and development services 97,180
Computer and peripheral equipment manufacturing 93,240
Software publishers 87,450
Computer systems design and related services 84,660
Data processing, hosting, and related services 78,270

According to the National Association of Colleges and Employers, starting salary offers for graduates with a bachelor's degree in computer engineering averaged $56,201 in 2007. Starting salary offers for graduates with a bachelor's degree in computer science averaged $53,396.

According to Robert Half Technology, starting salaries for software engineers in software development ranged from $66,500 to $99,750 in 2007. For network engineers, starting salaries ranged from $65,750 to $90,250.

Related Occupations

Other workers who use mathematics and logic extensively include computer systems analysts, computer scientists and database administrators, computer programmers, computer hardware engineers, computer support specialists and systems administrators, engineers, commercial and industrial designers, statisticians, mathematicians, and actuaries.

Sources of Additional Information

Additional information on a career in computer software engineering is available from the following organizations:

- Association for Computing Machinery (ACM), 2 Penn Plaza, Suite 701, NY 10121-0701. Internet: http://www.acm.org
- Institute of Electronics and Electrical Engineers Computer Society, Headquarters Office, 1730 Massachusetts Ave. NW, Washington, DC 20036-1992. Internet: http://www.computer.org
- National Workforce Center for Emerging Technologies, 3000 Landerholm Circle SE, Bellevue, WA 98007. Internet: http://www.nwcet.org
- University of Washington Computer Science and Engineering Department, AC101 Paul G. Allen Center, Box 352350, 185 Stevens Way, Seattle, WA 98195-2350. Internet: http://www.cs.washington.edu/WhyCSE

Projections data from the National Employment Matrix

Occupational Title	SOC Code	Employment, 2006	Projected employment, 2016	Change, 2006-2016	
				Number	Percent
Computer software engineers	15-1030	857,000	1,181,000	324,000	38
Computer software engineers, applications	15-1031	507,000	733,000	226,000	45
Computer software engineers, systems software	15-1032	350,000	449,000	99,000	28

NOTE: Data in this table are rounded.

STEM Computer Support Specialists and Systems Administrators

(O*NET 15-1041.00, 15-1071.00, and 15-1071.01)

Significant Points

- Growth in computer support specialist jobs will be about as fast as the average, while growth in network and computer system administrator jobs will be much faster than average.
- There are many paths of entry to these occupations.
- Job prospects should be best for college graduates with relevant skills and experience; certifications and practical experience are essential for people without degrees.

Nature of the Work

In the last decade, computers have become an integral part of everyday life at home, work, school, and nearly everywhere else. Of course, almost every computer user encounters a problem occasionally, whether it is the annoyance of a forgotten password or the disaster of a crashing hard drive. The explosive use of computers has created demand for specialists who provide advice to users, as well as for the day-to-day administration, maintenance, and support of computer systems and networks.

Computer support specialists provide technical assistance, support, and advice to customers and other users. This occupational group includes *technical support specialists* and *help-desk technicians.* These troubleshooters interpret problems and provide technical support for hardware, software, and systems. They answer telephone calls, analyze problems by using automated diagnostic programs, and resolve recurring difficulties. Support specialists work either within a company that uses computer systems or directly for a computer hardware or software vendor. Increasingly, these specialists work for help-desk or support services firms, for which they provide computer support to clients on a contract basis.

Technical support specialists respond to inquiries from their organizations' computer users and may run automatic diagnostics programs to resolve problems. They also install, modify, clean, and repair computer hardware and software. In addition, they may write training manuals and train computer users in how to use new computer hardware and software. These workers also oversee the daily performance of their company's computer systems and evaluate how useful software programs are.

Help-desk technicians respond to telephone calls and e-mail messages from customers looking for help with computer problems. In responding to these inquiries, help-desk technicians must listen carefully to the customer, ask questions to diagnose the nature of the problem, and then patiently walk the customer through the problem-solving steps.

Help-desk technicians deal directly with customer issues and companies value them as a source of feedback on their products. They are consulted for information about what gives customers the most trouble, as well as other customer concerns. Most computer support specialists start out at the help desk.

Network and *computer systems administrators* design, install, and support an organization's computer systems. They are responsible for local-area networks (LAN), wide-area networks (WAN), network segments, and Internet and intranet systems. They work in a variety of environments, including professional offices, small businesses, government organizations, and large corporations. They maintain network hardware and software, analyze problems, and monitor networks to ensure their availability to system users. These workers gather data to identify customer needs and then use the information to identify, interpret, and evaluate system and network requirements. Administrators also may plan, coordinate, and implement network security measures.

Systems administrators are responsible for maintaining network efficiency. They ensure that the design of an organization's computer system allows all of the components, including computers, the network, and software, to work properly together. Furthermore, they monitor and adjust the performance of existing networks and continually survey the current computer site to determine future network needs. Administrators also troubleshoot problems reported by users and by automated network monitoring systems and make recommendations for future system upgrades.

In some organizations, *computer security specialists* may plan, coordinate, and implement the organization's information security. These workers educate users about computer security, install security software, monitor networks for security breaches, respond to cyber attacks, and, in some cases, gather data and evidence to be used in prosecuting cyber crime. The responsibilities of computer security specialists have increased in recent years as cyber attacks have become more common. This and other growing specialty occupations reflect an increasing emphasis on client-server applications, the expansion of Internet and intranet applications, and the demand for more end-user support.

Work environment. Computer support specialists and systems administrators normally work in well-lighted, comfortable offices or computer laboratories. They usually work about 40 hours a week, but if their employer requires computer support over extended hours, they may be "on call" for rotating evening or weekend work. Overtime may be necessary when unexpected technical problems arise. Like other workers who type on a keyboard for long periods, computer support specialists and systems administrators are susceptible to eyestrain, back discomfort, and hand and wrist problems such as carpal tunnel syndrome.

Computer support specialists and systems administrators constantly interact with customers and fellow employees as they answer questions and give advice. Those who work as consultants are away from their offices much of the time, sometimes spending months working in a client's office.

As computer networks expand, more computer support specialists and systems administrators may be able to provide technical support from remote locations. This capability would reduce or eliminate travel to the customer's workplace. Systems administrators also can administer and configure networks and servers remotely, although this practice is not as common as it is among computer support specialists.

Training, Other Qualifications, and Advancement

A college degree is required for some computer support specialist positions, but certification and relevant experience may be sufficient for others. A bachelor's degree is required for many network and computer systems administrator positions. For both occupations, strong analytical and communication skills are essential.

Education and training. Due to the wide range of skills required, there are many paths of entry to a job as a computer support specialist or systems administrator. Training requirements for computer support specialist positions vary, but many employers prefer to hire applicants with some formal college education. A bachelor's degree in computer science or information systems is a prerequisite for some jobs; other jobs, however, may require only a computer-related associate degree. And for some jobs, relevant computer experience and certifications may substitute for formal education. For systems administrator jobs, many employers seek applicants with bachelor's degrees, although not necessarily in a computer-related field.

A number of companies are becoming more flexible about requiring a college degree for support positions. In the absence of a degree, however, certification and practical experience are essential. Certification training programs, offered by a variety of vendors and product makers, may help some people to qualify for entry-level positions.

Other qualifications. People interested in becoming a computer support specialist or systems administrator must have strong problem-solving, analytical, and communication skills because troubleshooting and helping others are vital parts of the job. The constant interaction with other computer personnel, customers, and employees requires computer support specialists and systems administrators to communicate effectively on paper, via e-mail, over the phone, or in person. Strong writing skills are useful in preparing manuals for employees and customers.

Advancement. Beginning computer support specialists usually work for organizations that deal directly with customers or in-house users. Support specialists may advance into positions in which they use what they have learned from customers to improve the design and efficiency of future products. Job promotions usually depend more on performance than on formal education. Eventually, some computer support specialists become software engineers, designing products rather than assisting users. Computer support specialists in hardware and software companies often enjoy great upward mobility; advancement sometimes comes within months of becoming employed.

Entry-level network and computer systems administrators are involved in routine maintenance and monitoring of computer systems, typically working behind the scenes in an organization. After gaining experience and expertise, they often are able to advance to more senior-level positions. For example, senior network and computer systems administrators may make presentations to executives and managers on the security of the company computer network. They also may translate the needs of an organization into a set of technical requirements based on the available technology. As with support specialists, administrators may become software engineers involved in system and network design.

As technology continues to improve, computer support specialists and systems administrators must strive to acquire new skills. Many continuing education programs are provided by employers, hardware and software vendors, colleges and universities, and private training institutions. Professional development seminars offered by computing services firms also can enhance skills and advancement opportunities.

Employment

Computer support specialists and systems administrators held about 862,000 jobs in 2006. Of these, approximately 552,000 were computer support specialists and about 309,000 were network and computer systems administrators. Although they worked in a wide range of industries, about 23 percent of all computer support specialists and systems administrators were employed in professional, scientific, and technical services industries, principally computer systems design and related services. Substantial numbers of these workers were also employed in administrative and support services companies, financial institutions, insurance companies, government agencies, educational institutions, software publishers, telecommunications organizations, health care organizations, and management of companies and enterprises.

Employers of computer support specialists and systems administrators range from startup companies to established industry leaders. As computer networks become an integral part of business, industries not typically associated with computers—such as construction—increasingly need computer support workers.

Job Outlook

Employment of computer support specialists and systems administrators is expected to increase faster than the average. Job prospects should be best for those with a college degree and relevant experience.

Employment change. Employment of computer support specialists and systems administrators is expected to increase by 18 percent from 2006 to 2016, which is much faster than the average for all occupations. In addition, this occupation is expected to add 155,000 jobs over the projection decade.

Employment of computer support specialists is expected to increase by 13 percent from 2006 to 2016, which is about as fast as the average for all occupations. Demand for these workers will result as organizations and individuals continue to adopt increasingly sophisticated technology. Job growth will continue to be driven by the ongoing expansion of the computer system design and related services industry, which is projected to remain one of the fastest-growing industries in the U.S. economy. Growth will not be as explosive as during the previous decade, however, because the information technology industry is maturing and because some of these jobs are expected to be outsourced offshore where prevailing wages are lower. Physical location is not as important for computer support specialists as it is for other occupations because these workers can provide assistance remotely and support services are provided around the clock across time zones.

Job growth among computer support specialists reflects the rapid evolution of technology. As computers and software become more complex, support specialists will be needed to provide technical assistance to customers and other users. The adoption of new mobile technologies, such as the wireless Internet, will continue to create a need for these workers to familiarize and educate computer users. Consulting jobs for computer support specialists also should continue to increase as businesses seek help managing, upgrading, and customizing ever more complex computer systems.

Employment of network and computer systems administrators is expected to increase by 27 percent from 2006 to 2016, which is much faster than the average for all occupations. Computer networks have become an integral part of business, and demand for

Projections data from the National Employment Matrix

Occupational Title	SOC Code	Employment, 2006	Projected employment, 2016	Change, 2006-2016	
				Number	Percent
Computer support specialists and systems administrators	—	862,000	1,016,000	155,000	18
Computer support specialists	15-1041	552,000	624,000	71,000	13
Network and computer systems administrators	15-1071	309,000	393,000	83,000	27

NOTE: Data in this table are rounded.

these workers will increase as firms continue to invest in new technologies. The wide use of electronic commerce and the increasing adoption of mobile technologies mean that more establishments will use the Internet to conduct business online. This growth translates into a need for systems administrators who can help organizations use technology to communicate with employees, clients, and consumers.

Demand for computer security specialists will grow as businesses and government continue to invest heavily in "cyber security," protecting vital computer networks and electronic infrastructures from attack. The information security field is expected to generate many new system administrator jobs over the next decade as firms across all industries place a high priority on safeguarding their data and systems.

Employment of network and computer systems administrators, however, may be tempered somewhat by offshore outsourcing, as firms transfer work to countries with lower-prevailing wages and highly skilled work forces. Systems administrators may increasingly be able to manage computer systems from remote locations as technology advances.

Job prospects. Job prospects should be best for college graduates who possess the latest technological skills, particularly graduates who have supplemented their formal education with relevant work experience. Employers will continue to seek computer specialists who possess strong fundamental computer skills combined with good interpersonal and communication skills. Due to the demand for computer support specialists and systems administrators over the next decade, those who have strong computer skills but do not have a college degree should continue to qualify for some entry-level positions.

Earnings

Median annual earnings of wage-and-salary computer support specialists were $41,470 in May 2006. The middle 50 percent earned between $32,110 and $53,640. The lowest 10 percent earned less than $25,290, and the highest 10 percent earned more than $68,540. Median annual earnings in the industries employing the largest numbers of computer support specialists in May 2006 were as follows:

Software publishers $46,270
Management of companies and enterprises 42,770
Computer systems design and related services 42,510
Colleges, universities, and professional schools 40,130
Elementary and secondary schools 37,880

Median annual earnings of wage-and-salary network and computer systems administrators were $62,130 in May 2006. The middle 50 percent earned between $48,520 and $79,160. The lowest 10 percent earned less than $38,610, and the highest 10 percent earned more than $97,080. Median annual earnings in the industries employing the largest numbers of network and computer systems administrators in May 2006 were as follows:

Wired telecommunications carriers $70,790
Computer systems design and related services 66,680
Management of companies and enterprises 66,020
Colleges, universities, and professional schools 54,590
Elementary and secondary schools 53,750

According to Robert Half Technology, starting salaries in 2007 ranged from $27,500 to $37,000 for help-desk workers. Starting salaries for desktop support analysts ranged from $46,500 to $65,250. For systems administrators, starting salaries ranged from $50,000 to $75,750.

Related Occupations

Other computer specialists include computer programmers, computer software engineers, computer systems analysts, and computer scientists and database administrators. Other workers who respond to customer inquiries are customer service representatives.

Sources of Additional Information

For additional information about a career as a computer support specialist, contact

- Association of Support Professionals, 122 Barnard Ave., Watertown, MA 02472.

For additional information about a career as a systems administrator, contact

- The League of Professional System Administrators, 15000 Commerce Parkway, Suite C, Mount Laurel, NJ 08054. Internet: http://lopsa.org/
- National Workforce Center for Emerging Technologies, 3000 Landerholm Circle SE, Bellevue, WA 98007. Internet: http://www.nwcet.org

STEM Computer Systems Analysts

(O*NET 15-1051.00, 15-1099.01, 15-1099.02, and 15-1099.03)

Significant Points

- Employers generally prefer applicants who have at least a bachelor's degree in computer science, information science, or management information systems (MIS).
- Employment is expected to increase much faster than the average and more new jobs are expected to arise than in all but a few other occupations.

- Very good job prospects are expected as organizations continue to adopt increasingly sophisticated technologies.

Nature of the Work

All organizations rely on computer and information technology to conduct business and operate efficiently. Computer systems analysts help organizations to use technology effectively and to incorporate rapidly changing technologies into their existing systems. The work of computer systems analysts evolves rapidly, reflecting new areas of specialization and changes in technology.

Computer systems analysts solve computer problems and use computer technology to meet the needs of an organization. They may design and develop new computer systems by choosing and configuring hardware and software. They may also devise ways to apply existing systems' resources to additional tasks. Most systems analysts work with specific types of computer systems—for example, business, accounting, or financial systems or scientific and engineering systems—that vary with the kind of organization. Analysts who specialize in helping an organization select the proper system software and infrastructure are often called *system architects*. Analysts who specialize in developing and fine-tuning systems often are known as *systems designers*.

To begin an assignment, systems analysts consult managers and users to define the goals of the system. Analysts then design a system to meet those goals. They specify the inputs that the system will access, decide how the inputs will be processed, and format the output to meet users' needs. Analysts use techniques such as structured analysis, data modeling, information engineering, mathematical model building, sampling, and cost accounting to make sure their plans are efficient and complete. They also may prepare cost-benefit and return-on-investment analyses to help management decide whether implementing the proposed technology would be financially feasible.

When a system is approved, systems analysts determine what computer hardware and software will be needed to set it up. They coordinate tests and observe the initial use of the system to ensure that it performs as planned. They prepare specifications, flow charts, and process diagrams for computer programmers to follow; then they work with programmers to "debug," or eliminate errors, from the system. Systems analysts who do more in-depth testing may be called *software quality assurance analysts*. In addition to running tests, these workers diagnose problems, recommend solutions, and determine whether program requirements have been met.

In some organizations, *programmer-analysts* design and update the software that runs a computer. They also create custom applications tailored to their organization's tasks. Because they are responsible for both programming and systems analysis, these workers must be proficient in both areas. (A separate section on computer programmers appears elsewhere in this book.) As this dual proficiency becomes more common, analysts are increasingly working with databases, object-oriented programming languages, client–server applications, and multimedia and Internet technology.

One challenge created by expanding computer use is the need for different computer systems to communicate with each other. Systems analysts work to make the computer systems within an organization, or across organizations, compatible so that information can be shared. Many systems analysts are involved with these "networking" tasks, connecting all the computers internally, in an individual office, department, or establishment, or externally, as when setting up e-commerce networks to facilitate business among companies.

Work environment. Computer systems analysts work in offices or laboratories in comfortable surroundings. They usually work about 40 hours a week—about the same as many other professional or office workers. Evening or weekend work may be necessary, however, to meet deadlines or solve specific problems. Many analysts telecommute, using computers to work from remote locations.

Like other workers who spend long periods typing on a computer, computer systems analysts are susceptible to eyestrain, back discomfort, and hand and wrist problems such as carpal tunnel syndrome or cumulative trauma disorder.

Training, Other Qualifications, and Advancement

Training requirements for computer systems analysts vary depending on the job, but many employers prefer applicants who have a bachelor's degree. Relevant work experience also is very important. Advancement opportunities are good for those with the necessary skills and experience.

Education and training. When hiring computer systems analysts, employers usually prefer applicants who have at least a bachelor's degree. For more technically complex jobs, people with graduate degrees are preferred.

The level and type of education that employers require reflects changes in technology. Employers often scramble to find workers capable of implementing the newest technologies. Workers with formal education or experience in information security, for example, are currently in demand because of the growing use of computer networks, which must be protected from threats.

For jobs in a technical or scientific environment, employers often seek applicants who have at least a bachelor's degree in a technical field, such as computer science, information science, applied mathematics, engineering, or the physical sciences. For jobs in a business environment, employers often seek applicants with at least a bachelor's degree in a business-related field such as management information systems (MIS). Increasingly, employers are seeking individuals who have a master's degree in business administration (MBA) with a concentration in information systems.

Despite the preference for technical degrees, however, people who have degrees in other majors may find employment as systems analysts if they also have technical skills. Courses in computer science or related subjects combined with practical experience can qualify people for some jobs in the occupation.

Employers generally look for people with expertise relevant to the job. For example, systems analysts who wish to work for a bank should have some expertise in finance, and systems analysts who wish to work for a hospital should have some knowledge of health management.

Technological advances come so rapidly in the computer field that continuous study is necessary to remain competitive. Employers, hardware and software vendors, colleges and universities, and private training institutions offer continuing education to help workers attain the latest skills. Additional training may come from professional development seminars offered by professional computing societies.

Other qualifications. Employers usually look for people who have broad knowledge and experience related to computer systems and technologies, strong problem-solving and analytical skills, and the ability to think logically. In addition, because they often deal with a number of tasks simultaneously, the ability to concentrate and pay close attention to detail is important. Although these workers sometimes work independently, they frequently work in teams on large projects. Therefore, they must have good interpersonal skills and be able to communicate effectively with computer personnel, users, and other staff who may have no technical background.

Advancement. With experience, systems analysts may be promoted to senior or lead systems analyst. Those who possess leadership ability and good business skills also can become computer and information systems managers or can advance into other management positions such as manager of information systems or chief information officer. Those with work experience and considerable expertise in a particular subject or application may find lucrative opportunities as independent consultants, or may choose to start their own computer consulting firms.

Employment

Computer systems analysts held about 504,000 jobs in 2006. Although they are increasingly employed in every sector of the economy, the greatest concentration of these workers is in the computer systems design and related services industry. Computer systems analysts are also employed by governments; insurance companies; financial institutions; hospitals; management, scientific, and technical consulting services firms; data processing services firms; professional and commercial equipment wholesalers; universities; and management of companies and enterprises.

A growing number of systems analysts are employed on a temporary or contract basis; many of these individuals are self-employed, working independently as contractors or consultants. About 29,000 computer systems analysts were self-employed in 2006.

Job Outlook

Employment is expected to grow much faster than the average for all occupations. As a result of this rapid growth, job prospects should be very good.

Employment change. Employment of computer systems analysts is expected to grow by 29 percent from 2006 to 2016, which is much faster than the average for all occupations. In addition, the 146,000 new jobs that are expected to arise over the projections decade will be substantial. Demand for these workers will increase as organizations continue to adopt and integrate increasingly sophisticated technologies. Job growth will not be as rapid as during the preceding decade, however, as the information technology sector matures and as routine work is increasingly outsourced offshore to foreign countries with lower prevailing wages.

The growth of electronic commerce and the integration of Internet technologies into business have resulted in a growing need for specialists who can develop and support Internet and intranet applications. Moreover, falling prices of computer hardware and software should continue to induce more businesses to expand their computerized operations and incorporate new technologies.

The demand for computer networking within organizations will also drive demand for computer systems analysts. The introduction of the wireless Internet, known as WiFi, and of personal mobile computers has created a need for new systems that can integrate these technologies into existing networks. Explosive growth in these areas is expected to fuel demand for analysts who are knowledgeable about systems integration and network, data, and communications security.

As more sophisticated and complex technology is implemented across all organizations, demand for systems analysts will remain strong. These workers will be called upon to solve problems and to integrate new technologies with existing ones. Also, the increasing importance being placed on "cybersecurity"—the protection of electronic information—will result in a need for workers skilled in information security.

As with other information technology jobs, employment growth may be tempered somewhat as some computer systems analyst jobs are outsourced offshore. Firms may look to cut costs by shifting operations to foreign countries with lower prevailing wages and highly educated workers who have strong technical skills.

Job prospects. Job prospects should be very good. Job openings will occur as a result of strong job growth and from the need to replace workers who move into managerial positions or other occupations, or who leave the labor force. As technology becomes more sophisticated and complex, employers demand a higher level of skill and expertise from their employees. Individuals with an advanced degree in computer science or computer engineering or with an MBA with a concentration in information systems should have the best prospects. College graduates with a bachelor's degree in computer science, computer engineering, information science, or management information systems also should enjoy very good prospects, particularly if they have supplemented their formal education with practical experience. Because employers continue to seek computer specialists who can combine strong technical skills with good interpersonal and business skills, graduates with non-computer-science degrees who have had courses in computer programming, systems analysis, and other information technology subjects also should continue to find jobs in computer fields.

Earnings

Median annual earnings of wage-and-salary computer systems analysts were $69,760 in May 2006. The middle 50 percent earned between $54,320 and $87,600 a year. The lowest 10 percent earned less than $42,780, and the highest 10 percent earned more than $106,820. Median annual earnings in the industries employing the largest numbers of computer systems analysts in May 2006 were

Projections data from the National Employment Matrix

Occupational Title	SOC Code	Employment, 2006	Projected employment, 2016	Change, 2006-2016	
				Number	Percent
Computer systems analysts	15-1051	504,000	650,000	146,000	29

NOTE: Data in this table are rounded.

Professional and commercial equipment and supplies merchant wholesalers $81,080
Computer systems design and related services 71,680
Management of companies and enterprises 71,090
Insurance carriers 69,990
State government 61,340

According to the National Association of Colleges and Employers, starting offers for graduates with a bachelor's degree in computer science averaged $53,396. Starting offers for graduates with a bachelor's degree in information sciences and systems averaged $50,852. For those with a degree in management information systems/business data processing, starting offers averaged $47,648.

According to Robert Half Technology, starting salaries for systems analysts ranged from $64,000 to $87,000 in 2007. Starting salaries for business systems analysts ranged from $61,250 to $86,500. Starting salaries for developer/programmer analysts ranged from $55,250 to $90,250.

Related Occupations

Other workers who use computers extensively and who use logic and creativity to solve business and technical problems include computer programmers, computer software engineers, computer and information systems managers, engineers, mathematicians, statisticians, operations research analysts, management analysts, and actuaries.

Sources of Additional Information

Further information about computer careers is available from

- Association for Computing Machinery (ACM), 2 Penn Plaza, Suite 701,New York, NY 10121-0701. Internet: http://www.acm.org
- Institute of Electrical and Electronics Engineers Computer Society, Headquarters Office, 1730 Massachusetts Ave. NW, Washington, DC 20036-1992. Internet: http://www.computer.org
- National Workforce Center for Emerging Technologies, 3000 Landerholm Circle SE, Bellevue, WA 98007. Internet: http://www.nwcet.org
- University of Washington Computer Science and Engineering Department, AC101 Paul G. Allen Center, Box 352350, 185 Stevens Way, Seattle, WA 98195-2350. Internet: http://www.cs.washington.edu/WhyCSE

Computer, Automated Teller, and Office Machine Repairers

(O*NET 49-2011.00)

Significant Points

- Workers qualify for these jobs by receiving training in electronics from associate degree programs, the military, vocational schools, equipment manufacturers, or employers.
- Employment is expected to grow more slowly than the average for all occupations.
- Job prospects will be best for applicants with knowledge of electronics, and who have formal training and repair experience.

Nature of the Work

Computer, automated teller, and office machine repairers install, fix, and maintain many of the machines that are common to businesses and households. Some repairers travel to customers' workplaces or other locations to make the necessary repairs. These workers—known as *field technicians*—often have assigned areas in which they perform preventive maintenance on a regular basis. *Bench technicians* work in repair shops located in stores, factories, or service centers. In small companies, repairers may work both in repair shops and at customer locations.

Computer repairers, also known as *computer service technicians* or *data processing equipment repairers,* service mainframe, server, and personal computers; printers; and auxiliary computer equipment. These workers primarily perform hands-on repair, maintenance, and installation of computers and related equipment. Workers who provide technical assistance, in person or by telephone, to computer system users are known as computer support specialists or computer support technicians. (See the section on computer support specialists and systems administrators elsewhere in this book.)

Computer repairers usually replace subsystems instead of repairing them. Replacement is common because subsystems are inexpensive and businesses are reluctant to shut down their computers for time-consuming repairs. Subsystems commonly replaced by computer repairers include video cards, which transmit signals from the computer to the monitor; hard drives, which store data; and network cards, which allow communication over the network. Defective modules may be given to bench technicians, who use software programs to diagnose the problem and who may repair the modules, if possible.

Office machine and cash register servicers work on photocopiers, cash registers, mail-processing equipment, and fax machines. Newer models of office machinery include computerized components that allow them to function more effectively than earlier models.

Office machine repairers usually work on machinery at the customer's workplace. However, if the machines are small enough, customers may bring them to a repair shop for maintenance. Common malfunctions include paper misfeeds caused by worn or dirty parts, and poor-quality copy resulting from problems with lamps, lenses, or mirrors. These malfunctions usually can be resolved simply by cleaning the relevant components. Breakdowns also may result from the failure of commonly used parts. For example, heavy use of a photocopier may wear down the printhead, which applies ink to the final copy. In such cases, the repairer usually replaces the part instead of repairing it.

Automated teller machine servicers install and repair automated teller machines (ATMs). These machines allow customers to carry out bank transactions without the assistance of a teller. ATMs also provide a growing variety of other services, including stamp, phone card, and ticket sales.

When ATMs malfunction, computer networks recognize the problem and alert repairers. Common problems include worn magnetic heads on card readers, which prevent the equipment from recognizing customers' bankcards, and "pick failures," which prevent the equipment from dispensing the correct amount of cash. Field technicians travel to the locations of ATMs and usually repair equipment by removing and replacing defective components. Broken components are taken to a repair shop, where bench technicians make the necessary repairs. Field technicians perform routine maintenance on a regular basis, replacing worn parts and running diagnostic tests to ensure that the equipment functions properly.

To install large equipment, such as mainframe computers and ATMs, repairers connect the equipment to power sources and communication lines that allow the transmission of information over computer networks. For example, when an ATM dispenses cash, it transmits the withdrawal information to the customer's bank. Workers also may install operating software and peripheral equipment, checking that all components are configured to function together correctly.

Computer, automated teller, and office machine repairers use a variety of tools for diagnostic tests and repair. To diagnose malfunctions, they use multimeters to measure voltage, current, resistance, and other electrical properties; signal generators to provide test signals; and oscilloscopes to monitor equipment signals. To diagnose computerized equipment, repairers use software programs. To repair or adjust equipment, workers use handtools, such as pliers, screwdrivers, soldering irons, and wrenches.

Work environment. Repairers usually work in clean, well-lighted surroundings. Because computers and office machines are sensitive to extreme temperatures and humidity, repair shops usually are air-conditioned and well ventilated. Field repairers must travel frequently to various locations to install, maintain, or repair customers' equipment. ATM repairers may have to perform their jobs in small, confined spaces that house the equipment.

Because computers and ATMs are critical for many organizations to function efficiently, data processing equipment repairers and ATM field technicians often work around the clock. Their schedules may include evening, weekend, and holiday shifts, sometimes assigned on the basis of seniority. Office machine and cash register servicers usually work regular business hours because the equipment they repair is not as critical. Most repairers work about 40 hours per week, but about 12 percent work more than 50 hours per week.

Although their jobs are not strenuous, repairers must lift equipment and work in a variety of postures. Repairers of computer monitors need to discharge voltage from the equipment to avoid electrocution. Workers may have to wear protective goggles.

Training, Other Qualifications, and Advancement

Knowledge of electronics is required, and employers prefer workers with formal training. Office machine and ATM repairers usually have an associate degree. Certification is available for entry-level workers, as well as experienced workers seeking advancement.

Education and training. Knowledge of electronics is necessary for employment as a computer, automated teller, or office machine repairer. Employers prefer workers who are certified or who have training in electronics from an associate degree program, the military, a vocational school, or an equipment manufacturer. Employers generally provide some training to new repairers on specific equipment; however, workers are expected to arrive on the job with a basic understanding of equipment repair. Employers may send experienced workers to training sessions to keep up with changes in technology and service procedures.

Most office machine and ATM repairer positions require an associate degree in electronics. A basic understanding of mechanical equipment also is important because many of the parts that fail in office machines and ATMs, such as paper loaders, are mechanical. Entry-level employees at large companies normally receive on-the-job training lasting several months. Such training may include a week of classroom instruction, followed by a period of two weeks to several months assisting an experienced repairer.

Certification and other qualifications. Various organizations offer certification. Certification demonstrates a level of competency, and can make an applicant more attractive to employers.

Field technicians work closely with customers and must have good communications skills and a neat appearance. Employers may require that field technicians have a driver's license.

Certification and advancement. Newly hired computer repairers may work on personal computers or peripheral equipment. With experience, they can advance to positions maintaining more sophisticated systems, such as networking equipment and servers. Field repairers of ATMs may advance to bench technician positions responsible for more complex repairs. Experienced workers may become specialists who help other repairers diagnose difficult problems or who work with engineers in designing equipment and developing maintenance procedures. Experienced workers also may move into management positions responsible for supervising other repairers.

Because of their familiarity with equipment, experienced repairers may move into customer service or sales positions. Some experienced workers open their own repair shops or become wholesalers or retailers of electronic equipment.

Certification may also increase one's opportunities for advancement. Certification is available for workers with varying levels of skills and experience. To obtain certification, workers generally must pass an examination corresponding to their skill level.

Employment

Computer, automated teller, and office machine repairers held about 175,000 jobs in 2006. Wholesale trade establishments employed about 31 percent of the workers in this occupation; most of these establishments were wholesalers of professional and commercial equipment and supplies. Many workers also were employed in computer and software stores and office supply stores. Others worked in electronic and precision equipment repair shops and computer systems design firms. About 20 percent of computer, automated teller, and office machine repairers were self-employed, compared to 7 percent for all installation, maintenance, and repair occupations.

Job Outlook

Employment is expected to grow more slowly than the average for all occupations. Opportunities will be best for applicants with knowledge of electronics, formal training, and previous experience.

Employment change. Employment of computer, automated teller, and office machine repairers is expected to grow by 3 percent from 2006 to 2016, which is slower than the average for all occupations. Limited job growth will be driven by the increasing dependence of business and individuals on computers and other sophisticated office machines. The need to maintain this equipment will create new jobs for repairers.

Projections data from the National Employment Matrix

Occupational Title	SOC Code	Employment, 2006	Projected employment, 2016	Change, 2006-16	
				Number	Percent
Computer, automated teller, and office machine repairers...............	49-2011	175,000	180,000	5,200	3

NOTE: Data in this table are rounded.

Although computer equipment continues to become less expensive and more reliable, malfunctions still occur and can cause severe problems for users, most of whom lack the knowledge to make repairs. Computers are critical to most businesses today and will become even more so as companies increasingly engage in electronic commerce, and as individuals continue to bank, shop, and pay bills online.

People also are becoming increasingly reliant on ATMs. Besides offering bank and retail transactions, ATMs provide an increasing number of other services, such as employee information processing and distribution of government payments. The relatively slow rate at which new ATMs are installed, however, and the fact that they are becoming easier to repair, will limit demand for ATM repairers.

Conventional office machines, such as calculators, are inexpensive, and often are replaced instead of repaired. However, digital copiers and other, newer office machines are more costly and complex. This equipment often is computerized, designed to work on a network, and capable of performing multiple functions. But because this equipment is becoming more reliable, job growth in office machine repairers will be limited as well.

Job prospects. In addition to new job growth, a number of openings will result from the need to replace workers who retire or leave the occupation. Job prospects will be best for applicants with knowledge of electronics, formal training, and repair experience.

Earnings

Median hourly earnings of wage-and-salary computer, automated teller, and office machine repairers were $17.54 in May 2006. The middle 50 percent earned between $13.56 and $22.44. The lowest 10 percent earned less than $10.65, and the highest 10 percent earned more than $27.36. Median hourly earnings in the industries employing the largest numbers of computer, automated teller, and office machine repairers in May 2006 were

- Computer systems design and related services $19.41
- Professional and commercial equipment and supplies merchant wholesalers 19.09
- Office supplies, stationery, and gift stores 16.64
- Electronic and precision equipment repair and maintenance 15.82
- Computer and software stores 15.20
- Electronics and appliance stores 14.71

Related Occupations

Workers in other occupations who repair and maintain electronic equipment include electronic home entertainment equipment installers and repairers; home appliance repairers; broadcast and sound engineering technicians and radio operators; precision instrument and equipment repairers; electrical and electronics installers and repairers; electricians; radio and telecommunications equipment installers and repairers; coin, vending, and amusement machine servicers and repairers; industrial machinery mechanics and maintenance workers; and maintenance and repair workers, general.

Sources of Additional Information

For information on careers and certification, contact

- ACES International, 5241 Princess Anne Rd., Suite 110, Virginia Beach, VA 23462. Internet: http://www.acesinternational.org
- Electronics Technicians Association International, 5 Depot St., Greencastle, IN 46135. Internet: http://eta-i.org/
- International Society of Certified Electronics Technicians, 3608 Pershing Ave., Fort Worth, TX 76107-4527. Internet: http://www.iscet.org

STEM Conservation Scientists and Foresters

(O*NET 19-1031.00, 19-1031.01, 19-1031.02, 19-1031.03, and 19-1032.00)

Significant Points

- About 2 of 3 conservation scientists and foresters work for federal, state, or local governments.
- Workers in this occupation need, at a minimum, a bachelor's degree in forestry, environmental science, range management, or a related discipline.
- Slower than average job growth is projected; most new jobs will be in governments and in private sector forestry and conservation consulting.

Nature of the Work

Forests and rangelands supply wood products, livestock forage, minerals, and water. They serve as sites for recreational activities and provide habitats for wildlife. Conservation scientists and foresters manage the use and development of these lands and help to protect them. Some advise landowners on the use and management of their land. Conservation scientists and foresters often specialize in one area, such as wildlife management, soil conservation, urban forestry, pest management, native species, or forest economics. But most work falls into one of three categories: forestry, conservation science focusing on range lands, and conservation science focusing on farming and soil.

Foresters oversee our nation's forests and direct activities on them for economic, recreational, conservational, and environmental purposes. Individual landowners, the public, and industry own most of the forested land in this country, and they require the expertise of foresters to keep the forests healthy and sustainable. Often this means coming up with a plan to keep the forests free from disease, harmful insects, and damaging wildfires, for example, planning when and where to plant trees and vegetation and when to cut timber. It may also mean coming up with ways to make the land profitable but still protected for future generations.

Foresters have a wide range of duties, often depending on who they are working for. Some primary duties of foresters include drawing up plans to regenerate forested lands, monitoring their progress, and supervising harvests. Land management foresters choose and direct the preparation of sites on which trees will be planted. They oversee controlled burning and the use of bulldozers or herbicides to clear weeds, brush, and logging debris. They advise on the type, number, and placement of trees to be planted. Foresters then monitor the seedlings to ensure healthy growth and to determine the best time for harvesting. If they detect signs of disease or harmful insects, they consult with specialists in forest pest management to decide on the best course of treatment. When the trees reach a certain size, foresters decide which trees and how many should be harvested and sold to sawmills.

Procurement foresters make up a large share of foresters. Their job is to buy timber, typically for a sawmill or wood products manufacturer, by contacting local forest owners and negotiating a sale contract. This typically involves taking inventory of the type, amount, and location of all standing timber on the property, a process known as timber cruising. They then appraise the timber's worth, negotiate its purchase, and draw up a contract for purchase. The forester next subcontracts with loggers or pulpwood cutters for tree removal and to aid in laying out roads to access the timber. Throughout the process, foresters maintain close contact with the subcontractor and the landowner to ensure that the work meets the landowner's requirements and federal, state, and local environmental regulations.

Throughout the forest management and procurement processes, foresters are often responsible for conserving wildlife habitats and creek beds within forests, maintaining water quality and soil stability, and complying with environmental regulations. Foresters must balance the desire to conserve forested ecosystems with the need to use forest resources for recreational or economic purposes. For example, foresters are increasingly working with landowners to find ways to generate money from forested lands, such as for hunting or other recreational activity, without cutting down trees. An increasing concern of foresters is the prevention of devastating wildfires. Using a variety of techniques, including the thinning of forests or using controlled burns to clear brush, foresters work with governments and private landowners to minimize the impact of fire on the forest. During fires, they work with or supervise fire fighters and plan ways to attack the fire.

Some foresters, mostly in the federal government, perform research on issues facing forests and related natural resources. They may study tree improvement and harvesting techniques; global change; protection of forests from pests, diseases, and fire; improving wildlife habitats; forest recreation; and other topics. State foresters may perform some research but more often work with private landowners in developing forest management plans. Both federal and state foresters enforce relevant environmental laws, including laws on water quality and fire suppression.

Relatively new fields in forestry are urban forestry and conservation education. Urban foresters live and work in larger cities and manage urban forests. They are concerned with quality of life issues, such as air quality, shade, beautification, storm water runoff, and property values. Conservation education foresters train teachers and students about sound forest stewardship.

Foresters use a number of tools to perform their jobs. Clinometers measure the height of trees; diameter tapes measure tree diameter; and increment borers and bark gauges measure the growth of trees so that timber volumes can be computed and growth rates estimated. Remote sensing (aerial photographs and other imagery taken from airplanes and satellites) and Geographic Information Systems (GIS) data often are used for mapping large forest areas and for detecting widespread trends of forest and land use. Once a map is generated, data are digitized to create a computerized inventory of information required to manage the forest land and its resources. Moreover, hand-held computers, Global Positioning Systems (GPS), and Internet-based applications are used extensively.

Conservation scientists manage, improve, and protect the country's natural resources. They work with landowners and federal, state, and local governments to devise ways to use and improve the land while safeguarding the environment. Conservation scientists mainly advise farmers, farm managers, and ranchers on how they can improve their land for agricultural purposes and to control erosion. A growing number of conservation scientists are also advising landowners and governments on recreational uses for the land.

Two of the more common conservation scientists are range managers and soil conservationists. Range managers, also called range conservationists, range ecologists, or range scientists, study, manage, improve, and protect rangelands to maximize their use without damaging the environment. Rangelands cover hundreds of millions of acres of the United States, mostly in Western states and Alaska. They contain many natural resources, including grass and shrubs for animal grazing, wildlife habitats, water from vast watersheds, recreation facilities, and valuable mineral and energy resources. Range managers may inventory soils, plants, and animals; develop resource management plans; help to restore degraded ecosystems; or assist in managing a ranch. For example, they may help ranchers attain optimum livestock production by determining the number and kind of animals to graze, the grazing system to use, and the best season for grazing. At the same time, however, range managers maintain soil stability and vegetation for other uses such as wildlife habitats and outdoor recreation. They also plan and implement revegetation of disturbed sites.

Soil and water conservationists provide technical assistance to farmers, ranchers, forest managers, state and local agencies, and others concerned with the conservation of soil, water, and related natural resources. They develop programs for private landowners designed to make the most productive use of land without damaging it. Soil conservationists also assist landowners by visiting areas with erosion problems, finding the source of the problem, and helping landowners and managers develop management practices to combat it. Water conservationists also assist private landowners and federal, state, and local governments by advising on water quality, preserving water supplies, groundwater contamination, and management and conservation of water resources.

Work environment. Working conditions vary considerably. Some foresters and conservation scientists work regular hours in offices or labs, but others may split their time between fieldwork and office work. Independent consultants and new, less experienced workers spend the majority of their time outdoors overseeing or participating in hands-on work. Fieldwork can involve long hours alone.

The work can be physically demanding. Some conservation scientists and foresters work outdoors in all types of weather, sometimes in isolated areas, and consequently may need to walk long distances through densely wooded land to carry out their work. Natural disasters may also cause foresters and conservation scientists to work long hours during emergencies. For example, foresters often have to work long hours during fire season, and conservation scientists often are called to prevent erosion after a forest fire and to provide emergency help after floods, mudslides, and tropical storms.

Foresters employed by the federal government and the states usually work 40 hours a week, but not always on a standard schedule. In field positions, foresters often work for long blocks of time, working 10 days straight, followed by 4 days off, for example. Overtime may be necessary when working in fire fighting, law enforcement, or natural disaster response.

Training, Other Qualifications, and Advancement

Most forester and conservation scientist jobs require a bachelor's degree. Research and teaching positions usually need a graduate degree.

Education and training. A bachelor's degree in forestry, biology, natural resource management, environmental sciences, or a related discipline is the minimum educational requirement for careers in forestry. In the federal government, a combination of experience and appropriate education occasionally may substitute for a bachelor's degree, but competition for jobs makes this difficult. Foresters who wish to do research or to teach usually need an advanced degree, preferably a Ph.D.

Conservation scientists generally have at least a bachelor's degree in fields such as ecology, natural resource management, agriculture, biology, or environmental science. A master's degree or Ph.D. is usually required for teaching and research positions.

Most land-grant colleges and universities offer degrees in forestry. The Society of American Foresters accredits about 50 degree programs throughout the country. Curricula focus on four areas: forest ecology and biology, measurement of forest resources, management of forest resources, and public policy. Students should balance general science courses such as ecology, biology, tree physiology, taxonomy, and soil formation with technical forestry courses, such as forest inventory, wildlife habitat assessment, remote sensing, land surveying, GPS technology, integrated forest resource management, forest protection, and silviculture, which is the care and cultivation of forest trees. In addition, mathematics, statistics, and computer science courses are recommended. Courses in resource policy and administration, specifically forest economics and business administration, are also helpful. Forestry curricula increasingly include courses on wetlands analysis and sustainability and regulatory issues because prospective foresters need a strong grasp of federal, state, and local policy issues and an understanding of complex environmental regulations.

Many colleges require students to complete a field session either in a camp operated by the college or in a cooperative work-study program with a federal or state agency or with private industry. All schools encourage students to take summer jobs that provide experience in forestry or conservation work.

Range managers usually have a degree in range management or range science. Nine colleges and universities offer degrees in range management that are accredited by the Society of Range Management. More than 40 other schools offer coursework in range science or in a closely related discipline. Range management courses combine plant, animal, and soil sciences with principles of ecology and resource management. Desirable electives include statistics, forestry, hydrology, agronomy, wildlife, animal husbandry, computer science, and recreation. Selection of a minor in range management, such as wildlife ecology, watershed management, animal science, or agricultural economics, can often enhance qualifications for certain types of employment.

Very few colleges and universities offer degrees in soil conservation. Most soil conservationists have degrees in environmental studies, agronomy, general agriculture, hydrology, or crop or soil science; a few have degrees in related fields such as wildlife biology, forestry, and range management. Programs of study usually include 30 semester hours in natural resources or agriculture, including at least three hours in soil science.

Licensure. Sixteen states sponsor some type of credentialing process for foresters. Alabama, California, Connecticut, Maine, Maryland, Massachusetts, and New Hampshire have licensing statutes. Arkansas, Georgia, Mississippi, North Carolina, and South Carolina have mandatory registration statutes, and Michigan, New Jersey, Oklahoma, and West Virginia have voluntary registration statutes. Both licensing and registration requirements usually entail completing a four-year degree in forestry and several years of forestry work experience. Candidates pursuing licensing also may be required to pass a comprehensive written exam.

Other qualifications. Foresters and conservation scientists usually enjoy working outdoors, are able to tolerate extensive walking and other types of physical exertion, and are willing to relocate to find work. They also must work well with people and have good communication skills.

Certification and advancement. One option to advance in these occupations is to become certified. The Society of American Foresters certifies foresters who have at least a bachelor's degree from one of the 50 forestry programs accredited by the Society or from a forestry program that, though not accredited by the Society, is substantially equivalent. In addition, the candidate must have five years of qualifying professional experience and pass an examination.

The Society for Range Management offers two types of certification: one as a certified professional in rangeland management and another as a certified range management consultant. Candidates seeking certification must have at least a bachelor's degree in range science or a closely related field, a minimum of six years of full-time work experience, and a passing score on an exam.

Additionally, a graduate with the proper coursework in college can seek certification as a wetland scientist through the Society of Wetland Scientists.

Recent forestry and conservation scientist graduates usually work under the supervision of experienced foresters or scientists. After gaining experience, they may advance to more responsible positions. In the federal government, most entry-level foresters work in forest resource management. An experienced federal forester may supervise a ranger district and may advance to forest supervisor, regional forester, or a top administrative position in the national headquarters.

In private industry, foresters start by learning the practical and administrative aspects of the business and by acquiring comprehensive technical training. They are then introduced to contract writing,

timber harvesting, and decision making. Some foresters work their way up to top managerial positions. Foresters in management usually leave fieldwork behind, spending more of their time in an office, working with teams to develop management plans and supervising others. After gaining several years of experience, some foresters may become consultants, working alone or with one or several partners. They contract with state or local governments, private landowners, private industry, or other forestry consulting groups.

Soil conservationists usually begin working within one county or conservation district and, with experience, may advance to the area, state, regional, or national level. Also, soil conservationists can transfer to related occupations, such as farm or ranch management advisor or land appraiser.

Employment

Conservation scientists and foresters held about 33,000 jobs in 2006. Conservation scientist jobs are heavily concentrated in government where nearly 3 in 4 are employed. Soil conservationists are employed primarily in the U.S. Department of Agriculture's (USDA) Natural Resource Conservation Service. Most range managers work in the USDA's Forest Service, the U.S. Department of the Interior's Bureau of Land Management, and the Natural Resource Conservation Service. A small number are self-employed and others work for nonprofit organizations or in consulting firms.

More than half of all foresters work for federal, state and local governments. Federal government foresters are concentrated in the USDA's Forest Service. A few foresters are self-employed, generally working as consultants or procurement foresters. Others work for sawmills, wood products manufacturers, logging companies, and the forestry industry.

Although conservation scientists and foresters work in every state, employment of foresters is concentrated in the Western and Southeastern states, where many national and private forests and parks—and most of the lumber and pulpwood-producing forests—are located. Range managers work almost entirely in the Western states, where most of the rangeland is located. Soil conservationists, on the other hand, are employed in almost every county in the country. Besides the jobs described above, some foresters and conservation scientists held faculty positions in colleges and universities. (See the section on teachers—postsecondary elsewhere in this book.)

Job Outlook

Employment of conservation scientists and foresters is expected to grow more slowly than the average for all occupations through 2016. In addition to job openings from growth, many openings are expected as today's scientists and foresters retire.

Employment change. Employment of conservation scientists and foresters is expected to grow by 5 percent during the 2006–2016 decade, more slowly than the average for all occupations. Recent large-scale sales of forestlands by industry has resulted in a loss of jobs within the traditional forest industry while creating limited opportunities with Timber Investment Management Organizations and Real Estate Investment Trusts.

Fire prevention and suppression will become a main activity for some conservation scientists and foresters, especially within the federal government, as the human population spreads into previously uninhabited lands. The federal government employs more conservation scientists and foresters than any other industry. Overall employment of conservation scientists and foresters in the federal government is expected to grow more slowly than the average for all occupations, mostly because of budgetary constraints and the trend toward contracting these functions out to private consulting firms. Also, federal land management agencies, such as the United States Forest Service, have de-emphasized their timber programs and increasingly focused on wildfire suppression and law enforcement, which may require hiring people with other skills.

State governments are the second largest employer of conservation and forest workers, and they are expected to have little or no growth in their employment of conservation scientists and foresters due to budgetary restrictions. A few states are now working to provide market-based incentives to private landowners to encourage them to use forest land for the public benefit by cleaning watersheds, keeping trees, or doing other environmentally focused activities. More state foresters are being asked to design and help implement such eco-management plans.

The management of storm water and coastlines has created demand for people knowledgeable about runoff and erosion on farms and in cities and suburbs. The opening of federal lands to leasing by oil and gas companies is creating healthy demand for range scientists and range managers, who are finding work with consulting companies to help write environmental impact statements. Additionally, soil and water quality experts will still be needed as states design initiatives to improve water resources by preventing pollution by agricultural producers and industrial plants. A small number of new jobs will result from the need for range and soil conservationists to provide technical assistance to owners of grazing land through the Natural Resource Conservation Service. Salaried foresters working for private industry—such as paper companies, sawmills, and pulpwood mills—will be needed, though in smaller numbers than in the past, to provide technical assistance and management plans to landowners.

Establishments in management, scientific, and technical consulting services have increased their hiring of conservation scientists and foresters in recent years in response to demand for professionals to prepare environmental impact statements and erosion and sediment control plans, monitor water quality near logging sites, and advise on tree harvesting practices required by federal, state, or local regulations. Hiring by these firms should continue during the 2006–2016 decade.

Projections data from the National Employment Matrix

Occupational Title	SOC Code	Employment, 2006	Projected employment, 2016	Change, 2006-2016	
				Number	Percent
Conservation scientists and foresters	19-1030	33,000	35,000	1,700	5
Conservation scientists	19-1031	20,000	21,000	1,100	5
Foresters	19-1032	13,000	14,000	700	5

NOTE: Data in this table are rounded.

Job prospects. The federal government and some state governments expect a large number of workers to retire over the next decade. This is likely to create a large number of job openings for foresters and conservation scientists in government despite the projection for slower than average growth of this occupation in all state, local, and federal governments combined. However, the best opportunities for foresters and conservation scientists will be in consulting. Government and businesses are increasingly contracting out forestry and conservation services to companies that specialize in providing them.

Foresters involved with timber harvesting will find better opportunities in the Southeast, where much forested land is privately owned. However, the recent opening of public lands, especially in the West, to commercial activity will also help the outlook for foresters.

Earnings

Median annual earnings of conservation scientists in May 2006 were $54,970. The middle 50 percent earned between $40,950 and $68,460. The lowest 10 percent earned less than $29,860, and the highest 10 percent earned more than $80,260.

Median annual earnings of foresters in 2006 were $51,190. The middle 50 percent earned between $40,870 and $62,290. The lowest 10 percent earned less than $33,490, and the highest 10 percent earned more than $74,570.

In 2006, most bachelor's degree graduates entering the federal government as foresters, range managers, or soil conservationists started at $28,862 or $35,752, depending on academic achievement. Those with a master's degree could start at $43,731 or $52,912. Holders of doctorates could start at $63,417. Beginning salaries were slightly higher in selected areas where the prevailing local pay level was higher. In 2007, the average federal salary for foresters was $65,964; for soil conservationists, $64,284; and for rangeland managers, $60,828.

According to the National Association of Colleges and Employers, graduates with a bachelor's degree in conservation and renewable natural resources received an average starting salary offer of $34,678 in July 2007.

In private industry, starting salaries for students with a bachelor's degree were comparable with starting salaries in the federal government, but starting salaries in state and local governments were usually lower.

Conservation scientists and foresters who work for federal, state, and local governments and large private firms generally receive more generous benefits than do those working for smaller firms. Governments usually have good pension, health, and leave plans.

Related Occupations

Conservation scientists and foresters manage, develop, and protect natural resources. Other workers with similar responsibilities include environmental engineers, agricultural and food scientists, biological scientists, environmental scientists and hydrologists, geoscientists, and farmers, ranchers, and agricultural managers.

Sources of Additional Information

For information about forestry careers and schools offering education in forestry, send a self-addressed, stamped business envelope to

- Society of American Foresters, 5400 Grosvenor Ln., Bethesda, MD 20814-2198. Internet: http://www.safnet.org

Information about a career as a range manager, and a list of schools offering training, is available from

- Society for Range Management, 10030 West 27th Ave., Wheat Ridge, CO 80215-6601. Internet: http://www.rangelands.org/srm.shtml

Information on getting a job as a conservation scientist or forester with the federal government is available from the Office of Personnel Management (OPM) through USAJOBS, the federal government's official employment information system. This resource for locating and applying for job opportunities can be accessed through the Internet at http://www.usajobs.opm.gov or through an interactive voice response telephone system at (703) 724-1850 or TDD (978) 461-8404. These numbers are not toll free, and charges may result. For advice on how to find and apply for jobs, see the *Occupational Outlook Quarterly* article "How to get a job in the Federal Government," online at http://www.bls.gov/opub/ooq/2004/summer/art01.pdf.

Dental Assistants

(O*NET 31-9091.00)

Significant Points

- Job prospects should be excellent.
- Dentists are expected to hire more assistants to perform routine tasks so that they may devote their own time to more complex procedures.
- Many assistants learn their skills on the job, although an increasing number are trained in dental-assisting programs; most programs take 1 year or less to complete.

Nature of the Work

Dental assistants work closely with, and under the supervision of, dentists. (See the statement on dentists elsewhere in this book.) Assistants perform a variety of patient care, office, and laboratory duties.

Dental assistants should not be confused with dental hygienists, who are licensed to perform different clinical tasks. (See the statement on dental hygienists elsewhere in this book.)

Dental assistants sterilize and disinfect instruments and equipment, prepare and lay out the instruments and materials required to treat each patient, and obtain patients' dental records. Assistants make patients as comfortable as possible in the dental chair and prepare them for treatment. During dental procedures, assistants work alongside the dentist to provide assistance. They hand instruments and materials to dentists and keep patients' mouths dry and clear by using suction or other devices. They also instruct patients on postoperative and general oral health care.

Dental assistants may prepare materials for impressions and restorations, take dental x rays, and process x-ray film as directed by a dentist. They also may remove sutures, apply topical anesthetics to gums or cavity-preventive agents to teeth, remove excess cement used in the filling process, and place rubber dams on the teeth to isolate them for individual treatment. Some states are expanding dental assistants' duties to include tasks such as coronal polishing and restorative dentistry functions for those assistants that meet specific training and experience requirements.

Dental assistants with laboratory duties make casts of the teeth and mouth from impressions, clean and polish removable appliances, and make temporary crowns. Those with office duties schedule and confirm appointments, receive patients, keep treatment records, send bills, receive payments, and order dental supplies and materials.

Work environment. Dental assistants work in a well-lighted, clean environment. Their work area usually is near the dental chair so that they can arrange instruments, materials, and medication and hand them to the dentist when needed. Dental assistants must wear gloves, masks, eyewear, and protective clothing to protect themselves and their patients from infectious diseases. Assistants also follow safety procedures to minimize the risks associated with the use of x-ray machines.

About half of dental assistants have a 35- to 40-hour work week. Most of the rest work part-time or have variable schedules. Depending on the hours of the dental office where they work, assistants may have to work on Saturdays or evenings. Some dental assistants hold multiple jobs by working at dental offices that are open on different days or scheduling their work at a second office around the hours they work at their primary office.

Training, Other Qualifications, and Advancement

Many assistants learn their skills on the job, although an increasing number are trained in dental-assisting programs offered by community and junior colleges, trade schools, technical institutes, or the Armed Forces.

Education and training. High school students interested in a career as a dental assistant should take courses in biology, chemistry, health, and office practices. For those wishing to pursue further education, the Commission on Dental Accreditation within the American Dental Association (ADA) approved 269 dental-assisting training programs in 2006. Programs include classroom, laboratory, and preclinical instruction in dental-assisting skills and related theory. In addition, students gain practical experience in dental schools, clinics, or dental offices. Most programs take one year or less to complete and lead to a certificate or diploma. Two-year programs offered in community and junior colleges lead to an associate degree. All programs require a high school diploma or its equivalent, and some require science or computer-related courses for admission. A number of private vocational schools offer four- to six-month courses in dental assisting, but the Commission on Dental Accreditation does not accredit these programs.

A large number of dental assistants learn through on-the-job training. In these situations, the employing dentist or other dental assistants in the dental office teach the new assistant dental terminology, the names of the instruments, how to perform daily duties, how to interact with patients, and other things necessary to help keep the dental office running smoothly. While some things can be picked up easily, it may be a few months before new dental assistants are completely knowledgeable about their duties and comfortable doing all of their tasks without assistance.

A period of on-the-job training is often required even for those that have completed a dental-assisting program or have some previous experience. Different dentists may have their own styles of doing things that need to be learned before an assistant can be comfortable working with them. Office-specific information, such as where files are kept, will need to be learned at each new job. Also, as dental technology changes, dental assistants need to stay familiar with the tools and procedures that they will be using or helping dentists to use. On-the-job training is often sufficient to keep assistants up-to-date on these matters.

Licensure. Most states regulate the duties that dental assistants are allowed to perform. Some states require licensure or registration, which may include passing a written or practical examination. There are a variety of schools offering courses—approximately 10 to 12 months in length—that meet their state's requirements. Other states require dental assistants to complete state-approved education courses of four to 12 hours in length. Some states offer registration of other dental assisting credentials with little or no education required. Some states require continuing education to maintain licensure or registration. A few states allow dental assistants to perform any function delegated to them by the dentist.

Individual states have adopted different standards for dental assistants who perform certain advanced duties. In some states, for example, dental assistants who perform radiological procedures must complete additional training. Completion of the Radiation Health and Safety examination offered by Dental Assisting National Board (DANB) meets the standards in more than 30 states. Some states require completion of a state-approved course in radiology as well.

Certification and other qualifications. Certification is available through the Dental Assisting National Board (DANB) and is recognized or required in more than 30 states. Certification is an acknowledgment of an assistant's qualifications and professional competence and may be an asset when one is seeking employment. Candidates may qualify to take the DANB certification examination by graduating from an ADA-accredited dental assisting education program or by having two years of full-time, or four years of part-time, experience as a dental assistant. In addition, applicants must have current certification in cardiopulmonary resuscitation. For annual recertification, individuals must earn continuing education credits. Other organizations offer registration, most often at the state level.

Dental assistants must be a second pair of hands for a dentist; therefore, dentists look for people who are reliable, work well with others, and have good manual dexterity.

Advancement. Without further education, advancement opportunities are limited. Some dental assistants become office managers, dental-assisting instructors, dental product sales representatives, or insurance claims processors for dental insurance companies. Others go back to school to become dental hygienists. For many, this entry-level occupation provides basic training and experience and serves as a steppingstone to more highly skilled and higher paying jobs.

Employment

Dental assistants held about 280,000 jobs in 2006. Almost all jobs for dental assistants were in offices of dentists. A small number of jobs were in the federal, state, and local governments or in offices of physicians. About 35 percent of dental assistants worked part time, sometimes in more than one dental office.

Projections data from the National Employment Matrix

Occupational Title	SOC Code	Employment, 2006	Projected employment, 2016	Change, 2006-16 Number	Change, 2006-16 Percent
Dental assistants	31-9091	280,000	362,000	82,000	29

NOTE: Data in this table are rounded.

Job Outlook

Employment is expected to increase much faster than average; job prospects are expected to be excellent.

Employment change. Employment is expected to grow 29 percent from 2006 to 2016, which is much faster than the average for all occupations. In fact, dental assistants are expected to be among the fastest growing occupations over the 2006–2016 projection period.

Population growth, greater retention of natural teeth by middle-aged and older people, and an increased focus on preventative dental care for younger generations will fuel demand for dental services. Older dentists, who have been less likely to employ assistants or have employed fewer, are leaving the occupation and will be replaced by recent graduates, who are more likely to use one or more assistants. In addition, as dentists' workloads increase, they are expected to hire more assistants to perform routine tasks, so that they may devote their own time to more complex procedures.

Job prospects. Job prospects for dental assistants should be excellent. In addition to job openings due to employment growth, numerous job openings will arise out of the need to replace assistants who transfer to other occupations, retire, or leave for other reasons. Many opportunities for entry-level positions offer on-the-job training, but some dentists prefer to hire experienced assistants or those who have completed a dental-assisting program.

Earnings

Median hourly earnings of dental assistants were $14.53 in May 2006. The middle 50 percent earned between $11.94 and $17.44 an hour. The lowest 10 percent earned less than $9.87, and the highest 10 percent earned more than $20.69 an hour.

Benefits vary substantially by practice setting and may be contingent upon full-time employment. According to the American Dental Association, 87 percent of dentists offer reimbursement for continuing education courses taken by their assistants.

Related Occupations

Other workers supporting health practitioners include dental hygienists, medical assistants, surgical technologists, pharmacy aides, pharmacy technicians, occupational therapist assistants and aides, and physical therapist assistants and aides.

Sources of Additional Information

Information about career opportunities and accredited dental assistant programs is available from

- Commission on Dental Accreditation, American Dental Association, 211 East Chicago Ave., Suite 1814, Chicago, IL 60611. Internet: http://www.ada.org

For information on becoming a Certified Dental Assistant and a list of state boards of dentistry, contact

- Dental Assisting National Board, Inc., 676 North Saint Clair St., Suite 1880, Chicago, IL 60611. Internet: http://www.danb.org

For more information on a career as a dental assistant and general information about continuing education, contact

- American Dental Assistants Association, 35 East Wacker Dr., Suite 1730, Chicago, IL 60601. Internet: http://www.dentalassistant.org

For more information about continuing education courses, contact

- National Association of Dental Assistants, 900 South Washington St., Suite G-13, Falls Church, VA 22046.

Dental Hygienists

(O*NET 29-2021.00)

Significant Points

- A degree from an accredited dental hygiene school and a state license are required for this job.
- Dental hygienists rank among the fastest-growing occupations.
- Job prospects are expected to remain excellent.
- More than half work part time, and flexible scheduling is a distinctive feature of this job.

Nature of the Work

Dental hygienists remove soft and hard deposits from teeth, teach patients how to practice good oral hygiene, and provide other preventive dental care. They examine patients' teeth and gums, recording the presence of diseases or abnormalities.

Dental hygienists use an assortment of different tools to complete their tasks. Hand and rotary instruments and ultrasonic devices are used to clean and polish teeth, including removing calculus, stains, and plaque. Hygienists use X-ray machines to take dental pictures, and sometimes develop the film. They may use models of teeth to explain oral hygiene, perform root planning as a periodontal therapy, or apply cavity-preventative agents such as fluorides and pit and fissure sealants. In some states, hygienists are allowed to administer anesthetics, while in others they administer local anesthetics using syringes. Some states also allow hygienists to place and carve filling materials, temporary fillings, and periodontal dressings; remove sutures; and smooth and polish metal restorations.

Dental hygienists also help patients develop and maintain good oral health. For example, they may explain the relationship between diet and oral health or inform patients how to select toothbrushes and show them how to brush and floss their teeth.

Hygienists sometimes make a diagnosis and other times may prepare clinical and laboratory diagnostic tests for the dentist to interpret. Hygienists sometimes work chair side with the dentist during treatment.

Work environment. Dental hygienists work in clean, well-lighted offices. Important health safeguards include strict adherence to proper radiological procedures and the use of appropriate protective devices when administering anesthetic gas. Dental hygienists also wear safety glasses, surgical masks, and gloves to protect themselves and patients from infectious diseases.

Flexible scheduling is a distinctive feature of this job. Full-time, part-time, evening, and weekend schedules are widely available. Dentists frequently hire hygienists to work only two or three days a week, so hygienists may hold jobs in more than one dental office. More than half of all dental hygienists worked part time—less than 35 hours a week.

Training, Other Qualifications, and Advancement

Prospective dental hygienists must become licensed in the state in which they wish to practice. A degree from an accredited dental hygiene school is usually required along with licensure examinations.

Education and training. A high school diploma and college entrance test scores are usually required for admission to a dental hygiene program. High school students interested in becoming a dental hygienist should take courses in biology, chemistry, and mathematics. Also, some dental hygiene programs require applicants to have completed at least one year of college. Specific entrance requirements vary from one school to another.

In 2006, there were 286 dental hygiene programs accredited by the Commission on Dental Accreditation. Most dental hygiene programs grant an associate degree, although some also offer a certificate, a bachelor's degree, or a master's degree. A minimum of an associate degree or certificate in dental hygiene is generally required for practice in a private dental office. A bachelor's or master's degree usually is required for research, teaching, or clinical practice in public or school health programs.

Schools offer laboratory, clinical, and classroom instruction in subjects such as anatomy, physiology, chemistry, microbiology, pharmacology, nutrition, radiography, histology (the study of tissue structure), periodontology (the study of gum diseases), pathology, dental materials, clinical dental hygiene, and social and behavioral sciences.

Licensure. Dental hygienists must be licensed by the state in which they practice. Nearly all states require candidates to graduate from an accredited dental hygiene school and pass both a written and clinical examination. The American Dental Association's Joint Commission on National Dental Examinations administers the written examination, which is accepted by all states and the District of Columbia. State or regional testing agencies administer the clinical examination. In addition, most states require an examination on the legal aspects of dental hygiene practice. Alabama is the only state that allows candidates to take its examinations if they have been trained through a state-regulated on-the-job program in a dentist's office.

Other qualifications. Dental hygienists should work well with others because they work closely with dentists and dental assistants as well as dealing directly with patients. Hygienists also need good manual dexterity, because they use dental instruments within a patient's mouth, with little room for error.

Employment

Dental hygienists held about 167,000 jobs in 2006. Because multiple job holding is common in this field, the number of jobs exceeds the number of hygienists. Almost all jobs for dental hygienists were in offices of dentists. A very small number worked for employment services, offices of physicians, or other industries.

Job Outlook

Dental hygienists rank among the fastest growing occupations, and job prospects are expected to remain excellent.

Employment change. Employment of dental hygienists is expected to grow 30 percent through 2016, much faster than the average for all occupations. This projected growth ranks dental hygienists among the fastest growing occupations, in response to increasing demand for dental care and the greater use of hygienists.

The demand for dental services will grow because of population growth, older people increasingly retaining more teeth, and a growing focus on preventative dental care. To meet this demand, facilities that provide dental care, particularly dentists' offices, will increasingly employ dental hygienists, and more hygienists per office, to perform services that have been performed by dentists in the past.

Job prospects. Job prospects are expected to remain excellent. Older dentists, who have been less likely to employ dental hygienists, are leaving the occupation and will be replaced by recent graduates, who are more likely to employ one or more hygienists. In addition, as dentists' workloads increase, they are expected to hire more hygienists to perform preventive dental care, such as cleaning, so that they may devote their own time to more complex procedures.

Earnings

Median hourly earnings of dental hygienists were $30.19 in May 2006. The middle 50 percent earned between $24.63 and $35.67 an hour. The lowest 10 percent earned less than $19.45, and the highest 10 percent earned more than $41.60 an hour.

Earnings vary by geographic location, employment setting, and years of experience. Dental hygienists may be paid on an hourly, daily, salary, or commission basis.

Benefits vary substantially by practice setting and may be contingent upon full-time employment. According to the American Dental Association, 86 percent of hygienists receive hospital and medical benefits.

Related Occupations

Other workers supporting health practitioners in an office setting include dental assistants, medical assistants, occupational therapist assistants and aides, physical therapist assistants and aides, physi-

Projections data from the National Employment Matrix

Occupational Title	SOC Code	Employment, 2006	Projected employment, 2016	Change, 2006-2016	
				Number	Percent
Dental hygienists	29-2021	167,000	217,000	50,000	30

NOTE: Data in this table are rounded.

cian assistants, and registered nurses. Dental hygienists sometimes work with radiation technology, as do radiation therapists.

Sources of Additional Information

For information on a career in dental hygiene, including educational requirements, contact

- Division of Education, American Dental Hygienists Association, 444 N. Michigan Ave., Suite 3400, Chicago, IL 60611. Internet: http://www.adha.org

For information about accredited programs and educational requirements, contact

- Commission on Dental Accreditation, American Dental Association, 211 E. Chicago Ave., Suite 1814, Chicago, IL 60611. Internet: http://www.ada.org

The State Board of Dental Examiners in each state can supply information on licensing requirements.

Dentists

(O*NET 29-1021.00, 29-1022.00, 29-1023.00, 29-1024.00, and 29-1029.99)

Significant Points

- Most dentists are solo practitioners.
- Dentists usually complete at least eight years of education beyond high school.
- Average employment growth will generate some job openings, but most openings will result from the need to replace the large number of dentists expected to retire.
- Job prospects should be good.

Nature of the Work

Dentists diagnose and treat problems with teeth and tissues in the mouth, along with giving advice and administering care to help prevent future problems. They provide instruction on diet, brushing, flossing, the use of fluorides, and other aspects of dental care. They remove tooth decay, fill cavities, examine x rays, place protective plastic sealants on children's teeth, straighten teeth, and repair fractured teeth. They also perform corrective surgery on gums and supporting bones to treat gum diseases. Dentists extract teeth and make models and measurements for dentures to replace missing teeth. They also administer anesthetics and write prescriptions for antibiotics and other medications.

Dentists use a variety of equipment, including x-ray machines, drills, mouth mirrors, probes, forceps, brushes, and scalpels. They wear masks, gloves, and safety glasses to protect themselves and their patients from infectious diseases.

Dentists in private practice oversee a variety of administrative tasks, including bookkeeping and the buying of equipment and supplies. They may employ and supervise dental hygienists, dental assistants, dental laboratory technicians, and receptionists. (Two of these occupations are described elsewhere in this book.)

Most dentists are general practitioners, handling a variety of dental needs. Other dentists practice in any of nine specialty areas. *Orthodontists,* the largest group of specialists, straighten teeth by applying pressure to the teeth with braces or retainers. The next largest group, *oral and maxillofacial surgeons*, operates on the mouth and jaws. The remainder may specialize as *pediatric dentists* (focusing on dentistry for children); *periodontists* (treating gums and bone supporting the teeth); *prosthodontists* (replacing missing teeth with permanent fixtures, such as crowns and bridges, or with removable fixtures such as dentures); *endodontists* (performing root canal therapy); *public health dentists* (promoting good dental health and preventing dental diseases within the community); *oral pathologists* (studying oral diseases); or *oral and maxillofacial radiologists* (diagnosing diseases in the head and neck through the use of imaging technologies).

Work environment. Most dentists are solo practitioners, meaning that they own their own businesses and work alone or with a small staff. Some dentists have partners, and a few work for other dentists as associate dentists.

Most dentists work 4 or 5 days a week. Some work evenings and weekends to meet their patients' needs. The number of hours worked varies greatly among dentists. Most full-time dentists work between 35 and 40 hours a week. However, others, especially those who are trying to establish a new practice, work more. Also, experienced dentists often work fewer hours. It is common for dentists to continue in part-time practice well beyond the usual retirement age.

Training, Other Qualifications, and Advancement

All 50 states and the District of Columbia require dentists to be licensed. To qualify for a license in most states, candidates must graduate from an accredited dental school and pass written and practical examinations.

Education and training. In 2006, there were 56 dental schools accredited by the American Dental Association's (ADA's) Commission on Dental Accreditation. Dental schools require a minimum of two years of college-level predental education prior to admittance. Most dental students have at least a bachelor's degree before entering dental school, although a few applicants are accepted to dental school after two or three years of college and complete their bachelor's degree while attending dental school.

High school and college students who want to become dentists should take courses in biology, chemistry, physics, health, and mathematics. College undergraduates planning on applying to dental school are required to take many science courses. Because of this, some choose a major in a science, such as biology or chemistry, while others take the required science coursework while pursuing a major in another subject.

All dental schools require applicants to take the Dental Admissions Test (DAT). When selecting students, schools consider scores earned on the DAT, applicants' grade point averages, and information gathered through recommendations and interviews. Competition for admission to dental school is keen.

Dental school usually lasts four academic years. Studies begin with classroom instruction and laboratory work in science, including anatomy, microbiology, biochemistry, and physiology. Beginning courses in clinical sciences, including laboratory techniques, are also completed. During the last two years, students treat patients, usually in dental clinics, under the supervision of licensed dentists. Most dental schools award the degree of Doctor of Dental Surgery (DDS). Others award an equivalent degree, Doctor of Dental Medicine (DMD).

Some dental school graduates work for established dentists as associates for one to two years to gain experience and save money to equip an office of their own. Most dental school graduates, however, purchase an established practice or open a new one immediately after graduation.

Licensure. Licensing is required to practice as a dentist. In most states, licensure requires passing written and practical examinations in addition to having a degree from an accredited dental school. Candidates may fulfill the written part of the state licensing requirements by passing the National Board Dental Examinations. Individual states or regional testing agencies administer the written or practical examinations.

In 2006, 17 states licensed or certified dentists who intended to practice in a specialty area. Requirements include two to four years of postgraduate education and, in some cases, the completion of a special state examination. Most state licenses permit dentists to engage in both general and specialized practice.

Other qualifications. Dentistry requires diagnostic ability and manual skills. Dentists should have good visual memory, excellent judgment regarding space, shape, and color, a high degree of manual dexterity, and scientific ability. Good business sense, self-discipline, and good communication skills are helpful for success in private practice.

Advancement. Dentists who want to teach or conduct research usually spend an additional two to five years in advanced dental training, in programs operated by dental schools or hospitals. A recent survey by the American Dental Education Association showed that 11 percent of new graduates enrolled in postgraduate training programs to prepare for a dental specialty.

Employment

Dentists held about 161,000 jobs in 2006. Employment was distributed among general practitioners and specialists as follows:

- Dentists, general 136,000
- Orthodontists 9,200
- Oral and maxillofacial surgeons 7,700
- Prosthodontists...1,000
- Dentists, all other specialists 6,900

About one third of dentists were self-employed and not incorporated. Almost all dentists work in private practice. According to the ADA, about 3 out of 4 dentists in private practice are sole proprietors, and 1 in 7 belongs to a partnership. A few salaried dentists work in hospitals and offices of physicians.

Job Outlook

Average employment growth will generate some job openings, but most openings will result from the need to replace the large number of dentists expected to retire. Job prospects should be good as new dentists take over established practices or start their own.

Employment change. Employment of dentists is projected to grow nine percent through 2016, about as fast as the average for all occupations. The demand for dental services is expected to continue to increase. The overall population is growing, particularly the number of older people, which will increase the demand for dental care. As members of the baby-boom generation advance into middle age, a large number will need complicated dental work, such as bridges. In addition, elderly people are more likely to retain their teeth than were their predecessors, so they will require much more care than in the past. The younger generation will continue to need preventive checkups despite an overall increase in the dental health of the public over the last few decades. Recently, some private insurance providers have increased their dental coverage. If this trend continues, those with new or expanded dental insurance will be more likely to visit a dentist than in the past. Also, while they are currently a small proportion of dental expenditures, cosmetic dental services, such as fitting braces for adults as well as children and providing teeth-whitening treatments, have become increasingly popular.

However, employment of dentists is not expected to keep pace with the increased demand for dental services. Productivity increases from new technology, as well as having dental hygienists and assistants perform some tasks, will allow dentists to perform more work than they have in the past. As their practices expand, dentists are likely to hire more hygienists and dental assistants to handle routine services.

Dentists will increasingly provide care and instruction aimed at preventing the loss of teeth, rather than simply providing treatments such as fillings. Improvements in dental technology also will allow dentists to offer more effective and less painful treatment to their patients.

Job prospects. As an increasing number of dentists from the baby-boom generation reach retirement age, many of them will retire or work fewer hours. However, the number of applicants to, and graduates from, dental schools has increased in recent years. Therefore, younger dentists will be able to take over the work from older dentists who retire or cut back on hours, as well as provide dental services to accommodate the growing demand.

Demand for dental services tends to follow the business cycle, primarily because these services usually are paid for either by the patient or by private insurance companies. As a result, during slow times in the economy, demand for dental services can decrease; dentists may have difficulty finding employment, or if already in an

Projections data from the National Employment Matrix

Occupational Title	SOC Code	Employment, 2006	Projected employment, 2016	Change, 2006-2016	
				Number	Percent
Dentists	29-1020	161,000	176,000	15,000	9
Dentists, general	29-1021	136,000	149,000	13,000	9
Oral and maxillofacial surgeons	29-1022	7,700	8,400	700	9
Orthodontists	29-1023	9,200	10,000	800	9
Prosthodontists	29-1024	1,000	1,100	100	11
Dentists, all other specialists	29-1029	6,900	7,400	500	7

NOTE: Data in this table are rounded.

established practice, they may work fewer hours because of reduced demand.

Earnings

Median annual earnings of salaried dentists were $136,960 in May 2006. Earnings vary according to number of years in practice, location, hours worked, and specialty. Self-employed dentists in private practice tend to earn more than do salaried dentists.

Dentists who are salaried often receive benefits paid by their employer, with health insurance and malpractice insurance being among the most common. However, like other business owners, self-employed dentists must provide their own health insurance, life insurance, retirement plans, and other benefits.

Related Occupations

Dentists examine, diagnose, prevent, and treat diseases and abnormalities. Chiropractors, optometrists, physicians and surgeons, podiatrists, psychologists, and veterinarians do similar work.

Sources of Additional Information

For information on dentistry as a career, a list of accredited dental schools, and a list of state boards of dental examiners, contact

- American Dental Association, Commission on Dental Accreditation, 211 E. Chicago Ave., Chicago, IL 60611. Internet: http://www.ada.org

For information on admission to dental schools, contact

- American Dental Education Association, 1400 K St. NW, Suite 1100, Washington, DC 20005. Internet: http://www.adea.org

Persons interested in practicing dentistry should obtain the requirements for licensure from the board of dental examiners of the state in which they plan to work.

To obtain information on scholarships, grants, and loans, including federal financial aid, prospective dental students should contact the office of student financial aid at the schools to which they apply.

Desktop Publishers

(O*NET 43-9031.00)

Significant Points

- About 35 percent work for newspaper, periodical, book, and directory publishers, while almost 25 percent work in the printing industry.
- Overall employment is expected to experience little or no change over the 2006–2016 decade.
- Most employers prefer to hire experienced desktop publishers; among persons without experience, opportunities should be best for those with certificates or degrees in desktop publishing or graphic design.

Nature of the Work

Desktop publishers use computer software to format and combine text, data, photographs, charts, and other graphic art or illustrations into prototypes of pages and other documents that are to be printed. They then may print the document using a high resolution printer or they may send the materials, either in print form or electronically, to a commercial printer. Examples of materials produced by desktop publishers include books, brochures, calendars, magazines, newsletters and newspapers, packaging, and forms.

Desktop publishers typically design and create the graphics that accompany text, convert photographs and illustrations into digital images, and manipulate the text and images to display information in an attractive and readable format. They design page layouts, develop presentations and advertising campaigns, and do color separation of pictures and graphics material. Some desktop publishers may write some of the text or headlines used in newsletters or brochures. They also may translate electronic information onto film or other traditional media if the final product will be sent to an offset printer. As companies bring the production of marketing, promotional, and other kinds of materials in-house, they increasingly employ desktop publishers to produce such materials in house.

Desktop publishers use a computer and appropriate software to enter and select formatting properties, such as the size and style of type, column width, and spacing. Print formats are stored in the computer and displayed on a computer monitor. Images and text can be rearranged, column widths altered, or material enlarged or reduced. New information, such as charts, pictures, or additional text can be added. Scanners are used to capture photographs, images, or art as digital data that can be either incorporated directly into electronic page layouts or further manipulated with the use of computer software. The desktop publisher can make adjustments or compensate for deficiencies in the original color print or transparency. An entire newspaper, catalog, or book page, complete with artwork and graphics, can be created on the screen exactly as it will appear in print. Digital files are then used to produce printing plates. Like photographers and multimedia artists and animators, desktop publishers also can create special effects or other visual images using film, video, computers, or other electronic media. (A separate statement on photographers appears elsewhere in this book.)

Desktop publishing encompasses a number of different kinds of jobs. Personal computers enable desktop publishers to more easily perform many of the design and layout tasks that would otherwise require large and complicated equipment and extensive human effort. Advances in computer software and printing technology continue to enhance desktop publishing work, making desktop publishing more economical and efficient than before. For example, desktop publishers get the material as computer files delivered over the Internet or on a portable disk drive instead of receiving simple typed text and instructions from customers. Other innovations in the occupation include digital color page makeup systems, electronic page layout systems, and off-press color proofing systems. In addition, most materials are reproduced on the Internet as well as printed; therefore, desktop publishers may need to know electronic publishing software, such as Hypertext Markup Language (HTML) and may be responsible for converting text and graphics to an Internet-ready format.

Some desktop publishers may write and edit as well as lay out and design pages. For example, in addition to laying out articles for a newsletter, desktop publishers may be responsible for copyediting content or for writing original content themselves. Desktop publisher's writing and editing responsibilities may vary widely from project to project and employer to employer. Smaller firms typically use desktop publishers to perform a wide range of tasks, while desktop publishers at larger firms may specialize in a certain part of the publishing process.

Desktop publishers also may be called publications specialists, electronic publishers, DTP operators, desktop publishing editors, electronic prepress technicians, electronic publishing specialists, image designers, typographers, compositors, layout artists, and Web publications designers. The exact name may vary by the specific tasks performed or simply by personal preference.

Work environment. Desktop publishers usually work in clean, air-conditioned office areas with little noise. They generally work a standard work week; however, some may work night shifts, weekends, or holidays depending upon the production schedule for the project or to meet deadlines.

These workers often are subject to stress and the pressures of short deadlines and tight work schedules. Like other workers who spend long hours working in front of a computer monitor, desktop publishers may be susceptible to eyestrain, back discomfort, and hand and wrist problems.

Training, Other Qualifications, and Advancement

Most desktop publishers learn their skills by taking classes, completing a certificate program offered on line or through an accredited academic program, or through experience on the job. Experience is the best training and many desktop publishers get started just by experimenting with the software and developing a knack for designing and laying out material for publication.

Education and training. There is generally no educational requirement for the job of desktop publisher. Most people learn on the job or by taking classes on line or through local learning centers that teach the latest software. For those who are interested in pursuing a career in desktop publishing, an associate degree or a bachelor's degree in graphic arts, graphic communications, or graphic design is preferred. Graphic arts programs are a good way to learn about the desktop publishing software used to format pages; assign type characteristics; and import text and graphics into electronic page layouts. The programs teach print and graphic design fundamentals and provide an extensive background in imaging, prepress operations, print reproduction, and emerging media. Courses in other aspects of printing also are available at vocational-technical institutes, industry-sponsored update and retraining programs, and private trade and technical schools.

Other qualifications. Although formal training is not always required, those with certificates or degrees will have the best job opportunities. Most employers prefer to hire people who have at least a high school diploma and who possess good communication skills, basic computer skills, and a strong work ethic. Desktop publishers should be able to deal courteously with people, because they have to interact with customers and clients and be able to express design concepts and layout options with them. They also may have to do simple math calculations and compute ratios to scale graphics and artwork and estimate job costs. A basic understanding and facility with computers, printers, scanners, and other office equipment and technologies also is needed to work as a desktop publisher.

Desktop publishers need good manual dexterity, and they must be able to pay attention to detail and work independently. Good eyesight, including visual acuity, depth perception, a wide field of view, color vision, and the ability to focus quickly also are assets. Artistic ability often is a plus. Employers also seek persons who are even tempered and adaptable—important qualities for workers who often must meet deadlines and learn how to operate new equipment.

Advancement. Workers with limited training and experience assist more experienced staff on projects while they learn the software and gain practical experience. They advance on the basis of their demonstrated mastery of skills. Desktop publishing software continues to evolve and gain in technological sophistication. As a result, desktop publishers need to keep abreast of the latest developments and how to use new software and equipment. As they gain experience, they may advance to positions with greater responsibility. Some may move into supervisory or management positions. Other desktop publishers may start their own companies or work as independent consultants, while those with more artistic talent and further education may find job opportunities in graphic design or commercial art positions.

Employment

Desktop publishers held about 32,000 jobs in 2006. About 35 percent worked for newspaper, periodical, book, and directory publishers, while 24 percent worked in the printing and related support activities industry. Other desktop publishers work for professional, scientific, and technical services firms and in many other industries that produce printed or published materials.

The printing and publishing industries are two of the most geographically dispersed industries in the United States, and desktop publishing jobs are found throughout the country. Although most jobs are in large metropolitan cities, electronic communication networks and the Internet allow some desktop publishers to work from other locations.

Job Outlook

Employment of desktop publishers is expected to experience little or no change over the 2006–2016 decade because more people are learning basic desktop publishing skills as a part of their regular job functions in other occupations and because more organizations are formatting materials for display on the web rather than designing pages for print publication.

Employment change. Employment of desktop publishers is expected to grow 1 percent between 2006 and 2016, which is considered little or no change in employment. Desktop publishing has become a frequently used and common tool for designing and laying out printed matter, such as advertisements, brochures, newsletters, and forms. However, increased computer processing capacity and widespread availability of more elaborate desktop publishing

Projections data from the National Employment Matrix

Occupational Title	SOC Code	Employment, 2006	Projected employment, 2016	Change, 2006-16	
				Number	Percent
Desktop publishers	43-9031	32,000	32,000	300	1

NOTE: Data in this table are rounded.

software will make it easier and more affordable to use for people who are not printing professionals. As a result, the need for people who specialize in desktop publishing will slow, as more people are able to do this work.

In addition, organizations are increasingly moving their published material to the Internet to save the cost of printing and distributing materials. This change will slow the growth of desktop publishers, especially in smaller membership and trade organizations, which publish newsletters and small reports. Companies that produce large reports and rely on high quality and high resolution color and graphics within their publications, however, will continue to use desktop publishers to lay out publications for offset printing.

Job prospects. Despite the little to no change in projected employment, job opportunities for desktop publishers are expected to be good because of the need to replace workers who move into managerial positions, transfer to other occupations, or leave the labor force. However, job prospects will be better for those with experience as many employers prefer to hire experienced desktop publishers because of the long time it takes to become good at this work. Among individuals with little or no experience, opportunities should be best for those with computer backgrounds, certification in desktop publishing, or who have completed a postsecondary program in desktop publishing, graphic design, or web design.

Earnings

Earnings for desktop publishers vary according to level of experience, training, geographic location, and company size. Median annual earnings of desktop publishers were $34,130 in May 2006. The middle 50 percent earned between $26,270 and $44,360. The lowest 10 percent earned less than $20,550, and the highest 10 percent earned more than $55,040 a year. Median annual earnings of desktop publishers in May 2006 were $36,460 in printing and related support services and $31,450 in newspaper, periodical, book, and directory publishers.

Related Occupations

Desktop publishers use artistic and editorial skills in their work. These skills also are essential for artists and related workers; commercial and industrial designers; prepress technicians and workers; public relations specialists; and writers and editors.

Sources of Additional Information

Details about training programs may be obtained from local employers such as newspapers and printing shops or from local offices of the state employment service.

For information on careers and training in printing, desktop publishing, and graphic arts, write to

- Graphic Arts Education and Research Foundation, 1899 Preston White Dr., Reston, VA 20191-4367. Internet: http://www.gaerf.org
- Graphic Arts Information Network, 200 Deer Run Rd., Sewickley, PA 15143. Internet: http://www.gain.net

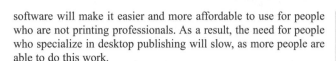

Diagnostic Medical Sonographers

(O*NET 29-2032.00)

Significant Points

- Job opportunities should be favorable.
- Employment growth is expected to be faster than average as sonography becomes an increasingly attractive alternative to radiologic procedures.
- More than half of all sonographers were employed by hospitals, and most of the rest were employed by offices of physicians, medical and diagnostic laboratories, and mobile imaging services.
- Sonographers may train in hospitals, vocational-technical institutions, colleges and universities, and the Armed Forces; employers prefer those who trained in accredited programs and who are registered.

Nature of the Work

Diagnostic imaging embraces several procedures that aid in diagnosing ailments. The most familiar procedures are the x ray and the magnetic resonance imaging; however, not all imaging technologies use ionizing radiation or radio waves. Sonography, or ultrasonography, is the use of sound waves to generate an image for the assessment and diagnosis of various medical conditions. Sonography commonly is associated with obstetrics and the use of ultrasound imaging during pregnancy, but this technology has many other applications in the diagnosis and treatment of medical conditions throughout the body.

Diagnostic medical sonographers use special equipment to direct nonionizing, high frequency sound waves into areas of the patient's body. Sonographers operate the equipment, which collects reflected echoes and forms an image that may be videotaped, transmitted, or photographed for interpretation and diagnosis by a physician.

Sonographers begin by explaining the procedure to the patient and recording any medical history that may be relevant to the condition being viewed. They then select appropriate equipment settings and direct the patient to move into positions that will provide the best view. To perform the exam, sonographers use a transducer, which transmits sound waves in a cone- or rectangle-shaped beam. Although techniques vary with the area being examined, sonographers usually spread a special gel on the skin to aid the transmission of sound waves.

Viewing the screen during the scan, sonographers look for subtle visual cues that contrast healthy areas with unhealthy ones. They decide whether the images are satisfactory for diagnostic purposes and select which ones to store and show to the physician. Sonographers take measurements, calculate values, and analyze the results in preliminary findings for the physicians.

In addition to working directly with patients, diagnostic medical sonographers keep patient records and adjust and maintain equipment. They also may prepare work schedules, evaluate equipment purchases, or manage a sonography or diagnostic imaging department.

Diagnostic medical sonographers may specialize in obstetric and gynecologic sonography (the female reproductive system), abdominal sonography (the liver, kidneys, gallbladder, spleen, and pancreas), neurosonography (the brain), or breast sonography. In addition, sonographers may specialize in vascular sonography or cardiac sonography. (Vascular sonographers and cardiac sonographers are covered in this book's statement on cardiovascular technologists and technicians.)

Obstetric and gynecologic sonographers specialize in the imaging of the female reproductive system. Included in the discipline is one of the more well-known uses of sonography: examining the fetus of a pregnant woman to track the baby's growth and health.

Abdominal sonographers inspect a patient's abdominal cavity to help diagnose and treat conditions primarily involving the gallbladder, bile ducts, kidneys, liver, pancreas, spleen, and male reproductive system. Abdominal sonographers also are able to scan parts of the chest, although studies of the heart using sonography usually are done by echocardiographers.

Neurosonographers focus on the nervous system, including the brain. In neonatal care, neurosonographers study and diagnose neurological and nervous system disorders in premature infants. They also may scan blood vessels to check for abnormalities indicating a stroke in infants diagnosed with sickle-cell anemia. Like other sonographers, neurosonographers operate transducers to perform the sonogram, but use frequencies and beam shapes different from those used by obstetric and abdominal sonographers.

Breast sonographers use sonography to study diseases of the breasts. Sonography aids mammography in the detection of breast cancer. Breast sonography can also track tumors, blood supply conditions, and assist in the accurate biopsy of breast tissue. Breast sonographers use high-frequency transducers, made exclusively to study breast tissue.

Work environment. Sonographers typically work in health care facilities that are clean. They usually work at diagnostic imaging machines in darkened rooms, but also may perform procedures at patients' bedsides. Sonographers may be on their feet for long periods of time and may have to lift or turn disabled patients. In addition, the nature of their work can put sonographers at an increased risk for musculoskeletal disorders such as carpel tunnel syndrome, neck and back strain, and eye strain: however, greater use of ergonomic equipment and an increasing awareness will continue to minimize such risks.

Some sonographers work as contract employees and may travel to several health care facilities in an area. Similarly, some sonographers work with mobile imaging service providers and travel to patients and use mobile diagnostic imaging equipment to provide service in areas that otherwise do not have the access to such services.

Most full-time sonographers work about 40 hours a week. Hospital-based sonographers may have evening and weekend hours and times when they are on call and must be ready to report to work on short notice.

Training, Other Qualifications, and Advancement

Diagnostic medical sonography is an occupation where there is no preferred level of education and several avenues of education are widely accepted by employers. Although no level of education is preferred, employers do prefer sonographers who trained in accredited programs and who are registered.

Education and training. There are several avenues for entry into the field of diagnostic medical sonography. Sonographers may train in hospitals, vocational-technical institutions, colleges and universities, and the Armed Forces. Some training programs prefer applicants with a background in science or experience in other health care professions. Some also may consider high school graduates with courses in mathematics and science, as well as applicants with liberal arts backgrounds, but this practice is infrequent.

Colleges and universities offer formal training in both two- and four-year programs, culminating in an associate or a bachelor's degree. Two-year programs are most prevalent. Course work includes classes in anatomy, physiology, instrumentation, basic physics, patient care, and medical ethics.

A few one-year programs that may result in a certificate also are accepted as proper education by employers. These programs typically are satisfactory education for workers already in health care who seek to increase their marketability by training in sonography. These programs are not accredited.

The Commission on Accreditation for Allied Health Education Programs (CAAHEP) accredited 147 training programs in 2006. These programs typically are the formal training programs offered by colleges and universities. Some hospital programs are accredited as well.

Certification and other qualifications. Although no state requires licensure in diagnostic medical sonography, organizations such as the American Registry for Diagnostic Medical Sonography (ARDMS) certify the skills and knowledge of sonographers through credentialing, including registration. Because registration provides an independent, objective measure of an individual's professional standing, many employers prefer to hire registered sonographers. Sonographers registered by the ARDMS are Registered Diagnostic Medical Sonographers (RDMS). Registration with ARDMS requires passing a general physical principles and instrumentation examination, in addition to passing an exam in a specialty such as obstetric and gynecologic sonography, abdominal sonography, or neurosonography. Sonographers must complete a required number of continuing education hours to maintain registration with the ARDMS and to stay abreast of technological advancements related to the occupation.

Sonographers need good communication and interpersonal skills because they must be able to explain technical procedures and results to their patients, some of whom may be nervous about the exam or the problems it may reveal. Good hand-eye coordination is particularly important to obtaining quality images. It is also important that sonographers enjoy learning because continuing education is the key to sonographers staying abreast of the ever-changing field of diagnostic medicine. A background in mathematics and science is helpful for sonographers as well.

Advancement. Sonographers specializing in one particular discipline often seek competency in others. For example, obstetric sonographers might seek training in abdominal sonography to broaden their opportunities and increase their marketability.

Sonographers may also have advancement opportunities in education, administration, research, sales, or technical advising.

Projections data from the National Employment Matrix

Occupational Title	SOC Code	Employment, 2006	Projected employment, 2016	Change, 2006-2016	
				Number	Percent
Diagnostic medical sonographers	29-2032	46,000	54,000	8,700	19

NOTE: Data in this table are rounded.

Employment

Diagnostic medical sonographers held about 46,000 jobs in 2006. More than half of all sonographer jobs were in public and private hospitals. The rest were typically in offices of physicians, medical and diagnostic laboratories, and mobile imaging services.

Job Outlook

Faster-than-average employment growth is expected. Job opportunities should be favorable.

Employment change. Employment of diagnostic medical sonographers is expected to increase by about 19 percent through 2016—faster than the average for all occupations—as the population ages, increasing the demand for diagnostic imaging and therapeutic technology.

Additional job growth is expected as sonography becomes an increasingly attractive alternative to radiologic procedures, as patients seek safer treatment methods. Unlike most diagnostic imaging methods, sonography does not involve radiation, so harmful side effects and complications from repeated use are less likely for both the patient and the sonographer. Sonographic technology is expected to evolve rapidly and to spawn many new sonography procedures, such as 3D- and 4D-sonography for use in obstetric and ophthalmologic diagnosis. However, high costs and approval by the federal government may limit the rate at which some promising new technologies are adopted.

Hospitals will remain the principal employer of diagnostic medical sonographers. However, employment is expected to grow more rapidly in offices of physicians and in medical and diagnostic laboratories, including diagnostic imaging centers. Healthcare facilities such as these are expected to grow very rapidly through 2016 because of the strong shift toward outpatient care, encouraged by third-party payers and made possible by technological advances that permit more procedures to be performed outside the hospital.

Job prospects. Job opportunities should be favorable. In addition to job openings from growth, some openings will arise from the need to replace sonographers who retire or leave the occupation permanently for some other reason. Pain caused by musculoskeletal disorders has made it difficult for sonographers to perform well. Some are forced to leave the occupation early because of this disorder.

Earnings

Median annual earnings of diagnostic medical sonographers were $57,160 in May 2006. The middle 50 percent earned between $48,890 and $67,670 a year. The lowest 10 percent earned less than $40,960, and the highest 10 percent earned more than $77,520. Median annual earnings of diagnostic medical sonographers in May 2006 were $56,970 in offices of physicians and $56,850 in general medical and surgical hospitals.

Related Occupations

Diagnostic medical sonographers operate sophisticated equipment to help physicians and other health practitioners diagnose and treat patients. Workers in related occupations include cardiovascular technologists and technicians, clinical laboratory technologists and technicians, nuclear medicine technologists, radiologic technologists and technicians, and respiratory therapists.

Sources of Additional Information

For information on a career as a diagnostic medical sonographer, contact

- Society of Diagnostic Medical Sonography, 2745 Dallas Pkwy., Suite 350, Plano, TX 75093-8730. Internet: http://www.sdms.org

For information on becoming a registered diagnostic medical sonographer, contact

- American Registry for Diagnostic Medical Sonography, 51 Monroe St., Plaza East 1, Rockville, MD 20850-2400. Internet: http://www.ardms.org

For more information on ultrasound in medicine, contact

- American Institute of Ultrasound in Medicine, 14750 Sweitzer Lane, Suite 100, Laurel, MD 20707-5906. Internet: http://www.aium.org

For a current list of accredited education programs in diagnostic medical sonography, contact

- Joint Review Committee on Education in Diagnostic Medical Sonography, 2025 Woodlane Dr., St. Paul, MN 55125-2998. Internet: http://www.jrcdms.org
- Commission on Accreditation for Allied Health Education Programs, 35 East Wacker Dr., Suite 1970, Chicago, IL 60601. Internet: http://www.caahep.org

Diesel Service Technicians and Mechanics

(O*NET 49-3031.00)

Significant Points

- A career in diesel engine repair can offer relatively high wages and the challenge of skilled repair work.
- Opportunities are expected to be very good for people who complete formal training programs.
- National certification is the recognized standard of achievement for diesel service technicians and mechanics.

Nature of the Work

Diesel-powered engines are more efficient and durable than their gasoline-burning counterparts. These powerful engines are standard in our nation's trucks, locomotives, and buses and are becoming more prevalent in light vehicles, including passenger vehicles, pickups, and other work trucks.

Diesel service technicians and mechanics, including *bus and truck mechanics and diesel engine specialists*, repair and maintain the diesel engines that power transportation equipment. Some diesel technicians and mechanics also work on other heavy vehicles and mobile equipment, including bulldozers, cranes, road graders, farm tractors, and combines. Other technicians repair diesel-powered passenger automobiles, light trucks, or boats. (For information on technicians and mechanics working primarily on gasoline-powered automobiles, heavy vehicles and mobile equipment, or boat engines, see this book's sections on automotive service technicians, heavy vehicle and mobile equipment service technicians, and small engine mechanics.)

Increasingly, diesel technicians must be versatile to adapt to customers' needs and new technologies. It is common for technicians to handle all kinds of repairs, working on a vehicle's electrical system one day and doing major engine repairs the next. Diesel maintenance is becoming increasingly complex, as more electronic components are used to control the operation of an engine. For example, microprocessors now regulate and manage fuel timing, increasing the engine's efficiency. Also, new emissions standards require mechanics to retrofit engines with emissions control systems, such as emission filters and catalysts, to comply with pollution regulations. In modern shops, diesel service technicians use hand-held or laptop computers to diagnose problems and adjust engine functions.

Technicians who work for organizations that maintain their own vehicles spend most of their time doing preventive maintenance. During a routine maintenance check, technicians follow a checklist that includes inspecting brake systems, steering mechanisms, wheel bearings, and other important parts. Following inspection, technicians repair or adjust parts that do not work properly or remove and replace parts that cannot be fixed.

Diesel service technicians use a variety of tools in their work, including power tools, such as pneumatic wrenches that remove bolts quickly; machine tools, such as lathes and grinding machines to rebuild brakes; welding and flame-cutting equipment to remove and repair exhaust systems; and jacks and hoists to lift and move large parts. Common handtools—screwdrivers, pliers, and wrenches—are used to work on small parts and get at hard-to-reach places. Diesel service technicians and mechanics also use a variety of computerized testing equipment to pinpoint and analyze malfunctions in electrical systems and engines. Employers typically furnish expensive power tools, computerized engine analyzers, and other diagnostic equipment, but workers usually accumulate their own hand tools over time.

Work environment. Technicians normally work in well-lighted and ventilated areas. However, some shops are drafty and noisy. Many employers provide lockers and shower facilities. Diesel technicians usually work indoors, although they occasionally repair vehicles on the road. Diesel technicians may lift heavy parts and tools, handle greasy and dirty parts, and stand or lie in awkward positions while making repairs. Minor cuts, burns, and bruises are common, although serious accidents can usually be avoided when safety procedures are followed. Technicians may work as a team or be assisted by an apprentice or helper when doing heavy work, such as removing engines and transmissions.

Most service technicians work a standard 40-hour week, although some work longer hours, particularly if they are self-employed. A growing number of shops have expanded their hours to speed repairs and offer more convenience to customers. Technicians employed by truck and bus firms providing service around the clock may work evenings, nights, and weekends.

Training, Other Qualifications, and Advancement

Employers prefer to hire graduates of formal training programs because those workers are able to advance quickly to the journey level of diesel service. Other workers who learn diesel engine repair through on-the-job training need three to four years of experience before becoming journey-level technicians.

Education and training. High school courses in automotive repair, electronics, English, mathematics, and physics provide a strong educational background for a career as a diesel service technician or mechanic. Many mechanics also have additional training after high school.

A large number of community colleges and trade and vocational schools offer programs in diesel engine repair. These programs usually last from six months to two years and may lead to a certificate of completion or an associate degree. Some offer about 30 hours per week of hands-on training with equipment; others offer more lab or classroom instruction. Formal training provides a foundation in the latest diesel technology and instruction in the service and repair of the equipment that technicians will encounter on the job. Training programs also teach technicians to interpret technical manuals and to communicate well with coworkers and customers. Increasingly, employers work closely with representatives of educational programs, providing instructors with the latest equipment, techniques, and tools and offering jobs to graduates.

Although formal training programs lead to the best prospects, some technicians and mechanics learn through on-the-job training. Unskilled beginners generally are assigned tasks such as cleaning parts, fueling and lubricating vehicles, and driving vehicles into and out of the shop. Beginners are usually promoted to trainee positions as they gain experience and as vacancies become available.

After a few months' experience, most trainees can perform routine service tasks and make minor repairs. These workers advance to increasingly difficult jobs as they prove their ability and competence. After technicians master the repair and service of diesel engines, they learn to work on related components, such as brakes, transmissions, and electrical systems. Generally, technicians with at least three to four years of on-the-job experience will qualify as journey-level diesel technicians.

Employers often send experienced technicians and mechanics to special training classes conducted by manufacturers and vendors, in which workers learn about the latest technology and repair techniques.

Other qualifications. Employers usually look for applicants who have mechanical aptitude and strong problem-solving skills and who are at least 18 years old and in good physical condition. Technicians need a state commercial driver's license to test-drive trucks or buses on public roads. Many companies also require applicants to pass a drug test. Practical experience in automobile repair at an automotive service station, in the Armed Forces, or as a hobby is valuable as well.

Projections data from the National Employment Matrix

Occupational Title	SOC Code	Employment, 2006	Projected employment, 2016	Change, 2006-16	
				Number	Percent
Bus and truck mechanics and diesel engine specialists	49-3031	275,000	306,000	32,000	11

NOTE: Data in this table are rounded.

Certification and advancement. Experienced diesel service technicians and mechanics with leadership ability may advance to shop supervisor or service manager, and some open their own repair shops. Technicians and mechanics with sales ability sometimes become sales representatives.

Although national certification is not required for employment, many diesel engine technicians and mechanics find that it increases their ability to advance. Certification by the National Institute for Automotive Service Excellence (ASE) is the recognized industry credential for diesel and other automotive service technicians and mechanics. Diesel service technicians may be certified as master medium/heavy truck technicians, master school bus technicians, or master truck equipment technicians. They may also be certified in specific areas of truck repair, such as drivetrains, brakes, suspension and steering, electrical and electronic systems, or preventive maintenance and inspection. For certification in each area, a technician must pass one or more of the ASE-administered exams and present proof of two years of relevant work experience. To remain certified, technicians must be retested every five years.

Employment

Diesel service technicians and mechanics held about 275,000 jobs in 2006. These workers were employed in almost every industry, particularly those that use trucks, buses, and equipment to haul, deliver, and transport materials, goods, and people. The largest employer, the truck transportation industry, employed 1 out of 6 diesel service technicians and mechanics. Less than 1 out of 10 were employed by local governments, mainly to repair school buses, waste removal trucks, and road equipment. A similar number were employed by automotive repair and maintenance facilities. The rest were employed throughout the economy, including construction, manufacturing, retail and wholesale trade, and automotive leasing. About 16,000, a relatively small number, were self-employed. Nearly every area of the country employs diesel service technicians and mechanics, although most work is found in towns and cities where trucking companies, bus lines, and other fleet owners have large operations.

Job Outlook

The number of jobs for diesel service technicians and mechanics is projected to grow about as fast as average. Opportunities should be very good for people who complete formal training in diesel mechanics.

Employment change. Employment of diesel service technicians and mechanics is expected to grow 11 percent from 2006 to 2016, about as fast as the average for all occupations. Additional trucks—and truck repairers—will be needed to keep pace with the increasing volume of freight shipped nationwide. Moreover, the greater durability and economy of the diesel engine relative to the gasoline engine is expected to increase the number of buses, trucks, and other vehicles powered by diesel engines. And because diesel engines are now cleaner burning and more efficient—to comply with emissions and environmental standards—they are expected to be used in more passenger vehicles, which will create jobs for diesel service technicians and mechanics over the long run. In fact, auto industry executives are projecting more sales of diesel passenger vehicles as gasoline prices increase. In the short-run, many older diesel engines in trucks must be retrofitted to comply with the new emissions regulations, creating more jobs for diesel engine mechanics.

Job prospects. People who enter diesel engine repair will find favorable opportunities, especially as the need to replace workers who retire increases over the next decade. Opportunities should be very good for people who complete formal training in diesel mechanics at community colleges or vocational and technical schools. Applicants without formal training will face stiffer competition for jobs.

Most people entering this occupation can expect relatively steady work because changes in economic conditions have less of an effect on the diesel repair business than on other sectors of the economy. During a downturn in the economy, however, employers may be reluctant to hire new workers.

Earnings

Median hourly earnings of bus and truck mechanics and diesel engine specialists, including incentive pay, were $18.11 in May 2006, more than the $17.65 median hourly earnings for all installation, maintenance, and repair occupations. The middle 50 percent earned between $14.48 and $22.07 an hour. The lowest 10 percent earned less than $11.71, and the highest 10 percent earned more than $26.50 an hour. Median hourly earnings in the industries employing the largest numbers of bus and truck mechanics and diesel engine specialists in May 2006 were as follows:

Local government $21.22
Motor vehicle and motor vehicle parts and
  supplies merchant wholesalers 18.27
Automotive repair and maintenance........................17.53
General freight trucking 17.14
Specialized freight trucking 16.15

Because many experienced technicians employed by truck fleet dealers and independent repair shops receive a commission related to the labor cost charged to the customer, weekly earnings depend on the amount of work completed. Beginners usually earn from 50 to 75 percent of the rate of skilled workers and receive increases as they become more skilled.

About 23 percent of diesel service technicians and mechanics are members of labor unions, including the International Association of Machinists and Aerospace Workers; the Amalgamated Transit Union; the International Union, United Automobile, Aerospace and Agricultural Implement Workers of America; the Transport Workers Union of America; the Sheet Metal Workers' International

Association; and the International Brotherhood of Teamsters. Labor unions may provide additional benefits for their members.

Related Occupations

Diesel service technicians and mechanics repair trucks, buses, and other diesel-powered equipment. Related technician and mechanic occupations include aircraft and avionics equipment mechanics and service technicians, automotive service technicians and mechanics, heavy vehicle and mobile equipment service technicians and mechanics, and small engine mechanics.

Sources of Additional Information

More details about work opportunities for diesel service technicians and mechanics may be obtained from local employers such as trucking companies, truck dealers, or buslines; locals of the unions previously mentioned; and local offices of your state employment service. Local state employment service offices also may have information about training programs. State boards of postsecondary career schools have information on licensed schools with training programs for diesel service technicians and mechanics.

For general information about a career as a diesel service technician or mechanic, write

- Association of Diesel Specialists, 10 Laboratory Dr., PO Box 13966, Research Triangle Park, NC 27709. Internet: http://www.diesel.org

Information on how to become a certified diesel technician of medium to heavy-duty vehicles or a certified bus technician is available from

- National Institute for Automotive Service Excellence (ASE), 101 Blue Seal Dr. SE, Suite 101, Leesburg, VA 20175. Internet: http://www.asecert.org

For a directory of accredited private trade and technical schools with training programs for diesel service technicians and mechanics, contact

- Accrediting Commission of Career Schools and Colleges of Technology, 2101 Wilson Blvd., Suite 302, Arlington, VA 22201. Internet: http://www.accsct.org
- National Automotive Technicians Education Foundation, 101 Blue Seal Dr. SE, Suite 101, Leesburg, VA 20175. Internet: http://www.natef.org

 Dietitians and Nutritionists

(O*NET 29-1031.00)

Significant Points

- Most jobs are in hospitals, nursing care facilities, outpatient care centers, and offices of physicians or other health practitioners.
- Dietitians and nutritionists need at least a bachelor's degree in dietetics, foods and nutrition, food service systems management, or a related area; licensure, certification, or registration requirements vary by state.
- Employment is projected to grow about as fast as the average for all occupations; however, growth may be constrained if employers substitute other workers for dietitians and if limitations are placed on insurance reimbursement for dietetic services.
- Good job opportunities are expected.

Nature of the Work

Dietitians and nutritionists plan food and nutrition programs, supervise meal preparation, and oversee the serving of meals. They prevent and treat illnesses by promoting healthy eating habits and recommending dietary modifications. For example, dietitians might teach a patient with high blood pressure how to use less salt when preparing meals, or create a diet reduced in fat and sugar for an overweight patient.

Dietitians manage food service systems for institutions such as hospitals and schools, promote sound eating habits through education, and conduct research. Many dietitians specialize, becoming a clinical dietitian, community dietitian, management dietitian, or consultant.

Clinical dietitians provide nutritional services to patients in hospitals, nursing care facilities, and other institutions. They assess patients' nutritional needs, develop and implement nutrition programs, and evaluate and report the results. They also confer with doctors and other health care professionals to coordinate medical and nutritional needs. Some clinical dietitians specialize in managing the weight of overweight patients or in the care of renal (kidney), diabetic, or critically ill patients. In addition, clinical dietitians in nursing care facilities, small hospitals, or correctional facilities may manage the food service department.

Community dietitians counsel individuals and groups on nutritional practices designed to prevent disease and promote health. Working in places such as public health clinics, home health agencies, and health maintenance organizations, community dietitians evaluate individual needs, develop nutritional care plans, and instruct individuals and their families. Dietitians working in home health agencies provide instruction on grocery shopping and food preparation to the elderly, children, and individuals with special needs.

Increased public interest in nutrition has led to job opportunities in food manufacturing, advertising, and marketing. In these areas, dietitians analyze foods, prepare literature for distribution, or report on issues such as dietary fiber, vitamin supplements, or the nutritional content of recipes.

Management dietitians oversee large-scale meal planning and preparation in health care facilities, company cafeterias, prisons, and schools. They hire, train, and direct other dietitians and food service workers; budget for and purchase food, equipment, and supplies; enforce sanitary and safety regulations; and prepare records and reports.

Consultant dietitians work under contract with health care facilities or in their own private practice. They perform nutrition screenings for their clients and offer advice on diet-related concerns such as weight loss and cholesterol reduction. Some work for wellness programs, sports teams, supermarkets, and other nutrition-related businesses. They may consult with food service managers, providing expertise in sanitation, safety procedures, menu development, budgeting, and planning.

Work environment. Dietitians and nutritionists usually work in clean, well-lighted, and well-ventilated areas. However, some work in hot, congested kitchens. Many dietitians and nutritionists are on their feet for much of the workday.

Most full-time dietitians and nutritionists work a regular 40-hour week, although some work weekends. About 1 in 3 worked part time in 2006.

Training, Other Qualifications, and Advancement

Dietitians and nutritionists need at least a bachelor's degree. Licensure, certification, or registration requirements vary by state.

Education and training. Becoming a dietitian or nutritionist usually requires at least a bachelor's degree in dietetics, foods and nutrition, food service systems management, or a related area. Graduate degrees also are available. College students in these majors take courses in foods, nutrition, institution management, chemistry, biochemistry, biology, microbiology, and physiology. Other suggested courses include business, mathematics, statistics, computer science, psychology, sociology, and economics. High school students interested in becoming a dietitian or nutritionist should take courses in biology, chemistry, mathematics, health, and communications.

As of 2007, there were 281 bachelor's degree programs and 22 master's degree programs approved by the American Dietetic Association's Commission on Accreditation for Dietetics Education.

Licensure. Of the 48 states and jurisdictions with laws governing dietetics, 35 require licensure, 12 require statutory certification, and one requires registration. Requirements vary by state. As a result, interested candidates should determine the requirements of the state in which they want to work before sitting for any exam.

In states that require licensure, only people who are licensed can work as dietitians and nutritionists. States that require statutory certification limit the use of occupational titles to people who meet certain requirements; individuals without certification can still practice as a dietitian or nutritionist but without using certain titles. Registration is the least restrictive form of state regulation of dietitians and nutritionists. Unregistered people are permitted to practice as a dietitian or nutritionist.

Certification and other qualifications. Although not required, the Commission on Dietetic Registration of the American Dietetic Association awards the Registered Dietitian credential to those who pass an exam after completing academic coursework and a supervised internship. This certification is different from the statutory certification regulated by some states and discussed in the previous section. To maintain a Registered Dietitian status, workers must complete at least 75 credit hours in approved continuing education classes every five years.

A supervised internship, required for certification, can be completed in one of two ways. The first requires the completion of a program accredited by the Commission on Dietetic Registration. As of 2007, there were 53 accredited programs that combined academic and supervised practice experience and generally lasted four to five years. The second option requires the completion of 900 hours of supervised practice experience in any of the 265 accredited internships. These internships may be full-time programs lasting six to 12 months or part-time programs lasting two years.

Advancement. Experienced dietitians may advance to management positions, such as assistant director, associate director, or director of a dietetic department, or may become self-employed. Some dietitians specialize in areas such as renal, diabetic, cardiovascular, or pediatric dietetics. Others leave the occupation to become sales representatives for equipment, pharmaceutical, or food manufacturers. A master's degree can help some workers to advance their careers, particularly in career paths related to research, advanced clinical positions, or public health.

Employment

Dietitians and nutritionists held about 57,000 jobs in 2006. More than half of all jobs were in hospitals, nursing care facilities, outpatient care centers, or offices of physicians and other health practitioners. State and local government agencies provided additional jobs—mostly in correctional facilities, health departments, and other public-health-related areas. Some dietitians and nutritionists were employed in special food services, an industry made up of firms providing food services on contract to facilities such as colleges and universities, airlines, correctional facilities, and company cafeterias.

Other jobs were in public and private educational services, community care facilities for the elderly (which includes assisted-living facilities), individual and family services, home health care services, and the federal government—mostly in the U.S. Department of Veterans Affairs. Some dietitians were self-employed, working as consultants to facilities such as hospitals and nursing care facilities or providing dietary counseling to individuals.

Job Outlook

Average employment growth is projected. Good job opportunities are expected, especially for dietitians with specialized training, an advanced degree, or certifications beyond the particular state's minimum requirement.

Employment change. Employment of dietitians and nutritionists is expected to increase 9 percent during the 2006–2016 projection decade, about as fast as the average for all occupations. Job growth will result from an increasing emphasis on disease prevention through improved dietary habits. A growing and aging population will boost demand for nutritional counseling and treatment in hospitals, residential care facilities, schools, prisons, community health programs, and home health care agencies. Public interest in nutrition and increased emphasis on health education and prudent lifestyles also will spur demand, especially in food service management.

Employment growth, however, may be constrained if some employers substitute other workers, such as health educators, food service managers, and dietetic technicians, to do work related to nutrition. Also, demand for nutritional therapy services is related to the ability of patients to pay, either out-of-pocket or through health insurance, and although more insurance plans now cover nutritional therapy services, the extent of such coverage varies among plans. Growth may be curbed by limitations on insurance reimbursement for dietetic services.

Hospitals will continue to employ a large number of dietitians and nutritionists to provide medical nutritional therapy and plan meals. But hospitals also will continue to contract with outside agencies for food service and move medical nutritional therapy to outpatient care facilities, slowing job growth in hospitals relative to food service, outpatient facilities, and other employers.

The number of dietitian positions in nursing care facilities is expected to decline, as these establishments continue to contract with outside agencies for food services. However, employment is

Projections data from the National Employment Matrix

Occupational Title	SOC Code	Employment, 2006	Projected employment, 2016	Change, 2006-2016	
				Number	Percent
Dietitians and nutritionists	29-1031	57,000	62,000	4,900	9

NOTE: Data in this table are rounded.

expected to grow rapidly in contract providers of food services, in outpatient care centers, and in offices of physicians and other health practitioners.

Finally, with increased public awareness of obesity and diabetes, Medicare coverage may be expanded to include medical nutrition therapy for renal and diabetic patients, creating job growth for dietitians and nutritionists specializing in those diseases.

Job prospects. In addition to employment growth, job openings will result from the need to replace experienced workers who retire or leave the occupation for other reasons. Overall, job opportunities will be good for dietitians and nutritionists, particularly for licensed and registered dietitians. Job opportunities should be particularly good in outpatient care facilities, offices of physicians, and food service management. Dietitians and nutritionists without a bachelor's degree will face keen competition for jobs.

Dietitians with specialized training, an advanced degree, or certifications beyond the particular state's minimum requirement will experience the best job opportunities. Those specializing in renal and diabetic nutrition or gerontological nutrition will benefit from the growing number of diabetics and the aging of the population.

Earnings

Median annual earnings of dietitians and nutritionists were $46,980 in May 2006. The middle 50 percent earned between $38,430 and $57,090. The lowest 10 percent earned less than $29,860, and the highest 10 percent earned more than $68,330. Median annual earnings in the industries employing the largest numbers of dietitians and nutritionists in May 2006 were

Outpatient care centers	$49,950
General medical and surgical hospitals	47,320
State government	46,690
Nursing care facilities	46,660
Local government	43,250

According to the American Dietetic Association, median annualized wages for registered dietitians in 2005 varied by practice area as follows: $53,800 in consultation and business; $60,000 in food and nutrition management; $60,200 in education and research; $48,800 in clinical nutrition/ambulatory care; $50,000 in clinical nutrition/long-term care; $44,800 in community nutrition; and $45,000 in clinical nutrition/acute care. Salaries also vary by years in practice, education level, and geographic region.

Related Occupations

Workers in other occupations who may apply the principles of dietetics include food service managers, health educators, dietetic technicians, and registered nurses.

Sources of Additional Information

For a list of academic programs, scholarships, and other information about dietetics, contact

- The American Dietetic Association, 120 South Riverside Plaza, Suite 2000, Chicago, IL 60606-6995. Internet: http://www.eatright.org

For information on the Registered Dietitian exam and other specialty credentials, contact

- The Commission on Dietetic Registration, 120 South Riverside Plaza, Suite 2000, Chicago, IL 60606-6995. Internet: http://www.cdrnet.org

STEM Drafters

(O*NET 17-3011.00, 17-3011.01, 17-3011.02, 17-3012.00, 17-3012.01, 17-3012.02, 17-3013.00, and 17-3019.99)

Significant Points

- The type and quality of training programs vary considerably so prospective students should be careful in selecting a program.
- Opportunities should be best for individuals with at least 2 years of postsecondary training in drafting and considerable skill and experience using computer-aided design and drafting systems.
- Employment is projected to grow more slowly than average.
- Demand for drafters varies by specialty and depends on the needs of local industry.

Nature of the Work

Drafters prepare technical drawings and plans, which are used to build everything from manufactured products such as toys, toasters, industrial machinery, and spacecraft to structures such as houses, office buildings, and oil and gas pipelines.

In the past, drafters sat at drawing boards and used pencils, pens, compasses, protractors, triangles, and other drafting devices to prepare a drawing by hand. Now, most drafters use Computer Aided Design and Drafting (CADD) systems to prepare drawings. Consequently, some drafters may be referred to as *CADD operators*.

With CADD systems, drafters can create and store drawings electronically so that they can be viewed, printed, or programmed directly into automated manufacturing systems. CADD systems also permit drafters to quickly prepare variations of a design. Although drafters use CADD extensively, it is only a tool. Drafters still need knowledge of traditional drafting techniques, in addition to CADD skills. Despite the nearly universal use of CADD systems, manual drafting and sketching are used in certain applications.

Drafters' drawings provide visual guidelines and show how to construct a product or structure. Drawings include technical details and specify dimensions, materials, and procedures. Drafters fill in technical details using drawings, rough sketches, specifications, and calculations made by engineers, surveyors, architects, or scientists. For example, drafters use their knowledge of standardized building techniques to draw in the details of a structure. Some use their understanding of engineering and manufacturing theory and standards to draw the parts of a machine; they determine design elements, such as the numbers and kinds of fasteners needed to assemble the machine. Drafters use technical handbooks, tables, calculators, and computers to complete their work.

Drafting work has many specialties:

Aeronautical drafters prepare engineering drawings detailing plans and specifications used in the manufacture of aircraft, missiles, and related parts.

Architectural drafters draw architectural and structural features of buildings and other structures. These workers may specialize in a type of structure, such as residential or commercial, or in a kind of material used, such as reinforced concrete, masonry, steel, or timber.

Civil drafters prepare drawings and topographical and relief maps used in major construction or civil engineering projects, such as highways, bridges, pipelines, flood control projects, and water and sewage systems.

Electrical drafters prepare wiring and layout diagrams used by workers who erect, install, and repair electrical equipment and wiring in communication centers, power plants, electrical distribution systems, and buildings.

Electronics drafters draw wiring diagrams, circuit board assembly diagrams, schematics, and layout drawings used in the manufacture, installation, and repair of electronic devices and components.

Mechanical drafters prepare drawings showing the detail and assembly of a wide variety of machinery and mechanical devices, indicating dimensions, fastening methods, and other requirements.

Process piping or pipeline drafters prepare drawings used in the layout, construction, and operation of oil and gas fields, refineries, chemical plants, and process piping systems.

Work environment. Drafters usually work in comfortable offices. They may sit at adjustable drawing boards or drafting tables when doing manual drawings, although most drafters work at computer terminals much of the time. Because they spend long periods in front of computers doing detailed work, drafters may be susceptible to eyestrain, back discomfort, and hand and wrist problems. Most drafters work a standard 40-hour week; only a small number work part time.

Training, Other Qualifications, and Advancement

Employers prefer applicants who have completed postsecondary school training in drafting, which is offered by technical institutes, community colleges, and some four-year colleges and universities. Employers are most interested in applicants with well-developed drafting and mechanical drawing skills; knowledge of drafting standards, mathematics, science, and engineering technology; and a solid background in CADD techniques.

Education and training. High school courses in mathematics, science, computer technology, design, computer graphics, and, where available, drafting are useful for people considering a drafting career. Employers prefer applicants who have also completed training after high school at a technical institute, community college, or four-year college or university.

The kind and quality of drafting training programs vary considerably so prospective students should be careful in selecting a program. They should contact prospective employers to ask which schools they prefer and contact schools to ask for information about the kinds of jobs their graduates have, the type and condition of instructional facilities and equipment, and teacher qualifications.

Technical institutes offer intensive technical training, but they provide a less general education than do community colleges. Either certificates or diplomas may be awarded. Many technical institutes offer two-year associate degree programs, which are similar to, or part of, the programs offered by community colleges or state university systems. Their programs vary considerably in length and in the type of courses offered. Some public vocational-technical schools serve local students and emphasize the type of training preferred by local employers. Most require a high school diploma or its equivalent for admission. Other technical institutes are run by private, often for-profit, organizations sometimes called proprietary schools.

Community colleges offer courses similar to those in technical institutes but include more classes in theory and liberal arts. Often, there is little or no difference between technical institute and community college programs. However, courses taken at community colleges are more likely to be accepted for credit at four-year colleges. After completing a two-year associate degree program, graduates may obtain jobs as drafters or continue their education in a related field at a four-year college. Most four-year colleges do not offer training in drafting, but they do offer classes in engineering, architecture, and mathematics that are useful for obtaining a job as a drafter.

Technical training obtained in the Armed Forces also can be applied in civilian drafting jobs. Some additional training may be necessary, depending on the technical area or military specialty.

Training differs somewhat within the drafting specialties, although the basics, such as mathematics, are similar. In an electronics drafting program, for example, students learn how to depict electronic components and circuits in drawings. In architectural drafting, they learn the technical specifications of buildings.

Certification and other qualifications. Mechanical ability and visual aptitude are important for drafters. Prospective drafters should be able to draw well and perform detailed work accurately and neatly. Artistic ability is helpful in some specialized fields, as is knowledge of manufacturing and construction methods. In addition, prospective drafters should have good interpersonal skills because they work closely with engineers, surveyors, architects, and other professionals and, sometimes, with customers.

The American Design Drafting Association (ADDA) has established a certification program for drafters. Although employers usually do not require drafters to be certified, certification demonstrates knowledge and an understanding of nationally recognized practices. Individuals who wish to become certified must pass the Drafter Certification Test, administered periodically at ADDA-authorized sites. Applicants are tested on basic drafting concepts, such as geometric construction, working drawings, and architectural terms and standards.

Advancement. Entry-level or junior drafters usually do routine work under close supervision. After gaining experience, they may become intermediate drafters and progress to more difficult work with less supervision. At the intermediate level, they may need to exercise more judgment and perform calculations when preparing and modifying drawings. Drafters may eventually advance to senior drafter, designer, or supervisor. Many employers pay for continuing education, and, with appropriate college degrees, drafters may go on to become engineering technicians, engineers, or architects.

Employment

Drafters held about 253,000 jobs in 2006. Architectural and civil drafters held 46 percent of all jobs for drafters, mechanical drafters held about 31 percent, and electrical and electronics drafters held about 14 percent.

About 49 percent of all jobs for drafters were in architectural, engineering, and related services firms that design construction projects or do other engineering work on a contract basis for other industries. Another 25 percent of jobs were in manufacturing industries such as machinery manufacturing, including metalworking and other general machinery; fabricated metal products manufacturing, including architectural and structural metals; computer and electronic products manufacturing, including navigational, measuring, electromedical, and control instruments; and transportation equipment manufacturing, including aerospace products and parts manufacturing, as well as ship and boat building. Most of the rest were employed in construction, government, wholesale trade, utilities, and employment services. Approximately 5 percent were self-employed in 2006.

Job Outlook

Drafters can expect slower than average employment growth through 2016, with the best opportunities expected for those with 2 years of professional training.

Employment change. Employment of drafters is expected to grow by 6 percent between 2006 and 2016, which is slower than the average for all occupations. Industrial growth and increasingly complex design problems associated with new products and manufacturing processes will increase the demand for drafting services. Furthermore, drafters are beginning to break out of the traditional drafting role and do work traditionally performed by engineers and architects, also increasing demand. However, drafters tend to be concentrated in slow-growing or declining manufacturing industries. In addition, CADD systems that are more powerful and easier to use are also expected to limit demand for lesser skilled drafters because simple tasks will be made easier or able to be done by other technical professionals. Employment growth also should be slowed by the offshore outsourcing to other countries of some drafting work because some drafting can be done by sending CADD files over the Internet.

Although growth is expected to be greatest for mechanical, architectural, and civil drafters, demand for particular drafting specialties varies throughout the country because employment usually is contingent on the needs of local industry.

Job prospects. Most job openings are expected to arise from the need to replace drafters who transfer to other occupations, leave the labor force, or retire.

Opportunities should be best for individuals with at least 2 years of postsecondary training in a drafting program that provides strong technical skills and considerable experience with CADD systems. CADD has increased the complexity of drafting applications while enhancing the productivity of drafters. It also has enhanced the nature of drafting by creating more possibilities for design and drafting. As technology continues to advance, employers will look for drafters with a strong background in fundamental drafting principles, a high level of technical sophistication, and the ability to apply their knowledge to a broader range of responsibilities.

Employment of drafters remains highly concentrated in industries that are sensitive to cyclical changes in the economy, primarily manufacturing industries. During recessions, drafters may be laid off. However, a growing number of drafters should continue to find employment on a temporary or contract basis as more companies turn to the employment services industry to meet their changing needs.

Earnings

Drafters' earnings vary by specialty, location, and level of responsibility. Median annual earnings of architectural and civil drafters were $41,960 in May 2006. The middle 50 percent earned between $33,550 and $52,220. The lowest 10 percent earned less than $27,010, and the highest 10 percent earned more than $63,310.

Median annual earnings of mechanical drafters were $43,700 in May 2006. The middle 50 percent earned between $34,680 and $55,130. The lowest 10 percent earned less than $28,230, and the highest 10 percent earned more than $67,860. Median annual earnings for mechanical drafters in architectural, engineering, and related services were $44,120.

Median annual earnings of electrical and electronics drafters were $46,830 in May 2006. The middle 50 percent earned between $36,660 and $60,160. The lowest 10 percent earned less than $29,290, and the highest 10 percent earned more than $74,490. In architectural, engineering, and related services, median annual earnings for electrical and electronics drafters were $44,140.

Related Occupations

Other workers who prepare or analyze detailed drawings and make precise calculations and measurements include architects, except landscape and naval; landscape architects; commercial and industrial designers; engineers; engineering technicians; science techni-

Projections data from the National Employment Matrix

Occupational Title	SOC Code	Employment, 2006	Projected employment, 2016	Change, 2006-2016 Number	Change, 2006-2016 Percent
Drafters	17-3010	253,000	268,000	15,000	6
Architectural and civil drafters	17-3011	116,000	123,000	7,000	6
Electrical and electronics drafters	17-3012	35,000	36,000	1,400	4
Mechanical drafters	17-3013	78,000	82,000	4,100	5
Drafters, all other	17-3019	25,000	27,000	2,700	11

NOTE: Data in this table are rounded.

cians; and surveyors, cartographers, photogrammetrists, and surveying technicians.

Sources of Additional Information

Information on schools offering programs in drafting and related fields is available from

- Accrediting Commission of Career Schools and Colleges of Technology, 2101 Wilson Blvd., Suite 302, Arlington, VA 22201. Internet: http://www.accsct.org

Information about certification is available from

- American Design Drafting Association, 105 E. Main St., Newbern, TN 38059. Internet: http://www.adda.org

Economists

(O*NET 19-3011.00)

Significant Points

- Slower than average job growth is expected as firms increasingly employ workers with titles that reflect specialized duties rather than the general title of economist.
- Job seekers with a background in economics should have opportunities in various occupations.
- Candidates who hold a master's or Ph.D. degree in economics will have the best employment prospects and advancement opportunities.
- Quantitative skills are important in all economics specialties.

Nature of the Work

Economists study how society distributes resources, such as land, labor, raw materials, and machinery, to produce goods and services. They may conduct research, collect and analyze data, monitor economic trends, or develop forecasts. Economists research a wide variety of issues including energy costs, inflation, interest rates, exchange rates, business cycles, taxes, and employment levels, among others.

Economists develop methods for obtaining the data they need. For example, sampling techniques may be used to conduct a survey and various mathematical modeling techniques may be used to develop forecasts. Preparing reports, including tables and charts, on research results also is an important part of an economist's job. Presenting economic and statistical concepts in a clear and meaningful way is particularly important for economists whose research is intended for managers and others who do not have a background in economics. Some economists also perform economic analysis for the media.

Many economists specialize in a particular area of economics, although general knowledge of basic economic principles is essential. *Microeconomists* study the supply and demand decisions of individuals and firms, such as how profits can be maximized and the quantity of a good or service that consumers will demand at a certain price. *Industrial economists* or *organizational economists* study the market structure of particular industries in terms of the number of competitors within those industries and examine the market decisions of competitive firms and monopolies. These economists also may be concerned with antitrust policy and its impact on market structure. *Macroeconomists* study historical trends in the whole economy and forecast future trends in areas such as unemployment, inflation, economic growth, productivity, and investment. Doing similar work as macroeconomists are *monetary economists* or *financial economists*, who study the money and banking system and the effects of changing interest rates. *International economists* study international financial markets, exchange rates, and the effects of various trade policies such as tariffs. *Labor economists* or *demographic economists* study the supply and demand for labor and the determination of wages. These economists also try to explain the reasons for unemployment and the effects of changing demographic trends, such as an aging population and increasing immigration, on labor markets. *Public finance economists* are involved primarily in studying the role of the government in the economy and the effects of tax cuts, budget deficits, and welfare policies. *Econometricians* investigate all areas of economics and apply mathematical techniques such as calculus, game theory, and regression analysis to their research. With these techniques, they formulate economic models that help explain economic relationships and that can be used to develop forecasts about business cycles, the effects of a specific rate of inflation on the economy, the effects of tax legislation on unemployment levels, and other economic phenomena.

Many economists apply these areas of economics to health, education, agriculture, urban and regional economics, law, history, energy, the environment, or other issues. Most economists are concerned with practical applications of economic policy. Economists working for corporations are involved primarily in microeconomic issues, such as forecasting consumer demand and sales of the firm's products. Some analyze their competitors' growth and market share and advise their company on how to handle the competition. Others monitor legislation passed by Congress, such as environmental and worker safety regulations, and assess how the new laws will affect the corporation. Corporations with many international branches or subsidiaries might employ economists to monitor the economic situations in countries where they do business or to provide a risk assessment of a country into which the company is considering expanding.

Economists working in economic consulting or research firms sometimes perform the same tasks as economists working for corporations. However, economists in consulting firms also perform much of the macroeconomic analysis and forecasting conducted in the United States. These economists collect data on various economic indicators, maintain databases, analyze historical trends, and develop models to forecast growth, inflation, unemployment, or interest rates. Their analyses and forecasts are frequently published in newspapers and journal articles.

Another large employer of economists is the government. Economists in the federal government administer most of the surveys and collect the majority of the economic data about the United States. For example, economists in the U.S. Department of Commerce collect and analyze data on the production, distribution, and consumption of commodities produced in the United States and overseas, and economists employed by the U.S. Department of Labor collect and analyze data on the domestic economy, including data on prices, wages, employment, productivity, and safety and health.

Economists who work for government agencies also assess economic conditions in the United States or abroad to estimate the effects of specific changes in legislation or public policy. Government economists advise policy makers in areas such as the deregu-

lation of industries, the effects of changes to Social Security, the effects of tax cuts on the budget deficit, and the effectiveness of imposing tariffs on imported goods. An economist working in state or local government might analyze data on the growth of school-age or prison populations and on employment and unemployment rates in order to project future spending needs.

Work environment. Economists have structured work schedules. They often work alone, writing reports, preparing statistical charts, and using computers, but they also may be an integral part of a research team. Most work under pressure of deadlines and tight schedules, which may require overtime. Their routine may be interrupted by special requests for data and by the need to attend meetings or conferences. Frequent travel may be necessary.

Training, Other Qualifications, and Advancement

Some entry-level positions for economists are available to those with a bachelor's degree, but higher degrees are required for many positions. Prospective economists need good quantitative skills.

Education and training. A master's or Ph.D. degree in economics is required for many private sector economist jobs and for advancement to more responsible positions. In the federal government, candidates for entry-level economist positions must have a bachelor's degree with a minimum of 21 semester hours of economics and three hours of statistics, accounting, or calculus.

Economics includes numerous specialties at the graduate level, such as econometrics, international economics, and labor economics. Students should select graduate schools that are strong in the specialties that interest them. Some schools help graduate students find internships or part-time employment in government agencies, economic consulting or research firms, or financial institutions before graduation.

Undergraduate economics majors can choose from a variety of courses, ranging from microeconomics, macroeconomics, and econometrics to more philosophical courses, such as the history of economic thought. Because of the importance of quantitative skills to economists, courses in mathematics, statistics, econometrics, sampling theory and survey design, and computer science are extremely helpful.

Whether working in government, industry, research organizations, or consulting firms, economists with a bachelor's degree usually qualify for entry-level positions as a research assistant, for administrative or management trainee positions, or for various sales jobs. A master's degree usually is required to qualify for more responsible research and administrative positions. A Ph.D. is necessary for top economist positions in many organizations. Also, many corporation and government executives have a strong background in economics.

Aspiring economists should gain experience gathering and analyzing data, conducting interviews or surveys, and writing reports on their findings while in college. This experience can prove invaluable later in obtaining a full-time position in the field because much of the economist's work, especially in the beginning, may center on these duties. With experience, economists eventually are assigned their own research projects. Related job experience, such as work as a stock or bond trader, might be advantageous.

Other qualifications.Those considering careers as economists should be able to pay attention to details because much time is spent on precise data analysis. Candidates also should have strong computer and quantitative skills and be able to perform complex research. Patience and persistence are necessary qualities, given that economists must spend long hours on independent study and problem solving. Good communication skills also are useful, as economists must be able to present their findings, both orally and in writing, in a clear, concise manner.

Advancement. With experience or an advanced degree, economists may advance into positions of greater responsibility, including administration and independent research.

Many people with an economics background become teachers. (See the statement on teachers—postsecondary elsewhere in this book.) A master's degree usually is the minimum requirement for a job as an instructor in a junior or community college. In most colleges and universities, however, a Ph.D. is necessary for appointment as an instructor. A Ph.D. and extensive publications in academic journals are required for a professorship, tenure, and promotion.

Employment

Economists held about 15,000 jobs in 2006. Government employed 52 percent of economists, in a wide range of agencies, with 32 percent in federal government and 20 percent in state and local government. The remaining jobs were spread throughout private industry, particularly in scientific research and development services and management, scientific, and technical consulting services. A number of economists combine a full-time job in government, academia, or business with part-time or consulting work in another setting.

Employment of economists is concentrated in large cities. Some work abroad for companies with major international operations, for U.S. Government agencies, and for international organizations, such as the World Bank, International Monetary Fund, and United Nations.

In addition to the previously mentioned jobs, economists hold faculty positions in colleges and universities. Economics faculties have flexible work schedules and may divide their time among teaching, research, consulting, and administration. These workers are counted as postsecondary teachers, not economists.

Job Outlook

Employment of economists is expected to grow about as fast as the average for all occupations. The demand for workers who have knowledge and skill in economics is projected to grow faster, but these workers are often in occupations other than economist. Job prospects will be best for those with graduate degrees in economics.

Employment change. Employment of economists is expected to grow seven percent from 2006 to 2016, about as fast as the average for all occupations. Demand for economic analysis should grow, but the increase in the number of economist jobs will be tempered as firms hire workers for more specialized jobs with specialized titles. Many workers with economic backgrounds will work in related occupations with more specific job titles, such as financial analyst, market analyst, public policy consultant, researcher or research assistant, and purchasing manager. Overall employment growth also will be slowed because of the relatively high number of economists employed in slow growing or declining government sectors. Employment in federal government agencies is expected to decrease, and employment in state and local government is expected to grow more slowly than employment in the private sector.

Projections data from the National Employment Matrix

Occupational Title	SOC Code	Employment, 2006	Projected employment, 2016	Change, 2006-2016	
				Number	Percent
Economists	19-3011	15,000	16,000	1,100	7

NOTE: Data in this table are rounded.

Employment growth should be fastest in private industry, especially in management, scientific, and technical consulting services. Rising demand for economic analysis in virtually every industry should stem from the growing complexity of the global economy, the effects of competition on businesses, and increased reliance on quantitative methods for analyzing and forecasting business, sales, and other economic trends. Some corporations choose to hire economic consultants to fill these needs, rather than keeping an economist on staff. This practice should result in more economists being employed in consulting services.

Job prospects. In addition to job openings from growth, the need to replace experienced workers who transfer to other occupations or who retire or leave the labor force for other reasons will create openings for economists.

Individuals with a background in economics should have opportunities in various occupations. As indicated earlier, some examples of job titles often held by those with an economics background are financial analyst, market analyst, public policy consultant, researcher or research assistant, and purchasing manager.

People who have a master's or Ph.D. degree in economics, who are skilled in quantitative techniques and their application to economic modeling and forecasting, and who also have good communications skills, should have the best job opportunities. Like those in many other disciplines, some economists leave the occupation to become professors, but competition for tenured teaching positions is expected to be keen.

Bachelor's degree holders may face competition for the limited number of economist positions for which they qualify. However, they will qualify for a number of other positions that can use their economic knowledge. Many graduates with bachelor's degrees will find jobs in industry and business as management or sales trainees. Bachelor's degree holders with good quantitative skills and a strong background in mathematics, statistics, survey design, and computer science also may be hired as researchers. Some will find jobs in government.

Candidates who meet state certification requirements may become high school economics teachers. The demand for secondary school economics teachers is expected to grow, as economics becomes an increasingly important and popular course.

Earnings

Median annual wage and salary earnings of economists were $77,010 in May 2006. The middle 50 percent earned between $55,740 and $103,500. The lowest 10 percent earned less than $42,280, and the highest 10 percent earned more than $136,550.

In the federal government, the starting salary for economists having a bachelor's degree was $35,752 in 2007. Those having a master's degree could qualify for positions with an annual salary of $43,731. Those with a Ph.D. could begin at $52,912, and some individuals with experience and an advanced degree could start at $63,417. Starting salaries were higher in selected geographical areas where the prevailing local pay was higher. The average annual salary for economists employed by the federal government was $94,098 a year in 2007.

Related Occupations

Economists are concerned with understanding and interpreting financial matters, among other subjects. Other occupations in this area include accountants and auditors; actuaries; budget analysts; cost estimators; financial analysts and personal financial advisors; financial managers; insurance underwriters; loan officers; and purchasing managers, buyers, and purchasing agents. Economists also rely heavily on quantitative analysis, as do mathematicians, statisticians, and operations research analysts. Other occupations involved in market research and data collection are management analysts and market and survey researchers. Economists also study consumer behavior, similar to the work of sociologists.

Sources of Additional Information

For information on careers in business economics, contact

- National Association for Business Economics, 1233 20th St. NW, Suite 505, Washington, DC 20036.

Information on obtaining positions as economists with the federal government is available from the Office of Personnel Management through USAJOBS, the federal government's official employment information system. This resource for locating and applying for job opportunities can be accessed through the Internet at http://www.usajobs.opm.gov or through an interactive voice response telephone system at (703) 724-1850 or TDD (978) 461-8404. These numbers are not toll free, and charges may result. For advice on how to find and apply for federal jobs, see the *Occupational Outlook Quarterly* article "How to get a job in the Federal Government," online at http://www.bls.gov/opub/ooq/2004/summer/art01.pdf.

Electrical and Electronics Installers and Repairers

(O*NET 49-2092.00, 49-2093.00, 49-2094.00, 49-2095.00, and 49-2096.00)

Significant Points

- Knowledge of electrical equipment and electronics is necessary for employment; employers often prefer applicants with an associate degree in electronics.
- Employment is projected to grow more slowly than average for all occupations.
- Job opportunities will be best for applicants with an associate degree, certification, and related experience.

Nature of the Work

Businesses and other organizations depend on complex electronic equipment for a variety of functions. Industrial controls automatically monitor and direct production processes on the factory floor. Transmitters and antennae provide communication links for many organizations. Electric power companies use electronic equipment to operate and control generating plants, substations, and monitoring equipment. The federal government uses radar and missile control systems to provide for the national defense and to direct commercial air traffic. These complex pieces of electronic equipment are installed, maintained, and repaired by electrical and electronics installers and repairers.

Installers and repairers, known as *field technicians*, often travel to factories or other locations to repair equipment. These workers usually have assigned areas in which they perform preventive maintenance on a regular basis. When equipment breaks down, field technicians go to a customer's site to repair the equipment. *Bench technicians* work in repair shops located in factories and service centers, fixing components that cannot be repaired on the factory floor.

Electrical and electronic equipment are two distinct types of industrial equipment, although much equipment contains both electrical and electronic components. In general, electrical portions provide the power for the equipment, while electronic components control the device, although many types of equipment still are controlled with electrical devices.

Some industrial electronic equipment is self-monitoring and alerts repairers to malfunctions. When equipment breaks down, repairers will first check for common causes of trouble, such as loose connections or obviously defective components. If routine checks do not locate the trouble, repairers may refer to schematics and manufacturers' specifications that show connections and provide instructions on how to locate problems. Automated electronic control systems are becoming increasingly complex, making diagnosis more challenging. With these systems, repairers use software programs and testing equipment to diagnose malfunctions. Among their diagnostic tools are multimeters, which measure voltage, current, and resistance, and advanced multimeters, which measure capacitance, inductance, and current gain of transistors. Repairers also use signal generators, which provide test signals, and oscilloscopes, which display signals graphically. Finally, repairers use handtools such as pliers, screwdrivers, soldering irons, and wrenches to replace faulty parts and adjust equipment.

Because repairing components is a complex activity and factories cannot allow production equipment to stand idle, repairers on the factory floor usually remove and replace defective units, such as circuit boards, instead of fixing them. Defective units are discarded or returned to the manufacturer or a specialized shop for repair. Bench technicians at these locations have the training, tools, and parts needed to thoroughly diagnose and repair circuit boards or other complex components. These workers also locate and repair circuit defects, such as poorly soldered joints, blown fuses, or malfunctioning transistors.

Electrical and electronics installers often fit older manufacturing equipment with new automated control devices. Older manufacturing machines are frequently in good working order but are limited by inefficient control systems for which replacement parts are no longer available. Installers replace old electronic control units with new programming logic controls (PLCs). Setting up and installing a new PLC involves connecting it to different sensors and electrically powered devices (electric motors, switches, and pumps) and writing a computer program to operate the PLC. Electronics installers coordinate their efforts with those of other workers who are installing and maintaining equipment. (See the section on industrial machinery mechanics and maintenance workers elsewhere in this book.)

Electrical and electronics installers and repairers, transportation equipment install, adjust, or maintain mobile electronic communication equipment, including sound, sonar, security, navigation, and surveillance systems on trains, watercraft, or other vehicles. *Electrical and electronics repairers, powerhouse, substation, and relay* inspect, test, maintain, or repair electrical equipment used in generating stations, substations, and in-service relays. These workers may be known as powerhouse electricians, relay technicians, or power transformer repairers. *Electric motor, power tool, and related repairers*—such as armature winders, generator mechanics, and electric golf cart repairers—specialize in installing, maintaining, and repairing electric motors, wiring, or switches.

Electronic equipment installers and repairers, motor vehicles have a significantly different job. They install, diagnose, and repair communication, sound, security, and navigation equipment in motor vehicles. Most installation work involves either new alarm or sound systems. New sound systems vary significantly in cost and complexity of installation. Replacing a head unit (radio) with a new CD player is simple, requiring the removal of a few screws and the connection of a few wires. Installing a new sound system with a subwoofer, amplifier, and fuses is far more complicated. The installer builds a fiberglass or wood box designed to hold the subwoofer and to fit inside the unique dimensions of the automobile. Installing sound-deadening material, which often is necessary with more powerful speakers, requires an installer to remove many parts of a car (for example, seats, carpeting, or interiors of doors), add sound-absorbing material in empty spaces, and reinstall the interior parts. The installer also runs new speaker and electrical cables. The new system may require additional fuses, a new electrical line to be run from the battery through a newly drilled hole in the firewall into the interior of the vehicle, or an additional or more powerful alternator or battery. Motor vehicle installers and repairers work with an increasingly complex range of electronic equipment, including DVD players, satellite navigation equipment, passive security systems, and active security systems.

Work environment. Many electrical and electronics installers and repairers work on factory floors, where they are subject to noise, dirt, vibration, and heat. Bench technicians primarily work in repair shops, where the surroundings are relatively quiet, comfortable, and well lighted.

Installers and repairers may have to do heavy lifting and work in a variety of positions. They must follow safety guidelines and often wear protective goggles and hardhats. When working on ladders or on elevated equipment, repairers must wear harnesses to avoid falls. Before repairing a piece of machinery, these workers must follow procedures to ensure that others cannot start the equipment during the repair process. They also must take precautions against electric shock by locking off power to the unit under repair.

Motor vehicle electronic equipment installers and repairers normally work indoors in well-ventilated and well-lighted repair shops. Minor cuts and bruises are common, but serious accidents usually are avoided when safety practices are observed.

Training, Other Qualifications, and Advancement

Applicants with an associate degree in electronics are preferred, and professional certification often is required.

Education and training. Knowledge of electrical equipment and electronics is necessary for employment. Employers often prefer applicants with an associate degree from a community college or technical school, although a high school diploma may be sufficient for some jobs. Entry-level repairers may begin by working with experienced technicians who provide technical guidance, and work independently only after developing the necessary skills.

Certification and other qualifications. Many employers require applicants to be certified. Certification is available from various professional and education organizations, and usually requires applicants to pass an exam demonstrating their level of expertise.

Installers and repairers should have good eyesight and color perception to work with the intricate components used in electronic equipment. Field technicians work closely with customers and should have good communication skills and a neat appearance. Employers also may require that field technicians have a driver's license.

Certification and advancement. Certification can also serve as a form of advancement. Workers who become certified in a specialty area may gain additional responsibilities and be awarded higher pay.

Experienced repairers with advanced training may become specialists or troubleshooters who help other repairers diagnose difficult problems. Workers with leadership ability may become supervisors of other repairers. Some experienced workers open their own repair shops.

Employment

Electrical and electronics installers and repairers held about 169,000 jobs in 2006. The following tabulation breaks down their employment by occupational specialty:

Electrical and electronics repairers, commercial and industrial equipment 80,000

Electric motor, power tool, and related repairers 25,000

Electrical and electronics repairers, powerhouse, substation, and relay 22,000

Electrical and electronics installers and repairers, transportation equipment.................................21,000

Electronic equipment installers and repairers, motor vehicles 20,000

Many repairers worked for utilities; building equipment contractors; machinery and equipment repair shops; electrical and electronics wholesalers; electronics and appliance retailers; motor vehicle and parts dealers; manufacturers of electrical, electronic, and transportation equipment; and federal, state, and local government.

Job Outlook

Employment is expected to increase more slowly than the average through the year 2016. Job prospects should be best for applicants with an associate degree, certification, and related experience.

Employment change. Overall employment of electrical and electronics installers and repairers is expected to grow by 3 percent through the year 2016, which is slower than the average for all occupations. Growth rates will vary by occupational specialty.

Employment of electrical and electronics installers and repairers of commercial and industrial equipment is expected to grow by 7 percent, which is about as fast as the average for all occupations. This equipment will become more sophisticated and will be used more frequently as businesses strive to lower costs by increasing and improving automation. Companies will install electronic controls, robots, sensors, and other equipment to automate processes such as assembly and testing. In addition, as prices decline, this equipment will be used more frequently throughout a number of industries, including services, utilities, and construction, as well as manufacturing. Improved reliability of equipment should not constrain employment growth, however: companies increasingly will rely on repairers because malfunctions that idle commercial and industrial equipment will continue to be costly.

Employment of motor vehicle electronic equipment installers and repairers is expected to grow by 5 percent, which is slower than the average for all occupations. As motor vehicle manufacturers install more and better sound, security, entertainment, and navigation systems in new vehicles, and as newer electronic systems require progressively less maintenance, employment growth for aftermarket electronic equipment installers will be limited.

Employment of electric motor, power tool, and related repairers is expected to decline slowly, decreasing by 4 percent. Improvements in electrical and electronic equipment design, as well as the increased use of disposable tool parts should suppress job growth.

Employment of electrical and electronic installers and repairers of transportation equipment is expected to grow by 4 percent, which is slower than the average for all occupations. Declining employment in the rail transportation industry will dampen growth in this occupational specialty.

Employment of electrical and electronics installers and repairers, powerhouse, substation, and relay is expected to decline slowly, decreasing by 5 percent. Consolidation and privatization in utilities industries should improve productivity, reducing employment. Newer equipment will be more reliable and easier to repair, further limiting employment.

Job prospects. Job opportunities should be best for applicants with an associate degree in electronics, certification, and related experience. In addition to employment growth, the need to replace workers who transfer to other occupations or leave the labor force will result in some openings.

Earnings

Median hourly earnings of wage-and-salary electrical and electronics repairers, commercial and industrial equipment were $21.72 in May 2006. The middle 50 percent earned between $17.18 and $26.59. The lowest 10 percent earned less than $13.43, and the highest 10 percent earned more than $30.90. In May 2006, median hourly earnings were $23.49 in the federal government and $19.92 in building equipment contractors, the industries employing the largest numbers of electrical and electronics repairers, commercial and industrial equipment.

Median hourly earnings of wage-and-salary electric motor, power tool, and related repairers were $15.80 in May 2006. The middle 50 percent earned between $12.56 and $20.24. The lowest 10 percent earned less than $9.97, and the highest 10 percent earned more than

Projections data from the National Employment Matrix

Occupational Title	SOC Code	Employment, 2006	Projected employment, 2016	Change, 2006-16	
				Number	Percent
Electrical and electronics installers and repairers	—	169,000	174,000	5,200	3
Electric motor, power tool, and related repairers	49-2092	25,000	24,000	-1,100	-4
Electrical and electronics installers and repairers, transportation equipment	49-2093	21,000	22,000	900	4
Electrical and electronics repairers, commercial and industrial equipment	49-2094	80,000	86,000	5,500	7
Electrical and electronics repairers, powerhouse, substation, and relay	49-2095	22,000	21,000	-1,000	-5
Electronic equipment installers and repairers, motor vehicles	49-2096	20,000	21,000	900	5

NOTE: Data in this table are rounded.

$25.37. In May 2006, median hourly earnings were $15.32 in commercial and industrial machinery and equipment (except automotive and electronic) repair and maintenance, the industry employing the largest number of electronic motor, power tool, and related repairers.

Median hourly earnings of wage-and-salary electrical and electronics repairers, powerhouse, substation, and relay were $27.60 in May 2006. The middle 50 percent earned between $23.62 and $32.07. The lowest 10 percent earned less than $19.42, and the highest 10 percent earned more than $35.49. In May 2006, median hourly earnings were $28.30 in electric power generation, transmission, and distribution, the industry employing the largest number of these repairers.

Median hourly earnings of wage-and-salary electronics installers and repairers, motor vehicles were $13.57 in May 2006. The middle 50 percent earned between $10.78 and $17.41. The lowest 10 percent earned less than $9.13, and the highest 10 percent earned more than $23.45.

Median hourly earnings of wage-and-salary electrical and electronics repairers, transportation equipment were $20.72 in May 2006. The middle 50 percent earned between $16.79 and $25.10. The lowest 10 percent earned less than $13.24, and the highest 10 percent earned more than $28.78.

Related Occupations

Workers in other occupations who install and repair electronic equipment include broadcast and sound engineering technicians and radio operators; computer, automated teller, and office machine repairers; electronic home entertainment equipment installers and repairers; radio and telecommunications equipment installers and repairers; electricians; elevator installers and repairers; aircraft and avionics equipment mechanics and service technicians; coin, vending, and amusement machine servicers and repairers; and maintenance and repair workers, general. Industrial machinery mechanics and maintenance workers also install, maintain, and repair industrial machinery.

Sources of Additional Information

For information on careers and certification, contact any of the following organizations:

- ACES International, 5241 Princess Anne Rd., Suite 110, Virginia Beach, VA 23462. Internet: http://www.acesinternational.org
- Electronics Technicians Association International, 5 Depot St., Greencastle, IN 46135. Internet: http://eta-i.org/
- International Society of Certified Electronics Technicians, 3608 Pershing Ave., Fort Worth, TX 76107-4527. Internet: http://www.iscet.org

Electronic Home Entertainment Equipment Installers and Repairers

(O*NET 49-2097.00)

Significant Points

- Employers prefer applicants who have basic knowledge and skills in electronics; many applicants gain these skills at vocational training programs and community colleges.
- Employment is expected to grow more slowly than the average for all occupations because it often is cheaper to replace equipment than to repair it.
- Job opportunities will be best for applicants with knowledge of electronics, related hands-on experience, and good customer service skills.

Nature of the Work

Electronic home entertainment equipment installers and repairers—also called *service technicians*—repair a variety of equipment. They may specialize in one type of product, or may be trained in many different ones. The most common products include televisions and radios, stereo components, video and audio disc players, and video cameras. They also install and repair home security systems, intercom equipment, satellite television dishes, and home theater systems, which consist of large-screen televisions and sophisticated surround-sound audio components.

Customers usually bring small, portable equipment to repair shops for servicing. Repairers at these locations, known as *bench technicians*, are equipped with a full array of electronic tools and parts. When larger, less mobile equipment breaks down, customers may pay repairers to come to their homes. These repairers, known as *field technicians*, travel with a limited set of tools and parts, and attempt to complete the repair at the customer's location. If the job is complex, technicians may bring defective components back to the shop for diagnosis and repair.

When equipment breaks down, repairers check for common causes of trouble, such as dirty or defective components. Many repairs consist simply of cleaning and lubricating equipment. If routine checks do not locate the trouble, repairers may refer to schematics and manufacturers' specifications that provide instructions on how to locate problems. Repairers use a variety of test equipment to diagnose and identify malfunctions. Multimeters detect short circuits, failed capacitors, and blown fuses by measuring voltage, current, and resistance. Color-bar and dot generators provide onscreen test patterns, signal generators test signals, and oscilloscopes and digital storage scopes measure complex waveforms produced by electronic equipment. Repairs may involve removing and replacing a failed capacitor, transistor, or fuse. Repairers use hand tools, such as pliers, screwdrivers, soldering irons, and wrenches, to replace faulty parts. They also make adjustments to equipment, such as focusing and converging the picture of a television set or balancing the audio on a surround-sound system.

Improvements in technology have miniaturized and digitized many audio and video recording devices. Miniaturization has made repair work significantly more difficult because both the components and the acceptable tolerances are smaller. Also, components now are mounted on the surface of circuit boards, instead of plugged into slots, requiring more precise soldering when a new part is installed. Improved technologies have lowered the price of electronic home entertainment equipment to the point where customers often replace broken equipment instead of repairing it.

Work environment. Most repairers work in well-lighted electrical repair shops. Field technicians, however, spend much time traveling in service vehicles and working in customers' residences.

Repairers may have to work in a variety of positions and carry heavy equipment. Although the work of repairers is comparatively safe, they must take precautions against minor burns and electric shock. Because television monitors carry high voltage even when they are turned off, repairers need to discharge the voltage before servicing such equipment.

Training, Other Qualifications, and Advancement

Employers prefer applicants who have basic electronics skills, good problem-solving skills, and previous repair experience. Good customer service skills are essential for field technicians, as they spend a majority of their time working in customers' homes.

Education and training. Employers prefer applicants who have basic knowledge and skills in electronics as well as previous repair experience. Many applicants gain these skills at vocational training programs and community colleges. Training programs should include both hands-on experience and theoretical education in digital consumer electronics. Entry-level repairers may work closely with more experienced technicians, who provide technical guidance.

Other qualifications. Field technicians work closely with customers and must have good communication skills and a neat appearance. Repairers also must have good problem solving skills, as their main duty is to diagnose and solve problems. Employers also may require that field technicians have a driver's license.

Certification and advancement. Various organizations offer certification for electronic home entertainment equipment installers and repairers. Repairers may specialize in a variety of skill areas, including consumer electronics. To receive certification, repairers must pass qualifying exams corresponding to their level of training and experience.

Experienced repairers with advanced training may become specialists or troubleshooters, helping other repairers to diagnose difficult problems. Workers with leadership ability may become supervisors of other repairers. Some experienced workers open their own repair shops.

Employment

Electronic home entertainment equipment installers and repairers held about 40,000 jobs in 2006. Many repairers worked in electronics and appliance stores that sell and service electronic home entertainment products or in electronic and precision equipment repair and maintenance shops. About 12 percent of electronic home entertainment equipment installers and repairers were self-employed, compared to 7 percent for all installation, maintenance, and repair occupations.

Job Outlook

Employment is expected to increase more slowly than the average for all occupations. Job prospects will be best for applicants with knowledge of electronics, related experience, and good customer service skills.

Employment change. Employment of electronic home entertainment equipment installers and repairers is expected to grow by 3 percent from 2006 to 2016, which is slower than the average for all occupations. Demand will be driven by the rising sales of home entertainment equipment.

The need for repairers is expected to grow slowly, however, because home entertainment equipment is less expensive than in the past. As technological developments have lowered the price and improved the reliability of equipment, the demand for repair services has decreased. When a malfunction does occur, it often is cheaper for consumers to replace equipment than to pay for repairs.

Employment growth will be spurred somewhat by the introduction of sophisticated digital equipment, such as high-definition digital televisions and digital camcorders. So long as the price of such equipment remains high, purchasers will be willing to hire repairers when malfunctions occur. There also will be demand to install sophisticated home entertainment systems, such as home theaters.

Job prospects. Job openings will come about because of employment growth and from the need to replace workers who retire or who leave the occupation. Opportunities will be best for applicants with knowledge of electronics and who have related hands-on experience and good customer service skills.

Earnings

Median hourly earnings of wage-and-salary electronic home entertainment equipment installers and repairers were $14.42 in May 2006. The middle 50 percent earned between $11.52 and $18.24. The lowest 10 percent earned less than $8.96, and the highest 10 percent earned more than $22.42. In May 2006, median hourly earnings of electronic home entertainment equipment installers and repairers were $14.46 in electronics and appliance stores and $13.18 in electronic and precision equipment repair and maintenance.

Projections data from the National Employment Matrix

Occupational Title	SOC Code	Employment, 2006	Projected employment, 2016	Change, 2006-16	
				Number	Percent
Electronic home entertainment equipment installers and repairers ..	49-2097	40,000	41,000	1,200	3

NOTE: Data in this table are rounded.

Related Occupations

Other workers who install, repair, and maintain electronic equipment include computer, automated teller, and office machine repairers; electrical and electronics installers and repairers; radio and telecommunications equipment installers and repairers; precision instrument and equipment repairers; home appliance repairers; coin, vending, and amusement machine servicers and repairers; maintenance and repair workers, general; and electricians.

Sources of Additional Information

For information on careers and certification, contact

- ACES International, 5241 Princess Anne Rd., Suite 110, Virginia Beach, VA 23462. Internet: http://www.acesinternational.org
- Electronics Technicians Association International, 5 Depot St., Greencastle, IN 46135. Internet: http://www.eta-i.org
- International Society of Certified Electronics Technicians, 3608 Pershing Ave., Fort Worth, TX 76107-4527. Internet: http://www.iscet.org

Elevator Installers and Repairers

(O*NET 47-4021.00)

Significant Points

- Most workers belong to a union and enter the occupation through a 4-year apprenticeship program.
- Excellent employment opportunities are expected.
- Elevator installers and repairers are less affected by downturns in the economy and inclement weather than other construction trades workers.

Nature of the Work

Elevator installers and repairers—also called *elevator constructors* or *elevator mechanics*—assemble, install, and replace elevators, escalators, chairlifts, dumbwaiters, moving walkways, and similar equipment in new and old buildings. Once the equipment is in service, they maintain and repair it as well. They also are responsible for modernizing older equipment.

To install, repair, and maintain modern elevators, which are almost all electronically controlled, elevator installers and repairers must have a thorough knowledge of electronics, electricity, and hydraulics. Many elevators are controlled with microprocessors, which are programmed to analyze traffic conditions in order to dispatch elevators in the most efficient manner. With these controls, it is possible to get the greatest amount of service with the fewest number of cars.

Elevator installers and repairers usually specialize in installation, maintenance, or repair work. Maintenance and repair workers generally need greater knowledge of electricity and electronics than do installers because a large part of maintenance and repair work is troubleshooting.

When installing a new elevator, installers and repairers begin by studying blueprints to determine the equipment needed to install rails, machinery, car enclosures, motors, pumps, cylinders, and plunger foundations. Then, they begin equipment installation. Working on scaffolding or platforms, installers bolt or weld steel rails to the walls of the shaft to guide the elevator.

Elevator installers put in electrical wires and controls by running tubing, called conduit, along a shaft's walls from floor to floor. Once the conduit is in place, mechanics pull plastic-covered electrical wires through it. They then install electrical components and related devices required at each floor and at the main control panel in the machine room.

Installers bolt or weld together the steel frame of an elevator car at the bottom of the shaft; install the car's platform, walls, and doors; and attach guide shoes and rollers to minimize the lateral motion of the car as it travels through the shaft. They also install the outer doors and door frames at the elevator entrances on each floor.

For cabled elevators, these workers install geared or gearless machines with a traction drive wheel that guides and moves heavy steel cables connected to the elevator car and counterweight. (The counterweight moves in the opposite direction from the car and balances most of the weight of the car to reduce the weight that the elevator's motor must lift.) Elevator installers also install elevators in which a car sits on a hydraulic plunger that is driven by a pump. The plunger pushes the elevator car up from underneath, similar to a lift in an auto service station.

Installers and repairers also install escalators. They place the steel framework, the electrically powered stairs, and the tracks and install associated motors and electrical wiring. In addition to elevators and escalators, installers and repairers also may install devices such as dumbwaiters and material lifts—which are similar to elevators in design—as well as moving walkways, stair lifts, and wheelchair lifts.

Once an elevator is operating properly, it must be maintained and serviced regularly to keep it in safe working condition. Elevator installers and repairers generally do preventive maintenance—such as oiling and greasing moving parts, replacing worn parts, testing equipment with meters and gauges, and adjusting equipment for optimal performance. They insure that the equipment and rooms are clean. They also troubleshoot and may be called to do emergency repairs. Unlike most elevator installers, those who specialize in elevator maintenance are on their own most of the day and typically service the same elevators periodically.

A service crew usually handles major repairs—for example, replacing cables, elevator doors, or machine bearings. This may require the use of cutting torches or rigging equipment—tools that an elevator repairer would not normally carry. Service crews also do major modernization and alteration work, such as moving and replacing electrical motors, hydraulic pumps, and control panels.

The most highly skilled elevator installers and repairers, called "adjusters," specialize in fine-tuning all the equipment after installation. Adjusters make sure that an elevator works according to specifications and stops correctly at each floor within a specified time. Adjusters need a thorough knowledge of electricity, electronics, and computers to ensure that newly installed elevators operate properly.

Work environment. Elevator installers lift and carry heavy equipment and parts, and they may work in cramped spaces or awkward positions. Potential hazards include falls, electrical shock, muscle strains, and other injuries related to handling heavy equipment. Most of their work is performed indoors in existing buildings or buildings under construction.

Most elevator installers and repairers work a 40-hour week. However, overtime is required when essential equipment must be repaired, and some workers are on 24-hour call. Because most of their work is performed indoors in buildings, elevator installers and repairers lose less work time due to inclement weather than do other construction trades workers.

Training, Other Qualifications, and Advancement

Most elevator installers receive their education through an apprenticeship program. High school classes in mathematics, science, and shop may help applicants compete for apprenticeship openings.

Education and training. Most elevators installers and repairers learn their trade in an apprenticeship program administered by local joint educational committees representing the employers and the union—the International Union of Elevator Constructors. In nonunion shops, workers may complete training programs sponsored by independent contractors.

Apprenticeship programs teach a range of skills, usually during a four-year period. Programs combine paid on-the-job training with classroom instruction in blueprint reading, electrical and electronic theory, mathematics, applications of physics, and safety.

Most apprentices assist experienced elevator installers and repairers. Beginners carry materials and tools, bolt rails to walls, and assemble elevator cars. Eventually, apprentices learn more difficult tasks such as wiring.

Applicants for apprenticeship positions must have a high school diploma or the equivalent. High school courses in electricity, mathematics, and physics provide a useful background. As elevators become increasingly sophisticated, workers may need to get more advanced education—for example, a certificate or associate degree in electronics. Workers with education beyond high school usually advance more quickly than their counterparts without a degree.

Many elevator installers and repairers receive additional training in their particular company's equipment.

Licensure. Most cities and states require elevator installers and repairers to pass a licensing examination. Other requirements for licensure vary.

Certification and other qualifications. Workers who also complete an apprenticeship registered by the U.S. Department of Labor or their state board earn a journeyworker certificate recognized Nationwide. Applicants for apprenticeship positions must be at least 18 years old, have a high school diploma or equivalent, and pass a drug test and an aptitude test. Good physical condition and mechanical aptitude also are important.

Jobs with many employers require membership in the union. To be considered fully qualified by the union, workers must complete an apprenticeship and pass a standard exam administered by the National Elevator Industry Educational Program.

The National Association of Elevator Contractors also offers certification as a Certified Elevator Technician or Certified Accessibility and Private Residence Lift Technician.

Advancement. Ongoing training is very important if a worker is to keep up with technological developments in elevator repair. In fact, union elevator installers and repairers typically receive training throughout their careers, through correspondence courses, seminars, or formal classes. This training greatly improves one's chances for promotion and retention.

Some installers may receive further training in specialized areas and advance to the position of mechanic-in-charge, adjuster, supervisor, or elevator inspector. Adjusters, for example, may be picked for their position because they possess particular skills or are electronically inclined. Other workers may move into management, sales, or product design jobs.

Employment

Elevator installers and repairers held about 22,000 jobs in 2006. Most were employed by specialty trades contractors, particularly elevator maintenance and repair contractors. Others were employed by field offices of elevator manufacturers, machinery wholesalers, government agencies, or businesses that do their own elevator maintenance and repair.

Job Outlook

Even with average job growth, excellent job opportunities are expected in this occupation.

Employment change. Employment of elevator installers and repairers is expected to increase 9 percent during the 2006–2016 decade, about as fast as the average for all occupations. Demand for additional elevator installers depends greatly on growth in nonresidential construction, such as commercial office buildings and stores that have elevators and escalators. This sector of the construction industry is expected to grow during the decade as the economy expands. In addition, the need to continually update and repair old equipment, provide access to the disabled, and install increasingly sophisticated equipment and controls should add to the demand for elevator installers and repairers. The demand for elevator installers and repairers will also increase as a growing number of the elderly require easier access to their homes through stair lifts and residential elevators.

Job prospects. Workers should have excellent opportunities when seeking to enter this occupation. Elevator installer and repairer jobs have relatively high earnings and good benefits. However, the dangerous and physically challenging nature of this occupation and the significant training it requires reduces the number of applicants and creates better opportunities for those who apply. Job prospects should be best for those with postsecondary education in electronics or experience in the military.

Elevators, escalators, lifts, moving walkways, and related equipment need to be kept in good working condition year round, so

Projections data from the National Employment Matrix

Occupational Title	SOC Code	Employment, 2006	Projected employment, 2016	Change, 2006-16	
				Number	Percent
Elevator installers and repairers	47-4021	22,000	24,000	1,900	9

NOTE: Data in this table are rounded.

employment of elevator repairers is less affected by economic downturns and seasonality than other construction trades.

Earnings

Earnings of elevator installers and repairers are among the highest of all construction trades. Median hourly earnings of wage and salary elevator installers and repairers were $30.59 in May 2006. The middle 50 percent earned between $23.90 and $35.76. The lowest 10 percent earned less than $17.79, and the top 10 percent earned more than $42.14. Median hourly earnings in the building equipment contractors industry were $30.74.

Earnings for members of the International Union of Elevator Constructors vary based on the local and specialty. Check with a local in your area for exact wages.

About 3 out of 4 elevator installers and repairers were members of unions or covered by a union contract, one of the highest proportions of all occupations. The largest numbers were members of the International Union of Elevator Constructors. In addition to free continuing education, elevator installers and repairers receive basic benefits enjoyed by most other workers.

Related Occupations

Elevator installers and repairers combine electrical and mechanical skills with construction skills, such as welding, rigging, measuring, and blueprint reading. Other occupations that require many of these skills are boilermakers; electricians; electrical and electronics installers and repairers; industrial machinery mechanics and maintenance workers; millwrights; sheet metal workers; and structural and reinforcing iron and metal workers.

Sources of Additional Information

For information about apprenticeships or job opportunities as an elevator mechanic, contact local contractors, a local chapter of the International Union of Elevator Constructors, a local joint union-management apprenticeship committee, or the nearest office of your state employment service or apprenticeship agency. You can also find information on the registered apprenticeship system with links to state apprenticeship programs on the U.S. Department of Labor's Web site: http://www.doleta.gov/atels_bat. Apprenticeship information is also available from the U.S. Department of Labor's toll free helpline: (877) 872-5627.

For further information on opportunities as an elevator installer and repairer, contact

- International Union of Elevator Constructors, 7154 Columbia Gateway Dr., Columbia, MD 21046. Internet: http://www.iuec.org

For additional information about the Certified Elevator Technician (CET) program or the Certified Accessibility and Private Residence Lift Technician (CAT) program, contact

- National Association of Elevator Contractors, 1298 Wellbrook Circle, Suite A, Conyers, GA 30012. Internet: http://www.naec.org

For general information on apprenticeships and how to get them, see the *Occupational Outlook Quarterly* article "Apprenticeships: Career training, credentials—and a paycheck in your pocket," online at http://www.bls.gov/opub/ooq/2002/summer/art01.pdf and in print at many libraries and career centers.

Emergency Medical Technicians and Paramedics

(O*NET 29-2041.00)

Significant Points

- Employment is projected to grow faster than the average as paid positions replace unpaid volunteers.
- Emergency medical technicians and paramedics need formal training and certification, but requirements vary by state.
- Emergency services function 24 hours a day so emergency medical technicians and paramedics have irregular working hours.
- Opportunities will be best for those who have earned advanced certifications.

Nature of the Work

People's lives often depend on the quick reaction and competent care of emergency medical technicians (EMTs) and paramedics. Incidents as varied as automobile accidents, heart attacks, slips and falls, childbirth, and gunshot wounds all require immediate medical attention. EMTs and paramedics provide this vital service as they care for and transport the sick or injured to a medical facility.

In an emergency, EMTs and paramedics are typically dispatched by a 911 operator to the scene, where they often work with police and fire fighters. Once they arrive, EMTs and paramedics assess the nature of the patient's condition while trying to determine whether the patient has any pre-existing medical conditions. Following medical protocols and guidelines, they provide appropriate emergency care and, when necessary, transport the patient. Some paramedics are trained to treat patients with minor injuries on the scene of an accident or they may treat them at their home without transporting them to a medical facility. Emergency treatment is carried out under the medical direction of physicians.

EMTs and paramedics may use special equipment, such as backboards, to immobilize patients before placing them on stretchers and securing them in the ambulance for transport to a medical facility. These workers generally work in teams. During the transport of a patient, one EMT or paramedic drives while the other monitors the patient's vital signs and gives additional care as needed. Some paramedics work as part of a helicopter's flight crew to transport critically ill or injured patients to hospital trauma centers.

At the medical facility, EMTs and paramedics help transfer patients to the emergency department, report their observations and actions to emergency department staff, and may provide additional emergency treatment. After each run, EMTs and paramedics replace used supplies and check equipment. If a transported patient had a contagious disease, EMTs and paramedics decontaminate the interior of the ambulance and report cases to the proper authorities.

EMTs and paramedics also provide transportation for patients from one medical facility to another, particularly if they work for private ambulance services. Patients often need to be transferred to a hospital that specializes in their injury or illness or to a nursing home.

Beyond these general duties, the specific responsibilities of EMTs and paramedics depend on their level of qualification and training. The National Registry of Emergency Medical Technicians (NREMT) certifies emergency medical service providers at five levels: First Responder; EMT-Basic; EMT-Intermediate, which has two levels called 1985 and 1999; and Paramedic. Some states, however, have their own certification programs and use distinct names and titles.

The EMT-Basic represents the first component of the emergency medical technician system. An EMT trained at this level is prepared to care for patients at the scene of an accident and while transporting patients by ambulance to the hospital under medical direction. The EMT-Basic has the emergency skills to assess a patient's condition and manage respiratory, cardiac, and trauma emergencies.

The EMT-Intermediate has more advanced training. However, the specific tasks that those certified at this level are allowed to perform varies greatly from state to state.

EMT-Paramedics provide the most extensive pre-hospital care. In addition to carrying out the procedures of the other levels, paramedics may administer drugs orally and intravenously, interpret electrocardiograms (EKGs), perform endotracheal intubations, and use monitors and other complex equipment. However, like EMT-Intermediate, what paramedics are permitted to do varies by state.

Work environment. EMTs and paramedics work both indoors and out, in all types of weather. They are required to do considerable kneeling, bending, and heavy lifting. These workers risk noise-induced hearing loss from sirens and back injuries from lifting patients. In addition, EMTs and paramedics may be exposed to diseases such as hepatitis-B and AIDS, as well as violence from mentally unstable patients. The work is not only physically strenuous but can be stressful, sometimes involving life-or-death situations and suffering patients. Nonetheless, many people find the work exciting and challenging and enjoy the opportunity to help others.

EMTs and paramedics employed by fire departments work about 50 hours a week. Those employed by hospitals frequently work between 45 and 60 hours a week, and those in private ambulance services, between 45 and 50 hours. Some of these workers, especially those in police and fire departments, are on call for extended periods. Because emergency services function 24 hours a day, EMTs and paramedics have irregular working hours.

Training, Other Qualifications, and Advancement

Generally, a high school diploma is required to enter a training program to become an EMT or paramedic. Workers must complete a formal training and certification process.

Education and training. A high school diploma is usually required to enter a formal emergency medical technician training program. Training is offered at progressive levels: EMT-Basic, EMT-Intermediate, and EMT-Paramedic.

At the EMT-Basic level, coursework emphasizes emergency skills, such as managing respiratory, trauma, and cardiac emergencies, and patient assessment. Formal courses are often combined with time in an emergency room or ambulance. The program provides instruction and practice in dealing with bleeding, fractures, airway obstruction, cardiac arrest, and emergency childbirth. Students learn how to use and maintain common emergency equipment, such as backboards, suction devices, splints, oxygen delivery systems, and stretchers. Graduates of approved EMT-Basic training programs must pass a written and practical examination administered by the state certifying agency or the NREMT.

At the EMT-Intermediate level, training requirements vary by state. The nationally defined levels (EMT-Intermediate 1985 and EMT-Intermediate 1999) typically require 30 to 350 hours of training based on scope of practice. Students learn advanced skills such the use of advanced airway devices, intravenous fluids, and some medications.

The most advanced level of training for this occupation is EMT-Paramedic. At this level, the caregiver receives training in anatomy and physiology as well as advanced medical skills. Most commonly, the training is conducted in community colleges and technical schools over one to two years and may result in an associate's degree. Such education prepares the graduate to take the NREMT examination and become certified as a Paramedic. Extensive related coursework and clinical and field experience is required. Refresher courses and continuing education are available for EMTs and paramedics at all levels.

Licensure. All 50 states require certification for each of the EMT levels. In most states and the District of Columbia registration with the NREMT is required at some or all levels of certification. Other states administer their own certification examination or provide the option of taking either the NREMT or state examination. To maintain certification, EMTs and paramedics must recertify, usually every two years. Generally, they must be working as an EMT or paramedic and meet a continuing education requirement.

Other qualifications. EMTs and paramedics should be emotionally stable, have good dexterity, agility, and physical coordination, and be able to lift and carry heavy loads. They also need good eyesight (corrective lenses may be used) with accurate color vision.

Advancement. Paramedics can become supervisors, operations managers, administrative directors, or executive directors of emergency services. Some EMTs and paramedics become instructors, dispatchers, or physician assistants; others move into sales or marketing of emergency medical equipment. A number of people become EMTs and paramedics to test their interest in health care before training as registered nurses, physicians, or other health workers.

Employment

EMTs and paramedics held about 201,000 jobs in 2006. Most career EMTs and paramedics work in metropolitan areas. Volunteer EMTs and paramedics are more common in small cities, towns, and rural areas. These individuals volunteer for fire departments, emergency medical services, or hospitals and may respond to only a few calls

Projections data from the National Employment Matrix

Occupational Title	SOC Code	Employment, 2006	Projected employment, 2016	Change, 2006-2016	
				Number	Percent
Emergency medical technicians and paramedics	29-2041	201,000	240,000	39,000	19

NOTE: Data in this table are rounded.

per month. About 30 percent of EMTs or paramedics belong to a union.

Paid EMTs and paramedics were employed in a number of industries. About 4 out of 10 worked as employees of private ambulance services. About 3 out of 10 worked in local government for fire departments, public ambulance services, and emergency medical services. Another 2 out of 10 worked full time in hospitals within the medical facility or responded to calls in ambulances or helicopters to transport critically ill or injured patients. The remainder worked in various industries providing emergency services.

Job Outlook

Employment for EMTs and paramedics is expected to grow faster than the average for all occupations through 2016. Job prospects should be good, particularly in cities and private ambulance services.

Employment change. Employment of emergency medical technicians and paramedics is expected to grow by 19 percent between 2006 and 2016, which is faster than the average for all occupations. Full-time paid EMTs and paramedics will be needed to replace unpaid volunteers. It is becoming increasing difficult for emergency medical services to recruit and retain unpaid volunteers because of the amount of training and the large time commitment these positions require. As a result, more paid EMTs and paramedics are needed. Furthermore, as a large segment of the population—aging members of the baby boom generation—becomes more likely to have medical emergencies, demand will increase for EMTs and paramedics. There also will still be demand for part-time, volunteer EMTs and paramedics in rural areas and smaller metropolitan areas.

Job prospects. Job prospects should be favorable. Many job openings will arise from growth and from the need to replace workers who leave the occupation because of the limited potential for advancement, as well as the modest pay and benefits in private-sector jobs.

Job opportunities should be best in private ambulance services. Competition will be greater for jobs in local government, including fire, police, and independent third-service rescue squad departments which tend to have better salaries and benefits. EMTs and paramedics who have advanced education and certifications, such as Paramedic level certification, should enjoy the most favorable job prospects as clients and patients demand higher levels of care before arriving at the hospital.

Earnings

Earnings of EMTs and paramedics depend on the employment setting and geographic location of their jobs, as well as their training and experience. Median annual earnings of EMTs and paramedics were $27,070 in May 2006. The middle 50 percent earned between $21,290 and $35,210. The lowest 10 percent earned less than $17,300, and the highest 10 percent earned more than $45,280. Median annual earnings in the industries employing the largest numbers of EMTs and paramedics in May 2006 were $23,250 in general medical and surgical hospitals and $20,350 in ambulance services.

Those in emergency medical services who are part of fire or police departments typically receive the same benefits as firefighters or police officers. For example, many are covered by pension plans that provide retirement at half pay after 20 or 25 years of service or if the worker is disabled in the line of duty.

Related Occupations

Other workers in occupations that require quick and level-headed reactions to life-or-death situations are air traffic controllers, firefighting occupations, physician assistants, police and detectives, and registered nurses.

Sources of Additional Information

General information about emergency medical technicians and paramedics is available from

- National Association of Emergency Medical Technicians, P.O. Box 1400, Clinton, MS 39060-1400. Internet: http://www.naemt.org
- National Highway Traffic Safety Administration, EMS Division, 400 7th St. SW, NTS-14, Washington, DC 20590. Internet: http://www.nhtsa.dot.gov/portal/site/nhtsa/menuitem.2a0771e91315babbbf30811060008a0c/
- National Registry of Emergency Medical Technicians, Rocco V. Morando Bldg., 6610 Busch Blvd., P.O. Box 29233, Columbus, OH 43229. Internet: http://www.nremt.org

STEM Engineering and Natural Sciences Managers

(O*NET 11-9041.00 and 11-9121.00)

Significant Points

- Most engineering and natural sciences managers have formal education and work experience as engineers, scientists, or mathematicians.
- Projected employment growth for engineering and natural sciences managers is closely related to growth in employment of the engineers and scientists they supervise and the industries in which they work.
- Opportunities will be best for workers with strong communication and business management skills.

Nature of the Work

Engineering and natural sciences managers plan, coordinate, and direct research, design, and production activities. They may supervise engineers, scientists, and technicians, along with support personnel. These managers use their knowledge of engineering and natural sciences to oversee a variety of activities. They determine scientific and technical goals within broad outlines provided by top executives. These goals may include improving manufacturing processes, advancing scientific research, or developing new products. Managers make detailed plans to accomplish these goals. For example, they may develop the overall concepts of a new product or identify technical problems preventing the completion of a project.

To perform effectively, these managers also must apply knowledge of administrative procedures, such as budgeting, hiring, and supervision. They propose budgets for projects and programs and determine staff, training, and equipment needs. They hire and assign scientists, engineers, and support personnel to carry out specific parts of each project. They also supervise the work of these employees, check the technical accuracy of their work and the soundness of their methods, review their output, and establish administrative procedures and policies—including environmental standards, for example.

In addition, these managers use communication skills extensively. They spend a great deal of time coordinating the activities of their unit with those of other units or organizations. They confer with higher levels of management; with financial, production, marketing, and other managers; and with contractors and equipment and materials suppliers.

Engineering managers may supervise people who design and develop machinery, products, systems, and processes. They might also direct and coordinate production, operations, quality assurance, testing, or maintenance in industrial plants. Many are plant engineers, who direct and coordinate the design, installation, operation, and maintenance of equipment and machinery in industrial plants. Others manage research and development teams that produce new products and processes or improve existing ones.

Natural sciences managers oversee the work of life and physical scientists, including agricultural scientists, chemists, biologists, geologists, medical scientists, and physicists. These managers direct research and development projects and coordinate activities such as testing, quality control, and production. They may work on basic research projects or on commercial activities. Science managers sometimes conduct their own research in addition to managing the work of others.

Work environment. Engineering and natural sciences managers spend most of their time in an office. Some managers, however, also may work in laboratories, where they may be exposed to the same conditions as research scientists, or in industrial plants, where they may be exposed to the same conditions as production workers. Most managers work at least 40 hours a week and may work much longer on occasion to meet project deadlines. Some may experience considerable pressure to meet technical or scientific goals on a short deadline or within a tight budget.

Training, Other Qualifications, and Advancement

Strong technical knowledge is essential for engineering and natural sciences managers, who must understand and guide the work of their subordinates and explain the work in nontechnical terms to senior management and potential customers. Therefore, most managers have formal education and work experience as an engineer, scientist, or mathematician.

Education and training. These managers usually have education similar to that of the workers they supervise. Most engineering managers, for example, begin their careers as engineers after completing a bachelor's degree in the field. Many engineers gain business management skills by completing a master's degree in engineering management (MEM) or business administration (MBA). Employers often pay for such training. In large firms, some courses required in these degree programs may be offered onsite. Typically, engineers who prefer to manage in technical areas pursue an MEM, and those interested in less technical management earn an MBA.

Similarly, many science managers begin their careers as scientists, such as chemists, biologists, geologists, or mathematicians. Most scientists and mathematicians engaged in basic research have a Ph.D. degree; some who work in applied research and other activities may have a bachelor's or master's degree. Graduate programs allow scientists to augment their undergraduate training with instruction in other fields, such as management or computer technology. Natural science managers interested in more technical management may earn traditional master's or Ph.D. degrees in natural sciences or master's degrees in science that incorporate business management skills. Those interested in more general management may pursue an MBA. Given the rapid pace of scientific developments, science managers must continuously upgrade their knowledge.

Other qualifications. Engineering and natural sciences managers must be specialists in the work they supervise. To advance to these positions, engineers and scientists generally must gain experience and assume management responsibility. To fill management positions, employers seek engineers and scientists who possess administrative and communication skills in addition to technical knowledge in their specialty. In fact, because engineering and natural sciences managers must effectively lead groups and coordinate projects, they usually need excellent communication and administrative skills.

Advancement. Engineering and natural sciences managers may advance to progressively higher leadership positions within their disciplines. Some may become managers in nontechnical areas such as marketing, human resources, or sales. In high-technology firms, managers in nontechnical areas often must possess the same specialized knowledge as do managers in technical areas. For example, employers in an engineering firm may prefer to hire experienced engineers as sales workers because the complex services offered by the firm can be marketed only by someone with specialized engineering knowledge. Such sales workers could eventually advance to jobs as sales managers.

Employment

Engineering and natural sciences managers held about 228,000 jobs in 2006. Manufacturing industries employed 38 percent of engineering and natural sciences managers. Manufacturing industries with the largest employment are those that produce computer and electronic equipment and those that produce transportation equipment, including aerospace products and parts. Another 31 percent worked in professional, scientific, and technical services industries, primarily for firms providing architectural, engineering, and related services and firms providing scientific research and development services. Other large employers include federal, state, and local government agencies.

Projections data from the National Employment Matrix

Occupational Title	SOC Code	Employment, 2006	Projected employment, 2016	Change, 2006-16	
				Number	Percent
Engineering and natural sciences managers	—	228,000	246,000	18,000	8
Engineering managers	11-9041	187,000	201,000	14,000	7
Natural sciences managers	11-9121	41,000	45,000	4,600	11

NOTE: Data in this table are rounded.

Job Outlook

Employment of engineering and natural sciences managers is projected to grow about as fast as the average for all occupations, similar to the growth rate of engineers and life and physical scientists. Opportunities will be best for workers with strong communication and business management skills.

Employment change. Employment of engineering and natural sciences managers is expected to grow 8 percent over the 2006–2016 decade, about as fast as the average for all occupations. Projected employment growth for engineering and natural sciences managers should be in line with the growth of the engineers and scientists they supervise and the industries in which they work. Because many employers find it more efficient to contract engineering and science work to specialty firms, there should be strong demand for engineering managers in the scientific research and development services industry and for both engineering and natural science managers in the architectural, engineering, and related services industry.

Job prospects. Opportunities for engineering managers should be better in rapidly growing areas of engineering, such as environmental and biomedical engineering, than in more slowly growing areas, such as electronics and materials engineering. Opportunities for natural sciences managers should likewise be best in the rapidly growing medical and environmental sciences. (See the statements on engineers and life and physical scientists elsewhere in this book.) Engineers and scientists with advanced technical knowledge and strong communication skills will be in the best position to become managers. Because engineering and natural sciences managers are involved in the financial, production, and marketing activities of their firm, business management skills are also advantageous for those seeking management positions. In addition to those openings resulting from employment growth, job openings will result from the need to replace managers who retire or move into other occupations.

Earnings

Earnings for engineering and natural sciences managers vary by specialty and by level of responsibility. Median annual earnings of wage and salary engineering managers were $105,430 in May 2006. The middle 50 percent earned between $84,090 and $130,170. Median annual earnings in the industries employing the largest numbers of engineering managers were

Semiconductor and other electronic component manufacturing $120,740
Federal executive branch 116,140
Navigational, measuring, electromedical, and control instruments manufacturing 115,150
Aerospace product and parts manufacturing..........111,020
Engineering services..103,570

Median annual earnings of wage and salary natural sciences managers were $100,080 in May 2006. The middle 50 percent earned between $77,320 and $130,900. Median annual earnings in the industries employing the largest numbers of natural sciences managers were

Research and development in the physical, engineering, and life sciences $120,780
Pharmaceutical and medicine manufacturing 111,070
Federal executive branch 96,100
Architectural, engineering, and related services......88,990
State government 65,570

In addition, engineering and natural sciences managers, especially those at higher levels, often receive more benefits—such as expense accounts, stock option plans, and bonuses—than do nonmanagerial workers in their organizations.

Related Occupations

The work of engineering and natural sciences managers is closely related to that of engineers; mathematicians; and physical and life scientists, including agricultural and food scientists, atmospheric scientists, biological scientists, conservation scientists and foresters, chemists and materials scientists, environmental scientists and hydrologists, geoscientists, medical scientists, and physicists and astronomers. It also is related to the work of other managers, especially top executives.

Sources of Additional Information

For information about a career as an engineering and natural sciences manager, contact the sources of additional information for engineers, life scientists, and physical scientists that are listed at the end of statements on these occupations elsewhere in this book.

Additional information on science and engineering master's degrees is available from

- Commission on Professionals in Science and Technology, 1200 New York Ave. NW, Suite 113, Washington, DC 20005. Internet: http://www.sciencemasters.org

To learn more about managing scientists and engineers in research and development, see the *Occupational Outlook Quarterly* article "Careers for scientists—and others—in scientific research and development," online at http://www.bls.gov/opub/ooq/2005/summer/art04.htm and in print at many libraries and career centers.

STEM Engineering Technicians

(O*NET 17-3021.00, 17-3022.00, 17-3023.00, 17-3023.01, 17-3023.02, 17-3023.03, 17-3024.00, 17-3025.00, 17-3026.00, 17-3027.00, and 17-3029.99)

Significant Points

- Because the type and quality of training programs vary considerably, prospective students should carefully investigate training programs before enrolling.
- Electrical and electronic engineering technicians make up 33 percent of all engineering technicians.
- Employment of engineering technicians often is influenced by the same economic conditions that affect engineers; as a result, job outlook varies by specialty.
- Opportunities will be best for individuals with an associate degree or extensive job training in engineering technology.

Nature of the Work

Engineering technicians use the principles and theories of science, engineering, and mathematics to solve technical problems in research and development, manufacturing, sales, construction, inspection, and maintenance. Their work is more narrowly focused and application-oriented than that of scientists and engineers. Many engineering technicians assist engineers and scientists, especially in research and development. Others work in quality control, inspecting products and processes, conducting tests, or collecting data. In manufacturing, they may assist in product design, development, or production.

Engineering technicians who work in research and development build or set up equipment; prepare and conduct experiments; collect data; calculate or record results; and help engineers or scientists in other ways, such as making prototype versions of newly designed equipment. They also assist in design work, often using computer-aided design and drafting (CADD) equipment.

Most engineering technicians specialize, learning skills and working in the same disciplines as engineers. Occupational titles, therefore, tend to reflect this similarity. This book does not cover in detail some branches of engineering technology, such as chemical engineering technology (the development of new chemical products and processes) and bioengineering technology (the development and implementation of biomedical equipment), for which there are accredited programs of study.

Aerospace engineering and operations technicians construct, test, and maintain aircraft and space vehicles. They may calibrate test equipment and determine causes of equipment malfunctions. Using computer and communications systems, aerospace engineering and operations technicians often record and interpret test data.

Civil engineering technicians help civil engineers plan and oversee the building of highways, buildings, bridges, dams, wastewater treatment systems, and other structures and do related research. Some estimate construction costs and specify materials to be used, and some may even prepare drawings or perform land-surveying duties. Others may set up and monitor instruments used to study traffic conditions. (Drafters and surveying occupations are covered elsewhere in this book.)

Electrical and electronics engineering technicians help design, develop, test, and manufacture electrical and electronic equipment such as communication equipment; radar, industrial, and medical monitoring or control devices; navigational equipment; and computers. They may work in product evaluation and testing, using measuring and diagnostic devices to adjust, test, and repair equipment. (Workers whose jobs primarily involve repairing electrical and electronic equipment are often are referred to as electronics technicians, but they are included with electrical and electronics installers and repairers discussed elsewhere in this book.)

Electromechanical engineering technicians combine knowledge of mechanical engineering technology with knowledge of electrical and electronic circuits to design, develop, test, and manufacture electronic and computer-controlled mechanical systems. Their work often overlaps that of both electrical and electronics engineering technicians and mechanical engineering technicians.

Environmental engineering technicians work closely with environmental engineers and scientists in developing methods and devices used in the prevention, control, or correction of environmental hazards. They inspect and maintain equipment related to air pollution and recycling. Some inspect water and wastewater treatment systems to ensure that pollution control requirements are met.

Industrial engineering technicians study the efficient use of personnel, materials, and machines in factories, stores, repair shops, and offices. They prepare layouts of machinery and equipment, plan the flow of work, conduct statistical studies of production time or quality, and analyze production costs.

Mechanical engineering technicians help engineers design, develop, test, and manufacture industrial machinery, consumer products, and other equipment. They may assist in product tests by, for example, setting up instrumentation for auto crash tests. They may make sketches and rough layouts, record and analyze data, make calculations and estimates, and report on their findings. When planning production, mechanical engineering technicians prepare layouts and drawings of the assembly process and of parts to be manufactured. They estimate labor costs, equipment life, and plant space. Some test and inspect machines and equipment or work with engineers to eliminate production problems.

Work environment. Most engineering technicians work 40 hours a week in laboratories, offices, manufacturing or industrial plants, or on construction sites. Some may be exposed to hazards from equipment, chemicals, or toxic materials.

Training, Other Qualifications, and Advancement

Most engineering technicians enter the occupation with an associate degree in engineering technology. Training is available at technical institutes, community colleges, extension divisions of colleges and universities, public and private vocational-technical schools, and in the Armed Forces. Because the type and quality of training programs vary considerably, prospective students should carefully investigate training programs before enrolling.

Education and training. Although it may be possible to qualify for certain engineering technician jobs without formal training, most employers prefer to hire someone with at least a two-year associate degree in engineering technology. People with college courses in science, engineering, and mathematics may qualify for some positions but may need additional specialized training and experience. Prospective engineering technicians should take as many high school science and math courses as possible to prepare for programs in engineering technology after high school.

Most two-year associate degree programs accredited by the Technology Accreditation Commission of the Accreditation Board for

Engineering and Technology (ABET) include at least college algebra and trigonometry and one or two basic science courses. Depending on the specialty, more math or science may be required. About 710 ABET-accredited programs are offered in engineering technology specialties.

The type of technical courses required depends on the specialty. For example, prospective mechanical engineering technicians may take courses in fluid mechanics, thermodynamics, and mechanical design; electrical engineering technicians may need classes in electrical circuits, microprocessors, and digital electronics; and those preparing to work in environmental engineering technology need courses in environmental regulations and safe handling of hazardous materials.

Many publicly and privately operated schools provide technical training, but the type and quality of training vary considerably. Therefore, prospective students should carefully select a program in line with their goals. They should ascertain prospective employers' preferences and ask schools to provide information about the kinds of jobs obtained by program graduates, about instructional facilities and equipment, and about faculty qualifications. Graduates of ABET-accredited programs usually are recognized as having achieved an acceptable level of competence in the mathematics, science, and technical courses required for this occupation.

Technical institutes offer intensive technical training through application and practice, but they provide less theory and general education than do community colleges. Many technical institutes offer two-year associate degree programs and are similar to or part of a community college or state university system. Other technical institutes are run by private organizations, with programs that vary considerably in length and types of courses offered.

Community colleges offer curriculums that are similar to those in technical institutes but include more theory and liberal arts. There may be little or no difference between programs at technical institutes and community colleges, as both offer associate degrees. After completing the two-year program, some graduates get jobs as engineering technicians, whereas others continue their education at four-year colleges. However, an associate degree in pre-engineering is different from one in engineering technology. Students who enroll in a two-year pre-engineering program may find it very difficult to find work as an engineering technician if they decide not to enter a four-year engineering program because pre-engineering programs usually focus less on hands-on applications and more on academic preparatory work. Conversely, graduates of two-year engineering technology programs may not receive credit for some of the courses they have taken if they choose to transfer to a four-year engineering program. Colleges having four-year programs usually do not offer engineering technician training, but college courses in science, engineering, and mathematics are useful for obtaining a job as an engineering technician. Many four-year colleges offer bachelor's degrees in engineering technology, but graduates of these programs often are hired to work as technologists or applied engineers, not technicians.

Area vocational-technical schools, another source of technical training, include postsecondary public institutions that serve local students and emphasize training needed by local employers. Most require a high school diploma or its equivalent for admission.

Other training in technical areas may be obtained in the Armed Forces. Many military technical training programs are highly regarded by employers. However, skills acquired in military programs are often narrowly focused and may be of limited applicability in civilian industry, which often requires broader training. Therefore, some additional training may be needed, depending on the acquired skills and the kind of job.

Other qualifications. Because many engineering technicians assist in design work, creativity is desirable. Good communication skills and the ability to work well with others also are important as engineering technicians are typically part of a team of engineers and other technicians.

Certification and advancement. Although employers usually do not require engineering technicians to be certified, such certification may provide jobseekers a competitive advantage. The National Institute for Certification in Engineering Technologies has established voluntary certification programs for several engineering technology specialties. Certification is available at various levels, each level combining a written examination in a specialty with a certain amount of job-related experience, a supervisory evaluation, and a recommendation.

Engineering technicians usually begin by performing routine duties under the close supervision of an experienced technician, technologist, engineer, or scientist. As they gain experience, they are given more difficult assignments with only general supervision. Some engineering technicians eventually become supervisors.

Employment

Engineering technicians held 511,000 jobs in 2006. Approximately 33 percent were electrical and electronics engineering technicians, as indicated by the following tabulation.

Electrical and electronic engineering technicians	170,000
Civil engineering technicians	91,000
Industrial engineering technicians	75,000
Mechanical engineering technicians	48,000
Environmental engineering technicians	21,000
Electro-mechanical technicians	16,000
Aerospace engineering and operations technicians	8,500
Engineering technicians, except drafters, all other	82,000

About 35 percent of all engineering technicians worked in manufacturing, mainly in the computer and electronic equipment, transportation equipment, and machinery manufacturing industries. Another 25 percent worked in professional, scientific, and technical service industries, mostly in engineering or business services companies that do engineering work on contract for government, manufacturing firms, or other organizations.

In 2006, the federal government employed 37,000 engineering technicians. State governments employed 29,000, and local governments employed 25,000.

Job Outlook

Overall employment of engineering technicians is expected to grow about as fast as the average for all occupations, but projected growth and job prospects vary by specialty. Opportunities will be best for individuals with an associate degree or extensive job training in engineering technology.

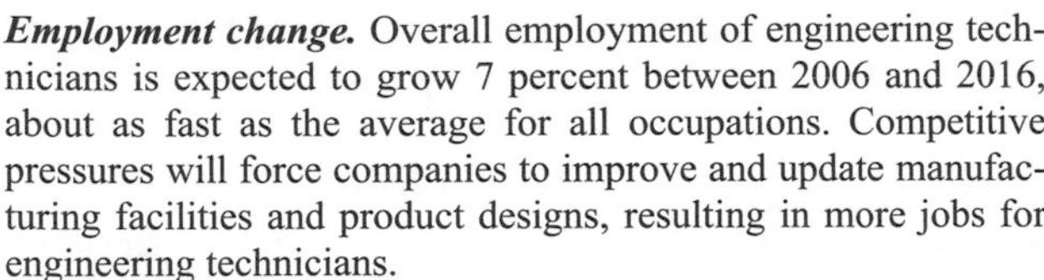

Employment change. Overall employment of engineering technicians is expected to grow 7 percent between 2006 and 2016, about as fast as the average for all occupations. Competitive pressures will force companies to improve and update manufacturing facilities and product designs, resulting in more jobs for engineering technicians.

Growth of engineering technician employment in some design functions may be dampened by increasing globalization of the development process. To reduce costs and speed project completion, some companies may relocate part of their development operations to facilities overseas, impacting both engineers and engineering technicians—particularly in electronics and computer-related specialties. However, much of the work of engineering technicians requires on-site presence, so demand for engineering technicians within the U.S. should continue to grow—particularly in the environmental, civil, and industrial specialties.

Because engineering technicians work closely with engineers, employment of engineering technicians is often influenced by the same local and national economic conditions that affect engineers. As a result, the employment outlook varies with industry and specialization.

Aerospace engineering and operations technicians are expected to have 10 percent employment growth between 2006 and 2016, about as fast as the average for all occupations. Increases in the number and scope of military aerospace projects likely will generate new jobs. New technologies to be used on commercial aircraft produced during the next decade should also spur demand for these workers.

Civil engineering technicians are expected to have 10 percent employment growth between 2006 and 2016, about as fast as the average for all occupations. Spurred by population growth and the related need to improve the nation's infrastructure, more civil engineering technicians will be needed to expand transportation, water supply, and pollution control systems, as well as large buildings and building complexes. They also will be needed to repair or replace existing roads, bridges, and other public structures.

Electrical and electronic engineering technicians are expected to have 4 percent employment growth between 2006 and 2016, more slowly than the average for all occupations. Although rising demand for electronic goods—including communications equipment, defense-related equipment, medical electronics, and consumer products—should continue to drive demand, foreign competition in design and manufacturing will limit employment growth.

Electro-mechanical technicians are expected to have 3 percent employment growth between 2006 and 2016, more slowly than the average for all occupations. As with the closely-related electrical and electronic engineering technicians and mechanical engineering technicians, job growth should be driven by increasing demand for electro-mechanical products such as unmanned aircraft and robotic equipment. However, growth will be tempered by advances in productivity and strong foreign competition.

Environmental engineering technicians are expected to have 25 percent employment growth between 2006 and 2016, much faster than the average for all occupations. More environmental engineering technicians will be needed to comply with environmental regulations and to develop methods of cleaning up existing hazards. A shift in emphasis toward preventing problems rather than controlling those that already exist, as well as increasing public health concerns resulting from population growth, also will spur demand.

Industrial engineering technicians are expected to have 10 percent employment growth between 2006 and 2016, about as fast as the average for all occupations. As firms continue to seek new means of reducing costs and increasing productivity, demand for industrial engineering technicians to analyze and improve production processes should increase. This should lead to some job growth even in manufacturing industries with slowly growing or declining employment.

Mechanical engineering technicians are expected to have 6 percent employment growth between 2006 and 2016, more slowly than the average for all occupations. As mechanical products and components become increasingly complex, demand for improvements in these products should drive employment growth of mechanical engineering technicians. However, growth is expected to be limited by foreign competition in both design services and manufacturing.

Job prospects. Job prospects will vary by specialty and location, depending on the health and composition of local industry. In general, opportunities will be best for individuals with an associate degree or extensive job training in engineering technology. As technology becomes more sophisticated, employers will continue to look for technicians who are skilled in new technology and require little additional training. An increase in the number of jobs related to public health and safety should create job opportunities for engineering technicians with the appropriate training and certification. In addition to openings from job growth, many job openings will stem from the need to replace technicians who retire or leave the labor force.

Projections data from the National Employment Matrix

Occupational Title	SOC Code	Employment, 2006	Projected employment, 2016	Change, 2006-2016	
				Number	Percent
Engineering technicians, except drafters	17-3020	511,000	545,000	34,000	7
Aerospace engineering and operations technicians	17-3021	8,500	9,400	900	10
Civil engineering technicians	17-3022	91,000	100,000	9,200	10
Electrical and electronic engineering technicians	17-3023	170,000	177,000	6,100	4
Electro-mechanical technicians	17-3024	16,000	16,000	400	3
Environmental engineering technicians	17-3025	21,000	26,000	5,200	25
Industrial engineering technicians	17-3026	75,000	82,000	7,500	10
Mechanical engineering technicians	17-3027	48,000	51,000	3,100	6
Engineering technicians, except drafters, all other	17-3029	82,000	83,000	1,600	2

NOTE: Data in this table are rounded.

Earnings

Median annual earnings in May 2006 of engineering technicians by specialty are shown in the following tabulation.

Aerospace engineering and operations technicians	$53,300
Electrical and electronic engineering technicians	50,660
Industrial engineering technicians	46,810
Mechanical engineering technicians	45,850
Electro-mechanical technicians	44,720
Civil engineering technicians	40,560
Environmental engineering technicians	40,560

Median annual earnings of wage-and-salary electrical and electronics engineering technicians were $50,660 in May 2006. The middle 50 percent earned between $39,270 and $60,470. The lowest 10 percent earned less than $30,120, and the highest 10 percent earned more than $73,200. Median annual earnings in the industries employing the largest numbers of electrical and electronics engineering technicians are:

Wired telecommunications carriers	$54,780
Engineering services	48,330
Semiconductor and other electronic component manufacturing	45,720
Navigational, measuring, electromedical, and control instruments manufacturing	45,140
Employment services	38,910

Median annual earnings of wage-and-salary civil engineering technicians were $40,560 in May 2006. The middle 50 percent earned between $31,310 and $51,230. The lowest 10 percent earned less than $25,250, and the highest 10 percent earned more than $62,920. Median annual earnings in the industries employing the largest numbers of civil engineering technicians are:

Local government	$45,800
Architectural services	42,310
Engineering services	41,180
State government	35,870
Testing laboratories	31,800

In May 2006, the median annual salary for aerospace engineering and operations technicians in the aerospace products and parts manufacturing industry was $52,060, and the median annual salary for environmental engineering technicians in the architectural, engineering, and related services industry was $38,060. The median annual salary for industrial engineering technicians in the aerospace product and parts manufacturing industry was $57,330. In the architectural, engineering, and related services industry, the median annual salary for mechanical engineering technicians was $43,920. Electro-mechanical technicians earned a median salary of $41,550 in the navigational, measuring, electromedical, and control instruments manufacturing industry.

Related Occupations

Engineering technicians apply scientific and engineering skills usually gained in postsecondary programs below the bachelor's degree level. Similar occupations include science technicians; drafters; surveyors, cartographers, photogrammetrists, and surveying technicians; and broadcast and sound engineering technicians and radio operators.

Sources of Additional Information

For information about careers in engineering technology, contact

- JETS (Junior Engineering Technical Society) Guidance, 1420 King St., Suite 405, Alexandria, VA 22314. Internet: http://www.jets.org

Information on engineering technology programs accredited by the Accreditation Board for Engineering and Technology is available from

- ABET, Inc., 111 Market Place, Suite 1050, Baltimore, MD 21202. Internet: http://www.abet.org

Information on certification, as well as job and career information, is available from

- National Institute for Certification in Engineering Technologies, 1420 King St., Alexandria, VA 22314. Internet: http://www.nicet.org

STEM Engineers

(O*NET 17-2011.00, 17-2021.00, 17-2031.00, 17-2041.00, 17-2051.00, 17-2061.00, 17-2071.00, 17-2072.00, 17-2081.00, 17-2111.00, 17-2111.01, 17-2111.02, 17-2111.03, 17-2112.00, 17-2121.00, 17-2121.01, 17-2121.02, 17-2131.00, 17-2141.00, 17-2151.00, 17-2161.00, 17-2171.00, and 17-2199.99)

Significant Points

- Overall job opportunities in engineering are expected to be good, but will vary by specialty.
- A bachelor's degree in engineering is required for most entry-level jobs.
- Starting salaries are among the highest of all college graduates.
- Continuing education is critical for engineers as technology evolves.

Nature of the Work

Engineers apply the principles of science and mathematics to develop economical solutions to technical problems. Their work is the link between scientific discoveries and the commercial applications that meet societal and consumer needs.

Many engineers develop new products. During this process, they consider several factors. For example, in developing an industrial robot, engineers precisely specify the functional requirements; design and test the robot's components; integrate the components to produce the final design; and evaluate the design's overall effectiveness, cost, reliability, and safety. This process applies to the development of many different products, such as chemicals, computers, power plants, helicopters, and toys.

In addition to design and development, many engineers work in testing, production, or maintenance. These engineers supervise production in factories, determine the causes of component failure, and test manufactured products to maintain quality. They also estimate the time and cost to complete projects. Supervisory engineers are responsible for major components or entire projects. (See the statement on engineering and natural sciences managers elsewhere in this book.)

Engineers use computers extensively to produce and analyze designs; to simulate and test how a machine, structure, or system operates; to generate specifications for parts; and to monitor product quality and control process efficiency. Nanotechnology, which involves the creation of high-performance materials and components by integrating atoms and molecules, also is introducing entirely new principles to the design process.

Most engineers specialize. Following are details on the 17 engineering specialties covered in the federal government's Standard Occupational Classification (SOC) system. Numerous other specialties are recognized by professional societies, and each of the major branches of engineering has numerous subdivisions. Civil engineering, for example, includes structural and transportation engineering, and materials engineering includes ceramic, metallurgical, and polymer engineering. Engineers also may specialize in one industry, such as motor vehicles, or in one type of technology, such as turbines or semiconductor materials.

Aerospace engineers design, develop, and test aircraft, spacecraft, and missiles and supervise the manufacture of these products. Those who work with aircraft are called *aeronautical engineers,* and those working specifically with spacecraft are *astronautical engineers*. Aerospace engineers develop new technologies for use in aviation, defense systems, and space exploration, often specializing in areas such as structural design, guidance, navigation and control, instrumentation and communication, or production methods. They also may specialize in a particular type of aerospace product, such as commercial aircraft, military fighter jets, helicopters, spacecraft, or missiles and rockets, and may become experts in aerodynamics, thermodynamics, celestial mechanics, propulsion, acoustics, or guidance and control systems.

Agricultural engineers apply knowledge of engineering technology and science to agriculture and the efficient use of biological resources. Because of this, they are also referred to as *biological and agricultural engineers*. They design agricultural machinery, equipment, sensors, processes, and structures, such as those used for crop storage. Some engineers specialize in areas such as power systems and machinery design; structures and environment engineering; and food and bioprocess engineering. They develop ways to conserve soil and water and to improve the processing of agricultural products. Agricultural engineers often work in research and development, production, sales, or management.

Biomedical engineers develop devices and procedures that solve medical and health-related problems by combining their knowledge of biology and medicine with engineering principles and practices. Many do research, along with life scientists, chemists, and medical scientists, to develop and evaluate systems and products such as artificial organs, prostheses (artificial devices that replace missing body parts), instrumentation, medical information systems, and health management and care delivery systems. Biomedical engineers may also design devices used in various medical procedures, imaging systems such as magnetic resonance imaging (MRI), and devices for automating insulin injections or controlling body functions. Most engineers in this specialty need a sound background in another engineering specialty, such as mechanical or electronics engineering, in addition to specialized biomedical training. Some specialties within biomedical engineering include biomaterials, biomechanics, medical imaging, rehabilitation engineering, and orthopedic engineering.

Chemical engineers apply the principles of chemistry to solve problems involving the production or use of chemicals and biochemicals. They design equipment and processes for large-scale chemical manufacturing, plan and test methods of manufacturing products and treating byproducts, and supervise production. Chemical engineers also work in a variety of manufacturing industries other than chemical manufacturing, such as those producing energy, electronics, food, clothing, and paper. They also work in health care, biotechnology, and business services. Chemical engineers apply principles of physics, mathematics, and mechanical and electrical engineering, as well as chemistry. Some may specialize in a particular chemical process, such as oxidation or polymerization. Others specialize in a particular field, such as nanomaterials, or in the development of specific products. They must be aware of all aspects of chemicals manufacturing and how the manufacturing process affects the environment and the safety of workers and consumers.

Civil engineers design and supervise the construction of roads, buildings, airports, tunnels, dams, bridges, and water supply and sewage systems. They must consider many factors in the design process, from the construction costs and expected lifetime of a project to government regulations and potential environmental hazards such as earthquakes and hurricanes. Civil engineering, considered one of the oldest engineering disciplines, encompasses many specialties. The major ones are structural, water resources, construction, environmental, transportation, and geotechnical engineering. Many civil engineers hold supervisory or administrative positions, from supervisor of a construction site to city engineer. Others may work in design, construction, research, and teaching.

Computer hardware engineers research, design, develop, test, and oversee the manufacture and installation of computer hardware. Hardware includes computer chips, circuit boards, computer systems, and related equipment such as keyboards, modems, and printers. (Computer software engineers—often simply called computer engineers—design and develop the software systems that control computers. These workers are covered elsewhere in this book.) The work of computer hardware engineers is very similar to that of electronics engineers in that they may design and test circuits and other electronic components, but computer hardware engineers do that work only as it relates to computers and computer-related equipment. The rapid advances in computer technology are largely a result of the research, development, and design efforts of these engineers.

Electrical engineers design, develop, test, and supervise the manufacture of electrical equipment. Some of this equipment includes electric motors; machinery controls, lighting, and wiring in buildings; automobiles; aircraft; radar and navigation systems; and power generation, control, and transmission devices used by electric utilities. Although the terms electrical and electronics engineering often are used interchangeably in academia and industry, electrical engineers have traditionally focused on the generation and supply of power, whereas electronics engineers have worked on applications of electricity to control systems or signal processing. Electrical engineers specialize in areas such as power systems engineering or electrical equipment manufacturing.

Electronics engineers, except computer are responsible for a wide range of technologies, from portable music players to the global positioning system (GPS), which can continuously provide the location, for example, of a vehicle. Electronics engineers design, develop, test, and supervise the manufacture of electronic equipment such as broadcast and communications systems. Many electronics engineers also work in areas closely related to computers. However, engineers whose work is related exclusively to computer hardware are considered computer hardware engineers. Electronics engineers specialize in areas such as communications, signal processing, and control systems or have a specialty within one of these areas—control systems or aviation electronics, for example.

Environmental engineers develop solutions to environmental problems using the principles of biology and chemistry. They are involved in water and air pollution control, recycling, waste disposal, and public health issues. Environmental engineers conduct hazardous-waste management studies in which they evaluate the significance of the hazard, advise on treatment and containment, and develop regulations to prevent mishaps. They design municipal water supply and industrial wastewater treatment systems. They conduct research on the environmental impact of proposed construction projects, analyze scientific data, and perform quality-control checks. Environmental engineers are concerned with local and worldwide environmental issues. They study and attempt to minimize the effects of acid rain, global warming, automobile emissions, and ozone depletion. They may also be involved in the protection of wildlife. Many environmental engineers work as consultants, helping their clients to comply with regulations, to prevent environmental damage, and to clean up hazardous sites.

Health and safety engineers, except mining safety engineers and inspectors prevent harm to people and property by applying knowledge of systems engineering and mechanical, chemical, and human performance principles. Using this specialized knowledge, they identify and measure potential hazards, such as the risk of fires or the dangers involved in handling of toxic chemicals. They recommend appropriate loss prevention measures according to the probability of harm and potential damage. Health and safety engineers develop procedures and designs to reduce the risk of illness, injury, or damage. Some work in manufacturing industries to ensure the designs of new products do not create unnecessary hazards. They must be able to anticipate, recognize, and evaluate hazardous conditions, as well as develop hazard control methods.

Industrial engineers determine the most effective ways to use the basic factors of production—people, machines, materials, information, and energy—to make a product or provide a service. They are primarily concerned with increasing productivity through the management of people, methods of business organization, and technology. To maximize efficiency, industrial engineers carefully study the product requirements and design manufacturing and information systems to meet those requirements with the help of mathematical methods and models. They develop management control systems to aid in financial planning and cost analysis, and design production planning and control systems to coordinate activities and ensure product quality. They also design or improve systems for the physical distribution of goods and services and determine the most efficient plant locations. Industrial engineers develop wage and salary administration systems and job evaluation programs. Many industrial engineers move into management positions because the work is closely related to the work of managers.

Marine engineers and naval architects are involved in the design, construction, and maintenance of ships, boats, and related equipment. They design and supervise the construction of everything from aircraft carriers to submarines, and from sailboats to tankers. Naval architects work on the basic design of ships, including hull form and stability. Marine engineers work on the propulsion, steering, and other systems of ships. Marine engineers and naval architects apply knowledge from a range of fields to the entire design and production process of all water vehicles. Other workers who operate or supervise the operation of marine machinery on ships and other vessels sometimes may be called marine engineers or, more frequently, ship engineers, but they do different work.

Materials engineers are involved in the development, processing, and testing of the materials used to create a range of products, from computer chips and aircraft wings to golf clubs and snow skis. They work with metals, ceramics, plastics, semiconductors, and composites to create new materials that meet certain mechanical, electrical, and chemical requirements. They also are involved in selecting materials for new applications. Materials engineers have developed the ability to create and then study materials at an atomic level, using advanced processes to replicate the characteristics of materials and their components with computers. Most materials engineers specialize in a particular material. For example, metallurgical engineers specialize in metals such as steel, and ceramic engineers develop ceramic materials and the processes for making them into useful products such as glassware or fiber optic communication lines.

Mechanical engineers research, design, develop, manufacture, and test tools, engines, machines, and other mechanical devices. Mechanical engineering is one of the broadest engineering disciplines. Engineers in this discipline work on power-producing machines such as electric generators, internal combustion engines, and steam and gas turbines. They also work on power-using machines such as refrigeration and air-conditioning equipment, machine tools, material handling systems, elevators and escalators, industrial production equipment, and robots used in manufacturing. Mechanical engineers also design tools that other engineers need for their work. In addition, mechanical engineers work in manufacturing or agriculture production, maintenance, or technical sales; many become administrators or managers.

Mining and geological engineers, including mining safety engineers find, extract, and prepare coal, metals, and minerals for use by manufacturing industries and utilities. They design open-pit and underground mines, supervise the construction of mine shafts and tunnels in underground operations, and devise methods for transporting minerals to processing plants. Mining engineers are responsible for the safe, economical, and environmentally sound operation of mines. Some mining engineers work with geologists and metallurgical engineers to locate and appraise new ore deposits. Others develop new mining equipment or direct mineral-processing operations that separate minerals from the dirt, rock, and other materials with which they are mixed. Mining engineers frequently specialize in the mining of one mineral or metal, such as coal or gold. With increased emphasis on protecting the environment, many mining engineers work to solve problems related to land reclamation and water and air pollution. Mining safety engineers use their knowledge of mine design and practices to ensure the safety of workers and to comply with state and federal safety regulations. They inspect walls and roof surfaces, monitor air quality, and examine mining equipment for compliance with safety practices.

Nuclear engineers research and develop the processes, instruments, and systems used to derive benefits from nuclear energy and radiation. They design, develop, monitor, and operate nuclear plants to generate power. They may work on the nuclear fuel cycle—the production, handling, and use of nuclear fuel and the safe disposal of waste produced by the generation of nuclear energy—or on the development of fusion energy. Some specialize in the development of nuclear power sources for naval vessels or spacecraft; others find industrial and medical uses for radioactive materials, as in equipment used to diagnose and treat medical problems.

Petroleum engineers search the world for reservoirs containing oil or natural gas. Once these resources are discovered, petroleum engineers work with geologists and other specialists to understand the geologic formation and properties of the rock containing the reservoir, determine the drilling methods to be used, and monitor drilling and production operations. They design equipment and processes to achieve the maximum profitable recovery of oil and gas. Because only a small proportion of oil and gas in a reservoir flows out under natural forces, petroleum engineers develop and use various enhanced recovery methods. These include injecting water, chemicals, gases, or steam into an oil reservoir to force out more of the oil and doing computer-controlled drilling or fracturing to connect a larger area of a reservoir to a single well. Because even the best techniques in use today recover only a portion of the oil and gas in a reservoir, petroleum engineers research and develop technology and methods to increase recovery and lower the cost of drilling and production operations.

Work environment. Most engineers work in office buildings, laboratories, or industrial plants. Others may spend time outdoors at construction sites and oil and gas exploration and production sites, where they monitor or direct operations or solve onsite problems. Some engineers travel extensively to plants or worksites here and abroad.

Many engineers work a standard 40-hour week. At times, deadlines or design standards may bring extra pressure to a job, requiring engineers to work longer hours.

Training, Other Qualifications, and Advancement

Engineers typically enter the occupation with a bachelor's degree in an engineering specialty, but some basic research positions may require a graduate degree. Engineers offering their services directly to the public must be licensed. Continuing education to keep current with rapidly changing technology is important for engineers.

Education and training. A bachelor's degree in engineering is required for almost all entry-level engineering jobs. College graduates with a degree in a natural science or mathematics occasionally may qualify for some engineering jobs, especially in specialties in high demand. Most engineering degrees are granted in electrical, electronics, mechanical, or civil engineering. However, engineers trained in one branch may work in related branches. For example, many aerospace engineers have training in mechanical engineering. This flexibility allows employers to meet staffing needs in new technologies and specialties in which engineers may be in short supply. It also allows engineers to shift to fields with better employment prospects or to those that more closely match their interests.

Most engineering programs involve a concentration of study in an engineering specialty, along with courses in both mathematics and the physical and life sciences. Many programs also include courses in general engineering. A design course, sometimes accompanied by a computer or laboratory class or both, is part of the curriculum of most programs. General courses not directly related to engineering, such as those in the social sciences or humanities, are also often required.

In addition to the standard engineering degree, many colleges offer two-year or four-year degree programs in engineering technology. These programs, which usually include various hands-on laboratory classes that focus on current issues in the application of engineering principles, prepare students for practical design and production work, rather than for jobs that require more theoretical and scientific knowledge. Graduates of four-year technology programs may get jobs similar to those obtained by graduates with a bachelor's degree in engineering. Engineering technology graduates, however, are not qualified to register as professional engineers under the same terms as graduates with degrees in engineering. Some employers regard technology program graduates as having skills between those of a technician and an engineer.

Graduate training is essential for engineering faculty positions and many research and development programs, but is not required for the majority of entry-level engineering jobs. Many experienced engineers obtain graduate degrees in engineering or business administration to learn new technology and broaden their education. Many high-level executives in government and industry began their careers as engineers.

About 1,830 programs at colleges and universities offer bachelor's degrees in engineering that are accredited by the Accreditation Board for Engineering and Technology (ABET), Inc., and there are another 710 accredited programs in engineering technology. ABET accreditation is based on a program's faculty, curriculum, and facilities; the achievement of a program's students; program improvements; and institutional commitment to specific principles of quality and ethics. Although most institutions offer programs in the major branches of engineering, only a few offer programs in the smaller specialties. Also, programs of the same title may vary in content. For example, some programs emphasize industrial practices, preparing students for a job in industry, whereas others are more theoretical and are designed to prepare students for graduate work. Therefore, students should investigate curriculums and check accreditations carefully before selecting a college.

Admissions requirements for undergraduate engineering schools include a solid background in mathematics (algebra, geometry, trigonometry, and calculus) and science (biology, chemistry, and physics), with courses in English, social studies, and humanities. Bachelor's degree programs in engineering typically are designed to last four years, but many students find that it takes between four and five years to complete their studies. In a typical four-year college curriculum, the first two years are spent studying mathematics, basic sciences, introductory engineering, humanities, and social sciences. In the last two years, most courses are in engineering, usually with a concentration in one specialty. Some programs offer a general engineering curriculum; students then specialize on the job or in graduate school.

Some engineering schools have agreements with two-year colleges whereby the college provides the initial engineering education, and the engineering school automatically admits students for their last two years. In addition, a few engineering schools have arrangements that allow students who spend three years in a liberal arts college studying pre-engineering subjects and two years in an engineering school studying core subjects to receive a bachelor's degree from each school. Some colleges and universities offer five-year master's degree programs. Some five-year or even six-year cooperative plans combine classroom study and practical work, permitting students to gain valuable experience and to finance part of their education.

Licensure. All 50 states and the District of Columbia require licensure for engineers who offer their services directly to the public. Engineers who are licensed are called professional engineers (PE). This licensure generally requires a degree from an ABET-accredited engineering program, four years of relevant work experience, and successful completion of a state examination. Recent graduates can start the licensing process by taking the examination in two stages. The initial Fundamentals of Engineering (FE) examination can be taken upon graduation. Engineers who pass this examination commonly are called engineers in training (EIT) or engineer interns (EI). After acquiring suitable work experience, EITs can take the second examination, the Principles and Practice of Engineering exam. Several states have imposed mandatory continuing education requirements for relicensure. Most states recognize licensure from other states, provided that the manner in which the initial license was obtained meets or exceeds their own licensure requirements. Many civil, electrical, mechanical, and chemical engineers are licensed PEs. Independent of licensure, various certification programs are offered by professional organizations to demonstrate competency in specific fields of engineering.

Other qualifications. Engineers should be creative, inquisitive, analytical, and detail oriented. They should be able to work as part of a team and to communicate well, both orally and in writing. Communication abilities are becoming increasingly important as engineers frequently interact with specialists in a wide range of fields outside engineering.

Certification and advancement. Beginning engineering graduates usually work under the supervision of experienced engineers and, in large companies, also may receive formal classroom or seminar-type training. As new engineers gain knowledge and experience, they are assigned more difficult projects with greater independence to develop designs, solve problems, and make decisions. Engineers may advance to become technical specialists or to supervise a staff or team of engineers and technicians. Some may eventually become engineering managers or enter other managerial or sales jobs. In sales, an engineering background enables them to discuss a product's technical aspects and assist in product planning, installation, and use. (See the statements under management and business and financial operations occupations, and the statement on sales engineers elsewhere in this book.)

Numerous professional certifications for engineers exist and may be beneficial for advancement to senior technical or managerial positions. Many certification programs are offered by the professional societies listed as sources of additional information for engineering specialties at the end of this statement.

Employment

In 2006, engineers held about 1.5 million jobs. The distribution of employment by engineering specialty follows:

Civil engineers 256,000
Mechanical engineers 227,000
Industrial engineers 201,000
Electrical engineers 153,000
Electronics engineers, except computer 138,000
Aerospace engineers 90,000
Computer hardware engineers 79,000
Environmental engineers 54,000
Chemical engineers 30,000
Health and safety engineers, except mining safety engineers and inspectors 25,000
Materials engineers 22,000
Petroleum engineers 17,000
Nuclear engineers 15,000
Biomedical engineers 14,000
Marine engineers and naval architects 9,200
Mining and geological engineers, including mining safety engineers 7,100
Agricultural engineers 3,100
All other engineers 170,000

About 37 percent of engineering jobs were found in manufacturing industries and another 28 percent were in the professional, scientific, and technical services sector, primarily in architectural, engineering, and related services. Many engineers also worked in the construction, telecommunications, and wholesale trade industries.

Federal, state, and local governments employed about 12 percent of engineers in 2006. About half of these were in the federal government, mainly in the U.S. Departments of Defense, Transportation, Agriculture, Interior, and Energy, and in the National Aeronautics and Space Administration. Most engineers in state and local government agencies worked in highway and public works departments. In 2006, about 3 percent of engineers were self-employed, many as consultants.

Engineers are employed in every state, in small and large cities and in rural areas. Some branches of engineering are concentrated in particular industries and geographic areas—for example, petroleum engineering jobs tend to be located in areas with sizable petroleum deposits, such as Texas, Louisiana, Oklahoma, Alaska, and California. Others, such as civil engineering, are widely dispersed, and engineers in these fields often move from place to place to work on different projects.

Engineers are employed in every major industry. The industries employing the most engineers in each specialty are given in table 1, along with the percent of occupational employment in the industry.

Job Outlook

Employment of engineers is expected to grow about as fast as the average for all occupations over the next decade, but growth will vary by specialty. Environmental engineers should experience the fastest growth, while civil engineers should see the largest employment increase. Overall job opportunities in engineering are expected to be good.

Overall employment change. Overall engineering employment is expected to grow by 11 percent over the 2006–2016 decade, about as fast as the average for all occupations. Engineers have traditionally been concentrated in slower growing or declining manufacturing industries, in which they will continue to be needed to design, build, test, and improve manufactured products. However, increasing employment of engineers in faster growing service industries should generate most of the employment growth. Job outlook varies by engineering specialty, as discussed later.

Table 1. Percent concentration of engineering specialty employment in key industries, 2006

Specialty	Industry	Percent
Aerospace engineers	Aerospace product and parts manufacturing	49
Agricultural engineers	Food manufacturing	25
	Architectural, engineering, and related services	15
Biomedical engineers	Medical equipment and supplies manufacturing	20
	Scientific research and development services	20
Chemical engineers	Chemical manufacturing	29
	Architectural, engineering, and related services	15
Civil engineers	Architectural, engineering, and related services	49
Computer hardware engineers	Computer and electronic product manufacturing	41
	Computer systems design and related services	19
Electrical engineers	Architectural, engineering, and related services	21
Electronics engineers, except computer	Computer and electronic product manufacturing	26
	Telecommunications	15
Environmental engineers	Architectural, engineering, and related services	29
	State and local government	21
Health and safety engineers, except mining safety engineers and inspectors	State and local government	10
Industrial engineers	Transportation equipment manufacturing	18
	Machinery manufacturing	8
Marine engineers and naval architects	Architectural, engineering, and related services	29
Materials engineers	Primary metal manufacturing	11
	Semiconductor and other electronic component manufacturing	9
Mechanical engineers	Architectural, engineering, and related services	22
	Transportation equipment manufacturing	14
Mining and geological engineers, including mining safety engineers	Mining	58
Nuclear engineers	Research and development in the physical, engineering, and life sciences	30
	Electric power generation, transmission, and distribution	27
Petroleum engineers	Oil and gas extraction	43

Competitive pressures and advancing technology will force companies to improve and update product designs and to optimize their manufacturing processes. Employers will rely on engineers to increase productivity and expand output of goods and services. New technologies continue to improve the design process, enabling engineers to produce and analyze various product designs much more rapidly than in the past. Unlike in some other occupations, however, technological advances are not expected to substantially limit employment opportunities in engineering because engineers will continue to develop new products and processes that increase productivity.

Offshoring of engineering work will likely dampen domestic employment growth to some degree. There are many well-trained, often English-speaking engineers available around the world willing to work at much lower salaries than U.S. engineers. The rise of the Internet has made it relatively easy for part of the engineering work previously done by engineers in this country to be done by engineers in other countries, a factor that will tend to hold down employment growth. Even so, there will always be a need for onsite engineers to interact with other employees and clients.

Overall job outlook. Overall job opportunities in engineering are expected to be good because the number of engineering graduates should be in rough balance with the number of job openings between 2006 and 2016. In addition to openings from job growth, many openings will be created by the need to replace current engineers who retire; transfer to management, sales, or other occupations; or leave engineering for other reasons.

Many engineers work on long-term research and development projects or in other activities that continue even during economic slowdowns. In industries such as electronics and aerospace, however, large cutbacks in defense expenditures and in government funding for research and development have resulted in significant layoffs of engineers in the past. The trend toward contracting for engineering work with engineering services firms, both domestic and foreign, has also made engineers more vulnerable to layoffs during periods of lower demand.

It is important for engineers, as it is for workers in other technical and scientific occupations, to continue their education throughout their careers because much of their value to their employer depends on their knowledge of the latest technology. Engineers in high-technology areas, such as biotechnology or information technology, may find that technical knowledge becomes outdated rapidly. By keeping current in their field, engineers are able to deliver the best solutions and greatest value to their employers. Engineers who have not kept current in their field may find themselves at a disadvantage when seeking promotions or during layoffs.

Employment change and job outlook by engineering specialty.

Aerospace engineers are expected to have 10 percent growth in employment over the projections decade, about as fast as the average for all occupations. Increases in the number and scope of military aerospace projects likely will generate new jobs. In addition, new technologies expected to be used on commercial aircraft produced during the next decade should spur demand for aerospace engineers. The employment outlook for aerospace engineers appears favorable. The number of degrees granted in aerospace engineering has declined for many years because of a perceived lack of opportunities in this field. Although this trend has reversed, new graduates continue to be needed to replace aerospace engineers who retire or leave the occupation for other reasons.

Agricultural engineers are expected to have employment growth of 9 percent over the projections decade, about as fast as the average for all occupations. More engineers will be needed to meet the increasing demand for using biosensors to determine the optimal treatment of crops. Employment growth should also result from the need to increase crop yields to feed an expanding population and produce crops used as renewable energy sources. Moreover, engineers will be needed to develop more efficient agricultural production and conserve resources.

Biomedical engineers are expected to have 21 percent employment growth over the projections decade, much faster than the average for all occupations. The aging of the population and the focus on health issues will drive demand for better medical devices and equipment designed by biomedical engineers. Along with the demand for more sophisticated medical equipment and procedures, an increased concern for cost-effectiveness will boost demand for biomedical engineers, particularly in pharmaceutical manufacturing and related industries. However, because of the growing interest in this field, the number of degrees granted in biomedical engineering has increased greatly. Biomedical engineers, particularly those with only a bachelor's degree, may face competition for jobs. Unlike many other engineering specialties, a graduate degree is recommended or required for many entry-level jobs.

Chemical engineers are expected to have employment growth of 8 percent over the projections decade, about as fast as the average for all occupations. Although overall employment in the chemical manufacturing industry is expected to decline, chemical companies will continue to research and develop new chemicals and more efficient processes to increase output of existing chemicals. Among manufacturing industries, pharmaceuticals may provide the best opportunities for jobseekers. However, most employment growth for chemical engineers will be in service-providing industries such as professional, scientific, and technical services, particularly for research in energy and the developing fields of biotechnology and nanotechnology.

Civil engineers are expected to experience 18 percent employment growth during the projections decade, faster than the average for all occupations. Spurred by general population growth and the related need to improve the nation's infrastructure, more civil engineers will be needed to design and construct or expand transportation, water supply, and pollution control systems and buildings and building complexes. They also will be needed to repair or replace existing roads, bridges, and other public structures. Because construction industries and architectural, engineering and related services employ many civil engineers, employment opportunities will vary by geographic area and may decrease during economic slowdowns, when construction is often curtailed.

Computer hardware engineers are expected to have 5 percent employment growth over the projections decade, slower than the average for all occupations. Although the use of information technology continues to expand rapidly, the manufacture of computer hardware is expected to be adversely affected by intense foreign competition. As computer and semiconductor manufacturers contract out more of their engineering needs to both domestic and foreign design firms, much of the growth in employment of hardware engineers is expected in the computer systems design and related services industry.

Electrical engineers are expected to have employment growth of 6 percent over the projections decade, slower than the average for all occupations. Although strong demand for electrical devices—including electric power generators, wireless phone transmitters, high-density batteries, and navigation systems—should spur job growth, international competition and the use of engineering services performed in other countries will limit employment growth. Electrical engineers working in firms providing engineering expertise and design services to manufacturers should have better job prospects.

Electronics engineers, except computer are expected to have employment growth of 4 percent during the projections decade, slower than the average for all occupations. Although rising demand for electronic goods—including communications equipment, defense-related equipment, medical electronics, and consumer products—should continue to increase demand for electronics engineers, foreign competition in electronic products development and the use of engineering services performed in other countries will limit employment growth. Growth is expected to be fastest in service-providing industries—particularly in firms that provide engineering and design services.

Environmental engineers should have employment growth of 25 percent during the projections decade, much faster than the average for all occupations. More environmental engineers will be needed to comply with environmental regulations and to develop methods of cleaning up existing hazards. A shift in emphasis toward preventing problems rather than controlling those that already exist, as well as increasing public health concerns resulting from population growth, also are expected to spur demand for environmental engineers. Because of this employment growth, job opportunities should be good even as more students earn degrees. Even though employment of environmental engineers should be less affected by economic conditions than most other types of engineers, a significant economic downturn could reduce the emphasis on environmental protection, reducing job opportunities.

Health and safety engineers, except mining safety engineers and inspectors are projected to experience 10 percent employment growth over the projections decade, about as fast as the average for all occupations. Because health and safety engineers make production processes and products as safe as possible, their services should be in demand as concern increases for health and safety within work environments. As new technologies for production or processing are developed, health and safety engineers will be needed to ensure that they are safe.

Industrial engineers are expected to have employment growth of 20 percent over the projections decade, faster than the average for all occupations. As firms look for new ways to reduce costs and raise productivity, they increasingly will turn to industrial engineers to develop more efficient processes and reduce costs, delays, and waste. This should lead to job growth for these engineers, even in manufacturing industries with slowly growing or declining employment overall. Because their work is similar to that done in management occupations, many industrial engineers leave the occupation to become managers. Many openings will be created by the need to replace industrial engineers who transfer to other occupations or leave the labor force.

Marine engineers and naval architects are expected to experience employment growth of 11 percent over the projections decade, about as fast as the average for all occupations. Strong demand for naval vessels and recreational small craft should more than offset the long-term decline in the domestic design and construction of large ocean-going vessels. Good prospects are expected for marine engineers and naval architects because of growth in employment, the need to replace workers who retire or take other jobs, and the limited number of students pursuing careers in this occupation.

Materials engineers are expected to have employment growth of 4 percent over the projections decade, slower than the average for all occupations. Although employment is expected to decline in many of the manufacturing industries in which materials engineers are concentrated, growth should be strong for materials engineers working on nanomaterials and biomaterials. As manufacturing firms contract for their materials engineering needs, employment growth is expected in professional, scientific, and technical services industries also.

Mechanical engineers are projected to have 4 percent employment growth over the projections decade, slower than the average for all occupations. This is because total employment in manufacturing industries—in which employment of mechanical engineers is concentrated—is expected to decline. Some new job opportunities will be created due to emerging technologies in biotechnology, materials science, and nanotechnology. Additional opportunities outside of mechanical engineering will exist because the skills acquired through earning a degree in mechanical engineering often can be applied in other engineering specialties.

Mining and geological engineers, including mining safety engineers are expected to have 10 percent employment growth over the projections decade, about as fast as the average for all occupations. Following a lengthy period of decline, strong growth in demand for minerals and increased use of mining engineers in the oil and gas extraction industry is expected to create some employment growth over the 2006–2016 period. Moreover, many mining engineers currently employed are approaching retirement age, a factor that should create additional job openings. Furthermore, relatively few schools offer mining engineering programs, resulting in good job opportunities for graduates. The best opportunities may require frequent travel or even living overseas for extended periods of time as mining operations around the world recruit graduates of U.S. mining engineering programs.

Nuclear engineers are expected to have employment growth of 7 percent over the projections decade, about as fast as the average for all occupations. Most job growth will be in research and development and engineering services. Although no commercial nuclear power plants have been built in the United States for many years, nuclear engineers will be needed to operate existing plants and design new ones, including researching future nuclear power sources. They also will be needed to work in defense-related areas, to develop nuclear medical technology, and to improve and enforce waste management and safety standards. Nuclear engineers are expected to have good employment opportunities because the small number of nuclear engineering graduates is likely to be in rough balance with the number of job openings.

Petroleum engineers are expected to have 5 percent employment growth over the projections decade, more slowly than the average for all occupations. Even though most of the potential petroleum-producing areas in the United States already have been explored, petroleum engineers will increasingly be needed to

Projections data from the National Employment Matrix

Occupational Title	SOC Code	Employment, 2006	Projected employment, 2016	Change, 2006-2016	
				Number	Percent
Engineers	17-2000	1,512,000	1,671,000	160,000	11
Aerospace engineers	17-2011	90,000	99,000	9,200	10
Agricultural engineers	17-2021	3,100	3,400	300	9
Biomedical engineers	17-2031	14,000	17,000	3,000	21
Chemical engineers	17-2041	30,000	33,000	2,400	8
Civil engineers	17-2051	256,000	302,000	46,000	18
Computer hardware engineers	17-2061	79,000	82,000	3,600	5
Electrical and electronics engineers	17-2070	291,000	306,000	15,000	5
Electrical engineers	17-2071	153,000	163,000	9,600	6
Electronics engineers, except computer	17-2072	138,000	143,000	5,100	4
Environmental engineers	17-2081	54,000	68,000	14,000	25
Industrial engineers, including health and safety	17-2110	227,000	270,000	43,000	19
Health and safety engineers, except mining safety engineers and inspectors	17-2111	25,000	28,000	2,400	10
Industrial engineers	17-2112	201,000	242,000	41,000	20
Marine engineers and naval architects	17-2121	9,200	10,000	1,000	11
Materials engineers	17-2131	22,000	22,000	900	4
Mechanical engineers	17-2141	226,000	235,000	9,400	4
Mining and geological engineers, including mining safety engineers	17-2151	7,100	7,800	700	10
Nuclear engineers	17-2161	15,000	16,000	1,100	7
Petroleum engineers	17-2171	17,000	18,000	900	5
Engineers, all other	17-2199	170,000	180,000	9,400	6

NOTE: Data in this table are rounded.

Table 2: Earnings distribution by engineering specialty, May 2006

Specialty	Lowest 10%	Lowest 25%	Median	Highest 25%	Highest 10%
Aerospace engineers	59,610	71,360	87,610	106,450	124,550
Agricultural engineers	42,390	53,040	66,030	80,370	96,270
Biomedical engineers	44,930	56,420	73,930	93,420	116,330
Chemical engineers	50,060	62,410	78,860	98,100	118,670
Civil engineers	44,810	54,520	68,600	86,260	104,420
Computer hardware engineers	53,910	69,500	88,470	111,030	135,260
Electrical engineers	49,120	60,640	75,930	94,050	115,240
Electronics engineers, except computer	52,050	64,440	81,050	99,630	119,900
Environmental engineers	43,180	54,150	69,940	88,480	106,230
Health and safety engineers, except mining safety engineers and inspectors	41,050	51,630	66,290	83,240	100,160
Industrial engineers	44,790	55,060	68,620	84,850	100,980
Marine engineers and naval architects	45,200	56,280	72,990	90,790	113,320
Materials engineers	46,120	57,850	73,990	92,210	112,140
Mechanical engineers	45,170	55,420	69,850	87,550	104,900
Mining and geological engineers, including mining safety engineers	42,040	54,390	72,160	94,110	128,410
Nuclear engineers	65,220	77,920	90,220	105,710	124,510
Petroleum engineers	57,960	75,880	98,380	123,130	145,600+
All other engineers	46,080	62,710	81,660	100,320	120,610

develop new methods of extracting more resources from existing sources. Favorable opportunities are expected for petroleum engineers because the number of job openings is likely to exceed the relatively small number of graduates. Petroleum engineers work around the world and, in fact, the best employment opportunities may include some work in other countries.

Earnings

Earnings for engineers vary significantly by specialty, industry, and education. Variation in median earnings and in the earnings distributions for engineers in various specialties is especially significant. Table 2 shows wage-and-salary earnings distributions in May 2006 for engineers in specialties covered in this statement.

In the federal government, mean annual salaries for engineers ranged from $75,144 in agricultural engineering to $107,546 in ceramic engineering in 2007.

As a group, engineers earn some of the highest average starting salaries among those holding bachelor's degrees. Table 3 shows average starting salary offers for engineers, according to a 2007 survey by the National Association of Colleges and Employers.

Table 3: Average starting salary by engineering specialty and degree, 2007

Curriculum	Bachelor's	Master's	Ph.D.
Aerospace/aeronautical/ astronautical	$53,408	$62,459	$73,814
Agricultural	49,764	—	—
Architectual	48,664	—	—
Bioengineering and biomedical	51,356	59,240	—
Chemical	59,361	68,561	73,667
Civil	48,509	48,280	62,275
Computer	56,201	60,000	92,500
Electrical/electronics and communications	55,292	66,309	75,982
Environmental/ environmental health	47,960	—	—
Industrial/manufacturing	55,067	64,759	77,364
Materials	56,233	—	—
Mechanical	54,128	62,798	72,763
Mining and mineral	54,381	—	—
Nuclear	56,587	59,167	—
Petroleum	60,718	57,000	—

Source: National Association of Colleges and Employers

Related Occupations

Engineers apply the principles of physical science and mathematics in their work. Other workers who use scientific and mathematical principles include architects, except landscape and naval; engineering and natural sciences managers; computer and information systems managers; computer programmers; computer software engineers; mathematicians; drafters; engineering technicians; sales engineers; science technicians; and physical and life scientists, including agricultural and food scientists, biological scientists, conservation scientists and foresters, atmospheric scientists, chemists and materials scientists, environmental scientists and hydrologists, geoscientists, and physicists and astronomers.

Sources of Additional Information

Information about careers in engineering is available from:

- JETS, 1420 King St., Suite 405, Alexandria, VA 22314. Internet: http://www.jets.org

Information on ABET-accredited engineering programs is available from

- ABET, Inc., 111 Market Place, Suite 1050, Baltimore, MD 21202. Internet: http://www.abet.org

Those interested in information on the Professional Engineer licensure should contact

- National Council of Examiners for Engineering and Surveying, P.O. Box 1686, Clemson, SC 29633. Internet: http://www.ncees.org

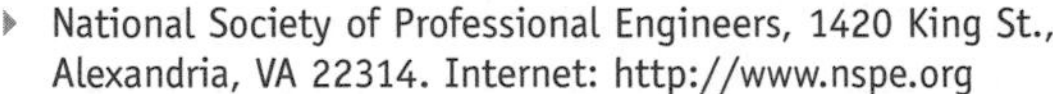

- National Society of Professional Engineers, 1420 King St., Alexandria, VA 22314. Internet: http://www.nspe.org

Information on general engineering education and career resources is available from

- American Society for Engineering Education, 1818 N St. NW, Suite 600, Washington, DC 20036. Internet: http://www.asee.org

Information on obtaining engineering positions with the federal government is available from the Office of Personnel Management through USAJOBS, the federal government's official employment information system. This resource for locating and applying for job opportunities can be accessed through the Internet at http://www.usajobs.opm.gov or through an interactive voice response telephone system at (703) 724-1850 or TDD (978) 461-8404. These numbers are not toll free, and charges may result. For advice on how to find and apply for federal jobs, see the Occupational Outlook Quarterly article "How to get a job in the Federal Government," online at http://www.bls.gov/opub/ooq/2004/summer/art01.pdf.

For more detailed information on an engineering specialty, contact societies representing the individual branches of engineering. Each can provide information about careers in the particular branch.

Aerospace engineers

- Aerospace Industries Association, 1000 Wilson Blvd., Suite 1700, Arlington, VA 22209. Internet: http://www.aia-aerospace.org
- American Institute of Aeronautics and Astronautics, Inc., 1801 Alexander Bell Dr., Suite 500, Reston, VA 20191. Internet: http://www.aiaa.org

Agricultural engineers

- American Society of Agricultural and Biological Engineers, 2950 Niles Rd., St. Joseph, MI 49085. Internet: http://www.asabe.org

Biomedical engineers

- Biomedical Engineering Society, 8401 Corporate Dr., Suite 140, Landover, MD 20785. Internet: http://www.bmes.org

Chemical engineers

- American Chemical Society, Department of Career Services, 1155 16th St. NW, Washington, DC 20036. Internet: http://www.chemistry.org
- American Institute of Chemical Engineers, 3 Park Ave., New York, NY 10016. Internet: http://www.aiche.org

Civil engineers

- American Society of Civil Engineers, 1801 Alexander Bell Dr., Reston, VA 20191. Internet: http://www.asce.org

Computer hardware engineers

- IEEE Computer Society, 1730 Massachusetts Ave. NW, Washington, DC 20036. Internet: http://www.computer.org

Electrical and electronics engineers

- Institute of Electrical and Electronics EngineersûUSA, 1828 L St. NW, Suite 1202, Washington, DC 20036. Internet: http://www.ieeeusa.org

Environmental engineers

- American Academy of Environmental Engineers, 130 Holiday Court, Suite 100, Annapolis, MD 21401. Internet: http://www.aaee.net

Health and safety engineers

- American Society of Safety Engineers, 1800 E Oakton St., Des Plaines, IL 60018. Internet: http://www.asse.org
- Board of Certified Safety Professionals, 208 Burwash Ave., Savoy, IL 61874. Internet: http://www.bcsp.org

Industrial engineers

- Institute of Industrial Engineers, 3577 Parkway Lane, Suite 200, Norcross, GA 30092. Internet: http://www.iienet.org

Marine engineers and naval architects

- Society of Naval Architects and Marine Engineers, 601 Pavonia Ave., Jersey City, NJ 07306. Internet: http://www.sname.org

Materials engineers

- ASM International, 9639 Kinsman Rd., Materials Park, OH 44073. Internet: http://www.asminternational.org
- Minerals, Metals, and Materials Society, 184 Thorn Hill Rd., Warrendale, PA 15086. Internet: http://www.tms.org

Mechanical engineers

- American Society of Heating, Refrigerating, and Air-Conditioning Engineers, Inc., 1791 Tullie Circle NE, Atlanta, GA 30329. Internet: http://www.ashrae.org
- American Society of Mechanical Engineers, 3 Park Ave., New York, NY 10016. Internet: http://www.asme.org
- SAE International, 400 Commonwealth Dr., Warrendale, PA 15096. Internet: http://www.sae.org

Mining and geological engineers, including mining safety engineers

- Society for Mining, Metallurgy, and Exploration, Inc., 8307 Shaffer Parkway, Littleton, CO 80127. Internet: http://www.smenet.org

Nuclear engineers

- American Nuclear Society, 555 North Kensington Ave., La Grange Park, IL 60526. Internet: http://www.ans.org

Petroleum engineers

- Society of Petroleum Engineers, P.O. Box 833836, Richardson, TX 75083. Internet: http://www.spe.org

STEM Environmental Scientists and Hydrologists

(O*NET 19-2041.00 and 19-2043.00)

Significant Points

- Environmental scientists and hydrologists often work in offices, laboratories, and field sites.
- Federal, state, and local governments employ 43 percent of all environmental scientists and hydrologists.
- Although a bachelor's degree in an earth science is adequate for a few entry-level jobs, employers prefer a master's degree; a Ph.D. degree generally is required for research or college teaching positions.
- Job prospects are expected to be favorable, particularly for hydrologists.

Nature of the Work

Environmental scientists and hydrologists use their knowledge of the physical makeup and history of the Earth to protect the environment, study the properties of underground and surface waters, locate water and energy resources, predict water-related geologic hazards, and provide environmental site assessments and advice on indoor air quality and hazardous-waste-site remediation.

Environmental scientists conduct research to identify, abate, and eliminate hazards that affect people, wildlife, and their environments. These workers analyze measurements or observations of air, food, water, and soil to determine the way to clean and preserve the environment. Understanding the issues involved in protecting the environment—degradation, conservation, recycling, and replenishment—is central to the work of environmental scientists. They often use this understanding to design and monitor waste disposal sites, preserve water supplies, and reclaim contaminated land and water to comply with federal environmental regulations. They also write risk assessments, describing the likely affect of construction and other environmental changes; write technical proposals; and give presentations to managers and regulators.

Hydrologists study the quantity, distribution, circulation, and physical properties of bodies of water. Often, they specialize in either underground water or surface water. They examine the form and intensity of precipitation, its rate of infiltration into the soil, its movement through the Earth, and its return to the ocean and atmosphere. Hydrologists use sophisticated techniques and instruments. For example, they may use remote sensing technology, data assimilation, and numerical modeling to monitor the change in regional and global water cycles. Some surface-water hydrologists use sensitive stream-measuring devices to assess flow rates and water quality.

Many environmental scientists and hydrologists work at consulting firms, helping businesses and government agencies comply with environmental policy, particularly with regard to ground-water decontamination and flood control. They are usually hired to solve problems. Most consulting firms fall into two categories: large multidisciplinary engineering companies, the largest of which may employ thousands of workers, and small niche firms that may employ only a few workers. When looking for jobs, environmental scientists and hydrologists should consider the type of firm and the scope of the projects it undertakes. In larger firms, environmental scientists are more likely to engage in large, long-term projects in which they will work with people in other scientific disciplines. In smaller specialty firms, however, they work more often with business professionals and clients in government and the private sector.

Environmental scientists who work on policy formation may help identify ways that human behavior can be modified in the future to avoid such problems as ground-water contamination and depletion of the ozone layer. Some environmental scientists work in managerial positions, usually after spending some time performing research or learning about environmental laws and regulations.

Many environmental scientists do work and have training that is similar to other physical or life scientists, but they focus on environmental issues. Many specialize in subfields such as environmental ecology and conservation, environmental chemistry, environmental biology, or fisheries science. Specialties affect the specific activities that environmental scientists perform, although recent understandings of the interconnectedness of life processes have blurred some traditional classifications. For example, *environmental ecologists* study the relationships between organisms and their environments and the effects of factors such as population size, pollutants, rainfall, temperature, and altitude, on both. They may collect, study, and report data on air, soil, and water using their knowledge of various scientific disciplines. *Ecological modelers* study ecosystems, pollution control, and resource management using mathematical modeling, systems analysis, thermodynamics, and computer techniques. *Environmental chemists* study the toxicity of various chemicals, that is, how those chemicals affect plants, animals, and people. (Information on geoscientists, who also study the Earth, is located elsewhere in this book.)

Environmental scientists and hydrologists in research positions with the federal government or in colleges and universities often have to find funding for their work by writing grant proposals. Consultants face similar pressures to market their skills and write proposals so that they will have steady work.

Work environment. Most entry-level environmental scientists and hydrologists spend the majority of their time in the field, while more experienced workers generally devote more time to office or laboratory work. Many beginning hydrologists and some environmental scientists, such as environmental ecologists and environmental chemists, often take field trips that involve physical activity. Environmental scientists and hydrologists in the field may work in warm or cold climates, in all kinds of weather. In their research, they may dig or chip with a hammer, scoop with a net, come in contact with water, and carry equipment. Travel often is required to meet with prospective clients or investors.

Researchers and consultants might face stress when looking for funding. Occasionally, those who write technical reports to business clients and regulators may be under pressure to meet deadlines and thus have to work long hours.

Training, Other Qualifications, and Advancement

Most environmental scientists and hydrologists need a master's degree. A Ph.D. is usually necessary for jobs in college teaching or research.

Education and training. A bachelor's degree in an earth science is adequate for a few entry-level positions, but environmental scientists increasingly need a master's degree in environmental science, hydrology, or a related natural science. A master's degree also is the minimum educational requirement for most entry-level applied research positions in private industry, in state and federal agencies, and at state geological surveys. A doctoral degree generally is necessary for college teaching and most research positions.

Some environmental scientists have a degree in environmental science. Many, however, earn degrees in life science, chemistry, geology, geophysics, atmospheric science, or physics and then apply their education to the environment. They often need research or work experience related to environmental science.

A bachelor's degree in environmental science offers an interdisciplinary approach to the natural sciences, with an emphasis on biology, chemistry, and geology. Undergraduate environmental science majors typically focus on data analysis and physical geography, which are particularly useful in studying pollution abatement, water resources, or ecosystem protection, restoration, and management. Understanding the geochemistry of inorganic compounds is becoming increasingly important in developing remediation goals. Students interested in working in the environmental or regulatory fields, either in environmental consulting firms or for federal or state governments, should take courses in hydrology, hazardous-waste management, environmental legislation, chemistry, fluid mechanics, and geologic logging, which is the gathering of geologic data. An understanding of environmental regulations and government permit issues also is valuable for those planning to work in mining and oil and gas extraction.

Students interested in hydrology should take courses in the physical sciences, geophysics, chemistry, engineering science, soil science, mathematics, aquatic biology, atmospheric science, geology, oceanography, hydrogeology, and the management or conservation of water resources. In some cases, a bachelor's degree in a hydrologic science is sufficient for positions consulting about water quality or wastewater treatment.

For environmental scientists and hydrologists who consult, courses in business, finance, marketing, or economics may be useful. In addition, combining environmental science training with other disciplines such as engineering or business, qualifies these scientists for the widest range of jobs.

Other qualifications. Computer skills are essential for prospective environmental scientists and hydrologists. Students who have some experience with computer modeling, data analysis and integration, digital mapping, remote sensing, and Geographic Information Systems (GIS) will be the most prepared to enter the job market. Familiarity with the Global Positioning System (GPS)—a locator system that uses satellites—is vital.

Environmental scientists and hydrologists must have good interpersonal skills, because they usually work as part of a team with other scientists, engineers, and technicians. Strong oral and written communication skills also are essential because writing technical reports and research proposals and communicating results to company managers, regulators, and the public are important aspects of the work. Because international work is becoming increasingly pervasive, knowledge of a second language can be an advantage. Those involved in fieldwork must have physical stamina.

Certification and advancement. Environmental scientists and hydrologists often begin their careers in field exploration or, occasionally, as research assistants or technicians in laboratories or offices. They are given more difficult assignments as they gain experience. Eventually, they may be promoted to project leader, program manager, or some other management and research position. (Information on engineering and natural sciences managers is located elsewhere in this book.)

The American Institute of Hydrology offers certification programs in professional hydrology. Certification may be beneficial for those seeking advancement.

Employment

Environmental scientists and hydrologists held about 92,000 jobs in 2006. Jobs for hydrologists accounted for only 9 percent of the total. Many more individuals held environmental science faculty positions in colleges and universities, but they are classified as postsecondary teachers. (See the statement on teachers—postsecondary elsewhere in this book.)

About 35 percent of environmental scientists were employed in state and local governments; 21 percent in management, scientific, and technical consulting services; 15 percent in architectural, engineering and related services; and 8 percent in the federal government. About 2 percent were self-employed.

Among hydrologists, 26 percent were employed in architectural, engineering, and related services, and 18 percent worked for management, scientific, and technical consulting services. In 2006, the federal government employed about 28 percent of hydrologists, mostly within the U.S. Department of the Interior for the U.S. Geological Survey (USGS) and within the U.S. Department of Defense. Another 21 percent worked for state agencies, such as state geological surveys and state departments of conservation. About 2 percent of hydrologists were self-employed, most as consultants to industry or government.

Job Outlook

Employment of environmental scientists and hydrologists is expected to grow much faster than the average for all occupations. Job prospects are expected to be favorable, particularly for hydrologists.

Employment change. Employment of environmental scientists is expected to increase by 25 percent between 2006 and 2016, much faster than the average for all occupations. Over the same period, employment of hydrologists should increase by 24 percent, also much faster than the average. Job growth for environmental scientists and hydrologists should be strongest in private-sector consulting firms. Growth in employment of environmental scientists and hydrologists will be spurred largely by the increasing demands placed on the environment and water resources by population growth. Further demand should result from the need to comply with complex environmental laws and regulations, particularly those regarding ground-water decontamination, clean air, and flood control.

Much job growth will result from a continued need to monitor the quality of the environment, to interpret the impact of human actions on terrestrial and aquatic ecosystems, and to develop strategies for restoring ecosystems. In addition, environmental scientists will be needed to help planners develop and construct buildings, transportation corridors, and utilities that protect water resources and reflect efficient and beneficial land use.

Demand for hydrologists should also be strong as the population increases and moves to more environmentally sensitive locations. As people increasingly migrate toward coastal regions, for example, hydrologists will be needed to assess building sites for potential geologic hazards and to mitigate the effects of natural hazards such as floods, landslides, and hurricanes. Hydrologists also will be needed to study hazardous-waste sites and determine the effect of pollutants on soil and ground water so that engineers can design remediation systems. Increased government regulations, such as those regarding the management of storm water, and issues related to water conservation, deteriorating coastal environments, and rising sea levels also will stimulate employment growth for these workers.

Many environmental scientists and hydrologists work in consulting. Consulting firms have hired these scientists to help businesses and government address issues related to underground tanks, land disposal areas, and other hazardous-waste-management facilities. Currently, environmental consulting is evolving from investigations to creating remediation and engineering solutions. At the same time, the regulatory climate is moving from a rigid structure to a more flexible risk-based approach. These factors, coupled with new federal and state initiatives that integrate environmental activities into the business process itself, will result in a greater focus on waste minimization, resource recovery, pollution prevention, and the consideration of environmental effects during product development. This shift in focus to preventive management will provide many new opportunities for environmental scientists and hydrologists in consulting roles.

Job prospects. In addition to job openings due to growth, there will be additional demand for new environmental scientists and

Projections data from the National Employment Matrix

Occupational Title	SOC Code	Employment, 2006	Projected employment, 2016	Change, 2006-2016	
				Number	Percent
Environmental scientists and hydrologists	—	92,000	114,000	23,000	25
Environmental scientists and specialists, including health	19-2041	83,000	104,000	21,000	25
Hydrologists	19-2043	8,300	10,000	2,000	24

NOTE: Data in this table are rounded.

hydrologists to replace those who retire, advance to management positions, or change careers. Job prospects for hydrologists should be favorable, particularly for those with field experience. Demand for hydrologists who understand both the scientific and engineering aspects of waste remediation should be strong. Few colleges and universities offer programs in hydrology, so the number of qualified workers may be limited.

Job prospects for environmental scientists also will be good, but less favorable than for hydrologists because of the larger number of workers seeking to enter the field.

Funding for federal and state geological surveys depend largely on the political climate and the current budget. Thus, job security for environmental scientists and hydrologists may vary. During periods of economic recession, layoffs of environmental scientists and hydrologists may occur in consulting firms; layoffs are much less likely in government.

Earnings

Median annual earnings of environmental scientists were $56,100 in May 2006. The middle 50 percent earned between $42,840 and $74,480. The lowest 10 percent earned less than $34,590, and the highest 10 percent earned more than $94,670.

Median annual earnings of hydrologists were $66,260 in 2006, with the middle 50 percent earning between $51,370 and $82,140, the lowest 10 percent earning less than $42,080, and the highest 10 percent earning more than $98,320.

Median annual earnings in the industries employing the largest number of environmental scientists in 2006 were as follows:

- Federal executive branch $82,490
- Management, scientific, and technical consulting services 57,280
- Engineering services 56,080
- Local government 52,100
- State government 50,590

According to the National Association of Colleges and Employers, beginning salary offers in July 2007 for graduates with bachelor's degrees in an environmental science averaged $38,336 a year.

In 2007, the federal government's average salary for hydrologists was $82,217.

Related Occupations

Environmental scientists and hydrologists perform investigations for the purpose of abating or eliminating pollutants or hazards that affect the environment or plants, animals, and humans. Many other occupations deal with preserving or researching the natural environment, including conservation scientists and foresters, atmospheric scientists, and some biological scientists, science technicians, and engineering technicians. Environmental scientists and hydrologists have extensive training in physical sciences, and many apply their knowledge of chemistry, physics, biology, and mathematics to the study of the Earth, work closely related to that of geoscientists.

Using problem-solving skills, physicists; chemists; engineers; mathematicians; surveyors, cartographers, photogrammetrists, and surveying technicians; computer systems analysts; and computer scientists and database administrators may also perform similar work related to the environment.

Sources of Additional Information

Information on training and career opportunities for environmental scientists is available from

- American Geological Institute, 4220 King St., Alexandria, VA 22302. Internet: http://www.agiweb.org

For information on careers in hydrology, contact

- American Institute of Hydrology, 300 Village Green Circle, Suite #201, Smyrna, GA 30080. Internet: http://www.aihydro.org

Information on obtaining a position as a hydrologist or an environmental protection specialist with the federal government is available from the Office of Personnel Management through USAJOBS, the federal government's official employment information system. This resource for locating and applying for job opportunities can be accessed through the Internet at http://www.usajobs.opm.gov or through an interactive voice response telephone system at (703) 724-1850 or TDD (978) 461-8404. These numbers are not toll free, and charges may result.

STEM Geoscientists

(O*NET 19-2042.00)

Significant Points

- Work at remote field sites is common.
- Federal, state, and local governments employ 18 percent of all geoscientists.
- Employers prefer applicants with a master's degree for most positions; a Ph.D. degree is required for most high-level research and college teaching positions.
- Excellent job opportunities are expected for graduates with a master's degree.

Nature of the Work

Geoscientists study the composition, structure, and other physical aspects of the Earth. They study the Earth's geologic past and present by using sophisticated instruments to analyze the composition of earth, rock, and water. Many geoscientists help to search for natural

resources such as groundwater, metals, and petroleum. Others work closely with environmental and other scientists to preserve and clean up the environment.

Geoscientists usually study and work in one of several closely related fields of geoscience. *Geologists* study the composition, processes, and history of the Earth. They try to find out how rocks were formed and what has happened to them since their formation. They also study the evolution of life by analyzing plant and animal fossils. *Geophysicists* use the principles of physics, mathematics, and chemistry to study not only the Earth's surface, but also its internal composition, ground and surface waters, atmosphere, oceans, and magnetic, electrical, and gravitational forces.

Within these two major disciplines of geology and geophysics are numerous subspecialties. For example, *petroleum geologists* map the subsurface of the ocean or land as they explore the terrain for oil and gas deposits. They use sophisticated instrumentation and computers to interpret geological information. *Engineering geologists* apply geologic principles to the fields of civil and environmental engineering, offering advice on major construction projects and assisting in environmental remediation and natural hazard-reduction projects. *Mineralogists* analyze and classify minerals and precious stones according to their composition and structure. They study the environment surrounding rocks in order to find new mineral resources. *Sedimentologists* study the nature, origin, distribution, and alteration of sediments, such as sand, silt, and mud. These sediments may contain oil, gas, coal, and many other mineral deposits. *Paleontologists* study fossils found in geological formations to trace the evolution of plant and animal life and the geologic history of the Earth. *Stratigraphers* examine the formation and layering of rocks to understand the environment which formed them. *Volcanologists* investigate volcanoes and volcanic phenomena to try to predict the potential for future eruptions and hazards to human health and welfare. *Glacial geologists* study the physical properties and movement of glaciers and ice sheets. *Geochemists* study the nature and distribution of chemical elements in groundwater and earth materials.

Geophysicists specialize in areas such as geodesy, seismology, and magnetic geophysics. *Geodesists* study the Earth's size, shape, gravitational field, tides, polar motion, and rotation. *Seismologists* interpret data from seismographs and other geophysical instruments to detect earthquakes and locate earthquake-related faults. *Geomagnetists* measure the Earth's magnetic field and use measurements taken over the past few centuries to devise theoretical models that explain the Earth's origin. *Paleomagnetists* interpret fossil magnetization in rocks and sediments from the continents and oceans to record the spreading of the sea floor, the wandering of the continents, and the many reversals of polarity that the Earth's magnetic field has undergone through time. Other geophysicists study atmospheric sciences and space physics. (See the statement on atmospheric scientists, and physicists and astronomers, elsewhere in this book.)

Oceanographers use their knowledge of geology and geophysics, in addition to biology and chemistry, to study the world's oceans and coastal waters. They study the motion and circulation of the ocean waters; the physical and chemical properties of the oceans; and how these properties affect coastal areas, climate, and weather. Oceanographers are further broken down according to their areas of expertise. For example, *physical oceanographers* study the tides, waves, currents, temperatures, density, and salinity of the ocean. They examine the interaction of various forms of energy, such as light, radar, sound, heat, and wind, with the sea, in addition to investigating the relationship between the sea, weather, and climate. *Chemical oceanographers* study the distribution of chemical compounds and chemical interactions that occur in the ocean and on the sea floor. They may investigate how pollution affects the chemistry of the ocean. *Geological and geophysical oceanographers* study the topographic features and the physical makeup of the ocean floor. Their knowledge can help companies find oil and gas off coastal waters. (*Biological oceanographers,* often called marine biologists, study the distribution and migration patterns of the many diverse forms of sea life in the ocean; the statement on biological scientists discusses this occupation elsewhere in this book.)

Geoscientists in research positions with the federal government or in colleges and universities frequently are required to design programs and write grant proposals in order to fund their research. Geoscientists in consulting jobs face similar pressures to market their skills and write proposals so that they will have steady work.

Work environment. Geoscientists can spend a large part of their time in the field, identifying and examining rocks, studying information collected by remote sensing instruments in satellites, conducting geological surveys, constructing field maps, and using instruments to measure the Earth's gravity and magnetic field. They often perform seismic studies, for example, which involve bouncing energy waves off buried layers of rock, to search for oil and gas or to understand the structure of the subsurface layers. Similarly, they use seismic signals generated by an earthquake to determine the earthquake's location and intensity. In laboratories, geologists and geophysicists examine the chemical and physical properties of specimens. They study fossil remains of animal and plant life or experiment with the flow of water and oil through rocks.

Some geoscientists spend the majority of their time in an office, but many others divide their time between fieldwork and office or laboratory work. Work at remote field sites is common. Many geoscientists, such as volcanologists, often take field trips that involve physical activity. Geoscientists in the field may work in warm or cold climates and in all kinds of weather. In their research, they may dig or chip with a hammer, scoop with a net, and carry equipment in a backpack. Oceanographers may spend considerable time at sea on academic research ships. Geologists frequently travel to remote field sites by helicopter or 4-wheel-drive vehicles and cover large areas on foot. Many exploration geologists and geophysicists work in foreign countries, sometimes in remote areas and under difficult conditions. Travel often is required to meet with prospective clients or investors. Fieldwork often requires working long hours.

Training, Other Qualifications, and Advancement

A master's degree is the primary educational requirement for most entry-level positions. A Ph.D. is necessary for most high-level research and college teaching positions, but a master's degree is preferred for most other geoscience jobs.

Education and training. A bachelor's degree is adequate for a few entry-level positions, but most geoscientists need a master's degree in geology or earth science. A master's degree is the preferred educational requirement for most entry-level research positions in private industry, federal agencies, and state geological surveys. A Ph.D. is necessary for most high-level research and college teaching positions, but it may not be preferred for other jobs.

Many colleges and universities offer a bachelor's or higher degree in a geoscience. Traditional geoscience courses emphasizing classical geologic methods and topics (such as mineralogy, petrology, paleontology, stratigraphy, and structural geology) are important for all geoscientists. People who study physics, chemistry, biology, mathematics, engineering, or computer science may also qualify for some geoscience positions if their course work includes geology.

Licensure. A number of states require geoscientists who offer their services directly to the public, particularly geologists, to obtain a license from a state licensing board. Licensing requirements vary but often include education, experience, and a passing score on an examination.

Other qualifications. Computer skills are essential for prospective geoscientists; students who have experience with computer modeling, data analysis and integration, digital mapping, remote sensing, and Geographic Information Systems (GIS) will be the most prepared entering the job market. Knowledge of the Global Positioning System (GPS)—a locator system that uses satellites—has also become essential. Some employers seek applicants with field experience, so a summer internship is often helpful.

Geoscientists must have good interpersonal skills because they usually work as part of a team with other geoscientists and with environmental scientists, engineers, and technicians. Strong oral and written communication skills also are important because writing technical reports and research proposals and explaining research results in person are important aspects of the work. Because many jobs require foreign travel, knowledge of a second language is becoming increasingly beneficial.

Geoscientists must be inquisitive, able to think logically, and capable of complex analytical thinking, including spatial visualization and the ability to infer conclusions from sparse data. Those involved in fieldwork must have physical stamina.

Advancement. Geoscientists often begin their careers in field exploration or as research assistants or technicians in laboratories or offices. As they gain experience, they get more assignments that are difficult. Eventually, some are promoted to project leader, program manager, or to a senior research position. Those who choose to work in management will spend more time scheduling, budgeting, and reporting to top executives or clients. (See the statement on engineering and natural sciences managers elsewhere in this book.)

Employment

Geoscientists held about 31,000 jobs in 2006. Many more individuals held geoscience faculty positions in colleges and universities, but they are classified as college and university faculty. (See the statement on teachers—postsecondary elsewhere in this book.)

About 24 percent of geoscientists were employed in architectural, engineering, and related services, and 18 percent worked for oil and gas extraction companies. In 2006, state agencies such as state geological surveys and state departments of conservation employed about 2,900 geoscientists. Another 2,600 worked for the federal government, including geologists, geophysicists, and oceanographers, mostly within the U.S. Department of the Interior for the U.S. Geological Survey (USGS) and within the U.S. Department of Defense. About 2 percent of geoscientists were self-employed, most as consultants to industry or government.

Job Outlook

Although employment growth will vary by industry, overall employment of geoscientists is expected to grow much faster than the average for all occupations. Graduates with a master's degree can expect excellent job opportunities; very few geoscientist jobs are available to bachelor's degree holders. Ph.D.s should face competition for basic research and college teaching jobs.

Employment change. Employment growth of 22 percent for geoscientists is expected between 2006 and 2016, much faster than the average for all occupations. The need for energy, environmental protection, and responsible land and water management will spur employment demand. Employment in management, scientific, and technical consulting services should continue to grow as more geoscientists work as consultants. These services have increased their hiring of geoscientists in recent years because of increased government contracting, and private corporations' need for technical assistance and environmental management plans. Moreover, many geoscientists monitor the quality of the environment, including aquatic ecosystems, deteriorating coastal environments, and rising sea levels—all of which will create employment growth for them. An expected increase in highway building and other infrastructure projects will also be a source of jobs for engineering geologists.

Employment is also expected to increase in the oil and gas extraction industry. Many geoscientists work in the exploration and production of oil and gas. Historically, employment of petroleum geologists, geophysicists, and some other geoscientists has been cyclical and affected considerably by the price of oil and gas. When prices are low, oil and gas producers curtail exploration activities and lay off geologists. When prices were higher, companies had the funds and incentive to renew exploration efforts and to hire geoscientists in larger numbers. In recent years, however, a growing worldwide demand for oil and gas and for new exploration and recovery techniques—particularly in deep water and previously inaccessible sites in Alaska and the Gulf of Mexico—has created some stability to the petroleum industry. Geoscientists who speak a foreign language and who are willing to work abroad should enjoy the best opportunities, as the need for energy, construction materials, and a broad range of geoscience expertise grows in developing nations.

Job prospects. Graduates with a master's degree should have excellent opportunities, especially in the management, scientific and technical consulting industry and in the engineering services industries. In addition to demand resulting from job growth, replacing those who leave the occupation for retirement, managerial positions, or other careers will generate a number of jobs. With relatively few students earning master's degrees in the geosciences, job openings may exceed the number of qualified job seekers over the 2006–2016 projection decade. However, geoscientists with doctoral degrees, who primarily work as college and university faculty or do basic research, may face competition. There are few openings for new graduates with only a bachelor's degree in geoscience, but these graduates may have favorable opportunities in related occupations, such as high school science teacher or science technician.

There will be fewer opportunities for geoscientists in federal and state government, mostly because of budget constraints at key agencies, such as the USGS, and the trend among governments toward contracting out to consulting firms instead of hiring new government employees. However, departures of geoscientists who retire or

Projections data from the National Employment Matrix

Occupational Title	SOC Code	Employment, 2006	Projected employment, 2016	Change, 2006-2016	
				Number	Percent
Geoscientists, except hydrologists and geographers	19-2042	31,000	38,000	6,800	22

NOTE: Data in this table are rounded.

leave the government for other reasons will result in some job openings over the next decade.

Geoscientists may face layoffs during periods of economic recession. Especially vulnerable are those in consulting and, to a lesser extent, workers in Government. Employment for those working in the production of oil and gas, however, will largely be dictated by the cyclical nature of the energy sector and changes in government policy, although less so than in the past.

Earnings

Median annual earnings of geoscientists were $72,660 in May 2006. The middle 50 percent earned between $51,860 and $100,650; the lowest 10 percent earned less than $39,740, the highest 10 percent more than $135,950.

The petroleum, mineral, and mining industries offer higher salaries, but less job security, than other industries because economic downturns sometimes cause layoffs.

According to the National Association of Colleges and Employers, beginning salary offers in July 2007 for graduates with bachelor's degrees in geology and related sciences averaged $40,786 a year.

In 2007, the federal government's average salary was $87,392 for geologists, $100,585 for geophysicists, and 93,461 for oceanographers.

Related Occupations

Many geoscientists work in the petroleum and natural gas industry, an industry that also employs numerous other workers whose jobs deal with the scientific and technical aspects of the exploration and extraction of petroleum and natural gas. Among these other workers are engineering technicians; science technicians; petroleum engineers; and surveyors, cartographers, photogrammetrists, and surveying technicians. Also, some physicists and astronomers, chemists and materials scientists, atmospheric scientists, biological scientists, and environmental scientists and hydrologists perform related work both in the exploration and extraction of petroleum and natural gas and in activities having to do with the environment.

Sources of Additional Information

Information on training and career opportunities for geologists is available from either of the following organizations:

- American Association of Petroleum Geologists, P.O. Box 979, Tulsa, OK 74101. Internet: http://www.aapg.org
- American Geological Institute, 4220 King St., Alexandria, VA 22302-1502. Internet: http://www.agiweb.org

Information on obtaining a position as a geologist, geophysicist, or oceanographer with the federal government is available from the Office of Personnel Management through USAJOBS, the federal government's official employment information system. This resource for locating and applying for job opportunities can be accessed through the Internet at http://www.usajobs.opm.gov or through an interactive voice response telephone system at (703) 724-1850 or TDD (978) 461-8404. These numbers are not toll free, and charges may result.

Heating, Air-Conditioning, and Refrigeration Mechanics and Installers

(O*NET 49-9021.00, 49-9021.01, and 49-9021.02)

Significant Points

- Employment is projected to grow as fast as the average.
- Job prospects are expected to be excellent.
- Employers prefer to hire those who have completed technical school training or a formal apprenticeship.

Nature of the Work

Heating and air-conditioning systems control the temperature, humidity, and the total air quality in residential, commercial, industrial, and other buildings. Refrigeration systems make it possible to store and transport food, medicine, and other perishable items. Heating, air-conditioning, and refrigeration mechanics and installers—also called technicians—install, maintain, and repair such systems. Because heating, ventilation, air-conditioning, and refrigeration systems often are referred to as HVACR systems, these workers also may be called HVACR technicians.

Heating, air-conditioning, and refrigeration systems consist of many mechanical, electrical, and electronic components, such as motors, compressors, pumps, fans, ducts, pipes, thermostats, and switches. In central forced air heating systems, for example, a furnace heats air, which is then distributed via a system of metal or fiberglass ducts. Technicians must be able to maintain, diagnose, and correct problems throughout the entire system. To do this, they adjust system controls to recommended settings and test the performance of the system using special tools and test equipment.

Technicians often specialize in either installation or maintenance and repair, although they are trained to do both. They also may specialize in doing heating work or air-conditioning or refrigeration work. Some specialize in one type of equipment—for example, hydronics (water-based heating systems), solar panels, or commercial refrigeration. Some technicians also sell service contracts to their clients. Service contracts provide for regular maintenance of the heating and cooling systems and they help to reduce the seasonal fluctuations of this type of work.

Technicians follow blueprints or other specifications to install oil, gas, electric, solid-fuel, and multiple-fuel heating systems and air-conditioning systems. After putting the equipment in place, they install fuel and water supply lines, air ducts and vents, pumps, and other components. They may connect electrical wiring and controls and check the unit for proper operation. To ensure the proper functioning of the system, furnace installers often use combustion test equipment, such as carbon dioxide testers, carbon monoxide testers, combustion analyzers, and oxygen testers. These tests ensure that the system will operate safely and at peak efficiency.

After a furnace or air-conditioning unit has been installed, technicians often perform routine maintenance and repair work to keep the systems operating efficiently. They may adjust burners and blowers and check for leaks. If the system is not operating properly, they check the thermostat, burner nozzles, controls or other parts to diagnose and correct the problem.

Technicians also install and maintain heat pumps, which are similar to air conditioners but can be reversed so that they both heat and cool a home. Because of the added complexity and the fact that they run both in summer and winter, these systems often require more maintenance and need to be replaced more frequently than traditional furnaces and air conditioners.

During the summer, when heating systems are not being used, heating equipment technicians do maintenance work, such as replacing filters, ducts, and other parts of the system that may accumulate dust and impurities during the operating season. During the winter, air-conditioning mechanics inspect the systems and do required maintenance, such as overhauling compressors.

Refrigeration mechanics install, service, and repair industrial and commercial refrigerating systems and a variety of refrigeration equipment. They follow blueprints, design specifications, and manufacturers' instructions to install motors, compressors, condensing units, evaporators, piping, and other components. They connect this equipment to the ductwork, refrigerant lines, and electrical power source. After making the connections, they charge the system with refrigerant, check it for proper operation and leaks, and program control systems.

When air-conditioning and refrigeration technicians service equipment, they must use care to conserve, recover, and recycle the refrigerants used in air-conditioning and refrigeration systems. The release of these refrigerants can be harmful to the environment. Technicians conserve the refrigerant by making sure that there are no leaks in the system; they recover it by venting the refrigerant into proper cylinders; they recycle it for reuse with special filter-dryers; or they ensure that the refrigerant is properly disposed of.

Heating, air-conditioning, and refrigeration mechanics and installers are adept at using a variety of tools, including hammers, wrenches, metal snips, electric drills, pipe cutters and benders, measurement gauges, and acetylene torches, to work with refrigerant lines and air ducts. They use voltmeters, thermometers, pressure gauges, manometers, and other testing devices to check airflow, refrigerant pressure, electrical circuits, burners, and other components.

Other craft workers sometimes install or repair cooling and heating systems. For example, on a large air-conditioning installation job, especially where workers are covered by union contracts, ductwork might be done by sheet metal workers and duct installers; electrical work by electricians; and installation of piping, condensers, and other components by pipelayers, plumbers, pipefitters, and steamfitters. Home appliance repairers usually service room air-conditioners and household refrigerators.

Work environment. Heating, air-conditioning, and refrigeration mechanics and installers work in homes, retail establishments, hospitals, office buildings, and factories—anywhere there is climate-control equipment that needs to be installed, repaired, or serviced. They may be assigned to specific job sites at the beginning of each day or may be dispatched to a variety of locations if they are making service calls.

Technicians may work outside in cold or hot weather or in buildings that are uncomfortable because the air-conditioning or heating equipment is broken. In addition, technicians might work in awkward or cramped positions and sometimes are required to work in high places. Hazards include electrical shock, burns, muscle strains, and other injuries from handling heavy equipment. Appropriate safety equipment is necessary when handling refrigerants because contact can cause skin damage, frostbite, or blindness. Inhalation of refrigerants when working in confined spaces also is a possible hazard.

The majority of mechanics and installers work at least a 40-hour week. During peak seasons, they often work overtime or irregular hours. Maintenance workers, including those who provide maintenance services under contract, often work evening or weekend shifts and are on call. Most employers try to provide a full work week year-round by scheduling both installation and maintenance work, and many manufacturers and contractors now provide or even require year-round service contracts. In most shops that service both heating and air-conditioning equipment, employment is stable throughout the year.

Training, Other Qualifications, and Advancement

Because of the increasing sophistication of heating, air-conditioning, and refrigeration systems, employers prefer to hire those who have completed technical school training or a formal apprenticeship. Some mechanics and installers, however, still learn the trade informally on the job.

Education and training. Many secondary and postsecondary technical and trade schools, junior and community colleges, and the U.S. Armed Forces offer six-month to two-year programs in heating, air-conditioning, and refrigeration. Students study theory of temperature control, equipment design and construction, and electronics. They also learn the basics of installation, maintenance, and repair. Three accrediting agencies have set academic standards for HVACR programs. These accrediting bodies are HVAC Excellence, the National Center for Construction Education and Research, and the Partnership for Air-Conditioning, Heating, and Refrigeration Accreditation. After completing these programs, new technicians generally need between an additional six months and two years of field experience before they are considered proficient.

Many technicians train through apprenticeships. Apprenticeship programs frequently are run by joint committees representing local chapters of the Air-Conditioning Contractors of America, the Mechanical Contractors Association of America, Plumbing-Heating-Cooling Contractors—National Association, and locals of the sheet metal workers' International Association or the United Association of Journeymen and Apprentices of the Plumbing and Pipefitting Industry of the United States and Canada. Local chapters of the Associated Builders and Contractors and the National Association of Home Builders sponsor other apprenticeship programs. Formal apprenticeship programs normally last three to five years and combine paid on-the-job training with classroom instruction. Classes include subjects such as the use and care of tools, safety practices, blueprint reading, and the theory and design of heating, ventilation, air-conditioning, and refrigeration systems. In addition to understanding how systems work, technicians must learn about refrigerant products and the legislation and regulations that govern their use.

Applicants for apprenticeships must have a high school diploma or equivalent. Math and reading skills are essential. After completing an apprenticeship program, technicians are considered skilled trades workers and capable of working alone. These programs are also a pathway to certification and, in some cases, college credits.

Those who acquire their skills on the job usually begin by assisting experienced technicians. They may begin by performing simple tasks such as carrying materials, insulating refrigerant lines, or cleaning furnaces. In time, they move on to more difficult tasks, such as cutting and soldering pipes and sheet metal and checking electrical and electronic circuits.

Several organizations have begun to offer basic self-study, classroom, and Internet courses for individuals with limited experience.

Licensure. Heating, air-conditioning, and refrigeration mechanics and installers are required to be licensed by some states and localities. Requirements for licensure vary greatly, but all states or localities that require a license have a test that must be passed. The contents of these tests vary by state or locality, with some requiring extensive knowledge of electrical codes and others focusing more on HVACR-specific knowledge. Completion of an apprenticeship program or two to five years of experience are also common requirements.

In addition, all technicians who purchase or work with refrigerants must be certified in their proper handling. To become certified to purchase and handle refrigerants, technicians must pass a written examination specific to the type of work in which they specialize. The three possible areas of certification are: Type I—servicing small appliances; Type II—high-pressure refrigerants; and Type III—low-pressure refrigerants. Exams are administered by organizations approved by the U.S. Environmental Protection Agency, such as trade schools, unions, contractor associations, or building groups.

Other qualifications. High school courses in shop math, mechanical drawing, applied physics and chemistry, electronics, blueprint reading, and computer applications provide a good background for those interested in entering this occupation. Some knowledge of plumbing or electrical work also is helpful. A basic understanding of electronics is becoming more important because of the increasing use of electronics in equipment controls. Because technicians frequently deal directly with the public, they should be courteous and tactful, especially when dealing with an aggravated customer. They also should be in good physical condition because they sometimes have to lift and move heavy equipment.

Certification and advancement. Throughout the learning process, technicians may have to take a number of tests that measure their skills. For those with relevant coursework and less than one year of experience, the industry has developed a series of exams to test basic competency in residential heating and cooling, light commercial heating and cooling, and commercial refrigeration. These are referred to as "Entry-level" certification exams and are commonly conducted at both secondary and post-secondary technical and trade schools. HVACR technicians who have at least one year of experience performing installations and two years of experience performing maintenance and repair can take a number of different tests to certify their competency in working with specific types of equipment, such as oil-burning furnaces. These tests are offered through the Refrigeration Service Engineers Society, HVAC Excellence, Carbon Monoxide Safety Association, Air-Conditioning and Refrigeration Safety Coalition, and North American Technician Excellence, Inc., among others. Employers increasingly recommend taking and passing these tests and obtaining certification; doing so may increase advancement opportunities.

Advancement usually takes the form of higher wages. Some technicians, however, may advance to positions as supervisor or service manager. Others may move into sales and marketing. Still others may become building superintendents, cost estimators, system test and balance specialists, or, with the necessary certification, teachers. Those with sufficient money and managerial skill can open their own contracting business.

Employment

Heating, air-conditioning, and refrigeration mechanics and installers held about 292,000 jobs in 2006; about 55 percent worked for plumbing, heating, and air-conditioning contractors. The rest were employed in a variety of industries throughout the country, reflecting a widespread dependence on climate-control systems. Some worked for fuel oil dealers, refrigeration and air-conditioning service and repair shops, schools, and stores that sell heating and air-conditioning systems. Local governments, the federal government, hospitals, office buildings, and other organizations that operate large air-conditioning, refrigeration, or heating systems also employed these workers. About 13 percent of these workers were self-employed.

Job Outlook

With average job growth and numerous expected retirements, heating, air-conditioning, and refrigeration mechanics and installers should have excellent employment opportunities.

Employment change. Employment of heating, air-conditioning, and refrigeration mechanics and installers is projected to increase 9 percent during the 2006–2016 decade, as fast as the average for all occupations. As the population and stock of buildings grows, so does the demand for residential, commercial, and industrial climate-control systems. Residential HVACR systems generally need replacement after 10 to 15 years; the large number of homes built in recent years will enter this replacement timeframe by 2016. The increased complexity of HVACR systems, which increases the possibility that equipment may malfunction, also will create opportunities for service technicians. A growing focus on improving indoor air quality and the increasing use of refrigerated equipment by a growing number of stores and gasoline stations that sell food should also create more jobs for heating, air-conditioning, and refrigeration technicians.

Concern for the environment has prompted the development of new energy-saving heating and air-conditioning systems. An emphasis on better energy management should lead to the replacement of older systems and the installation of newer, more efficient systems in existing homes and buildings. Also, demand for maintenance and service work should increase as businesses and homeowners strive to keep increasingly complex systems operating at peak efficiency. Regulations prohibiting the discharge and production of older types of refrigerants that pollute the atmosphere should continue to result in the need to replace many existing air conditioning systems or to modify them to use new environmentally safe refrigerants. The pace of replacement in the commercial and industrial sectors will quicken if Congress or individual states change tax rules designed to encourage companies to buy new HVACR equipment.

Job prospects. Job prospects for heating, air-conditioning, and refrigeration mechanics and installers are expected to be excellent, particularly for those who have completed training from an accredited technical school or a formal apprenticeship. Job opportunities should be best in the fastest growing areas of the country. A growing number of retirements of highly skilled technicians are expected to generate many job openings. Many contractors have reported problems finding enough workers to meet the demand for service and installation of HVACR systems.

Technicians who specialize in installation work may experience periods of unemployment when the level of new construction activity declines, but maintenance and repair work usually remains relatively stable. People and businesses depend on their climate-control or refrigeration systems and must keep them in good working order, regardless of economic conditions.

Earnings

Median hourly wage-and-salary earnings of heating, air-conditioning, and refrigeration mechanics and installers were $18.11 in May 2006. The middle 50 percent earned between $14.12 and $23.32 an hour. The lowest 10 percent earned less than $11.38, and the top 10 percent earned more than $28.57. Median hourly earnings in the industries employing the largest numbers of heating, air-conditioning, and refrigeration mechanics and installers were

Hardware, and plumbing and heating equipment and supplies merchant wholesalers $20.53
Commercial and industrial machinery and equipment (except automotive and electronic) repair and maintenance 19.95
Direct selling establishments 19.12
Plumbing, heating, and air-conditioning contractors 17.46
Electrical contractors 16.74

Apprentices usually begin at about 50 percent of the wage rate paid to experienced workers. As they gain experience and improve their skills, they receive periodic increases until they reach the wage rate of experienced workers.

Heating, air-conditioning, and refrigeration mechanics and installers enjoy a variety of employer-sponsored benefits. In addition to typical benefits such as health insurance and pension plans, some employers pay for work-related training and provide uniforms, company vans, and tools.

About 14 percent of heating, air-conditioning, and refrigeration mechanics and installers are members of a union. The unions to which the greatest numbers of mechanics and installers belong are the sheet metal workers International Association and the United Association of Journeymen and Apprentices of the Plumbing and Pipefitting Industry of the United States and Canada.

Related Occupations

Heating, air-conditioning, and refrigeration mechanics and installers work with sheet metal and piping, and repair machinery, such as electrical motors, compressors, and burners. Other workers who have similar skills include boilermakers; home appliance repairers; electricians; sheet metal workers; and pipelayers, plumbers, pipefitters, and steamfitters.

Sources of Additional Information

For more information about opportunities for training, certification, and employment in this trade, contact local vocational and technical schools; local heating, air-conditioning, and refrigeration contractors; a local of the unions or organizations previously mentioned; a local joint union-management apprenticeship committee; or the nearest office of the state employment service or apprenticeship agency. You can also find information on the registered apprenticeship system with links to state apprenticeship programs on the U.S. Department of Labor's Web site: http://www.doleta.gov/atles_bat. Apprenticeship information is also available from the U.S. Department of Labor's toll free helpline: (877) 872-5627.

For information on career opportunities, training, and technician certification, contact

- Air-Conditioning Contractors of America, 2800 Shirlington Rd., Suite 300, Arlington, VA 22206. Internet: http://www.acca.org
- Air-Conditioning and Refrigeration Institute, 4100 North Fairfax Dr., Suite 200, Arlington, VA 22203. Internet: http://www.coolcareers.org and http://www.ari.org
- Associated Builders and Contractors, Workforce Development Department, 4250 North Fairfax Dr., 9th Floor, Arlington, VA 22203. Internet: http://www.trytools.org
- Carbon Monoxide Safety Association, P.O. Box 669, Eastlake, CO 80614. Internet: http://www.cosafety.org
- Home Builders Institute, National Association of Home Builders, 1201 15th St. NW, 6th Floor, Washington, DC 20005. Internet: http://www.hbi.org
- HVAC Excellence, P.O. Box 491, Mt. Prospect, IL 60056. Internet: http://www.hvacexcellence.org
- Mechanical Contractors Association of America, Mechanical Service Contractors of America, 1385 Piccard Dr., Rockville, MD 20850. Internet: http://www.mcaa.org and http://www.mcaa.org/msca
- National Center for Construction Education and Research, P.O. Box 141104, Gainesville, FL 32601. Internet: http://www.nccer.org
- National Occupational Competency Testing Institute. Internet: http://www.nocti.org

Projections data from the National Employment Matrix

Occupational Title	SOC Code	Employment, 2006	Projected employment, 2016	Change, 2006-16 Number	Change, 2006-16 Percent
Heating, air conditioning, and refrigeration mechanics and installers	49-9021	292,000	317,000	25,000	9

NOTE: Data in this table are rounded.

- North American Technician Excellence, 4100 North Fairfax Dr., Suite 210, Arlington, VA 22203. Internet: http://www.natex.org
- Plumbing-Heating-Cooling Contractors, 180 S. Washington, St., P.O. Box 6808, Falls Church, VA 22046. Internet: http://www.phccweb.org org
- Refrigeration Service Engineers Society, 1666 Rand Rd., Des Plaines, IL 60016. Internet: http://www.rses.org
- Sheet Metal and Air-Conditioning Contractors National Association, 4201 Lafayette Center Dr., Chantilly, VA 20151. Internet: http://www.smacna.org
- United Association of Journeymen and Apprentices of the Plumbing and Pipefitting Industry, 901 Massachusetts Ave. NW, Washington, DC 20001. Internet: http://www.ua.org

Heavy Vehicle and Mobile Equipment Service Technicians and Mechanics

(O*NET 49-3041.00, 49-3042.00, and 49-3043.00)

Significant Points

- Opportunities should be excellent for people with formal post-secondary training in diesel or heavy equipment mechanics; those without formal training will face keen competition.
- This occupation offers relatively high wages and the challenge of skilled repair work.
- Skill in using computerized diagnostic equipment is important in this occupation.

Nature of the Work

Heavy vehicles and mobile equipment are indispensable to many industrial activities from construction to railroads. Various types of equipment move materials, till land, lift beams, and dig earth to pave the way for development and production. Heavy vehicle and mobile equipment service technicians and mechanics repair and maintain engines and hydraulic, transmission, and electrical systems for this equipment. Farm machinery, cranes, bulldozers, and railcars are all examples of heavy vehicles that require such service. (For information on service technicians specializing in diesel engines, see the section on diesel service technicians and mechanics elsewhere in this book.)

Service technicians perform routine maintenance checks on agricultural, industrial, construction, and rail equipment. They service fuel, brake, and transmission systems to ensure peak performance, safety, and longevity of the equipment. Maintenance checks and comments from equipment operators usually alert technicians to problems. After locating the problem, these technicians rely on their training and experience to use the best possible technique to solve the problem.

With many types of modern heavy and mobile equipment, technicians can plug diagnostic computers into onboard computers to diagnose a component needing adjustment or repair. If necessary, they may partially dismantle affected components to examine parts for damage or excessive wear. Then, using hand-held tools, they repair, replace, clean, and lubricate parts as necessary. In some cases, technicians re-calibrate systems by typing codes into the onboard computer. After reassembling the component and testing it for safety, they put it back into the equipment and return the equipment to the field.

Many types of heavy and mobile equipment use hydraulics to raise and lower movable parts. When hydraulic components malfunction, technicians examine them for fluid leaks, ruptured hoses, or worn gaskets on fluid reservoirs. Occasionally, the equipment requires extensive repairs, as when a defective hydraulic pump needs replacing.

Service technicians diagnose electrical problems and adjust or replace defective components. They also disassemble and repair undercarriages and track assemblies. Occasionally, technicians weld broken equipment frames and structural parts, using electric or gas welders.

Technicians use a variety of tools in their work: power tools, such as pneumatic wrenches to remove bolts quickly; machine tools, like lathes and grinding machines, to rebuild brakes; welding and flame-cutting equipment to remove and repair exhaust systems; and jacks and hoists to lift and move large parts. Service technicians also use common hand tools—screwdrivers, pliers, and wrenches—to work on small parts and to get at hard-to-reach places. They may use a variety of computerized testing equipment to pinpoint and analyze malfunctions in electrical systems and other essential systems. Tachometers and dynamometers, for example, serve to locate engine malfunctions. Service technicians also use ohmmeters, ammeters, and voltmeters when working on electrical systems. Employers typically furnish expensive power tools, computerized engine analyzers, and other diagnostic equipment, but hand tools are normally accumulated with experience, and many experienced technicians have thousands of dollars invested in them.

It is common for technicians in large shops to specialize in one or two types of repair. For example, a shop may have individual specialists in major engine repair, transmission work, electrical systems, and suspension or brake systems. Technicians in smaller shops, on the other hand, generally perform multiple functions.

Technicians also specialize in types of equipment. *Mobile heavy equipment mechanics and service technicians*, for example, keep construction and surface mining equipment, such as bulldozers, cranes, graders, and excavators in working order. Typically, these workers are employed by equipment wholesale distribution and leasing firms, large construction and mining companies, local and federal governments, and other organizations operating and maintaining heavy machinery and equipment fleets. Service technicians employed by the federal government may work on tanks and other armored equipment.

Farm equipment mechanics service, maintain, and repair farm equipment, as well as smaller lawn and garden tractors sold to suburban homeowners. What once was a general repairer's job around the farm has evolved into a specialized technical career. Farmers have increasingly turned to farm equipment dealers to service and repair their equipment because the machinery has grown in complexity. Modern equipment uses more computers, electronics, and hydraulics, making it difficult to perform repairs without specialized training and tools.

Railcar repairers specialize in servicing railroad locomotives and other rolling stock, streetcars and subway cars, or mine cars. Most railcar repairers work for railroads, public and private transit companies, and railcar manufacturers.

Work environment. Heavy vehicle and mobile equipment service technicians usually work indoors. To repair vehicles and equipment, technicians often lift heavy parts and tools, handle greasy and dirty parts, and stand or lie in awkward positions. Minor cuts, burns, and bruises are common, but serious accidents normally are avoided when safety practices are observed. Although some shops are drafty and noisy, technicians usually work in well-lighted and ventilated areas. Many employers provide uniforms, locker rooms, and shower facilities. Mobile heavy equipment mechanics and railcar repairers generally work a standard 40 hour week.

When heavy or mobile equipment breaks down at a construction site, it may be too difficult or expensive to bring into a repair shop, so the shop will send a field service technician to the site to make repairs. Field service technicians work outdoors and spend much of their time away from the shop. Generally, the more experienced service technicians specialize in field service. They drive trucks specially equipped with replacement parts and tools. On occasion, they must travel many miles to reach disabled machinery.

The hours of work for farm equipment mechanics vary according to the season of the year. During the busy planting and harvesting seasons, farm equipment mechanics often work 6 or 7 days a week, 10 to 12 hours daily. In slow winter months, however, mechanics may work fewer than 40 hours a week.

Training, Other Qualifications, and Advancement

Although industry experts recommend that applicants complete a formal diesel or heavy equipment mechanic training program after graduating from high school, many people qualify for service technician jobs by training on the job. Employers seek people with mechanical aptitude who are knowledgeable about diesel engines, transmissions, electrical systems, computers, and hydraulics.

Education and training. High school courses in automobile repair, physics, chemistry, and mathematics provide a strong foundation for a career as a service technician or mechanic. After high school, those interested in heavy vehicle repair can choose to attend many community colleges and vocational schools that offer programs in diesel technology. Some of these schools tailor programs to heavy equipment mechanics. These programs teach the basics of analytical and diagnostic techniques, electronics, and hydraulics. The increased use of electronics and computers makes training in electronics essential for new heavy and mobile equipment mechanics. Some one- to two-year programs lead to a certificate of completion, whereas others lead to an associate degree in diesel or heavy equipment mechanics. Formal training programs enable trainee technicians to advance to the journey, or experienced worker, level sooner than with informal ones.

Entry-level workers with no formal background in heavy vehicle repair begin to perform routine service tasks and make minor repairs after a few months of on-the-job training. As they prove their ability and competence, workers advance to harder jobs. After trainees master the repair and service of diesel engines, they learn to work on related components, such as brakes, transmissions, and electrical systems. Generally, a service technician with at least three to four years of on-the-job experience is accepted as fully qualified.

Many employers send trainee technicians to training sessions conducted by heavy equipment manufacturers. The sessions, which typically last up to one week, provide intensive instruction in the repair of the manufacturer's equipment. Some sessions focus on particular components found in the equipment, such as diesel engines, transmissions, axles, or electrical systems. Other sessions focus on particular types of equipment, such as crawler-loaders and crawler-dozers. When appropriate, experienced technicians attend training sessions to gain familiarity with new technology or equipment.

Other qualifications. Technicians must read and interpret service manuals, so reading ability and communication skills are both important skills to have. The technology used in heavy equipment is becoming more sophisticated, and technicians should feel comfortable with computers and electronics because hand-held diagnostic computers are often used to make engine adjustments and diagnose problems. Experience in the Armed Forces working on diesel engines and heavy equipment provides valuable background for these positions.

Certification and advancement. Industry certification often allows workers to advance faster. Voluntary certification by the National Institute for Automotive Service Excellence is the recognized industry credential for heavy vehicle and mobile equipment service technicians, who may be certified as master medium/heavy truck technicians or in a specific area of heavy-duty equipment repair, such as brakes, electrical systems, or suspension and steering. For certification in each area, technicians must pass a written examination and have at least two years of experience. High school, vocational or trade school, or community or junior college training in gasoline or diesel engine repair may substitute for up to one year of experience. To remain certified, technicians must be retested every five years.

Experienced technicians may advance to field service jobs, where they have a greater opportunity to tackle problems independently and earn additional pay. Field positions may require a commercial driver's license and a clean driving record. Technicians with administrative ability may become shop supervisors or service managers. Some technicians open their own repair shops or invest in a franchise.

Employment

Heavy vehicle and mobile equipment service technicians and mechanics held about 188,000 jobs in 2006. Approximately 131,000 were mobile heavy equipment mechanics, 31,000 were farm equipment mechanics, and 27,000 were railcar repairers.

About 29 percent were employed by machinery, equipment, and supplies merchant wholesalers. About 14 percent worked in construction, primarily for specialty trade contractors and highway, street, and bridge construction companies; another 13 percent were employed by federal, state, and local governments. Other service technicians worked in agriculture; mining; rail transportation and support activities; and commercial and industrial machinery and equipment rental, leasing, and repair. A small number repaired equipment for machinery and railroad rolling stock manufacturers or lawn and garden equipment and supplies stores. About 5 percent of service technicians were self-employed.

Nearly every area of the country employs heavy and mobile equipment service technicians and mechanics, although most work in towns and cities where equipment dealers, equipment rental and leasing companies, and construction companies have repair facilities.

Job Outlook

The number of heavy vehicle and mobile equipment service technicians and mechanics is expected to grow about as fast as average. Those who have completed postsecondary training programs should find excellent opportunities, but those without a formal background in diesel engine or heavy vehicle repair will face keen competition.

Employment change. Employment of heavy vehicle and mobile equipment service technicians and mechanics is expected to grow by 10 percent through the year 2016, about as fast as the average for all occupations. Increasing numbers of heavy duty and mobile equipment service technicians will be required to support growth in the construction and mining industries. Additionally, the agriculture and railroad industries are projected to see more demand over the decade, potentially generating new jobs for farm equipment and railcar repairers, although job opportunities for these repairers will not be as numerous. Finally, as this equipment becomes more complex, repairs increasingly must be made by specially trained technicians. In large part, these service jobs will be with wholesale equipment dealers and rental and leasing companies who do much of the repair work associated with heavy vehicles and mobile equipment.

Job prospects. Opportunities for heavy vehicle and mobile equipment service technicians and mechanics should be excellent for those who have completed formal training programs in diesel or heavy equipment mechanics. People without formal training are expected to encounter growing difficulty entering these jobs.

Most job openings for mobile, rail, and farm equipment technicians will arise from the need to replace experienced repairers who retire. Employers report difficulty finding candidates with formal postsecondary training to fill available service technician positions. This is often because young people with mechanic training and experience opt to take jobs as automotive service technicians or diesel service technicians—jobs that offer more openings and a wider variety of locations in which to work.

Construction and mining operations, which use large numbers of heavy vehicles and mobile equipment, are particularly sensitive to changes in the level of economic activity. While the increased use of such equipment increases the need for periodic service and repair, heavy and mobile equipment may be idle during downturns. Thus, opportunities for service technicians that work on construction and mining equipment may fluctuate with the nation's economic cycle. In addition, opportunities for farm equipment mechanics are seasonal and are best in warmer months.

Earnings

Median hourly earnings of mobile heavy equipment mechanics were $19.44 in May 2006, as compared to $17.65 per hour for all installation, maintenance, and repair occupations. The middle 50 percent earned between $15.65 and $23.45. The lowest 10 percent earned less than $12.64, and the highest 10 percent earned more than $28.18. Median hourly earnings in the industries employing the largest numbers of mobile heavy equipment mechanics were as follows:

- Federal government $21.96
- Local government 20.33
- Machinery, equipment, and supplies merchant wholesalers 19.15
- Commercial and industrial machinery and equipment rental and leasing 18.73
- Other specialty trade contractors...........................18.63

Median hourly earnings of farm equipment mechanics were $14.16 in May 2006. The middle 50 percent earned between $11.34 and $17.35. The lowest 10 percent earned less than $9.30, and the highest 10 percent earned more than $20.77. In machinery, equipment, and supplies merchant wholesalers, the industry employing the largest number of farm equipment mechanics, median earnings were $14.37.

Median hourly earnings of railcar repairers were $20.82 in May 2006. The middle 50 percent earned between $16.75 and $24.71. The lowest 10 percent earned less than $12.48, and the highest 10 percent earned more than $28.02. Median hourly earnings were $21.63 in rail transportation, the industry employing the largest number of railcar repairers.

Field technicians normally earn a higher wage than their counterparts because they are required to make on-the-spot decisions to serve their customers.

About 23 percent of heavy vehicle and mobile equipment service technicians and mechanics are members of unions, including the International Association of Machinists and Aerospace Workers, the International Union of Operating Engineers, and the International Brotherhood of Teamsters. Members may enjoy job benefits in addition to what employers provide.

Related Occupations

Workers in related repair occupations include aircraft and avionics equipment mechanics and service technicians; automotive service technicians and mechanics; diesel service technicians and mechanics; industrial machinery mechanics and maintenance workers; and small engine mechanics.

Sources of Additional Information

More details about job openings for heavy vehicle and mobile equipment service technicians and mechanics may be obtained from

Projections data from the National Employment Matrix

Occupational Title	SOC Code	Employment, 2006	Projected employment, 2016	Change, 2006-16 Number	Change, 2006-16 Percent
Heavy vehicle and mobile equipment service technicians and mechanics	49-3040	188,000	206,000	18,000	10
Farm equipment mechanics	49-3041	31,000	31,000	400	1
Mobile heavy equipment mechanics, except engines	49-3042	131,000	147,000	16,000	12
Rail car repairers	49-3043	27,000	28,000	1,300	5

NOTE: Data in this table are rounded.

local heavy and mobile equipment dealers and distributors, construction contractors, and government agencies. Local offices of the state employment service also may have information on job openings and training programs.

For general information about a career as a heavy vehicle and mobile equipment service technician or mechanic, contact

- The AED Foundation (Associated Equipment Dealers affiliate), 615 W. 22nd St., Oak Brook, IL 60523. Internet: http://www.aedcareers.com

A list of certified diesel service technician training programs can be obtained from

- National Automotive Technician Education Foundation (NATEF), 101 Blue Seal Dr., Suite 101, Leesburg, VA 20175. Internet: http://www.natef.org

Information on certification as a heavy-duty diesel service technician is available from

- National Institute for Automotive Service Excellence (ASE), 101 Blue Seal Dr. SE, Suite 101, Leesburg, VA 20175. Internet: http://www.asecert.org

Industrial Machinery Mechanics and Maintenance Workers

(O*NET 49-9041.00 and 49-9043.00)

Significant Points

- Most of these workers are employed in manufacturing, but a growing number work for industrial equipment dealers and repair shops.
- Machinery maintenance workers learn on the job, while industrial machinery mechanics usually need some education after high school plus experience working on specific machines.
- Applicants with broad skills in machine repair and maintenance should have favorable job prospects.

Nature of the Work

Imagine an automobile assembly line: a large conveyor system moves unfinished automobiles down the line, giant robotic welding arms bond the different body panels together, hydraulic lifts move the motor into the body of the car, and giant presses stamp body parts from flat sheets of steel. All of these machines—the hydraulic lifts, the robotic welders, the conveyor system, and the giant presses—sometimes break down. When the assembly line stops because a machine breaks down, it costs the company money. Industrial machinery mechanics and machinery maintenance workers maintain and repair these very different, and often very expensive, machines.

The most basic tasks are performed by *machinery maintenance workers*. These employees are responsible for cleaning and lubricating machinery, performing basic diagnostic tests, checking performance, and testing damaged machine parts to determine whether major repairs are necessary. In carrying out these tasks, maintenance workers must follow machine specifications and adhere to maintenance schedules. Maintenance workers may perform minor repairs, but major repairs are generally left to machinery mechanics.

Industrial machinery mechanics, also called industrial machinery repairers or maintenance machinists, are highly skilled workers who maintain and repair machinery in a plant or factory. To do this effectively, they must be able to detect minor problems and correct them before they become major. Machinery mechanics use technical manuals, their understanding of the equipment, and careful observation to discover the cause of the problem. For example, after hearing a vibration from a machine, the mechanic must decide whether it is due to worn belts, weak motor bearings, or some other problem. Mechanics need years of training and experience to diagnose problems, but computerized diagnostic systems and vibration analysis techniques provide aid in determining the nature of the problem.

After diagnosing the problem, the industrial machinery mechanic disassembles the equipment to repair or replace the necessary parts. When repairing electronically controlled machinery, mechanics may work closely with electronic repairers or electricians who maintain the machine's electronic parts. (Electrical and electronics installers and repairers are described elsewhere in this book.) Increasingly, mechanics are expected to have the electrical, electronics, and computer programming skills to repair sophisticated equipment on their own. Once a repair is made, mechanics perform tests to ensure that the machine is running smoothly.

Primary responsibilities of industrial machinery mechanics also often include preventive maintenance and the installation of new machinery. For example, they adjust and calibrate automated manufacturing equipment, such as industrial robots. Part of setting up equipment is programming the programmable logic control (PLC), a frequently used type of computer used as the control system for automated industrial machines. Situating and installing machinery has traditionally been the job of millwrights, but as plants retool and invest in new equipment, companies increasingly rely on mechanics to do this task for some machinery. (A section on millwrights appears elsewhere in this book.)

Industrial machinery mechanics and machinery maintenance workers use a variety of tools to perform repairs and preventive maintenance. They may use handtools to adjust a motor or a chain hoist to lift a heavy printing press off the ground. When replacements for broken or defective parts are not readily available, or when a machine must be quickly returned to production, mechanics may create a new part using lathes, grinders, or drill presses. Mechanics use catalogs to order replacement parts and often follow blueprints, technical manuals, and engineering specifications to maintain and fix equipment. By keeping complete and up-to-date records, mechanics try to anticipate trouble and service equipment before factory production is interrupted.

Work environment. In production facilities, these workers are subject to common shop injuries such as cuts, bruises, and strains. They also may work in awkward positions, including on top of ladders or in cramped conditions under large machinery, which exposes them to additional hazards. They often use protective equipment such as hardhats, safety glasses, steel-tipped shoes, hearing protectors, and belts.

Because factories and other facilities cannot afford to have industrial machinery out of service for long periods, mechanics may be on call or assigned to work nights or on weekends. Overtime is common among full-time industrial machinery mechanics; about 30 percent work over 40 hours a week.

Training, Other Qualifications, and Advancement

Machinery maintenance workers can usually get a job with little more than a high school diploma or its equivalent—most learn on the job. Industrial machinery mechanics, on the other hand, usually need some education after high school plus experience working on specific machines before they can be considered a mechanic.

Education and training. Employers prefer to hire those who have taken courses in mechanical drawing, mathematics, blueprint reading, computer programming, or electronics. Entry-level machinery maintenance worker positions generally require a high school diploma, GED, or its equivalent. However, employers increasingly prefer to hire machinery maintenance workers with some training in industrial technology or an area of it, such as fluid power. Machinery maintenance workers typically receive on-the-job training lasting a few months to a year to perform routine tasks, such as setting up, cleaning, lubricating, and starting machinery. This training may be offered by experienced workers, professional trainers, or representatives of equipment manufacturers.

Industrial machinery mechanics usually need a year or more of formal education and training after high school to learn the growing range of mechanical and technical skills that they need. While mechanics used to specialize in one area, such as hydraulics or electronics, many factories now require every mechanic to have knowledge of electricity, electronics, hydraulics, and computer programming.

Workers can get this training in a number of different ways. Experience in the military repairing equipment, particularly ships, is highly valued by employers. Also, two-year associate degree programs in industrial maintenance are good preparation. Some employers offer four-year apprenticeship programs that combine classroom instruction with paid on-the-job-training. Apprenticeship programs usually are sponsored by a local trade union. Other mechanics may start as helpers or in other factory jobs and learn the skills of the trade informally and by taking courses offered through their employer. Classroom instruction focuses on subjects such as shop mathematics, blueprint reading, welding, electronics, and computer training. In addition to classroom training, it is important that mechanics train on the specific machines they will repair. They can get this training on the job, through dealer or manufacturer's representatives or in a classroom.

Other qualifications. Mechanical aptitude and manual dexterity are important for workers in this occupation. Good reading comprehension is also necessary to understand the technical manuals of a wide range of machines. And, good physical conditioning and agility are necessary because repairers sometimes have to lift heavy objects or climb to reach equipment.

Advancement. Opportunities for advancement vary by specialty. Machinery maintenance workers, if they take classes and gain additional skills, may advance to industrial machinery mechanic or supervisor. Industrial machinery mechanics also advance by working with more complicated equipment and gaining additional repair skills. The most highly skilled repairers can be promoted to supervisor, master mechanic, or millwright.

Employment

Industrial machinery mechanics and maintenance workers held about 345,000 jobs in 2006. Of these, 261,000 were held by the more highly skilled industrial machinery mechanics, while machinery maintenance workers accounted for 84,000 jobs. The majority of both types of workers were employed in the manufacturing sector in industries such as food processing and chemical, fabricated metal product, machinery, and motor vehicle and parts manufacturing. Additionally, about 9 percent work in wholesale trade, mostly for dealers of industrial equipment. Manufacturers often rely on these dealers to make complex repairs to specific machines. About 7 percent of mechanics work for the commercial and industrial machinery and equipment repair and maintenance industry, often making site visits to companies to repair equipment. Local governments employ a number of machinery maintenance workers, but few mechanics.

Job Outlook

Employment of industrial machinery mechanics and maintenance workers is projected to grow about as fast as average, and job prospects should be favorable for those with a variety of repair skills.

Employment change. Employment of industrial machinery mechanics and maintenance workers is expected to grow 7 percent from 2006 to 2016, about as fast as the average for all occupations. As factories become increasingly automated, these workers will be needed to maintain and repair the automated equipment. However, many new machines are more reliable and capable of self-diagnosis, making repairs easier and quicker and somewhat slowing the growth of repairer jobs.

Industrial machinery mechanics and maintenance workers are not as affected by changes in production levels as other manufacturing workers. During slack periods, when some plant workers are laid off, mechanics often are retained to do major overhaul jobs and to keep expensive machinery in working order. In addition, replacing highly skilled and experienced industrial maintenance workers is quite difficult, which discourages lay-offs.

Job prospects. Applicants with broad skills in machine repair and maintenance should have favorable job prospects. Many mechanics are expected to retire in coming years, and employers have reported difficulty in recruiting young workers with the necessary skills to be

Projections data from the National Employment Matrix

Occupational Title	SOC Code	Employment, 2006	Projected employment, 2016	Change, 2006-16	
				Number	Percent
Industrial machinery mechanics and maintenance workers	—	345,000	368,000	23,000	7
Industrial machinery mechanics	49-9041	261,000	284,000	24,000	9
Maintenance workers, machinery	49-9043	84,000	83,000	-900	-1

NOTE: Data in this table are rounded.

industrial machinery mechanics. In addition to openings from growth, most job openings will stem from the need to replace workers who transfer to other occupations or who retire or leave the labor force for other reasons.

Earnings

Median hourly wage-and-salary earnings of industrial machinery mechanics were $19.74 in May 2006. The middle 50 percent earned between $15.87 and $24.46. The lowest 10 percent earned less than $12.84, and the highest 10 percent earned more than $29.85.

Machinery maintenance workers earned somewhat less than the higher skilled industrial machinery mechanics. Median hourly wage-and-salary earnings of machinery maintenance workers were $16.61 in May 2006. The middle 50 percent earned between $12.91 and $21.53. The lowest 10 percent earned less than $10.29, and the highest 10 percent earned more than $26.46.

Earnings vary by industry and geographic region. Median hourly wage-and-salary earnings in the industries employing the largest numbers of industrial machinery mechanics are:

Electric power generation, transmission, and distribution	$26.02
Motor vehicle parts manufacturing	24.97
Machinery, equipment, and supplies merchant wholesalers	18.94
Plastics product manufacturing	18.79
Commercial and industrial machinery and equipment (except automotive and electronic) repair and maintenance	17.78

About 18 percent of industrial machinery mechanics and maintenance workers are union members. Labor unions that represent these workers include the United Steelworkers of America; the United Auto Workers; the International Association of Machinists and Aerospace Workers; the United Brotherhood of Carpenters and Joiners of America; and the International Union of Electronic, Electrical, Salaried, Machine, and Furniture Workers-Communications Workers of America.

Related Occupations

Other occupations that involve repairing and maintaining industrial machinery include machinists; maintenance and repair workers, general; millwrights; electrical and electronics installers and repairers; electricians; and pipelayers, plumbers, pipefitters, and steamfitters.

Sources of Additional Information

Information about employment and apprenticeship opportunities may be obtained from local employers and from local offices of the state employment service. For further information on apprenticeship programs, write to the Apprenticeship Council of your state's labor department or local firms that employ machinery mechanics and repairers. You can also find information on registered apprenticeships, together with links to state apprenticeship programs, on the U.S. Department of Labor's Web site: http://www.doleta.gov/atels_bat. Apprenticeship information is also available from the U.S. Department of Labor's toll free helpline: (877) 872-5627.

Licensed Practical and Licensed Vocational Nurses

(O*NET 29-2061.00)

Significant Points

- Most training programs, lasting about 1 year, are offered by vocational or technical schools or community or junior colleges.
- Overall job prospects are expected to be very good, but job outlook varies by industry.
- Replacement needs will be a major source of job openings, as many workers leave the occupation permanently.

Nature of the Work

Licensed practical nurses (LPNs), or licensed vocational nurses (LVNs), care for people who are sick, injured, convalescent, or disabled under the direction of physicians and registered nurses. (The work of physicians and surgeons and of registered nurses is described elsewhere in this book.) The nature of the direction and supervision required varies by state and job setting.

LPNs care for patients in many ways. Often, they provide basic bedside care. Many LPNs measure and record patients' vital signs such as height, weight, temperature, blood pressure, pulse, and respiration. They also prepare and give injections and enemas, monitor catheters, dress wounds, and give alcohol rubs and massages. To help keep patients comfortable, they assist with bathing, dressing, and personal hygiene, moving in bed, standing, and walking. They might also feed patients who need help eating. Experienced LPNs may supervise nursing assistants and aides.

As part of their work, LPNs collect samples for testing, perform routine laboratory tests, and record food and fluid intake and output. They clean and monitor medical equipment. Sometimes, they help physicians and registered nurses perform tests and procedures. Some LPNs help to deliver, care for, and feed infants.

LPNs also monitor their patients and report adverse reactions to medications or treatments. LPNs gather information from patients, including their health history and how they are currently feeling. They may use this information to complete insurance forms, preauthorizations, and referrals, and they share information with registered nurses and doctors to help determine the best course of care for a patient.

LPNs often teach family members how to care for a relative or teach patients about good health habits.

Most LPNs are generalists and work in all areas of health care. However, some work in a specialized setting, such as a nursing home, a doctor's office, or in home health care. LPNs in nursing care facilities help to evaluate residents' needs, develop care plans, and supervise the care provided by nursing aides. In doctors' offices and clinics, they may be responsible for making appointments, keeping records, and performing other clerical duties. LPNs who work in home health care may prepare meals and teach family members simple nursing tasks.

In some states, LPNs are permitted to administer prescribed medicines, start intravenous fluids, and provide care to ventilator-dependent patients.

Work environment. Most licensed practical nurses in hospitals and nursing care facilities work a 40-hour week, but because patients need round-the-clock care, some work nights, weekends, and holidays. They often stand for long periods and help patients move in bed, stand, or walk.

LPNs may face hazards from caustic chemicals, radiation, and infectious diseases. They are subject to back injuries when moving patients. They often must deal with the stress of heavy workloads. In addition, the patients they care for may be confused, agitated, or uncooperative.

Training, Other Qualifications, and Advancement

Most training programs, lasting about one year, are offered by vocational or technical schools or community or junior colleges. LPNs must be licensed to practice. Successful completion of a practical nurse program and passing an examination are required to become licensed.

Education and training. All states and the District of Columbia require LPNs to pass a licensing examination, known as the NCLEX-PN, after completing a state-approved practical nursing program. A high school diploma or its equivalent usually is required for entry, although some programs accept candidates without a diploma, and some programs are part of a high school curriculum.

In 2006, there were more than 1,500 state-approved training programs in practical nursing. Most training programs are available from technical and vocational schools or community and junior colleges. Other programs are available through high schools, hospitals, and colleges and universities.

Most year-long practical nursing programs include both classroom study and supervised clinical practice (patient care). Classroom study covers basic nursing concepts and subjects related to patient care, including anatomy, physiology, medical-surgical nursing, pediatrics, obstetrics, psychiatric nursing, the administration of drugs, nutrition, and first aid. Clinical practice usually is in a hospital but sometimes includes other settings.

Licensure. The NCLEX-PN licensing exam is required in order to obtain licensure as an LPN. The exam is developed and administered by the National Council of State Boards of Nursing. The NCLEX-PN is a computer-based exam and varies in length. The exam covers four major categories: safe and effective care environment, health promotion and maintenance, psychosocial integrity, and physiological integrity.

Other qualifications. LPNs should have a caring, sympathetic nature. They should be emotionally stable because working with the sick and injured can be stressful. They also need to be observant, and to have good decision-making and communication skills. As part of a health-care team, they must be able to follow orders and work under close supervision.

Advancement. In some employment settings, such as nursing homes, LPNs can advance to become charge nurses who oversee the work of other LPNs and of nursing aides. Some LPNs also choose to become registered nurses through numerous LPN-to-RN training programs.

Employment

Licensed practical nurses held about 749,000 jobs in 2006. About 26 percent of LPNs worked in hospitals, 26 percent in nursing care facilities, and another 12 percent in offices of physicians. Others worked for home health care services; employment services; residential care facilities; community care facilities for the elderly; outpatient care centers; and federal, state, and local government agencies. About 19 percent worked part time.

Job Outlook

Employment of LPNs is projected to grow faster than average. Overall job prospects are expected to be very good, but job outlook varies by industry. The best job opportunities will occur in nursing care facilities and home health care services, while applicants for jobs in hospitals may face competition.

Employment change. Employment of LPNs is expected to grow 14 percent between 2006 and 2016, faster than the average for all occupations, in response to the long-term care needs of an increasing elderly population and the general increase in demand for health care services.

Many procedures once performed only in hospitals are being performed in physicians' offices and in outpatient care centers such as ambulatory surgical and emergency medical centers, largely because of advances in technology. LPNs care for patients who undergo these and other procedures, so employment of LPNs is projected to decline in traditional hospitals, but is projected to grow faster than average in most settings outside of hospitals. However, some hospitals are assigning a larger share of nursing duties to LPNs, which will temper the employment decline in the industry.

Employment of LPNs is expected to grow much faster than average in home health care services. Home health care agencies will offer a large number of new jobs for LPNs because of an increasing number of older people with functional disabilities, consumer preference for care in the home, and technological advances that make it possible to bring increasingly complex treatments into the home.

Employment of LPNs in nursing care facilities is expected to grow faster than average, and provide the most new jobs for LPNs, because of the growing number of people who are aged and disabled and in need of long-term care. In addition, LPNs in nursing care facilities will be needed to care for the increasing number of patients who have been discharged from the hospital but who have not recovered enough to return home.

Projections data from the National Employment Matrix

Occupational Title	SOC Code	Employment, 2006	Projected employment, 2016	Change, 2006-2016 Number	Change, 2006-2016 Percent
Licensed practical and licensed vocational nurses	29-2061	749,000	854,000	105,000	14

NOTE: Data in this table are rounded.

Job prospects. Replacement needs will be a major source of job openings, as many workers leave the occupation permanently. Very good job opportunities are expected. Rapid employment growth is projected in most health care industries, with the best job opportunities occurring in nursing care facilities and in home health care services. However, applicants for jobs in hospitals may face competition as the number of hospital jobs for LPNs declines.

Earnings

Median annual earnings of licensed practical nurses were $36,550 in May 2006. The middle 50 percent earned between $31,080 and $43,640. The lowest 10 percent earned less than $26,380, and the highest 10 percent earned more than $50,480. Median annual earnings in the industries employing the largest numbers of licensed practical nurses in May 2006 were

Employment services	$42,110
Nursing care facilities	38,320
Home health care services	37,880
General medical and surgical hospitals	35,000
Offices of physicians	32,710

Related Occupations

LPNs work closely with people while helping them. So do emergency medical technicians and paramedics; medical assistants; nursing, psychiatric, and home health aides; registered nurses; athletic trainers; social and human service assistants; pharmacy technicians; pharmacy aides; and surgical technologists.

Sources of Additional Information

For information about practical nursing, contact the following organizations:

- National Association for Practical Nurse Education and Service, Inc., P.O. Box 25647, Alexandria, VA 22313. Internet: http://www.napnes.org
- National Federation of Licensed Practical Nurses, Inc., 605 Poole Dr., Garner, NC 27529. Internet: http://www.nflpn.org
- National League for Nursing, 61 Broadway, New York, NY 10006. Internet: http://www.nln.org

Information on the NCLEX-PN licensing exam is available from

- National Council of State Boards of Nursing, 111 East Wacker Dr., Suite 2900, Chicago, IL 60611. Internet: http://www.ncsbn.org

A list of state-approved LPN programs is available from individual state boards of nursing.

Machinists

(O*NET 51-4041.00)

Significant Points

- Machinists learn in apprenticeship programs, informally on the job, in vocational high schools, and in community or technical colleges.
- Many entrants previously have worked as machine setters, operators, or tenders.
- Although employment is projected to decline, job opportunities are expected to be good.

Nature of the Work

Machinists use machine tools, such as lathes, milling machines, and machining centers, to produce precision metal parts. Although they may produce large quantities of one part, precision machinists often produce small batches or one-of-a-kind items. They use their knowledge of the working properties of metals and their skill with machine tools to plan and carry out the operations needed to make machined products that meet precise specifications.

Machinists first review electronic or written blueprints or specifications for a job before they machine a part. Next, they calculate where to cut or bore into the workpiece—the piece of steel, aluminum, titanium, plastic, silicon or any other material that is being shaped. They determine how fast to feed the workpiece into the machine and how much material to remove. They then select tools and materials for the job, plan the sequence of cutting and finishing operations, and mark the workpiece to show where cuts should be made.

After this layout work is completed, machinists perform the necessary machining operations. They position the workpiece on the machine tool—drill press, lathe, milling machine, or other type of machine—set the controls, and make the cuts. During the machining process, they must constantly monitor the feed rate and speed of the machine. Machinists also ensure that the workpiece is properly lubricated and cooled because the machining of metal products generates a significant amount of heat. The temperature of the workpiece is a key concern because most metals expand when heated; machinists must adjust the size of their cuts relative to the temperature.

During the cutting process, machinists detect problems by listening for specific sounds—for example, that of a dull cutting tool or excessive vibration. Dull cutting tools are removed and replaced. Cutting speeds are adjusted to compensate for harmonic vibrations, which can decrease the accuracy of cuts, particularly on newer high-speed spindles and lathes. After the work is completed, machinists use both simple and highly sophisticated measuring tools to check the accuracy of their work against blueprints.

Some machinists, often called production machinists, may produce large quantities of one part, especially parts requiring the use of complex operations and great precision. Many modern machine tools are computer numerically controlled (CNC). CNC machines, following a computer program, control the cutting tool speed, change dull tools, and perform all of the necessary cuts to create a part. Frequently, machinists work with computer control programmers to determine how the automated equipment will cut a part. (See the section on computer control programmers and operators elsewhere in this book.) The machinist determines the cutting path, speed of the cut and the feed rate, and the programmer converts path, speed, and feed information into a set of instructions for the CNC machine tool.

Because most machinists train in CNC programming, they may write basic programs themselves and often modify programs in response to problems encountered during test runs. Modifications, called offsets, not only fix problems, but they also improve efficiency by reducing manufacturing time and tool wear. After the production process is designed, computer control operators implement it by performing relatively simple and repetitive operations.

Some manufacturing techniques employ automated parts loaders, automatic tool changers, and computer controls, allowing machines to operate without anyone present. One production machinist, working 8 hours a day, might monitor equipment, replace worn cutting tools, check the accuracy of parts being produced, adjust offsets, and perform other tasks on several CNC machines that operate 24 hours a day. In the off-hours, during what is known as "lights-out manufacturing," a factory may need only a few machinists to monitor the entire factory.

Maintenance machinists repair or make new parts for existing machinery. After an industrial machinery mechanic or maintenance worker discovers the broken part of a machine, they give the broken part to the machinist. (See the section on industrial machinery mechanics and maintenance workers elsewhere in this book.) To replace broken parts, maintenance machinists refer to blueprints and perform the same machining operations that were needed to create the original part. While production machinists are concentrated in a few industries, maintenance machinists work in many manufacturing industries.

Because the technology of machining is changing rapidly, machinists must learn to operate a wide range of machines. Some newer machines use lasers, water jets, or electrified wires to cut the workpiece. While some of the computer controls are similar to other machine tools, machinists must understand the unique cutting properties of these different machines. As engineers create new types of machine tools and new materials to machine, machinists must constantly learn new machining properties and techniques.

Work environment. Today, most machine shops are relatively clean, well lit, and ventilated. Many computer-controlled machines are partially or totally enclosed, minimizing the exposure of workers to noise, debris, and the lubricants used to cool workpieces during machining. Nevertheless, working around machine tools presents certain dangers, and workers must follow safety precautions. Machinists wear protective equipment, such as safety glasses to shield against bits of flying metal and earplugs to dampen machinery noise. They also must exercise caution when handling hazardous coolants and lubricants, although many common water-based lubricants present little hazard. The job requires stamina because machinists stand most of the day and, at times, may need to lift moderately heavy workpieces. Modern factories use autoloaders and overhead cranes to reduce heavy lifting.

Many machinists work a 40-hour week. Evening and weekend shifts are becoming more common as companies extend hours of operation to make better use of expensive machines. However, this trend is somewhat offset by lights-out manufacturing that uses fewer machinists and the use of machine operators for less desirable shifts. Overtime is common during peak production periods.

Training, Other Qualifications, and Advancement

Machinists train in apprenticeship programs, vocational schools, or community or technical colleges, or informally on the job. Many entrants previously have worked as machine setters, operators, or tenders.

Education and training. There are many different ways to become a skilled machinist. Many entrants previously have worked as machine setters, operators, or tenders. In high school, students should take math courses, especially trigonometry, and, if available, courses in blueprint reading, metalworking, and drafting. After high school, some machinists learn entirely on the job, but most acquire their skills in a mix of classroom and on-the-job training. Formal apprenticeship programs, typically sponsored by a union or manufacturer, are an excellent way to learn the job of machinist, but are often hard to get into. Apprentices usually must have a high school diploma, GED, or the equivalent, and most have taken algebra and trigonometry classes.

Apprenticeship programs consist of paid shop training and related classroom instruction lasting up to four years. In shop training, apprentices work almost full time and are supervised by an experienced machinist while learning to operate various machine tools. Classroom instruction includes math, physics, materials science, blueprint reading, mechanical drawing, and quality and safety practices. In addition, as machine shops have increased their use of computer-controlled equipment, training in the operation and programming of CNC machine tools has become essential. Apprenticeship classes are often taught in cooperation with local community colleges or vocational-technical schools. A growing number of machinists are learning the trade through two-year associate degree programs at community or technical colleges. Graduates of these programs still need significant on-the-job experience before they are fully qualified.

Certification and other qualifications. People interested in becoming machinists should be mechanically inclined, have good problem-solving abilities, be able to work independently, and be able to do highly accurate work (tolerances may reach 50 millionths of an inch) that requires concentration and physical effort. Experience working with machine tools is helpful. In fact, many entrants have worked as machine setters, operators, or tenders.

To boost the skill level of machinists and to create a more uniform standard of competency, a number of training facilities, state apprenticeship boards, and colleges are implementing curriculums that incorporate national skills standards developed by the National Institute of Metalworking Skills (NIMS). After completing such a curriculum and passing practical and written exams, trainees are granted a NIMS credential. Completing a recognized certification program provides a machinist with better career opportunities and helps employers better judge the abilities of new hires. Journeyworker certification can be obtained from state apprenticeship boards after completing an apprenticeship.

As new automation is introduced, machinists normally receive additional training to update their skills. This training usually is provided by a representative of the equipment manufacturer or a local technical school. Some employers offer tuition reimbursement for job-related courses.

Advancement. Machinists can advance in several ways. Experienced machinists may become CNC programmers, tool and die makers, or mold makers, or be promoted to supervisory or administrative positions in their firms. A few open their own machine shops.

Employment

Machinists held about 397,000 jobs in 2006. About 78 percent of machinists work in manufacturing industries, such as machine shops and machinery, motor vehicle and parts, aerospace products and parts, and other transportation equipment manufacturing. Mainte-

Projections data from the National Employment Matrix

Occupational Title	SOC Code	Employment, 2006	Projected employment, 2016	Change, 2006-16	
				Number	Percent
Machinists	51-4041	397,000	384,000	-12,000	-3

NOTE: Data in this table are rounded.

nance machinists work in most industries that use production machinery.

Job Outlook

Although employment of machinists is projected to decline slowly, job prospects are expected to be good.

Employment change. Employment of machinists is projected to decline slowly by 3 percent over the 2006–2016 decade because of rising productivity among these workers and strong foreign competition in the manufacture of goods. Machinists will become more efficient as a result of the expanded use of and improvements in technologies such as CNC machine tools, autoloaders, and high-speed machining. This allows fewer machinists to accomplish the same amount of work. Technology is not expected to affect the employment of machinists as significantly as that of some other production workers, however, because machinists monitor and maintain many automated systems. Due to modern production techniques, employers prefer workers, such as machinists, who have a wide range of skills and are capable of performing almost any task in a machine shop.

Job prospects. Despite the projected decline in employment, job opportunities for machinists should continue to be good as employers value the wide-ranging skills of these workers. Also, many young people with the necessary educational and personal qualifications needed to become machinists prefer to attend college or may not wish to enter production occupations. Therefore, the number of workers learning to be machinists is expected to be less than the number of job openings arising each year from the need to replace experienced machinists who retire or transfer to other occupations.

Employment levels in this occupation are influenced by economic cycles—as the demand for machined goods falls, machinists involved in production may be laid off or forced to work fewer hours. Employment of machinists involved in plant maintenance, however, often is more stable because proper maintenance and repair of costly equipment remains critical to manufacturing operations, even when production levels fall.

Earnings

Median hourly wage-and-salary earnings of machinists were $16.71 in May 2006. The middle 50 percent earned between $13.14 and $20.82. The lowest 10 percent earned less than $10.29, while the top 10 percent earned more than $25.31. Median hourly wage-and-salary earnings in the manufacturing industries employing the largest number of machinists were

Aerospace product and parts manufacturing $18.46
Motor vehicle parts manufacturing..........................18.27
Metalworking machinery manufacturing 17.36
Machine shops; turned product; and screw, nut, and bolt manufacturing 16.24
Employment services 11.98

Apprentices earn much less than experienced machinists, but earnings increase quickly as they improve their skills. Also most employers pay for apprentices' training classes.

Related Occupations

Occupations most closely related to that of machinist are other machining occupations, which include tool and die makers; machine setters, operators, and tenders—metal and plastic; and computer control programmers and operators. Maintenance machinists work closely with industrial machinery mechanics and maintenance workers.

Sources of Additional Information

For general information about a career in machining, contact

- Precision Machine Products Association, 6700 West Snowville Rd., Brecksville, OH 44141. Internet: http://www.pmpa.org

For a list of training centers and apprenticeship programs, contact

- National Tooling and Machining Association, 9300 Livingston Rd., Fort Washington, MD 20744.

For more information on credential standards and apprenticeship, contact

- The National Institute for Metalworking Skills, 10565 Fairfax Blvd., Suite 203, Fairfax, VA 22030. Internet: http://www.nims-skills.org/home/index.htm

Information on the registered apprenticeship system with links to state apprenticeship programs may also be found on the U.S. Department of Labor's Web site: http://www.doleta.gov/atels_bat. Apprenticeship information is also available from the U.S. Department of Labor's toll free helpline: (877) 872-5627.

STEM Mathematicians

(O*NET 15-2021.00)

Significant Points

- A Ph.D. in mathematics usually is the minimum educational requirement, except in the federal government.
- Master's degree and Ph.D. holders with a strong background in mathematics and a related field, such as computer science or engineering, should have better employment opportunities in related occupations.
- Average employment growth is expected for mathematicians.

Nature of the Work

Mathematics is one of the oldest and most fundamental sciences. Mathematicians use mathematical theory, computational techniques, algorithms, and the latest computer technology to solve economic, scientific, engineering, physics, and business problems. The work of mathematicians falls into two broad classes—theoretical (pure) mathematics and applied mathematics. These classes, however, are not sharply defined and often overlap.

Theoretical mathematicians advance mathematical knowledge by developing new principles and recognizing previously unknown relationships between existing principles of mathematics. Although these workers seek to increase basic knowledge without necessarily considering its practical use, such pure and abstract knowledge has been instrumental in producing or furthering many scientific and engineering achievements. Many theoretical mathematicians are employed as university faculty, dividing their time between teaching and conducting research. (See the statement on teachers—postsecondary elsewhere in this book.)

Applied mathematicians, on the other hand, use theories and techniques, such as mathematical modeling and computational methods, to formulate and solve practical problems in business, government, engineering, and the physical, life, and social sciences. For example, they may analyze the most efficient way to schedule airline routes between cities, the effects and safety of new drugs, the aerodynamic characteristics of an experimental automobile, or the cost-effectiveness of alternative manufacturing processes.

Applied mathematicians working in industrial research and development may develop or enhance mathematical methods when solving a difficult problem. Some mathematicians, called cryptanalysts, analyze and decipher encryption systems—codes—designed to transmit military, political, financial, or law enforcement-related information.

Applied mathematicians start with a practical problem, envision its separate elements, and then reduce the elements to mathematical variables. They often use computers to analyze relationships among the variables and solve complex problems by developing models with alternative solutions.

Individuals with titles other than mathematician do much of the work in applied mathematics. In fact, because mathematics is the foundation on which so many other academic disciplines are built, the number of workers using mathematical techniques is much greater than the number formally called mathematicians. For example, engineers, computer scientists, physicists, and economists are among those who use mathematics extensively. Some professionals, including statisticians, actuaries, and operations research analysts, are actually specialists in a particular branch of mathematics. (For more information, see the statements on actuaries, operations research analysts, and statisticians elsewhere in this book.) Applied mathematicians are frequently required to collaborate with other workers in their organizations to find common solutions to problems.

Work environment. Mathematicians usually work in comfortable offices. They often are part of interdisciplinary teams that may include economists, engineers, computer scientists, physicists, technicians, and others. Deadlines, overtime work, special requests for information or analysis, and prolonged travel to attend seminars or conferences may be part of their jobs.

Mathematicians who work in academia usually have a mix of teaching and research responsibilities. These mathematicians may conduct research alone or in close collaboration with other mathematicians. Collaborators may work together at the same institution or from different locations, using technology such as e-mail to communicate. Mathematicians in academia also may be aided by graduate students.

Training, Other Qualifications, and Advancement

A Ph.D. degree in mathematics usually is the minimum educational requirement for prospective mathematicians, except in the federal government.

Education and training. In the federal government, entry-level job candidates usually must have at least a bachelor's degree with a major in mathematics or 24 semester hours of mathematics courses. Outside the federal government, bachelor's degree holders in mathematics usually are not qualified for most jobs, and many seek advanced degrees in mathematics or a related discipline.

Most colleges and universities offer a bachelor's degree in mathematics. Courses usually required for this degree include calculus, differential equations, and linear and abstract algebra. Additional courses might include probability theory and statistics, mathematical analysis, numerical analysis, topology, discrete mathematics, and mathematical logic. Many colleges and universities advise or require students majoring in mathematics to take courses in a closely related field, such as computer science, engineering, life science, physical science, or economics. A double major in mathematics and another related discipline is particularly desirable to many employers. High school students who are prospective college mathematics majors should take as many mathematics courses as possible while in high school.

In private industry, candidates for mathematician jobs typically need a Ph.D., although there may be opportunities for those with a master's degree. Most of the positions designated for mathematicians are in research and development laboratories, as part of technical teams.

In 2007, there were more than 300 graduate programs, offering both master's and doctoral degrees, in pure or applied mathematics around the country. In graduate school, students conduct research and take advanced courses, usually specializing in a subfield of mathematics.

Other qualifications. For jobs in applied mathematics, training in the field in which mathematics will be used is very important. Mathematics is used extensively in physics, actuarial science, statistics, engineering, and operations research. Computer science, business and industrial management, economics, finance, chemistry, geology, life sciences, and behavioral sciences are likewise dependent on applied mathematics. Mathematicians also should have substantial knowledge of computer programming, because most complex mathematical computation and much mathematical modeling are done on a computer.

Mathematicians need to have good reasoning to identify, analyze, and apply basic principles to technical problems. Communication skills also are important, as mathematicians must be able to interact and discuss proposed solutions with people who may not have extensive knowledge of mathematics.

Advancement. Bachelor's degree holders who meet state certification requirements may become primary or secondary school mathematics teachers.

The majority of those with a master's degree in mathematics who work in private industry do so not as mathematicians but in related fields such as computer science, where they have titles such as computer programmer, systems analyst, or systems engineer.

Employment

Mathematicians held about 3,000 jobs in 2006. Many people with mathematical backgrounds also worked in other occupations. For example, there were about 54,000 jobs as postsecondary mathematical science teachers in 2006.

Many mathematicians work for federal or state governments. The U.S. Department of Defense is the primary federal employer, accounting for about 37 percent of the mathematicians employed by the federal government. Many of the other mathematicians employed by the federal government work for the National Aeronautics and Space Administration (NASA).

In the private sector, major employers include scientific research and development services and management, scientific, and technical consulting services. Some mathematicians also work for software publishers, insurance companies, and in aerospace or pharmaceutical manufacturing.

Job Outlook

Employment of mathematicians is expected to grow as fast as the average. However, keen competition for jobs is expected.

Employment change. Employment of mathematicians is expected to increase by 10 percent during the 2006–16 decade, as fast as the average for all occupations. Advancements in technology usually lead to expanding applications of mathematics, and more workers with knowledge of mathematics will be required in the future. However, jobs in industry and government often require advanced knowledge of related scientific disciplines in addition to mathematics. The most common fields in which mathematicians study and find work are computer science and software development, physics, engineering, and operations research. More mathematicians also are becoming involved in financial analysis.

Job prospects. Job competition will remain keen because employment in this occupation is relatively small and few new jobs are expected. Master's degree and Ph.D. holders with a strong background in mathematics and a related discipline, such as engineering or computer science, and who apply mathematical theory to real-world problems will have the best job prospects in related occupations.

Holders of a master's degree in mathematics will face very strong competition for jobs in theoretical research. Because the number of Ph.D. degrees awarded in mathematics continues to exceed the number of available university positions—especially those that are tenure tracked—many graduates will need to find employment in industry and government.

Additionally, employment in theoretical mathematical research is sensitive to general economic fluctuations and to changes in government spending. Job prospects will be greatly influenced by changes in public and private funding for research and development.

Earnings

Median annual earnings of mathematicians were $86,930 in May 2006. The middle 50 percent earned between $62,970 and $106,250. The lowest 10 percent had earnings of less than $43,500, while the highest 10 percent earned more than $132,190.

In early 2007, the average annual salary for mathematicians employed by the federal government in supervisory, nonsupervisory, and managerial positions was $93,539; for mathematical statisticians, $96,121; and for cryptanalysts, the average was $90,435.

Related Occupations

Other occupations that require extensive knowledge of mathematics or, in some cases, a degree in mathematics include actuaries, statisticians, computer programmers, computer systems analysts, computer scientists and database administrators, computer software engineers, and operations research analysts. A strong background in mathematics also facilitates employment as teachers—postsecondary; teachers—preschool, kindergarten, elementary, middle, and secondary; engineers; economists; market and survey researchers; financial analysts and personal financial advisors; and physicists and astronomers.

Sources of Additional Information

For more information about careers and training in mathematics, especially for doctoral-level employment, contact

- American Mathematical Society, 201 Charles St., Providence, RI 02904-2294. Internet: http://www.ams.org

For specific information on careers in applied mathematics, contact

- Society for Industrial and Applied Mathematics, 3600 University City Science Center, Philadelphia, PA 19104-2688. Internet: http://www.siam.org

Information on obtaining positions as mathematicians with the federal government is available from the Office of Personnel Management through USAJOBS, the federal government's official employment information system. This resource for locating and applying for job opportunities can be accessed through the Internet at http://www.usajobs.gov or through an interactive voice response telephone system at (703) 724-1850 or TDD (978) 461-8404. These numbers are not toll free, and charges may result.

For advice on how to find and apply for federal jobs, see the *Occupational Outlook Quarterly* article "How to get a job in the Federal Government," online at http://www.bls.gov/opub/ooq/2004/summer/art01.pdf.

Projections data from the National Employment Matrix

Occupational Title	SOC Code	Employment, 2006	Projected employment, 2016	Change, 2006-2016	
				Number	Percent
Mathematicians	15-2021	3,000	3,300	300	10

NOTE: Data in this table are rounded.

Medical and Health Services Managers

(O*NET 11-9111.00)

Significant Points

- Job opportunities will be good, especially for applicants with work experience in health care and strong business and management skills.
- A master's degree is the standard credential, although a bachelor's degree is adequate for some entry-level positions.
- Medical and health services managers typically work long hours and may be called at all hours to deal with problems.

Nature of the Work

Health care is a business and, like every business, it needs good management to keep it running smoothly. Medical and health services managers, also referred to as *health-care executives* or *health-care administrators*, plan, direct, coordinate, and supervise the delivery of health care. These workers are either specialists in charge of a specific clinical department or generalists who manage an entire facility or system.

The structure and financing of health care are changing rapidly. Future medical and health services managers must be prepared to deal with the integration of health-care delivery systems, technological innovations, an increasingly complex regulatory environment, restructuring of work, and an increased focus on preventive care. They will be called on to improve efficiency in health-care facilities and the quality of the care provided.

Large facilities usually have several assistant administrators who aid the top administrator and handle daily decisions. Assistant administrators direct activities in clinical areas such as nursing, surgery, therapy, medical records, or health information.

In smaller facilities, top administrators handle more of the details of daily operations. For example, many nursing home administrators manage personnel, finances, facility operations, and admissions while also providing resident care.

Clinical managers have training or experience in a specific clinical area and, accordingly, have more specific responsibilities than do generalists. For example, directors of physical therapy are experienced physical therapists, and most health information and medical record administrators have a bachelor's degree in health information or medical record administration. Clinical managers establish and implement policies, objectives, and procedures for their departments; evaluate personnel and work quality; develop reports and budgets; and coordinate activities with other managers.

Health information managers are responsible for the maintenance and security of all patient records. Recent regulations enacted by the federal government require that all health-care providers maintain electronic patient records and that these records be secure. As a result, health information managers must keep up with current computer and software technology and with legislative requirements. In addition, as patient data become more frequently used for quality management and in medical research, health information managers ensure that databases are complete, accurate, and available only to authorized personnel.

In group medical practices, managers work closely with physicians. Whereas an office manager might handle business affairs in small medical groups, leaving policy decisions to the physicians themselves, larger groups usually employ a full-time administrator to help formulate business strategies and coordinate day-to-day business.

A small group of 10 to 15 physicians might employ 1 administrator to oversee personnel matters, billing and collection, budgeting, planning, equipment outlays, and patient flow. A large practice of 40 to 50 physicians might have a chief administrator and several assistants, each responsible for different areas.

Medical and health services managers in managed care settings perform functions similar to those of their counterparts in large group practices, except that they could have larger staffs to manage. In addition, they might do more community outreach and preventive care than do managers of a group practice.

Some medical and health services managers oversee the activities of a number of facilities in health systems. Such systems might contain both inpatient and outpatient facilities and offer a wide range of patient services.

Work environment. Some managers work in comfortable, private offices; others share space with other staff. Most medical and health services managers work long hours. Nursing care facilities and hospitals operate around the clock; administrators and managers may be called at all hours to deal with problems. They also travel to attend meetings or inspect satellite facilities.

Training, Other Qualifications, and Advancement

A master's degree in one of a number of fields is the standard credential for most generalist positions as a medical or health-care manager. A bachelor's degree is sometimes adequate for entry-level positions in smaller facilities and departments. In physicians' offices and some other facilities, on-the-job experience may substitute for formal education.

Education and training. Medical and health services managers must be familiar with management principles and practices. A master's degree in health services administration, long-term care administration, health sciences, public health, public administration, or business administration is the standard credential for most generalist positions in this field. However, a bachelor's degree is adequate for some entry-level positions in smaller facilities, at the departmental level within health-care organizations, and in health information management. Physicians' offices and some other facilities hire those with on-the-job experience instead of formal education.

Bachelor's, master's, and doctoral degree programs in health administration are offered by colleges; universities; and schools of public health, medicine, allied health, public administration, and business administration. In 2007, 72 schools had accredited programs leading to the master's degree in health services administration, according to the Commission on Accreditation of Healthcare Management Education.

For people seeking to become heads of clinical departments, a degree in the appropriate field and work experience may be sufficient early in their career. However, a master's degree in health services administration or a related field might be required to advance. For example, nursing service administrators usually are chosen from among supervisory registered nurses with administrative abilities and graduate degrees in nursing or health services administration.

Health information managers require a bachelor's degree from an accredited program. In 2007, there were 42 accredited bachelor's degree programs and three master's degree programs in health information management, according to the Commission on Accreditation for Health Informatics and Information Management Education.

Some graduate programs seek students with undergraduate degrees in business or health administration; however, many graduate programs prefer students with a liberal arts or health profession background. Candidates with previous work experience in health care also may have an advantage. Competition for entry into these programs is keen, and applicants need above-average grades to gain admission. Graduate programs usually last between two and three years. They may include up to one year of supervised administrative experience and coursework in areas such as hospital organization and management, marketing, accounting and budgeting, human resources administration, strategic planning, law and ethics, biostatistics or epidemiology, health economics, and health information systems. Some programs allow students to specialize in one type of facility—hospitals, nursing care facilities, mental health facilities, or medical groups. Other programs encourage a generalist approach to health administration education.

Licensure. All states and the District of Columbia require nursing care facility administrators to have a bachelor's degree, pass a licensing examination, complete a state-approved training program, and pursue continuing education. Some states also require licenses for administrators in assisted living facilities. A license is not required in other areas of medical and health services management.

Certification and other qualifications. Medical and health services managers often are responsible for facilities and equipment worth millions of dollars and for hundreds of employees. To make effective decisions, they need to be open to different opinions and good at analyzing contradictory information. They must understand finance and information systems and be able to interpret data. Motivating others to implement their decisions requires strong leadership abilities. Tact, diplomacy, flexibility, and communication skills are essential because medical and health services managers spend most of their time interacting with others.

Health information managers who have a bachelor's degree or post-baccalaureate from an approved program and who pass an exam can earn certification as a Registered Health Information Administrator from the American Health Information Management Association.

Advancement. Medical and health services managers advance by moving into more responsible and higher-paying positions, such as assistant or associate administrator, department head, or chief executive officer, or by moving to larger facilities. Some experienced managers also may become consultants or professors of health-care management.

New graduates with master's degrees in health services administration may start as department managers or as supervisory staff. The level of the starting position varies with the experience of the applicant and the size of the organization. Hospitals and other health facilities offer postgraduate residencies and fellowships, which usually are staff positions. Graduates from master's degree programs also take jobs in large medical group practices, clinics, mental health facilities, nursing care corporations, and consulting firms.

Graduates with bachelor's degrees in health administration usually begin as administrative assistants or assistant department heads in larger hospitals. They also may begin as department heads or assistant administrators in small hospitals or nursing care facilities.

Employment

Medical and health services managers held about 262,000 jobs in 2006. About 37 percent worked in hospitals, and another 22 percent worked in offices of physicians or in nursing and residential care facilities. Most of the remainder worked in home health care services, federal government health care facilities, outpatient care centers, insurance carriers, and community care facilities for the elderly.

Job Outlook

Employment of medical and health services managers is expected to grow faster than average. Job opportunities should be good, especially for applicants with work experience in the health care field and strong business management skills.

Employment change. Employment of medical and health services managers is expected to grow 16 percent from 2006 to 2016, faster than the average for all occupations. The health care industry will continue to expand and diversify, requiring managers to help ensure smooth business operations.

Managers in all settings will be needed to improve the quality and efficiency of health care while controlling costs, as insurance companies and Medicare demand higher levels of accountability. Managers also will be needed to oversee the computerization of patient records and to ensure their security as required by law. Additional demand for managers will stem from the need to recruit workers and increase employee retention, to comply with changing regulations, to implement new technology, and to help improve the health of their communities by emphasizing preventive care.

Hospitals will continue to employ the most medical and health services managers over the 2006–2016 decade. However, the number of new jobs created is expected to increase at a slower rate in hospitals than in many other industries because of the growing use of clinics and other outpatient care sites. Despite relatively slow employment growth, a large number of new jobs will be created because of the industry's large size.

Employment will grow fastest in practitioners' offices and in home health care agencies. Many services previously provided in hospitals will continue to shift to these settings, especially as medical technologies improve. Demand in medical group practice management will grow as medical group practices become larger and more complex.

Medical and health services managers also will be employed by health-care management companies that provide management services to hospitals and other organizations and to specific departments such as emergency, information management systems, managed care contract negotiations, and physician recruiting.

Job prospects. Job opportunities will be good, and applicants with work experience in the health care field and strong business management skills should have the best opportunities. Medical and health services managers with experience in large hospital facilities will enjoy an advantage in the job market as hospitals become larger and more complex. Competition for jobs at the highest management levels will be keen because of the high pay and prestige.

Projections data from the National Employment Matrix

Occupational Title	SOC Code	Employment, 2006	Projected employment, 2016	Change, 2006-16	
				Number	Percent
Medical and health services managers	11-9111	262,000	305,000	43,000	16

NOTE: Data in this table are rounded.

Earnings

Median annual earnings of wage and salary medical and health services managers were $73,340 in May 2006. The middle 50 percent earned between $57,240 and $94,780. The lowest 10 percent earned less than $45,050, and the highest 10 percent earned more than $127,830. Median annual earnings in the industries employing the largest numbers of medical and health services managers in May 2006 were

General medical and surgical hospitals $78,660
Outpatient care centers 67,920
Offices of physicians 67,540
Nursing care facilities 66,730
Home health care services 66,720

Earnings of medical and health services managers vary by type and size of the facility and by level of responsibility. For example, the Medical Group Management Association reported that, in 2006, median salaries for administrators were $72,875 in practices with 6 or fewer physicians, $95,766 in practices with 7 to 25 physicians, and $132,955 in practices with 26 or more physicians.

According to a survey by the Professional Association of Health Care Office Management, 2006 average total compensation for office managers in specialty physicians' practices was $70,474 in gastroenterology, $70,599 in dermatology, $76,392 in cardiology, $67,317 in ophthalmology, $67,222 in obstetrics and gynecology, $77,621 in orthopedics, $62,125 in pediatrics, $66,853 in internal medicine, and $60,040 in family practice.

Related Occupations

Medical and health services managers have training or experience in both health and management. Other occupations requiring knowledge of both fields are insurance underwriters and social and community service managers.

Sources of Additional Information

Information about undergraduate and graduate academic programs in this field is available from

- Association of University Programs in Health Administration, 2000 North 14th St., Suite 780, Arlington, VA 22201. Internet: http://www.aupha.org

For a list of accredited graduate programs in medical and health services administration, contact

- Commission on Accreditation of Healthcare Management Education, 2000 North 14th St., Suite 780, Arlington, VA 22201. Internet: http://www.cahme.org

For information about career opportunities in health care management, contact

- American College of Healthcare Executives, One N. Franklin St., Suite 1700, Chicago, IL 60606. Internet: http://www.healthmanagementcareers.org

For information about career opportunities in long-term care administration, contact

- American College of Health Care Administrators, 300 N. Lee St., Suite 301, Alexandria, VA 22314. Internet: http://www.achca.org

For information about career opportunities in medical group practices and ambulatory care management, contact

- Medical Group Management Association, 104 Inverness Terrace East, Englewood, CO 80112. Internet: http://www.mgma.org

For information about medical and health care office managers, contact

- Professional Association of Health Care Office Management, 461 East Ten Mile Rd., Pensacola, FL 32534.

For information about career opportunities in health information management, contact

- American Health Information Management Association, 233 N. Michigan Ave., Suite 2150, Chicago, IL 60601. Internet: http://www.ahima.org

Medical Records and Health Information Technicians

(O*NET 29-2071.00)

Significant Points

- Employment is expected to grow faster than average.
- Job prospects should be very good; technicians with a strong background in medical coding will be in particularly high demand.
- Entrants usually have an associate degree.
- This is one of the few health occupations in which there is little or no direct contact with patients.

Nature of the Work

Every time a patient receives health care, a record is maintained of the observations, medical or surgical interventions, and treatment outcomes. This record includes information that the patient provides concerning his or her symptoms and medical history, the results of examinations, reports of x rays and laboratory tests, diagnoses, and treatment plans. Medical records and health information technicians organize and evaluate these records for completeness and accuracy.

Technicians assemble patients' health information, making sure that patients' initial medical charts are complete, that all forms are completed and properly identified and authenticated, and that all necessary information is in the computer. They regularly communicate with physicians and other health care professionals to clarify diagnoses or to obtain additional information. Technicians regularly use computer programs to tabulate and analyze data to improve patient care, better control cost, provide documentation for use in legal actions, or use in research studies.

Medical records and health information technicians' duties vary with the size of the facility where they work. In large to medium-size facilities, technicians might specialize in one aspect of health information or might supervise health information clerks and transcriptionists while a medical records and health information administrator manages the department. (See the statement on medical and health services managers elsewhere in this book.) In small facilities, a credentialed medical records and health information technician may have the opportunity to manage the department.

Some medical records and health information technicians specialize in coding patients' medical information for insurance purposes. Technicians who specialize in coding are called *health information coders, medical record coders, coder/abstractors*, or *coding specialists*. These technicians assign a code to each diagnosis and procedure, relying on their knowledge of disease processes. Technicians then use classification systems software to assign the patient to one of several hundred "diagnosis-related groups," or DRGs. The DRG determines the amount for which the hospital will be reimbursed if the patient is covered by Medicare or other insurance programs using the DRG system. In addition to the DRG system, coders use other coding systems, such as those required for ambulatory settings, physician offices, or long-term care.

Medical records and health information technicians also may specialize in cancer registry. *Cancer* (or tumor) *registrars* maintain facility, regional, and national databases of cancer patients. Registrars review patient records and pathology reports, and assign codes for the diagnosis and treatment of different cancers and selected benign tumors. Registrars conduct annual followups on all patients in the registry to track their treatment, survival, and recovery. Physicians and public health organizations then use this information to calculate survivor rates and success rates of various types of treatment, locate geographic areas with high incidences of certain cancers, and identify potential participants for clinical drug trials. Public health officials also use cancer registry data to target areas for the allocation of resources to provide intervention and screening.

Work environment. Medical records and health information technicians work in pleasant and comfortable offices. This is one of the few health-related occupations in which there is little or no direct contact with patients. Because accuracy is essential in their jobs, technicians must pay close attention to detail. Technicians who work at computer monitors for prolonged periods must guard against eyestrain and muscle pain.

Medical records and health information technicians usually work a 40-hour week. Some overtime may be required. In hospitals—where health information departments often are open 24 hours a day, 7 days a week—technicians may work day, evening, and night shifts.

Training, Other Qualifications, and Advancement

Medical records and health information technicians entering the field usually have an associate degree from a community or junior college. Many employers favor technicians who have become Registered Health Information Technicians (RHIT). Advancement opportunities for medical record and health information technicians are typically achieved by specialization or promotion to a management position.

Education and training. Medical records and health information technicians generally obtain an associate degree from a community or junior college. Typically, community and junior colleges offer flexible course scheduling or online distance learning courses. In addition to general education, coursework includes medical terminology, anatomy and physiology, legal aspects of health information, health data standards, coding and abstraction of data, statistics, database management, quality improvement methods, and computer science. Applicants can improve their chances of admission into a program by taking biology, math, chemistry, health, and computer science courses in high school.

Certification and other qualifications. Most employers prefer to hire Registered Health Information Technicians (RHIT), who must pass a written examination offered by the American Health Information Management Association (AHIMA). To take the examination, a person must graduate from a two-year associate degree program accredited by the Commission on Accreditation for Health Informatics and Information Management Education (CAHIIM). Technicians trained in non-CAHIIM-accredited programs or trained on the job are not eligible to take the examination. In 2007, there were about 245 CAHIIM accredited programs in Health Informantics and Information Management Education.

Some employers prefer candidates with experience in a health care setting. Experience is valuable in demonstrating certain skills or desirable qualities. It is beneficial for health information technicians to possess good communication skills, as they often serve as a liaison between health care facilities, insurance companies, and other establishments. Accuracy is also essential to technicians because they must pay close attention to detail. A candidate who exhibits proficiency with computers will become more valuable as health care facilities continue to adopt electronic medical records.

Certification and advancement. Experienced medical records and health information technicians usually advance in one of two ways—by specializing or by moving into a management position. Many senior technicians specialize in coding, in cancer registry, or in privacy and security. Most coding and registry skills are learned on the job. A number of schools offer certificate programs in coding or include coding as part of the associate degree program for health information technicians, although there are no formal degree programs in coding. For cancer registry, there are a few formal two-year certificate programs approved by the National Cancer Registrars Association (NCRA). Some schools and employers offer intensive one- to two-week training programs in either coding or cancer registry.

Certification in coding is available from several organizations. Coding certification within specific medical specialty areas is available from the Board of Medical Specialty Coding and the Professional Association of Healthcare Coding Specialist (PAHCS). The American Academy of Professional Coders (AAPC) offers three distinct certification programs in coding. The AHIMA also offers certification for Certified Healthcare Privacy and Security because of growing concerns for the security of electronic medical records. Certification in cancer registry is available from the NCRA. Continuing education units are typically required to renew credentials.

In large medical records and health information departments, experienced technicians may advance to section supervisor, overseeing the work of the coding, correspondence, or discharge sections, for example. Senior technicians with RHIT credentials may become director or assistant director of a medical records and health information department in a small facility. However, in larger institu-

Projections data from the National Employment Matrix

Occupational Title	SOC Code	Employment, 2006	Projected employment, 2016	Change, 2006-2016	
				Number	Percent
Medical records and health information technicians	29-2071	170,000	200,000	30,000	18

NOTE: Data in this table are rounded.

tions, the director usually is an administrator with a bachelor's degree in medical records and health information administration.

Hospitals sometimes advance promising health information clerks to jobs as medical records and health information technicians, although this practice may be less common in the future. Advancement usually requires two to four years of job experience and completion of a hospital's in-house training program.

Employment

Medical records and health information technicians held about 170,000 jobs in 2006. About 2 out of 5 jobs were in hospitals. The rest were mostly in offices of physicians, nursing care facilities, outpatient care centers, and home health care services. Insurance firms that deal in health matters employ a small number of health information technicians to tabulate and analyze health information. Public health departments also employ technicians to supervise data collection from health care institutions and to assist in research.

Job Outlook

Employment is expected to grow faster than average. Job prospects should be very good; technicians with a strong background in medical coding will be in particularly high demand.

Employment change. Employment of medical records and health information technicians is expected to increase by 18 percent through 2016—faster than the average for all occupations—because of rapid growth in the number of medical tests, treatments, and procedures that will be increasingly scrutinized by health insurance companies, regulators, courts, and consumers. Also, technicians will be needed to enter patient information into computer databases to comply with federal legislation mandating the use of electronic medical records.

New jobs are expected in offices of physicians as a result of increasing demand for detailed records, especially in large group practices. New jobs also are expected in home health care services, outpatient care centers, and nursing and residential care facilities. Although employment growth in hospitals will not keep pace with growth in other health care industries, many new jobs will, nevertheless, be created.

Cancer registrars should experience job growth. As the population continues to age, the incidence of cancer may increase.

Job prospects. Job prospects should be very good. In addition to job growth, openings will result from the need to replace technicians who retire or leave the occupation permanently.

Technicians with a strong background in medical coding will be in particularly high demand. Changing government regulations and the growth of managed care have increased the amount of paperwork involved in filing insurance claims. Additionally, health care facilities are having some difficulty attracting qualified workers, primarily because employers prefer trained and experienced technicians prepared to work in an increasingly electronic environment with the integration of electronic health records. Job opportunities may be especially good for coders employed through temporary help agencies or by professional services firms.

Earnings

Median annual earnings of medical records and health information technicians were $28,030 in May 2006. The middle 50 percent earned between $22,420 and $35,990. The lowest 10 percent earned less than $19,060, and the highest 10 percent earned more than $45,260. Median annual earnings in the industries employing the largest numbers of medical records and health information technicians in May 2006 were

General medical and surgical hospitals $29,400
Nursing care facilities 28,410
Outpatient care centers 26,680
Offices of physicians 24,170

Related Occupations

Medical records and health information technicians need a strong clinical background to analyze the contents of medical records. Medical secretaries and medical transcriptionists also must be knowledgeable about medical terminology, anatomy, and physiology even though they have little or no direct contact with patients.

Sources of Additional Information

Information on careers in medical records and health information technology, and a list of accredited training programs is available from

- American Health Information Management Association, 233 N. Michigan Ave., Suite 2150, Chicago, IL 60601-5800. Internet: http://www.ahima.org

Information on training and certification for medical coders is available from

- American Academy of Professional Coders, 2480 South 3850 West, Suite B, Salt Lake City, UT 84120. Internet: http://www.aapc.com

Information on cancer registrars is available from

- National Cancer Registrars Association, 1340 Braddock Place Suite 203, Alexandria, VA 22314. Internet: http://www.ncra-usa.org

STEM Medical Scientists

(O*NET 19-1041.00 and 19-1042.00)

Significant Points

- Most medical scientists need a Ph.D. in a biological science; some hold a medical degree.
- Epidemiologists typically need a master's degree in public health or, in some cases, a Ph.D. or medical degree.

- Competition is expected for most positions; however, those with both a Ph.D. and M.D. are likely to have very good opportunities.

Nature of the Work

Medical scientists research human diseases to improve human health. Most medical scientists conduct biomedical research and development to advance knowledge of life processes and living organisms, including viruses, bacteria, and other infectious agents. Past research has resulted in advances in diagnosis, treatment, and prevention of many diseases. Basic medical research continues to build the foundation for new vaccines, drugs, and treatment procedures. Medical scientists engage in laboratory research, clinical investigation, technical writing, drug application review, and related activities.

Medical scientists study biological systems to understand the causes of disease and other health problems. They develop treatments and design research tools and techniques that have medical applications. Some try to identify changes in cells or in chromosomes that signal the development of medical problems. For example, medical scientists involved in cancer research may formulate a combination of drugs that will lessen the effects of the disease. Medical scientists who are also physicians can administer these drugs to patients in clinical trials, monitor their reactions, and observe the results. They may draw blood, excise tissue, or perform other invasive procedures. Those who are not physicians normally collaborate with physicians who deal directly with patients. Medical scientists examine the results of clinical trials and adjust the dosage levels to reduce negative side effects or to induce better results. In addition to developing treatments for medical conditions, medical scientists attempt to discover ways to prevent health problems. For example, they may study the link between smoking and lung cancer or between alcoholism and liver disease.

Medical scientists who work in applied research or product development use knowledge discovered through basic research to develop new drugs and medical treatments. They usually have less autonomy than basic medical researchers do to choose the emphasis of their research. They spend more time working on marketable treatments to meet the business goals of their employers. Medical scientists doing applied research and product development in private industry may also be required to explain their research plans or results to nonscientists who are in a position to reject or approve their ideas. These scientists must consider the business effects of their work. Scientists increasingly work as part of teams, interacting with engineers, scientists of other disciplines, business managers, and technicians.

Swift advances in basic medical knowledge related to genetics and organic molecules have spurred growth in the field of biotechnology. Discovery of important drugs, including human insulin and growth hormone, is the result of research using biotechnology techniques, such as recombining DNA. Many other substances not previously available in large quantities are now produced by biotechnological means; some may one day be useful in treating diseases such as Parkinson's or Alzheimer's. Today, many medical scientists are involved in the science of genetic engineering—isolating, identifying, and sequencing human genes to determine their functions. This work continues to lead to the discovery of genes associated with specific diseases and inherited health risks, such as sickle cell anemia. These advances in biotechnology have opened up research opportunities in almost all areas of medical science.

Some medical scientists specialize in epidemiology. This branch of medical science investigates and describes the causes and spread of disease and develops the means for prevention or control. Epidemiologists may study many different illnesses, often focusing on major infectious diseases such as influenza or cholera. Epidemiologists can be separated into two groups—research and clinical.

Research epidemiologists conduct research in an effort to eradicate or control infectious diseases. Many work on illnesses that affect the entire body, such as AIDS or typhus, while others focus on localized infections such as those of the brain, lungs, or digestive tract. Research epidemiologists work at colleges and universities, schools of public health, medical schools, and independent research firms. For example, federal government agencies, such as the U.S. Department of Defense, may contract with a research firm to evaluate the incidence of malaria in certain parts of the world. Other research epidemiologists may work as college and university faculty and are counted as postsecondary teachers.

Clinical epidemiologists work primarily in consulting roles at hospitals, informing the medical staff of infectious outbreaks and providing containment solutions. These epidemiologists sometimes are referred to as infection control professionals, and some of them are also physicians. Clinical epidemiologists who are not also physicians often collaborate with physicians to find ways to contain outbreaks of diseases. In addition to traditional duties of studying and controlling diseases, clinical epidemiologists also may be required to develop standards and guidelines for the treatment and control of communicable diseases. Some clinical epidemiologists may work in outpatient settings.

Work environment. Many medical scientists work independently in private industry, university, or government laboratories, exploring new areas of research or expanding on specialized research that they began in graduate school. Medical scientists working in colleges and universities, hospitals, and nonprofit medical research organizations typically submit grant proposals to obtain funding for their projects. Colleges and universities, private industry, and federal government agencies—particularly the National Institutes of Health and the National Science Foundation—provide the primary support for researchers whose proposals are determined to be financially feasible and to have the potential to advance new ideas or processes. Medical scientists who rely on grant money may be under pressure to meet deadlines and to conform to rigid grant-writing specifications when preparing proposals to seek new or extended funding.

Medical scientists who conduct research usually work in laboratories and use a wide variety of equipment. Some may work directly with individual patients or larger groups as they administer drugs and monitor patients during clinical trials. Often, these medical scientists also spend time working in clinics and hospitals.

Medical scientists usually are not exposed to unsafe or unhealthy conditions; however, those scientists who work with dangerous organisms or toxic substances must follow strict safety procedures to avoid contamination.

Medical scientists typically work regular hours in offices or laboratories, but longer hours are not uncommon. Researchers may be required to work odd hours in laboratories or other locations, depending on the nature of their research. On occasion, epidemiologists may be required to travel to meetings and hearings for medical investigations.

Training, Other Qualifications, and Advancement

A Ph.D. in a biological science is the minimum education required for most prospective medical scientists, except epidemiologists. However, some medical scientists pursue medical degrees to perform clinical work. Epidemiologists typically need at least a master's degree in public health, but some work requires a Ph.D. or medical degree. A period of postdoctoral work in the laboratory of a senior researcher is becoming increasingly common for medical scientists.

Education and training. A Ph.D. typically qualifies people to research basic life processes or particular medical problems and to analyze the results of experiments. Some medical scientists obtain a medical degree instead of a Ph.D., but some do not become licensed physicians because they prefer research to clinical practice. It is particularly helpful for medical scientists to earn both a Ph.D. and a medical degree.

Students planning careers as medical scientists should have a bachelor's degree in a biological science. In addition to required courses in chemistry and biology, undergraduates should study allied disciplines, such as mathematics, engineering, physics, and computer science, or courses in their field of interest. Once they have completed undergraduate studies, they can then select a specialty for their advanced degree, such as cytology, bioinformatics, genomics, or pathology.

The minimum educational requirement for epidemiologists is a master's degree from a school of public health. Some jobs may require a Ph.D. or medical degree, depending on the work performed. Epidemiologists who work in hospitals and health care centers often must have a medical degree with specific training in infectious diseases. Some employees in research epidemiology positions are required to be licensed physicians because they must administer drugs in clinical trials.

Few students select epidemiology for undergraduate study. Undergraduates, nonetheless, should study biological sciences and should have a solid background in chemistry, mathematics, and computer science. Once a student is prepared for graduate studies, he or she can choose a specialty within epidemiology. For example, those interested in studying environmental epidemiology should focus on environmental coursework, such as water pollution, air pollution, pesticide use, toxicology, and molecular biology. Other specialties include occupational epidemiology, infection processes, infection control precautions, surveillance methodology, and outbreak investigation. Some epidemiologists begin their careers in other health care occupations, such as registered nurse or medical technologist.

In addition to formal education, medical scientists usually spend some time in a postdoctoral position before they apply for permanent jobs. Postdoctoral work provides valuable laboratory experience, including experience in specific processes and techniques such as gene splicing, which is transferable to other research projects. In some institutions, the postdoctoral position can lead to a permanent job.

Licensure. Medical scientists who administer drug or gene therapy to human patients, or who otherwise interact medically with patients—drawing blood, excising tissue, or performing other invasive procedures—must be licensed physicians. To be licensed, physicians must graduate from an accredited medical school, pass a licensing examination, and complete one to seven years of graduate medical education. (See the statement on physicians and surgeons elsewhere in this book.)

Epidemiologists who perform laboratory tests often require the knowledge and expertise of a licensed physician to administer drugs to patients in clinical trials. Epidemiologists who are not physicians frequently work closely with one.

Other qualifications. Medical scientists should be able to work independently or as part of a team and be able to communicate clearly and concisely, both orally and in writing. Those in private industry, especially those who aspire to consulting and administrative positions, should possess strong communication skills so that they can provide instruction and advice to physicians and other health care professionals.

Certification and advancement. The Association for Professionals in Infection Control and Epidemiology offers continuing education courses and certification programs in infection prevention and control and applied epidemiology. To become certified as an infection control professional, applicants must pass an examination. Certification can be an advantage for those seeking advancement in this rapidly evolving field.

Advancement among medical scientists usually takes the form of greater independence in their work, larger budgets, or tenure in university positions. Others choose to move into managerial positions and become natural science managers (see engineering and natural sciences managers elsewhere in this book). Those who pursue management careers spend more time preparing budgets and schedules.

Employment

Medical scientists held about 92,000 jobs in 2006. Epidemiologists accounted for only 5 percent of that total. In addition, many medical scientists held faculty positions in colleges and universities, but they are classified as college or university faculty. (See teachers—postsecondary, elsewhere in this book.)

About 34 percent of medical scientists, except epidemiologists, were employed in colleges and universities. About 28 percent were employed in scientific research and development services firms; 12 percent were employed in pharmaceutical and medicine manufacturing; 9 percent were employed in hospitals; and most of the remainder were employed in private educational services and ambulatory health care services.

Among epidemiologists, 57 percent were employed in government; 12 percent were employed in hospitals; 11 percent were employed in colleges and universities; and 9 percent were employed in scientific research and development services.

Job Outlook

Medical scientists can expect to face competition for most jobs, in part because of the attractiveness of the career. However, those with both a Ph.D. and M.D. are likely to experience very good opportunities.

Employment change. Employment of medical scientists is expected to increase 20 percent over the 2006–2016 decade, faster than the average for all occupations. The federal government funds much basic research and development, including many areas of medical research. Although previous budget increases at the National Institutes of Health have led to large increases in the number of grants awarded to researchers, the increase in expenditures has slowed significantly, causing

Projections data from the National Employment Matrix

Occupational Title	SOC Code	Employment, 2006	Projected employment, 2016	Change, 2006-2016	
				Number	Percent
Medical scientists	19-1040	92,000	110,000	18,000	20
Epidemiologists	19-1041	4,500	5,100	600	14
Medical scientists, except epidemiologists	19-1042	87,000	105,000	18,000	20

NOTE: Data in this table are rounded.

expected future employment growth to be more modest than in the past despite the faster than average projected growth.

Medical scientists enjoyed rapid gains in employment since the 1980s—reflecting, in part, the growth of biotechnology companies. Job growth should be dampened somewhat as fewer new biotechnology firms are founded and as existing firms merge or are absorbed by larger biotechnology or pharmaceutical firms. Some companies may conduct a portion of their research and development in other lower-wage countries, further limiting employment growth. However, much of the basic medical research done in recent years has resulted in new knowledge, including the isolation and identification of new genes. Medical scientists will be needed to take this knowledge to the next stage—understanding how certain genes function within an entire organism—so that medical treatments can be developed for various diseases. Even pharmaceutical and other firms not solely engaged in biotechnology have largely adopted biotechnology techniques, thus creating employment for medical scientists.

Employment growth should also occur as a result of the expected expansion in research related to illnesses such as AIDS, cancer, and avian influenza, along with growing treatment problems such as antibiotic resistance. Moreover, environmental conditions such as overcrowding and the increasing frequency of international travel will tend to spread existing diseases and give rise to new ones. Medical scientists will continue to be needed because they greatly contribute to the development of treatments and medicines that improve human health.

An increasing focus on monitoring patients at hospitals and health care centers to ensure positive patient outcomes will contribute to job growth for epidemiologists. In addition, a heightened awareness of bioterrorism and rare, but infectious diseases such as West Nile Virus or severe acute respiratory syndrome (SARS) should spur demand for these workers. As hospitals enhance their infection control programs, many will seek to boost the quality and quantity of their staff.

Job prospects. Besides job openings due to employment growth, openings will arise as workers leave the labor force or transfer to other occupations. However, doctoral degree holders can expect to face considerable competition for basic research positions and for research grants. If the number of advanced degrees awarded continues to grow, applicants are likely to face even more competition.

Although medical scientists can expect competition for jobs, those with both doctoral and medical degrees are likely to experience very good opportunities. As funding for research becomes more difficult to obtain, those with both a biological and professional medical background will have a distinct advantage. Opportunities in epidemiology also should be highly competitive, as the number of available positions will continue to be limited.

Medical scientists and epidemiologists are less likely to lose their jobs during recessions than are those in many other occupations because they are employed on long-term research projects. However, a recession could influence the amount of money allocated to new research and development, particularly in areas of risky or innovative medical research. A recession also could limit extensions or renewals of existing projects.

Earnings

Median annual earnings of wage and salary medical scientists, except epidemiologists, were $61,680 in May 2006. The middle 50 percent of these workers earned between $44,830 and $88,130. The lowest 10 percent earned less than $35,490, and the highest 10 percent earned more than $117,520. Median annual earnings in the industries employing the largest numbers of medical scientists were

Pharmaceutical and medicine manufacturing $82,640
Research and development in the physical, engineering, and life sciences 71,490
Offices of physicians 70,000
General medical and surgical hospitals 64,700
Colleges, universities, and professional schools 44,600

Median annual earnings of wage and salary epidemiologists were $56,670 in May 2006. The middle 50 percent earned between $45,220 and $71,080. The lowest 10 percent earned less than $36,920, and the highest 10 percent earned more than $87,300.

Related Occupations

Many other occupations deal with living organisms and require a level of training similar to that of medical scientists. These occupations include biological scientists, agricultural and food scientists, pharmacists, engineering and natural sciences managers, and health occupations such as physicians and surgeons, dentists, and veterinarians.

Sources of Additional Information

For information on pharmaceutical scientists, contact

- American Association of Pharmaceutical Scientists (AAPS), 2107 Wilson Blvd., Suite 700, Arlington, VA 22201. Internet: http://www.aapspharmaceutica.org

For information on careers in microbiology, contact

- American Society for Microbiology, Career Information—Education Department, 1752 N St. NW, Washington, DC 20036. Internet: http://www.asm.org

For information on infectious diseases training programs, contact

- Infectious Diseases Society of America, Guide to Training Programs, 66 Canal Center Plaza, Suite 600, Alexandria, VA 22314. Internet: http://www.idsociety.org

Information on obtaining a medical scientist position with the federal government is available from the Office of Personnel

Management through USAJOBS, the federal government's official employment information system. This resource for locating and applying for job opportunities can be accessed through the Internet at http://www.usajobs.opm.gov or through an interactive voice response telephone system at (703) 724-1850 or TDD (978) 461-8404. These numbers are not toll free, and charges may result. For advice on how to find and apply for federal jobs, see the *Occupational Outlook Quarterly* article "How to get a job in the Federal Government," online at http://www.bls.gov/opub/ooq/2004/summer/art01.pdf.

Medical Transcriptionists

(O*NET 31-9094.00)

Significant Points

- Job opportunities will be good.
- Employers prefer medical transcriptionists who have completed a postsecondary training program.
- Many medical transcriptionists telecommute from home-based offices.
- About 41 percent worked in hospitals, and another 29 percent worked in offices of physicians.

Nature of the Work

Medical transcriptionists listen to dictated recordings made by physicians and other health care professionals and transcribe them into medical reports, correspondence, and other administrative material. They generally listen to recordings on a headset, using a foot pedal to pause the recording when necessary, and key the text into a personal computer or word processor, editing as necessary for grammar and clarity. The documents they produce include discharge summaries, medical history and physical examination reports, operative reports, consultation reports, autopsy reports, diagnostic imaging studies, progress notes, and referral letters. Medical transcriptionists return transcribed documents to the physicians or other health care professionals who dictated them for review and signature or correction. These documents eventually become part of patients' permanent files.

To understand and accurately transcribe dictated reports, medical transcriptionists must understand medical terminology, anatomy and physiology, diagnostic procedures, pharmacology, and treatment assessments. They also must be able to translate medical jargon and abbreviations into their expanded forms. To help identify terms appropriately, transcriptionists refer to standard medical reference materials—both printed and electronic; some of these are available over the Internet. Medical transcriptionists must comply with specific standards that apply to the style of medical records and to the legal and ethical requirements for keeping patient information confidential.

Experienced transcriptionists spot mistakes or inconsistencies in a medical report and check to correct the information. Their ability to understand and correctly transcribe patient assessments and treatments reduces the chance of patients receiving ineffective or even harmful treatments and ensures high-quality patient care.

Currently, most health care providers transmit dictation to medical transcriptionists using either digital or analog dictating equipment. The Internet has grown to be a popular mode for transmitting documentation. Many transcriptionists receive dictation over the Internet and are able to quickly return transcribed documents to clients for approval. Another increasingly popular method uses speech recognition technology, which electronically translates sound into text and creates drafts of reports. Transcriptionists then format the reports; edit them for mistakes in translation, punctuation, or grammar; and check for consistency and any wording that doesn't make sense medically. Transcriptionists working in specialties, such as radiology or pathology, with standardized terminology are more likely to use speech recognition technology. However, speech recognition technology will become more widespread in all specialties as the technology becomes more sophisticated, that is, better able to recognize and more accurately transcribe diverse modes of speech.

Medical transcriptionists who work in physicians' offices may have other office duties, such as receiving patients, scheduling appointments, answering the telephone, and handling incoming and outgoing mail. Medical secretaries also may transcribe as part of their jobs.

Work environment. The majority of these workers are employed in comfortable settings, such as hospitals, physicians' offices, transcription service offices, clinics, laboratories, medical libraries, government medical facilities, or their own homes. Many medical transcriptionists telecommute from home-based offices.

Workers usually sit in the same position for long periods. They can suffer wrist, back, neck, or eye problems due to strain and risk repetitive motion injuries such as carpal tunnel syndrome. The constant pressure to be accurate and productive also can be stressful.

Many medical transcriptionists work a standard 40-hour week. Self-employed medical transcriptionists are more likely to work irregular hours—including part time, evenings, weekends, or on call at any time.

Training, Other Qualifications, and Advancement

Postsecondary training in medical transcription is preferred by employers; writing and computer skills also are important.

Education and training. Employers prefer to hire transcriptionists who have completed postsecondary training in medical transcription offered by many vocational schools, community colleges, and distance-learning programs.

Completion of a two-year associate degree or one-year certificate program—including coursework in anatomy, medical terminology, legal issues relating to health care documentation, and English grammar and punctuation—is highly recommended, but not always required. Many of these programs include supervised on-the-job experience. Some transcriptionists, especially those already familiar with medical terminology from previous experience as a nurse or medical secretary, become proficient through refresher courses and training.

Formal accreditation is not required for medical transcription programs. However, the Approval Committee for Certificate Programs (AACP)—established by the Association for Healthcare Documentation Integrity (AHDI) and the American Health Information Management Association—offers voluntary accreditation for medical transcription programs. Although voluntary, completion of an ACCP approved program may be required for transcriptionists seeking certification.

Certification and other qualifications. The AHDI awards two voluntary designations, the Registered Medical Transcriptionist (RMT) and the Certified Medical Transcriptionist (CMT). Medical transcriptionists who are recent graduates of medical transcription educational programs, or have fewer than two years experience in acute care, may become a registered RMT. The RMT credential is awarded upon successfully passing the AHDI level 1 registered medical transcription exam. The CMT designation requires at least two years of acute care experience working in multiple specialty surgery areas using different format, report, and dictation types. Candidates also must earn a passing score on a certification examination. Because medicine is constantly evolving, medical transcriptionists are encouraged to update their skills regularly. RMTs and CMTs must earn continuing education credits every three years to be recertified. As in many other fields, certification is recognized as a sign of competence.

Graduates of an ACCP approved program who earn the RMT credential are eligible to participate in the Registered Apprenticeship Program sponsored by the Medical Transcription Industry Association through the U.S. Department of Labor. The Registered Apprenticeship program offers structured on-the-job learning and related technical instruction for qualified medical transcriptionists entering the profession.

In addition to understanding medical terminology, transcriptionists must have good English grammar and punctuation skills and proficiency with personal computers and word processing software. Normal hearing acuity and good listening skills also are necessary. Employers usually require applicants to take pre-employment tests.

Advancement. With experience, medical transcriptionists can advance to supervisory positions, home-based work, editing, consulting, or teaching. Some become owners of medical transcription businesses. With additional education or training, some become medical records and health information technicians, medical coders, or medical records and health information administrators.

Employment

Medical transcriptionists held about 98,000 jobs in 20006. About 41 percent worked in hospitals and another 29 percent worked in offices of physicians. Others worked for business support services; medical and diagnostic laboratories; outpatient care centers; and offices of physical, occupational, and speech therapists, and audiologists.

Job Outlook

Employment of medical transcriptionists is projected to grow faster than the average; job opportunities should be good, especially for those who are certified.

Employment change. Employment of medical transcriptionists is projected to grow 14 percent from 2006 to 2016, faster than the average for all occupations. Demand for medical transcription services will be spurred by a growing and aging population. Older age groups receive proportionately greater numbers of medical tests, treatments, and procedures that require documentation. A high level of demand for transcription services also will be sustained by the continued need for electronic documentation that can be shared easily among providers, third-party payers, regulators, consumers, and health information systems. Growing numbers of medical transcriptionists will be needed to amend patients' records, edit documents from speech recognition systems, and identify discrepancies in medical reports.

Contracting out transcription work overseas and advancements in speech recognition technology are not expected to significantly reduce the need for well-trained medical transcriptionists. Outsourcing transcription work abroad—to countries such as India, Pakistan, Philippines, and the Caribbean—has grown more popular as transmitting confidential health information over the Internet has become more secure; however, the demand for overseas transcription services is expected only to supplement the demand for well-trained domestic medical transcriptionists. In addition, reports transcribed by overseas medical transcription services usually require editing for accuracy by domestic medical transcriptionists before they meet U.S. quality standards.

Speech-recognition technology allows physicians and other health professionals to dictate medical reports to a computer that immediately creates an electronic document. In spite of the advances in this technology, the software has been slow to grasp and analyze the human voice and the English language, and the medical vernacular with all its diversity. As a result, there will continue to be a need for skilled medical transcriptionists to identify and appropriately edit the inevitable errors created by speech recognition systems, and to create a final document.

Job prospects. Job opportunities will be good, especially for those who are certified. Hospitals will continue to employ a large percentage of medical transcriptionists, but job growth there will not be as fast as in other industries. An increasing demand for standardized records should result in rapid employment growth in physicians' offices, especially in large group practices.

Earnings

Wage-and-salary medical transcriptionists had median hourly earnings of $14.40 in May 2006. The middle 50 percent earned between $12.17 and $17.06. The lowest 10 percent earned less than $10.22, and the highest 10 percent earned more than $20.15. Median hourly earnings in the industries employing the largest numbers of medical transcriptionists were

Medical and diagnostic laboratories $15.68
General medical and surgical hospitals 14.62
Business support services 14.34
Outpatient care centers 14.31
Offices of physicians 14.00

Projections data from the National Employment Matrix

Occupational Title	SOC Code	Employment, 2006	Projected employment, 2016	Change, 2006-16 Number	Change, 2006-16 Percent
Medical transcriptionists	31-9094	98,000	112,000	13,000	14

NOTE: Data in this table are rounded.

Compensation methods for medical transcriptionists vary. Some are paid based on the number of hours they work or on the number of lines they transcribe. Others receive a base pay per hour with incentives for extra production. Employees of transcription services and independent contractors almost always receive production-based pay. Independent contractors earn more than do transcriptionists who work for others, but independent contractors have higher expenses than their corporate counterparts, receive no benefits, and may face higher risk of termination than do wage-and-salary transcriptionists.

Related Occupations

Workers in other occupations also type, record information, and process paperwork. Among these are court reporters; human resources assistants, except payroll and timekeeping; receptionists and information clerks; and secretaries and administrative assistants. Other workers who provide medical support include medical assistants and medical records and health information technicians.

Sources of Additional Information

For information on a career as a medical transcriptionist, contact

- Association for Healthcare Documentation Integrity, 4230 Kiernan Ave., Suite 130, Modesto, CA 95356. Internet: http://www.ahdionline.org

State employment service offices can provide information about job openings for medical transcriptionists.

Medical, Dental, and Ophthalmic Laboratory Technicians

(O*NET 51-9081.00, 51-9082.00, and 51-9083.00)

Significant Points

- Around 55 percent of salaried jobs are in medical equipment and supply manufacturing laboratories, which usually are small, privately owned businesses with fewer than 5 employees.
- Most technicians learn their craft on the job, but many employers prefer to hire those with formal training.
- Slower-than-average employment growth is expected for dental and ophthalmic laboratory technicians, while average employment growth is expected for medical appliance technicians.
- Job opportunities should be favorable because few people seek these positions.

Nature of the Work

When patients require a medical device to help them see clearly, chew and speak well, or walk, their health care providers send requests to medical, dental, and ophthalmic laboratory technicians. These technicians produce a variety of implements to help patients.

Medical appliance technicians construct, fit, maintain, and repair braces, artificial limbs, joints, arch supports, and other surgical and medical appliances. They follow prescriptions or detailed instructions from podiatrists or orthotists, who request braces, supports, corrective shoes, or other devises; prosthetists, who order prostheses—replacement limbs, such as an arm, leg, hand, or foot—for patients who need them due to a birth defect, accident, or amputation; or other health care professionals. Medical appliance technicians who work with these types of devices are called orthotic and prosthetic technicians. Other medical appliance technicians work with appliances that help correct other medical problems, such as hearing aids.

Creating medical devices takes several steps. To make arch supports, for example, technicians first make a wax or plastic impression of the patient's foot. Then they bend and form a material so that it conforms to prescribed contours required to fabricate structural components. If a support is mainly required to correct the balance of a patient with legs of different lengths, a rigid material is used. If the support is primarily intended to protect those with arthritic or diabetic feet, a soft material is used. Supports and braces are polished with grinding and buffing wheels. Technicians may cover arch supports with felt to make them more comfortable.

For prostheses, technicians construct or receive a plaster cast of the patient's limb to use as a pattern. Then, they lay out parts and use precision measuring instruments to measure them. Technicians may use wood, plastic, metal, or other material for the parts of the artificial limb. Next, they carve, cut, or grind the material using hand or power tools. Then, they drill holes for rivets and glue, rivet, or weld the parts together. They are able to do very precise work using common tools. Next, technicians use grinding and buffing wheels to smooth and polish artificial limbs. Lastly, they may cover or pad the limbs with rubber, leather, felt, plastic, or another material. Also, technicians may mix pigments according to formulas to match the patient's skin color and apply the mixture to the artificial limb.

After fabrication, medical appliance technicians test devices for proper alignment, movement, and biomechanical stability using meters and alignment fixtures. They also may fit the appliance on the patient and adjust them as necessary. Over time the appliance will wear down, so technicians must repair and maintain the device. They also may service and repair the machinery used for the fabrication of orthotic and prosthetic devices.

Dental laboratory technicians fill prescriptions from dentists for crowns, bridges, dentures, and other dental prosthetics. First, dentists send a specification of the item to be manufactured, along with an impression or mold of the patient's mouth or teeth. With new technology, a technician may receive a digital impression rather than a physical mold. Then dental laboratory technicians, also called dental technicians, create a model of the patient's mouth by pouring plaster into the impression and allowing it to set. They place the model on an apparatus that mimics the bite and movement of the patient's jaw. The model serves as the basis of the prosthetic device. Technicians examine the model, noting the size and shape of the adjacent teeth, as well as gaps within the gumline. Based upon these observations and the dentist's specifications, technicians build and shape a wax tooth or teeth model, using small hand instruments called wax spatulas and wax carvers. The wax model is used to cast the metal framework for the prosthetic device.

After the wax tooth has been formed, dental technicians pour the cast and form the metal and, using small hand-held tools, prepare the surface to allow the metal and porcelain to bond. They then apply porcelain in layers, to arrive at the precise shape and color of a tooth. Technicians place the tooth in a porcelain furnace to bake the porcelain onto the metal framework, and then adjust the shape and color, with subsequent grinding and addition of porcelain to achieve a sealed finish. The final product is a nearly exact replica of the lost tooth or teeth.

In some laboratories, technicians perform all stages of the work, whereas in other labs, each technician does only a few. Dental laboratory technicians can specialize in 1 of 5 areas: orthodontic appliances, crowns and bridges, complete dentures, partial dentures, or ceramics. Job titles can reflect specialization in these areas. For example, technicians who make porcelain and acrylic restorations are called *dental ceramists*.

Ophthalmic laboratory technicians—also known as manufacturing opticians, optical mechanics, or optical goods workers—make prescription eyeglass or contact lenses. Prescription lenses are curved in such a way that light is correctly focused onto the retina of the patient's eye, improving his or her vision. Some ophthalmic laboratory technicians manufacture lenses for other optical instruments, such as telescopes and binoculars. Ophthalmic laboratory technicians cut, grind, edge, and finish lenses according to specifications provided by dispensing opticians, optometrists, or ophthalmologists and may insert lenses into frames to produce finished glasses. Although some lenses still are produced by hand, technicians are increasingly using automated equipment to make lenses.

Ophthalmic laboratory technicians should not be confused with workers in other vision care occupations. Ophthalmologists and optometrists are "eye doctors" who examine eyes, diagnose and treat vision problems, and prescribe corrective lenses. Ophthalmologists are physicians who also perform eye surgery. Dispensing opticians, who also may do the work of ophthalmic laboratory technicians, help patients select frames and lenses, and adjust finished eyeglasses. (See the statement on physicians and surgeons, which includes ophthalmologists, as well as the statement on optometrists and opticians, dispensing, elsewhere in this book.)

Ophthalmic laboratory technicians read prescription specifications, select standard glass or plastic lens blanks, and then mark them to indicate where the curves specified on the prescription should be ground. They place the lens in the lens grinder, set the dials for the prescribed curvature, and start the machine. After a minute or so, the lens is ready to be "finished" by a machine that rotates it against a fine abrasive, to grind it and smooth out rough edges. The lens is then placed in a polishing machine with an even finer abrasive, to polish it to a smooth, bright finish.

Next, the technician examines the lens through a lensometer, an instrument similar in shape to a microscope, to make sure that the degree and placement of the curve are correct. The technician then cuts the lenses and bevels the edges to fit the frame, dips each lens into dye if the prescription calls for tinted or coated lenses, polishes the edges, and assembles the lenses and frame parts into a finished pair of glasses.

In small laboratories, technicians usually handle every phase of the operation. In large ones, in which virtually every phase of the operation is automated, technicians may be responsible for operating computerized equipment. Technicians also inspect the final product for quality and accuracy.

Work environment. Medical, dental, and ophthalmic laboratory technicians generally work in clean, well-lighted, and well-ventilated laboratories. They have limited contact with the public. Salaried laboratory technicians usually work 40 hours a week, but some work part time. At times, technicians wear goggles to protect their eyes, gloves to handle hot objects, or masks to avoid inhaling dust. They may spend a great deal of time standing.

Dental technicians usually have their own workbenches, which can be equipped with Bunsen burners, grinding and polishing equipment, and hand instruments, such as wax spatulas and wax carvers. Some dental technicians have computer-aided milling equipment to assist them with creating artificial teeth.

Training, Other Qualifications, and Advancement

Most medical, dental, and ophthalmic laboratory technicians learn their craft on the job; however, many employers prefer to hire those with formal training.

Education and training. High school students interested in becoming medical appliance technicians should take mathematics, metal and wood shop, and drafting. Medical appliance technicians usually begin as helpers and gradually learn new skills as they gain experience.

Formal training is also available. In 2006, there were four orthotic and prosthetic technician programs accredited by the National Commission on Orthotic and Prosthetic Education (NCOPE). These programs offer either an associate degree or a one-year certificate for orthotic or prosthetic technicians. The programs instruct students on human anatomy and physiology, orthotic and prosthetic equipment and materials, and applied biomechanical principles to customize orthotics or prostheses. The programs also include clinical rotations to provide hands-on experience.

Dental laboratory technicians begin by learning simple tasks, such as pouring plaster into an impression, and progress to more complex procedures, such as making porcelain crowns and bridges. Becoming a fully trained technician requires an average of three to four years, depending upon the individual's aptitude and ambition, but it may take a few years more to become an accomplished technician. High school students interested in becoming dental laboratory technicians should take courses in art, metal and wood shop, drafting, and sciences. Courses in management and business may help those wishing to operate their own laboratories.

Training in dental laboratory technology also is available through community and junior colleges, vocational-technical institutes, and the Armed Forces. Formal training programs vary greatly both in length and in the level of skill they impart. In 2006, 20 programs in dental laboratory technology were accredited by the Commission on Dental Accreditation in conjunction with the American Dental Association. These programs provide classroom instruction in dental materials science, oral anatomy, fabrication procedures, ethics, and related subjects. In addition, each student is given supervised practical experience in a school or an associated dental laboratory. Accredited programs normally take two years to complete and lead to an associate degree. A few programs take about four years to complete and offer a bachelor's degree in dental technology. Graduates of two-year training programs need additional hands-on experience to become fully qualified.

Each dental laboratory owner operates in a different way, and classroom instruction does not necessarily expose students to techniques and procedures favored by individual laboratory owners. Students who have taken enough courses to learn the basics of the craft usually are considered good candidates for training, regardless of whether they have completed a formal program. Many employers will train someone without any classroom experience.

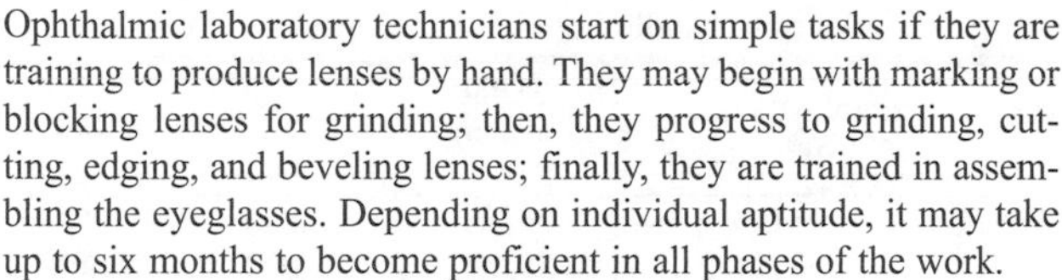

Ophthalmic laboratory technicians start on simple tasks if they are training to produce lenses by hand. They may begin with marking or blocking lenses for grinding; then, they progress to grinding, cutting, edging, and beveling lenses; finally, they are trained in assembling the eyeglasses. Depending on individual aptitude, it may take up to six months to become proficient in all phases of the work.

Employers filling trainee jobs prefer applicants who are high school graduates. Courses in science, mathematics, and computers are valuable; manual dexterity and the ability to do precision work are essential. Technicians using automated systems will find computer skills valuable.

A few ophthalmic laboratory technicians learn their trade in the Armed Forces or in the few programs in optical technology offered by vocational-technical institutes or trade schools. These programs have classes in optical theory, surfacing and lens finishing, and the reading and applying of prescriptions. Programs vary in length from six months to one year and award certificates or diplomas.

Other qualifications. A high degree of manual dexterity, good vision, and the ability to recognize very fine color shadings and variations in shape also are necessary for dental technicians. An artistic aptitude for detailed and precise work also is important.

Certification and advancement. Voluntary certification for orthotic and prosthetic technicians is available through the American Board for Certification in Orthotics and Prosthetics (ABC). Applicants are eligible for an exam after completing a program accredited by NCOPE or obtaining two years of experience as a technician under the direct supervision of an ABC-certified practitioner. After successfully passing the appropriate exam, technicians receive the Registered Orthotic Technician, Registered Prosthetic Technician, or Registered Prosthetic-Orthotic Technician credential. Certification may help those orthotic and prosthetic technicians seeking to advance.

With additional formal education, medical appliance technicians who make orthotics and prostheses can advance to become orthotists or prosthetists, technicians who work with patients who need braces, artificial limbs, or related devices and help to determine the specifications for those devices.

In large dental laboratories, dental technicians may become supervisors or managers. Experienced technicians may teach or take jobs with dental suppliers in such areas as product development, marketing, and sales. Opening one's own laboratory is another, and more common, way to advance and earn more.

The National Board for Certification, an independent board established by the National Association of Dental Laboratories, offers certification in dental laboratory technology. Certification, which is voluntary except in three states, can be obtained in five specialty areas: crowns and bridges, ceramics, partial dentures, complete dentures, and orthodontic appliances. Certification may increase chances of advancement.

Ophthalmic laboratory technicians can become supervisors and managers. Some become dispensing opticians, although further education or training generally is required in that occupation.

Employment

Medical, dental, and ophthalmic laboratory technicians held about 95,000 jobs in 2006. About 55 percent of salaried jobs were in medical equipment and supply manufacturing laboratories, which usually are small, privately owned businesses with fewer than 5 employees. However, some laboratories are large; a few employ more than 1,000 workers. The following tabulation shows employment by detailed occupation:

Dental laboratory technicians 53,000
Opthalmic laboratory technicians 29,000
Medical appliance technicians 12,000

In addition to manufacturing laboratories, many medical appliance technicians worked in health and personal care stores, while others worked in public and private hospitals, professional and commercial equipment and supplies merchant wholesalers, or consumer goods rental centers. Some were self-employed.

In addition to manufacturing laboratories, many dental laboratory technicians worked in offices of dentists. Some dental laboratory technicians open their own offices.

Most ophthalmic laboratory technician jobs were in medical equipment and supplies manufacturing laboratories, about 29 percent. Another 29 percent of jobs were in health and personal care stores, such as optical goods stores that manufacture and sell prescription glasses and contact lenses. Some jobs were in offices of optometrists or ophthalmologists, while others worked at professional and commercial equipment and supplies merchant wholesalers. A few worked in commercial and service industry machine manufacturing firms that produce lenses for other optical instruments, such as telescopes and binoculars.

Job Outlook

Overall, slower-than-average growth is expected for employment of medical, dental, and ophthalmic laboratory technicians. However, job opportunities should be favorable because few people seek these positions.

Employment change. Overall employment for these occupations is expected to grow five percent from 2006 to 2016, slower than the average for all occupations.

Medical appliance technicians will grow at nine percent, about as fast as the average for all occupations, because of the increasing prevalence of the two leading causes of limb loss—diabetes and cardiovascular disease. In addition, advances in technology may spur demand for prostheses that allow for greater movement.

Employment of dental laboratory technicians is expected to grow more slowly than average, at four percent. During the last few years, demand has arisen from an aging public that is growing increasingly interested in cosmetic prostheses. For example, many dental laboratories are filling orders for composite fillings that are the same shade of white as natural teeth to replace older, less attractive fillings. However, job growth for dental laboratory technicians will be limited. The overall dental health of the population has improved because of fluoridation of drinking water and greater emphasis on preventive dental care, which has reduced the incidence of dental cavities. As a result, full dentures will be less common, as most people will need only a bridge or crown.

Ophthalmic laboratory technicians are expected to experience employment growth of seven percent, about as fast as the average for all occupations. Demographic trends make it likely that many more Americans will need vision care in the years ahead. Not only will the population grow, but also the proportion of middle-aged and older adults is projected to increase rapidly. Middle age is a time when many people use corrective lenses for the first time, and eld-

Projections data from the National Employment Matrix

Occupational Title	SOC Code	Employment, 2006	Projected employment, 2016	Change, 2006-16	
				Number	Percent
Medical, dental, and ophthalmic laboratory technicians	51-9080	95,000	100,000	5,000	5
Dental laboratory technicians	51-9081	53,000	55,000	2,000	4
Medical appliance technicians	51-9082	12,000	13,000	1,200	9
Ophthalmic laboratory technicians	51-9083	29,000	31,000	1,900	7

NOTE: Data in this table are rounded.

erly persons usually require more vision care than others. However, the increasing use of automated machinery will temper job growth for ophthalmic laboratory technicians.

Job prospects. Job opportunities for medical, dental, and ophthalmic laboratory technicians should be favorable, despite expected slower-than-average growth. Few people seek these jobs, reflecting the relatively limited public awareness and low starting wages. In addition to openings from job growth, many job openings also will arise from the need to replace technicians who transfer to other occupations or who leave the labor force.

Earnings

Median hourly earnings of wage-and-salary medical appliance technicians were $14.99 in May 2006. The middle 50 percent earned between $11.34 and $19.65 an hour. The lowest 10 percent earned less than $8.93, and the highest 10 percent earned more than $27.00 an hour.

Median hourly earnings of wage-and-salary dental laboratory technicians were $15.67 in May 2006. The middle 50 percent earned between $11.61 and $20.57 an hour. The lowest 10 percent earned less than $9.16, and the highest 10 percent earned more than $26.13 an hour. In the two industries that employed the most dental laboratory technicians, medical equipment and supplies manufacturing and offices of dentists, median hourly earnings were $15.09 and $17.74, respectively.

Median hourly earnings of wage-and-salary ophthalmic laboratory technicians were $12.24 in May 2006. The middle 50 percent earned between $9.86 and $15.82 an hour. The lowest 10 percent earned less than $8.38, and the highest 10 percent earned more than $19.98 an hour. Median hourly earnings were $11.63 in medical equipment and supplies manufacturing and $11.49 in health and personal care stores, the two industries that employ the most ophthalmic laboratory technicians.

Related Occupations

Medical, dental, and ophthalmic laboratory technicians manufacture and work with the same devices that are used by dispensing opticians and orthotists and prosthetists. Other occupations that work with or manufacture goods using similar tools and skills are precision instrument and equipment repairers and textile, apparel, and furnishings occupations.

Sources of Additional Information

For information on careers in orthotics and prosthetics, contact

- American Academy of Orthotists and Prosthetists, 526 King St., Suite 201, Alexandria, VA 22314. Internet: http://www.opcareers.org

For a list of accredited programs for orthotic and prosthetic technicians, contact

- National Commission on Orthotic and Prosthetic Education, 330 John Carlyle St., Suite 200, Alexandria, VA 22314. Internet: http://www.ncope.org

For information on requirements for certification of orthotic and prosthetic technicians, contact

- American Board for Certification in Orthotics and Prosthetics, 330 John Carlyle St., Suite 210, Alexandria, VA 22314. Internet: http://www.abcop.org

For a list of accredited programs in dental laboratory technology, contact

- Commission on Dental Accreditation, American Dental Association, 211 E. Chicago Ave., Chicago, IL 60611. Internet: http://www.ada.org

For information on requirements for certification of dental laboratory technicians, contact

- National Board for Certification in Dental Technology, 325 John Knox Rd., L103, Tallahassee, FL 32303. Internet: http://www.nbccert.org

For information on career opportunities in commercial dental laboratories, contact

- National Association of Dental Laboratories, 325 John Knox Rd., L103, Tallahassee, FL 32303. Internet: http://www.nadl.org

For information on an accredited program in ophthalmic laboratory technology, contact

- Commission on Opticianry Accreditation, P.O. Box 4342, Chapel Hill, NC 27515.

General information on grants and scholarships is available from individual schools. State employment service offices can provide information about job openings for medical, dental, and ophthalmic laboratory technicians.

Millwrights

(O*NET 49-9044.00)

Significant Points

- Millwrights usually train in 4-year to 5-year apprenticeships; some learn through community college programs coupled with informal paid on-the-job training.
- Despite projected slower-than-average employment growth, well-qualified applicants should have excellent job opportunities.
- About 50 percent of millwrights belong to labor unions, one of the highest rates of membership in the economy.

Nature of the Work

Millwrights install, replace, dismantle, and repair machinery and heavy equipment used in power generation, including wind power, hydroelectric damns, and natural gas turbines, and in manufacturing plants, construction sites, and mining operations. The development of new technologies requires millwrights to work with new industry-specific and highly complex precision machines. Some of these machines have tolerances smaller than the width of a human hair.

The millwright's responsibilities begin before a new piece of machinery arrives at the jobsite. Millwrights consult with production managers, industrial engineers, and others to determine the optimal placement of the machine in the plant. Some equipment, such as a metal forging press, is so heavy that it must be placed on a new foundation. Millwrights either prepare the foundation themselves or supervise its construction. As a result, they must know how to read blueprints and to work with a variety of building materials.

When the new machine arrives, millwrights unload, inspect, and move the equipment into position. To lift and move light machinery, millwrights use rigging and hoisting devices, such as pulleys and cables. With heavier equipment, they may use hydraulic-lift trucks or cranes. Lifting such heavy equipment requires millwrights to understand the load properties of cables, ropes, hoists, and cranes. Parts of power plant turbines and other machinery can weigh more than 100 tons and must be precisely positioned; even nuts and bolts can weigh a few hundred pounds each and require a crane to move.

Next, millwrights assemble the machinery. They fit bearings, align gears and wheels, attach motors, and connect belts, according to the manufacturer's blueprints and drawings. Precision leveling and alignment are important in the assembly process, so millwrights measure angles, material thickness, and small distances with calipers, squares, micrometers, and other tools. When a high level of precision is required, they use devices such as lasers and ultrasonic measuring and alignment tools. Millwrights also work with hand and power tools, such as cutting torches, welding machines, hydraulic torque wrenches, hydraulic stud tensioners, soldering guns, and with metalworking equipment, including lathes and grinding machines.

In addition to installing and dismantling machinery, many millwrights work with industrial mechanics and maintenance workers to repair and maintain equipment. This includes preventive maintenance, such as lubrication and fixing or replacing worn parts. If a spare part is unavailable, a millwright may use a lathe or other machine tool to cut a new part. (For further information on machinery maintenance, see the section on industrial machinery mechanics and maintenance workers elsewhere in this book.)

Increasingly sophisticated automation means more complicated machines for millwrights to install and maintain, requiring millwrights to specialize in certain machines or machine brands. For example, some millwrights specialize in installing and maintaining turbines in power plants that can weigh hundreds of tons and contain thousands of parts. This machinery requires special care and knowledge, so millwrights receive additional training and are required to be certified by the turbine manufacturer.

Work environment. Millwrights in manufacturing often work in a machine shop and use protective equipment, such as safety belts, protective glasses, and hardhats, to avoid injuries from falling objects or machinery. Those employed in construction may work outdoors in difficult weather conditions.

Millwrights at construction sites may travel long distances to worksites. For example, millwrights who specialize in turbine installation travel to wherever new power plants are being built.

Advanced equipment, such as hydraulic wrenches and hydraulic stud tensioners, have made the work safer and eliminated the need for millwrights to use sledge hammers to pound bolts into position. Other equipment has reduced the strenuous tasks that caused injuries in the past.

Millwrights work independently or as part of a team. Because disabled machinery costs time and money, many millwrights work overtime and some work in shifts; about 39 percent of millwrights report working more than 40 hours during a typical week. During power outages or other emergencies, millwrights often work overtime.

Training, Other Qualifications, and Advancement

Millwrights usually train in four-year to five-year apprenticeships that combine paid on-the-job training with classroom instruction. Some learn through community college programs coupled with informal paid on-the-job training.

Education and training. Employers prefer applicants who have a high school diploma, GED, or the equivalent and some vocational training or experience. Courses in science, mathematics, mechanical drawing, computers, and machine shop practice are useful. Once hired, millwrights are trained through four-year to five-year apprenticeship programs that combine on-the-job training with classroom instruction, or through community college programs coupled with informal on-the-job training.

Apprenticeships include training in dismantling, moving, erecting, and repairing machinery. Trainees also might learn carpentry, welding, use of concrete, sheet-metal work, and other skills related to installation and repair. Millwright apprentices often attend about one week of classes every three months. Classroom instruction covers mathematics, blueprint reading, hydraulics, vibration analysis, conveyor systems, electricity, computers, electronics, machining, and instruction in specific machinery. Millwrights are expected to keep their skills up-to-date and may need additional training on technological advances, such as laser shaft alignment.

Other qualifications. Because millwrights assemble and disassemble complicated machinery, mechanical aptitude is very important. Strength and agility also are necessary for lifting and climbing. Millwrights need good interpersonal and communication skills to work as part of a team and to effectively give detailed instructions to others.

Advancement. Advancement for millwrights usually takes the form of higher wages. Some advance to the position of supervisor or superintendent; others may become self-employed contractors.

Employment

Millwrights held about 55,000 jobs in 2006. About half work in manufacturing, primarily in industries such as transportation equipment manufacturing and primary metals manufacturing. About 40 percent of millwrights are employed in construction, where most work for contracting firms that assemble and maintain machinery and equipment for the manufacturing and utility industries, among others. Although millwrights work in every state, employment is concentrated in heavily industrialized areas.

Projections data from the National Employment Matrix

Occupational Title	SOC Code	Employment, 2006	Projected employment, 2016	Change, 2006-16	
				Number	Percent
Millwrights	49-9044	55,000	58,000	3,200	6

NOTE: Data in this table are rounded.

Job Outlook

Employment of millwrights is projected to grow more slowly than average. Opportunities for well-qualified applicants should be excellent, however, as many experienced millwrights retire.

Employment change. Employment of millwrights is projected to grow 6 percent during the 2006–2016 decade, slower than the average for all occupations. To remain competitive in coming years, firms will continue to need millwrights to dismantle old equipment and install new high-technology machinery. Highly automated systems that are installed and maintained by millwrights often allow manufacturing companies to remain competitive with producers in lower-wage countries. Warehouse and distribution companies also are deploying highly automated conveyor systems, which are assembled and maintained by millwrights. In addition, growth in both power generation, including wind power and turbines for natural gas and coal plants, and oil and gas extraction and refining will help drive employment growth.

Employment growth will be dampened somewhat by foreign competition in manufacturing. In addition, the demand for millwrights will be adversely affected as other workers, such as industrial machinery mechanics and maintenance workers, assume some installation and maintenance duties.

Job prospects. The large number of expected retirements and the difficulty of recruiting new workers will create excellent job opportunities for well-qualified applicants. Job prospects should be especially good for those who have experience in machining, welding, or doing mechanical work. Employment prospects for millwrights are better than for some other manufacturing workers because they work across a wide range of industries, including power generation, paper mills, mining, and motor vehicle parts manufacturing. When a downturn occurs in one industry, millwrights can more easily switch to another industry. There will always be a need to maintain and repair existing machinery, dismantle old machinery, and install new equipment.

Earnings

Median hourly wage-and-salary earnings of millwrights were $21.94 in May 2006. The middle 50 percent earned between $17.13 and $29.42. The lowest 10 percent earned less than $13.84, and the highest 10 percent earned more than $34.39. Earnings vary by industry and geographic location. Median hourly wage-and-salary earnings in the industries employing the largest numbers of millwrights were

Pulp, paper, and paperboard mills	$25.43
Iron and steel mills and ferroalloy manufacturing	20.91
Nonresidential building construction	20.34
Building equipment contractors	19.67
Sawmills and wood preservation	17.55

About 50 percent of millwrights belong to labor unions, one of the highest rates of membership in the economy.

Related Occupations

Other workers who install and maintain manufacturing equipment include industrial machinery mechanics and maintenance workers; tool and die makers; aircraft and avionics equipment mechanics and service technicians; structural and reinforcing iron and metal workers; boilermakers; and assemblers and fabricators. Millwrights also machine parts and operate computer-controlled machine tools as do machinists and computer control programmers and operators. Millwrights often use welding and soldering to assemble and repair machines as do welding, soldering, and brazing workers.

Sources of Additional Information

For further information on apprenticeship programs, write to the Apprenticeship Council of your state's labor department, local offices of your state employment service, or local firms that employ millwrights. You can also find information on the registered apprenticeships, together with links to state apprenticeship programs, on the U.S. Department of Labor's Web site: http://www.doleta.gov/atels_bat. Apprenticeship information is also available from the U.S. Department of Labor's toll-free helpline: (877) 872-5627.

In addition, you may contact

- Associated Builders and Contractors, Workforce Development Dept., 4250 N. Fairfax Dr., 9th Floor, Arlington, VA 22203. Internet: http://www.trytools.org
- United Brotherhood of Carpenters and Joiners of America, 6801 Placid St., Las Vegas, NV 89119. Internet: http://www.ubcmillwrights.org

STEM Nuclear Medicine Technologists

(O*NET 29-2033.00)

Significant Points

- Two-thirds of nuclear medicine technologists worked in hospitals.
- Nuclear medicine technology programs range in length from 1 to 4 years and lead to a certificate, an associate degree, or a bachelor's degree.
- Faster-than-average job growth will arise from an increase in the number of middle-aged and elderly persons, who are the primary users of diagnostic and treatment procedures.
- The number of job openings each year will be relatively low because the occupation is small; technologists who also are trained in other diagnostic methods, such as radiologic technology or diagnostic medical sonography, will have the best prospects.

Nature of the Work

Diagnostic imaging embraces several procedures that aid in diagnosing ailments, the most familiar being the x ray. In nuclear medicine, radionuclides—unstable atoms that emit radiation spontaneously—are used to diagnose and treat disease. Radionuclides are purified and compounded to form radiopharmaceuticals. Nuclear medicine technologists administer radiopharmaceuticals to patients and then monitor the characteristics and functions of tissues or organs in which the drugs localize. Abnormal areas show higher-than-expected or lower-than-expected concentrations of radioactivity. Nuclear medicine differs from other diagnostic imaging technologies because it determines the presence of disease on the basis of metabolic changes rather than changes in organ structure.

Nuclear medicine technologists operate cameras that detect and map the radioactive drug in a patient's body to create diagnostic images. After explaining test procedures to patients, technologists prepare a dosage of the radiopharmaceutical and administer it by mouth, injection, inhalation, or other means. They position patients and start a gamma scintillation camera, or "scanner," which creates images of the distribution of a radiopharmaceutical as it localizes in, and emits signals from, the patient's body. The images are produced on a computer screen or on film for a physician to interpret.

When preparing radiopharmaceuticals, technologists adhere to safety standards that keep the radiation exposure as low as possible to workers and patients. Technologists keep patient records and document the amount and type of radionuclides that they receive, use, and discard.

Work environment. Physical stamina is important because nuclear medicine technologists are on their feet much of the day and may have to lift or turn disabled patients. In addition, technologists must operate complicated equipment that requires mechanical ability and manual dexterity.

Although the potential for radiation exposure exists in this field, it is minimized by the use of shielded syringes, gloves, and other protective devices and by adherence to strict radiation safety guidelines. The amount of radiation in a nuclear medicine procedure is comparable to that received during a diagnostic x-ray procedure. Technologists also wear badges that measure radiation levels. Because of safety programs, badge measurements rarely exceed established safety levels.

Nuclear medicine technologists generally work a 40-hour week, perhaps including evening or weekend hours, in departments that operate on an extended schedule. Opportunities for part-time and shift work also are available. In addition, technologists in hospitals may have on-call duty on a rotational basis, and those employed by mobile imaging services may be required to travel to several locations.

Training, Other Qualifications, and Advancement

Nuclear medicine technology programs range in length from one to four years and lead to a certificate, an associate degree, or a bachelor's degree. Many employers and an increasing number of states require certification or licensure. Aspiring nuclear medicine technologists should check the requirements of the state in which they plan to work.

Education and training. Completion of a nuclear medicine technology program takes one to four years and leads to a certificate, an associate degree, or a bachelor's degree. Generally, certificate programs are offered in hospitals, associate degree programs in community colleges, and bachelor's degree programs in four-year colleges and universities. Courses cover the physical sciences, biological effects of radiation exposure, radiation protection and procedures, the use of radiopharmaceuticals, imaging techniques, and computer applications.

One-year certificate programs are for health professionals who already possess an associate degree—especially radiologic technologists and diagnostic medical sonographers—but who wish to specialize in nuclear medicine. The programs also attract medical technologists, registered nurses, and others who wish to change fields or specialize.

The Joint Review Committee on Education Programs in Nuclear Medicine Technology accredits most formal training programs in nuclear medicine technology. In 2006, there were about 100 accredited programs in the continental United States and Puerto Rico.

Licensure and certification. Educational requirements for nuclear medicine technologists vary from state to state, so it is important that aspiring technologists check the requirements of the state in which they plan to work. More than half of all states require certification or licensing of nuclear medicine technicians. Certification is available from the American Registry of Radiologic Technologists (ARRT) and from the Nuclear Medicine Technology Certification Board (NMTCB). Although not required, some workers receive certification from both agencies. Nuclear medicine technologists must meet the minimum federal standards on the administration of radioactive drugs and the operation of radiation detection equipment.

The most common way to become eligible for certification by ARRT or NMTCB is to complete a training program recognized by those organizations. Other ways to become eligible are completing a bachelor's or associate degree in biological science or related health field, such as registered nursing, or acquiring, under supervision, a certain number of hours of experience in nuclear medicine technology. ARRT and NMTCB have different requirements, but in all cases, one must pass a comprehensive exam to become certified.

In addition to the general certification requirements, certified technicians also must complete a certain number of continuing education hours. Continuing education is required primarily because of the frequent technological and innovative changes in the field of nuclear medicine. Typically, technologists must register annually with both the ARRT and the NMTCB.

Other qualifications. Nuclear medicine technologists should have excellent communication skills, be detail-oriented, and have a desire to continue learning. Technologists must effectively interact with patients and their families and should be sensitive to patients' physical and psychological needs. Nuclear medicine technologists must be able to work independently as they usually have little direct supervision. Technologists also must be detailed-oriented and meticulous when performing procedures to assure that all regulations are being followed.

Advancement. Technologists may advance to supervisor, then to chief technologist, and to department administrator or director. Some technologists specialize in a clinical area such as nuclear cardiology or computer analysis or leave patient care to take positions in research laboratories. Some become instructors in, or directors of,

Projections data from the National Employment Matrix

Occupational Title	SOC Code	Employment, 2006	Projected employment, 2016	Change, 2006-2016	
				Number	Percent
Nuclear medicine technologists	29-2033	20,000	23,000	2,900	15

NOTE: Data in this table are rounded.

nuclear medicine technology programs, a step that usually requires a bachelor's or master's degree in the subject. Others leave the occupation to work as sales or training representatives for medical equipment and radiopharmaceutical manufacturing firms or as radiation safety officers in regulatory agencies or hospitals.

Employment

Nuclear medicine technologists held about 20,000 jobs in 2006. About 67 percent of all nuclear medicine technologists jobs were in hospitals—private and government. Most of the rest were in offices of physicians or in medical and diagnostic laboratories, including diagnostic imaging centers.

Job Outlook

Faster-than-average job growth will arise from an increase in the number of middle-aged and elderly persons, who are the primary users of diagnostic and treatment procedures. However, the number of job openings each year will be relatively low because the occupation is small.

Employment change. Employment of nuclear medicine technologists is expected to increase by 15 percent from 2006 to 2016, faster than the average for all occupations. Growth will arise from technological advancement, the development of new nuclear medicine treatments, and an increase in the number of middle-aged and older persons, who are the primary users of diagnostic procedures, including nuclear medicine tests.

Technological innovations may increase the diagnostic uses of nuclear medicine. New nuclear medical imaging technologies, including positron emission tomography (PET) and single photon emission computed tomography (SPECT), are expected to be used increasingly and to contribute further to employment growth. The wider use of nuclear medical imaging to observe metabolic and biochemical changes during neurology, cardiology, and oncology procedures also will spur demand for nuclear medicine technologists.

Nonetheless, cost considerations will affect the speed with which new applications of nuclear medicine grow. Some promising nuclear medicine procedures, such as positron emission tomography, are extremely costly, and hospitals contemplating these procedures will have to consider equipment costs, reimbursement policies, and the number of potential users.

Job prospects. In spite of fast growth in nuclear medicine, the number of openings into the occupation each year will be relatively low because of the small size of the occupation. Technologists who have additional training in other diagnostic methods, such as radiologic technology or diagnostic medical sonography, will have the best prospects.

Earnings

Median annual earnings of nuclear medicine technologists were $62,300 in May 2006. The middle 50 percent earned between $53,530 and $72,410. The lowest 10 percent earned less than $46,490, and the highest 10 percent earned more than $82,310. Median annual earnings of nuclear medicine technologists in 2006 were $61,230 in general medical and surgical hospitals.

Related Occupations

Nuclear medical technologists operate sophisticated equipment to help physicians and other health practitioners diagnose and treat patients. Cardiovascular technologists and technicians, clinical laboratory technologists and technicians, diagnostic medical sonographers, radiation therapists, radiologic technologists and technicians, and respiratory therapists perform similar functions.

Sources of Additional Information

Additional information on a career as a nuclear medicine technologist is available from

- American Society of Radiologic Technologists, 15000 Central Ave. SE, Albuquerque, NM 87123-3917. Internet: http://www.asrt.org
- American Registry of Radiologic Technologists, 1255 Northland Dr., St. Paul, MN 55120-1155. Internet: http://www.arrt.org
- Society of Nuclear Medicine Technologists, 1850 Samuel Morse Dr., Reston, VA 20190-5316. Internet: http://www.snm.org

For a list of accredited programs in nuclear medicine technology, contact

- Joint Review Committee on Educational Programs in Nuclear Medicine Technology, 716 Black Point Rd., Polson, MT 59860. Internet: http://www.jrcnmt.org

Information on certification is available from

- Nuclear Medicine Technology Certification Board, 2970 Clairmont Rd., Suite 935, Atlanta, GA 30329-4421. Internet: http://www.nmtcb.org

Occupational Health and Safety Specialists and Technicians

(O*NET 29-9011.00 and 29-9012.00)

Significant Points

- About 2 out of 5 specialists and technicians worked in federal, state, and local government agencies that enforce rules on safety, health, and the environment.
- Some specialist jobs require a bachelor's degree in occupational health, safety, or a related field.
- Projected average employment growth reflects a balance of continuing public demand for a safe and healthy work environment against the desire for smaller government and fewer regulations.

Nature of the Work

Occupational health and safety specialists and technicians, also known as *safety and health professionals* or *occupational health and safety inspectors*, help prevent harm to workers, property, the environment, and the general public. For example, they might design safe work spaces, inspect machines, or test air quality. In addition to making workers safer, specialists and technicians aim to increase worker productivity by reducing absenteeism and equipment downtime—and to save money by lowering insurance premiums and workers' compensation payments, and preventing government fines. Some specialists and technicians work for governments, conducting safety inspections and imposing fines.

Occupational health and safety specialists analyze work environments and design programs to control, eliminate, and prevent disease or injury. They look for chemical, physical, radiological, and biological hazards, and they work to make more equipment ergonomic—designed to promote proper body positioning, increase worker comfort, and decrease fatigue. Specialists may conduct inspections and inform an organization's management of areas not in compliance with state and federal laws or employer policies. They also advise management on the cost and effectiveness of safety and health programs. Some provide training on new regulations and policies or on how to recognize hazards.

Sometimes, specialists develop methods to predict hazards from historical data and other information sources. They use these methods and their own knowledge and experience to evaluate current equipment, products, facilities, or processes and those planned for use in the future. For example, they might uncover patterns in injury data that show that many injuries are caused by a specific type of system failure, human error, or weakness in procedures. They evaluate the probability and severity of accidents and identify where controls need to be implemented to reduce or eliminate risk. If a new program or practice is required, they propose it to management and monitor results if it is implemented. Specialists also might conduct safety training for management, supervisors, and workers. Training sessions might show how to recognize hazards, for example, or explain new regulations and production processes.

Some specialists, often called *loss prevention specialists*, work for insurance companies, inspecting the facilities that they insure and suggesting and helping to implement improvements.

Occupational health and safety technicians often focus on testing air, water, machines, and other elements of the work environment. They collect data that occupational health and safety specialists then analyze. Usually working under the supervision of specialists, they also help to implement and evaluate safety programs.

To measure hazards, such as noise or radiation, occupational health and safety technicians prepare and calibrate scientific equipment. They must properly collect and handle samples of dust, gases, vapors, and other potentially toxic materials to ensure personal safety and accurate test results. Occupational health and safety specialists also may perform this work, especially if it is complex.

To ensure that machinery and equipment complies with appropriate safety regulations, occupational health and safety specialists and technicians both may examine and test machinery and equipment, such as lifting devices, machine guards, or scaffolding. They may check that personal protective equipment, such as masks, respirators, protective eyewear, or hardhats, is being used according to regulations. They also check that hazardous materials are stored correctly. They test and identify work areas for potential accident and health hazards, such as toxic vapors, mold, mildew, and explosive gas-air mixtures and help implement appropriate control measures, such as adjustments to ventilation systems. Their inspection of the workplace might involve talking with workers and observing their work, as well as inspecting elements in their work environment, such as lighting, tools, and equipment.

If an injury or illness occurs, occupational health and safety specialists and technicians help investigate, studying its causes and recommending remedial action. Some occupational health and safety specialists and technicians help workers to return to work after accidents and injuries.

Occupational health and safety specialists and technicians frequently communicate with management about the status of health and safety programs. They also might consult with engineers or physicians.

Specialists and technicians write reports, including accident reports, and enter information on Occupational Safety and Health Administration recordkeeping forms. They may prepare documents used in legal proceedings and give testimony in court. Those who develop expertise in specific areas may develop occupational health and safety systems, including policies, procedures, and manuals.

The responsibilities of occupational health and safety specialists and technicians vary by industry, workplace, and types of hazards affecting employees. Mine examiners, for example, are technicians who inspect mines for proper air flow and health hazards such as the buildup of methane or other noxious gases. Environmental protection officers evaluate and coordinate the storage and handling of hazardous waste, the cleanup of contaminated soil or water, or other activities that affect the environment. Ergonomists consider the design of industrial, office, and other equipment to maximize worker comfort, safety, and productivity. Health physicists work in places that use radiation and radioactive material, helping to protect people and the environment from hazardous radiation exposure. And industrial hygienists examine the workplace for health hazards, such as exposure to lead, asbestos, pesticides, or communicable diseases.

Work environment. Occupational health and safety specialists and technicians work in a variety of settings from offices and factories to mines. Their jobs often involve considerable fieldwork, and some require frequent travel.

Occupational health and safety specialists and technicians may be exposed to many of the same strenuous, dangerous, or stressful conditions faced by industrial employees. They may find themselves in an adversarial role if an organization disagrees with their recommendations. Many occupational health and safety specialists and technicians work long, and often irregular, hours.

Training, Other Qualifications, and Advancement

All occupational health and safety specialists and technicians are trained in the applicable laws or inspection procedures through some combination of classroom and on-the-job training.

Education and training. Some employers require occupational health and safety specialists to have a bachelor's degree in occupational health, safety, or a related field, such as engineering, biology, or chemistry. For some positions, a master's degree in industrial hygiene or a related subject is required. There also are associate degree and one-year certificate programs, which primarily are intended for technicians.

As of February 2007, the Accreditation Board for Engineering and Technology accredited 45 programs in health physics, industrial hygiene, and safety.

Certification and other qualifications. Although voluntary, many employers encourage certification. Certification is available through several organizations. The Board of Certified Safety Professionals offers the Certified Safety Professional (CSP) credential. The American Board of Industrial Hygiene offers the Certified Industrial Hygienist (CIH) credential. Also, the Council on Certification of Health, Environmental, and Safety Technologists certifies people as Occupational Health and Safety Technologists (OHST), who may be called Certified Loss Control Specialists (CLCS), Construction Health and Safety Technicians (CHST), and Safety Trained Supervisors (STS). The Indoor Air Quality Association awards the Certified Indoor Environmentalist (CIE) credential. The Board of Certification in Professional Ergonomics offers the Certified Professional Ergonomist (CPE) and the Certified Ergonomics Associate (CEA) credentials. The American Board of Health Physicists awards the Certified Health Physicist (CHP) credential.

Requirements for these credentials differ. Usually, they include specific education and experience, passing an examination, and completing periodic continuing education for recertification.

In general, people who want to enter this occupation should be responsible and like detailed work. Occupational health and safety specialists and technicians also should be able to communicate well. Recommended high school courses include English, mathematics, chemistry, biology, and physics. Experience as an occupational health and safety professional is also a prerequisite for many positions.

Advancement. Occupational health and safety specialists and technicians who work for the federal government advance through their career ladder to a specified full-performance level if their work is satisfactory. For positions above this level, usually supervisory positions, advancement is competitive and based on agency needs and individual merit. Advancement opportunities in state and local governments and the private sector are often similar to those in the federal government.

Specialists and technicians with broad education and experience and those who are well versed in numerous business functions usually have the best advancement opportunities. One way to keep up with current professional developments is to join a professional society, such as those that offer the certifications mentioned earlier. These organizations offer journals, continuing education courses, and conferences, which offer learning and networking opportunities and can help workers and students to advance.

With an advanced degree, professionals can become professors or do research. Promotion to senior specialist positions is likely to require an advanced degree and substantial experience in several areas of practice.

Employment

Occupational health and safety specialists and technicians held about 56,000 jobs in 2006. While the majority of jobs were spread throughout the private sector; about 2 out of 5 specialists worked for government agencies. Local governments employed 15 percent, the federal government employed 13 percent, and state governments employed 12 percent.

Within the federal government, most jobs are as Occupational Safety and Health Administration inspectors, who enforce U.S. Department of Labor regulations and impose fines. Within the U.S. Department of Health and Human Services, the National Institute of Occupational Safety and Health hires occupational health and safety specialists to offer companies help in evaluating safety without the risk of fines. Most large government agencies also employ occupational health and safety specialists and technicians who work to protect agency employees.

Most private companies either employ their own occupational health and safety workers or contract with them. Most contract work is done through consulting companies, but some specialists and technicians are self-employed.

In addition to working for governments, occupational health and safety specialists and technicians were employed in manufacturing firms; private general medical and surgical hospitals; private colleges, universities, and professional schools; scientific and technical consulting services; research and development in the physical, engineering, and life sciences; and electric power generation, transmission, and distribution. Insurance companies and technical consulting services also often employed specialists, whereas employment services and testing laboratories often employed technicians.

Job Outlook

Average employment growth is expected; additional opportunities will arise from the need to replace workers who leave the occupation.

Employment change. Employment of occupational health and safety specialists and technicians is expected to increase 9 percent during the 2006–2016 decade, about as fast as the average for all occupations, reflecting a balance of continuing public demand for a safe and healthy work environment against the desire for smaller government and fewer regulations. Emergency preparedness will continue to increase in importance, creating demand for these workers. More specialists will be needed to cope with technological advances in safety equipment and threats, changing regulations, and increasing public expectations. In private industry, employment growth will reflect overall business growth and continuing self-enforcement of government and company regulations and policies.

Over the past two decades, insurance and worker's compensation costs have risen and have become a financial concern for many employers and insurance companies. As a result, job growth should be good for those specializing in loss prevention, especially in construction safety and in ergonomics.

Job prospects. In addition to job openings from growth, job openings will arise from the need to replace workers who transfer to other occupations, retire, or leave for other reasons. An aging population paired with a decline in the number of postsecondary students studying the sciences, especially health physics, will create opportunities for those with technical skill.

Employment of occupational health and safety specialists and technicians in the private sector is somewhat affected by general economic fluctuations. Federal, state, and local governments, which employ about 2 out of 5 of all specialists and technicians, provide considerable job security; workers are less likely to be affected by changes in the economy.

Projections data from the National Employment Matrix

Occupational Title	SOC Code	Employment, 2006	Projected employment, 2016	Change, 2006-2016	
				Number	Percent
Occupational health and safety specialists and technicians	29-9010	56,000	61,000	5,200	9
Occupational health and safety specialists	29-9011	45,000	49,000	3,700	8
Occupational health and safety technicians	29-9012	10,000	12,000	1,500	15

NOTE: Data in this table are rounded.

Earnings

Median annual earnings of occupational health and safety specialists and technicians were $54,920 in May 2006. The middle 50 percent earned between $41,800 and $70,230. The lowest 10 percent earned less than $32,230, and the highest 10 percent earned more than $83,720. Median annual earnings in the industries employing the largest numbers of occupational health and safety specialists and technicians in May 2006 were

Federal government $68,890
Management, scientific, and technical consulting services 63,130
General medical and surgical hospitals 59,200
Local government 52,110
State government 49,690

Most occupational health and safety specialists and technicians work in large private firms or for federal, state, and local governments, most of which generally offer benefits more generous than those offered by smaller firms.

Related Occupations

Occupational health and safety specialists and technicians help to ensure that laws and regulations are obeyed. Others who enforce laws and regulations include agricultural inspectors, construction and building inspectors, correctional officers, financial examiners, fire inspectors, police and detectives, and transportation inspectors. Occupational health and safety specialists also analyze work environments and processes, topics that industrial engineers also study.

Sources of Additional Information

Information about jobs in federal, state, and local governments and in private industry is available from state employment service offices.

For information on a career as an industrial hygienist, including a list of colleges and universities offering industrial hygiene and related degrees, contact

- American Industrial Hygiene Association, 2700 Prosperity Ave., Suite 250, Fairfax, VA 22031. Internet: http://www.aiha.org

For information on the Certified Industrial Hygienist or Certified Associate Industrial Hygienist credential, contact

- American Board of Industrial Hygiene, 6015 West St. Joseph Hwy., Suite 102, Lansing, MI 48917. Internet: http://www.abih.org

For more information on professions in safety, a list of safety and related academic programs, and the Certified Safety Professional credential, contact

- Board of Certified Safety Professionals, 208 Burwash Ave., Savoy, IL 61874. Internet: http://www.bcsp.org

For information on the Occupational Health and Safety Technologist, Construction Health and Safety Technician credentials, and Safety Trained Supervisors, contact

- Council on Certification of Health, Environmental, and Safety Technologists, 208 Burwash Ave., Savoy, IL 61874. Internet: http://www.cchest.org

For information on a career as a health physicist, contact

- Health Physics Society, 1313 Dolley Madison Blvd., Suite 402, McLean, VA 22101. Internet: http://www.hps.org

For additional career information, contact

- U.S. Department of Health and Human Services, Center for Disease Control and Prevention, National Institute of Occupational Safety and Health, Hubert H. Humphrey Bldg., 200 Independence Ave. SW, Room 715H, Washington, DC 20201. Internet: http://www.cdc.gov/niosh
- U.S. Department of Labor, Occupational Safety and Health Administration, Office of Communication, 200 Constitution Ave. NW, Washington, DC 20210. Internet: http://www.osha.gov

Information on obtaining positions as occupational health and safety specialists and technicians with the federal government is available from the Office of Personnel Management through USAJOBS, the federal government's official employment information system. This resource for locating and applying for job opportunities can be accessed through the Internet at http://www.usajobs.opm.gov or through an interactive voice response telephone system at (703) 724-1850 or TDD (978) 461-8404. These numbers are not toll free, and charges may result.

Occupational Therapist Assistants and Aides

(O*NET 31-2011.00 and 31-2012.00)

Significant Points

- Occupational therapist assistants generally must complete an associate degree or a certificate program; in contrast, occupational therapist aides usually receive most of their training on the job.
- Employment is projected to grow much faster than the average as demand for occupational therapy services rises and as occupational therapists increasingly use assistants and aides.
- Job prospects should be very good for occupational therapist assistants; job seekers holding only a high school diploma might face keen competition for occupational therapist aide jobs.

Nature of the Work

Occupational therapist assistants and aides work under the direction of occupational therapists to provide rehabilitative services to persons with mental, physical, emotional, or developmental impairments. The ultimate goal is to improve clients' quality of life and ability to perform daily activities. For example, occupational therapist assistants help injured workers re-enter the labor force by teaching them how to compensate for lost motor skills or help individuals with learning disabilities increase their independence.

Occupational therapist assistants, commonly known as *occupational therapy assistants*, help clients with rehabilitative activities and exercises outlined in a treatment plan developed in collaboration with an occupational therapist. Activities range from teaching the proper method of moving from a bed into a wheelchair to the best way to stretch and limber the muscles of the hand. Assistants monitor an individual's activities to make sure that they are performed correctly and to provide encouragement. They also record their client's progress for the occupational therapist. If the treatment is not having the intended effect, or the client is not improving as expected, the therapist may alter the treatment program in hopes of obtaining better results. In addition, occupational therapist assistants document the billing of the client's health insurance provider.

Occupational therapist aides typically prepare materials and assemble equipment used during treatment. They are responsible for a range of clerical tasks, including scheduling appointments, answering the telephone, restocking or ordering depleted supplies, and filling out insurance forms or other paperwork. Aides are not licensed, so the law does not allow them to perform as wide a range of tasks as occupational therapist assistants.

Work environment. Occupational therapist assistants and aides need to have a moderate degree of strength because of the physical exertion required to assist patients. For example, assistants and aides may need to lift patients. Constant kneeling, stooping, and standing for long periods also are part of the job.

The hours and days that occupational therapist assistants and aides work vary by facility and with whether they are full- or part time. For example, many outpatient therapy offices and clinics have evening and weekend hours to coincide with patients' schedules.

Training, Other Qualifications, and Advancement

An associate degree or a certificate from an accredited community college or technical school is generally required to qualify for occupational therapist assistant jobs. In contrast, occupational therapist aides usually receive most of their training on the job.

Education and training. There were 126 accredited occupational therapist assistant programs in 2007. The first year of study typically involves an introduction to health care, basic medical terminology, anatomy, and physiology. In the second year, courses are more rigorous and usually include occupational therapist courses in areas such as mental health, adult physical disabilities, gerontology, and pediatrics. Students also must complete 16 weeks of supervised fieldwork in a clinic or community setting.

Applicants to occupational therapist assistant programs can improve their chances of admission by taking high school courses in biology and health and by performing volunteer work in nursing care facilities, occupational or physical therapists' offices, or other health care settings.

Occupational therapist aides usually receive most of their training on the job. Qualified applicants must have a high school diploma, strong interpersonal skills, and a desire to help people in need. Applicants may increase their chances of getting a job by volunteering their services, thus displaying initiative and aptitude to the employer.

Licensure. In most states, occupational therapist assistants are regulated and must pass a national certification examination after they graduate. Those who pass the test are awarded the title "Certified Occupational Therapy Assistant."

Other qualifications. Assistants and aides must be responsible, patient, and willing to take directions and work as part of a team. Furthermore, they should be caring and want to help people who are not able to help themselves.

Advancement. Occupational therapist assistants may advance into administration positions. They might organize all the assistants in a large occupational therapy department or act as the director for a specific department such as sports medicine. Some assistants go on to teach classes in accredited occupational therapist assistant academic programs or lead health risk reduction classes for the elderly.

Employment

Occupational therapist assistants and aides held about 33,000 jobs in 2006. Occupational therapist assistants held about 25,000 jobs, and occupational therapist aides held approximately 8,000. About 29 percent of jobs for assistants and aides were in hospitals, 23 percent were in offices of occupational therapists, and 21 percent were in nursing and residential care facilities. The rest were primarily in community care facilities for the elderly, home health care services, individual and family services, and state government agencies.

Job Outlook

Employment is expected to grow much faster than average as demand for occupational therapy services rises and as occupational therapists increasingly use assistants and aides. Job prospects should be very good for occupational therapist assistants. Job seekers holding only a high school diploma might face keen competition for occupational therapist aide jobs.

Employment change. Employment of occupational therapist assistants and aides is expected to grow 25 percent from 2006 to 2016, much faster than the average for all occupations. In the short run, the impact of proposed federal legislation imposing limits on reimbursement for therapy services may adversely affect the job market for occupational therapist assistants and aides. Over the long run, however, demand for occupational therapist assistants and aides will continue to rise because of the increasing number of individuals with disabilities or limited function.

The growing elderly population is particularly vulnerable to chronic and debilitating conditions that require therapeutic services. These patients often need additional assistance in their treatment, making the roles of assistants and aides vital. Also, the large baby-boom generation is entering the prime age for heart attacks and strokes, further increasing the demand for cardiac and physical rehabilitation. In addition, future medical developments should permit an increased percentage of trauma victims to survive, creating added demand for therapy services. An increase of sensory disorders in children will also spur demand for occupational therapy services.

Projections data from the National Employment Matrix

Occupational Title	SOC Code	Employment, 2006	Projected employment, 2016	Change, 2006-16	
				Number	Percent
Occupational therapist assistants and aides	31-2010	33,000	41,000	8,200	25
Occupational therapist assistants	31-2011	25,000	31,000	6,400	25
Occupational therapist aides	31-2012	8,200	10,000	1,800	22

NOTE: Data in this table are rounded.

Occupational therapists are expected to increasingly utilize assistants and aides to reduce the cost of occupational therapy services. Once a patient is evaluated and a treatment plan is designed by the therapist, the occupational therapist assistant can provide many aspects of treatment, as prescribed by the therapist.

Job prospects. Opportunities for individuals interested in becoming occupational therapist assistants are expected to be very good. In addition to employment growth, job openings will result from the need to replace occupational therapist assistants and aides who leave the occupation permanently over the 2006–2016 period. Occupational therapist assistants and aides with prior experience working in an occupational therapy office or other health care setting will have the best job opportunities. However, individuals with only a high school diploma may face keen competition for occupational therapist aide jobs.

Earnings

Median annual earnings of occupational therapist assistants were $42,060 in May 2006. The middle 50 percent earned between $34,130 and $50,230. The lowest 10 percent earned less than $26,050, and the highest 10 percent earned more than $58,270. Median annual earnings in the industries employing the largest numbers of occupational therapist assistants in May 2006 were

Offices of physical, occupational and speech therapists, and audiologists $45,130
Nursing care facilities 43,280
General medical and surgical hospitals 40,060

Median annual earnings of occupational therapist aides were $25,020 in May 2006. The middle 50 percent earned between $20,460 and $32,160. The lowest 10 percent earned less than $17,060, and the highest 10 percent earned more than $44,130. Median annual earnings in the industries employing the largest numbers of occupational therapist aides in May 2006 were

Offices of physical, occupational and speech therapists, and audiologists $26,960
General medical and surgical hospitals 26,360
Nursing care facilities 25,520

Related Occupations

Occupational therapist assistants and aides work under the supervision and direction of occupational therapists. Other workers in the health care field who work under similar supervision include dental assistants; medical assistants; nursing, psychiatric, and home health aides; personal and home care aides; pharmacy aides; pharmacy technicians; and physical therapist assistants and aides.

Sources of Additional Information

For information on a career as an occupational therapist assistant or aide, and a list of accredited programs, contact

- American Occupational Therapy Association, 4720 Montgomery Lane, Bethesda, MD 20824-1220. Internet: http://www.aota.org

Occupational Therapists

(O*NET 29-1122.00)

Significant Points

- Employment is expected to grow much faster than average and job opportunities should be good, especially for therapists treating the elderly.
- Occupational therapists must be licensed, requiring a master's degree in occupational therapy, 6 months of supervised fieldwork, and passing scores on national and state examinations.
- Occupational therapists are increasingly taking on supervisory roles, allowing assistants and aides to work more closely with clients under the guidance of a therapist.
- More than a quarter of occupational therapists work part time.

Nature of the Work

Occupational therapists help patients improve their ability to perform tasks in living and working environments. They work with individuals who suffer from a mentally, physically, developmentally, or emotionally disabling condition. Occupational therapists use treatments to develop, recover, or maintain the daily living and work skills of their patients. The therapist helps clients not only to improve their basic motor functions and reasoning abilities, but also to compensate for permanent loss of function. The goal is to help clients have independent, productive, and satisfying lives.

Occupational therapists help clients to perform all types of activities, from using a computer to caring for daily needs such as dressing, cooking, and eating. Physical exercises may be used to increase strength and dexterity, while other activities may be chosen to improve visual acuity or the ability to discern patterns. For example, a client with short-term memory loss might be encouraged to make lists to aid recall, and a person with coordination problems might be assigned exercises to improve hand-eye coordination. Occupational therapists also use computer programs to help clients improve decision-making, abstract-reasoning, problem-solving, and perceptual skills, as well as memory, sequencing, and coordination—all of which are important for independent living.

Patients with permanent disabilities, such as spinal cord injuries, cerebral palsy, or muscular dystrophy, often need special instruction to master certain daily tasks. For these individuals, therapists demonstrate the use of adaptive equipment, including wheelchairs, orthoses, eating aids, and dressing aids. They also design or build special equipment needed at home or at work, including computer-aided adaptive equipment. They teach clients how to use the equipment to improve communication and control various situations in their environment.

Some occupational therapists treat individuals whose ability to function in a work environment has been impaired. These practitioners might arrange employment, evaluate the work space, plan work activities, and assess the client's progress. Therapists also may collaborate with the client and the employer to modify the work environment so that the client can successfully complete the work.

Assessing and recording a client's activities and progress is an important part of an occupational therapist's job. Accurate records are essential for evaluating clients, for billing, and for reporting to physicians and other health care providers.

Occupational therapists may work exclusively with individuals in a particular age group or with a particular disability. In schools, for example, they evaluate children's capabilities, recommend and provide therapy, modify classroom equipment, and help children participate in school activities. A therapist may work with children individually, lead small groups in the classroom, consult with a teacher, or serve on an administrative committee. Some therapists provide early intervention therapy to infants and toddlers who have, or are at risk of having, developmental delays. Therapies may include facilitating the use of the hands and promoting skills for listening, following directions, social play, dressing, or grooming.

Other occupational therapists work with elderly patients. These therapists help the elderly lead more productive, active, and independent lives through a variety of methods. Therapists with specialized training in driver rehabilitation assess an individual's ability to drive using both clinical and on-the-road tests. The evaluations allow the therapist to make recommendations for adaptive equipment, training to prolong driving independence, and alternative transportation options. Occupational therapists also work with clients to assess their homes for hazards and to identify environmental factors that contribute to falls.

Occupational therapists in mental health settings treat individuals who are mentally ill, developmentally challenged, or emotionally disturbed. To treat these problems, therapists choose activities that help people learn to engage in and cope with daily life. Activities might include time management skills, budgeting, shopping, homemaking, and the use of public transportation. Occupational therapists also work with individuals who are dealing with alcoholism, drug abuse, depression, eating disorders, or stress-related disorders.

Work environment. In large rehabilitation centers, therapists may work in spacious rooms equipped with machines, tools, and other devices generating noise. The work can be tiring because therapists are on their feet much of the time. Those providing home health care services may spend time driving from appointment to appointment. Therapists also face hazards such as back strain from lifting and moving clients and equipment.

Occupational therapists in hospitals and other health care and community settings usually work a 40-hour week. Those in schools may participate in meetings and other activities during and after the school day. In 2006, more than a quarter of occupational therapists worked part time.

Training, Other Qualifications, and Advancement

Occupational therapists must be licensed, requiring a master's degree in occupational therapy, six months of supervised fieldwork, and passing scores on national and state examinations.

Education and training. A master's degree or higher in occupational therapy is the minimum requirement for entry into the field. In 2007, 124 master's degree programs offered entry-level education, 66 programs offered a combined bachelor's and master's degree, and five offered an entry-level doctoral degree. Most schools have full-time programs, although a growing number are offering weekend or part-time programs as well. Coursework in occupational therapy programs include the physical, biological, and behavioral sciences as well as the application of occupational therapy theory and skills. Programs also require the completion of six months of supervised fieldwork.

People considering this profession should take high school courses in biology, chemistry, physics, health, art, and the social sciences. College admissions offices also look favorably on paid or volunteer experience in the health care field. Relevant undergraduate majors include biology, psychology, sociology, anthropology, liberal arts, and anatomy.

Licensure. All states, Puerto Rico, Guam, and the District of Columbia regulate the practice of occupational therapy. To obtain a license, applicants must graduate from an accredited educational program and pass a national certification examination. Those who pass the exam are awarded the title "Occupational Therapist Registered (OTR)." Some states have additional requirements for therapists who work in schools or early intervention programs. These requirements may include education-related classes, an education practice certificate, or early intervention certification.

Other qualifications. Occupational therapists need patience and strong interpersonal skills to inspire trust and respect in their clients. Patience is necessary because many clients may not show rapid improvement. Ingenuity and imagination in adapting activities to individual needs are assets. Those working in home health care services also must be able to adapt to a variety of settings.

Advancement. Occupational therapists are expected to continue their professional development by participating in continuing education courses and workshops. In fact, a number of states require continuing education as a condition of maintaining licensure.

Therapists are increasingly taking on supervisory roles. Because of rising health care costs, third-party payers are beginning to encourage occupational therapist assistants and aides to take more hands-on responsibility for clients. Occupational therapists can choose to advance their careers by taking on administrative duties and supervising assistants and aides.

Occupational therapists also can advance by specializing in a clinical area and gaining expertise in treating a certain type of patient or ailment. Therapists have specialized in gerontology, mental health, pediatrics, and physical rehabilitation. In addition, some occupational therapists choose to teach classes in accredited occupational therapy educational programs.

Employment

Occupational therapists held about 99,000 jobs in 2006. About 1 in 10 occupational therapists held more than one job. The largest num-

Projections data from the National Employment Matrix

Occupational Title	SOC Code	Employment, 2006	Projected employment, 2016	Change, 2006-2016	
				Number	Percent
Occupational therapists	29-1122	99,000	122,000	23,000	23

NOTE: Data in this table are rounded.

ber of jobs was in hospitals. Other major employers were offices of other health practitioners (including offices of occupational therapists), public and private educational services, and nursing care facilities. Some occupational therapists were employed by home health care services, outpatient care centers, offices of physicians, individual and family services, community care facilities for the elderly, and government agencies.

A small number of occupational therapists were self-employed in private practice. These practitioners treated clients referred by other health professionals. They also provided contract or consulting services to nursing care facilities, schools, adult day care programs, and home health care agencies.

Job Outlook

Employment of occupational therapists is expected to grow much faster than the average for all occupations. Job opportunities should be good, especially for occupational therapists treating the elderly.

Employment change. Employment of occupational therapists is expected to increase 23 percent between 2006 and 2016, much faster than the average for all occupations. The increasing elderly population will drive growth in the demand for occupational therapy services. In the short run, the impact of proposed federal legislation imposing limits on reimbursement for therapy services may adversely affect the job market for occupational therapists. However, over the long run, the demand for occupational therapists should continue to rise as a result of the increasing number of individuals with disabilities or limited function who require therapy services. The baby-boom generation's movement into middle age, a period when the incidence of heart attack and stroke increases, will spur demand for therapeutic services. Growth in the population 75 years and older—an age group that suffers from high incidences of disabling conditions—also will increase demand for therapeutic services. In addition, medical advances now enable more patients with critical problems to survive—patients who ultimately may need extensive therapy.

Hospitals will continue to employ a large number of occupational therapists to provide therapy services to acutely ill inpatients. Hospitals also will need occupational therapists to staff their outpatient rehabilitation programs.

Employment growth in schools will result from the expansion of the school-age population, the extension of services for disabled students, and an increasing prevalence of sensory disorders in children. Therapists will be needed to help children with disabilities prepare to enter special education programs.

Job prospects. Job opportunities should be good for licensed occupational therapists in all settings, particularly in acute hospital, rehabilitation, and orthopedic settings because the elderly receive most of their treatment in these settings. Occupational therapists with specialized knowledge in a treatment area also will have increased job prospects. Driver rehabilitation and fall-prevention training for the elderly are emerging practice areas for occupational therapy.

Earnings

Median annual earnings of occupational therapists were $60,470 in May 2006. The middle 50 percent earned between $50,450 and $73,710. The lowest 10 percent earned less than $40,840, and the highest 10 percent earned more than $89,450. Median annual earnings in the industries employing the largest numbers of occupational therapists in May 2006 were

Home health care services....................................$67,600
Nursing care facilities 64,750
Offices of physical, occupational and speech therapists, and audiologists 62,290
General medical and surgical hospitals 61,610
Elementary and secondary schools 54,260

Related Occupations

Occupational therapists use specialized knowledge to help individuals perform daily living skills and achieve maximum independence. Other workers performing similar duties include athletic trainers, audiologists, chiropractors, physical therapists, recreational therapists, rehabilitation counselors, respiratory therapists, and speech-language pathologists.

Sources of Additional Information

For more information on occupational therapy as a career, contact

- American Occupational Therapy Association, 4720 Montgomery Lane, Bethesda, MD 20824-1220. Internet: http://www.aota.org

For information regarding the requirements to practice as an occupational therapist in schools, contact the appropriate occupational therapy regulatory agency for your state.

STEM Operations Research Analysts

(O*NET 15-2031.00)

Significant Points

- While a bachelor's degree is the minimum requirement, employers generally prefer applicants with at least a master's degree in operations research or a closely related field.
- Computer programming skills and keeping up to date with technological advances and improvements in analytical methods are essential.
- Employment growth is projected to be as fast as the average for all occupations.

- Individuals with a master's or Ph.D. degree in operations research or a closely related subject should find opportunities in a number of occupations that use their computer, mathematical, and problem-solving skills.

Nature of the Work

"Operations research" and "management science" are terms that are used interchangeably to describe the discipline of using advanced analytical techniques to make better decisions and to solve problems. The procedures of operations research were first formalized by the military. They have been used in wartime to effectively deploy radar, search for enemy submarines, and get supplies to where they are most needed. In peacetime and in private enterprises, operations research is used in planning business ventures and analyzing options by using statistical analysis, data and computer modeling, linear programming, and other mathematical techniques.

Large organizations are very complex. They must effectively manage money, materials, equipment, and people. Operations research analysts find better ways to coordinate these elements by applying analytical methods from mathematics, science, and engineering. Analysts often find many possible solutions for meeting the goals of a project. These potential solutions are presented to managers, who choose the course of action that they think best.

Operations research analysts are often involved in top-level strategizing, planning, and forecasting. They help to allocate resources, measure performance, schedule, design production facilities and systems, manage the supply chain, set prices, coordinate transportation and distribution, or analyze large databases.

The duties of the operations research analyst vary according to the structure and management of the organization they are assisting. Some firms centralize operations research in one department; others use operations research in each division. Operations research analysts also may work closely with senior managers to identify and solve a variety of problems. Analysts often have one area of specialization, such as working in the transportation or the financial services industry.

Operations research analysts start a project by listening to managers describe a problem. Then, analysts ask questions and formally define the problem. For example, an operations research analyst for an auto manufacturer may be asked to determine the best inventory level for each of the parts needed on a production line and to ascertain the optimal number of windshields to be kept in stock. Too many windshields would be wasteful and expensive, whereas too few could halt production.

Analysts would study the problem, breaking it into its components. Then they would gather information from a variety of sources. To determine the optimal inventory, operations research analysts might talk with engineers about production levels, discuss purchasing arrangements with buyers, and examine storage-cost data provided by the accounting department.

Relevant information in hand, the analysts determine the most appropriate analytical technique. Techniques used may include a Monte Carlo simulation, linear and nonlinear programming, dynamic programming, queuing and other stochastic-process models, Markov decision processes, econometric methods, data envelopment analysis, neural networks, expert systems, decision analysis, and the analytic hierarchy process. Nearly all of these techniques involve the construction of a mathematical model that attempts to describe the system being studied. So, the problem of the windshields, for example, would be described as a set of equations that try to model real-world conditions.

The use of models enables the analyst to explicitly describe the different components and clarify the relationships among them. The descriptions can be altered to examine what may happen to the system under different circumstances. In most cases, a computer program is developed to numerically evaluate the model.

Usually the model chosen is modified and run repeatedly to obtain different solutions. A model for airline flight scheduling, for example, might stipulate such things as connecting cities, the amount of fuel required to fly the routes, projected levels of passenger demand, varying ticket and fuel prices, pilot scheduling, and maintenance costs. By assessing different possible schedules, the analyst is able to determine the best flight schedule consistent with particular assumptions.

Based on the results of the analysis, the operations research analyst presents recommendations to managers. The analyst may need to modify and rerun the computer program to consider different assumptions before presenting the final recommendation. Once managers reach a decision, the analyst usually works with others in the organization to ensure the plan's successful implementation.

Work environment. Operations research analysts generally work regular hours in an office environment. However, because they work on projects that are of immediate interest to top managers, operations research analysts often are under pressure to meet deadlines and may work more than 40 hours a week.

Training, Other Qualifications, and Advancement

A college degree in operations research generally is required. Computer programming skills are essential.

Education and training. Employers generally prefer applicants with at least a master's degree in operations research or a closely related field—such as computer science, engineering, business, mathematics, information systems, or management science—coupled with a bachelor's degree in computer science or a quantitative discipline such as economics, mathematics, or statistics. Dual graduate degrees in operations research and computer science are especially attractive to employers. There are more than 130 programs in operations research and related studies in colleges and universities across the United States.

Continuing education is important for operations research analysts. Keeping up to date with technological advances and improvements in analytical methods is vital for maintaining their problem-solving skills.

Other qualifications. Computers are the most important tools used by operations research analysts, so analysts must have training and experience in programming. Analysts typically also need to be proficient in database collection and management, and the development and use of sophisticated software packages.

Operations research analysts must be able to think logically, work well with people, and write and speak well.

Advancement. Beginning analysts usually perform routine work under the supervision of more experienced analysts. As novices gain knowledge and experience, they are assigned more complex tasks and are given greater autonomy to design models and solve problems.

Projections data from the National Employment Matrix

Occupational Title	SOC Code	Employment, 2006	Projected employment, 2016	Change, 2006-2016	
				Number	Percent
Operations research analysts	15-2031	58,000	65,000	6,200	11

NOTE: Data in this table are rounded.

Operations research analysts can advance by becoming technical specialists or supervisors on more complicated projects. Analysts also gain valuable insights into the industry where they work and may assume higher level managerial or administrative positions. Operations research analysts with significant experience or expertise may become consultants, and some open their own consulting practices.

Employment

Operations research analysts held about 58,000 jobs in 2006. Major employers include computer systems design firms; insurance carriers and other financial institutions; telecommunications companies; management, scientific, and technical consulting services firms; and federal, state, and local governments. Most operations research analysts in the federal government work for the Department of Defense, and many in private industry work directly or indirectly on national defense.

Job Outlook

Employment of operations research analysts is projected to grow as fast as the average for all occupations. Individuals with a master's or Ph.D. degree in operations research or a closely related subject should find job opportunities in a number of occupations that use their computer, mathematical, and problem-solving skills.

Employment change. Employment of operations research analysts is expected to grow 11 percent, as fast as the average for all occupations between 2006 and 2016. Demand for operations research analysis should continue to grow. Organizations increasingly will be faced with the pressure of growing domestic and international competition and must work to make their operations as effective as possible. As a result, businesses increasingly will rely on operations research analysts to optimize profits by improving productivity and reducing costs. As new technology is introduced into the marketplace, operations research analysts will be needed to determine how to use the technology in the best way.

Additionally, technological advancements have extended the availability of data access and storage, making information more readily available. Advancements in computing capabilities and analytical software have made it cheaper and faster for analysts to solve problems. As problem solving becomes cheaper and faster with technological advances, more firms will have the ability to employ or consult with analysts.

Job prospects. Graduates with degrees in operations research or closely related fields should find opportunities in a number of occupations where their computer, mathematical, and problem-solving skills are needed—operations research analyst, systems analyst, computer scientist, or management analyst, for example. In addition to job growth, some openings will result from the need to replace analysts retiring or leaving the occupation permanently for other reasons. Analysts who keep up with the latest technological advancements and software will have the best opportunities.

Jobs for operations research analysts exist in almost every industry because of the diversity of applications for their work. As businesses and government agencies continue to contract out jobs to cut costs, opportunities for operations research analysts will be best in management, scientific, and technical consulting firms. Opportunities in the military exist as well, but will depend on the size of future military budgets. Military leaders rely on operations research analysts to test and evaluate the accuracy and effectiveness of new weapons systems and strategies. (See this book's statement on the Armed Forces.)

Earnings

Median annual earnings of operations research analysts were $64,650 in May 2006. The middle 50 percent earned between $48,820 and $85,760. The lowest 10 percent had earnings of less than $38,760, while the highest 10 percent earned more than $108,290. Median annual earnings of operations research analysts working in management, scientific, and technical consulting services were $69,870.

The average annual salary for operations research analysts in the federal government in nonsupervisory, supervisory, and managerial positions was $91,207 in 2007.

Employer-sponsored training is often another part of an analyst's compensation. Some analysts attend advanced university classes on these subjects at their employer's expense.

Related Occupations

Operations research analysts apply advanced analytical methods to large, complicated problems. Economists, computer systems analysts, mathematicians, and engineers also use advanced analysis and often apply the principles of operations research. Workers in other occupations that also stress advanced analysis include computer scientists and database administrators, computer programmers, statisticians, and market and survey researchers. Because its goal is improved organizational effectiveness, operations research also is closely allied to managerial occupations such as computer and information systems managers, and management analysts.

Sources of Additional Information

For information on career opportunities and a list of degree programs for operations research analysts, contact

- Institute for Operations Research and the Management Sciences, 7240 Parkway Dr., Suite 310, Hanover, MD 21076. Internet: http://www.informs.org

For information on operations research careers and degree programs in the Armed Forces, contact

- Military Operations Research Society, 1703 N. Beauregard St., Suite 450, Alexandria, VA 22311. Internet: http://www.mors.org

Information on obtaining positions as operations research analysts with the federal government is available from the Office of Personnel

Management through USAJOBS, the federal government's official employment information system. This resource for locating and applying for job opportunities can be accessed through the Internet at http://www.usajobs.opm.gov or through an interactive voice response telephone system at (703) 724-1850 or TDD (978) 461-8404. These numbers are not toll free, and charges may result. For advice on how to find and apply for federal jobs, see the *Occupational Outlook Quarterly* article "How to get a job in the Federal Government," online at http://www.bls.gov/opub/ooq/2004/summer/art01.pdf.

Opticians, Dispensing

(O*NET 29-2081.00)

Significant Points

- Most dispensing opticians receive training on the job or through apprenticeships lasting 2 or more years, but some employers seek graduates of postsecondary training programs in opticianry.
- A license to practice is required by 22 states.
- Employment growth is projected to be average and reflect the steady demand for corrective lenses and fashionable eyeglass frames.

Nature of the Work

Helping people see better and look good at the same time is the job of a dispensing optician. Dispensing opticians help select and then fit eyeglasses and contact lenses for people with eye problems, following prescriptions written by ophthalmologists or optometrists. (The work of optometrists is described elsewhere in this book. See the section on physicians and surgeons for information about ophthalmologists.) Dispensing opticians recommend eyeglass frames, lenses, and lens coatings after considering the prescription and the customer's occupation, habits, and facial features. They measure clients' eyes, including the distance between the centers of the pupils and the distance between the ocular surface and the lens. For customers without prescriptions, dispensing opticians may use a focimeter to record eyeglass measurements in order to duplicate their existing eyeglasses. They also may obtain a customer's previous record to re-make eyeglasses or contact lenses, or they may verify a prescription with the examining optometrist or ophthalmologist.

Dispensing opticians prepare work orders that give ophthalmic laboratory technicians the information they need to grind and insert lenses into a frame. The work order includes prescriptions for lenses and information on their size, material, color, and style. Some dispensing opticians grind and insert lenses themselves. They may also apply tint to glasses. After the glasses are made, dispensing opticians verify that the lenses have been ground to specifications. Then they may reshape or bend the frame by hand or using pliers so that the eyeglasses fit the customer properly and comfortably.

Many opticians also spend time fixing, adjusting, and refitting broken frames. They instruct clients about adapting to, wearing, or caring for eyeglasses. Additionally, administrative duties have become a major part of their work, including keeping records on customers' prescriptions, work orders, and payments, and tracking inventory and sales.

Some dispensing opticians, after additional education and training, specialize in fitting contacts, artificial eyes, or cosmetic shells to cover blemished eyes. To fit contact lenses, dispensing opticians measure the shape and size of the eye, select the type of contact lens material, and prepare work orders specifying the prescription and lens size. Fitting contact lenses requires considerable skill, care, and patience. Dispensing opticians observe customers' eyes, corneas, lids, and contact lenses with specialized instruments and microscopes. During several follow-up visits, opticians teach proper insertion, removal, and care of contact lenses.

Work environment. Dispensing opticians work indoors mainly in medical offices, optical stores, or in large department or club stores. Opticians spend a fair amount of time on their feet. If they prepare lenses, they need to take precautions against the hazards of glass cutting, chemicals, and machinery. Most dispensing opticians work about 40 hours a week, although a few work longer hours. Those in retail stores may work evenings and weekends. Some work part time.

Training, Other Qualifications, and Advancement

Most workers entering this occupation receive their training on the job, mainly through apprenticeship programs that may last two years or longer. Some employers, though, prefer to hire people who have graduated from an opticianry program.

Education and training. A high school diploma is all that is required to get into this occupation, but most workers have completed at least some college courses or a degree. Classes in physics, basic anatomy, algebra, and trigonometry as well as experience with computers are particularly valuable. These prepare dispensing opticians to learn job skills, including optical mathematics, optical physics, and the use of precision measuring instruments and other machinery and tools.

Most applicants for optician positions do not have any background in the field and learn mainly on the job. Large employers usually offer structured apprenticeship programs; small employers provide more informal, on-the-job training. Apprentices receive technical training and also learn office management and sales. Under the supervision of an experienced optician, optometrist, or ophthalmologist, apprentices work directly with patients, fitting eyeglasses and contact lenses.

Formal training in the field is offered in community colleges and in a few four-year colleges and universities. As of 2007, the Commission on Opticianry Accreditation accredited 21 associate degree programs. Graduation from an accredited program in opticianry provides a nationally recognized credential. There also are shorter programs of one year or less.

Licensure. Twenty-one states require dispensing opticians to be licensed. States may require individuals to pass one or more of the following for licensure: a state practical examination, a state written examination, and certification examinations offered by the American Board of Opticianry (ABO) and the National Contact Lens Examiners (NCLE). To qualify for the examinations, states often require applicants to complete postsecondary training or work as apprentices for two to four years.

Some states that license dispensing opticians allow graduates of opticianry programs to take the licensure exam immediately upon graduation; others require a few months to a year of experience.

Projections data from the National Employment Matrix

Occupational Title	SOC Code	Employment, 2006	Projected employment, 2016	Change, 2006-2016	
				Number	Percent
Opticians, dispensing	29-2081	66,000	72,000	5,700	9

NOTE: Data in this table are rounded.

Continuing education is commonly required for licensure renewal. Information about specific licensing requirements is available from the state board of occupational licensing.

Certification and other qualifications. Any optician can apply to the ABO and the NCLE for certification of their skills, whether or not their state requires it. Certification signifies to customers and employers that an optician has a certain level of expertise. All applicants age 18 or older who have a high school diploma or equivalent are eligible for the exam, but some state licensing boards have additional eligibility requirements. Certification must be renewed every three years through continuing education. The state of Texas offers voluntary registration for the occupation.

Dispensing opticians deal directly with the public, so they should be tactful, pleasant, and communicate well. Manual dexterity and the ability to do precision work are essential.

Advancement. Many experienced dispensing opticians open their own optical stores. Others become managers of optical stores or sales representatives for wholesalers or manufacturers of eyeglasses or lenses.

Employment

Dispensing opticians held about 66,000 jobs in 2006. About one-third of dispensing opticians worked in offices of optometrists. Nearly one-third worked in health and personal care stores, including optical goods stores. Many of these stores offer one-stop shopping. Customers may have their eyes examined, choose frames, and have glasses made on the spot. Some opticians work in optical departments of department stores or other general merchandise stores, such as warehouse clubs and superstores. Eleven percent worked in offices of physicians, primarily ophthalmologists, who sell glasses directly to patients. Two percent were self-employed and ran their own unincorporated businesses.

Job Outlook

Employment of dispensing opticians is expected to grow about as fast as average for all occupations through 2016, as the population ages and demand for corrective lenses increases. Good job prospects are expected, but the occupation will remain relatively small.

Employment change. Employment in this occupation is expected to rise 9 percent over the 2006–2016 decade. Middle age is a time when many individuals use corrective lenses for the first time, and elderly persons generally require more vision care than others. As the share of the population in these older age groups increases, more opticians will be needed to provide service to them. In addition, awareness is increasing of the importance of regular eye exams across all age groups. A small, but growing number of states require children as young as 5 to get eye exams, which is expected to increase the need for eye care services in those states. Fashion also influences demand. Frames come in a growing variety of styles, colors, and sizes, encouraging people to buy more than one pair.

Moderating the need for optician services is the increasing use of laser surgery to correct vision problems. Although the surgery remains relatively more expensive than eyewear, patients who successfully undergo this surgery may not require glasses or contact lenses for several years. Also, new technology is allowing people with minimal training to make the measurements needed to fit glasses and may allow dispensing opticians to work faster, limiting the need for more workers. There also is proposed legislation that, if passed, may require contact lens manufacturers to make lenses available to nonoptical retail outlets, which may allow them to be sold over the Internet, reducing the need for opticians to provide contact lens services.

Job prospects. Job prospects for entering the profession should be good as there is a regular need to replace those who leave the occupation or retire. Nevertheless, the number of job openings will be limited because the occupation is small. Also, dispensing opticians are vulnerable to changes in the business cycle because eyewear purchases often can be deferred for a time. Job prospects will be best for those who have taken formal opticianry classes and those who master new technology, including new refraction systems, framing materials, and edging techniques.

Earnings

Median annual earnings of dispensing opticians were $30,300 in May 2006. The middle 50 percent earned between $23,560 and $38,950. The lowest 10 percent earned less than $19,290, and the highest 10 percent earned more than $47,630. Median annual earnings in the industries employing the largest numbers of dispensing opticians in May 2006 were

Offices of physicians	$32,770
Health and personal care stores	31,850
Offices of health practitioner	29,200
Offices of optometrists	29,190

Benefits for opticians are generally determined by the industries in which they are employed. In general, those who work part-time or in small retail shops generally have fewer benefits than those who may work for large optical chains or department stores. Self-employed opticians must provide their own benefits.

Related Occupations

Other workers who deal with customers and perform delicate work include jewelers and precious stone and metal workers, orthotists and prosthetists, and precision instrument and equipment repairers. Ophthalmic laboratory technicians also perform many of the tasks that opticians perform. And because many opticians work in the retail industry, retail salesworkers also perform some of the same duties.

Sources of Additional Information

To learn about voluntary certification for opticians who fit eyeglasses, as well as a list of state licensing boards for opticians, contact

- American Board of Opticianry, 6506 Loisdale Rd., Suite 209, Springfield, VA 22150. Internet: http://www.abo.org

For information on voluntary certification for dispensing opticians who fit contact lenses, contact

- National Contact Lens Examiners, 6506 Loisdale Rd., Suite 209, Springfield, VA 22150. Internet: http://www.abo-ncle.org

Optometrists

(O*NET 29-1041.00)

Significant Points

- Admission to optometry school is competitive.
- To be licensed, optometrists must earn a Doctor of Optometry degree from an accredited optometry school and pass the appropriate exams administered by the National Board of Examiners in Optometry.
- Employment is expected to grow as fast as average in response to the vision care needs of a growing and aging population.

Nature of the Work

Optometrists, also known as *doctors of optometry*, or *ODs*, are the main providers of vision care. They examine people's eyes to diagnose vision problems, such as nearsightedness and farsightedness, and they test patients' depth and color perception and ability to focus and coordinate the eyes. Optometrists may prescribe eyeglasses or contact lenses, or they may prescribe or provide other treatments, such as vision therapy or low-vision rehabilitation.

Optometrists also test for glaucoma and other eye diseases and diagnose conditions caused by systemic diseases such as diabetes and high blood pressure, referring patients to other health practitioners as needed. They administer drugs to patients to aid in the diagnosis of vision problems and to treat eye diseases. Optometrists often provide preoperative and postoperative care to cataract patients, as well as to patients who have had laser vision correction or other eye surgery.

Most optometrists are in general practice. Some specialize in work with the elderly, children, or partially sighted persons who need specialized visual devices. Others develop and implement ways to protect workers' eyes from on-the-job strain or injury. Some specialize in contact lenses, sports vision, or vision therapy. A few teach optometry, perform research, or consult.

Most optometrists are private practitioners who also handle the business aspects of running an office, such as developing a patient base, hiring employees, keeping paper and electronic records, and ordering equipment and supplies. Optometrists who operate franchise optical stores also may have some of these duties.

Optometrists should not be confused with ophthalmologists or dispensing opticians. *Ophthalmologists* are physicians who perform eye surgery, as well as diagnose and treat eye diseases and injuries. Like optometrists, they also examine eyes and prescribe eyeglasses and contact lenses. *Dispensing opticians* fit and adjust eyeglasses and, in some states, may fit contact lenses according to prescriptions written by ophthalmologists or optometrists. (See the sections on physicians and surgeons; and opticians, dispensing, elsewhere in this book.)

Work environment. Optometrists work in places—usually their own offices—that are clean, well lighted, and comfortable. Most full-time optometrists work about 40 hours a week. Many work weekends and evenings to suit the needs of patients. Emergency calls, once uncommon, have increased with the passage of therapeutic-drug laws expanding optometrists' ability to prescribe medications.

Optometrists who work in solo practice or with a partner tend to work longer hours because they must tend to administrative duties in addition to their medical ones. According to the American Optometric Association surveys, optometrists worked about 49 hours per week, on average, in 2004, and were available to see patients about 38 hours per week.

Training, Other Qualifications, and Advancement

The Doctor of Optometry degree requires the completion of a four-year program at an accredited optometry school, preceded by at least three years of preoptometric study at an accredited college or university. All states require optometrists to be licensed.

Education and training. Optometrists need a Doctor of Optometry degree, which requires the completion of a four-year program at an accredited optometry school. In 2006, there were 16 colleges of optometry in the U.S. and one in Puerto Rico that offered programs accredited by the Accreditation Council on Optometric Education of the American Optometric Association. Requirements for admission to optometry schools include college courses in English, mathematics, physics, chemistry, and biology. Because a strong background in science is important, many applicants to optometry school major in a science, such as biology or chemistry as undergraduates. Others major in another subject and take many science courses offering laboratory experience.

Admission to optometry school is competitive. Applicants must take the Optometry Admissions Test, which measures academic ability and scientific comprehension. As a result, most applicants take the test after their sophomore or junior year in college, allowing them an opportunity to take the test again and raise their score. A few applicants are accepted to optometry school after three years of college and complete their bachelor's degree while attending optometry school. However, most students accepted by a school or college of optometry have completed an undergraduate degree. Each institution has its own undergraduate prerequisites, so applicants should contact the school or college of their choice for specific requirements.

Optometry programs include classroom and laboratory study of health and visual sciences and clinical training in the diagnosis and treatment of eye disorders. Courses in pharmacology, optics, vision science, biochemistry, and systemic diseases are included.

One-year postgraduate clinical residency programs are available for optometrists who wish to obtain advanced clinical competence. Specialty areas for residency programs include family practice optometry, pediatric optometry, geriatric optometry, vision therapy and rehabilitation, low-vision rehabilitation, cornea and contact lenses, refractive and ocular surgery, primary eye care optometry, and ocular disease.

Licensure. All states and the District of Columbia require that optometrists be licensed. Applicants for a license must have a Doctor of Optometry degree from an accredited optometry school and must pass both a written National Board examination and a National, regional, or state clinical examination. The written and

Projections data from the National Employment Matrix

Occupational Title	SOC Code	Employment, 2006	Projected employment, 2016	Change, 2006-2016	
				Number	Percent
Optometrists	29-1041	33,000	36,000	3,700	11

NOTE: Data in this table are rounded.

clinical examinations of the National Board of Examiners in Optometry usually are taken during the student's academic career. Many states also require applicants to pass an examination on relevant state laws. Licenses must be renewed every one to three years and, in all states, continuing education credits are needed for renewal.

Other qualifications. Business ability, self-discipline, and the ability to deal tactfully with patients are important for success. The work of optometrists also requires attention to detail and manual dexterity.

Advancement. Optometrists wishing to teach or conduct research may study for a master's degree or Ph.D. in visual science, physiological optics, neurophysiology, public health, health administration, health information and communication, or health education.

Employment

Optometrists held about 33,000 jobs in 2006. Salaried jobs for optometrists were primarily in offices of optometrists; offices of physicians, including ophthalmologists; and health and personal care stores, including optical goods stores. A few salaried jobs for optometrists were in hospitals, the federal government, or outpatient care centers including health maintenance organizations. Nearly 25 percent of optometrists are self-employed. According to a 2005 survey by the American Optometric Association most self-employed optometrists worked in private practice or in partnership with other health care professionals. A small number worked for optical chains or franchises or as independent contractors.

Job Outlook

Employment of optometrists is expected to grow as fast as average for all occupations through 2016, in response to the vision care needs of a growing and aging population. Greater recognition of the importance of vision care, along with growth in employee vision care plans, will also spur job growth.

Employment change.

Employment of optometrists is projected to grow 11 percent between 2006 and 2016. A growing population that recognizes the importance of good eye care will increase demand for optometrists. Also, an increasing number of health insurance plans that include vision care, should generate more job growth.

As the population ages, there will likely be more visits to optometrists and ophthalmologists because of the onset of vision problems that occur at older ages, such as cataracts and glaucoma. In addition, increased incidences of diabetes and hypertension in the general population as well as in the elderly will generate greater demand for optometric services as these diseases often affect eyesight.

Employment of optometrists would grow more rapidly if not for productivity gains expected to allow each optometrist to see more patients. These expected gains stem from greater use of optometric assistants and other support personnel, who can reduce the amount of time optometrists need with each patient.

The increasing popularity of laser surgery to correct some vision problems may reduce some of the demand for optometrists as patients often do not require eyeglasses afterward. But optometrists still will be needed to provide preoperative and postoperative care for laser surgery patients.

Job prospects. Job opportunities for optometrists should be very good over the next decade. Demand is expected to be much higher, and because there are only 16 schools of optometry, the number of students who can get a degree in optometry is limited. In addition to growth, the need to replace optometrists who retire or leave the occupation for other reasons will create more employment opportunities.

Earnings

Median annual earnings of salaried optometrists were $91,040 in May 2006. The middle 50 percent earned between $66,530 and $118,490. Median annual earnings of salaried optometrists in offices of optometrists were $86,760. Salaried optometrists tend to earn more initially than do optometrists who set up their own practices. In the long run, however, those in private practice usually earn more.

According to the American Optometric Association, median net annual income for all optometrists, including the self-employed, was $105,000 in 2006. The middle 50 percent earned between $84,000 and $150,000.

Self-employed optometrists, including those working in partnerships, must provide their own benefits. Optometrists employed by others typically enjoy paid vacation, sick leave, and pension contributions.

Related Occupations

Other workers who apply scientific knowledge to prevent, diagnose, and treat disorders and injuries are chiropractors, dentists, physicians and surgeons, psychologists, podiatrists, and veterinarians.

Sources of Additional Information

For information on optometry as a career and a list of accredited optometric institutions of education, contact

- Association of Schools and Colleges of Optometry, 6110 Executive Blvd., Suite 510, Rockville, MD 20852. Internet: http://www.opted.org

Additional career information is available from

- American Optometric Association, Educational Services, 243 North Lindbergh Blvd., St. Louis, MO 63141. Internet: http://www.aoa.org

The board of optometry in each state can supply information on licensing requirements.

For information on specific admission requirements and sources of financial aid, contact the admissions officers of individual optometry schools.

Pharmacists

(O*NET 29-1051.00)

Significant Points

- Excellent job opportunities are expected.
- Earnings are high, but some pharmacists are required to work nights, weekends, and holidays.
- Pharmacists are becoming more involved in counseling patients and planning drug therapy programs.
- A license is required; the prospective pharmacist must graduate from an accredited college of pharmacy and pass a series of examinations.

Nature of the Work

Pharmacists distribute prescription drugs to individuals. They also advise their patients, as well as physicians and other health practitioners, on the selection, dosages, interactions, and side effects of medications. Pharmacists monitor the health and progress of patients to ensure the safe and effective use of medication. Compounding—the actual mixing of ingredients to form medications—is a small part of a pharmacist's practice, because most medicines are produced by pharmaceutical companies in a standard dosage and drug delivery form. Most pharmacists work in a community setting, such as a retail drugstore, or in a health care facility, such as a hospital, nursing home, mental health institution, or neighborhood health clinic.

Pharmacists in community pharmacies dispense medications, counsel patients on the use of prescription and over-the-counter medications, and advise physicians about patients' medication therapy. They also advise patients about general health topics such as diet, exercise, and stress management, and provide information on products such as durable medical equipment or home health care supplies. In addition, they may complete third-party insurance forms and other paperwork. Those who own or manage community pharmacies may sell non-health-related merchandise, hire and supervise personnel, and oversee the general operation of the pharmacy. Some community pharmacists provide specialized services to help patients with conditions such as diabetes, asthma, smoking cessation, or high blood pressure; others also are trained to administer vaccinations.

Pharmacists in health care facilities dispense medications and advise the medical staff on the selection and effects of drugs. They may make sterile solutions to be administered intravenously. They also plan, monitor and evaluate drug programs or regimens. They may counsel hospitalized patients on the use of drugs before the patients are discharged.

Pharmacists who work in home health care monitor drug therapy and prepare infusions—solutions that are injected into patients—and other medications for use in the home.

Some pharmacists specialize in specific drug therapy areas, such as intravenous nutrition support, oncology (cancer), nuclear pharmacy (used for chemotherapy), geriatric pharmacy, and psychiatric pharmacy (the use of drugs to treat mental disorders).

Most pharmacists keep confidential computerized records of patients' drug therapies to prevent harmful drug interactions. Pharmacists are responsible for the accuracy of every prescription that is filled, but they often rely upon Pharmacy technicians and pharmacy aides to assist them in the dispensing process. Thus, the pharmacist may delegate prescription-filling and administrative tasks and supervise their completion. Pharmacists also frequently oversee pharmacy students serving as interns.

Increasingly, pharmacists are pursuing nontraditional pharmacy work. Some are involved in research for pharmaceutical manufacturers, developing new drugs and testing their effects. Others work in marketing or sales, providing clients with expertise on the use, effectiveness, and possible side effects of drugs. Some pharmacists work for health insurance companies, developing pharmacy benefit packages and carrying out cost-benefit analyses on certain drugs. Other pharmacists work for the government, managed care organizations, public health care services, the armed services, or pharmacy associations. Finally, some pharmacists are employed full time or part time as college faculty, teaching classes and performing research in a wide range of areas.

Work environment. Pharmacists work in clean, well-lighted, and well-ventilated areas. Many pharmacists spend most of their workday on their feet. When working with sterile or dangerous pharmaceutical products, pharmacists wear gloves, masks, and other protective equipment.

Most full-time salaried pharmacists work approximately 40 hours a week, and about 10 percent work more than 50 hours. Many community and hospital pharmacies are open for extended hours or around the clock, so pharmacists may be required to work nights, weekends, and holidays. Consultant pharmacists may travel to nursing homes or other facilities to monitor patients' drug therapy. About 16 percent of pharmacists worked part time in 2006.

Training, Other Qualifications, and Advancement

A license is required in all states, the District of Columbia, and all U.S. territories. In order to obtain a license, pharmacists must earn a Doctor of Pharmacy (Pharm.D.) degree from a college of pharmacy and pass several examinations.

Education and training. Pharmacists must earn a Pharm.D. degree from an accredited college or school of pharmacy. The Pharm.D. degree has replaced the Bachelor of Pharmacy degree, which is no longer being awarded. To be admitted to a Pharm.D. program, an applicant must have completed at least two years of postsecondary study, although most applicants have completed three or more years. Other entry requirements usually include courses in mathematics and natural sciences, such as chemistry, biology, and physics, as well as courses in the humanities and social sciences. In 2007, 92 colleges and schools of pharmacy were accredited to confer degrees by the Accreditation Council for Pharmacy Education (ACPE). About 70 percent of Pharm.D. programs require applicants to take the Pharmacy College Admissions Test (PCAT).

Courses offered at colleges of pharmacy are designed to teach students about all aspects of drug therapy. In addition, students learn how to communicate with patients and other health care providers about drug information and patient care. Students also learn professional ethics, concepts of public health, and medication distribution systems management. In addition to receiving classroom instruction, students in Pharm.D. programs spend about one-forth of their time in a variety of pharmacy practice settings under the supervision of licensed pharmacists.

In the 2006–2007 academic year, 70 colleges of pharmacy also awarded the master-of-science degree or the Ph.D. degree. Both degrees are awarded after the completion of a Pharm.D. degree and are designed for those who want additional clinical, laboratory, and research experience. Areas of graduate study include pharmaceutics and pharmaceutical chemistry (physical and chemical properties of drugs and dosage forms), pharmacology (effects of drugs on the body), and pharmacy administration. Many master's and Ph.D. degree holders go on to do research for a drug company or teach at a university.

Other options for pharmacy graduates who are interested in further training include one-year or two-year residency programs or fellowships. Pharmacy residencies are postgraduate training programs in pharmacy practice and usually require the completion of a research project. These programs are often mandatory for pharmacists who wish to work in hospitals. Pharmacy fellowships are highly individualized programs that are designed to prepare participants to work in a specialized area of pharmacy, such clinical practice or research laboratories. Some pharmacists who own their own pharmacy obtain a master's degree in business administration (MBA). Others may obtain a degree in public administration or public health.

Licensure. A license to practice pharmacy is required in all states, the District of Columbia, and all U.S. territories. To obtain a license, a prospective pharmacist must graduate from a college of pharmacy that is accredited by the ACPE and pass a series of examinations. All states, U.S. territories, and the District of Columbia require the North American Pharmacist Licensure Exam (NAPLEX), which tests pharmacy skills and knowledge. Forty-four states and the District of Columbia also require the Multistate Pharmacy Jurisprudence Exam (MPJE), which tests pharmacy law. Both exams are administered by the National Association of Boards of Pharmacy (NABP). Each of the eight states and territories that do not require the MJPE has its own pharmacy law exam. In addition to the NAPLEX and MPJE, some states and territories require additional exams that are unique to their jurisdiction.

All jurisdictions except California currently grant license transfers to qualified pharmacists who already are licensed by another jurisdiction. Many pharmacists are licensed to practice in more than one jurisdiction. Most jurisdictions require continuing education for license renewal. Persons interested in a career as a pharmacist should check with individual jurisdiction boards of pharmacy for details on license renewal requirements and license transfer procedures.

Graduates of foreign pharmacy schools may also qualify for licensure in some U.S. states and territories. These individuals must apply for certification from the Foreign Pharmacy Graduate Examination Committee (FPGEC). Once certified, they must pass the Foreign Pharmacy Graduate Equivalency Examination (FPGEE), Test of English as a Foreign Language (TOEFL) exam, and Test of Spoken English (TSE) exam. They then must pass all of the exams required by the licensing jurisdiction, such as the NAPLEX and MJPE. Applicants who graduated from programs accredited by the Canadian Council for Accreditation of Pharmacy Programs (CCAPP) between 1993 and 2004 are exempt from FPGEC certification and examination requirements.

Other qualifications. Prospective pharmacists should have scientific aptitude, good interpersonal skills, and a desire to help others. They also must be conscientious and pay close attention to detail, because the decisions they make affect human lives.

Advancement. In community pharmacies, pharmacists usually begin at the staff level. Pharmacists in chain drugstores may be promoted to pharmacy supervisor or manager at the store level, then to manager at the district or regional level, and later to an executive position within the chain's headquarters. Hospital pharmacists may advance to supervisory or administrative positions. After they gain experience and secure the necessary capital, some pharmacists become owners or part owners of independent pharmacies. Pharmacists in the pharmaceutical industry may advance in marketing, sales, research, quality control, production, or other areas.

Employment

Pharmacists held about 243,000 jobs in 2006. About 62 percent worked in community pharmacies that were either independently owned or part of a drugstore chain, grocery store, department store, or mass merchandiser. Most community pharmacists were salaried employees, but some were self-employed owners. About 23 percent of pharmacists worked in hospitals. A small proportion worked in mail-order and Internet pharmacies, pharmaceutical wholesalers, offices of physicians, and the federal government.

Job Outlook

Employment is expected to increase much faster than the average through 2016. As a result of rapid growth and the need to replace workers who leave the occupation, job prospects should be excellent.

Employment change. Employment of pharmacists is expected to grow by 22 percent between 2006 and 2016, which is much faster than the average for all occupations. The increasing numbers of middle-aged and elderly people—who use more prescription drugs than younger people—will continue to spur demand for pharmacists throughout the projection period. Other factors likely to increase the demand for pharmacists include scientific advances that will make more drug products available and the coverage of prescription drugs by a greater number of health insurance plans and Medicare.

As the use of prescription drugs increases, demand for pharmacists will grow in most practice settings, such as community pharmacies, hospital pharmacies, and mail-order pharmacies. As the population ages, assisted living facilities and home care organizations should see particularly rapid growth. Demand will also increase as cost conscious insurers, in an attempt to improve preventative care, use pharmacists in areas such as patient education and vaccination administration.

Demand is also increasing in managed care organizations where pharmacists analyze trends and patterns in medication use, and in

Projections data from the National Employment Matrix

Occupational Title	SOC Code	Employment, 2006	Projected employment, 2016	Change, 2006-2016	
				Number	Percent
Pharmacists	29-1051	243,000	296,000	53,000	22

NOTE: Data in this table are rounded.

pharmacoeconomics—the cost and benefit analysis of different drug therapies. New jobs also are being created in disease management—the development of new methods for curing and controlling diseases—and in sales and marketing. Rapid growth is also expected in pharmacy informatics—the use of information technology to improve patient care.

Job prospects. Excellent opportunities are expected for pharmacists over the 2006 to 2016 period. Job openings will result from rapid employment growth, and from the need to replace workers who retire or leave the occupation for other reasons.

Earnings

Median annual of wage-and-salary pharmacists in May 2006 were $94,520. The middle 50 percent earned between $83,180 and $108,140 a year. The lowest 10 percent earned less than $67,860, and the highest 10 percent earned more than $119,480 a year. Median annual earnings in the industries employing the largest numbers of pharmacists in May 2006 were

Department stores	$99,050
Grocery stores	95,600
Pharmacies and drug stores	94,640
General medical and surgical hospitals	93,640

According to a 2006 survey by *Drug Topics Magazine*, pharmacists in retail settings earned an average of $92,291 per year, while pharmacists in institutional settings earned an average of $97,545. Full-time pharmacists earned an average of $102,336, while part-time pharmacists earned an average of $55,589.

Related Occupations

Pharmacy technicians and pharmacy aides also work in pharmacies. Persons in other professions who may work with pharmaceutical compounds include biological scientists, medical scientists, and chemists and materials scientists. Increasingly, pharmacists are involved in patient care and therapy, work that they have in common with physicians and surgeons.

Sources of Additional Information

For information on pharmacy as a career, preprofessional and professional requirements, programs offered by colleges of pharmacy, and student financial aid, contact

- American Association of Colleges of Pharmacy, 1426 Prince St., Alexandria, VA 22314. Internet: http://www.aacp.org

General information on careers in pharmacy is available from

- American Society of Health-System Pharmacists, 7272 Wisconsin Ave., Bethesda, MD 20814. Internet: http://www.ashp.org
- National Association of Chain Drug Stores, 413 N. Lee St., P.O. Box 1417-D49, Alexandria, VA 22313-1480. Internet: http://www.nacds.org
- Academy of Managed Care Pharmacy, 100 North Pitt St., Suite 400, Alexandria, VA 22314. Internet: http://www.amcp.org
- American Pharmacists Association, 1100 15th Street, NW Suite 400., Washington, DC 20005. Internet: http://www.aphanet.org

Information on the North American Pharmacist Licensure Exam (NAPLEX) and the Multistate Pharmacy Jurisprudence Exam (MPJE) is available from

- National Association of Boards of Pharmacy, 1600 Feehanville Dr., Mount Prospect, IL 60056. Internet: http://www.nabp.net

State licensure requirements are available from each state's board of pharmacy. Information on specific college entrance requirements, curriculums, and financial aid is available from any college of pharmacy.

Pharmacy Aides

(O*NET 31-9095.00)

Significant Points

- Job opportunities are expected to be good for full-time and part-time work, especially for those with related work experience.
- Many pharmacy aides work evenings, weekends, and holidays.
- About 82 percent work in retail pharmacies, grocery stores, department stores, or mass retailers.

Nature of the Work

Pharmacy aides perform administrative duties in pharmacies. Aides often are clerks or cashiers who primarily answer telephones, handle money, stock shelves, and perform other clerical duties. They work closely with pharmacy technicians. *Pharmacy technicians* usually perform more complex tasks than do aides, although in some states the duties and titles of the jobs overlap. (See the statement on pharmacy technicians elsewhere in this book.) Aides refer any questions regarding prescriptions, drug information, or health matters to a pharmacist. (See the statement on pharmacists elsewhere in this book.)

Pharmacy aides may establish and maintain patient profiles, prepare insurance claim forms, and stock and take inventory of prescription and over-the-counter medications. Accurate recordkeeping is necessary to help avert dangerous drug interactions. In addition, because many people have medical insurance to help pay for prescriptions, it is essential that pharmacy aides correspond efficiently and correctly with third-party insurance providers to obtain payment. Pharmacy aides also maintain inventory and inform the supervisor of stock needs so that the pharmacy does not run out of vital medications that customers need. Some aides also help with the maintenance of equipment and supplies.

Work environment. Pharmacy aides work in clean, organized, well-lighted, and well-ventilated areas. Most of their workday is spent on their feet. They may be required to lift heavy boxes or to use stepladders to retrieve supplies from high shelves.

Aides work the same hours that pharmacists do. These include evenings, nights, weekends, and some holidays, particularly in facilities that are open 24 hours a day such as hospitals and some retail pharmacies.

Training, Other Qualifications, and Advancement

Most pharmacy aides are trained on the job. Employers prefer applicants with previous experience and strong customer service skills. Many pharmacy aides go on to become pharmacy technicians.

Projections data from the National Employment Matrix

Occupational Title	SOC Code	Employment, 2006	Projected employment, 2016	Change, 2006-16	
				Number	Percent
Pharmacy aides	31-9095	50,000	45,000	-5,600	-11

NOTE: Data in this table are rounded.

Education and training. Most pharmacy aides receive informal on-the-job training, but employers favor those with at least a high school diploma. Prospective pharmacy aides with experience working as cashiers may have an advantage when applying for jobs. Employers also prefer applicants with experience managing inventories and using computers.

Pharmacy aides begin their training by observing a more experienced worker. After they become familiar with the store's equipment, policies, and procedures, they begin to work on their own. Once they become experienced, aides are not likely to receive additional training, except when new equipment is introduced or when policies or procedures change.

Other qualifications. Strong customer service and communication skills are essential, as pharmacy aides frequently interact with patients, fellow employees, and other health-care professionals. Aides entering the field also need strong spelling, reading, and mathematics skills. Successful pharmacy aides are organized, dedicated, friendly, and responsible. They should be willing and able to take directions. Candidates interested in becoming pharmacy aides cannot have prior records of drug or substance abuse.

Advancement. With experience or certification, many pharmacy aides go on to become pharmacy technicians. Some become pharmacists after completing a substantial amount of formal training.

Employment

Pharmacy aides held about 50,000 jobs in 2006. About 82 percent worked in retail pharmacies, most of which were in drug stores but some of which were in grocery stores, department stores, or mass retailers. About 7 percent of aides worked in hospitals.

Job Outlook

Employment of pharmacy aides is expected to decline rapidly from 2006 to 2016. Job prospects, however, should be good.

Employment change. Employment of pharmacy aides is expected to decline rapidly, decreasing by 11 percent over the 2006 to 2016 period. Demand for pharmacy aides will fall as pharmacy technicians become increasingly responsible for answering phones, stocking shelves, operating cash registers, and performing other administrative tasks. In addition, with increased training, many pharmacy aides will become pharmacy technicians, which will result in further declines in pharmacy aide jobs.

Job prospects. Despite declining employment, job opportunities for full-time and part-time work are expected to be good. The frequent need to replace workers who leave the occupation will create opportunities for interested applicants. Aides with related work experience in pharmacies, or as cashiers or stock clerks in other retail settings, should have the best opportunities.

Earnings

Median hourly earnings of wage-and-salary pharmacy aides were $9.35 in May 2006. The middle 50 percent earned between $7.89 and $11.58; the lowest 10 percent earned less than $6.92, and the highest 10 percent earned more than $14.64. Median hourly earnings in the industries employing the largest numbers of pharmacy aides in May 2006 were

General medical and surgical hospitals $11.53
Grocery stores 9.87
Pharmacies and drug stores 8.97

Related Occupations

The work of pharmacy aides is closely related to that of pharmacy technicians, cashiers, and stock clerks and order fillers.

Sources of Additional Information

For information on employment opportunities, contact local employers or local offices of the state employment service.

Pharmacy Technicians

(O*NET 29-2052.00)

Significant Points

- Job opportunities are expected to be good, especially for those with certification or previous work experience.
- Many technicians work evenings, weekends, and holidays.
- About 71 percent of jobs are in retail pharmacies, grocery stores, department stores, or mass retailers.

Nature of the Work

Pharmacy technicians help licensed pharmacists provide medication and other health care products to patients. Technicians usually perform routine tasks to help prepare prescribed medication, such as counting tablets and labeling bottles. They also perform administrative duties, such as answering phones, stocking shelves, and operating cash registers. Technicians refer any questions regarding prescriptions, drug information, or health matters to a *pharmacist*. (See the statement on pharmacists elsewhere in this book.)

Pharmacy technicians who work in retail or mail-order pharmacies have varying responsibilities, depending on state rules and regulations. Technicians receive written prescriptions or requests for prescription refills from patients. They also may receive prescriptions sent electronically from the doctor's office. They must verify that information on the prescription is complete and accurate. To prepare the prescription, technicians must retrieve, count, pour, weigh, measure, and sometimes mix the medication. Then, they prepare the prescription labels, select the type of prescription container, and affix the prescription and auxiliary labels to the container. Once the prescription is filled, technicians price and file the prescription, which must be checked by a pharmacist before it is given to the patient. Technicians may establish and maintain patient profiles, prepare insurance claim forms, and stock and take inventory of prescription and over-the-counter medications.

In hospitals, nursing homes, and assisted-living facilities, technicians have added responsibilities, including reading patients' charts and preparing the appropriate medication. After the pharmacist checks the prescription for accuracy, the pharmacy technician may deliver it to the patient. The technician then copies the information about the prescribed medication onto the patient's profile. Technicians also may assemble a 24-hour supply of medicine for every patient. They package and label each dose separately. The packages are then placed in the medicine cabinets of patients until the supervising pharmacist checks them for accuracy, and only then is the medication given to the patients.

Pharmacy aides work closely with pharmacy technicians. They often are clerks or cashiers who primarily answer telephones, handle money, stock shelves, and perform other clerical duties. (See the statement on pharmacy aides elsewhere in this book.) Pharmacy technicians usually perform more complex tasks than pharmacy aides, although in some states their duties and job titles may overlap.

Work environment. Pharmacy technicians work in clean, organized, well-lighted, and well-ventilated areas. Most of their workday is spent on their feet. They may be required to lift heavy boxes or to use stepladders to retrieve supplies from high shelves.

Technicians work the same hours that pharmacists work. These may include evenings, nights, weekends, and holidays, particularly in facilities that are open 24 hours a day such as hospitals and some retail pharmacies. As their seniority increases, technicians often acquire increased control over the hours they work. There are many opportunities for part-time work in both retail and hospital settings.

Training, Other Qualifications, and Advancement

Most pharmacy technicians are trained on-the-job, but employers favor applicants who have formal training, certification, or previous experience. Strong customer service skills also are important. Pharmacy technicians may become supervisors, may move into specialty positions or into sales, or may become pharmacists.

Education and training. Although most pharmacy technicians receive informal on-the-job training, employers favor those who have completed formal training and certification. However, there are currently few state and no federal requirements for formal training or certification of pharmacy technicians. Employers who have insufficient resources to give on-the-job training often seek formally educated pharmacy technicians. Formal education programs and certification emphasize the technician's interest in and dedication to the work. In addition to the military, some hospitals, proprietary schools, vocational or technical colleges, and community colleges offer formal education programs.

Formal pharmacy technician education programs require classroom and laboratory work in a variety of areas, including medical and pharmaceutical terminology, pharmaceutical calculations, pharmacy recordkeeping, pharmaceutical techniques, and pharmacy law and ethics. Technicians also are required to learn medication names, actions, uses, and doses. Many training programs include internships, in which students gain hands-on experience in actual pharmacies. After completion, students receive a diploma, a certificate, or an associate's degree, depending on the program.

Prospective pharmacy technicians with experience working as an aide in a community pharmacy or volunteering in a hospital may have an advantage. Employers also prefer applicants with experience managing inventories, counting tablets, measuring dosages, and using computers. In addition, a background in chemistry, English, and health education may be beneficial.

Certification and other qualifications. Two organizations, the Pharmacy Technician Certification Board and the Institute for the Certification of Pharmacy Technicians, administer national certification examinations. Certification is voluntary in most states, but is required by some states and employers. Some technicians are hired without formal training, but under the condition that they obtain certification within a specified period of time. To be eligible for either exam, candidates must have a high school diploma or GED, no felony convictions of any kind within five years of applying, and no drug or pharmacy related felony convictions at any point. Employers, often pharmacists, know that individuals who pass the exam have a standardized body of knowledge and skills. Many employers also will reimburse the costs of the exam.

Under both programs, technicians must be recertified every two years. Recertification requires 20 hours of continuing education within the two-year certification period. At least one hour must be in pharmacy law. Continuing education hours can be earned from several different sources, including colleges, pharmacy associations, and pharmacy technician training programs. Up to 10 hours of continuing education can be earned on the job under the direct supervision and instruction of a pharmacist.

Strong customer service and teamwork skills are needed because pharmacy technicians interact with patients, coworkers, and health care professionals. Mathematics, spelling, and reading skills also are important. Successful pharmacy technicians are alert, observant, organized, dedicated, and responsible. They should be willing and able to take directions, but be able to work independently without constant instruction. They must be precise; details are sometimes a matter of life and death. Candidates interested in becoming pharmacy technicians cannot have prior records of drug or substance abuse.

Advancement. In large pharmacies and health-systems, pharmacy technicians with significant training, experience and certification can be promoted to supervisory positions, mentoring and training pharmacy technicians with less experience. Some may advance into specialty positions such as chemo therapy technician and nuclear pharmacy technician. Others move into sales. With a substantial amount of formal training, some pharmacy technicians go on to become pharmacists.

Employment

Pharmacy technicians held about 285,000 jobs in 2006. About 71 percent of jobs were in retail pharmacies, either independently owned or part of a drugstore chain, grocery store, department store, or mass retailer. About 18 percent of jobs were in hospitals and a small proportion was in mail-order and Internet pharmacies, offices of physicians, pharmaceutical wholesalers, and the federal government.

Projections data from the National Employment Matrix

Occupational Title	SOC Code	Employment, 2006	Projected employment, 2016	Change, 2006-2016	
				Number	Percent
Pharmacy technicians	29-2052	285,000	376,000	91,000	32

NOTE: Data in this table are rounded.

Job Outlook

Employment is expected to increase much faster than the average through 2016, and job opportunities are expected to be good.

Employment change. Employment of pharmacy technicians is expected to increase by 32 percent from 2006 to 2016, which is much faster than the average for all occupations. The increased number of middle-aged and elderly people—who use more prescription drugs than younger people—will spur demand for technicians throughout the projection period. In addition, as scientific advances bring treatments for an increasing number of conditions, more pharmacy technicians will be needed to fill a growing number of prescriptions.

As cost-conscious insurers begin to use pharmacies as patient-care centers, pharmacy technicians will assume responsibility for some of the more routine tasks previously performed by pharmacists. In addition, they will adopt some of the administrative duties that were previously performed by pharmacy aides, such as answering phones and stocking shelves.

Reducing the need for pharmacy technicians to some degree, however, will be the growing use of drug dispensing machines. These machines increase productivity by completing some of the pharmacy technician's duties, namely counting pills and placing them into prescription containers. These machines are only used for the most common medications, however, and their effect on employment should be minimal.

Almost all states have legislated the maximum number of technicians who can safely work under a pharmacist at one time. Changes in these laws could directly affect employment.

Job prospects. Good job opportunities are expected for full-time and part-time work, especially for technicians with formal training or previous experience. Job openings for pharmacy technicians will result from employment growth, and from the need to replace workers who transfer to other occupations or leave the labor force.

Earnings

Median hourly earnings of wage-and-salary pharmacy technicians in May 2006 were $12.32. The middle 50 percent earned between $10.10 and $14.92. The lowest 10 percent earned less than $8.56, and the highest 10 percent earned more than $17.65. Median hourly earnings in the industries employing the largest numbers of pharmacy technicians in May 2006 were

General medical and surgical hospitals	$13.86
Grocery stores	12.78
Pharmacies and drug stores	11.50

Certified technicians may earn more. Shift differentials for working evenings or weekends also can increase earnings. Some technicians belong to unions representing hospital or grocery store workers.

Related Occupations

This occupation is most closely related to pharmacists and pharmacy aides. Workers in other medical support occupations include dental assistants, medical transcriptionists, medical records and health information technicians, occupational therapist assistants and aides, and physical therapist assistants and aides.

Sources of Additional Information

For information on pharmacy technician certification programs, contact

- Pharmacy Technician Certification Board, 2215 Constitution Ave. NW, Washington DC 20037-2985. Internet: http://www.ptcb.org
- Institute for the Certification of Pharmacy Technicians, 2536 S. Old Hwy 94, Suite 214, St. Charles, MO 63303. Internet: http://www.nationaltechexam.org

For a list of accredited pharmacy technician training programs, contact

- American Society of Health-System Pharmacists, 7272 Wisconsin Ave., Bethesda, MD 20814. Internet: http://www.ashp.org

For pharmacy technician career information, contact

- National Pharmacy Technician Association, P.O. Box 683148, Houston, TX 77268. Internet: http://www.pharmacytechnician.org

Photographers

(O*NET 27-4021.00)

Significant Points

- Competition for jobs is expected to be keen because the work is attractive to many people.
- Technical expertise, a "good eye," imagination, and creativity are essential.
- More than half of all photographers are self-employed, a much higher proportion than for most occupations.

Nature of the Work

Photographers produce and preserve images that paint a picture, tell a story, or record an event. To create commercial-quality photographs, photographers need technical expertise, creativity, and the appropriate professional equipment. Producing a successful picture requires choosing and presenting a subject to achieve a particular effect, and selecting the right cameras and other photographic enhancing tools. For example, photographers may enhance the subject's appearance with natural or artificial light, shoot the subject from an interesting angle, draw attention to a particular aspect of the subject by blurring the background, or use various lenses to produce desired levels of detail at various distances from the subject.

Today, most photographers use digital cameras instead of traditional silver-halide film cameras, although some photographers use both types, depending on their own preference and the nature of the assignment. Regardless of the camera they use, photographers also employ an array of other equipment—from lenses, filters, and tripods to flash attachments and specially constructed lighting equipment—to improve the quality of their work.

Digital cameras capture images electronically, allowing them to be edited on a computer. Images can be stored on portable memory devices such as compact disks or on smaller storage devices such as memory cards used in digital cameras and flash drives. Once the raw image has been transferred to a computer, photographers can use processing software to crop or modify the image and enhance it through color correction and other specialized effects. As soon as a photographer has finished editing the image, it can be sent anywhere in the world over the Internet.

Photographers also can create electronic portfolios of their work and display them on their own webpage, allowing them to reach prospective customers directly. Digital technology also allows the production of larger, more colorful, and more accurate prints or images for use in advertising, photographic art, and scientific research. Photographers who process their own digital images need to be proficient in the use of computers, high-quality printers, and editing software.

Photographers who use cameras with silver-halide film often send their film to laboratories for processing. Color film requires expensive equipment and exacting conditions for correct processing and printing. (See the statement on photographic process workers and processing machine operators elsewhere in this book.) Other photographers develop and print their own photographs using their own fully equipped darkrooms, especially if they use black and white film or seek to achieve special effects. Photographers who do their own film developing must invest in additional developing and printing equipment and acquire the technical skills to operate it.

Some photographers specialize in areas such as portrait, commercial and industrial, scientific, news, or fine arts photography. *Portrait photographers* take pictures of individuals or groups of people and often work in their own studios. Some specialize in weddings, religious ceremonies, or school photographs and may work on location. Portrait photographers who own and operate their own business have many responsibilities in addition to taking pictures. They must arrange for advertising, schedule appointments, set and adjust equipment, purchase supplies, keep records, bill customers, pay bills, and—if they have employees—hire, train, and direct their workers. Many also process their own images, design albums, and mount and frame the finished photographs.

Commercial and industrial photographers take pictures of various subjects, such as buildings, models, merchandise, artifacts, and landscapes. These photographs are used in a variety of media, including books, reports, advertisements, and catalogs. Industrial photographers often take pictures of equipment, machinery, products, workers, and company officials. The pictures are used for various purposes—for example, analysis of engineering projects, publicity, or records of equipment development or deployment, such as placement of an offshore oil rig. This photography frequently is done on location.

Scientific photographers take images of a variety of subjects to illustrate or record scientific or medical data or phenomena, using knowledge of scientific procedures. They typically possess additional knowledge in areas such as engineering, medicine, biology, or chemistry.

News photographers, also called *photojournalists*, photograph newsworthy people, places, and sporting, political, and community events for newspapers, journals, magazines, or television.

Fine arts photographers sell their photographs as fine artwork. In addition to technical proficiency, fine arts photographers need artistic talent and creativity.

Self-employed, or freelance, photographers usually specialize in one of the above fields. In addition to carrying out assignments under direct contract with clients, they may license the use of their photographs through stock-photo agencies or market their work directly to the public. Stock-photo agencies sell magazines and other customers the right to use photographs, and pay the photographer a commission. These agencies require an application from the photographer and a sizable portfolio of pictures. Once accepted, photographers usually are required to submit a large number of new photographs each year. Self-employed photographers must also have a thorough understanding of copyright laws in order to protect their work.

Most photographers spend only a small portion of their work schedule actually taking photographs. Their most common activities are editing images on a computer—if they use a digital camera—and looking for new business—if they are self-employed.

Work environment. Working conditions for photographers vary considerably. Photographers employed in government and advertising studios usually work a 5-day, 40-hour week. On the other hand, news photographers often work long, irregular hours and must be available to work on short notice. Many photographers work part time or on variable schedules.

Portrait photographers usually work in their own studios but also may travel to take photographs at the client's location, such as a school, a company office, or a private home. News and commercial photographers frequently travel locally, stay overnight on assignments, or travel to distant places for long periods.

Some photographers work in uncomfortable or even dangerous surroundings, especially news photographers covering accidents, natural disasters, civil unrest, or military conflicts. Many photographers must wait long hours in all kinds of weather for an event to take place and stand or walk for long periods while carrying heavy equipment. News photographers often work under strict deadlines.

Self-employment allows for greater autonomy, freedom of expression, and flexible scheduling. However, income can be uncertain and the continuous, time consuming search for new clients can be stressful. Some self-employed photographers hire assistants who help seek out new business.

Training, Other Qualifications, and Advancement

Employers usually seek applicants with a "good eye," imagination, and creativity, as well as a good technical understanding of photography. Photojournalists or industrial or scientific photographers generally need a college degree. Freelance and portrait photographers need technical proficiency, gained through a degree, training program, or experience.

Education and training. Entry-level positions in photojournalism or in industrial or scientific photography generally require a college degree in photography or in a field related to the industry in which the photographer seeks employment. Entry-level freelance or portrait photographers need technical proficiency. Some complete a college degree or vocational training programs.

Photography courses are offered by many universities, community and junior colleges, vocational-technical institutes, and private trade and technical schools. Basic courses in photography cover equipment, processes, and techniques. Learning good business skills is important and some bachelor's degree programs offer courses focusing on them. Art schools offer useful training in photographic design and composition.

Photographers may start out as assistants to experienced photographers. Assistants acquire the technical knowledge needed to be a successful photographer and also learn other skills necessary to run a portrait or commercial photography business.

Some photographers enter the field by submitting unsolicited a portfolio of photographs to magazines and to art directors at advertising agencies; for freelance photographers, a good portfolio is essential.

Individuals interested in a career in photography should try to develop contacts in the field by subscribing to photographic newsletters and magazines, joining camera clubs, and seeking summer or part-time employment in camera stores, newspapers, or photo studios.

Other qualifications. Photographers need good eyesight, artistic ability, and good hand-eye coordination. They should be patient, accurate, and detail-oriented and should be able to work well with others, as they frequently deal with clients, graphic designers, and advertising and publishing specialists. Photographers need to know how to use computer software programs and applications that allow them to prepare and edit images, and those who market directly to clients should know how to use the Internet to display their work.

Portrait photographers need the ability to help people relax in front of the camera. Commercial and fine arts photographers must be imaginative and original. News photographers must not only be good with a camera, but also understand the story behind an event so that their pictures match the story. They must be decisive in recognizing a potentially good photograph and act quickly to capture it.

Photographers who operate their own business, or freelance, need business skills as well as talent. These individuals must know how to prepare a business plan; submit bids; write contracts; keep financial records; market their work; hire models, if needed; get permission to shoot on locations that normally are not open to the public; obtain releases to use photographs of people; license and price photographs; and secure copyright protection for their work. To protect their rights and their work, self-employed photographers require basic knowledge of licensing and copyright laws, as well as knowledge of contracts and negotiation procedures.

Freelance photographers also should develop an individual style of photography to differentiate themselves from the competition.

Advancement. After several years of experience, magazine and news photographers may advance to photography or picture editor positions. Some photographers teach at technical schools, film schools, or universities.

Employment

Photographers held about 122,000 jobs in 2006. More than half were self-employed, a much higher proportion than for most occupations. Some self-employed photographers have contracts with advertising agencies, magazine publishers, or other businesses to do individual projects for a set fee, while others operate portrait studios or provide photographs to stock-photo agencies.

Most salaried photographers work in portrait or commercial photography studios; most of the others work for newspapers, magazines, and advertising agencies. Photographers work in all areas of the country, but most are employed in metropolitan areas.

Job Outlook

Employment of photographers is expected to grow about as fast as the average for all occupations through 2016. Photographers can expect keen competition for job openings because the work is attractive to many people.

Employment change. Demand for portrait photographers should increase as the population grows. Moreover, growth of Internet versions of magazines, journals, and newspapers will require increasing numbers of commercial photographers to provide digital images. The Internet and improved data management programs also should make it easier for freelancers to market directly to their customers, increasing opportunities for self-employment and decreasing reliance on stock photo agencies. As a result, employment of photographers is expected to grow 10 percent over the 2006–2016 projection period, about as fast as the average for all occupations.

Job growth, however, will be constrained somewhat by the widespread use of digital photography and the falling price of digital equipment. Improvements in digital technology reduce barriers of entry into this profession and allow more individual consumers and businesses to produce, store, and access photographic images on their own. Photojournalists may be adversely affected by the increase in "citizen journalism"—when newspapers buy images taken by non-professionals who happen to be at the scene of an event. Declines in the newspaper industry also will reduce demand for photographers to provide still images for print.

Job prospects. Photographers can expect keen competition for job openings because the work is attractive to many people. The number of individuals interested in positions as commercial and news photographers usually is much greater than the number of openings. Salaried jobs in particular may be difficult to find as more companies contract with freelancers rather than hire their own photographers. Those who succeed in landing a salaried job or attracting enough work to earn a living by freelancing are likely to be adept at operating a business and to be among the most creative. They will be able to find and exploit the new opportunities available from rapidly changing technologies. Related work experience, job-related

Projections data from the National Employment Matrix

Occupational Title	SOC Code	Employment, 2006	Projected employment, 2016	Change, 2006-2016	
				Number	Percent
Photographers	27-4021	122,000	135,000	13,000	10

NOTE: Data in this table are rounded.

training, or some unique skill or talent—such as a background in computers or electronics—also improve a photographer's job prospects.

Earnings

Median annual earnings of salaried photographers were $26,170 in May 2006. The middle 50 percent earned between $18,680 and $38,730. The lowest 10 percent earned less than $15,540, and the highest 10 percent earned more than $56,640. Median annual earnings in the industry employing the largest numbers of salaried photographers were $22,860 in the photographic services industry.

Salaried photographers—more of whom work full time—tend to earn more than those who are self-employed. Because most freelance and portrait photographers purchase their own equipment, they incur considerable expense acquiring and maintaining cameras and accessories. Unlike news and commercial photographers, few fine arts photographers are successful enough to support themselves solely through their art.

Related Occupations

Other occupations requiring artistic talent and creativity include architects, except landscape and naval; artists and related workers; commercial and industrial designers, fashion designers, and graphic designers; and television, video, and motion picture camera operators and editors. Photojournalists are often required to cover news stories much the same as news analysts, reporters, and correspondents. The processing work that photographers do on computers is similar to the work of prepress technicians and workers and desktop publishers.

Sources of Additional Information

Career information on photography is available from

- Professional Photographers of America, Inc., 229 Peachtree St. NE, Suite 2200, Atlanta, GA 30303. Internet: http://www.ppa.com
- National Press Photographers Association, Inc., 3200 Croasdaile Dr., Suite 306, Durham, NC 27705. Internet: http://www.nppa.org
- American Society of Media Photographers, Inc., 150 North Second St., Philadelphia, PA 19106. Internet: http://www.asmp.org

Photographic Process Workers and Processing Machine Operators

(O*NET 51-9131.00 and 51-9132.00)

Significant Points

- Most workers receive on-the-job training from their companies, manufacturers' representatives, and experienced workers.
- A rapid decline in employment is expected as digital photography becomes commonplace.
- Job opportunities will be best for individuals with experience using computers and digital technology.

Nature of the Work

Both amateur and professional photographers rely heavily on photographic process workers and processing machine operators to develop film, make prints or slides, and do related tasks, such as enlarging or retouching photographs. *Photographic processing machine operators* operate various machines, such as mounting presses and motion picture film printing, photographic printing, and film developing machines. *Photographic process workers* perform more delicate tasks, such as retouching photographic negatives, prints, and images to emphasize or correct specific features.

Processing machine operators who work with digital images first load the raw images onto a computer, either directly from the camera or, more commonly, from a storage device such as a flash card or CD. Most processing of the images is done automatically by software, but images may also be reviewed manually by the operator, who then selects the images the customer wants printed and the quantity. Some digital processors also upload images onto a Web site so that the customer can view them from a home computer and share them with others.

Photographic processing machine operators often have specialized jobs. *Film process technicians* operate machines that develop exposed photographic film or sensitized paper in a series of chemical and water baths to produce negative or positive images. First, technicians mix developing and fixing solutions, following a formula. They then load the film in the machine, which immerses the exposed film in the various solutions to bring out the image. Finally they rinse it in water to remove the chemicals. The technician then dries the film. In some cases, these steps are performed by hand.

Color printer operators control equipment that produces color prints from negatives. These workers read customer instructions to determine processing requirements. They load film into color printing equipment, examine negatives to determine equipment control settings, set controls, and produce a specified number of prints. Finally, they inspect the finished prints for defects, remove any that are found, and insert the processed negatives and prints into an envelope for return to the customer.

Photographic process workers, sometimes known as *digital imaging technicians*, use computer images of conventional negatives and specialized computer software to vary the contrast of images, remove unwanted background, or combine features from different photographs.

Although computers and digital technology are replacing much manual work, some photographic process workers, especially those who work in portrait studios, still perform many specialized tasks by hand directly on the photo or negative. *Airbrush artists* restore damaged and faded photographs, and may color or shade drawings to create photographic likenesses using an airbrush. *Photographic retouchers* alter photographic negatives, prints, or images to accentuate the subject. *Colorists* apply oil colors to portrait photographs to create natural, lifelike appearances. *Photographic spotters* remove imperfections on photographic prints and images.

Work environment. Photographic process workers and processing machine operators generally work in clean, appropriately lighted, well-ventilated, and air-conditioned offices, photofinishing laboratories, or one-hour minilabs. In recent years, more commercial photographic processing has been done on computers than in darkrooms, and this trend is expected to continue.

Projections data from the National Employment Matrix

Occupational Title	SOC Code	Employment, 2006	Projected employment, 2016	Change, 2006-16	
				Number	Percent
Photographic process workers and processing machine operators ...	51-9130	73,000	40,000	-33,000	-45
Photographic process workers ...	51-9131	24,000	15,000	-8,600	-36
Photographic processing machine operators...	51-9132	49,000	25,000	-25,000	-50

NOTE: Data in this table are rounded.

Some photographic process workers and processing machine operators are exposed to the chemicals and fumes associated with developing and printing. These workers must wear rubber gloves and aprons and take precautions against these hazards. Those who use computers for extended periods may experience back pain, eyestrain, or fatigue.

Photographic processing machine operators must do repetitive work accurately and at a rapid pace. Photographic process workers do detailed tasks, such as airbrushing and spotting, which can contribute to eye fatigue.

Training, Other Qualifications, and Advancement

Most photographic process workers and processing machine operators receive on-the-job training from their companies, manufacturers' representatives, and experienced workers. New employees gradually learn to use the machines and chemicals that develop and print film and the computer techniques to process and print digital images.

Education and training. Employers prefer applicants who are high school graduates or who have some experience in the field. Familiarity with computers is essential for photographic processing machine operators. The ability to perform simple mathematical calculations also is helpful.

Photography courses that include instruction in film processing are valuable preparation. Such courses are available through high schools, vocational-technical institutes, private trade schools, and colleges and universities; some colleges offer degrees in photographic technology.

On-the-job training in photographic processing occupations can range from just a few hours for print machine operators to several months for photographic processing workers such as airbrush artists and colorists. Some workers attend periodic training seminars to maintain a high level of skill. With much of the processing and editing work now being done on computers, employees must continually learn new programs as they become available.

Other qualifications. Manual dexterity, good hand-eye coordination, and good vision, including normal color perception, are important qualifications for photographic process workers.

Advancement. Photographic process machine workers can sometimes advance from jobs as machine operators to supervisory positions in laboratories or to management positions within retail stores.

Employment

Photographic process workers held about 24,000 jobs in 2006. Photographic processing machine operators held about 49,000 jobs in 2006.

About 20 percent of photographic process workers were employed in photographic services. An additional 13 percent were employed by electronic and appliance stores and drug stores, and 14 percent worked in the publishing, internet services, and motion picture industries.

About 70 percent of photographic processing machine operators worked in retail establishments, primarily in general merchandise stores and drug stores Small numbers were employed in the printing industry and in portrait studios and commercial laboratories that process the work of professional photographers.

Job Outlook

A rapid decline in employment is expected for photographic process workers and processing machine operators through the year 2016. Job opportunities will be best for individuals with experience using computers and digital technology.

Employment change. Employment of photographic process workers and processing machine operators is expected to decline rapidly by 45 percent over the 2006–2016 decade. Digital cameras, which use electronic memory rather than film to record images, have in recent years become standard among professional photographers. They are rapidly gaining in popularity among amateur photographers as well as the cost of these cameras continues to fall. This will continue to reduce the demand for traditional photographic processing machine operators. However, while many digital camera owners will choose to print their own pictures with their own equipment, a growing number of casual photographers are choosing not to acquire the needed equipment and skills to print the photos themselves. For them, self-service machines and online ordering services will be able to meet most of the demand, but there will still be some demand for professionals to print digital photos and operate the machines, as well as to develop and print photos from those who continue to use film cameras.

Digital photography also will reduce demand for photographic process workers. Using digital cameras and technology, consumers who have a personal computer and the proper software are able to download and view pictures on their computer, as well as to manipulate, correct, and retouch their own photographs. No matter what improvements occur in camera technology, though, some photographic processing tasks will still require skillful manual treatment.

Job prospects. Job opportunities will be best for individuals with experience using computers and digital technology. Employment fluctuates somewhat over the course of the year, typically peaking during school graduation and summer vacation periods.

Earnings

Earnings of photographic process workers vary greatly depending on skill level, experience, and geographic location. Median hourly earnings for photographic process workers were $11.19 in May 2006. The middle 50 percent earned between $8.61 and $15.12. The lowest 10 percent earned less than $7.32, and the highest 10 percent earned more than $21.43. Median hourly earnings were $11.65 in photographic services.

Median hourly earning for photographic processing machine operators were $9.38 in May 2006. The middle 50 percent earned between $8.01 and $11.44. The lowest 10 percent earned less than $7.16, and the highest 10 percent earned more than $14.92. Median hourly earnings in the two industries employing the largest numbers of photographic processing machine operators were $9.58 in photographic services and $8.50 in health and personal care stores.

Related Occupations

Photographic process workers and processing machine operators need specialized knowledge of the photo developing process. Other workers who apply specialized technical knowledge include clinical laboratory technologists and technicians, computer operators, jewelers and precious stone and metal workers, prepress technicians and workers, printing machine operators, and science technicians.

Sources of Additional Information

For information about employment opportunities in photographic laboratories and schools that offer degrees in photographic technology, contact

- Photo Marketing Association International, 3000 Picture Place, Jackson, MI 49201. Internet: http://www.pmai.org

Physical Therapist Assistants and Aides

(O*NET 31-2021.00 and 31-2022.00)

Significant Points

- Employment is projected to increase much faster than average.
- Assistants should have very good job prospects; on the other hand, aides may face keen competition from the large pool of qualified applicants.
- Aides usually learn skills on the job, while assistants generally have an associate degree; some states require licensing for assistants.
- About 71 percent of jobs are in offices of physical therapists or in hospitals.

Nature of the Work

Physical therapist assistants and aides help physical therapists to provide treatment that improves patient mobility, relieves pain, and prevents or lessens physical disabilities of patients. A physical therapist might ask an assistant to help patients exercise or learn to use crutches, for example, or an aide to gather and prepare therapy equipment. Patients include accident victims and individuals with disabling conditions such as lower-back pain, arthritis, heart disease, fractures, head injuries, and cerebral palsy.

Physical therapist assistants perform a variety of tasks. Under the direction and supervision of physical therapists, they provide part of a patient's treatment. This might involve exercises, massages, electrical stimulation, paraffin baths, hot and cold packs, traction, and ultrasound. Physical therapist assistants record the patient's responses to treatment and report the outcome of each treatment to the physical therapist.

Physical therapist aides help make therapy sessions productive, under the direct supervision of a physical therapist or physical therapist assistant. They usually are responsible for keeping the treatment area clean and organized and for preparing for each patient's therapy. When patients need assistance moving to or from a treatment area, aides push them in a wheelchair or provide them with a shoulder to lean on. Because they are not licensed, aides do not perform the clinical tasks of a physical therapist assistant in states where licensure is required.

The duties of aides include some clerical tasks, such as ordering depleted supplies, answering the phone, and filling out insurance forms and other paperwork. The extent to which an aide or an assistant performs clerical tasks depends on the size and location of the facility.

Work environment. Physical therapist assistants and aides need a moderate degree of strength because of the physical exertion required in assisting patients with their treatment. In some cases, assistants and aides need to lift patients. Frequent kneeling, stooping, and standing for long periods also are part of the job.

The hours and days that physical therapist assistants and aides work vary with the facility. About 23 percent of all physical therapist assistants and aides work part time. Many outpatient physical therapy offices and clinics have evening and weekend hours, to coincide with patients' personal schedules.

Training, Other Qualifications, and Advancement

Most physical therapist aides are trained on the job, but most physical therapist assistants earn an associate degree from an accredited physical therapist assistant program. Some states require licensing for physical therapist assistants.

Education and training. Employers typically require physical therapist aides to have a high school diploma. They are trained on the job, and most employers provide clinical on-the-job training.

In many states, physical therapist assistants are required by law to hold at least an associate degree. According to the American Physical Therapy Association, there were 233 accredited physical therapist assistant programs in the United States as of 2006. Accredited programs usually last two years, or four semesters, and culminate in an associate degree.

Programs are divided into academic study and hands-on clinical experience. Academic course work includes algebra, anatomy and physiology, biology, chemistry, and psychology. Clinical work includes certifications in CPR and other first aid and field experience in treatment centers. Both educators and prospective employers view clinical experience as essential to ensuring that students understand the responsibilities of a physical therapist assistant.

Licensure. Licensing is not required to practice as a physical therapist aide. However, some states require licensure or registration in order to work as a physical therapist assistant. states that require licensure stipulate specific educational and examination criteria. Additional requirements may include certification in cardiopulmonary resuscitation (CPR) and other first aid and a minimum number of hours of clinical experience. Complete information on regulations can be obtained from state licensing boards.

Projections data from the National Employment Matrix

Occupational Title	SOC Code	Employment, 2006	Projected employment, 2016	Change, 2006-16	
				Number	Percent
Physical therapist assistants and aides	31-2020	107,000	137,000	31,000	29
Physical therapist assistants	31-2021	60,000	80,000	20,000	32
Physical therapist aides	31-2022	46,000	58,000	11,000	24

NOTE: Data in this table are rounded.

Other qualifications. Physical therapist assistants and aides should be well-organized, detail oriented, and caring. They usually have strong interpersonal skills and a desire to help people in need.

Advancement. Some physical therapist aides advance to become therapist assistants after gaining experience and, often, additional education. Sometimes, this education is required by law.

Some physical therapist assistants advance by specializing in a clinical area. They gain expertise in treating a certain type of patient, such as geriatric or pediatric, or a type of ailment, such as sports injuries. Many physical therapist assistants advance to administration positions. These positions might include organizing all the assistants in a large physical therapy organization or acting as the director for a specific department such as sports medicine. Other assistants go on to teach in an accredited physical therapist assistant academic program, lead health risk reduction classes for the elderly, or organize community activities related to fitness and risk reduction.

Employment

Physical therapist assistants and aides held about 107,000 jobs in 2006. Physical therapist assistants held about 60,000 jobs; physical therapist aides, approximately 46,000. Both work with physical therapists in a variety of settings. About 71 percent of jobs were in offices of physical therapists or in hospitals. Others worked primarily in nursing care facilities, offices of physicians, home health care services, and outpatient care centers.

Job Outlook

Employment is expected to grow much faster than average because of increasing consumer demand for physical therapy services. Job prospects for physical therapist assistants are expected to be very good. Aides should experience keen competition for jobs.

Employment change. Employment of physical therapist assistants and aides is expected to grow by 29 percent over the 2006–2016 decade, much faster than the average for all occupations. The impact of federal limits on Medicare and Medicaid reimbursement for therapy services may adversely affect the short-term job outlook for physical therapist assistants and aides. However, long-term demand for physical therapist assistants and aides will continue to rise, as the number of individuals with disabilities or limited function grows.

The increasing number of people who need therapy reflects, in part, the increasing elderly population. The elderly population is particularly vulnerable to chronic and debilitating conditions that require therapeutic services. These patients often need additional assistance in their treatment, making the roles of assistants and aides vital. In addition, the large baby-boom generation is entering the prime age for heart attacks and strokes, further increasing the demand for cardiac and physical rehabilitation. Moreover, future medical developments should permit an increased percentage of trauma victims to survive, creating added demand for therapy services.

Physical therapists are expected to increasingly use assistants to reduce the cost of physical therapy services. Once a patient is evaluated and a treatment plan is designed by the physical therapist, the physical therapist assistant can provide many parts of the treatment, as approved by the therapist.

Job prospects. Opportunities for individuals interested in becoming physical therapist assistants are expected to be very good. Physical therapist aides may face keen competition from the large pool of qualified individuals. In addition to employment growth, job openings will result from the need to replace workers who leave the occupation permanently. Physical therapist assistants and aides with prior experience working in a physical therapy office or other health care setting will have the best job opportunities.

Earnings

Median annual earnings of physical therapist assistants were $41,360 in May 2006. The middle 50 percent earned between $33,840 and $49,010. The lowest 10 percent earned less than $26,190, and the highest 10 percent earned more than $57,220. Median annual earnings in the industries employing the largest numbers of physical therapist assistants in May 2006 were

- Home health care services $46,390
- Nursing care facilities 44,460
- Offices of physical, occupational and speech therapists, and audiologists 40,780
- General medical and surgical hospitals 40,670
- Offices of physicians 39,290

Median annual earnings of physical therapist aides were $22,060 in May 2006. The middle 50 percent earned between $18,550 and $26,860. The lowest 10 percent earned less than $15,850, and the highest 10 percent earned more than $32,600. Median annual earnings in the industries employing the largest numbers of physical therapist aides in May 2006 were

- Nursing care facilities.......................................$24,170
- Offices of physicians 22,680
- General medical and surgical hospitals 22,680
- Offices of physical, occupational and speech therapists, and audiologists 21,230

Related Occupations

Physical therapist assistants and aides work under the supervision of physical therapists. Other workers in the health care field who work under similar supervision include dental assistants; medical assistants; occupational therapist assistants and aides; pharmacy aides; pharmacy technicians; nursing, psychiatric, and home health aides; personal and home care aides; and social and human service assistants.

Sources of Additional Information

Career information on physical therapist assistants and a list of schools offering accredited programs can be obtained from

- The American Physical Therapy Association, 1111 North Fairfax St., Alexandria, VA 22314-1488. Internet: http://www.apta.org

Physical Therapists

(O*NET 29-1123.00)

Significant Points

- Employment is expected to increase much faster than average.
- Job opportunities should be good, particularly in acute hospital, rehabilitation, and orthopedic settings.
- Physical therapists need a master's degree from an accredited physical therapy program and a state license, requiring passing scores on national and state examinations.
- About 6 out of 10 physical therapists work in hospitals or in offices of physical therapists.

Nature of the Work

Physical therapists provide services that help restore function, improve mobility, relieve pain, and prevent or limit permanent physical disabilities of patients suffering from injuries or disease. They restore, maintain, and promote overall fitness and health. Their patients include accident victims and individuals with disabling conditions such as low-back pain, arthritis, heart disease, fractures, head injuries, and cerebral palsy.

Therapists examine patients' medical histories and then test and measure the patients' strength, range of motion, balance and coordination, posture, muscle performance, respiration, and motor function. Next, physical therapists develop plans describing a treatment strategy and its anticipated outcome.

Treatment often includes exercise, especially for patients who have been immobilized or who lack flexibility, strength, or endurance. Physical therapists encourage patients to use their muscles to increase their flexibility and range of motion. More advanced exercises focus on improving strength, balance, coordination, and endurance. The goal is to improve how an individual functions at work and at home.

Physical therapists also use electrical stimulation, hot packs or cold compresses, and ultrasound to relieve pain and reduce swelling. They may use traction or deep-tissue massage to relieve pain and improve circulation and flexibility. Therapists also teach patients to use assistive and adaptive devices, such as crutches, prostheses, and wheelchairs. They also may show patients how to do exercises at home to expedite their recovery.

As treatment continues, physical therapists document the patient's progress, conduct periodic examinations, and modify treatments when necessary.

Physical therapists often consult and practice with a variety of other professionals, such as physicians, dentists, nurses, educators, social workers, occupational therapists, speech-language pathologists, and audiologists.

Some physical therapists treat a wide range of ailments; others specialize in areas such as pediatrics, geriatrics, orthopedics, sports medicine, neurology, and cardiopulmonary physical therapy.

Work environment. Physical therapists practice in hospitals, clinics, and private offices that have specially equipped facilities. They also treat patients in hospital rooms, homes, or schools. These jobs can be physically demanding because therapists often have to stoop, kneel, crouch, lift, and stand for long periods. In addition, physical therapists move heavy equipment and lift patients or help them turn, stand, or walk.

In 2006, most full-time physical therapists worked a 40-hour week; some worked evenings and weekends to fit their patients' schedules. About 1 in 5 physical therapists worked part time.

Training, Other Qualifications, and Advancement

Physical therapists need a master's degree from an accredited physical therapy program and a state license, requiring passing scores on national and state examinations.

Education and training. According to the American Physical Therapy Association, there were 209 accredited physical therapist education programs in 2007. Of the accredited programs, 43 offered master's degrees and 166 offered doctoral degrees. Only master's degree and doctoral degree programs are accredited, in accordance with the Commission on Accreditation in Physical Therapy Education. In the future, a doctoral degree might be the required entry-level degree. Master's degree programs typically last two years, and doctoral degree programs last three years.

Physical therapist education programs start with basic science courses such as biology, chemistry, and physics and then introduce specialized courses, including biomechanics, neuroanatomy, human growth and development, manifestations of disease, examination techniques, and therapeutic procedures. Besides getting classroom and laboratory instruction, students receive supervised clinical experience.

Among the undergraduate courses that are useful when one applies to a physical therapist education program are anatomy, biology, chemistry, social science, mathematics, and physics. Before granting admission, many programs require volunteer experience in the physical therapy department of a hospital or clinic. For high school students, volunteering with the school athletic trainer is a good way to gain experience.

Licensure. All states require physical therapists to pass national and state licensure exams before they can practice. They must also graduate from an accredited physical therapist education program.

Other qualifications. Physical therapists should have strong interpersonal skills so that they can educate patients about their physical therapy treatments and communicate with patients' families. Physical therapists also should be compassionate and possess a desire to help patients.

Advancement. Physical therapists are expected to continue their professional development by participating in continuing education courses and workshops. In fact, a number of states require continuing education as a condition of maintaining licensure.

Employment

Physical therapists held about 173,000 jobs in 2006. The number of jobs is greater than the number of practicing physical therapists

Projections data from the National Employment Matrix

Occupational Title	SOC Code	Employment, 2006	Projected employment, 2016	Change, 2006-2016	
				Number	Percent
Physical therapists..	29-1123	173,000	220,000	47,000	27

NOTE: Data in this table are rounded.

because some physical therapists hold two or more jobs. For example, some may work in a private practice, but also work part time in another health care facility.

About 6 out of 10 physical therapists worked in hospitals or in offices of physical therapists. Other jobs were in the home health care services industry, nursing care facilities, outpatient care centers, and offices of physicians. Some physical therapists were self-employed in private practices, seeing individual patients and contracting to provide services in hospitals, rehabilitation centers, nursing care facilities, home health care agencies, adult day care programs, and schools. Physical therapists also teach in academic institutions and conduct research.

Job Outlook

Employment of physical therapists is expected to grow much faster than average. Job opportunities will be good, especially in acute hospital, rehabilitation, and orthopedic settings.

Employment change. Employment of physical therapists is expected to grow 27 percent from 2006 to 2016, much faster than the average for all occupations. The impact of proposed federal legislation imposing limits on reimbursement for therapy services may adversely affect the short-term job outlook for physical therapists. However, the long-run demand for physical therapists should continue to rise as new treatments and techniques expand the scope of physical therapy practices. Moreover, demand will be spurred by the increasing numbers of individuals with disabilities or limited function.

The increasing elderly population will drive growth in the demand for physical therapy services. The elderly population is particularly vulnerable to chronic and debilitating conditions that require therapeutic services. Also, the baby-boom generation is entering the prime age for heart attacks and strokes, increasing the demand for cardiac and physical rehabilitation. And increasing numbers of children will need physical therapy as technological advances save the lives of a larger proportion of newborns with severe birth defects.

Future medical developments also should permit a higher percentage of trauma victims to survive, creating additional demand for rehabilitative care. In addition, growth may result from advances in medical technology that could permit the treatment of an increasing number of disabling conditions that were untreatable in the past.

Widespread interest in health promotion also should increase demand for physical therapy services. A growing number of employers are using physical therapists to evaluate worksites, develop exercise programs, and teach safe work habits to employees.

Job prospects. Job opportunities will be good for licensed physical therapists in all settings. Job opportunities should be particularly good in acute hospital, rehabilitation, and orthopedic settings, where the elderly are most often treated. Physical therapists with specialized knowledge of particular types of treatment also will have excellent job prospects.

Earnings

Median annual earnings of physical therapists were $66,200 in May 2006. The middle 50 percent earned between $55,030 and $78,080. The lowest 10 percent earned less than $46,510, and the highest 10 percent earned more than $94,810. Median annual earnings in the industries employing the largest numbers of physical therapists in May 2006 were

Home health care services.................................$70,920
Nursing care facilities 68,650
General medical and surgical hospitals 66,630
Offices of physicians 65,900
Offices of physical, occupational and speech therapists, and audiologists 65,150

Related Occupations

Physical therapists rehabilitate people with physical disabilities. Others who work in the rehabilitation field include audiologists, chiropractors, occupational therapists, recreational therapists, rehabilitation counselors, respiratory therapists, and speech-language pathologists.

Sources of Additional Information

Additional career information and a list of accredited educational programs in physical therapy are available from

- American Physical Therapy Association, 1111 North Fairfax St, Alexandria, VA 22314-1488. Internet: http://www.apta.org

Physician Assistants

(O*NET 29-1071.00)

Significant Points

- Physician assistant programs usually last at least 2 years; admission requirements vary by program, but many require at least 2 years of college and some health care experience.
- All states require physician assistants to complete an accredited education program and to pass a national exam in order to obtain a license.
- Employment is projected to grow much faster than average as health care establishments increasingly use physician assistants to contain costs.
- Job opportunities should be good, particularly in rural and inner-city clinics.

Nature of the Work

Physician assistants (PAs) practice medicine under the supervision of physicians and surgeons. They should not be confused with medical assistants, who perform routine clinical and clerical tasks. PAs are formally trained to provide diagnostic, therapeutic, and preventive health care services, as delegated by a physician. Working as members of the health care team, they take medical histories, examine and treat patients, order and interpret laboratory tests and x rays, and make diagnoses. They also treat minor injuries, by suturing, splinting, and casting. PAs record progress notes, instruct and counsel patients, and order or carry out therapy. In 48 states and the District of Columbia, physician assistants may prescribe some medications. In some establishments, a PA is responsible for managerial duties, such as ordering medical supplies or equipment and supervising technicians and assistants.

Physician assistants work under the supervision of a physician. However, PAs may be the principal care providers in rural or inner city clinics where a physician is present for only one or two days each week. In such cases, the PA confers with the supervising physician and other medical professionals as needed and as required by law. PAs also may make house calls or go to hospitals and nursing care facilities to check on patients, after which they report back to the physician.

The duties of physician assistants are determined by the supervising physician and by state law. Aspiring PAs should investigate the laws and regulations in the states in which they wish to practice.

Many PAs work in primary care specialties, such as general internal medicine, pediatrics, and family medicine. Other specialty areas include general and thoracic surgery, emergency medicine, orthopedics, and geriatrics. PAs specializing in surgery provide preoperative and postoperative care and may work as first or second assistants during major surgery.

Work environment. Although PAs usually work in a comfortable, well-lighted environment, those in surgery often stand for long periods. At times, the job requires a considerable amount of walking. Schedules vary according to the practice setting, and often depend on the hours of the supervising physician. The work week of hospital-based PAs may include weekends, nights, or early morning hospital rounds to visit patients. These workers also may be on call. PAs in clinics usually work a 40-hour week.

Training, Other Qualifications, and Advancement

Physician assistant programs usually last at least two years. Admission requirements vary by program, but many require at least two years of college and some health care experience. All states require that PAs complete an accredited, formal education program and pass a national exam to obtain a license.

Education and training. Physician assistant education programs usually last at least two years and are full time. Most programs are in schools of allied health, academic health centers, medical schools, or four-year colleges; a few are in community colleges, the military, or hospitals. Many accredited PA programs have clinical teaching affiliations with medical schools.

In 2007, 136 education programs for physician assistants were accredited or provisionally accredited by the American Academy of Physician Assistants. More than 90 of these programs offered the option of a master's degree, and the rest offered either a bachelor's degree or an associate degree. Most applicants to PA educational programs already have a bachelor's degree.

Admission requirements vary, but many programs require two years of college and some work experience in the health care field. Students should take courses in biology, English, chemistry, mathematics, psychology, and the social sciences. Many PAs have prior experience as registered nurses, and others come from varied backgrounds, including military corpsman or medics and allied health occupations such as respiratory therapists, physical therapists, and emergency medical technicians and paramedics.

PA education includes classroom instruction in biochemistry, pathology, human anatomy, physiology, microbiology, clinical pharmacology, clinical medicine, geriatric and home health care, disease prevention, and medical ethics. Students obtain supervised clinical training in several areas, including family medicine, internal medicine, surgery, prenatal care and gynecology, geriatrics, emergency medicine, psychiatry, and pediatrics. Sometimes, PA students serve one or more of these rotations under the supervision of a physician who is seeking to hire a PA. The rotations often lead to permanent employment.

Licensure. All states and the District of Columbia have legislation governing the qualifications or practice of physician assistants. All jurisdictions require physician assistants to pass the Physician Assistant National Certifying Examination, administered by the National Commission on Certification of Physician Assistants (NCCPA) and open only to graduates of accredited PA education programs. Only those successfully completing the examination may use the credential "Physician Assistant-Certified." To remain certified, PAs must complete 100 hours of continuing medical education every two years. Every six years, they must pass a recertification examination or complete an alternative program combining learning experiences and a take-home examination.

Other qualifications. Physician assistants must have a desire to serve patients and be self-motivated. PAs also must have a good bedside manner, emotional stability, and the ability to make decisions in emergencies. Physician assistants must be willing to study throughout their career to keep up with medical advances.

Certification and advancement. Some PAs pursue additional education in a specialty such as surgery, neonatology, or emergency medicine. PA postgraduate educational programs are available in areas such as internal medicine, rural primary care, emergency medicine, surgery, pediatrics, neonatology, and occupational medicine. Candidates must be graduates of an accredited program and be certified by the NCCPA.

As they attain greater clinical knowledge and experience, PAs can advance to added responsibilities and higher earnings. However, by the very nature of the profession, clinically practicing PAs always are supervised by physicians.

Employment

Physician assistants held about 66,000 jobs in 2006. The number of jobs is greater than the number of practicing PAs because some hold two or more jobs. For example, some PAs work with a supervising physician, but also work in another practice, clinic, or hospital. According to the American Academy of Physician Assistants, about 15 percent of actively practicing PAs worked in more than one clinical job concurrently in 2006.

More than half of jobs for PAs were in the offices of physicians. About a quarter were in hospitals, public or private. The rest were mostly in outpatient care centers, including health maintenance

Projections data from the National Employment Matrix

Occupational Title	SOC Code	Employment, 2006	Projected employment, 2016	Change, 2006-2016	
				Number	Percent
Physician assistants	29-1071	66,000	83,000	18,000	27

NOTE: Data in this table are rounded.

organizations; the federal government; and public or private colleges, universities, and professional schools. A few were self-employed.

Job Outlook

Employment is expected to grow much faster than the average as health care establishments increasingly use physician assistants to contain costs. Job opportunities for PAs should be good, particularly in rural and inner city clinics, as these settings typically have difficulty attracting physicians.

Employment change. Employment of physician assistants is expected to grow 27 percent from 2006 to 2016, much faster than the average for all occupations. Projected rapid job growth reflects the expansion of health care industries and an emphasis on cost containment, which results in increasing use of PAs by health care establishments.

Physicians and institutions are expected to employ more PAs to provide primary care and to assist with medical and surgical procedures because PAs are cost-effective and productive members of the health care team. Physician assistants can relieve physicians of routine duties and procedures. Telemedicine—using technology to facilitate interactive consultations between physicians and physician assistants—also will expand the use of physician assistants.

Besides working in traditional office-based settings, PAs should find a growing number of jobs in institutional settings such as hospitals, academic medical centers, public clinics, and prisons. PAs also may be needed to augment medical staffing in inpatient teaching hospital settings as the number of hours physician residents are permitted to work is reduced, encouraging hospitals to use PAs to supply some physician resident services.

Job prospects. Job opportunities for PAs should be good, particularly in rural and inner-city clinics because those settings have difficulty attracting physicians. In addition to job openings from employment growth, openings will result from the need to replace physician assistants who retire or leave the occupation permanently during the 2006–2016 decade. Opportunities will be best in states that allow PAs a wider scope of practice, such as allowing PAs to prescribe medications.

Earnings

Median annual earnings of wage-and-salary physician assistants were $74,980 in May 2006. The middle 50 percent earned between $62,430 and $89,220. The lowest 10 percent earned less than $43,100, and the highest 10 percent earned more than $102,230. Median annual earnings in the industries employing the largest numbers of physician assistants in May 2006 were

Outpatient care centers	$80,960
General medical and surgical hospitals	76,710
Offices of physicians	74,160

According to the American Academy of Physician Assistants, median income for physician assistants in full-time clinical practice was $80,356 in 2006; median income for first-year graduates was $69,517. Income varies by specialty, practice setting, geographical location, and years of experience. Employers often pay for their employees' liability insurance, registration fees with the Drug Enforcement Administration, state licensing fees, and credentialing fees.

Related Occupations

Other health care workers who provide direct patient care that requires a similar level of skill and training include audiologists, occupational therapists, physical therapists, registered nurses, and speech-language pathologists.

Sources of Additional Information

For information on a career as a physician assistant, including a list of accredited programs, contact

- American Academy of Physician Assistants Information Center, 950 North Washington St., Alexandria, VA 22314. Internet: http://www.aapa.org

For eligibility requirements and a description of the Physician Assistant National Certifying Examination, contact

- National Commission on Certification of Physician Assistants, Inc., 12000 Findley Rd., Suite 200, Duluth, GA 30097. Internet: http://www.nccpa.net

Physicians and Surgeons

(O*NET 29-1061.00, 29-1062.00, 29-1063.00, 29-1064.00, 29-1065.00, 29-1066.00, 29-1067.00, and 29-1069.99)

Significant Points

- Many physicians and surgeons work long, irregular hours; more than one-third of full-time physicians worked 60 hours or more a week in 2006.
- Acceptance to medical school is highly competitive.
- Formal education and training requirements are among the most demanding of any occupation, but earnings are among the highest.
- Job opportunities should be very good, particularly in rural and low-income areas.

Nature of the Work

Physicians and surgeons diagnose illnesses and prescribe and administer treatment for people suffering from injury or disease. Physicians examine patients, obtain medical histories, and order, perform, and interpret diagnostic tests. They counsel patients on diet, hygiene, and preventive health care.

There are two types of physicians: M.D.—Doctor of Medicine—and D.O.—Doctor of Osteopathic Medicine. M.D.s also are known as allopathic physicians. While both M.D.s and D.O.s may use all accepted methods of treatment, including drugs and surgery, D.O.s place special emphasis on the body's musculoskeletal system, preventive medicine, and holistic patient care. D.O.s are most likely to be primary care specialists although they can be found in all specialties. About half of D.O.s practice general or family medicine, general internal medicine, or general pediatrics.

Physicians work in one or more of several specialties, including, but not limited to, anesthesiology, family and general medicine, general internal medicine, general pediatrics, obstetrics and gynecology, psychiatry, and surgery.

Anesthesiologists focus on the care of surgical patients and pain relief. Like other physicians, they evaluate and treat patients and direct the efforts of their staffs. Through continual monitoring and assessment, these critical care specialists are responsible for maintenance of the patient's vital life functions—heart rate, body temperature, blood pressure, breathing—during surgery. They also work outside of the operating room, providing pain relief in the intensive care unit, during labor and delivery, and for those who suffer from chronic pain. Anesthesiologists confer with other physicians and surgeons about appropriate treatments and procedures before, during, and after operations.

Family and general practitioners often provide the first point of contact for people seeking health care, by acting as the traditional family doctor. They assess and treat a wide range of conditions, from sinus and respiratory infections to broken bones. Family and general practitioners typically have a base of regular, long-term patients. These doctors refer patients with more serious conditions to specialists or other health care facilities for more intensive care.

General internists diagnose and provide nonsurgical treatment for a wide range of problems that affect internal organ systems, such as the stomach, kidneys, liver, and digestive tract. Internists use a variety of diagnostic techniques to treat patients through medication or hospitalization. Like general practitioners, general internists commonly act as primary care specialists. They treat patients referred from other specialists, and, in turn they refer patients to other specialists when more complex care is required.

General pediatricians care for the health of infants, children, teenagers, and young adults. They specialize in the diagnosis and treatment of a variety of ailments specific to young people and track patients' growth to adulthood. Like most physicians, pediatricians work with different health care workers, such as nurses and other physicians, to assess and treat children with various ailments. Most of the work of pediatricians involves treating day-to-day illnesses—minor injuries, infectious diseases, and immunizations—that are common to children, much as a general practitioner treats adults. Some pediatricians specialize in pediatric surgery or serious medical conditions, such as autoimmune disorders or serious chronic ailments.

Obstetricians and gynecologists (OB/GYNs) specialize in women's health. They are responsible for women's general medical care, and they also provide care related to pregnancy and the reproductive system. Like general practitioners, OB/GYNs attempt to prevent, diagnose, and treat general health problems, but they focus on ailments specific to the female anatomy, such as cancers of the breast or cervix, urinary tract and pelvic disorders, and hormonal disorders. OB/GYNs also specialize in childbirth, treating and counseling women throughout their pregnancy, from giving prenatal diagnoses to assisting with delivery and providing postpartum care.

Psychiatrists are the primary caregivers in the area of mental health. They assess and treat mental illnesses through a combination of psychotherapy, psychoanalysis, hospitalization, and medication. Psychotherapy involves regular discussions with patients about their problems; the psychiatrist helps them find solutions through changes in their behavioral patterns, the exploration of their past experiences, or group and family therapy sessions. Psychoanalysis involves long-term psychotherapy and counseling for patients. In many cases, medications are administered to correct chemical imbalances that cause emotional problems. Psychiatrists also may administer electroconvulsive therapy to those of their patients who do not respond to, or who cannot take, medications.

Surgeons specialize in the treatment of injury, disease, and deformity through operations. Using a variety of instruments, and with patients under anesthesia, a surgeon corrects physical deformities, repairs bone and tissue after injuries, or performs preventive surgeries on patients with debilitating diseases or disorders. Although a large number perform general surgery, many surgeons choose to specialize in a specific area. One of the most prevalent specialties is orthopedic surgery: the treatment of the musculoskeletal system. Others include neurological surgery (treatment of the brain and nervous system), cardiovascular surgery, otolaryngology (treatment of the ear, nose, and throat), and plastic or reconstructive surgery. Like other physicians, surgeons also examine patients, perform and interpret diagnostic tests, and counsel patients on preventive health care.

Other physicians and surgeons work in a number of other medical and surgical specialists, including allergists, cardiologists, dermatologists, emergency physicians, gastroenterologists, ophthalmologists, pathologists, and radiologists.

Work environment. Many physicians—primarily general and family practitioners, general internists, pediatricians, OB/GYNs, and psychiatrists—work in small private offices or clinics, often assisted by a small staff of nurses and other administrative personnel. Increasingly, physicians are practicing in groups or health care organizations that provide backup coverage and allow for more time off. Physicians in a group practice or health care organization often work as part of a team that coordinates care for a number of patients; they are less independent than the solo practitioners of the past. Surgeons and anesthesiologists usually work in well-lighted, sterile environments while performing surgery and often stand for long periods. Most work in hospitals or in surgical outpatient centers.

Many physicians and surgeons work long, irregular hours. Over one-third of full-time physicians and surgeons worked 60 hours or more a week in 2006. Only 8 percent of all physicians and surgeons worked part-time, compared with 15 percent for all occupations. Physicians and surgeons must travel frequently between office and hospital to care for their patients. While on call, a physician will deal with many patients' concerns over the phone and make emergency visits to hospitals or nursing homes.

Training, Other Qualifications, and Advancement

The common path to practicing as a physician requires eight years of education beyond high school and three to eight additional years of internship and residency. All states, the District of Columbia, and U.S. territories license physicians.

Education and training. Formal education and training requirements for physicians are among the most demanding of any occupation—four years of undergraduate school, four years of medical school, and three to eight years of internship and residency, depending on the specialty selected. A few medical schools offer combined undergraduate and medical school programs that last six years rather than the customary eight years.

Premedical students must complete undergraduate work in physics, biology, mathematics, English, and inorganic and organic chemistry. Students also take courses in the humanities and the social sciences. Some students volunteer at local hospitals or clinics to gain practical experience in the health professions.

The minimum educational requirement for entry into medical school is three years of college; most applicants, however, have at least a bachelor's degree, and many have advanced degrees. There are 146 medical schools in the United States—126 teach allopathic medicine and award a Doctor of Medicine (M.D.) degree; 20 teach osteopathic medicine and award the Doctor of Osteopathic Medicine (D.O.) degree.

Acceptance to medical school is highly competitive. Applicants must submit transcripts, scores from the Medical College Admission Test, and letters of recommendation. Schools also consider an applicant's character, personality, leadership qualities, and participation in extracurricular activities. Most schools require an interview with members of the admissions committee.

Students spend most of the first two years of medical school in laboratories and classrooms, taking courses such as anatomy, biochemistry, physiology, pharmacology, psychology, microbiology, pathology, medical ethics, and laws governing medicine. They also learn to take medical histories, examine patients, and diagnose illnesses. During their last two years, students work with patients under the supervision of experienced physicians in hospitals and clinics, learning acute, chronic, preventive, and rehabilitative care. Through rotations in internal medicine, family practice, obstetrics and gynecology, pediatrics, psychiatry, and surgery, they gain experience in the diagnosis and treatment of illness.

Following medical school, almost all M.D.s enter a residency—graduate medical education in a specialty that takes the form of paid on-the-job training, usually in a hospital. Most D.O.s serve a 12-month rotating internship after graduation and before entering a residency, which may last two to six years.

A physician's training is costly. According to the Association of American Medical Colleges, in 2004 more than 80 percent of medical school graduates were in debt for educational expenses.

Licensure and certification. All states, the District of Columbia, and U.S. territories license physicians. To be licensed, physicians must graduate from an accredited medical school, pass a licensing examination, and complete one to seven years of graduate medical education. Although physicians licensed in one state usually can get a license to practice in another without further examination, some states limit reciprocity. Graduates of foreign medical schools generally can qualify for licensure after passing an examination and completing a U.S. residency.

M.D.s and D.O.s seeking board certification in a specialty may spend up to seven years in residency training, depending on the specialty. A final examination immediately after residency or after one or two years of practice also is necessary for certification by a member board of the American Board of Medical Specialists (ABMS) or the American Osteopathic Association (AOA). The ABMS represents 24 boards related to medical specialties ranging from allergy and immunology to urology. The AOA has approved 18 specialty boards, ranging from anesthesiology to surgery. For certification in a subspecialty, physicians usually need another one to two years of residency.

Other qualifications. People who wish to become physicians must have a desire to serve patients, be self-motivated, and be able to survive the pressures and long hours of medical education and practice. Physicians also must have a good bedside manner, emotional stability, and the ability to make decisions in emergencies. Prospective physicians must be willing to study throughout their career to keep up with medical advances.

Advancement. Some physicians and surgeons advance by gaining expertise in specialties and subspecialties and by developing a reputation for excellence among their peers and patients. Many physicians and surgeons start their own practice or join a group practice. Others teach residents and other new doctors, and some advance to supervisory and managerial roles in hospitals, clinics, and other settings.

Employment

Physicians and surgeons held about 633,000 jobs in 2006; approximately 15 percent were self-employed. About half of wage-and-salary physicians and surgeons worked in offices of physicians, and 18 percent were employed by hospitals. Others practiced in federal, state, and local governments, including colleges, universities, and professional schools; private colleges, universities, and professional schools; and outpatient care centers.

According to 2005 data from the American Medical Association (AMA), about one half of physicians in patient care were in primary care, but not in a subspecialty of primary care. (See table 1.)

Table 1. Percent distribution of active physicians in patient care by specialty, 2005

	Percent
Total	100.0
Primary care	40.4
Family medicine and general practice	12.3
Internal medicine	15.0
Obstetrics & gynecology	5.5
Pediatrics	7.5
Specialties	59.6
Anesthesiology	5.2
Psychiatry	5.1
Surgical specialties, selected	10.8
All other specialties	38.5

SOURCE: American Medical Association, Physician Characteristics and Distribution in the US, 2007.

A growing number of physicians are partners or wage-and-salary employees of group practices. Organized as clinics or as associations of physicians, medical groups can more easily afford expensive medical equipment, can share support staff, and benefit from other business advantages.

Projections data from the National Employment Matrix

Occupational Title	SOC Code	Employment, 2006	Projected employment, 2016	Change, 2006-2016	
				Number	Percent
Physicians and surgeons	29-1060	633,000	723,000	90,000	14

NOTE: Data in this table are rounded.

According to the AMA, the New England and Middle Atlantic states have the highest ratio of physicians to population; the South Central and Mountain states have the lowest. D.O.s are more likely than M.D.s to practice in small cities and towns and in rural areas. M.D.s tend to locate in urban areas, close to hospitals and education centers.

Job Outlook

Employment of physicians and surgeons is expected to grow faster than the average for all occupations. Job opportunities should be very good, especially for physicians and surgeons willing to practice in specialties—including family practice, internal medicine, and OB/GYN—or in rural and low-income areas where there is a perceived shortage of medical practitioners.

Employment change. Employment of physicians and surgeons is projected to grow 14 percent from 2006 to 2016, faster than the average for all occupations. Job growth will occur because of continued expansion of health care related industries. The growing and aging population will drive overall growth in the demand for physician services, as consumers continue to demand high levels of care using the latest technologies, diagnostic tests, and therapies.

Demand for physicians' services is highly sensitive to changes in consumer preferences, health care reimbursement policies, and legislation. For example, if changes to health coverage result in consumers facing higher out-of-pocket costs, they may demand fewer physician services. Patients relying more on other health care providers—such as physician assistants, nurse practitioners, optometrists, and nurse anesthetists—also may temper demand for physician services. In addition, new technologies will increase physician productivity. These technologies include electronic medical records, test and prescription orders, billing, and scheduling.

Job prospects. Opportunities for individuals interested in becoming physicians and surgeons are expected to be very good. In addition to job openings from employment growth, numerous openings will result from the need to replace physicians and surgeons who retire over the 2006–2016 decade.

Unlike their predecessors, newly trained physicians face radically different choices of where and how to practice. New physicians are much less likely to enter solo practice and more likely to take salaried jobs in group medical practices, clinics, and health networks.

Reports of shortages in some specialties, such as general or family practice, internal medicine, and OB/GYN, or in rural or low-income areas should attract new entrants, encouraging schools to expand programs and hospitals to increase available residency slots. However, because physician training is so lengthy, employment change happens gradually. In the short term, to meet increased demand, experienced physicians may work longer hours, delay retirement, or take measures to increase productivity, such as using more support staff to provide services. Opportunities should be particularly good in rural and low-income areas, as some physicians find these areas unattractive because of less control over work hours, isolation from medical colleagues, or other reasons.

Earnings

Earnings of physicians and surgeons are among the highest of any occupation. The Medical Group Management Association's Physician Compensation and Production Survey, reports that median total compensation for physicians in 2005 varied by specialty, as shown in table 2. Total compensation for physicians reflects the amount reported as direct compensation for tax purposes, plus all voluntary salary reductions. Salary, bonus and incentive payments, research stipends, honoraria, and distribution of profits were included in total compensation.

Table 2. Median compensation for physicians, 2005

Specialty	Less than two years in specialty	Over one year in specialty
Anesthesiology	$259,948	$321,686
Surgery: General	228,839	282,504
Obstetrics/gynecology: General	203,270	247,348
Psychiatry: General	173,922	180,000
Internal medicine: General	141,912	166,420
Pediatrics: General	132,953	161,331
Family practice (without obstetrics)	137,119	156,010

SOURCE: Medical Group Management Association, Physician Compensation and Production Report, 2005.

Self-employed physicians—those who own or are part owners of their medical practice—generally have higher median incomes than salaried physicians. Earnings vary according to number of years in practice, geographic region, hours worked, skill, personality, and professional reputation. Self-employed physicians and surgeons must provide for their own health insurance and retirement.

Related Occupations

Physicians work to prevent, diagnose, and treat diseases, disorders, and injuries. Other health care practitioners who need similar skills and who exercise critical judgment include chiropractors, dentists, optometrists, physician assistants, podiatrists, registered nurses, and veterinarians.

Sources of Additional Information

For a list of medical schools and residency programs, as well as general information on premedical education, financial aid, and medicine as a career, contact

- American Association of Colleges of Osteopathic Medicine, 5550 Friendship Blvd., Suite 310, Chevy Chase, MD 20815. Internet: http://www.aacom.org
- Association of American Medical Colleges, Section for Student Services, 2450 N St. NW, Washington, DC 20037. Internet: http://www.aamc.org/students

For general information on physicians, contact

- American Medical Association, 515 N. State St., Chicago, IL 60610. Internet: http://www.ama-assn.org
- American Osteopathic Association, Department of Communications, 142 East Ontario St., Chicago, IL 60611. Internet: http://www.osteopathic.org

For information about various medical specialties, contact

- American Academy of Family Physicians, Resident Student Activities Department, 11400 Tomahawk Creek Pkwy., Leawood, KS 66211. Internet: http://fmignet.aafp.org
- American Academy of Pediatrics, 141 Northwest Point Blvd., Elk Grove Village, IL 60007. Internet: http://www.aap.org
- American Board of Medical Specialties, 1007 Church St., Suite 404, Evanston, IL 60201. Internet: http://www.abms.org
- American College of Obstetricians and Gynecologists, 409 12th St. SW, P.O. Box 96920, Washington, DC 20090. Internet: http://www.acog.org
- American College of Physicians, 190 North Independence Mall West, Philadelphia, PA 19106. Internet: http://www.acponline.org
- American College of Surgeons, Division of Education, 633 North Saint Clair St., Chicago, IL 60611. Internet: http://www.facs.org
- American Psychiatric Association, 1000 Wilson Blvd., Suite 1825, Arlington, VA 22209. Internet: http://www.psych.org
- American Society of Anesthesiologists, 520 N. Northwest Hwy., Park Ridge, IL 60068. Internet: http://www.asahq.org/career/homepage.htm

Information on federal scholarships and loans is available from the directors of student financial aid at schools of medicine. Information on licensing is available from state boards of examiners.

Physicists and Astronomers

(O*NET 19-2011.00 and 19-2012.00)

Significant Points

- Scientific research and development services firms and the federal government employ over half of all physicists and astronomers.
- Most jobs are in basic research, usually requiring a doctoral degree; master's degree holders qualify for some jobs in applied research and development; bachelor's degree holders often qualify as research assistants or for other physics-related occupations, such as technicians.
- Applicants may face competition for basic research positions due to limited funding; however, those with a background in physics or astronomy may have good opportunities in related occupations.

Nature of the Work

Physicists and astronomers conduct research to understand the nature of the universe and everything in it. These researchers observe, measure, interpret, and develop theories to explain celestial and physical phenomena using mathematics. From the vastness of space to the infinitesimal scale of subatomic particles, they study the fundamental properties of the natural world and apply the knowledge gained to design new technologies.

Physicists explore and identify basic principles and laws governing the motion, energy, structure, and interactions of matter. Some physicists study theoretical areas, such as the nature of time and the origin of the universe; others apply their knowledge of physics to practical areas, such as the development of advanced materials, electronic and optical devices, and medical equipment.

Physicists design and perform experiments with lasers, particle accelerators, electron microscopes, mass spectrometers, and other equipment. On the basis of their observations and analysis, they attempt to discover and explain laws describing the forces of nature, such as gravity, electromagnetism, and nuclear interactions. Experiments also help physicists find ways to apply physical laws and theories to problems in nuclear energy, electronics, optics, materials, communications, aerospace technology, and medical instrumentation.

Astronomers use the principles of physics and mathematics to learn about the fundamental nature of the universe, including the sun, moon, planets, stars, and galaxies. As such, astronomy is sometimes considered a subfield of physics. They also apply their knowledge to solve problems in navigation, space flight, and satellite communications and to develop the instrumentation and techniques used to observe and collect astronomical data.

Most physicists work in research and development. Some do basic research to increase scientific knowledge. Others conduct applied research to build upon the discoveries made through basic research and work to develop new devices, products, and processes. For example, basic research in solid-state physics led to the development of transistors and, then, integrated circuits used in computers.

Physicists also design research equipment, which often has additional unanticipated uses. For example, lasers are used in surgery, microwave devices function in ovens, and measuring instruments can analyze blood or the chemical content of foods.

A small number of physicists work in inspection, testing, quality control, and other production-related jobs in industry.

Much physics research is done in small or medium-sized laboratories. However, experiments in plasma, nuclear, and high-energy physics, as well as in some other areas of physics, require extremely large, expensive equipment, such as particle accelerators. Physicists in these subfields often work in large teams. Although physics research may require extensive experimentation in laboratories, research physicists still spend much time in offices planning, recording, analyzing, and reporting on research.

Physicists generally specialize in one of many subfields: elementary particle physics, nuclear physics, atomic and molecular physics, condensed matter physics (solid-state physics), optics, acoustics, space physics, plasma physics, or the physics of fluids. Some specialize in a subdivision of one of these subfields. For example, within condensed-matter physics, specialties include superconductivity, crystallography, and semiconductors. However, all physics involves the same fundamental principles, so specialties may overlap, and physicists may switch from one subfield to another. Also, growing numbers of physicists work in interdisciplinary fields, such as biophysics, chemical physics, and geophysics.

Almost all astronomers do research. Some are theoreticians, working on the laws governing the structure and evolution of astronomical objects. Others analyze large quantities of data gathered by observatories and satellites and write scientific papers or reports on their findings. Some astronomers actually operate large space-based or ground-based telescopes, usually as part of a team. However, astronomers may spend only a few weeks each year making observations with optical telescopes, radio telescopes, and other instruments.

For many years, satellites and other space-based instruments, such as the Hubble space telescope, have provided prodigious amounts of astronomical data. New technology has lead to improvements in analytical techniques and instruments, such as computers and optical telescopes and mounts, and is creating a resurgence in ground-based research.

A small number of astronomers work in museums housing planetariums. These astronomers develop and revise programs presented to the public and may direct planetarium operations.

Work environment. Most physicists and astronomers do not encounter unusual hazards in their work. Some physicists temporarily work away from home at national or international facilities with unique equipment, such as particle accelerators. Astronomers who make observations with ground-based telescopes may spend many hours working in observatories; this work usually involves travel to remote locations and may require working at night. Physicists and astronomers whose work depends on grant money often are under pressure to write grant proposals to keep their work funded.

Physicists often work regular hours in laboratories and offices. At times, however, those who are deeply involved in research may work long or irregular hours. Astronomers may need to work at odd hours to observe celestial phenomena, particularly those working with ground-based telescopes.

Training, Other Qualifications, and Advancement

Because most jobs are in basic research and development, a doctoral degree is the usual educational requirement for physicists and astronomers. Master's degree holders qualify for some jobs in applied research and development, whereas bachelor's degree holders often qualify as research assistants or for other occupations related to physics.

Education and training. A Ph.D. degree in physics or closely related fiends is typically required for basic research positions, independent research in industry, faculty positions, and advancement to managerial positions. This prepares students for a career in research through rigorous training in theory, methodology, and mathematics. Most physicists specialize in a subfield during graduate school and continue working in that area afterwards.

Additional experience and training in a postdoctoral research appointment, although not required, is important for physicists and astronomers aspiring to permanent positions in basic research in universities and government laboratories. Many physics and astronomy Ph.D. holders ultimately teach at the college or university level.

Master's degree holders usually do not qualify for basic research positions, but may qualify for many kinds of jobs requiring a physics background, including positions in manufacturing and applied research and development. Increasingly, many master's degree programs are specifically preparing students for physics-related research and development that does not require a Ph.D. degree. These programs teach students specific research skills that can be used in private-industry jobs. In addition, a master's degree coupled with state certification usually qualifies one for teaching jobs in high schools or at two-year colleges.

Those with bachelor's degrees in physics are rarely qualified to fill positions in research or in teaching at the college level. They are, however, usually qualified to work as technicians or research assistants in engineering-related areas, in software development and other scientific fields, or in setting up computer networks and sophisticated laboratory equipment. Increasingly, some may qualify for applied research jobs in private industry or take on nontraditional physics roles, often in computer science, such as systems analysts or database administrators. Some become science teachers in secondary schools.

Holders of a bachelor's or master's degree in astronomy often enter an unrelated field. However, they are also qualified to work in planetariums running science shows, to assist astronomers doing research, and to operate space-based and ground-based telescopes and other astronomical instrumentation. (See the statements on engineers, geoscientists, computer programmers, computer scientists and database administrators, computer software engineers, and computer systems analysts elsewhere in this book.)

About 760 colleges and universities offer a bachelor's degree in physics. Undergraduate programs provide a broad background in the natural sciences and mathematics. Typical physics courses include electromagnetism, optics, thermodynamics, atomic physics, and quantum mechanics.

Approximately 185 colleges and universities have departments offering Ph.D. degrees in physics; about 70 additional colleges offer a master's as their highest degree in physics. Graduate students usually concentrate in a subfield of physics, such as elementary particles or condensed matter. Many begin studying for their doctorate immediately after receiving their bachelor's degree.

About 80 universities grant degrees in astronomy, either through an astronomy, physics, or combined physics-astronomy department. Currently, about 40 astronomy departments are combined with physics departments, and the same number are administered separately. With about 40 doctoral programs in astronomy, applicants face considerable competition for available slots. Those planning a career in the subject should have a strong physics background. In fact, an undergraduate degree in either physics or astronomy is excellent preparation, followed by a Ph.D. in astronomy.

Many physics and astronomy Ph.D. holders begin their careers in a postdoctoral research position, in which they may work with experienced physicists as they continue to learn about their specialties or develop a broader understanding of related areas of research. Initial work may be under the close supervision of senior scientists. As they gain experience, physicists perform increasingly complex tasks and achieve greater independence in their work. Experience, either in academic laboratories or through internships, fellowships, or work-study programs in industry, also is useful. Some employers of research physicists, particularly in the information technology industry, prefer to hire individuals with several years of postdoctoral experience.

Other qualifications. Mathematical ability, problem-solving and analytical skills, an inquisitive mind, imagination, and initiative are important traits for anyone planning a career in physics or astronomy. Prospective physicists who hope to work in industrial laboratories applying physics knowledge to practical problems should broaden their educational background to include courses outside of physics, such as economics, information technology, and business management. Good oral and written communication skills also are important because many physicists work as part of a team, write research papers or proposals, or have contact with clients or customers with nonphysics backgrounds.

Advancement. Advancement among physicists and astronomers usually takes the form of greater independence in their work, larger budgets, or tenure in university positions. Others choose to move into managerial positions and become natural science managers (described elsewhere in this book). Those who pursue management careers spend more time preparing budgets and schedules. Those who develop new products or processes sometimes form their own companies or join new firms to develop these ideas.

Employment

Physicists and astronomers held about 18,000 jobs in 2006. Physicists accounted for about 17,000 of these, while astronomers accounted for only about 1,700 jobs. Many physicists and astronomers held faculty positions in colleges and universities. Those classified as postsecondary teachers are not included in these employment numbers. (See the statement on teachers—postsecondary elsewhere in this book.)

About 38 percent of physicists and astronomers worked for scientific research and development services firms. The federal government employed 21 percent, mostly in the U.S. Department of Defense, but also in the National Aeronautics and Space Administration (NASA) and in the U.S. Departments of Commerce, Health and Human Services, and Energy. Other physicists and astronomers worked in colleges and universities in nonfaculty, usually research, positions, or for state governments, information technology companies, pharmaceutical and medicine manufacturing companies, or electronic equipment manufacturers.

Although physicists and astronomers are employed in all parts of the country, most work in areas in which universities, large research laboratories, or observatories are located.

Job Outlook

Physicists and astronomers should experience average job growth but may face competition for basic research positions due to limited funding. However, those with a background in physics or astronomy may have good opportunities in related occupations.

Employment change. Employment of physicists and astronomers is expected to grow at 7 percent, about as fast as the average for all occupations during the 2006–2016 decade. The need to replace physicists and astronomers who retire or otherwise leave the occupation permanently will account for many additional expected job openings.

Federal research expenditures are the major source of physics- and astronomy-related research funds, especially for basic research. Although these expenditures are expected to increase over the 2006–2016 projection period, resulting in some growth in employment and opportunities, the limited science research funds available still will result in competition for basic research jobs among Ph.D. holders. However, research relating to biotechnology and nanotechnology should continue to see strong growth.

Although research and development expenditures in private industry will continue to grow, many research laboratories in private industry are expected to continue to reduce basic research, which includes much physics research, in favor of applied or manufacturing research and product and software development. Nevertheless, people with a physics background continue to be in demand in information technology, semiconductor technology, and other applied sciences. This trend is expected to continue; however, many of the new workers will have job titles such as computer software engineer, computer programmer, or systems analyst or developer, rather than physicist.

Job prospects. In recent years the number of doctorates granted in physics has been somewhat greater than the number of job openings for traditional physics research positions in colleges and universities and in research centers. Recent increases in undergraduate physics enrollments may also lead to growth in enrollments in graduate physics programs, so that there may be an increase in the number of doctoral degrees granted that could intensify the competition for basic research positions. However, demand has grown in other related occupations for those with advanced training in physics. Prospects should be favorable for physicists in applied research, development, and related technical fields.

Opportunities should also be numerous for those with a master's degree, particularly graduates from programs preparing students for related work in applied research and development, product design, and manufacturing positions in private industry. Many of these positions, however, will have titles other than physicist, such as engineer or computer scientist.

People with only a bachelor's degree in physics or astronomy are usually not qualified for physics or astronomy research jobs, but they may qualify for a wide range of positions related to engineering, mathematics, computer science, environmental science, and some nonscience fields, such as finance. Those who meet state certification requirements can become high school physics teachers, an occupation in strong demand in many school districts. Some states require new teachers to obtain a master's degree in education within a certain time. Despite competition for traditional physics and astronomy research jobs, graduates with a physics or astronomy degree at any level will find their knowledge of science and mathematics useful for entry into many other occupations.

Despite their small numbers, astronomers can expect good job prospects in government and academia over the projection period.

Projections data from the National Employment Matrix

Occupational Title	SOC Code	Employment, 2006	Projected employment, 2016	Change, 2006-2016	
				Number	Percent
Astronomers and physicists	19-2010	18,000	19,000	1,200	7
Astronomers	19-2011	1,700	1,700	100	6
Physicists	19-2012	17,000	18,000	1,100	7

NOTE: Data in this table are rounded.

Since astronomers are particularly dependent upon government funding, federal budgetary decisions will have a sizable influence on job prospects for astronomers.

Earnings

Median annual earnings of physicists were 94,240 in May 2006. The middle 50 percent earned between $72,910 and $117,080. The lowest 10 percent earned less than $52,070, and the highest 10 percent earned 143,570.

Median annual earnings of astronomers were $95,740 in 2006. The middle 50 percent earned between $62,050 and $125,420, the lowest 10 percent less than $44,590, and the highest 10 percent more than $145,600.

According to a 2007 National Association of Colleges and Employers survey, the average annual starting salary offer to physics doctoral degree candidates was $52,469.

The American Institute of Physics reported a median annual salary of $80,000 in 2006 for its members with Ph.D.'s (excluding those in postdoctoral positions) who were employed by a university on a 9-10 month salary; the median was $112,700 for those who held a Ph.D. and worked at a federally funded research and development center; and $110,000 for self-employed physicists who hold a Ph.D. Those working in temporary postdoctoral positions earned significantly less.

The average annual salary for physicists employed by the federal government was $111,769 in 2007; for astronomy and space scientists, it was $117,570.

Related Occupations

The work of physicists and astronomers relates closely to that of engineers, chemists and materials scientists, atmospheric scientists, environmental scientists and hydrologists, geoscientists, computer systems analysts, computer scientists and database administrators, computer programmers, mathematicians, and engineering and natural sciences managers.

Sources of Additional Information

Further information on career opportunities in physics is available from the following organizations:

- American Institute of Physics, Career Services Division and Education and Employment Division, One Physics Ellipse, College Park, MD 20740-3843. Internet: http://www.aip.org
- American Physical Society, One Physics Ellipse, College Park, MD 20740-3844. Internet: http://www.aps.org

Podiatrists

(O*NET 29-1081.00)

Significant Points

- Podiatrists must be licensed, requiring 3 to 4 years of undergraduate education, the completion of a 4-year podiatric college program, and passing scores on national and state examinations.
- While the occupation is small, job opportunities should be good for entry-level graduates of accredited podiatric medicine programs.
- Opportunities for newly trained podiatrists will be better in group medical practices, clinics, and health networks than in traditional, solo practices.
- Podiatrists enjoy very high earnings.

Nature of the Work

Americans spend a great deal of time on their feet. As the nation becomes more active across all age groups, the need for foot care will become increasingly important.

The human foot is a complex structure. It contains 26 bones—plus muscles, nerves, ligaments, and blood vessels—and is designed for balance and mobility. The 52 bones in the feet make up about one-fourth of all the bones in the human body. Podiatrists, also known as *doctors of podiatric medicine* (DPMs), diagnose and treat disorders, diseases, and injuries of the foot and lower leg.

Podiatrists treat corns, calluses, ingrown toenails, bunions, heel spurs, and arch problems; ankle and foot injuries, deformities, and infections; and foot complaints associated with diabetes and other diseases. To treat these problems, podiatrists prescribe drugs and physical therapy, set fractures, and perform surgery. They also fit corrective shoe inserts called orthotics, design plaster casts and strappings to correct deformities, and design custom-made shoes. Podiatrists may use a force plate or scanner to help design the orthotics: patients walk across a plate connected to a computer that "reads" their feet, picking up pressure points and weight distribution. From the computer readout, podiatrists order the correct design or recommend another kind of treatment.

To diagnose a foot problem, podiatrists also order x rays and laboratory tests. The foot may be the first area to show signs of serious conditions such as arthritis, diabetes, and heart disease. For example, patients with diabetes are prone to foot ulcers and infections because of poor circulation. Podiatrists consult with and refer patients to other health practitioners when they detect symptoms of these disorders.

Most podiatrists have a solo practice, although more are forming group practices with other podiatrists or health practitioners. Some specialize in surgery, orthopedics, primary care, or public health. Besides these board-certified specialties, podiatrists may practice other specialties, such as sports medicine, pediatrics, dermatology, radiology, geriatrics, or diabetic foot care.

Podiatrists who are in private practice are responsible for running a small business. They may hire employees, order supplies, and keep records, among other tasks. In addition, some educate the community on the benefits of foot care through speaking engagements and advertising.

Work environment. Podiatrists usually work in small private offices or clinics, sometimes supported by a small staff of assistants and other administrative personnel. They also may spend time visiting patients in nursing homes or performing surgery at hospitals or ambulatory surgical centers. Podiatrists with private practices set their own hours but may work evenings and weekends to accommodate their patients. Podiatrists usually treat fewer emergencies than other doctors.

Training, Other Qualifications, and Advancement

Podiatrists must be licensed, requiring three to four years of undergraduate education, the completion of a four-year podiatric college program, and passing scores on national and state examinations.

Education and training. Prerequisites for admission to a college of podiatric medicine include the completion of at least 90 semester hours of undergraduate study, an acceptable grade point average, and suitable scores on the Medical College Admission Test. (Some colleges also may accept the Dental Admission Test or the Graduate Record Exam.)

Admission to podiatric colleges usually requires at least eight semester hours each of biology, inorganic chemistry, organic chemistry, and physics and at least six hours of English. The science courses should be those designed for premedical students. Extracurricular and community activities, personal interviews, and letters of recommendation are also important. About 95 percent of podiatric students have at least a bachelor's degree.

In 2007, there were seven colleges of podiatric medicine fully accredited by the Council on Podiatric Medical Education. Colleges of podiatric medicine offer a four-year program whose core curriculum is similar to that in other schools of medicine. During the first two years, students receive classroom instruction in basic sciences, including anatomy, chemistry, pathology, and pharmacology. Third-year and fourth-year students have clinical rotations in private practices, hospitals, and clinics. During these rotations, they learn how to take general and podiatric histories, perform routine physical examinations, interpret tests and findings, make diagnoses, and perform therapeutic procedures. Graduates receive the degree of Doctor of Podiatric Medicine (DPM).

Most graduates complete a hospital-based residency program after receiving a DPM. Residency programs last from two to four years. Residents receive advanced training in podiatric medicine and surgery and serve clinical rotations in anesthesiology, internal medicine, pathology, radiology, emergency medicine, and orthopedic and general surgery. Residencies lasting more than one year provide more extensive training in specialty areas.

Licensure. All states and the District of Columbia require a license for the practice of podiatric medicine. Each state defines its own licensing requirements, although many states grant reciprocity to podiatrists who are licensed in another state. Applicants for licensure must be graduates of an accredited college of podiatric medicine and must pass written and oral examinations. Some states permit applicants to substitute the examination of the National Board of Podiatric Medical Examiners, given in the second and fourth years of podiatric medical college, for part or all of the written state examination. In general, states require a minimum of two years of postgraduate residency training in an approved health care institution. For licensure renewal, most states require continuing education.

Other qualifications. People planning a career in podiatry should have scientific aptitude, manual dexterity, interpersonal skills, and a friendly bedside manner. In private practice, podiatrists also should have good business sense.

Certification and advancement. There are a number of certifying boards for the podiatric specialties of orthopedics, primary medicine, and surgery. Certification has requirements beyond licensure. Each board requires advanced training, the completion of written and oral examinations, and experience as a practicing podiatrist. Most managed-care organizations prefer board-certified podiatrists.

Podiatrists may advance to become professors at colleges of podiatric medicine, department chiefs in hospitals, or general health administrators.

Employment

Podiatrists held about 12,000 jobs in 2006. About 24 percent of podiatrists were self-employed. Most podiatrists were solo practitioners, although more are entering group practices with other podiatrists or other health practitioners. Solo practitioners primarily were unincorporated self-employed workers, although some also were incorporated wage and salary workers in offices of other health practitioners. Other podiatrists were employed by hospitals, long-term care facilities, the federal government, and municipal health departments.

Job Outlook

Employment is expected to increase about as fast as average because of increasing consumer demand for podiatric medicine services. Job prospects should be good.

Employment change. Employment of podiatrists is expected to increase 9 percent from 2006 to 2016, about as fast as the average for all occupations. More people will turn to podiatrists for foot care because of the rising number of injuries sustained by a more active and increasingly older population.

Medicare and most private health insurance programs cover acute medical and surgical foot services, as well as diagnostic x rays and leg braces. Details of such coverage vary among plans. However, routine foot care, including the removal of corns and calluses, is not usually covered unless the patient has a systemic condition that has resulted in severe circulatory problems or areas of desensitization in the legs or feet. Like dental services, podiatric care is often discretionary and, therefore, more dependent on disposable income than some other medical services.

Employment of podiatrists would grow even faster were it not for continued emphasis on controlling the costs of specialty health care. Insurers will balance the cost of sending patients to podiatrists against the cost and availability of substitute practitioners, such as physicians and physical therapists.

Job prospects. Although the occupation is small and most podiatrists continue to practice until retirement, job opportunities should be good for entry-level graduates of accredited podiatric medicine

Projections data from the National Employment Matrix

Occupational Title	SOC Code	Employment, 2006	Projected employment, 2016	Change, 2006-2016	
				Number	Percent
Podiatrists	29-1081	12,000	13,000	1,100	9

NOTE: Data in this table are rounded.

programs. Job growth and replacement needs should create enough job openings for the supply of new podiatric medicine graduates. Opportunities will be better for board-certified podiatrists because many managed-care organizations require board certification. Newly trained podiatrists will find more opportunities in group medical practices, clinics, and health networks than in traditional solo practices. Establishing a practice will be most difficult in the areas surrounding colleges of podiatric medicine, where podiatrists concentrate.

Earnings

Podiatrists enjoy very high earnings. Median annual earnings of salaried podiatrists were $108,220 in 2006. Additionally, a survey by *Podiatry Management Magazine* reported median net income of $114,000 in 2006. Podiatrists in partnerships tended to earn higher net incomes than those in solo practice. A salaried podiatrist typically receives heath insurance and retirement benefits from their employer, whereas self-employed chiropractors must provide for their own health insurance and retirement. Also, solo practitioners must absorb the costs of running their own offices.

Related Occupations

Other workers, who apply medical knowledge to prevent, diagnose, and treat muscle and bone disorders and injuries include athletic trainers, chiropractors, massage therapists, occupational therapists, physical therapists, and physicians and surgeons. Workers who specialize in developing orthopedic shoe inserts, braces, and prosthetic limbs are orthotists and prosthetists.

Sources of Additional Information

For information on a career in podiatric medicine, contact

- American Podiatric Medical Association, 9312 Old Georgetown Rd., Bethesda, MD 20814-1621. Internet: http://www.apma.org

Information on colleges of podiatric medicine and their entrance requirements, curricula, and student financial aid is available from

- American Association of Colleges of Podiatric Medicine, 15850 Crabbs Branch Way, Suite 320, Rockville, MD 20855-2622. Internet: http://www.aacpm.org

Power Plant Operators, Distributors, and Dispatchers

(O*NET 51-8011.00, 51-8012.00, and 51-8013.00)

Significant Points

- Job prospects are expected to be good as many workers retire and new plants are built.
- Most entry-level workers start as helpers or laborers, and several years of training and experience are required to become fully qualified.
- Familiarity with computers and a basic understanding of science and math is helpful for those entering the field.

Nature of the Work

Electricity is vital for most everyday activities. From the moment you flip the first switch each morning, you are connecting to a huge network of people, electric lines, and generating equipment. Power plant operators control the machinery that generates electricity. Power plant distributors and dispatchers control the flow of electricity from the power plant, over a network of transmission lines, to industrial plants and substations, and, finally, over distribution lines to residential users.

Power plant operators control and monitor boilers, turbines, generators, and auxiliary equipment in power-generating plants. Operators distribute power demands among generators, combine the current from several generators, and monitor instruments to maintain voltage and regulate electricity flows from the plant. When power requirements change, these workers start or stop generators and connect or disconnect them from circuits. They often use computers to keep records of switching operations and loads on generators, lines, and transformers. Operators also may use computers to prepare reports of unusual incidents, malfunctioning equipment, or maintenance performed during their shift.

Operators in plants with automated control systems work mainly in a central control room and usually are called *control room operators* or *control room operator trainees* or *assistants*. In older plants, the controls for the equipment are not centralized; *switchboard operators* control the flow of electricity from a central point, while *auxiliary equipment operators* work throughout the plant, operating and monitoring valves, switches, and gauges.

In nuclear power plants, most operators start working as *equipment operators* or *auxiliary operators*. They help the more senior workers with equipment maintenance and operation while learning the basics of plant operation. With experience and training they may be licensed by the Nuclear Regulatory Commission as *reactor operators* and authorized to control equipment that affects the power of the reactor in a nuclear power plant. *Senior reactor operators* supervise the operation of all controls in the control room. At least one senior operator must be on duty during each shift to act as the plant supervisor.

Power distributors and dispatchers, also called *load dispatchers* or *systems operators*, control the flow of electricity through transmission lines to industrial plants and substations that supply residential needs for electricity. They monitor and operate current converters, voltage transformers, and circuit breakers. Dispatchers also monitor other distribution equipment and record readings at a pilot board—a map of the transmission grid system showing the status of transmission circuits and connections with substations and industrial plants.

Dispatchers also anticipate power needs, such as those caused by changes in the weather. They call control room operators to start or stop boilers and generators, in order to bring production into balance with needs. Dispatchers handle emergencies such as transformer or transmission line failures and route current around affected areas. In substations, they also operate and monitor equipment that increases or decreases voltage, and they operate switchboard levers to control the flow of electricity in and out of the substations.

Work environment. Operators, distributors, and dispatchers who work in control rooms generally sit or stand at a control station. This work is not physically strenuous, but it does require constant attention. Operators who work outside the control room may be exposed to danger from electric shock, falls, and burns.

Nuclear power plant operators are subject to random drug and alcohol tests, as are most workers at such plants. Additionally, they have to pass a medical examination every two years and may be exposed to small amounts of ionizing radiation as part of their jobs.

Because electricity is provided around the clock, operators, distributors, and dispatchers usually work one of three 8-hour shifts or one of two 12-hour shifts on a rotating basis. Shift assignments may change periodically, so that all operators share less desirable shifts. Work on rotating shifts can be stressful and fatiguing because of the constant change in living and sleeping patterns.

Training, Other Qualifications, and Advancement

Power plant operators, dispatchers, and distributors generally need a combination of education, on-the-job training, and experience. Candidates with strong computer and technical skills are generally preferred.

Education and training. Employers often seek recent high school graduates for entry-level operator, distributor, and dispatcher positions. Workers with college or vocational school degrees will have more advancement opportunities, especially in nuclear power plants. Although it is not a prerequisite, many senior reactor operators have a bachelor's degree in engineering or the physical sciences.

Workers selected for training as power plant operators or distributors undergo extensive on-the-job and classroom instruction. Several years of training and experience are required for a worker to become a fully qualified control room operator or power plant distributor.

In addition to receiving initial training to become fully qualified as a power plant operator, distributor, or dispatcher, most workers are given periodic refresher training—especially the nuclear power plant operators. Refresher training usually is taken on plant simulators designed specifically to replicate procedures and situations that might be encountered at the trainee's plant.

Licensure. Power plant operators, distributors, and dispatchers may need licenses depending on jurisdiction and specific job function. Requirements vary greatly from place to place and may be administered by state, county, or local governments.

Extensive training and experience are necessary to pass the Nuclear Regulatory Commission (NRC) examinations required for nuclear reactor operators and senior nuclear reactor operators. Before beginning training, a nuclear power plant worker must have three years of power plant experience. At least six months of this must be on-site at the nuclear power plant where the operator is to be licensed. Training generally takes at least one year, after which the worker must take an NRC-administered examination. To maintain their licenses, reactor operators must pass an annual practical plant operation exam and a biennial written exam administered by their employers. Reactor operators can upgrade their licenses to the senior reactor operator level after a year of licensed experience at the plant by taking another examination given by the NRC. Training may include simulator and on-the-job training, classroom instruction, and individual study. Experience in other power plants or with Navy nuclear propulsion plants also is helpful.

Advancement. Most entry-level workers start as helpers or laborers and advance to more responsible positions as they become comfortable in the plant. In many cases, there are mandatory waiting times between starting a position and advancing to the next level due to licensing requirements. With sufficient training and experience, workers can become shift supervisors or, in nuclear power plants, senior reactor operators.

Because power plants have different systems and safety mechanisms, it is often very difficult to advance by changing companies or plants. Most utilities promote from within; most workers advance within a particular plant or by moving to another plant owned by the same utility.

Employment

Power plant operators, distributors, and dispatchers held about 47,000 jobs in 2006, of which 3,800 were nuclear power plant operators, 8,600 were power distributors and dispatchers, and 35,000 were other power plant operators. Jobs were located throughout the country. About 70 percent of jobs were in electric power generation, transmission, and distribution. About 16 percent worked in government, mainly in local government. Others worked for manufacturing establishments that produced electricity for their own use.

Job Outlook

Employment of power plant operators, distributors, and dispatchers is projected to experience little or no employment change, but job opportunities are expected to be very good due to the large number of retiring workers who must be replaced, increased demand for energy, and recent legislation which paves the way for a number of new plants.

Employment change. Between 2006 and 2016, employment of power plant operators, distributors, and dispatchers is projected to experience little or no employment change, growing by about 2 percent. Electric utilities are expected to build new power plants in response to the Energy Policy Act of 2005, which provides a number of subsidies. Growth will be tempered by a continued emphasis on cost reduction and automation. Although new power plants will require fewer workers than their older counterparts, the machinery in the new plants will be more technologically complex and environmental regulations will require much closer attention to emissions, so workers will be required to have higher skill levels.

Projections data from the National Employment Matrix

Occupational Title	SOC Code	Employment, 2006	Projected employment, 2016	Change, 2006-16	
				Number	Percent
Power plant operators, distributors, and dispatchers	51-8010	47,000	48,000	900	2
Nuclear power reactor operators	51-8011	3,800	4,200	400	11
Power distributors and dispatchers	51-8012	8,600	8,200	-400	-5
Power plant operators	51-8013	35,000	36,000	900	3

NOTE: Data in this table are rounded.

Job prospects. Job opportunities are expected to be very good for people who are interested in becoming power plant operators, distributors, and dispatchers. During the 1990s, the emphasis on cost cutting among utilities led to hiring freezes and the laying off of younger workers. The result is an aging workforce, half of which is expected to retire within the next 10 years. Utilities have responded by setting up new education programs at community colleges and high schools throughout the country. Prospects should be especially good for people with computer skills and a basic understanding of science and mathematics.

Earnings

Median annual earnings of power plant operators were $55,000 in May 2006. The middle 50 percent earned between $45,110 and $65,460. The lowest 10 percent earned less than $35,590, and the highest 10 percent earned more than $75,240.

Median annual earnings of nuclear power reactor operators were $69,370 in May 2006. The middle 50 percent earned between $61,590 and $78,150. The lowest 10 percent earned less than $54,180, and the highest 10 percent earned more than $92,240.

Median annual earnings of power distributors and dispatchers were $62,590 in May 2006. The middle 50 percent earned between $52,510 and $73,920. The lowest 10 percent earned less than $42,370, and the highest 10 percent earned more than $85,740.

Related Occupations

Other workers who monitor and operate plant and system equipment include chemical plant and system operators; petroleum pump system operators, refinery operators, and gaugers; stationary engineers and boiler operators; and water and liquid waste treatment plant and system operators.

Sources of Additional Information

For information about employment opportunities, contact local electric utility companies, local unions, and state employment service offices.

For general information about power plant operators, nuclear power reactor operators, and power plant distributors and dispatchers, contact

- American Public Power Association, 2301 M St. NW, Washington, DC 20037-1484. Internet: http://www.appanet.org
- International Brotherhood of Electrical Workers, 1125 15th St. NW, Washington, DC 20005.
- National Association of Power Engineers, Inc., 1 Springfield St., Chicopee, MA 01013.

Information on licensing for nuclear reactor operators and senior reactor operators is available from

- Nuclear Regulatory Commission, Washington, DC 20555-0001. Internet: http://www.nrc.gov

Precision Instrument and Equipment Repairers

(O*NET 49-9061.00, 49-9062.00, 49-9063.00, 49-9064.00, and 49-9069.99)

Significant Points

- Training requirements include a high school diploma and, in most cases, postsecondary education, coupled with significant on-the-job training.
- Overall employment is expected to grow about as fast as average, and good opportunities are expected for most types of jobs.
- About 1 out of 6 are self-employed.

Nature of the Work

Repairing and maintaining watches, cameras, musical instruments, medical equipment, and other precision instruments requires a high level of skill and attention to detail. Some devices contain tiny gears that must be manufactured to within one one-hundredth of a millimeter of design specifications, and other devices contain sophisticated electronic controls. Job descriptions vary greatly, depending on the type of instrument being repaired.

Camera and photographic equipment repairers fix broken cameras and other optical devices. The repairer must first determine whether a repair should be attempted, because many inexpensive cameras cost more to repair than to replace. The most complicated or expensive repairs are usually referred back to the manufacturer or to a large repair center. If the repairer decides to proceed with the job, the problem must be diagnosed, often by disassembling numerous small parts in order to reach the source. The defective parts are then replaced or repaired. Many problems are caused by the electronic circuits used in cameras, and fixing these circuits requires an understanding of electronics. Camera repairers also maintain cameras by removing and replacing broken or worn parts and cleaning and lubricating gears and springs. Because many of the components involved are extremely small, repairers must have a great deal of manual dexterity. Frequently, older camera parts are no longer available, requiring repairers to build replacement parts or to strip junked cameras. When machining new parts, workers often use a small lathe, a grinding wheel, and other metalworking tools.

Repairs on digital cameras are similar to those on conventional cameras, but because digital cameras have no film to wind, they have fewer moving parts. Digital cameras rely on software, so any repair to the lens requires that it be calibrated with the use of software and by connecting the camera to a personal computer. Because digital cameras are generally more expensive and more widely used than film cameras, they are quickly becoming the most important source of business for camera repairers.

Watch and clock repairers work almost exclusively on expensive and antique timepieces, because moderately priced timepieces are cheaper to replace than to repair. Electrically powered clocks and quartz watches and clocks function with almost no moving parts, limiting necessary maintenance to replacing the battery. Many expensive timepieces still employ old-style mechanical movements and a manual or automatic winding mechanism. This type of timepiece must be regularly adjusted and maintained. Repair and maintenance work on a mechanical timepiece requires using hand tools to disassemble many fine gears and components. Each part is inspected for signs of wear. Some gears or springs may need to be replaced or machined. Exterior portions of the watch may require polishing and buffing. Specialized machines are used to clean all of

the parts with ultrasonic waves and a series of baths in cleaning agents. Reassembling a watch often requires lubricating key parts.

As with older cameras, replacement parts are frequently unavailable for antique watches or clocks. In such cases, watch repairers must machine their own parts. They employ small lathes and other machines in creating tiny parts.

Musical instrument repairers and tuners combine their love of music with a highly skilled craft. These artisans, often referred to as technicians, work in four specialties: Band instruments, pianos and organs, orchestral string instruments, and guitars. (Repairers and tuners who work on electronic organs are discussed in this book's profile of electronic home entertainment equipment installers and repairers.)

Band instrument repairers, *brass and wind instrument repairers*, and *percussion instrument repairers* focus on woodwind, brass, reed, and percussion instruments damaged through deterioration or by accident. In most cases, the problem with the instrument will be clear, but in some cases the repairers must diagnose the issue. They may unscrew and remove rod pins, keys, worn cork pads, and pistons and remove soldered parts by means of gas torches. Using filling techniques or a mallet, they repair dents in metal and wood. They also use gas torches, grinding wheels, lathes, shears, mallets, and small hand tools and, are skilled in metalworking and woodworking.

Violin and guitar repairers adjust and repair stringed instruments. Some repairers work on both stringed and band instruments. Initially, repairers play and inspect the instrument to find any defects. They replace or repair cracked or broken sections and damaged parts. They also restring the instruments and repair damage to their finish. Because the specifications of all types of instruments vary greatly, custom parts machining is considered an essential skill.

Piano tuners and repairers use different techniques, skills, and tools. Most workers in this group are tuners; only a few workers in this occupation specialize in refurbishing older pianos. Tuning involves tightening and loosening different strings to achieve the proper tone or pitch. Pitch matching is usually done by ear—an experienced tuner can compare the sound of a pitch with a tuning fork, and then with other pitches on the piano to make sure it is tuned properly. Tuners must make house calls, as piano tuning is sensitive to movement and most pianos cannot be transported easily. Some repairers specialize in restoring older pianos. Restoration is complicated work, often involving replacing many of the parts, which number more than 12,000 in some pianos. With proper maintenance and restoration, pianos often survive more than 100 years.

Pipe organ repairers do work similar to that of piano repairers, but with organ pipes rather than piano strings. Tuning pipe organs is very complicated, as most organs have thousands of pipes, and different pipes are tuned in different ways. Additionally, many repairers assemble new organs or expand organs with new ranks of pipes. Even with repairers working in teams or with assistants, organ maintenance can take several weeks or even months, depending upon the size of the organ.

Medical equipment repairers, also known as *biomedical equipment technicians*, maintain, adjust, calibrate, and repair electronic, electromechanical, and hydraulic equipment used in hospitals and other medical environments. They use various tools, including multimeters, specialized software, and computers designed to communicate with specific pieces of hardware. These repairers use hand tools, soldering irons, and other electronic tools to repair and adjust equipment. Among the tools they use is equipment designed to simulate water or air pressure. Faulty circuit boards and other parts are normally removed and replaced. Medical equipment repairers must maintain careful, detailed logs of all maintenance and repair that they perform on each piece of equipment.

Medical equipment repairers work on medical equipment such as defibrillators, heart monitors, medical imaging equipment (x-rays, CAT scanners, and ultrasound equipment), voice-controlled operating tables, and electric wheelchairs. Because most equipment repairs take place within a hospital, medical equipment repairers must be comfortable working around patients. In some cases, repairs may take place while equipment is being used. When this is the case, the repairer must take great care to make sure that repairs do not disturb the patient.

Other precision instrument and equipment repairers service, repair, and replace a wide range of equipment associated with automated or instrument-controlled manufacturing processes. For most of these repairers, the emphasis is on determining the problem and how to best approach the solution. In many cases, replacement is preferable to repair, since precision parts are often very sensitive and may cost more to repair than replace. Replacement parts are not always available, so repairers sometimes machine or fabricate new parts. Repairers may also be responsible for preventive maintenance and calibration, which involves regular lubrication, cleaning, and adjustment of many measuring devices. Increasingly, it also involves solving computer software problems as more control devices, such as valves, are controlled by software. To adjust a control device, a technician may need to connect a laptop computer to the control device's computer and make adjustments through changes to the software commands.

Work environment. Camera, watch, and musical instrument repairers work under fairly similar solitary, low-stress conditions with minimal supervision. A quiet, well-lit workshop or repair shop is typical. Piano and organ tuners must travel to the instruments being repaired. Often, these workers can adjust their schedules, allowing for second jobs as needed. Musical instrument repairer jobs are attractive to many professional musicians and retirees because the flexible hours common to repair work allow these individuals time for other pursuits.

Medical equipment and other precision instrument and equipment repairers normally work daytime hours, but are often expected to be on call. Still, like other hospital and factory employees, some repairers work irregular hours. Medical equipment repairers must work in a patient environment, which has the potential to expose them to diseases and other health risks, but occupational injuries are relatively uncommon.

Precision instrument repairers work under a wide array of conditions, from hot, dirty, noisy factories, to air-conditioned workshops, to the outdoors on fieldwork. Attention to safety is essential, as the work sometimes involves dangerous machinery, toxic chemicals, or radiation. Due to the individualized nature of the work, supervision is fairly minimal.

Training, Other Qualifications, and Advancement

For most precision equipment repairers, the most significant source of postsecondary education is on-the-job training. Even in positions where an associate or bachelor's degree is required, an internship or apprenticeship is generally required before a technician is fully qualified. In some cases, learning these trades can take as many as seven years.

Education and training. Most employers require at least a high school diploma for beginning precision instrument and equipment repairers. Many employers prefer applicants with some postsecondary education.

The educational background required for camera and photographic equipment repairers varies, but some knowledge of electronics is necessary. Some workers complete postsecondary training, such as an associate degree, in electronics. The job requires the ability to read electronic schematic diagrams and comprehend other technical information, in addition to manual dexterity. New employees are trained on the job in two stages over about a year. First, they learn to repair a single product over a couple of weeks. Then, they learn to repair other products and refine their skills for six to 12 months while working under the close supervision of an experienced repairer. Finally, repairers continually teach themselves through studying manuals and attending manufacturer-sponsored seminars on the specifics of new models.

Training also varies for watch and clock repairers. Several associations, including the American Watchmakers-Clockmakers Institute and the National Association of Watch and Clock Collectors, offer certifications. Some certifications can be completed in a few months; others require simply passing an examination; the most demanding certifications require 3,000 hours, taken over two years, of classroom time in technical institutes or colleges. Those who have earned the most demanding certifications are usually the most sought-after by employers. Clock repairers generally require less training than do watch repairers, because watches have smaller components and require greater precision. Some repairers opt to learn through assisting a master watch repairer. Nevertheless, developing proficiency in watch or clock repair requires several years of education and experience.

For musical instrument repairers and tuners, employers prefer individuals with post-high school training in music repair technology. According to a Piano Technicians Guild membership survey, the overwhelming majority of respondents had at least some college education; most had a bachelor's or higher degree, although not always in music repair technology. Almost all repairers have a strong musical background; many are musicians themselves. Also, a basic ability to play the instruments being repaired is normally required. Courses in instrument repair are offered only at a few technical schools and colleges. Correspondence courses are common for piano tuners. Graduates of these programs normally receive additional training on the job, working with an experienced repairer. Many musical instrument repairers and tuners begin learning their trade on the job as assistants or apprentices. Trainees perform a variety of tasks around the shop. Full qualification usually requires two to five years of training and practice. Musical instrument repair and tuning requires good manual dexterity, a strong sense of pitch, and good hand-eye coordination.

Medical equipment repairers' training includes on-the-job training, manufacturer training classes, and associate degree programs. While an associate degree in electronics or medical technology is normally required, training varies by specialty. For those with a background in electronics, on-the-job training is more common for workers repairing less electronically sophisticated equipment, such as hospital beds or electric wheelchairs. An associate or even a bachelor's degree, often in medical technology or engineering, and a passing grade on a certification exam is likely to be required of persons repairing more complicated equipment, such as CAT scanners and defibrillators. Many repairers are trained in the military. New repairers begin by observing and assisting an experienced worker over a period of three to six months, learning a single piece of equipment at a time. Gradually, they begin working independently, while still under close supervision. Biomedical equipment repairers are constantly learning new technologies and equipment through seminars, self-study, and certification exams.

Educational requirements for other precision instrument and equipment repair jobs also vary, but include a high school diploma, with a focus on mathematics and science courses. Because repairers need to understand blueprints, electrical schematic diagrams, and electrical, hydraulic, and electromechanical systems, most employers require an associate or sometimes a bachelor's degree in instrumentation and control, electronics, or a related engineering field. In addition to formal education, a year or two of on-the-job training is required before a repairer is considered fully qualified. Many instrument and equipment repairers begin by working in a factory in another capacity, such as repairing electrical equipment. As companies seek to improve efficiency, other types of repair workers are trained to repair precision measuring equipment.

Certification and other qualifications. Much training takes place on the job. The ability to read and understand technical manuals is important. Necessary physical qualities include good fine-motor skills and acute vision. Those working with musical instruments must also have good hearing. Also, precision equipment repairers must be able to pay close attention to details, enjoy problem solving, and have the desire to disassemble machines to see how they work. Most precision equipment repairers must be able to work alone with minimal supervision.

Because many precision instrument and equipment repairers are self-employed, they must also have business skills. Although business most often comes from word-of-mouth advertising, repairers must nevertheless work to establish themselves in the industry. Further, they must manage their business operations, which may mean purchasing insurance and managing their own accounting.

Although most of the positions in this field do not require certification, it may be helpful in finding a job or demonstrating competency to prospective clients. There are several certifications possible in this diverse group of repairers. Information on various certifications is available from the sources of additional information at the end of the statement.

Advancement. Advancement opportunities vary greatly among precision instrument and equipment repairers. For self-employed repairers, advancement may mean the ability to charge more for their services. For workers who are employed by firms, supervisory opportunities are available. In both cases, an experienced worker may become a mentor to someone who is new to the field.

Employment

Precision instrument and equipment repairers held 68,000 jobs in 2006. Employment was distributed among the detailed occupations as follows:

Medical equipment repairers 38,000
Musical instrument repairers and tuners 6,000

Camera and photographic equipment repairers..........4,400
Watch repairers..3,800
Precision instrument and equipment repairers,
all other 16,000

Medical equipment repairers often work for hospitals or wholesale equipment suppliers, while those in the occupation titled "all other precision instrument repairers" frequently work for manufacturing companies and wholesalers of durable goods. About 1 out of 6 precision instrument and equipment repairers was self-employed—most are proprietors of jewelry, camera, medical equipment, or music repair services.

Job Outlook

Good opportunities are expected for most types of precision instrument and equipment repairer jobs. Overall employment growth is projected to be about as fast as the average for all occupations over the 2006–2016 period; however, projected growth varies by detailed occupation.

Employment change. Projected employment growth for precision instrument and equipment repairers varies greatly by specialty.

Employment of camera and photographic equipment repairers is projected to decline by about 2 percent between 2006 and 2016, and employment of watch repairers is projected to decline 5 percent over the same period. These occupations are in decline primarily because the products they service are often less expensive to replace than to repair. Most of the workers who remain in this industry will specialize in repair of expensive watches and cameras, as well as antiques.

Over the same time period, the employment of musical instrument repairers and tuners is projected to increase 3 percent, which is slower than average. Band and orchestra programs in high schools continue to provide most of the business for these workers, and they have been declining for several years. With fewer new musicians, there will be a slump in instrument rentals, purchases, and repairs. In the meantime, however, there continues to be a demand for these services, and new opportunities should continue to arise as the population grows.

The medical equipment repairer occupation is projected to increase 22 percent between 2006 and 2016, which is much faster than the average for all occupations, as a result of increased demand for medical services and increasing complexity of the equipment used in hospitals and clinics. Opportunities should be increasingly good for those who have a strong understanding of software and electronics, as many new medical devices are increasingly reliant on computers.

Over the same time period, employment of other precision instrument and equipment repairers is projected to increase 4 percent, more slowly than average, as most of them work in declining manufacturing industries. Nevertheless, these workers can expect to play an increasingly large role in those industries, as automation continues to dominate modern manufacturing.

Job prospects. Despite varying levels of growth in the various occupations, almost all workers in these fields can expect good job prospects over the next decade. As the baby boomer generation nears retirement, many skilled workers in these occupations are expected to leave the workforce. Additionally, many technical schools and other programs offering courses in these occupations have closed, leading to a shortage of qualified workers. Individuals with strong apprenticeships or internships should have the best prospects as instrumentation continues to become more complex and requires ever greater skill to repair.

Earnings

The following tabulation shows median annual earnings for various precision instrument and equipment repairers in May 2006:

Medical equipment repairers $40,580
Camera and photographic equipment repairers........34,850
Watch repairers...30,900
Musical instrument repairers and tuners 29,200
Precision instrument and equipment repairers,
all other 46,250

Earnings ranged from less than $16,230 for the lowest 10 percent of musical instrument repairers and tuners to more than $69,280 for the highest 10 percent in the occupation all other precision instrument and equipment repairers in May 2006.

Earnings within the different occupations vary significantly, depending upon skill levels. For example, a lesser skilled watch and clock repairer may simply change batteries and replace worn wrist straps, while a highly skilled watch and clock repairer with years of training and experience may rebuild and replace worn parts.

Related Occupations

Many precision instrument and equipment repairers work with precision mechanical and electronic equipment. Other workers who repair precision mechanical and electronic equipment include computer, automated teller, and office machine repairers and coin, vending, and amusement machine servicers and repairers. Other workers who make precision items include medical, dental, and ophthalmic laboratory technicians. Some precision instrument and equipment repairers work with a wide array of industrial equipment. Their work environment and responsibilities are similar to those of industrial machinery mechanics and maintenance workers. Much of the work of watch repairers is similar to that of jewelers and precious stone

Projections data from the National Employment Matrix

Occupational Title	SOC Code	Employment, 2006	Projected employment, 2016	Change, 2006-16 Number	Change, 2006-16 Percent
Precision instrument and equipment repairers	49-9060	68,000	77,000	8,700	13
Camera and photographic equipment repairers	49-9061	4,400	4,300	-100	-2
Medical equipment repairers	49-9062	38,000	46,000	8,200	22
Musical instrument repairers and tuners	49-9063	6,000	6,200	200	3
Watch repairers	49-9064	3,800	3,600	-200	-5
Precision instrument and equipment repairers, all other	49-9069	16,000	17,000	700	4

NOTE: Data in this table are rounded.

and metal workers. Camera repairers' work is similar to that of electronic home entertainment equipment installers and repairers; both occupations work with consumer electronics that are based around a circuit board, but that also involve numerous moving mechanical parts.

Sources of Additional Information

For information on musical instrument repair, including schools offering training, contact

- National Association of Professional Band Instrument Repair Technicians (NAPBIRT), P.O. Box 51, Normal, IL 61761. Internet: http://www.napbirt.org

For additional information on piano tuning and repair work, contact

- Piano Technicians Guild, 4444 Forest Ave., Kansas City, KS 66106. Internet: http://www.ptg.org

For information about training, mentoring programs, employers, and schools with programs in precision instrumentation, automation, and control, contact

- ISA-The Instrumentation, Systems, and Automation Society, 67 Alexander Dr, Research Triangle Park, NC 27709. Internet: http://www.isa.org

For information about watch and clock repair and a list of schools with related programs of study, contact

- American Watchmakers-Clockmakers Institute (AWI), 701 Enterprise Dr., Harrison, OH 45030-1696. Internet: http://www.awi-net.org
- National Association of Watch and Clock Collectors, 514 Poplar St., Columbia, PA 17512-2130. Internet: http://www.nawcc.org

For information about medical equipment technicians and a list of schools with related programs of study, contact

- Association for the Advancement of Medical Instrumentation (AAMI), 1110 North Glebe Rd., Suite 220, Arlington, VA 22201-4795. Internet: http://www.aami.org

Prepress Technicians and Workers

(O*NET 51-5021.00 and 51-5022.00)

Significant Points

- Most prepress technician jobs now require formal postsecondary graphic communications training in the various types of computer software used in digital imaging.
- Employment is projected to decline rapidly as the increased use of computers in typesetting and page layout requires fewer prepress technicians.

Nature of the Work

The printing process has three stages: prepress, press, and binding or finishing. While workers in small print shops are usually responsible for all three stages, in most printing firms, formatting print jobs and correcting layout errors before the job goes to print is the responsibility of a specialized group of workers. *Prepress technicians and workers* are responsible for this prepress work. They perform a variety of tasks to help transform text and pictures into finished pages and prepare the pages for print.

Prepress technicians receive images from in-house graphic designers or directly from customers and see the job through the process of preparing print-ready pages to create a finished printing plate. Printing plates are thin sheets of metal that carry the final image to be printed. Printing presses use this plate to copy the image to the printed products we see every day. Once a printing plate has been created, prepress technicians collaborate with printing machine operators to check for any potential printing problems. Several plates may be needed if a job requires color, but advanced printing technology does not require plates.

For a long time, prepress workers used a photographic process to make printing plates. This is a complex process involving ultraviolet light and chemical exposure through which the text and images of a print job harden on a metal plate and become water repellent. These hard, water repellent portions of the metal plate are in the form of the text and images that will be printed on paper. More recently, the printing industry has largely moved to technology known as "direct-to-plate", by which the prepress technicians send the data directly to a plating system, by-passing the need for the photographic technique.

The direct-to-plate technique is just one example of digital imaging technology that has largely replaced cold type print technology. Prepress technicians known as "preflight technicians" or production coordinators are using digital imaging technology to complete more and more print jobs. Using this technology, technicians take electronic files received from customers and check them for completeness. They then format the jobs using electronic page layout software in order to fit the pages to dimensions of the paper stock to be used. When color printing is required, the technicians produce an electronic image of the printed pages and then print a copy, or "proof," of the pages as they will appear when printed. The technician then has the proofs delivered or mailed to the customer for a final check. Once the customer approves the proofs, technicians use laser "imagesetters" to expose digital images of the pages directly onto the thin metal printing plates.

Advances in computer software and printing technology continue to change prepress work. Today, customers of print shops often use their own computers to do much of the typesetting and page layout work formerly done by prepress technicians. This process, called "desktop publishing," provides printers with pages of material that look like the desired finished product. This work is usually done by desktop publishers or graphic designers with knowledge of publishing software. (A section on desktop publishers appears elsewhere in this book.) As a result, prepress workers often receive files from customers on a computer disk or via e-mail that contain typeset material already laid out in pages. Other more advanced technologies now allow prepress technicians to send printing files directly to the printer and skip the plate-making process altogether. Despite the shortcuts that technological advancements allow, workers still need to understand the basic processes behind prepress, press, and finishing operations. Some workers, known as *job printers,* perform prepress and print operations. Job printers often are found in small establishments where work combines several job skills.

Work environment. Prepress technicians and workers usually work in clean, air-conditioned areas with little noise. Some workers may develop eyestrain from working in front of a video display terminal or other minor problems, such as backaches. Those platemakers who still work with toxic chemicals face the hazard of skin irritations. Workers are often subject to stress and the pressures of deadlines and tight work schedules.

Prepress employees usually work an 8-hour day. Some workers—particularly those employed by newspapers—work night shifts. Weekend and holiday work may be required, particularly when a print job is behind schedule. Part-time prepress technicians made up 12 percent of this occupation in 2006.

Training, Other Qualifications, and Advancement

Employers prefer workers with formal training in printing or publishing. Familiarity with the printing process, including the technology used, and attention to detail are the qualities that employers will seek most in job applicants.

Education and training. Many employers consider the best candidates for prepress jobs to be individuals with a combination of work experience in the printing industry and formal training in the new digital technology. The experience of these applicants provides them with an understanding of how printing plants operate and demonstrates their interest in advancing within the industry.

Traditionally, prepress technicians and workers started as helpers and were trained on the job. Some of these jobs required years of experience performing detailed manual work to become skillful enough to perform the most difficult tasks. Today, however, employers expect workers to have some formal postsecondary graphic communications training in the various types of computer software used in digital imaging and will train workers on the job as needed.

For beginners, two-year associate degree programs offered by community colleges, junior colleges, and technical schools teach the latest prepress skills and allow students to practice applying them. There are also four-year bachelor's degree programs in graphic design aimed primarily at students who plan to move into management positions in printing or design. For workers who do not wish to enroll in a degree program, prepress-related courses are offered at many community colleges, junior colleges, four-year colleges and universities, vocational-technical institutes, and private trade and technical schools. Workers with experience in other printing jobs can take a few college-level graphic communications courses to upgrade their skills and qualify for prepress jobs.

Other qualifications. Employers prefer workers with good communication skills, both oral and written. When prepress problems arise, prepress technicians and workers should be able to deal courteously with customers to resolve them. Also, in small shops, they may take customer orders. Persons interested in working for firms using advanced printing technology need to be comfortable with electronics and computers. At times, prepress personnel may have to perform computations in order to estimate job costs or operate many of the electronics used to run modern equipment.

Prepress technicians and workers need manual dexterity and accurate eyesight. Good color vision helps workers find mistakes and locate potential problems. It is essential for prepress workers to be able to pay attention to detail and work independently. Artistic ability is often a plus. Employers also seek persons who are comfortable with the pressures of meeting deadlines, using new software, and operating new equipment.

Advancement. Employers may send experienced technicians to industry-sponsored update and retraining programs to develop new skills or hone current ones. This kind of prepress training is sometimes offered in-house or through unions in the printing industry.

Employment

Prepress technicians and workers overall held about 119,000 jobs in 2006. Most prepress jobs are found in the printing industry, while newspaper publishing employs the second largest number of prepress technicians and workers.

The printing and publishing industries are two of the most geographically dispersed in the United States. While prepress jobs are found throughout the country, large numbers are concentrated in large printing centers such as Chicago, Los Angeles–Long Beach, New York City, Minneapolis–St. Paul, Philadelphia, Boston, and Washington, DC.

Job Outlook

Employment of prepress technicians and workers is projected to decline rapidly through 2016, because of improvements in printing technology that require fewer of these workers. Despite this, job prospects are good for prepress technicians with good computer and customer service skills.

Employment change. Overall employment of prepress technicians and workers is expected to decline by 16 percent over the 2006–2016 period. Demand for printed material should continue to grow, spurred by rising levels of personal income, increasing school enrollments, higher levels of educational attainment, and expanding markets. But the use of computers and publishing software—often by the clients of the printing company—will result in rising productivity of prepress technicians, and thus halting the creation of new jobs.

Computer software now allows office workers at a desktop computer terminal to specify text typeface and style and to format pages. This development shifts traditional prepress functions away from printing plants into advertising and public relations agencies, graphic design firms, and large corporations. As page layout and graphic design capabilities of computer software have become less expensive and more user-friendly, many companies are turning to in-house desktop publishing. Some firms also are finding it less costly to prepare their own newsletters and other reports. At newspapers, writers and editors also are doing more composition using publishing software. This rapid growth in the use of desktop publishing software has eliminated most prepress typesetting and composition technician jobs associated with the older printing technologies. In addition, new technology is increasing the amount of automation that printing companies can employ, which leaves less work for prepress workers. The duties of prepress workers will likely begin to merge with those of other printing industry workers—such as those of customer service representatives—which will also curb prepress job growth.

Job prospects. Despite a decline in the number of new prepress positions, opportunities will be favorable for workers with strong computer and customer service skills, such as preflight technicians who electronically check materials prepared by clients and adapt them for printing.

In order to compete in the desktop publishing environment, commercial printing companies are adding desktop publishing and electronic prepress work to the list of services they provide. Electronic prepress technicians, digital proofers, platemakers, and graphic designers are using new equipment and ever-improving software to design and lay out publications and complete their printing more quickly. The increasing range of services offered by printing

Projections data from the National Employment Matrix

Occupational Title	SOC Code	Employment, 2006	Projected employment, 2016	Change, 2006-16	
				Number	Percent
Prepress technicians and workers	—	119,000	100,000	-19,000	-16
Job printers	51-5021	48,000	44,000	-4,500	-9
Prepress technicians and workers	51-5022	71,000	56,000	-15,000	-21

NOTE: Data in this table are rounded.

companies using new digital technologies mean that opportunities in prepress work will be best for those with computer backgrounds who have completed postsecondary programs in printing technology or graphic communications. Workers with this background will be better able to adapt to the continuing evolution of publishing and printing technology.

Earnings

While wage rates for prepress technicians and workers depend on basic factors such as employer, education, and location, the median hourly earnings of prepress technicians and workers were $16.01 in May 2006, compared to $13.16 per hour for all production occupations. The middle 50 percent earned between $11.98 and $20.69 an hour. The lowest 10 percent earned less than $9.37, and the highest 10 percent earned more than $25.71 an hour. Median hourly earnings in printing and related support activities, the industry employing the largest number of prepress technicians and workers, were $16.44 in May 2006, while workers in the newspaper, periodical, and book publishing industry earned $15.17 an hour.

For job printers, median hourly earnings were $15.58 in May 2006. The middle 50 percent earned between $12.15 and $19.83 an hour. The lowest 10 percent earned less than $9.56, and the highest 10 percent earned more than $24.70 an hour. Median hourly earnings in the industries employing the largest numbers of job printers May 2006 were $16.19 in the newspaper, periodical, and book publishing industry and $15.76 in printing and related support activities.

Related Occupations

Prepress technicians and workers use artistic skills in their work. These skills also are essential for artists and related workers, graphic designers, and desktop publishers. Moreover, many of the skills used in Web site design also are employed in prepress technology. Prepress technicians' work also is tied in closely with that of printing machine operators.

Sources of Additional Information

Details about training programs may be obtained from local employers such as newspapers and printing shops, or from local offices of the state employment service.

For information on careers and training in printing and the graphic arts, write to

- Graphic Arts Education and Research Foundation, 1899 Preston White Dr., Reston, VA 20191-5468. Internet: http://www.makeyourmark.org
- Graphic Communications Conference of the International Brotherhood of Teamsters, 1900 L St. NW, Washington, DC 20036-5007.
- Printing Industries of America/Graphic Arts Technical Foundation, 200 Deer Run Rd., Sewickley, PA 15143-2324.

Printing Machine Operators

(O*NET 51-5023.00, 51-5023.01, 51-5023.02, 51-5023.03, 51-5023.04, 51-5023.05, 51-5023.06, 51-5023.07, 51-5023.08, and 51-5023.09)

Significant Points

- Most printing machine operators are trained on the job.
- Retirements of older press operators are expected to create openings for skilled workers.
- Rising demand for customized print jobs will mean those skilled in digital printing operations will have the best job opportunities.

Nature of the Work

Printing machine operators, also known as press operators, prepare, operate, and maintain printing presses. Duties of printing machine operators vary according to the type of press they operate. Traditional printing methods, such as offset lithography, gravure, flexography, and letterpress, use a plate or roller that carries the final image that is to be printed and copies the image to paper. In addition to the traditional printing processes, plateless or nonimpact processes are coming into general use. Plateless processes—including digital, electrostatic, and ink-jet printing—are used for copying, duplicating, and document and specialty printing. Plateless processes usually are done by quick printing shops and smaller in-house printing shops, but increasingly are being used by commercial printers for short-run or customized printing jobs.

Machine operators' jobs differ from one shop to another because of differences in the types and sizes of presses. Small commercial shops can be operated by one person and tend to have relatively small presses, which print only one or two colors at a time. Large newspaper, magazine, and book printers use giant "in-line web" presses that require a crew of several press operators and press assistants.

After working with prepress technicians (who are covered in this book's statement on prepress technicians and workers) to identify and resolve any potential problems with a job, printing machine operators prepare machines for printing. To prepare presses, operators install the printing plate with the images to be printed and adjust the pressure at which the machine prints. Then they ink the presses, load paper, and adjust the press to the paper size. Operators ensure that paper and ink meet specifications, and adjust the flow of ink to the inking rollers accordingly. They then feed paper through the press cylinders and adjust feed and tension controls. New digital technology, in contrast, is able to automate much of this work.

While printing presses are running, printing machine operators monitor their operation and keep the paper feeders well stocked. They make adjustments to manage ink distribution, speed, and temperature in the drying chamber, if the press has one. If paper tears or jams and the press stops, which can happen with some offset presses, operators quickly correct the problem to minimize downtime. Similarly, operators working with other high-speed presses constantly look for problems, and when necessary make quick corrections to avoid expensive losses of paper and ink. Throughout the run, operators must regularly pull sheets to check for any printing imperfections. Most printers have, or will soon have, presses with computers and sophisticated instruments to control press operations, making it possible to complete printing jobs in less time. With this equipment, printing machine operators set up, monitor, and adjust the printing process on a control panel or computer monitor, which allows them to control the press electronically.

In most shops, machine operators also perform preventive maintenance. They oil and clean the presses and make minor repairs.

Work environment. Operating a press can be physically and mentally demanding, and sometimes tedious. Printing machine operators are on their feet most of the time. Often, operators work under pressure to meet deadlines. Most printing presses are capable of high printing speeds, and adjustments must be made quickly to avoid waste. Pressrooms are noisy, and workers in certain areas wear ear protection. Working with press machinery can be hazardous, but the threat of accidents has decreased with newer computerized presses that allow operators to make most adjustments from a control panel.

Many printing machine operators, particularly those who work for newspapers, work weekends, nights, and holidays as many presses operate continually. They also may work overtime to meet deadlines. The average operator worked 40 hours per week in 2006.

Training, Other Qualifications, and Advancement

Although employers prefer that beginners complete a formal apprenticeship or a postsecondary program in printing equipment operation, most printing machine operators are trained on the job. Attention to detail and familiarity with electronics and computers are essential for operators.

Education and training. Beginning printing machine operators load, unload, and clean presses. With time and training, they may become fully qualified to operate that type of press. Operators can gain experience on more than one kind of printing press during the course of their career.

Experienced operators will periodically receive retraining and skill updating. For example, printing plants that change from sheet-fed offset presses to digital presses have to retrain the entire press crew because skill requirements for the two types of presses are different.

Apprenticeships for printing machine operators, once the dominant method for preparing for this occupation, are becoming less prevalent. When they are offered by the employer, they include on-the-job instruction and some related classroom training or correspondence school courses.

Formal postsecondary programs in printing equipment operation offered by technical and trade schools, community colleges, and universities are growing in importance. Postsecondary courses in printing provide the theoretical and technical knowledge needed to operate advanced equipment that employers look for in an entry-level worker. Some postsecondary school programs require two years of study and award an associate degree.

Because of technical developments in the printing industry, courses in chemistry, electronics, color theory, and physics are helpful in secondary or postsecondary programs.

Other qualifications. Persons who wish to become printing machine operators need mechanical aptitude to make press adjustments and repairs. Workers need good vision and attention to detail to locate and fix problems with print jobs. Oral and written communication skills also are required. Operators should possess the mathematical skills necessary to compute percentages, weights, and measures, and to calculate the amount of ink and paper needed to do a job. Operators now also need basic computer skills to work with newer printing machines.

Certification and advancement. As printing machine operators gain experience, they may advance in pay and responsibility by working on a more complex printing press. For example, operators who have demonstrated their ability to work with a one-color sheet-fed press may be trained to operate a four-color sheet-fed press. Voluntarily earning a formal certification may also help advance a career in printing. An operator also may advance to pressroom supervisor and become responsible for an entire press crew. In addition, printing machine operators can draw on their knowledge of press operations to become cost estimators, providing estimates of printing jobs to potential customers.

Employment

Printing machine operators held about 198,000 jobs in 2006. Half of all operator jobs were in printing and related support activities. Paper manufacturers and newspaper publishers also were large employers. Additional jobs were in advertising agencies, employment services firms, and colleges and universities that do their own printing.

The printing and newspaper publishing industries are two of the most geographically dispersed in the United States. While printing machine operators can find jobs throughout the country, large numbers of jobs are concentrated in large printing centers such as Chicago, Los Angeles–Long Beach, New York, Minneapolis–St. Paul, Philadelphia, Boston, and Washington, DC.

Job Outlook

Employment of printing machine operators is projected to decline moderately through 2016, as newer printing presses require fewer operators. Despite this, job opportunities are expected to be favorable because a large number of these workers are expected to retire over the next decade. The best opportunities will be available to skilled operators.

Employment change. Employment of printing machine operators is expected to decline moderately by six percent over the 2006–2016 decade even as the output of printed materials is expected to increase. Employment will fall because of increasing automation in the printing industry and because of the outsourcing of some production to foreign countries.

Book and magazine circulation will increase as school enrollments rise and niche publications continue to enjoy success. Additional growth will also come from the increasing ability of the printing industry to profitably print smaller quantities, which should widen the market for printed materials as production costs decline.

Commercial printing will continue to be driven by increased expenditures for print advertising materials. New marketing techniques

Projections data from the National Employment Matrix

Occupational Title	SOC Code	Employment, 2006	Projected employment, 2016	Change, 2006-16	
				Number	Percent
Printing machine operators	51-5023	198,000	186,000	-11,000	-6

NOTE: Data in this table are rounded.

are leading advertisers to increase spending on messages targeted to specific audiences, and should continue to require the printing of a wide variety of catalogs, direct mail enclosures, newspaper inserts, and other kinds of print advertising.

However, employment will not grow at the same pace as output because increased use of new computerized printing equipment will require fewer operators. This will especially be true with the increasing automation of the large printing presses used in the newspaper industry. In addition, some companies are lowering their printing costs by having their work printed out of the country when it does not need to be completed quickly. New business practices within the publishing industry, such as printing-on-demand and electronic publishing, will reduce the size of print runs, further moderating output.

Job prospects. Opportunities for employment in printing machine operation should be favorable. Retirements of older printing machine operators and the need for workers trained on increasingly computerized printing equipment will create many job openings over the next decade. For example, small printing jobs will increasingly be run on sophisticated high-speed digital printing equipment that requires a complex set of operator skills, such as knowledge of database management software. Those who complete postsecondary training programs in printing and who are comfortable with computers will have the best employment opportunities.

Earnings

Median hourly earnings of printing machine operators were $14.90 in May 2006, as compared to $13.16 per hour for all production occupations. The middle 50 percent earned between $11.11 and $19.49 an hour. The lowest 10 percent earned less than $8.84, and the highest 10 percent earned more than $24.23 an hour. Median hourly earnings in the industries employing the largest numbers of printing machine operators in May 2006 were

Newspaper, periodical, book, and directory publishers	$17.27
Converted paper product manufacturing	16.37
Printing and related support activities	15.55
Plastics product manufacturing	13.81
Advertising and related services	11.95

The basic wage rate for a printing machine operator depends on the geographic area in which the work is located and on the size and complexity of the printing press being operated.

Related Occupations

Other workers who set up and operate production machinery include machine setters, operators, and tenders—metal and plastic; bookbinders and bindery workers; and various precision machine operators.

Sources of Additional Information

Details about apprenticeships and other training opportunities may be obtained from local employers, such as newspapers and printing shops, local offices of the Graphic Communications Conference of the International Brotherhood of Teamsters, local affiliates of Printing Industries of America/Graphic Arts Technical Foundation, or local offices of the state employment service.

For general information about printing machine operators, contact

- Graphic Communications Conference of the International Brotherhood of Teamsters, 1900 L St. NW, Washington, DC 20036-5007.

For information on careers and training in printing and the graphic arts contact

- NPES The Association for Suppliers of Printing Publishing, and Converting Technologies, 1899 Preston White Dr., Reston, VA 20191-4367. Internet: http://www.npes.org/education/index.html
- Printing Industry of America/Graphic Arts Technical Foundation, 200 Deer Run Rd., Sewickley, PA 15143.
- Graphic Arts Education and Research Foundation, 1899 Preston White Dr., Reston, VA 20191-5468. Internet: http://www.makeyourmark.org

Psychologists

(O*NET 19-3031.01, 19-3031.02, 19-3031.03, 19-3032.00, and 19-3039.99)

Significant Points

- About 34 percent of psychologists are self-employed, compared with only 8 percent of all workers.
- Competition for admission to graduate psychology programs is keen.
- Overall employment of psychologists is expected to grow faster than average.
- Job prospects should be the best for people who have a doctoral degree in an applied specialty, such as counseling or health, and those with a specialist or doctoral degree in school psychology.

Nature of the Work

Psychologists study the human mind and human behavior. Research psychologists investigate the physical, cognitive, emotional, or social aspects of human behavior. Psychologists in health service fields provide mental health care in hospitals, clinics, schools, or private settings. Psychologists employed in applied settings, such as business, industry, government, or nonprofit organizations, provide training, conduct research, design organizational systems, and act as advocates for psychology.

Like other social scientists, psychologists formulate hypotheses and collect data to test their validity. Research methods vary with the topic under study. Psychologists sometimes gather information through controlled laboratory experiments or by administering personality, performance, aptitude, or intelligence tests. Other methods include observation, interviews, questionnaires, clinical studies, and surveys.

Psychologists apply their knowledge to a wide range of endeavors, including health and human services, management, education, law, and sports. They usually specialize in one of a number of different areas.

Clinical psychologists—who constitute the largest specialty—work most often in counseling centers, independent or group practices, hospitals, or clinics. They help mentally and emotionally distressed clients adjust to life and may assist medical and surgical patients in dealing with illnesses or injuries. Some clinical psychologists work in physical rehabilitation settings, treating patients with spinal cord injuries, chronic pain or illness, stroke, arthritis, or neurological conditions. Others help people deal with personal crisis, such as divorce or the death of a loved one.

Clinical psychologists often interview patients and give diagnostic tests. They may provide individual, family, or group psychotherapy and may design and implement behavior modification programs. Some clinical psychologists collaborate with physicians and other specialists to develop and implement treatment and intervention programs that patients can understand and comply with. Other clinical psychologists work in universities and medical schools, where they train graduate students in the delivery of mental health and behavioral medicine services. Some administer community mental health programs.

Areas of specialization within clinical psychology include health psychology, neuropsychology, and geropsychology. *Health psychologists* study how biological, psychological, and social factors affect health and illness. They promote healthy living and disease prevention through counseling, and they focus on how patients adjust to illnesses and treatments and view their quality of life. *Neuropsychologists* study the relation between the brain and behavior. They often work in stroke and head injury programs. *Geropsychologists* deal with the special problems faced by the elderly. The emergence and growth of these specialties reflects the increasing participation of psychologists in direct services to special patient populations.

Often, clinical psychologists consult with other medical personnel regarding the best treatment for patients, especially treatment that includes medication. Clinical psychologists generally are not permitted to prescribe medication to treat patients; only psychiatrists and other medical doctors may prescribe most medications. (See the statement on physicians and surgeons elsewhere in this book.) However, two states—Louisiana and New Mexico—currently allow appropriately trained clinical psychologists to prescribe medication with some limitations.

Counseling psychologists use various techniques, including interviewing and testing, to advise people on how to deal with problems of everyday living, including career or work problems and problems faced in different stages of life. They work in settings such as university counseling centers, hospitals, and individual or group practices.

School psychologists work with students in early childhood and elementary and secondary schools. They collaborate with teachers, parents, and school personnel to create safe, healthy, and supportive learning environments for all students. School psychologists address students' learning and behavioral problems, suggest improvements to classroom management strategies or parenting techniques, and evaluate students with disabilities and gifted and talented students to help determine the best way to educate them.

They improve teaching, learning, and socialization strategies based on their understanding of the psychology of learning environments. They also may evaluate the effectiveness of academic programs, prevention programs, behavior management procedures, and other services provided in the school setting.

Industrial-organizational psychologists apply psychological principles and research methods to the workplace in the interest of improving productivity and the quality of worklife. They also are involved in research on management and marketing problems. They screen, train, and counsel applicants for jobs, as well as perform organizational development and analysis. An industrial psychologist might work with management to reorganize the work setting in order to improve productivity or quality of life in the workplace. Industrial psychologists frequently act as consultants, brought in by management to solve a particular problem.

Developmental psychologists study the physiological, cognitive, and social development that takes place throughout life. Some specialize in behavior during infancy, childhood, and adolescence, or changes that occur during maturity or old age. Developmental psychologists also may study developmental disabilities and their effects. Increasingly, research is developing ways to help elderly people remain independent as long as possible.

Social psychologists examine people's interactions with others and with the social environment. They work in organizational consultation, marketing research, systems design, or other applied psychology fields. Prominent areas of study include group behavior, leadership, attitudes, and perception.

Experimental or *research psychologists* work in university and private research centers and in business, nonprofit, and governmental organizations. They study the behavior of both human beings and animals, such as rats, monkeys, and pigeons. Prominent areas of study in experimental research include motivation, thought, attention, learning and memory, sensory and perceptual processes, effects of substance abuse, and genetic and neurological factors affecting behavior.

Work environment. Psychologists' work environments vary by subfield and place of employment. For example, clinical, school, and counseling psychologists in private practice frequently have their own offices and set their own hours. However, they usually offer evening and weekend hours to accommodate their clients. Those employed in hospitals, nursing homes, and other health care facilities may work shifts that include evenings and weekends, and those who work in schools and clinics generally work regular daytime hours. Most psychologists in government and industry have structured schedules.

Psychologists employed as faculty by colleges and universities divide their time between teaching and research and also may have administrative responsibilities; many have part-time consulting practices.

Increasingly, many psychologists work as part of a team, consulting with other psychologists and professionals. Many experience pressures because of deadlines, tight schedules, and overtime. Their routine may be interrupted frequently. Travel may be required in order to attend conferences or conduct research.

Training, Other Qualifications, and Advancement

A master's or doctoral degree, and a license, are required for most psychologists.

Education and training. A doctoral degree usually is required for independent practice as a psychologist. Psychologists with a Ph.D. or Doctor of Psychology (Psy.D.) qualify for a wide range of teaching, research, clinical, and counseling positions in universities, health care services, elementary and secondary schools, private industry, and government. Psychologists with a doctoral degree often work in clinical positions or in private practices, but they also sometimes teach, conduct research, or carry out administrative responsibilities.

A doctoral degree generally requires five to seven years of graduate study, culminating in a dissertation based on original research. Courses in quantitative research methods, which include the use of computer-based analysis, are an integral part of graduate study and are necessary to complete the dissertation. The Psy.D. degree may be based on practical work and examinations rather than a dissertation. In clinical, counseling, and school psychology, the requirements for the doctoral degree include at least a one-year internship.

A specialist degree or its equivalent is required in most states for an individual to work as a school psychologist, although a few states still credential school psychologists with master's degrees. A specialist (Ed.S.) degree in school psychology requires a minimum of three years of full-time graduate study (at least 60 graduate semester hours) and a one-year full-time internship. Because their professional practice addresses educational and mental health components of students' development, school psychologists' training includes coursework in both education and psychology.

People with a master's degree in psychology may work as industrial-organizational psychologists. They also may work as psychological assistants under the supervision of doctoral-level psychologists and may conduct research or psychological evaluations. A master's degree in psychology requires at least two years of full-time graduate study. Requirements usually include practical experience in an applied setting and a master's thesis based on an original research project.

Competition for admission to graduate psychology programs is keen. Some universities require applicants to have an undergraduate major in psychology. Others prefer only coursework in basic psychology with additional courses in the biological, physical, and social sciences and in statistics and mathematics.

A bachelor's degree in psychology qualifies a person to assist psychologists and other professionals in community mental health centers, vocational rehabilitation offices, and correctional programs. Bachelor's degree holders may also work as research or administrative assistants for psychologists. Some work as technicians in related fields, such as marketing research. Many find employment in other areas, such as sales, service, or business management.

In the federal government, candidates having at least 24 semester hours in psychology and one course in statistics qualify for entry-level positions. However, competition for these jobs is keen because this is one of the few ways in which one can work as a psychologist without an advanced degree.

The American Psychological Association (APA) presently accredits doctoral training programs in clinical, counseling, and school psychology, as well as institutions that provide internships for doctoral students in school, clinical, and counseling psychology. The National Association of School Psychologists, with the assistance of the National Council for Accreditation of Teacher Education, helps to approve advanced degree programs in school psychology.

Licensure. Psychologists in independent practice or those who offer any type of patient care—including clinical, counseling, and school psychologists—must meet certification or licensing requirements in all states and the District of Columbia. Licensing laws vary by state and by type of position and require licensed or certified psychologists to limit their practice to areas in which they have developed professional competence through training and experience. Clinical and counseling psychologists usually need a doctorate in psychology, an approved internship, and one to two years of professional experience. In addition, all states require that applicants pass an examination. Most state licensing boards administer a standardized test, and many supplement that with additional oral or essay questions. Some states require continuing education for renewal of the license.

The National Association of School Psychologists (NASP) awards the Nationally Certified School Psychologist (NCSP) designation, which recognizes professional competency in school psychology at a national, rather than state, level. Currently, 29 states recognize the NCSP and allow those with the certification to transfer credentials from one state to another without taking a new certification exam. In states that recognize the NCSP, the requirements for certification or licensure and those for the NCSP often are the same or similar. Requirements for the NCSP include the completion of 60 graduate semester hours in school psychology; a 1,200-hour internship, 600 hours of which must be completed in a school setting; and a passing score on the National School Psychology Examination.

Other qualifications. Aspiring psychologists who are interested in direct patient care must be emotionally stable, mature, and able to deal effectively with people. Sensitivity, compassion, good communication skills, and the ability to lead and inspire others are particularly important qualities for people wishing to do clinical work and counseling. Research psychologists should be able to do detailed work both independently and as part of a team. Patience and perseverance are vital qualities, because achieving results in the psychological treatment of patients or in research may take a long time.

Certification and advancement. The American Board of Professional Psychology (ABPP) recognizes professional achievement by awarding specialty certification in 13 different areas. Candidates for ABPP certification need a doctorate in psychology, postdoctoral training in their specialty, several years of experience, professional endorsements, and are required to pass the specialty board examination.

Psychologists can improve their advancement opportunities by earning an advanced degree and by participation in continuing education. Many psychologists opt to start their own practice after gaining experience working in the field.

Employment

Psychologists held about 166,000 jobs in 2006. Educational institutions employed about 29 percent of psychologists in positions other than teaching, such as counseling, testing, research, and administration. About 21 percent were employed in health care, primarily in offices of mental health practitioners, hospitals, physicians' offices, and outpatient mental health and substance abuse centers. Government agencies at the state and local levels employed psychologists in correctional facilities, law enforcement, and other settings.

After several years of experience, some psychologists—usually those with doctoral degrees—enter private practice or set up private research or consulting firms. About 34 percent of psychologists were self-employed in 2006, compared with only 8 percent of all professional workers.

In addition to the previously mentioned jobs, many psychologists held faculty positions at colleges and universities and as high school psychology teachers. (See the statement on teachers—postsecondary elsewhere in this book.)

Job Outlook

Faster-than-average employment growth is expected for psychologists. Job prospects should be the best for people who have a doctoral degree from a leading university in an applied specialty, such as counseling or health, and those with a specialist or doctoral degree in school psychology. Master's degree holders in fields other than industrial-organizational psychology will face keen competition. Opportunities will be limited for bachelor's degree holders.

Employment change. Employment of psychologists is expected to grow 15 percent from 2006 to 2016, faster than the average for all occupations. Employment will grow because of increased demand for psychological services in schools, hospitals, social service agencies, mental health centers, substance abuse treatment clinics, consulting firms, and private companies.

Employment growth will vary by specialty. Growing awareness of how students' mental health and behavioral problems, such as bullying, affect learning will increase demand for school psychologists to offer student counseling and mental health services.

The rise in health care costs associated with unhealthy lifestyles, such as smoking, alcoholism, and obesity, has made prevention and treatment more critical. An increase in the number of employee assistance programs, which help workers deal with personal problems, also should lead to employment growth for clinical and counseling specialties. Clinical and counseling psychologists also will be needed to help people deal with depression and other mental disorders, marriage and family problems, job stress, and addiction. The growing number of elderly will increase the demand for psychologists trained in geropsychology to help people deal with the mental and physical changes that occur as individuals grow older. There also will be increased need for psychologists to work with returning veterans.

Industrial-organizational psychologists also will be in demand to help to boost worker productivity and retention rates in a wide range of businesses. Industrial-organizational psychologists will help companies deal with issues such as workplace diversity and antidiscrimination policies. Companies also will use psychologists' expertise in survey design, analysis, and research to develop tools for marketing evaluation and statistical analysis.

Job prospects. Job prospects should be the best for people who have a doctoral degree from a leading university in an applied specialty, such as counseling or health, and those with a specialist or doctoral degree in school psychology. Psychologists with extensive training in quantitative research methods and computer science may have a competitive edge over applicants without such background.

Master's degree holders in fields other than industrial-organizational psychology will face keen competition for jobs because of the limited number of positions that require only a master's degree. Master's degree holders may find jobs as psychological assistants or counselors, providing mental health services under the direct supervision of a licensed psychologist. Still others may find jobs involving research and data collection and analysis in universities, government, or private companies.

Opportunities directly related to psychology will be limited for bachelor's degree holders. Some may find jobs as assistants in rehabilitation centers or in other jobs involving data collection and analysis. Those who meet state certification requirements may become high school psychology teachers.

Earnings

Median annual earnings of wage and salary clinical, counseling, and school psychologists in May 2006 were $59,440. The middle 50 percent earned between $45,300 and $77,750. The lowest 10 percent earned less than $35,280, and the highest 10 percent earned more than $102,730. Median annual earnings in the industries employing the largest numbers of clinical, counseling, and school psychologists were

Offices of mental health practitioners	$69,510
Elementary and secondary schools	61,290
Local government	58,770
Individual and family services	50,780
Outpatient care centers	50,310

Median annual earnings of wage and salary industrial-organizational psychologists in May 2006 were $86,420. The middle 50 percent earned between $66,310 and $115,000. The lowest 10 percent earned less than $48,380, and the highest 10 percent earned more than $139,620.

Related Occupations

Psychologists work with people, developing relationships and comforting them. Other occupations with similar duties include counselors, social workers, clergy, sociologists, special education teachers, funeral directors, market and survey researchers, recreation

Projections data from the National Employment Matrix

Occupational Title	SOC Code	Employment, 2006	Projected employment, 2016	Change, 2006-2016	
				Number	Percent
Psychologists	19-3030	166,000	191,000	25,000	15
Clinical, counseling, and school psychologists	19-3031	152,000	176,000	24,000	16
Industrial-organizational psychologists	19-3032	1,900	2,400	400	21
Psychologists, all other	19-3039	12,000	13,000	900	8

NOTE: Data in this table are rounded.

workers, and human resources, training, and labor relations managers and specialists. Psychologists also sometimes diagnose and treat problems and help patients recover. These duties are similar to those for physicians and surgeons, radiation therapists, audiologists, dentists, optometrists, and speech-language pathologists.

Sources of Additional Information

For information on careers, educational requirements, financial assistance, and licensing in all fields of psychology, contact

- American Psychological Association, Center for Psychology Workforce Analysis and Research and Education Directorate, 750 1st St. NE, Washington, DC 20002. Internet: http://www.apa.org/students

For information on careers, educational requirements, certification, and licensing of school psychologists, contact

- National Association of School Psychologists, 4340 East West Hwy., Suite 402, Bethesda, MD 20814. Internet: http://www.nasponline.org

Information about state licensing requirements is available from

- Association of State and Provincial Psychology Boards, P.O. Box 241245, Montgomery, AL 36124. Internet: http://www.asppb.org

Information about psychology specialty certifications is available from

- American Board of Professional Psychology, Inc., 300 Drayton St., 3rd Floor, Savannah, GA 31401. Internet: http://www.abpp.org

Radiation Therapists

(O*NET 29-1124.00)

Significant Points

- A bachelor's degree, associate degree, or certificate in radiation therapy is generally required.
- Good job opportunities are expected.
- Employment is projected to grow much faster than the average for all occupations.

Nature of the Work

Treating cancer in the human body is the principal use of radiation therapy. As part of a medical radiation oncology team, radiation therapists use machines—called linear accelerators—to administer radiation treatment to patients. Linear accelerators, used in a procedure called external beam therapy, project high-energy x rays at targeted cancer cells. As the x rays collide with human tissue, they produce highly energized ions that can shrink and eliminate cancerous tumors. Radiation therapy is sometimes used as the sole treatment for cancer, but is usually used in conjunction with chemotherapy or surgery.

The first step in the radiation therapy process is simulation. During simulation, the radiation therapist uses an x-ray imaging machine or computer tomography (CT) scan to pinpoint the location of the tumor. The therapist then positions the patient and adjusts the linear accelerator so that, when treatment begins, radiation exposure is concentrated on the tumor cells. The radiation therapist then develops a treatment plan in conjunction with a radiation oncologist (a physician who specializes in therapeutic radiology), and a dosimetrist (a technician who calculates the dose of radiation that will be used for treatment). The therapist later explains the treatment plan to the patient and answers any questions that the patient may have.

The next step in the process is treatment. To begin, the radiation therapist positions the patient and adjusts the linear accelerator according to the guidelines established in simulation. Then, from a separate room that is protected from the x-ray radiation, the therapist operates the linear accelerator and monitors the patient's condition through a TV monitor and an intercom system. Treatment can take anywhere from 10 to 30 minutes and is usually administered once a day, 5 days a week, for 2 to 9 weeks.

During the treatment phase, the radiation therapist monitors the patient's physical condition to determine if any adverse side effects are taking place. The therapist must also be aware of the patient's emotional wellbeing. Because many patients are under stress and are emotionally fragile, it is important for the therapist to maintain a positive attitude and provide emotional support.

Radiation therapists keep detailed records of their patients' treatments. These records include information such as the dose of radiation used for each treatment, the total amount of radiation used to date, the area treated, and the patient's reactions. Radiation oncologists and dosimetrists review these records to ensure that the treatment plan is working, to monitor the amount of radiation exposure that the patient has received, and to keep side effects to a minimum.

Radiation therapists also assist medical radiation physicists, workers who monitor and adjust the linear accelerator. Because radiation therapists often work alone during the treatment phase, they need to be able to check the linear accelerator for problems and make any adjustments that are needed. Therapists also may assist dosimetrists with routine aspects of dosimetry, the process used to calculate radiation dosages.

Work environment. Radiation therapists work in hospitals or in cancer treatment centers. These places are clean, well lighted, and well ventilated. Therapists do a considerable amount of lifting and must be able to help disabled patients get on and off treatment tables. They spend most of their time on their feet.

Radiation therapists generally work 40 hours a week, and unlike those in other health care occupations, they normally work only during the day. However, because radiation therapy emergencies do occur, some therapists are required to be on call and may have to work outside of their normal hours.

Working with cancer patients can be stressful, but many radiation therapists also find it rewarding. Because they work around radioactive materials, radiation therapists take great care to ensure that they are not exposed to dangerous levels of radiation. Following standard safety procedures can prevent overexposure.

Training, Other Qualifications, and Advancement

A bachelor's degree, associate degree, or certificate in radiation therapy generally is required. Many states also require radiation therapists to be licensed. With experience, therapists can advance to managerial positions.

Education and training. Employers usually require applicants to complete an associate or a bachelor's degree program in radiation therapy. Individuals also may become qualified by completing an associate or a bachelor's degree program in radiography, which is the study of radiological imaging, and then completing a 12-month certificate program in radiation therapy. Radiation therapy programs include core courses on radiation therapy procedures and the scientific theories behind them. In addition, such programs often include courses on human anatomy and physiology, physics, algebra, precalculus, writing, public speaking, computer science, and research methodology. In 2007 there were 123 radiation therapy programs accredited by the American Registry of Radiologic Technologists (ARRT).

Licensure. In 2007, 32 states required radiation therapists to be licensed by a state accrediting board. Licensing requirements vary by state, but many states require applicants to pass the ARRT certification examination. Further information is available from individual state licensing offices.

Certification and other qualifications. Some states, as well as many employers, require that radiation therapists be certified by ARRT. To become ARRT-certified, an applicant must complete an accredited radiation therapy program, adhere to ARRT ethical standards, and pass the ARRT certification examination. The examination and accredited academic programs cover radiation protection and quality assurance, clinical concepts in radiation oncology, treatment planning, treatment delivery, and patient care and education. Candidates also must demonstrate competency in several clinical practices including patient care activities; simulation procedures; dosimetry calculations; fabrication of beam modification devices; low-volume, high-risk procedures, and the application of radiation.

ARRT certification is valid for one year, after which therapists must renew their certification. Requirements for renewal include abiding by the ARRT ethical standards, paying annual dues, and satisfying continuing education requirements. Continuing education requirements must be met every two years and include either the completion of 24 credits of radiation therapy-related courses or the attainment of ARRT certification in a discipline other than radiation therapy. Certification renewal, however, may not be required by all states or employers that require initial certification.

All radiation therapists need good communication skills because their work involves a great deal of patient interaction. Individuals interested in becoming radiation therapists should be psychologically capable of working with cancer patients. They should be caring and empathetic because they work with patients who are ill and under stress. They should be able to keep accurate, detailed records. They also should be physically fit because they work on their feet for long periods and lift and move disabled patients.

Advancement. Experienced radiation therapists may advance to manage radiation therapy programs in treatment centers or other health care facilities. Managers generally continue to treat patients while taking on management responsibilities. Other advancement opportunities include teaching, technical sales, and research. With additional training and certification, therapists also can become dosimetrists, who use complex mathematical formulas to calculate proper radiation doses.

Employment

Radiation therapists held about 15,000 jobs in 2006. About 73 percent worked in hospitals, and about 17 percent worked in the offices of physicians. A small proportion worked in outpatient care centers.

Job Outlook

Employment is expected to increase much faster than the average from 2006 to 2016, and job prospects should be good.

Employment change. Employment of radiation therapists is projected to grow by 25 percent between 2006 and 2016, which is much faster than the average for all occupations. As the U.S. population grows and an increasing share of it is in the older age groups, the number of people needing treatment is expected to increase and to spur demand for radiation therapists. In addition, as radiation technology advances and is able to treat more types of cancer, radiation therapy will be prescribed more often.

Job prospects. Job prospects are expected to be good. Job openings will result from employment growth and from the need to replace workers who retire or leave the occupation for other reasons. Applicants who are certified should have the best opportunities.

Earnings

Median annual earnings of wage-and-salary radiation therapists were $66,170 in May 2006. The middle 50 percent earned between $54,170 and $78,550. The lowest 10 percent earned less than $44,840, and the highest 10 percent earned more than $92,110. Median annual earnings in the industries that employed the largest numbers of radiation therapists in May 2006 are as follows:

Outpatient care centers	$73,810
Offices of physicians	70,050
General medical and surgical hospitals	63,580

Some employers also reimburse their employees for the cost of continuing education.

Related Occupations

Radiation therapists use advanced machinery to administer medical treatment to patients. Other occupations that perform similar duties include radiologic technologists and technicians, diagnostic medical sonographers, nuclear medicine technologists, cardiovascular technologists and technicians, dental hygienists, respiratory therapists, physical therapist assistants and aides, registered nurses, and physicians and surgeons.

Other occupations that build relationships with patients and provide them with emotional support include nursing, psychiatric, and home health aides; counselors; psychologists; social workers; and social and human service assistants.

Projections data from the National Employment Matrix

Occupational Title	SOC Code	Employment, 2006	Projected employment, 2016	Change, 2006-2016	
				Number	Percent
Radiation therapists	29-1124	15,000	18,000	3,600	25

NOTE: Data in this table are rounded.

Sources of Additional Information

Information on certification by the American Registry of Radiologic Technologists and on accredited radiation therapy programs may be obtained from

- American Registry of Radiologic Technologists, 1255 Northland Dr., St. Paul, MN 55120. Internet: http://www.arrt.org

Information on careers in radiation therapy may be obtained from

- American Society of Radiologic Technologists, 15000 Central Ave. SE, Albuquerque, NM 87123. Internet: http://www.asrt.org

Radio and Telecommunications Equipment Installers and Repairers

(O*NET 49-2021.00 and 49-2022.00)

Significant Points

- Little or no change in employment is projected.
- Job opportunities vary by specialty; good opportunities are expected for central office installers and repairers, but station installers and repairers can expect keen competition.
- Applicants with computer skills and postsecondary electronics training should have the best opportunities.
- Repairers may be on-call around the clock in case of emergencies—night, weekend, and holiday hours are common.

Nature of the Work

Telephones, computers, and radios depend on a variety of equipment to transmit communications signals and connect to the Internet. From electronic and optical switches that route telephone calls and packets of data to their destinations to radio transmitters and receivers that relay signals from radios in airplanes, boats, and emergency vehicles, complex equipment is needed to keep us communicating. The workers who set up and maintain this sophisticated equipment are called radio and telecommunications equipment installers and repairers.

Telecommunications equipment installers and repairers have a range of skills and abilities, which vary by the type of work they do and where it is performed. Most work indoors. (Equipment installers who work mainly outdoors are classified as telecommunications line installers and repairers—a separate occupation.)

Central office installers and repairers—telecommunications equipment installers and repairers who work at switching hubs called central offices—do some of the most complex work. Switching hubs contain the switches and routers that direct packets of information to their destinations. Installers and repairers set up those switches and routers as well as cables and other equipment.

Although most telephone lines connecting houses to central offices and switching stations are still copper, the lines connecting central hubs to each other are fiber optic. Fiber optic lines, along with newer packet switching equipment, have greatly increased the transmission capacity of each line, allowing an ever increasing amount of information to pass through the lines. Switches and routers are used to transmit, process, amplify, and direct a massive amount of information. Installing and maintaining this equipment requires a high level of special technical knowledge.

The increasing reliability of switches and routers has simplified maintenance, however. New self-monitoring telecommunications switches alert central office repairers to malfunctions. Some switches allow repairers to diagnose and correct problems from remote locations. When faced with a malfunction, the repairer may refer to manufacturers' manuals that provide maintenance instructions.

As cable television and telecommunications technology converge, the equipment used in both technologies is becoming more similar. The distribution centers for cable television companies, which are similar to central offices in the telecommunications sector, are called headends. *Headend technicians* perform essentially the same work as central office technicians, but they work in the cable industry.

When problems with telecommunications equipment arise, telecommunications equipment repairers diagnose the source of the problem by testing each part of the equipment. This requires understanding how the software and hardware interact. Repairers often use spectrum analyzers, network analyzers, or both to locate the problem. A network analyzer sends a signal through the equipment to detect any distortion in the signal. The nature of the signal distortion often directs the repairer to the source of the problem. To fix the equipment, repairers may use small hand tools, including pliers and screwdrivers, to remove and replace defective components such as circuit boards or wiring. Newer equipment is easier to repair because whole boards and parts are designed to be quickly removed and replaced. Repairers also may install updated software or programs that maintain existing software.

Another type of telecommunications installer and repairer, *PBX installers and repairers* set up private branch exchange (PBX) switchboards, which relay incoming, outgoing, and interoffice telephone calls within a single location or organization. To install switches and switchboards, installers first connect the equipment to power lines and communications cables and install frames and supports. They test the connections to ensure that adequate power is available and that the communication links work properly. They also install equipment such as power systems, alarms, and telephone sets. New switches and switchboards are computerized and workers often need to install software or program the equipment to provide specific features. Finally, the installer performs tests to verify that the newly installed equipment functions properly. If a problem arises, PBX repairers determine whether it is located within the PBX system or whether it originates in the telephone lines maintained by the local telephone company. Newer installations use voice-over Internet protocol (VoIP) systems. VoIP systems operate like a PBX system, but they use a company's computer wiring to run Internet access, network applications, and telephone communications.

Station installers and repairers, telephone—commonly known as *home installers and repairers* or *telecommunications service technicians*—install and repair telecommunications wiring and equipment in customers' home or business premises. They install telephone, VoIP, Internet, and other communications services by installing wiring inside the home or connecting existing wiring to outside service lines. Depending upon the service required, they may setup television capability or connect modems and install software on a customer's computer. To complete the

connection to an outside service line, the installer may need to climb telephone poles or ladders and test the line. Later on, if a maintenance problem occurs, station repairers test the customer's lines to determine if the problem is located in the customer's premises or in the outside service lines and attempt to fix the problem if it is inside. If the problem is with the outside service lines, telecommunications line repairers are usually called to fix it.

Radio mechanics install and maintain radio transmitting and receiving equipment, excluding cellular communications systems. This includes stationary equipment mounted on transmission towers or tall buildings and mobile equipment, such as two-way radio communications systems in taxis, airplanes, ships, and emergency vehicles. Aviation and marine radio mechanics also may work on other electronic equipment, in addition to radios. Newer radio equipment is self-monitoring and may alert mechanics to potential malfunctions. When malfunctions occur, these mechanics examine equipment for damaged components and either fix them, replace the part, or make a software modification. They may use electrical measuring instruments to monitor signal strength, transmission capacity, interference, and signal delay, as well as hand tools to replace defective components and parts and to adjust equipment so that it performs within required specifications.

Work environment. Radio and telecommunications equipment installers and repairers generally work in clean, well-lighted, air-conditioned surroundings, such as a telecommunications company's central office, a customer's location, or an electronic repair shop or service center. Traveling to the site of the installation or repair is common among station installers and repairers, PBX and VoIP installers and repairers, and radio mechanics. The installation may require access to rooftops, ladders, and telephone poles to complete the repair. Radio mechanics may need to work on transmissions towers, which may be located on top of tall buildings or mountains, as well as aboard airplanes and ships. These workers are subject to a variety of weather conditions while working outdoors.

The work of most repairers involves lifting, reaching, stooping, crouching, and crawling. Adherence to safety precautions is important in order to guard against work hazards. These hazards include falls, minor burns, electrical shock, and contact with hazardous materials.

Nearly all radio and telecommunications equipment installers and repairers work full time. Many work regular business hours to meet the demand for repair services during the workday. Schedules are more irregular at employers that provide repair services 24 hours a day, such as for police radio communications operations or where installation and maintenance must take place after normal business hours. At these locations, mechanics work a variety of shifts, including weekend and holiday hours. Repairers may be on call around the clock, in case of emergencies, and may have to work overtime.

Training, Other Qualifications, and Advancement

Postsecondary education in electronics and computer technology is increasingly required for radio and telecommunications equipment installers and repairer jobs, and a few employers even prefer people with a bachelor's degree for some of the most complex types of work. About half of all radio and telecommunications equipment installers and repairers have completed some college courses or an associate degree.

Education and training. As telecommunications technology becomes more complex, the education required for radio and telecommunications equipment installers and repairer jobs has increased. Most employers prefer applicants with postsecondary training in electronics and familiarity with computers. The education needed for these jobs may vary from a certification to work on certain equipment to a two- or four-year degree in electronics or a related subject. Sources of training include two- and four-year college programs in electronics or communications technology, military experience in radios and electronics, trade schools, and programs offered by equipment and software manufacturers. Educational requirements are higher for central office installers and repairers and for those working in nonresidential settings.

Many in the telecommunications industry work their way up into this occupation by gaining experience at less difficult jobs. Experience as a telecommunications line installer or station installer is helpful before moving up to the job of central office installer and other more complex jobs, for example. Military experience with communications equipment is also valued by many employers in both telecommunications and radio repair.

Newly hired repairers usually receive some training from their employers. This may include formal classroom training in electronics, communications systems, or software and informal hands-on training assisting an experienced repairer. Large companies may send repairers to outside training sessions to learn about new equipment and service procedures. As networks have become more sophisticated—often including equipment from a variety of companies—the knowledge needed for installation and maintenance also has increased.

Licensure. Aviation and marine radio mechanics are required to have a license from the Federal Communications Commission before they can work on these types of radios. This requires passing several exams on radio law, electronics fundamentals, and maintenance practices.

Other qualifications. Familiarity with computers, being mechanically inclined, and being able to solve problems are traits that are highly regarded by employers. Repairers must also be able to distinguish colors, because wires are color-coded. For positions that require climbing poles and towers, workers must be in good physical shape and not afraid of heights. Repairers who handle assignments alone at a customer's site must be able to work without close supervision. For workers who frequently contact customers, a pleasant personality, neat appearance, and good communications skills also are important.

Certification and advancement. This is an occupation where the technology is changing rapidly. Workers must keep abreast of the latest equipment available and know how to repair it. Telecommunications equipment installers and repairers often need to be certified to perform certain tasks or to work on specific equipment. Certification often requires taking classes. Some of certifications are needed before entering an occupation; others are meant to improve one's current abilities or to advance in the occupation.

The Society of Cable and Telecommunications Engineers and the Telecommunications Industry Association offer voluntary certifications to workers in this field. Telecommunications equipment manufacturers also provide training on specific equipment.

Experienced repairers with advanced training may become specialists or troubleshooters who help other repairers diagnose difficult problems, or may work with engineers in designing equipment and developing maintenance procedures. Home installers may advance to wiring computer networks or working as a central office installer and repairer. Because of their familiarity with equipment, repairers are particularly well qualified to become manufacturers' sales workers. Workers with leadership ability also may become maintenance supervisors or service managers. Some experienced workers open their own repair services or shops, or become wholesalers or retailers of electronic equipment.

Employment

Radio and telecommunications equipment installers and repairers held about 205,000 jobs in 2006. About 198,000 were telecommunications equipment installers and repairers, except line installers. The remaining 6,500 were radio mechanics.

Telecommunications equipment installers and repairers work mostly in the telecommunications industry. Increasingly, however, they can be found in the construction industry working as contractors to the telecommunications industry.

Radio mechanics work in the electronic and precision equipment repair and maintenance industry, the telecommunications industry, electronics and appliance stores, government, and other industries.

Job Outlook

Little or no change in employment of radio and telecommunications equipment installers and repairers is projected. Job opportunities vary by specialty. Job prospects are best for those with computer skills and postsecondary training in electronics.

Employment change. Employment of radio and telecommunications equipment installers and repairers is expected to increase 2 percent, reflecting little or no change, during the 2006–2016 period. Over the next decade, telecommunications companies will provide faster Internet connections, provide video-on-demand, add hundreds of television stations, and many services that haven't even been invented yet. Although building the new networks required to provide these services will create jobs, these gains will be offset by a decline in maintenance work. The new equipment requires much less maintenance work because it is newer, more reliable, easier to repair, and more resistant to damage from the elements.

The increased reliability of radio equipment and the use of self-monitoring systems also will continue to lessen the need for radio mechanics. However, technological changes are also creating new wireless applications that create jobs for radio mechanics.

Job prospects. Applicants with computer skills and postsecondary training in electronics should have the best opportunities for radio and telecommunications equipment installer and repairer jobs, but opportunities will vary by specialty. Good opportunities should be available for central office and PBX installers and repairers experienced in current technology, as the growing popularity of VoIP, expanded multimedia offerings such as video on demand, and other telecommunications services continue to place additional demand on telecommunications networks. These new services require high data transfer rates, which can be achieved only by installing new optical switching and routing equipment. Extending high-speed communications from central offices to customers also will require telecommunications equipment installers to put in place more advanced switching and routing equipment, but opportunities for repairers will be limited by the increased reliability and automation of the new switching equipment.

Station installers and repairers can expect keen competition. Prewired buildings and the increasing reliability of telephone equipment will reduce the need for installation and maintenance of customers' telephones, as will the declining number of pay telephones in operation as use of cellular telephones grows. However, some of these losses should be offset by the need to upgrade internal lines in businesses and the wiring of new homes and businesses with fiber optic lines.

Radio mechanics should find good opportunities if they have a strong background in electronics and an ability to work independently. Increasing competition from cellular services is limiting the growth of radio services, but employers report difficulty finding adequate numbers of qualified radio mechanics to perform repair work.

Earnings

In May 2006, median hourly earnings of telecommunications equipment installers and repairers, except line installers were $25.21. The middle 50 percent earned between $20.43 and $28.66. The bottom 10 percent earned less than $14.96, whereas the top 10 percent earned more than $32.84. The median hourly earnings of these workers in the wired telecommunications carriers industry were $26.25 in May 2006.

Median hourly earnings of radio mechanics in May 2006 were $18.12. The middle 50 percent earned between 14.04 and $23.02. The bottom 10 percent earned less than $10.94, whereas the top 10 percent earned more than $28.54.

About 4 percent of radio and telecommunications equipment installers and repairers were self-employed. About 26 percent of radio and telecommunication equipment installers and repairers are members of unions, such as the Communications Workers of America (CWA) and the International Brotherhood of Electrical Workers (IBEW.)

Telecommunications equipment installers and repairers employed by large telecommunications companies who also belong to unions often have very good benefits, including health, dental, vision, and

Projections data from the National Employment Matrix

Occupational Title	SOC Code	Employment, 2006	Projected employment, 2016	Change, 2006-16 Number	Change, 2006-16 Percent
Radio and telecommunications equipment installers and repairers	49-2020	205,000	209,000	4,800	2
Radio mechanics	49-2021	6,500	6,300	-300	-4
Telecommunications equipment installers and repairers, except line installers	49-2022	198,000	203,000	5,000	3

NOTE: Data in this table are rounded.

life insurance. They also usually have good retirement and leave policies. Those working for small independent companies and contractors may get fewer benefits.

Radio mechanics tend to work for small electronics firms or government. Benefits vary widely depending upon the type of work and size of firm. Government jobs usually have good benefits.

Related Occupations

Related occupations that involve work with electronic equipment include broadcast and sound engineering technicians and radio operators; computer, automated teller, and office machine repairers; and electrical and electronics installers and repairers. Line installers and repairers also set up and install telecommunications equipment. Engineering technicians also may repair electronic equipment as part of their duties.

Sources of Additional Information

For information on career and training opportunities, contact

- International Brotherhood of Electrical Workers, Telecommunications Department, 900 7th St. NW, Washington, DC 20001.
- Communications Workers of America, 501 3rd St. NW, Washington, DC 20001. Internet: http://www.cwa-union.org/jobs

For information on training and professional certifications for those already employed by cable telecommunications firms, contact

- Society of Cable Telecommunications Engineers, Certification Department, 140 Phillips Rd., Exton, PA 19341-1318. Internet: http://www.scte.org

For information on training and licensing for aviation and marine radio mechanics, contact

- The Federal Communications Commission (FCC), 445 12th St. SW, Washington, DC 20554. Internet: http://wireless.fcc.gov/commoperators

For more information on employers, education, and training in marine electronics and radios, contact

- National Marine Electronics Association, 7 Riggs Ave., Severna Park, MD 21164. Internet: http://www.nmea.org

Radiologic Technologists and Technicians

(O*NET 29-2034.00, 29-2034.01, and 29-2034.02)

Significant Points

- Employment is projected to grow faster than average, and job opportunities are expected to be favorable.
- Formal training programs in radiography are offered in hospitals, colleges and universities, and less frequently at vocational-technical institutes; range in length from 1 to 4 years; and lead to a certificate, an associate degree, or a bachelor's degree.
- Although hospitals will remain the primary employer, a number of new jobs will be found in physicians' offices and diagnostic imaging centers.

Nature of the Work

Radiologic technologists take x rays and administer nonradioactive materials into patients' bloodstreams for diagnostic purposes.

Radiologic technologists also referred to as *radiographers,* produce x-ray films (radiographs) of parts of the human body for use in diagnosing medical problems. They prepare patients for radiologic examinations by explaining the procedure, removing jewelry and other articles through which x rays cannot pass, and positioning patients so that the parts of the body can be appropriately radiographed. To prevent unnecessary exposure to radiation, these workers surround the exposed area with radiation protection devices, such as lead shields, or limit the size of the x-ray beam. Radiographers position radiographic equipment at the correct angle and height over the appropriate area of a patient's body. Using instruments similar to a measuring tape, they may measure the thickness of the section to be radiographed and set controls on the x-ray machine to produce radiographs of the appropriate density, detail, and contrast. They place the x-ray film under the part of the patient's body to be examined and make the exposure. They then remove the film and develop it.

Radiologic technologists must follow physicians' orders precisely and conform to regulations concerning the use of radiation to protect themselves, their patients, and their coworkers from unnecessary exposure.

In addition to preparing patients and operating equipment, radiologic technologists keep patient records and adjust and maintain equipment. They also may prepare work schedules, evaluate purchases of equipment, or manage a radiology department.

Experienced radiographers may perform more complex imaging procedures. When performing fluoroscopies, for example, radiographers prepare a solution of contrast medium for the patient to drink, allowing the radiologist (a physician who interprets radiographs) to see soft tissues in the body.

Some radiographers specialize in computed tomography (CT), and are sometimes referred to as *CT technologists*. CT scans produce a substantial amount of cross-sectional x rays of an area of the body. From those cross-sectional x rays, a three-dimensional image is made. The CT uses ionizing radiation; therefore, it requires the same precautionary measures that radiographers use with other x rays.

Radiographers also can specialize in Magnetic Resonance Imaging as an *MR technologist*. MR, like CT, produces multiple cross-sectional images to create a 3-dimensional image. Unlike CT, MR uses non-ionizing radio frequency to generate image contrast.

Another common specialty for radiographers specialize in is mammography. Mammographers use low dose x-ray systems to produce images of the breast.

In addition to radiologic technologists, others who conduct diagnostic imaging procedures include cardiovascular technologists and technicians, diagnostic medical sonographers, and nuclear medicine technologists. (Each is discussed elsewhere in this book.)

Work environment. Physical stamina is important in this occupation because technologists are on their feet for long periods and may lift or turn disabled patients. Technologists work at diagnostic machines but also may perform some procedures at patients' bedsides. Some travel to patients in large vans equipped with sophisticated diagnostic equipment.

Although radiation hazards exist in this occupation, they are minimized by the use of lead aprons, gloves, and other shielding devices, as well as by instruments monitoring exposure to radiation. Technologists wear badges measuring radiation levels in the radiation area, and detailed records are kept on their cumulative lifetime dose.

Most full-time radiologic technologists work about 40 hours a week. They may, however, have evening, weekend, or on-call hours. Opportunities for part-time and shift work also are available.

Training, Other Qualifications, and Advancement

Preparation for this profession is offered in hospitals, colleges and universities, and less frequently at vocational-technical institutes. Hospitals employ most radiologic technologists. Employers prefer to hire technologists with formal training.

Education and training. Formal training programs in radiography range in length from one to four years and lead to a certificate, an associate degree, or a bachelor's degree. Two-year associate degree programs are most prevalent.

Some one-year certificate programs are available for experienced radiographers or individuals from other health occupations, such as medical technologists and registered nurses, who want to change fields. A bachelor's or master's degree in one of the radiologic technologies is desirable for supervisory, administrative, or teaching positions.

The Joint Review Committee on Education in Radiologic Technology accredits most formal training programs for the field. The committee accredited more than 600 radiography programs in 2007. Admission to radiography programs require, at a minimum, a high school diploma or the equivalent. High school courses in mathematics, physics, chemistry, and biology are helpful. The programs provide both classroom and clinical instruction in anatomy and physiology, patient care procedures, radiation physics, radiation protection, principles of imaging, medical terminology, positioning of patients, medical ethics, radiobiology, and pathology.

Licensure. Federal legislation protects the public from the hazards of unnecessary exposure to medical and dental radiation by ensuring that operators of radiologic equipment are properly trained. Under this legislation, the federal government sets voluntary standards that the states may use for accrediting training programs and licensing individuals who engage in medical or dental radiography. In 2007, 40 states required licensure for practicing radiologic technologists and technicians.

Certification and other qualifications. The American Registry of Radiologic Technologists (ARRT) offers voluntary certification for radiologic technologists. In addition, 35 states use ARRT-administered exams for state licensing purposes. To be eligible for certification, technologists generally must graduate from an accredited program and pass an examination. Many employers prefer to hire certified radiographers. To be recertified, radiographers must complete 24 hours of continuing education every two years.

Radiologic technologists should be sensitive to patients' physical and psychological needs. They must pay attention to detail, follow instructions, and work as part of a team. In addition, operating complicated equipment requires mechanical ability and manual dexterity.

Advancement. With experience and additional training, staff technologists may become specialists, performing CT scanning, MR, and angiography, a procedure during which blood vessels are x rayed to find clots. Technologists also may advance, with additional education and certification, to become a radiologist assistant.

Experienced technologists also may be promoted to supervisor, chief radiologic technologist, and, ultimately, department administrator or director. Depending on the institution, courses or a master's degree in business or health administration may be necessary for the director's position.

Some technologists progress by specializing in the occupation to become instructors or directors in radiologic technology programs; others take jobs as sales representatives or instructors with equipment manufacturers.

Employment

Radiologic technologists held about 196,000 jobs in 2006. More than 60 percent of all jobs were in hospitals. Most other jobs were in offices of physicians; medical and diagnostic laboratories, including diagnostic imaging centers; and outpatient care centers.

Job Outlook

Employment is projected to grow faster than average, and job opportunities are expected to be favorable.

Employment change. Employment of radiologic technologists is expected to increase by about 15 percent from 2006 to 2016, faster than the average for all occupations. As the population grows and ages, there will be an increasing demand for diagnostic imaging. Although health care providers are enthusiastic about the clinical benefits of new technologies, the extent to which they are adopted depends largely on cost and reimbursement considerations. As technology advances many imaging modalities are becoming less expensive and their adoption is becoming more widespread. For example, digital imaging technology can improve the quality of the images and the efficiency of the procedure, but it remains slightly more expensive than analog imaging, a procedure during which the image is put directly on film. Despite this, digital imaging is becoming more widespread in many imaging facilities because of the advantages it provides over analog.

Although hospitals will remain the principal employer of radiologic technologists, a number of new jobs will be found in offices of physicians and diagnostic imaging centers. Health facilities such as these are expected to grow through 2016, because of the shift toward outpatient care, encouraged by third-party payers and made possible by technological advances that permit more procedures to be performed outside the hospital.

Projections data from the National Employment Matrix

Occupational Title	SOC Code	Employment, 2006	Projected employment, 2016	Change, 2006-2016	
				Number	Percent
Radiologic technologists and technicians	29-2034	196,000	226,000	30,000	15

NOTE: Data in this table are rounded.

Job prospects. In addition to job growth, job openings also will arise from the need to replace technologists who leave the occupation. Radiologic technologists are willing to relocate and who also are experienced in more than one diagnostic imaging procedure—such as CT, MR, and mammography—will have the best employment opportunities as employers seek to control costs by using multi-credentialed employees.

CT is becoming a frontline diagnosis tool. Instead of taking x rays to decide whether a CT is needed, as was the practice before, it is often the first choice for imaging because of its accuracy. MR also is increasing in frequency of use. Technologists with credentialing in either of these specialties will be very marketable to employers.

Earnings

Median annual earnings of radiologic technologists were $48,170 in May 2006. The middle 50 percent earned between $39,840 and $57,940. The lowest 10 percent earned less than $32,750, and the highest 10 percent earned more than $68,920. Median annual earnings in the industries employing the largest numbers of radiologic technologists in 2006 were

Medical and diagnostic laboratories	$51,280
General medical and surgical hospitals	48,830
Offices of physicians	45,500

Related Occupations

Radiologic technologists operate sophisticated equipment to help physicians, dentists, and other health practitioners diagnose and treat patients. Workers in related occupations include cardiovascular technologists and technicians, clinical laboratory technologists and technicians, diagnostic medical sonographers, nuclear medicine technologists, radiation therapists, and respiratory therapists.

Sources of Additional Information

For information on careers in radiologic technology, contact

- American Society of Radiologic Technologists, 15000 Central Ave. SE, Albuquerque, NM 87123-3917. Internet: http://www.asrt.org

For the current list of accredited education programs in radiography, write to

- Joint Review Committee on Education in Radiologic Technology, 20 N. Wacker Dr., Suite 2850, Chicago, IL 60606-3182. Internet: http://www.jrcert.org

For certification information, contact

- American Registry of Radiologic Technologists, 1255 Northland Dr., St. Paul, MN 55120-1155. Internet: http://www.arrt.org

Registered Nurses

(O*NET 29-1111.00)

Significant Points

- Registered nurses constitute the largest health care occupation, with 2.5 million jobs.
- About 59 percent of jobs are in hospitals.
- The three major educational paths to registered nursing are a bachelor's degree, an associate degree, and a diploma from an approved nursing program.
- Registered nurses are projected to generate about 587,000 new jobs over the 2006–2016 period, one of the largest numbers among all occupations; overall job opportunities are expected to be excellent, but may vary by employment setting.

Nature of the Work

Registered nurses (RNs), regardless of specialty or work setting, treat patients, educate patients and the public about various medical conditions, and provide advice and emotional support to patients' family members. RNs record patients' medical histories and symptoms, help perform diagnostic tests and analyze results, operate medical machinery, administer treatment and medications, and help with patient follow-up and rehabilitation.

RNs teach patients and their families how to manage their illness or injury, explaining post-treatment home care needs; diet, nutrition, and exercise programs; and self-administration of medication and physical therapy. Some RNs work to promote general health by educating the public on warning signs and symptoms of disease. RNs also might run general health screening or immunization clinics, blood drives, and public seminars on various conditions.

When caring for patients, RNs establish a plan of care or contribute to an existing plan. Plans may include numerous activities, such as administering medication, including careful checking of dosages and avoiding interactions; starting, maintaining, and discontinuing intravenous (IV) lines for fluid, medication, blood, and blood products; administering therapies and treatments; observing the patient and recording those observations; and consulting with physicians and other health care clinicians. Some RNs provide direction to licensed practical nurses and nursing aids regarding patient care. RNs with advanced educational preparation and training may perform diagnostic and therapeutic procedures and may have prescriptive authority.

RNs can specialize in one or more areas of patient care. There generally are four ways to specialize. RNs can choose a particular work setting or type of treatment, such as perioperative nurses, who work in operating rooms and assist surgeons. RNs also may choose to specialize in specific health conditions, as do diabetes management nurses, who assist patients to manage diabetes. Other RNs specialize in working with one or more organs or body system types, such as dermatology nurses, who work with patients who have skin disorders. RNs also can choose to work with a well-defined population, such as geriatric nurses, who work with the elderly. Some RNs may combine specialties. For example, pediatric oncology nurses deal with children and adolescents who have cancer.

There are many options for RNs who specialize in a work setting or type of treatment. *Ambulatory care nurses* provide preventive care and treat patients with a variety of illnesses and injuries in physicians' offices or in clinics. Some ambulatory care nurses are involved in telehealth, providing care and advice through electronic communications media such as videoconferencing, the Internet, or by telephone. *Critical care nurses* provide care to patients with serious, complex, and acute illnesses or injuries that require very close monitoring and extensive medication protocols and therapies. Critical care nurses often work in critical or intensive care hospital units. *Emergency*, or *trauma, nurses* work in hospital or stand-alone emergency departments, providing initial assessments and care for patients with life-threatening conditions. Some emergency nurses may become qualified to serve as *transport nurses*, who provide medical care to patients who are transported by helicopter or airplane to the nearest medical facility. *Holistic nurses* provide care such as acupuncture, massage and aroma therapy, and biofeedback, which are meant to treat patients' mental and spiritual health in addition to their physical health. *Home health care nurses* provide at-home nursing care for patients, often as follow-up care after discharge from a hospital or from a rehabilitation, long-term care, or skilled nursing facility. *Hospice and palliative care nurses* provide care, most often in home or hospice settings, focused on maintaining quality of life for terminally ill patients. *Infusion nurses* administer medications, fluids, and blood to patients through injections into patients' veins. *Long- term care nurses* provide health care services on a recurring basis to patients with chronic physical or mental disorders, often in long-term care or skilled nursing facilities. *Medical-surgical nurses* provide health promotion and basic medical care to patients with various medical and surgical diagnoses. *Occupational health nurses* seek to prevent job-related injuries and illnesses, provide monitoring and emergency care services, and help employers implement health and safety standards. *Perianesthesia nurses* provide preoperative and postoperative care to patients undergoing anesthesia during surgery or other procedure. *Perioperative nurses* assist surgeons by selecting and handling instruments, controlling bleeding, and suturing incisions. Some of these nurses also can specialize in plastic and reconstructive surgery. *Psychiatric-mental health nurses* treat patients with personality and mood disorders. *Radiology nurses* provide care to patients undergoing diagnostic radiation procedures such as ultrasounds, magnetic resonance imaging, and radiation therapy for oncology diagnoses. *Rehabilitation nurses* care for patients with temporary and permanent disabilities. *Transplant nurses* care for both transplant recipients and living donors and monitor signs of organ rejection.

RNs specializing in a particular disease, ailment, or health care condition are employed in virtually all work settings, including physicians' offices, outpatient treatment facilities, home health care agencies, and hospitals. *Addictions nurses* care for patients seeking help with alcohol, drug, tobacco, and other addictions. *Intellectual and developmental disabilities nurses* provide care for patients with physical, mental, or behavioral disabilities; care may include help with feeding, controlling bodily functions, sitting or standing independently, and speaking or other communication. *Diabetes management nurses* help diabetics to manage their disease by teaching them proper nutrition and showing them how to test blood sugar levels and administer insulin injections. *Genetics nurses* provide early detection screenings, counseling, and treatment of patients with genetic disorders, including cystic fibrosis and Huntington's disease. *HIV/AIDS nurses* care for patients diagnosed with HIV and AIDS. *Oncology nurses* care for patients with various types of cancer and may assist in the administration of radiation and chemotherapies and follow-up monitoring. *Wound, ostomy, and continence nurses* treat patients with wounds caused by traumatic injury, ulcers, or arterial disease; provide postoperative care for patients with openings that allow for alternative methods of bodily waste elimination; and treat patients with urinary and fecal incontinence.

RNs specializing in treatment of a particular organ or body system usually are employed in hospital specialty or critical care units, specialty clinics, and outpatient care facilities. *Cardiovascular nurses* treat patients with coronary heart disease and those who have had heart surgery, providing services such as postoperative rehabilitation. *Dermatology nurses* treat patients with disorders of the skin, such as skin cancer and psoriasis. *Gastroenterology nurses* treat patients with digestive and intestinal disorders, including ulcers, acid reflux disease, and abdominal bleeding. Some nurses in this field also assist in specialized procedures such as endoscopies, which look inside the gastrointestinal tract using a tube equipped with a light and a camera that can capture images of diseased tissue. *Gynecology nurses* provide care to women with disorders of the reproductive system, including endometriosis, cancer, and sexually transmitted diseases. *Nephrology nurses* care for patients with kidney disease caused by diabetes, hypertension, or substance abuse. *Neuroscience nurses* care for patients with dysfunctions of the nervous system, including brain and spinal cord injuries and seizures. *Ophthalmic nurses* provide care to patients with disorders of the eyes, including blindness and glaucoma, and to patients undergoing eye surgery. *Orthopedic nurses* care for patients with muscular and skeletal problems, including arthritis, bone fractures, and muscular dystrophy. *Otorhinolaryngology nurses* care for patients with ear, nose, and throat disorders, such as cleft palates, allergies, and sinus disorders. *Respiratory nurses* provide care to patients with respiratory disorders such as asthma, tuberculosis, and cystic fibrosis. *Urology nurses* care for patients with disorders of the kidneys, urinary tract, and male reproductive organs, including infections, kidney and bladder stones, and cancers.

RNs who specialize by population provide preventive and acute care in all health care settings to the segment of the population in which they specialize, including newborns (neonatology), children and adolescents (pediatrics), adults, and the elderly (gerontology or geriatrics). RNs also may provide basic health care to patients outside of health care settings in such venues as including correctional facilities, schools, summer camps, and the military. Some RNs travel around the United States and abroad providing care to patients in areas with shortages of health care workers.

Most RNs work as staff nurses as members of a team providing critical health care . However, some RNs choose to become advanced practice nurses, who work independently or in collaboration with physicians, and may focus on the provision of primary care services. *Clinical nurse specialists* provide direct patient care and expert consultations in one of many nursing specialties, such as psychiatric-mental health. *Nurse anesthetists* provide anesthesia and related care before and after surgical, therapeutic, diagnostic and obstetrical procedures. They also provide pain management and emergency services, such as airway management. *Nurse-midwives* provide primary care to women, including gynecological exams, family planning advice, prenatal care, assistance in labor and delivery, and neonatal care. *Nurse practitioners* serve as primary and specialty care providers, providing a blend of nursing and health care services to patients and families. The most common specialty areas for nurse practitioners are family practice, adult practice, women's health, pediatrics, acute care, and geriatrics. However, there are a variety of other specialties that nurse practitioners can choose, including neonatology and mental health. Advanced practice nurses can prescribe medications in all states and in the District of Columbia.

Some nurses have jobs that require little or no direct patient care, but still require an active RN license. *Case managers* ensure that all of the medical needs of patients with severe injuries and severe or chronic illnesses are met. *Forensics nurses* participate in the scientific investigation and treatment of abuse victims, violence, criminal activity, and traumatic accident. *Infection control nurses* identify, track, and control infectious outbreaks in health care facilities and develop programs for outbreak prevention and response to biological terrorism. *Legal nurse consultants* assist lawyers in medical cases by interviewing patients and witnesses, organizing medical records, determining damages and costs, locating evidence, and educating lawyers about medical issues. *Nurse administrators* supervise nursing staff, establish work schedules and budgets, maintain medical supply inventories, and manage resources to ensure high-quality care. *Nurse educators* plan, develop, implement, and evaluate educational programs and curricula for the professional development of student nurses and RNs. *Nurse informaticists* manage and communicate nursing data and information to improve decision making by consumers, patients, nurses, and other health care providers. RNs also may work as health care consultants, public policy advisors, pharmaceutical and medical supply researchers and salespersons, and medical writers and editors.

Work environment. Most RNs work in well-lighted, comfortable health care facilities. Home health and public health nurses travel to patients' homes, schools, community centers, and other sites. RNs may spend considerable time walking, bending, stretching, and standing. Patients in hospitals and nursing care facilities require 24-hour care; consequently, nurses in these institutions may work nights, weekends, and holidays. RNs also may be on call—available to work on short notice. Nurses who work in offices, schools, and other settings that do not provide 24-hour care are more likely to work regular business hours. About 21 percent of RNs worked part time in 2006, and 7 percent held more than one job.

Nursing has its hazards, especially in hospitals, nursing care facilities, and clinics, where nurses may be in close contact with individuals who have infectious diseases and with toxic, harmful, or potentially hazardous compounds, solutions, and medications. RNs must observe rigid, standardized guidelines to guard against disease and other dangers, such as those posed by radiation, accidental needle sticks, chemicals used to sterilize instruments, and anesthetics. In addition, they are vulnerable to back injury when moving patients, shocks from electrical equipment, and hazards posed by compressed gases. RNs also may suffer emotional strain from caring for patients suffering unrelieved intense pain, close personal contact with patients' families, the need to make critical decisions, and ethical dilemmas and concerns.

Training, Other Qualifications, and Advancement

The three major educational paths to registered nursing are a bachelor's degree, an associate degree, and a diploma from an approved nursing program. Nurses most commonly enter the occupation by completing an associate degree or bachelor's degree program. Individuals then must complete a national licensing examination in order to obtain a nursing license. Further training or education can qualify nurses to work in specialty areas, and may help improve advancement opportunities.

Education and training. There are three major educational paths to registered nursing—a bachelor's of science degree in nursing (BSN), an associate degree in nursing (ADN), and a diploma. BSN programs, offered by colleges and universities, take about four years to complete. In 2006, 709 nursing programs offered degrees at the bachelor's level. ADN programs, offered by community and junior colleges, take about two to three years to complete. About 850 RN programs granted associate degrees. Diploma programs, administered in hospitals, last about three years. Only about 70 programs offered diplomas. Generally, licensed graduates of any of the three types of educational programs qualify for entry-level positions.

Many RNs with an ADN or diploma later enter bachelor's programs to prepare for a broader scope of nursing practice. Often, they can find an entry-level position and then take advantage of tuition reimbursement benefits to work toward a BSN by completing an RN-to-BSN program. In 2006, there were 629 RN-to-BSN programs in the United States. Accelerated master's degree in nursing (MSN) programs also are available by combining one year of an accelerated BSN program with two years of graduate study. In 2006, there were 149 RN-to-MSN programs.

Accelerated BSN programs also are available for individuals who have a bachelor's or higher degree in another field and who are interested in moving into nursing. In 2006, 197 of these programs were available. Accelerated BSN programs last 12 to 18 months and provide the fastest route to a BSN for individuals who already hold a degree. MSN programs also are available for individuals who hold a bachelor's or higher degree in another field.

Individuals considering nursing should carefully weigh the advantages and disadvantages of enrolling in a BSN or MSN program because, if they do, their advancement opportunities usually are broader. In fact, some career paths are open only to nurses with a bachelor's or master's degree. A bachelor's degree often is necessary for administrative positions and is a prerequisite for admission to graduate nursing programs in research, consulting, and teaching, and all four advanced practice nursing specialties—clinical nurse specialists, nurse anesthetists, nurse-midwives, and nurse practitioners. Individuals who complete a bachelor's receive more training in areas such as communication, leadership, and critical thinking, all of which are becoming more important as nursing care becomes more complex. Additionally, bachelor's degree programs offer more clinical experience in nonhospital settings. Education beyond a bachelor's degree can also help students looking to enter certain fields or increase advancement opportunities. In 2006, 448 nursing schools offered master's degrees, 108 offered doctoral degrees, and 58 offered accelerated BSN-to-doctoral programs.

All four advanced practice nursing specialties require at least a master's degree. Most programs include about two years of full-time study and require a BSN degree for entry; some programs require at least one to two years of clinical experience as an RN for admission. In 2006, there were 342 master's and post-master's programs offered for nurse practitioners, 230 master's and post-master's programs for clinical nurse specialists, 106 programs for nurse anesthetists, and 39 programs for nurse-midwives.

All nursing education programs include classroom instruction and supervised clinical experience in hospitals and other health care facilities. Students take courses in anatomy, physiology, microbiology, chemistry, nutrition, psychology and other behavioral sciences, and nursing. Coursework also includes the liberal arts for ADN and BSN students.

Supervised clinical experience is provided in hospital departments such as pediatrics, psychiatry, maternity, and surgery. A growing number of programs include clinical experience in nursing care facilities, public health departments, home health agencies, and ambulatory clinics.

Licensure and certification. In all states, the District of Columbia, and U.S. territories, students must graduate from an approved nursing program and pass a national licensing examination, known as the NCLEX-RN, in order to obtain a nursing license. Nurses may be licensed in more than one state, either by examination or by the endorsement of a license issued by another state. The Nurse Licensure Compact Agreement allows a nurse who is licensed and permanently resides in one of the member states to practice in the other member states without obtaining additional licensure. In 2006, 20 states were members of the Compact, while two more were pending membership. All states require periodic renewal of licenses, which may require continuing education.

Certification is common, and sometimes required, for the four advanced practice nursing specialties—clinical nurse specialists, nurse anesthetists, nurse-midwives, and nurse practitioners. Upon completion of their educational programs, most advanced practice nurses become nationally certified in their area of specialty. Certification also is available in specialty areas for all nurses. In some states, certification in a specialty is required in order to practice that specialty.

Foreign-educated and foreign-born nurses wishing to work in the United States must obtain a work visa. To obtain the visa, nurses must undergo a federal screening program to ensure that their education and licensure are comparable to that of a U.S. educated nurse, that they have proficiency in written and spoken English, and that they have passed either the Commission on Graduates of Foreign Nursing Schools (CGFNS) Qualifying Examination or the NCLEX-RN. CGFNS administers the VisaScreen Program. (The Commission is an immigration-neutral, nonprofit organization that is recognized internationally as an authority on credentials evaluation in the health care field.) Nurses educated in Australia, Canada (except Quebec), Ireland, New Zealand, and the United Kingdom, or foreign-born nurses who were educated in the United States, are exempt from the language proficiency testing. In addition to these national requirements, foreign-born nurses must obtain state licensure in order to practice in the United States. Each state has its own requirements for licensure.

Other qualifications. Nurses should be caring, sympathetic, responsible, and detail oriented. They must be able to direct or supervise others, correctly assess patients' conditions, and determine when consultation is required. They need emotional stability to cope with human suffering, emergencies, and other stresses.

Advancement. Some RNs start their careers as licensed practical nurses or nursing aides, and then go back to school to receive their RN degree. Most RNs begin as staff nurses in hospitals, and with experience and good performance often move to other settings or are promoted to more responsible positions. In management, nurses can advance from assistant unit manger or head nurse to more senior-level administrative roles of assistant director, director, vice president, or chief nurse. Increasingly, management-level nursing positions require a graduate or an advanced degree in nursing or health services administration. Administrative positions require leadership, communication and negotiation skills, and good judgment.

Some nurses move into the business side of health care. Their nursing expertise and experience on a health care team equip them to manage ambulatory, acute, home-based, and chronic care. Employers—including hospitals, insurance companies, pharmaceutical manufacturers, and managed care organizations, among others—need RNs for health planning and development, marketing, consulting, policy development, and quality assurance. Other nurses work as college and university faculty or conduct research.

Employment

As the largest health care occupation, registered nurses held about 2.5 million jobs in 2006. Hospitals employed the majority of RNs, with 59 percent of jobs. Other industries also employed large shares of workers. About 8 percent of jobs were in offices of physicians, 5 percent in home health care services, 5 percent in nursing care facilities, 4 percent in employment services, and 3 percent in outpatient care centers. The remainder worked mostly in government agencies, social assistance agencies, and educational services. About 21 percent of RNs worked part time.

Job Outlook

Overall job opportunities for registered nurses are expected to be excellent, but may vary by employment and geographic setting. Employment of RNs is expected to grow much faster than the average for all occupations through 2016 and, because the occupation is very large, many new jobs will result. In fact, registered nurses are projected to generate 587,000 new jobs, among the largest number of new jobs for any occupation. Additionally, hundreds of thousands of job openings will result from the need to replace experienced nurses who leave the occupation.

Employment change. Employment of registered nurses is expected to grow 23 percent from 2006 to 2016, much faster than the average for all occupations. Growth will be driven by technological advances in patient care, which permit a greater number of health problems to be treated, and by an increasing emphasis on preventive care. In addition, the number of older people, who are much more likely than younger people to need nursing care, is projected to grow rapidly.

However, employment of RNs will not grow at the same rate in every industry. The projected growth rates for RNs in the industries with the highest employment of these workers are:

Offices of physicians	39%
Home health care services	39
Outpatient care centers, except mental health and substance abuse	34
Employment services	27
General medical and surgical hospitals, public and private	22
Nursing care facilities	20

Employment is expected to grow more slowly in hospitals—health care's largest industry—than in most other health care industries. While the intensity of nursing care is likely to increase, requiring more nurses per patient, the number of inpatients (those who remain in the hospital for more than 24 hours) is not likely to grow by much. Patients are being discharged earlier, and more procedures are being done on an outpatient basis, both inside and outside hospitals. Rapid growth is expected in hospital outpatient facilities, such as those providing same-day surgery, rehabilitation, and chemotherapy.

More and more sophisticated procedures, once performed only in hospitals, are being performed in physicians' offices and in outpatient care centers, such as freestanding ambulatory surgical and emergency centers. Accordingly, employment is expected to grow very fast in these places as health care in general expands.

Employment in nursing care facilities is expected to grow because of increases in the number of elderly, many of whom require

Projections data from the National Employment Matrix

Occupational Title	SOC Code	Employment, 2006	Projected employment, 2016	Change, 2006-2016	
				Number	Percent
Registered nurses	29-1111	2,505,000	3,092,000	587,000	23

NOTE: Data in this table are rounded.

long-term care. However, this growth will be relatively slower than in other health care industries because of the desire of patients to be treated at home or in residential care facilities, and the increasing availability of that type of care. The financial pressure on hospitals to discharge patients as soon as possible should produce more admissions to nursing and residential care facilities and to home health care. Job growth also is expected in units that provide specialized long-term rehabilitation for stroke and head injury patients, as well as units that treat Alzheimer's victims.

Employment in home health care is expected to increase rapidly in response to the growing number of older persons with functional disabilities, consumer preference for care in the home, and technological advances that make it possible to bring increasingly complex treatments into the home. The type of care demanded will require nurses who are able to perform complex procedures.

Rapid employment growth in employment services industry is expected as hospitals, physician's offices, and other health care establishments utilize temporary workers to fill short-term staffing needs. And as the demand for nurses grows, temporary nurses will be needed more often, further contributing to employment growth in this industry.

Job prospects. Overall job opportunities are expected to be excellent for registered nurses. Employers in some parts of the country and in certain employment settings report difficulty in attracting and retaining an adequate number of RNs, primarily because of an aging RN workforce and a lack of younger workers to fill positions. Enrollments in nursing programs at all levels have increased more rapidly in the past few years as students seek jobs with stable employment. However, many qualified applicants are being turned away because of a shortage of nursing faculty. The need for nursing faculty will only increase as many instructors near retirement. Many employers also are relying on foreign-educated nurses to fill vacant positions.

Even though overall employment opportunities for all nursing specialties are expected to be excellent, they can vary by employment setting. Despite the slower employment growth in hospitals, job opportunities should still be excellent because of the relatively high turnover of hospital nurses. RNs working in hospitals frequently work overtime and night and weekend shifts and also treat seriously ill and injured patients, all of which can contribute to stress and burnout. Hospital departments in which these working conditions occur most frequently—critical care units, emergency departments, and operating rooms—generally will have more job openings than other departments. To attract and retain qualified nurses, hospitals may offer signing bonuses, family-friendly work schedules, or subsidized training. A growing number of hospitals also are experimenting with online bidding to fill open shifts, in which nurses can volunteer to fill open shifts at premium wages. This can decrease the amount of mandatory overtime that nurses are required to work.

Although faster employment growth is projected in physicians' offices and outpatient care centers, RNs may face greater competition for these positions because they generally offer regular working hours and more comfortable working environments. There also may be some competition for jobs in employment services, despite a high rate of employment growth, because a large number of workers are attracted by the industry's relatively high wages and the flexibility of the work in this industry.

Generally, RNs with at least a bachelor's degree will have better job prospects than those without a bachelor's. In addition, all four advanced practice specialties—clinical nurse specialists, nurse practitioners, nurse-midwives, and nurse anesthetists—will be in high demand, particularly in medically underserved areas such as inner cities and rural areas. Relative to physicians, these RNs increasingly serve as lower-cost primary care providers.

Earnings

Median annual earnings of registered nurses were $57,280 in May 2006. The middle 50 percent earned between $47,710 and $69,850. The lowest 10 percent earned less than $40,250, and the highest 10 percent earned more than $83,440. Median annual earnings in the industries employing the largest numbers of registered nurses in May 2006 were

Employment services	$64,260
General medical and surgical hospitals	58,550
Home health care services	54,190
Offices of physicians	53,800
Nursing care facilities	52,490

Many employers offer flexible work schedules, child care, educational benefits, and bonuses.

Related Occupations

Because of the number of specialties for registered nurses, and the variety of responsibilities and duties, many other health care occupations are similar in some aspect of the job. Other occupations that deal directly with patients when providing care include licensed practical and licensed vocational nurses, physicians and surgeons, athletic trainers, respiratory therapists, massage therapists, dietitians and nutritionists, occupational therapists, physical therapists, and emergency medical technicians and paramedics. Other occupations that use advanced medical equipment to treat patients include cardiovascular technologists and technicians, diagnostic medical sonographers, radiologic technologists and technicians, radiation therapists, and surgical technologists. Workers who also assist other health care professionals in providing care include nursing, psychiatric, and home health aides; physician assistants; and dental hygienists. Some nurses take on a management role, similar to medical and health services managers.

Sources of Additional Information

For information on a career as a registered nurse and nursing education, contact

- National League for Nursing, 61 Broadway, New York, NY 10006. Internet: http://www.nln.org

For information on baccalaureate and graduate nursing education, nursing career options, and financial aid, contact

- American Association of Colleges of Nursing, 1 Dupont Circle NW, Suite 530, Washington, DC 20036. Internet: http://www.aacn.nche.edu

For additional information on registered nurses, including credentialing, contact

- American Nurses Association, 8515 Georgia Ave., Suite 400, Silver Spring, MD 20910. Internet: http://nursingworld.org

For information on the NCLEX-RN exam and a list of individual state boards of nursing, contact

- National Council of State Boards of Nursing, 111 E. Wacker Dr., Suite 2900, Chicago, IL 60611. Internet: http://www.ncsbn.org

For information on the nursing population, including workforce shortage facts, contact

- Bureau of Health Professions, 5600 Fishers Lane, Room 8-05, Rockville, MD 20857. Internet: http://bhpr.hrsa.gov

For information on obtaining U.S. certification and work visas for foreign-educated nurses, contact

- Commission on Graduates of Foreign Nursing Schools, 3600 Market St., Suite 400, Philadelphia, PA 19104. Internet: http://www.cgfns.org

For a list of accredited clinical nurse specialist programs, contact

- National Association of Clinical Nurse Specialists, 2090 Linglestown Rd., Suite 107, Harrisburg, PA 17110. Internet: http://www.nacns.org

For information on nurse anesthetists, including a list of accredited programs, contact

- American Association of Nurse Anesthetists, 222 Prospect Ave., Park Ridge, IL 60068.

For information on nurse-midwives, including a list of accredited programs, contact

- American College of Nurse-Midwives, 8403 Colesville Rd., Suite 1550, Silver Spring, MD 20910. Internet: http://www.midwife.org

For information on nurse practitioners, including a list of accredited programs, contact

- American Academy of Nurse Practitioners, P.O. Box 12846, Austin, TX 78711. Internet: http://www.aanp.org

For information on nurse practitioners education, contact

- National Organization of Nurse Practitioner Faculties, 1522 K St. NW, Suite 702, Washington, DC 20005. Internet: http://www.nonpf.org

For information on critical care nurses, contact

- American Association of Critical-Care Nurses, 101 Columbia, Aliso Viejo, CA 92656. Internet: http://www.aacn.org

For additional information on registered nurses in all fields and specialties, contact

- American Society of Registered Nurses, 1001 Bridgeway, Suite 411, Sausalito, CA 94965. Internet: http://www.asrn.org

Respiratory Therapists

(O*NET 29-1126.00 and 29-2054.00)

Significant Points

- Job opportunities should be very good.
- An associate degree is the minimum educational requirement, but a bachelor's or master's degree may be important for advancement.
- All states, except Alaska and Hawaii, require respiratory therapists to be licensed.
- Hospitals will account for the vast majority of job openings, but a growing number of openings will arise in other settings.

Nature of the Work

Respiratory therapists and *respiratory therapy technicians*—also known as respiratory care practitioners—evaluate, treat, and care for patients with breathing or other cardiopulmonary disorders. Practicing under the direction of a physician, respiratory therapists assume primary responsibility for all respiratory care therapeutic treatments and diagnostic procedures, including the supervision of respiratory therapy technicians. Respiratory therapy technicians follow specific, well-defined respiratory care procedures under the direction of respiratory therapists and physicians.

In clinical practice, many of the daily duties of therapists and technicians overlap. However, therapists generally have greater responsibility than technicians. For example, respiratory therapists consult with physicians and other health care staff to help develop and modify patient care plans. Respiratory therapists also are more likely to provide complex therapy requiring considerable independent judgment, such as caring for patients on life support in intensive-care units of hospitals. In this job profile, the term *respiratory therapist* includes both respiratory therapists and respiratory therapy technicians.

Respiratory therapists evaluate and treat all types of patients, ranging from premature infants whose lungs are not fully developed to elderly people whose lungs are diseased. Respiratory therapists provide temporary relief to patients with chronic asthma or emphysema, and they give emergency care to patients who are victims of a heart attack, stroke, drowning, or shock.

To evaluate patients, respiratory therapists interview them, perform limited physical examinations, and conduct diagnostic tests. For example, respiratory therapists test a patient's breathing capacity and determine the concentration of oxygen and other gases in a patient's blood. They also measure a patient's pH, which indicates the acidity or alkalinity of the blood. To evaluate a patient's lung capacity, respiratory therapists have the patient breathe into an instrument that measures the volume and flow of oxygen during inhalation and exhalation. By comparing the reading with the norm for the patient's age, height, weight, and sex, respiratory therapists can provide information that helps determine whether the patient has any lung deficiencies. To analyze oxygen, carbon dioxide, and blood pH levels, therapists draw an arterial blood sample, place it in a blood gas analyzer, and relay the results to a physician, who then makes treatment decisions.

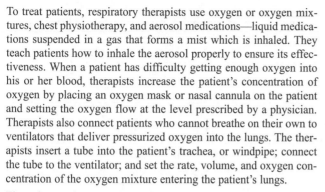

To treat patients, respiratory therapists use oxygen or oxygen mixtures, chest physiotherapy, and aerosol medications—liquid medications suspended in a gas that forms a mist which is inhaled. They teach patients how to inhale the aerosol properly to ensure its effectiveness. When a patient has difficulty getting enough oxygen into his or her blood, therapists increase the patient's concentration of oxygen by placing an oxygen mask or nasal cannula on the patient and setting the oxygen flow at the level prescribed by a physician. Therapists also connect patients who cannot breathe on their own to ventilators that deliver pressurized oxygen into the lungs. The therapists insert a tube into the patient's trachea, or windpipe; connect the tube to the ventilator; and set the rate, volume, and oxygen concentration of the oxygen mixture entering the patient's lungs.

Therapists perform regular assessments of patients and equipment. If a patient appears to be having difficulty breathing or if the oxygen, carbon dioxide, or pH level of the blood is abnormal, therapists change the ventilator setting according to the doctor's orders or check the equipment for mechanical problems.

Respiratory therapists perform chest physiotherapy on patients to remove mucus from their lungs and make it easier for them to breathe. Therapists place patients in positions that help drain mucus, and then vibrate the patients' rib cages, often by tapping on the chest, and tell the patients to cough. Chest physiotherapy may be needed after surgery, for example, because anesthesia depresses respiration. As a result, physiotherapy may be prescribed to help get the patient's lungs back to normal and to prevent congestion. Chest physiotherapy also helps patients suffering from lung diseases, such as cystic fibrosis, that cause mucus to collect in the lungs.

Therapists who work in home care teach patients and their families to use ventilators and other life-support systems. In addition, these therapists visit patients in their homes to inspect and clean equipment, evaluate the home environment, and ensure that patients have sufficient knowledge of their diseases and the proper use of their medications and equipment. Therapists also make emergency visits if equipment problems arise.

In some hospitals, therapists perform tasks that fall outside their traditional role. Therapists are becoming involved in areas such as pulmonary rehabilitation, smoking cessation counseling, disease prevention, case management, and polysomnography—the diagnosis of breathing disorders during sleep, such as apnea. Respiratory therapists also increasingly treat critical care patients, either as part of surface and air transport teams or as part of rapid-response teams in hospitals.

Work environment. Respiratory therapists generally work between 35 and 40 hours a week. Because hospitals operate around the clock, therapists may work evenings, nights, or weekends. They spend long periods standing and walking between patients' rooms. In an emergency, therapists work under the stress of the situation. Respiratory therapists employed in home health care must travel frequently to patients' homes.

Respiratory therapists are trained to work with gases stored under pressure. Adherence to safety precautions and regular maintenance and testing of equipment minimize the risk of injury. As in many other health occupations, respiratory therapists are exposed to infectious diseases, but by carefully following proper procedures they can minimize the risks.

Training, Other Qualifications, and Advancement

An associate degree is the minimum educational requirement, but a bachelor's or master's degree may be important for advancement. All states, except Alaska and Hawaii, require respiratory therapists to be licensed.

Education and training. An associate degree is required to become a respiratory therapist. Training is offered at the postsecondary level by colleges and universities, medical schools, vocational-technical institutes, and the Armed Forces. Most programs award associate or bachelor's degree and prepare graduates for jobs as advanced respiratory therapists. A limited number of associate degree programs lead to jobs as entry-level respiratory therapists. According to the Commission on Accreditation of Allied Health Education Programs (CAAHEP), 45 entry-level and 334 advanced respiratory therapy programs were accredited in the United States in 2006.

Among the areas of study in respiratory therapy programs are human anatomy and physiology, pathophysiology, chemistry, physics, microbiology, pharmacology, and mathematics. Other courses deal with therapeutic and diagnostic procedures and tests, equipment, patient assessment, cardiopulmonary resuscitation, the application of clinical practice guidelines, patient care outside of hospitals, cardiac and pulmonary rehabilitation, respiratory health promotion and disease prevention, and medical recordkeeping and reimbursement.

High school students interested in applying to respiratory therapy programs should take courses in health, biology, mathematics, chemistry, and physics. Respiratory care involves basic mathematical problem solving and an understanding of chemical and physical principles. For example, respiratory care workers must be able to compute dosages of medication and calculate gas concentrations.

Licensure and certification. A license is required to practice as a respiratory therapist, except in Alaska and Hawaii. Also, most employers require respiratory therapists to maintain a cardiopulmonary resuscitation (CPR) certification.

Licensure is usually based, in large part, on meeting the requirements for certification from the National Board for Respiratory Care (NBRC). The board offers the Certified Respiratory Therapist (CRT) credential to those who graduate from entry-level or advanced programs accredited by CAAHEP or the Committee on Accreditation for Respiratory Care (CoARC) and who also pass an exam.

The board also awards the Registered Respiratory Therapist (RRT) to CRTs who have graduated from advanced programs and pass two separate examinations. Supervisory positions and intensive-care specialties usually require the RRT.

Other qualifications. Therapists should be sensitive to a patient's physical and psychological needs. Respiratory care practitioners must pay attention to detail, follow instructions, and work as part of a team. In addition, operating advanced equipment requires proficiency with computers.

Advancement. Respiratory therapists advance in clinical practice by moving from general care to the care of critically ill patients who have significant problems in other organ systems, such as the heart or kidneys. Respiratory therapists, especially those with a bachelor's or master's degree, also may advance to supervisory or managerial positions in a respiratory therapy department. Respiratory therapists in home health care and equipment rental firms may become branch

Projections data from the National Employment Matrix

Occupational Title	SOC Code	Employment, 2006	Projected employment, 2016	Change, 2006-2016 Number	Change, 2006-2016 Percent
Respiratory therapists	—	122,000	145,000	23,000	19
Respiratory therapists	29-1126	102,000	126,000	23,000	23
Respiratory therapy technicians	29-2054	19,000	19,000	200	1

NOTE: Data in this table are rounded.

managers. Some respiratory therapists advance by moving into teaching positions. Some others use the knowledge gained as a respiratory therapist to work in another industry, such as developing, marketing, or selling pharmaceuticals and medical devices.

Employment

Respiratory therapists held about 122,000 jobs in 2006. About 79 percent of jobs were in hospitals, mainly in departments of respiratory care, anesthesiology, or pulmonary medicine. Most of the remaining jobs were in offices of physicians or other health practitioners, consumer-goods rental firms that supply respiratory equipment for home use, nursing care facilities, and home health care services. Holding a second job is relatively common for respiratory therapists. About 12 percent held another job, compared with 5 percent of workers in all occupations.

Job Outlook

Faster-than-average employment growth is projected for respiratory therapists. Job opportunities should be very good, especially for respiratory therapists with cardiopulmonary care skills or experience working with infants.

Employment change. Employment of respiratory therapists is expected to grow 19 percent from 2006 to 2016, faster than the average for all occupations. The increasing demand will come from substantial growth in the middle-aged and elderly population—a development that will heighten the incidence of cardiopulmonary disease. Growth in demand also will result from the expanding role of respiratory therapists in case management, disease prevention, emergency care, and the early detection of pulmonary disorders.

Older Americans suffer most from respiratory ailments and cardiopulmonary diseases such as pneumonia, chronic bronchitis, emphysema, and heart disease. As their numbers increase, the need for respiratory therapists is expected to increase as well. In addition, advances in inhalable medications and in the treatment of lung transplant patients, heart attack and accident victims, and premature infants (many of whom are dependent on a ventilator during part of their treatment) will increase the demand for the services of respiratory care practitioners.

Job prospects. Job opportunities are expected to be very good. The vast majority of job openings will continue to be in hospitals. However, a growing number of openings are expected to be outside of hospitals, especially in home health care services, offices of physicians or other health practitioners, consumer-goods rental firms, or in the employment services industry as a temporary worker in various settings.

Earnings

Median annual earnings of wage-and-salary respiratory therapists were $47,420 in May 2006. The middle 50 percent earned between $40,840 and $56,150. The lowest 10 percent earned less than $35,200, and the highest 10 percent earned more than $64,190.

Median annual earnings of wage-and-salary respiratory therapy technicians were $39,120 in May 2006. The middle 50 percent earned between $32,050 and $46,930. The lowest 10 percent earned less than $25,940, and the highest 10 percent earned more than $56,220.

Related Occupations

Under the supervision of a physician, respiratory therapists administer respiratory care and life support to patients with heart and lung difficulties. Other workers who care for, treat, or train people to improve their physical condition include registered nurses, occupational therapists, physical therapists, radiation therapists, and athletic trainers. Respiratory care practitioners work with advanced medical technology, as do other health care technicians including cardiovascular technologists and technicians, nuclear medicine technologists, radiologic technologists and technicians, and diagnostic medical sonographers.

Sources of Additional Information

Information concerning a career in respiratory care is available from

- American Association for Respiratory Care, 9425 N. MacArthur Blvd., Suite 100, Irving, TX 75063. Internet: http://www.aarc.org

For a list of accredited educational programs for respiratory care practitioners, contact either of the following organizations:

- Commission on Accreditation for Allied Health Education Programs, 1361 Park St., Clearwater, FL 33756. Internet: http://www.caahep.org
- Committee on Accreditation for Respiratory Care, 1248 Harwood Rd., Bedford, TX 76021.

Information on gaining credentials in respiratory care and a list of state licensing agencies can be obtained from

- National Board for Respiratory Care, Inc., 18000 W. 105th St., Olathe, KS 66061. Internet: http://www.nbrc.org

Sales Engineers

(O*NET 41-9031.00)

Significant Points

- A bachelor's degree in engineering usually is required; many sales engineers have previous work experience in an engineering specialty.
- Projected employment growth will stem from the increasing numbers of technical products and services for sale.
- More job opportunities are expected in independent sales agencies.

- Earnings are typically based on a combination of salary and commission.

Nature of the Work

Many products and services, especially those purchased by large companies and institutions, are highly complex. Sales engineers—who also may be called *manufacturers' agents, sales representatives*, or *technical sales support workers*—work with the production, engineering, or research and development departments of their companies, or with independent sales firms, to determine how products and services could be designed or modified to suit customers' needs. They also may advise customers on how best to use the products or services provided.

Sales engineers sell and consult on technologically and scientifically advanced products. They should possess extensive knowledge of these products, including their components and processes. Sales engineers then use their technical skills to demonstrate to potential customers how and why the products or services they are selling would suit the customer better than competitors' products. Often, there may not be a directly competitive product. In these cases, the job of the sales engineer is to demonstrate to the customer the usefulness of the product or service—for example, how much money new production machinery would save.

Engineers apply the theories and principles of science and mathematics to technical problems. Their work is the link between scientific discoveries and commercial applications. Many sales engineers specialize in products that are related to their engineering specialty. For example, sales engineers selling chemical products may have chemical engineering backgrounds, while those selling business software or information systems may have degrees in computer engineering. (Information on engineers, including 17 engineering specialties, appears elsewhere in this book.)

Many of the duties of sales engineers are similar to those of other salespersons. They must interest the client in purchasing their products, many of which are durable manufactured products such as turbines. Sales engineers often are teamed with other salespersons who concentrate on the marketing and sales, enabling the sales engineer to concentrate on the technical aspects of the job. By working on a sales team, each member is able to focus on his or her strengths and expertise.

Sales engineers tend to employ selling techniques that are different from those used by most other sales workers. They generally use a "consultative" style; that is, they focus on the client's problem and show how it could be solved or mitigated with their product or service. This selling style differs from the "benefits and features" method, whereby the salesperson describes the product and leaves the customer to decide how it would be useful.

In addition to maintaining current clients and attracting new ones, sales engineers help clients solve any problems that arise when the product is installed. Afterward, they may continue to serve as a liaison between the client and their company. Increasingly, sales engineers are asked to undertake tasks related to sales, such as market research, because of their familiarity with clients' purchasing needs. Drawing on this same familiarity, sales engineers may help identify and develop new products.

Work environment. Sales engineers may work directly for manufacturers or service providers, or they may work in small independent sales firms. In an independent firm, they may sell complementary products from several different suppliers.

Workers in this occupation can encounter pressure and stress because their income and job security often depend directly on their success in sales and customer service. Many sales engineers work more than 40 hours per week to meet sales goals and client needs. Although the hours may be long and often irregular, many sales engineers have the freedom to determine their own schedules. Consequently, they often can arrange their appointments so that they can have time off when they want it.

Some sales engineers have large territories and travel extensively. Because sales regions may cover several states, sales engineers may be away from home for several days or even weeks at a time. Others work near their home base and travel mostly by car. International travel to secure contracts with foreign clients is becoming more common.

Training, Other Qualifications, and Advancement

Most sales engineers have a bachelor's degree in engineering, and many have previous work experience in an engineering specialty. New sales engineers may need some on-the-job training in sales or may work closely with a sales mentor familiar with company policies and practices before they can work on their own.

Education and training. A bachelor's degree in engineering usually is required to become a sales engineer. However, some workers with previous experience in sales combined with technical experience or training sometimes hold the title of sales engineer. Also, workers who have a degree in a science, such as chemistry, or even a degree in business with little or no previous sales experience, may be termed sales engineers.

Admissions requirements for undergraduate engineering schools include a solid background in mathematics (algebra, geometry, trigonometry, and calculus) and the physical sciences (biology, chemistry, and physics), as well as basic courses in English, social studies, humanities, and computer science. University programs vary in content, though all require the development of computer skills. Once a university has been selected, a student must choose an area of engineering in which to specialize. Some programs offer a general engineering curriculum; students then specialize on the job or in graduate school. Most engineering degrees are granted in electrical, mechanical, or civil engineering. However, engineers trained in one branch may work in related branches.

New graduates with engineering degrees may need sales experience and training before they can work independently as sales engineers. Training may involve teaming with a sales mentor who is familiar with the employer's business practices, customers, procedures, and company culture. After the training period has been completed, sales engineers may continue to partner with someone who lacks technical skills, yet excels in the art of sales.

It is important for sales engineers to continue their engineering and sales education throughout their careers. Much of their value to their employers depends on their knowledge of and ability to sell the latest technologies. Sales engineers in high-technology fields, such as information technology or advanced electronics, may find that technical knowledge rapidly becomes obsolete.

Projections data from the National Employment Matrix

Occupational Title	SOC Code	Employment, 2006	Projected employment, 2016	Change, 2006-16	
				Number	Percent
Sales engineers	41-9031	76,000	82,000	6,500	9

NOTE: Data in this table are rounded.

Other qualifications. Many sales engineers first work as engineers. For some, engineering experience is necessary to obtain the technical background needed to sell their employers' products or services effectively. Others move into the occupation because it offers better earnings and advancement potential than engineering or because they are looking for a new challenge.

Advancement. Promotion may include a higher commission rate, larger sales territory, or elevation to the position of supervisor or marketing manager. Alternatively, sales engineers may leave their companies and form independent firms. Independent firms tend to be small, and relatively few sales engineers are self-employed.

Employment

Sales engineers held about 76,000 jobs in 2006. About 37 percent were employed in wholesale trade and another 26 percent were employed in the manufacturing industries. Smaller numbers of sales engineers worked in information industries, such as software publishing and telecommunications; professional, scientific, and technical services, such as computer systems design and related services; architectural, engineering, and related services; and other industries. Unlike workers in many other sales occupations, very few sales engineers are self-employed.

Job Outlook

Job growth for sales engineers is projected to be about average through 2016, and opportunities will be good in independent sales agencies because of the increase in outsourcing of sales departments by manufacturers.

Employment change. Employment of sales engineers is expected to grow by 9 percent between 2006 and 2016, which is about as fast as the average for all occupations. Projected employment growth stems from the increasing variety and technical nature of goods and services to be sold. Competitive pressures and advancing technology will force companies to improve and update product designs more frequently and to optimize their manufacturing and sales processes, and thus require the services of a sales engineer.

In wholesale trade, both outsourcing to independent sales agencies and the use of information technology are expected to create some job growth for sales engineers. Although outsourcing should lead to more jobs in independent agencies, employment growth for sales engineers in wholesale trade likely will be dampened by the increasing ability of businesses to find, order, and track shipments directly from wholesalers through the Internet, without assistance from sales engineers. However, since direct purchases from wholesalers are more likely to be non-scientific or non-technical products, their impact on sales engineers should remain somewhat limited.

Job prospects. Manufacturers, especially foreign manufacturers that sell their products in the United States, are expected to continue outsourcing more of their sales functions to independent sales agencies in an attempt to control costs. Additionally, since independent agencies can carry multiple lines of products, a single sales engineer can handle more products than the single product line they would have handled under a manufacturer. This should result in more job opportunities for sales engineers in independent agencies.

Employment opportunities may fluctuate from year to year because sales are affected by changing economic conditions, legislative issues, and consumer preferences. Prospects will be best for those with the appropriate knowledge or technical expertise, as well as the personal traits necessary for successful sales work. In addition to new positions created as companies expand their sales forces, some openings will arise each year from the need to replace sales engineers who transfer to other occupations or leave the labor force.

Earnings

Median annual earnings, including commissions, of wage and salary sales engineers were $77,720 in May 2006. The middle 50 percent earned between $59,490 and $100,280 a year. The lowest 10 percent earned less than $47,010, and the highest 10 percent earned more than $127,680 a year. Median annual earnings of those employed by firms in the computer systems design and related services industry were $90,950.

Compensation varies significantly by the type of firm and the product sold. Most employers offer a combination of salary and commission payments or a salary plus a bonus. Those working in independent sales companies may solely earn commissions. Commissions usually are based on the amount of sales, whereas bonuses may depend on individual performance, on the performance of all workers in the group or district, or on the company's performance. Earnings from commissions and bonuses may vary greatly from year to year, depending on sales ability, the demand for the company's products or services, and the overall economy.

In addition to their earnings, sales engineers who work for manufacturers usually are reimbursed for expenses such as transportation, meals, hotels, and customer entertainment. In addition to typical benefits, sales engineers may get personal use of a company car and frequent-flyer mileage. Some companies offer incentives such as free vacation trips or gifts for outstanding performance. Sales engineers who work in independent firms may have higher but less stable earnings and, often, relatively few benefits. Most independent sales engineers do not earn any income while on vacation.

Related Occupations

Sales engineers must have sales ability and knowledge of the products and services they sell, as well as technical and analytical skills. Other occupations that require similar skills include advertising, marketing, promotions, public relations, and sales managers; engineers; insurance sales agents; purchasing managers, buyers and purchasing agents; real estate brokers and sales agents; sales representatives, wholesale and manufacturing; and securities, commodities, and financial services sales agents.

Sources of Additional Information

Information on careers for manufacturers' representatives and agents is available from

- Manufacturers' Agents National Association, P.O. Box 3467, Laguna Hills, CA 92654. Internet: http://www.manaonline.org
- Manufacturers' Representatives Educational Research Foundation, 8329 Cole St., Arvada, CO 80005. Internet: http://www.mrerf.org

STEM Science Technicians

(O*NET 19-4011.00, 19-4011.01, 19-4011.02, 19-4021.00, 19-4031.00, 19-4041.00, 19-4041.01, 19-4041.02, 19-4051.00, 19-4051.01, 19-4051.02, 19-4091.00, 19-4092.00, 19-4093.00, and 19-4099.99)

Significant Points

- Science technicians in production jobs can be employed on day, evening, or night shifts; other technicians work outdoors, sometimes in remote locations.
- Most science technicians need an associate degree or a certificate in applied science or science-related technology; biological and forensic science technicians usually need a bachelor's degree.
- Projected job growth varies among occupational specialties; for example, forensic science technicians will grow much faster than average, while chemical technicians will grow more slowly than average.
- Job opportunities are expected to be best for graduates of applied science technology programs who are well trained on equipment used in laboratories or production facilities.

Nature of the Work

Science technicians use the principles and theories of science and mathematics to solve problems in research and development and to help invent and improve products and processes. However, their jobs are more practically oriented than those of scientists. Technicians set up, operate, and maintain laboratory instruments, monitor experiments, make observations, calculate and record results, and often develop conclusions. They must keep detailed logs of all of their work. Those who perform production work monitor manufacturing processes and may ensure quality by testing products for proper proportions of ingredients, for purity, or for strength and durability.

As laboratory instrumentation and procedures have become more complex, the role of science technicians in research and development has expanded. In addition to performing routine tasks, many technicians, under the direction of scientists, now develop and adapt laboratory procedures to achieve the best results, interpret data, and devise solutions to problems. Technicians must develop expert knowledge of laboratory equipment so that they can adjust settings when necessary and recognize when equipment is malfunctioning.

Most science technicians specialize, learning their skills and working in the same disciplines in which scientists work. Occupational titles, therefore, tend to follow the same structure as those for scientists.

Agricultural and food science technicians work with related scientists to conduct research, development, and testing on food and other agricultural products. Agricultural technicians are involved in food, fiber, and animal research, production, and processing. Some conduct tests and experiments to improve the yield and quality of crops or to increase the resistance of plants and animals to disease, insects, or other hazards. Other agricultural technicians breed animals for the purpose of investigating nutrition. Food science technicians assist food scientists and technologists in research and development, production technology, and quality control. For example, food science technicians may conduct tests on food additives and preservatives to ensure compliance with Food and Drug Administration regulations regarding color, texture, and nutrients. These technicians analyze, record, and compile test results; order supplies to maintain laboratory inventory; and clean and sterilize laboratory equipment.

Biological technicians work with biologists studying living organisms. Many assist scientists who conduct medical research—helping to find a cure for cancer or AIDS, for example. Those who work in pharmaceutical companies help develop and manufacture medicine. Those working in the field of microbiology generally work as laboratory assistants, studying living organisms and infectious agents. Biological technicians also analyze organic substances, such as blood, food, and drugs. Biological technicians working in biotechnology apply knowledge and techniques gained from basic research, including gene splicing and recombinant DNA, and apply them to product development.

Chemical technicians work with chemists and chemical engineers, developing and using chemicals and related products and equipment. Generally, there are two types of chemical technicians: research technicians who work in experimental laboratories and process control technicians who work in manufacturing or other industrial plants. Many chemical technicians working in research and development conduct a variety of laboratory procedures, from routine process control to complex research projects. For example, they may collect and analyze samples of air and water to monitor pollution levels, or they may produce compounds through complex organic synthesis. Most *process technicians* work in manufacturing, testing packaging for design, integrity of materials, and environmental acceptability. Often, process technicians who work in plants focus on quality assurance, monitoring product quality or production processes and developing new production techniques. A few work in shipping to provide technical support and expertise.

Environmental science and protection technicians perform laboratory and field tests to monitor environmental resources and determine the contaminants and sources of pollution in the environment. They may collect samples for testing or be involved in abating and controlling sources of environmental pollution. Some are responsible for waste management operations, control and management of hazardous materials inventory, or general activities involving regulatory compliance. Many environmental science technicians employed at private consulting firms work directly under the supervision of an environmental scientist.

Forensic science technicians investigate crimes by collecting and analyzing physical evidence. Often, they specialize in areas such as DNA analysis or firearm examination, performing tests on weapons or on substances such as fiber, glass, hair, tissue, and body fluids to determine their significance to the investigation. Proper collection and storage methods are important to protect the evidence. Forensic science technicians also prepare reports to document their findings and the laboratory techniques used, and they may provide information and expert opinions to investigators. When criminal cases come to trial, forensic science technicians often give testimony as expert witnesses on laboratory findings by identifying and classifying substances, materials, and other evidence collected at the scene of a crime. Some forensic science technicians work closely with other experts or technicians. For example, a forensic science technician may consult either a medical expert about the exact time and cause of a death or another technician who specializes in DNA typing in hopes of matching a DNA type to a suspect.

Forest and conservation technicians compile data on the size, content, and condition of forest land. These workers usually work in a forest under the supervision of a forester, doing specific tasks such as measuring timber, supervising harvesting operations, assisting in road building operations, and locating property lines and features. They also may gather basic information, such as data on populations of trees, disease and insect damage, tree seedling mortality, and conditions that may pose a fire hazard. In addition, forest and conservation technicians train and lead forest and conservation workers in seasonal activities, such as planting tree seedlings, and maintaining recreational facilities. Increasing numbers of forest and conservation technicians work in urban forestry—the study of individual trees in cities—and other nontraditional specialties, rather than in forests or rural areas.

Geological and petroleum technicians measure and record physical and geologic conditions in oil or gas wells, using advanced instruments lowered into the wells or analyzing the mud from the wells. In oil and gas exploration, technicians collect and examine geological data or test geological samples to determine their petroleum content and their mineral and element composition. Some petroleum technicians, called scouts, collect information about oil well and gas well drilling operations, geological and geophysical prospecting, and land or lease contracts.

Nuclear technicians operate nuclear test and research equipment, monitor radiation, and assist nuclear engineers and physicists in research. Some also operate remote controlled equipment to manipulate radioactive materials or materials exposed to radioactivity. Workers who control nuclear reactors are classified as *nuclear power reactor operators*, and are not included in this statement. (See the statement on power plant operators, distributors, and dispatchers elsewhere in this book.)

Other science technicians perform a wide range of activities. Some collect weather information or assist oceanographers; others work as laser technicians or radiographers.

Work environment. Science technicians work under a wide variety of conditions. Most work indoors, usually in laboratories, and have regular hours. Some occasionally work irregular hours to monitor experiments that cannot be completed during regular working hours. Production technicians often work in 8-hour shifts around the clock. Others, such as agricultural, forest and conservation, geological and petroleum, and environmental science and protection technicians, perform much of their work outdoors, sometimes in remote locations.

Advances in automation and information technology require technicians to operate more sophisticated laboratory equipment. Science technicians make extensive use of computers, electronic measuring equipment, and traditional experimental apparatus.

Some science technicians may be exposed to hazards from equipment, chemicals, or toxic materials. Chemical technicians sometimes work with toxic chemicals or radioactive isotopes; nuclear technicians may be exposed to radiation, and biological technicians sometimes work with disease-causing organisms or radioactive agents. Forensic science technicians often are exposed to human body fluids and firearms. However, these working conditions pose little risk if proper safety procedures are followed. For forensic science technicians, collecting evidence from crime scenes can be distressing and unpleasant.

Training, Other Qualifications, and Advancement

Most science technicians need an associate degree or a certificate in applied science or science-related technology. Biological and forensic science technicians usually need a bachelor's degree. Science technicians with a high school diploma and no college degree typically begin work as trainees under the direct supervision of a more experienced technician, and eventually earn a two-year degree in science technology.

Education and training. There are several ways to qualify for a job as a science technician. Many employers prefer applicants who have at least two years of specialized training or an associate degree in applied science or science-related technology. Because employers' preferences vary, however, some science technicians have a bachelor's degree in chemistry, biology, or forensic science or have completed several science and math courses at a four-year college.

Most biological technician jobs, for example, require a bachelor's degree in biology or a closely related field. Forensic science positions also typically require a bachelor's degree to work in the field. Knowledge and understanding of legal procedures also can be helpful. Chemical technician positions in research and development also often have a bachelor's degree, but most chemical process technicians have a two-year degree instead, usually an associate degree in process technology. In some cases, a high school diploma is sufficient. These workers usually receive additional on-the-job training. Entry-level workers whose college training encompasses extensive hands-on experience with a variety of diagnostic laboratory equipment generally require less on-the-job training.

Whatever their degree, science technicians usually need hands-on training either in school or on the job. Most can get good career preparation through two-year formal training programs that combine the teaching of scientific principles and theory with practical hands-on application in a laboratory setting with up-to-date equipment. Graduates of bachelor's degree programs in science who have considerable experience in laboratory-based courses, have completed internships, or have held summer jobs in laboratories also are well qualified for science technician positions and are preferred by some employers.

Job candidates, who have extensive hands-on experience with a variety of laboratory equipment, including computers and related equipment, usually require a short period of on-the-job training. Those with a high school diploma and no college degree typically begin work as trainees under the direct supervision of a more experienced technician. Many with a high school diploma eventually earn a two-year degree in science technology, often paid for by their employer.

Many technical and community colleges offer associate degrees in a specific technology or more general education in science and mathematics. A number of associate degree programs are designed to provide easy transfer to bachelor's degree programs at colleges or universities. Technical institutes usually offer technician training, but they provide less theory and general education than do community colleges. The length of programs at technical institutes varies, although one-year certificate programs and two-year associate degree programs are common. Prospective forestry and conservation technicians can choose from more than 20 associate degree programs in forest technology accredited by the Society of American Foresters.

Approximately 30 colleges and universities offer a bachelor's degree program in forensic science; about another 25 schools offer a bachelor's degree in a natural science with an emphasis on forensic science or criminology; a few additional schools offer a bachelor's degree with an emphasis in a specialty area, such as criminology, pathology, jurisprudence, investigation, odontology, toxicology, or forensic accounting.

Some schools offer cooperative-education or internship programs, allowing students the opportunity to work at a local company or some other workplace while attending classes during alternate terms. Participation in such programs can significantly enhance a student's employment prospects.

People interested in careers as science technicians should take as many high school science and math courses as possible. Science courses taken beyond high school, in an associate or bachelor's degree program, should be laboratory oriented, with an emphasis on bench skills. A solid background in applied chemistry, physics, and math is vital.

Other qualifications. Communication skills are important because technicians are often required to report their findings both orally and in writing. In addition, technicians should be able to work well with others. Because computers often are used in research and development laboratories, technicians should also have strong computer skills, especially in computer modeling. Organizational ability, an eye for detail, and skill in interpreting scientific results are important as well, as are a high mechanical aptitude, attention to detail, and analytical thinking.

Advancement. Technicians usually begin work as trainees in routine positions under the direct supervision of a scientist or a more experienced technician. As they gain experience, technicians take on more responsibility and carry out assignments under only general supervision, and some eventually become supervisors. However, technicians employed at universities often have job prospects tied to those of particular professors; when those professors retire or leave, these technicians face uncertain employment prospects.

Employment

Science technicians held about 267,000 jobs in 2006. As indicated by the following tabulation, chemical and biological technicians accounted for 52 percent of all jobs:

Occupation	Jobs
Biological technicians	79,000
Chemical technicians	61,000
Environmental science and protection technicians, including health	37,000
Forest and conservation technicians	34,000
Agricultural and food science technicians	26,000
Forensic science technicians	13,000
Geological and petroleum technicians	12,000
Nuclear technicians	6,500

About 30 percent of biological technicians worked in professional, scientific, or technical services firms; most other biological technicians worked in educational services, federal, state, and local governments, or pharmaceutical and medicine manufacturing. Chemical technicians held jobs in a wide range of manufacturing and service-providing industries. About 39 percent worked in chemical manufacturing and another 30 percent worked in professional, scientific, or technical services firms. Most environmental science and protection technicians worked for state and local governments and professional, scientific, and technical services firms. About 76 percent of forest and conservation technicians held jobs in the federal government, mostly in the Forest Service; another 17 percent worked for state governments. Around 32 percent of agricultural and food science technicians worked in educational services and 20 percent worked for food processing companies; most of the rest were employed in agriculture. Forensic science technicians worked primarily for state and local governments. Approximately 37 percent of all geological and petroleum technicians worked for oil and gas extraction companies and 49 percent of nuclear technicians worked for utilities.

Job Outlook

Employment of science technicians is projected to grow about as fast as the average, although employment change will vary by specialty. Job opportunities are expected to be best for graduates of applied science technology programs who are well trained on equipment used in laboratories or production facilities.

Employment change. Overall employment of science technicians is expected to grow 12 percent during the 2006–2016 decade, about as fast as the average for all occupations. The continued growth of scientific and medical research—particularly research related to biotechnology—will be the primary driver of employment growth, but the development and production of technical products should also stimulate demand for science technicians in many industries.

Employment of biological technicians should increase faster than the average, as the growing number of agricultural and medicinal products developed with the use of biotechnology techniques boosts demand for these workers. Also, an aging population and stronger competition among pharmaceutical companies are expected to contribute to the need for innovative and improved drugs, further spurring demand. Most growth in employment will be in professional, scientific, and technical services and in educational services.

Job growth for chemical technicians is projected to grow more slowly than the average. The chemical manufacturing industry, except pharmaceutical and medicine manufacturing, is anticipated to experience a decline in overall employment as companies downsize and turn to outside contractors to provide specialized services. Some of these contractors will be in other countries with lower average wages, further limiting employment growth. An increasing focus on quality assurance will require a greater number of process technicians, however, stimulating demand for these workers.

Employment of environmental science and protection technicians is expected to grow much faster than the average; these workers will be needed to help regulate waste products; to collect air, water, and soil samples for measuring levels of pollutants; to monitor compliance with environmental regulations; and to clean up contaminated sites. Over 80 percent of this growth is expected to be in

Projections data from the National Employment Matrix

Occupational Title	SOC Code	Employment, 2006	Projected employment, 2016	Change, 2006-2016	
				Number	Percent
Science technicians	—	267,000	300,000	33,000	12
Agricultural and food science technicians	19-4011	26,000	28,000	1,700	7
Biological technicians	19-4021	79,000	91,000	13,000	16
Chemical technicians	19-4031	61,000	65,000	3,600	6
Geological and petroleum technicians	19-4041	12,000	13,000	1,000	9
Nuclear technicians	19-4051	6,500	6,900	400	7
Environmental science and protection technicians, including health	19-4091	37,000	47,000	10,000	28
Forensic science technicians	19-4092	13,000	17,000	4,000	31
Forest and conservation technicians	19-4093	34,000	33,000	-700	-2

NOTE: Data in this table are rounded.

professional, scientific, and technical services as environmental monitoring, management, and regulatory compliance increase.

An expected decline in employment of forest and conservation technicians within the federal government will lead to little or no change in employment in this specialty, due to budgetary constraints and continued reductions in demand for timber management on federal lands. However, opportunities at state and local governments within specialties such as urban forestry may provide some new jobs. In addition, an increased emphasis on specific conservation issues, such as environmental protection, preservation of water resources, and control of exotic and invasive pests, may provide some employment opportunities.

Employment of agricultural and food science technicians is projected to grow about as fast as the average. Research in biotechnology and other areas of agricultural science will increase as it becomes more important to balance greater agricultural output with protection and preservation of soil, water, and the ecosystem. In particular, research will be needed to combat insects and diseases as they adapt to pesticides and as soil fertility and water quality continue to need improvement.

Jobs for forensic science technicians are expected to increase much faster than the average. Employment growth in state and local government should be driven by the increasing application of forensic science to examine, solve, and prevent crime. Crime scene technicians who work for state and county crime labs should experience favorable employment prospects resulting from strong job growth.

Average employment growth is expected for geological and petroleum technicians. Job growth should be strongest in professional, scientific, and technical services firms because geological and petroleum technicians will be needed to assist environmental scientists and geoscientists as they provide consultation services for companies regarding environmental policy and federal government mandates, such as those requiring lower sulfur emissions.

Nuclear technicians should grow about as fast as the average as more are needed to monitor the nation's aging fleet of nuclear reactors and research future advances in nuclear power. Although no new nuclear powerplants have been built for decades in the United States, energy demand has recently renewed interest in this form of electricity generation and may lead to future construction. Technicians also will be needed to work in defense-related areas, to develop nuclear medical technology, and to improve and enforce waste management and safety standards.

Job prospects. In addition to job openings created by growth, many openings should arise from the need to replace technicians who retire or leave the labor force for other reasons. Job opportunities are expected to be best for graduates of applied science technology programs who are well trained on equipment used in laboratories or production facilities. As the instrumentation and techniques used in industrial research, development, and production become increasingly more complex, employers will seek individuals with highly developed technical skills. Good communication skills are also increasingly sought by employers.

Job opportunities vary by specialty. The best opportunities for agricultural and food science technicians will be in agricultural biotechnology, specifically in research and development on biofuels. Geological and petroleum technicians should experience little competition for positions because of the relatively small number of new entrants. Forensic science technicians with a bachelor's degree in a forensic science will enjoy much better opportunities than those with an associate degree. During periods of economic recession, science technicians may be laid off.

Earnings

Median hourly earnings of science technicians in May 2006 were as follows:

Nuclear technicians $31.49
Geological and petroleum technicians 22.19
Forensic science technicians 21.79
Chemical technicians 18.87
Environmental science and protection technicians, including health 18.31
Biological technicians 17.17
Agricultural and food science technicians 15.26
Forest and conservation technicians.......................14.84

In 2007, the average annual salary in the federal government was $40,629 for biological science technicians; $53,026 for physical science technicians; $40,534 for forestry technicians; $54,081 for geodetic technicians; $50,337 for hydrologic technicians; and $63,396 for meteorological technicians.

Related Occupations

Other technicians who apply scientific principles and who usually have a 2-year associate degree include engineering technicians, broadcast and sound engineering technicians and radio operators, drafters, and health technologists and technicians—especially clinical laboratory technologists and technicians, diagnostic medical sonographers, and radiologic technologists and technicians.

Sources of Additional Information

For information about a career as a chemical technician, contact

- American Chemical Society, Education Division, Career Publications, 1155 16th St. NW, Washington, DC 20036. Internet: http://www.acs.org

For career information and a list of undergraduate, graduate, and doctoral programs in forensic sciences, contact

- American Academy of Forensic Sciences, P.O. Box 669, Colorado Springs, CO, 80901. Internet: http://www.aafs.org

For general information on forestry technicians and a list of schools offering education in forestry, send a self-addressed, stamped business envelope to

- Society of American Foresters, 5400 Grosvenor Ln., Bethesda, MD 20814. Internet: http://www.safnet.org

Semiconductor Processors

(O*NET 51-9141.00)

Significant Points

- Employment is expected to decline over the next 10 years because of increasing automation and the building of many new plants abroad.
- Opportunities will be best for applicants who have an associate degree in a relevant subject.

Nature of the Work

Semiconductors are unique substances, which, under different conditions, can act as either conductors or insulators of electricity. Semiconductor processors turn one of these substances—silicon—into microchips, also known as integrated circuits. These microchips contain millions of tiny electronic components and are used in a wide range of products, from personal computers and cellular telephones to airplanes and missile guidance systems.

To manufacture microchips, *semiconductor processors* start with cylinders of silicon called ingots. First, the ingots are sliced into thin wafers. Using automated equipment, workers or robots polish the wafers, imprint precise microscopic patterns of the circuitry onto them using photolithography, etch out patterns with acids, and replace the patterns with conductors, such as aluminum or copper. The wafers then receive a chemical bath to make them smooth, and the imprint process begins again on a new layer with the next pattern. A complex chip may contain more than 20 layers of circuitry. Once the process is complete, wafers are then cut into individual chips, which are enclosed in a casing and shipped to equipment manufacturers.

The manufacturing and slicing of wafers to create semiconductors takes place in cleanrooms—production areas that are kept free of all airborne matter because the circuitry on a chip is so small that even microscopic particles can make it unusable. All semiconductor processors working in cleanrooms must wear special lightweight outer garments known as "bunny suits". These garments fit over clothing to prevent lint and other particles from contaminating the cleanroom.

There are two types of semiconductor processors: operators and technicians. *Operators* start and monitor the equipment that performs the various production tasks. They spend the majority of their time at computer terminals, monitoring the operation of equipment to ensure that each of the tasks in the production of the wafer is performed correctly. Operators may also transfer wafer carriers from one station to the next, though the lifting of heavy wafer carriers is done by robots in most new fabricating plants.

Technicians are generally more experienced workers who troubleshoot production problems and make equipment adjustments and repairs. They take the lead in assuring quality control and in maintaining equipment. They also test completed chips to make sure they work properly. To keep equipment repairs to a minimum, technicians perform diagnostic analyses and run computations. For example, technicians may determine if a flaw in a chip is due to contamination and peculiar to that wafer, or if the flaw is inherent in the manufacturing process.

Work environment. The work pace in cleanrooms is deliberately slow. Limited movement keeps the air in cleanrooms as free as possible of dust and other particles, which can destroy microchips during their production. Because the machinery sets the operators' rate of work, workers maintain a relaxed pace. Although workers spend some time alone monitoring equipment, operators and technicians spend much of their time working in teams.

Technicians are on their feet most of the day, walking through the cleanroom to oversee production activities. Operators spend a great deal of time sitting or standing at workstations, monitoring computer readouts and indicators.

The temperature in the cleanrooms must be kept within a narrow range and is generally comfortable for workers. Although bunny suits cover virtually the entire body, their lightweight fabric keeps the temperature inside fairly comfortable. Entry and exit of workers from the cleanroom are controlled to minimize contamination, and workers must be reclothed in a clean bunny suit and decontaminated each time they return to the cleanroom.

Several highly toxic chemicals are used at various points in the process of manufacturing microchips. Workers who are exposed to such chemicals can be seriously harmed. However, fabrication plants are designed with safeguards to ensure that these chemicals are handled, used, and disposed of without exposing workers or the surrounding environment. Toxic chemicals are applied to wafers by computer-controlled machine tools in sealed chambers, and there is normally little risk of workers coming into contact with them.

Semiconductor fabricating plants operate around the clock. Night and weekend work is common. In some plants, workers maintain standard 8-hour shifts, 5 days a week. In other plants, employees are on duty for 12-hour shifts to minimize the disruption of cleanroom operations brought about by changes. Managers may also allow workers to alternate schedules, thereby distributing the overnight shift equitably.

Training, Other Qualifications, and Advancement

People interested in becoming semiconductor processors—either operators or technicians—need strong technical skills, an ability to solve problems intuitively, and an ability to work in teams.

Projections data from the National Employment Matrix

Occupational Title	SOC Code	Employment, 2006	Projected employment, 2016	Change, 2006-16	
				Number	Percent
Semiconductor processors	51-9141	42,000	37,000	-5,500	-13

NOTE: Data in this table are rounded.

Mathematics, including statistics, and physical science knowledge are also very useful. Communication skills and an understanding of manufacturing principles are also very important.

Education and training. For semiconductor processor jobs, employers prefer applicants who have completed an associate degree. However, experience plus completion of a one-year certificate program in semiconductor technology, offered by some community colleges, may also be sufficient. Some semiconductor technology programs at community colleges include internships at semiconductor fabricating plants. Other applicants may qualify by completing a degree in high-tech manufacturing. Hands-on training is an important part of degree and certificate programs.

To ensure that operators and technicians keep their skills current, employers provide regular on-the-job training. Some employers also provide financial assistance to employees who want to earn an associate or bachelor's degree, especially if the employee is working toward becoming a technician.

Advancement. Workers advance as they become more comfortable with the equipment and better understand the manufacturing process. Employees train workers for several months, after which they become entry-level operators or technicians. After a few years, as they become more knowledgeable about the operations of the plant, they generally advance to the intermediate level. This entails greater responsibilities. Over time, usually seven to 10 years, workers may become senior technicians, who lead teams of technicians and work directly with engineers to develop processes in the plant.

Employment

Semiconductor processors held approximately 42,000 jobs in 2006. Nearly all of them were employed in the computer and electronic product manufacturing industry.

Job Outlook

Employment of semiconductor processors is projected to decline through 2016. Opportunities will be best for those with a 2-year degree and experience working in high-tech manufacturing.

Employment change. Employment of semiconductor processors is projected to decline moderately, decreasing by 13 percent between 2006 and 2016. Although the demand for microchips is growing at a very rapid rate, employment levels in the industry will not increase over the next 10 years because of automation and the opening of fabricating plants in other countries. As the electrical components of chips become smaller, they become more sensitive. This means that chip manufacturers prefer precise robotics to human workers, who could potentially damage the chips. Additionally, there is a trend toward moving production to the areas where demand is most concentrated, thus, reducing the demand for U.S. exports of microchips. While this has not decreased U.S. production, fewer new plants are being constructed here.

Because of increased automation, most of the new positions created will be for technicians. While operator jobs will decline as older plants close and newer plants use more robotics, technician jobs will become more prevalent as the machinery becomes more complex and needs more monitoring. Technicians are responsible for understanding more of the fabrication process, so companies hiring new employees will expect a higher level of competency.

The demand for semiconductor chips remains very high, stemming from the many existing and future applications for semiconductors in computers, appliances, machinery, biotechnology, vehicles, cell phones, and other equipment.

Job prospects. Despite the decline in employment, some jobs will open up due to the need to replace workers who leave the occupation. Because specialized training is required to excel in this field, the number of openings is expected to remain in rough balance with the number of qualified job seekers. Prospects will be best for applicants with an associate degree and experience in high-tech manufacturing.

Earnings

Median annual earnings of wage-and-salary semiconductor processors were $32,860 in May 2006. The middle 50 percent earned between $26,680 and $40,620 an hour. The lowest 10 percent earned less than $21,700, and the top 10 percent earned more than $49,470 an hour.

Technicians with an associate degree in electronics or semiconductor technology generally start at higher salaries than those with less education.

Semiconductor processors generally received good benefits packages, including health care, disability plans and life insurance, stock options and retirement.

Related Occupations

Semiconductor processors do production work that resembles the work of precision assemblers and fabricators of other high-tech equipment. Also, many electronic semiconductor processors have academic training in semiconductor technology, which emphasizes scientific and engineering principles. Other occupations that require some college or postsecondary vocational training emphasizing such principles are engineering technicians, electrical engineers, and science technicians.

Sources of Additional Information

For more information on semiconductor processor careers, contact

- Maricopa Advanced Technology Education Center, 2323 West 14th St., Suite 540, Tempe, AZ 85281. Internet: http://www.matec.org
- Semiconductor Industry Association, 181 Metro Dr., Suite 450, San Jose, CA 95110. Internet: http://www.sia-online.org

Small Engine Mechanics

(O*NET 49-3051.00, 49-3052.00, and 49-3053.00)

Significant Points

- Job prospects should be excellent for people who complete formal training programs.
- Most mechanics learn their skills on the job or while working in related occupations.
- Use of motorcycles, motorboats, and outdoor power equipment is seasonal in many areas, so mechanics may service other types of equipment or work reduced hours in the winter.

Nature of the Work

Small engine mechanics repair and service power equipment ranging from jet skis to chainsaws. Mechanics usually specialize in the service and repair of one type of equipment, although they may work on closely-related products.

When a piece of equipment breaks down, mechanics use various techniques to diagnose the source and extent of the problem. The mark of a skilled mechanic is the ability to diagnose mechanical, fuel, and electrical problems and to make repairs quickly. Quick and accurate diagnosis requires problem-solving ability and a thorough knowledge of the equipment's operation.

Some jobs require minor adjustments or the replacement of a single item, whereas a complete engine overhaul requires hours to disassemble the engine and replace worn valves, pistons, bearings, and other internal parts. Some highly skilled mechanics use specialized components and the latest computerized equipment to customize and tune motorcycles and motorboats for racing.

Handtools are the most important work possessions of mechanics. Small engine mechanics use wrenches, pliers, and screwdrivers on a regular basis. Mechanics usually provide their own tools, although employers will furnish expensive power tools, computerized engine analyzers, and other diagnostic equipment. Computerized engine analyzers, compression gauges, ammeters and voltmeters, and other testing devices help mechanics locate faulty parts and tune engines. This equipment provides a systematic performance report of various components to compare against normal ratings. After pinpointing the problem, the mechanic makes the needed adjustments, repairs, or replacements.

Small engines also require periodic service to minimize the chance of breakdowns and to keep them operating at peak performance. During routine maintenance, mechanics follow a checklist that includes the inspection and cleaning of brakes, electrical systems, fuel injection systems, plugs, carburetors, and other parts. Following inspection, mechanics usually repair or adjust parts that do not work properly or replace unfixable parts.

Motorcycle mechanics specialize in the repair and overhaul of motorcycles, motor scooters, mopeds, dirt bikes, and all-terrain vehicles. Besides repairing engines, they may work on transmissions, brakes, and ignition systems and make minor body repairs. Mechanics often service just a few makes and models of motorcycles because most work for dealers that service only the products they sell.

Motorboat mechanics, or *marine equipment mechanics*, repair and adjust the electrical and mechanical equipment of inboard and outboard boat engines. Most small boats have portable outboard engines that are removed and brought into the repair shop. Larger craft, such as cabin cruisers and commercial fishing boats, are powered by diesel or gasoline inboard or inboard-outboard engines, which are removed only for major overhauls. Most of these repairs, therefore, are performed at docks or marinas. Motorboat mechanics also may work on propellers, steering mechanisms, marine plumbing, and other boat equipment.

Outdoor power equipment and other small engine mechanics service and repair outdoor power equipment such as lawnmowers, garden tractors, edge trimmers, and chain saws. They also may occasionally work on portable generators and go-carts. In addition, small engine mechanics in certain parts of the country may work on snowblowers and snowmobiles, but demand for this type of repair is both seasonal and regional.

Work environment. Small engine mechanics usually work in repair shops that are well lighted and ventilated but are sometimes noisy when engines are tested. Motorboat mechanics may work outdoors in poor weather conditions when making repairs aboard boats. They may also work in cramped or awkward positions to reach a boat's engine. Outdoor power equipment mechanics face similar conditions when they need to make on-site repairs.

During the winter months in the northern United States, mechanics may work fewer than 40 hours a week because the amount of repair and service work declines when lawnmowers, motorboats, and motorcycles are not in use. Many mechanics work full-time only during the busy spring and summer seasons. However, they often schedule time-consuming engine overhauls or work on snowmobiles and snowblowers during winter downtime. Mechanics may work considerably more than 40 hours a week when demand is strong.

Training, Other Qualifications, and Advancement

Due to the increasing complexity of motorcycles and motorboats, employers prefer to hire mechanics who have graduated from formal training programs. However, because the number of these specialized postsecondary programs is limited, most mechanics still learn their skills on the job or while working in related occupations.

Education and training. Employers prefer to hire high school graduates for trainee mechanic positions, but many will accept applicants with less education if they possess adequate reading, writing, and math skills. Helpful high school courses include small engine repair, automobile mechanics, science, and business math. Many equipment dealers employ high school students part time and during the summer to help assemble new equipment and perform minor repairs.

Once employed, trainees learn routine service tasks under the guidance of experienced mechanics by replacing ignition points and spark plugs or by taking apart, assembling, and testing new equipment. As they gain experience and proficiency, trainees progress to more difficult tasks, such as advanced computerized diagnosis and engine overhauls. Anywhere from three to five years of on-the-job training may be necessary before a novice worker becomes competent in all aspects of the repair of motorcycle and motorboat engines. Repair of outdoor equipment, because of fewer moving parts, requires less on-the-job training.

Projections data from the National Employment Matrix

Occupational Title	SOC Code	Employment, 2006	Projected employment, 2016	Change, 2006-16	
				Number	Percent
Small engine mechanics	49-3050	78,000	87,000	9,100	12
Motorboat mechanics	49-3051	24,000	29,000	4,600	19
Motorcycle mechanics	49-3052	21,000	24,000	2,600	12
Outdoor power equipment and other small engine mechanics	49-3053	33,000	35,000	1,800	6

NOTE: Data in this table are rounded.

A growing number of motorcycle and marine equipment mechanics graduate from formal motorcycle and motorboat postsecondary programs. Employers prefer to hire these workers for their advanced knowledge of small engine repair. These workers also tend to advance quickly to more demanding small engine repair jobs.

Employers often send mechanics and trainees to courses conducted by motorcycle, motorboat, and outdoor power equipment manufacturers or distributors. These courses, which can last up to two weeks, upgrade workers' skills and provide information on repairing new models. Manufacturer classes are usually a prerequisite for any mechanic who performs warranty work for manufacturers or insurance companies.

Other qualifications. For trainee jobs, employers hire people with mechanical aptitude who are knowledgeable about the fundamentals of small two- and four-stroke engines. Many trainees get their start by working on automobiles, motorcycles, motorboats, or outdoor power equipment as a hobby. Knowledge of basic electronics is essential because many parts of small vehicles and engines are electric.

Advancement. The skills needed for small engine repair can transfer to other occupations, such as automobile, diesel, or heavy vehicle and mobile equipment mechanics. Experienced mechanics with leadership ability may advance to shop supervisor or service manager jobs. Mechanics with sales ability sometimes become sales representatives or open their own repair shops.

Employment

Small engine mechanics held about 78,000 jobs in 2006. Motorcycle mechanics held around 21,000 jobs. Motorboat mechanics held approximately 24,000 and outdoor power equipment and other small engine mechanics about 33,000. Almost half, 47 percent, of small engine mechanics worked for either other motor vehicle dealers—an industry that includes retail dealers of motorcycles, boats, and miscellaneous vehicles—or for retail hardware, lawn, and garden stores. Most of the remainder were employed by independent repair shops, marinas and boatyards, equipment rental companies, wholesale distributors, and landscaping services. About 23 percent were self-employed, compared to about 7 percent of workers in all installation, maintenance, and repair occupations.

Job Outlook

Average employment growth is projected for of small engine mechanics. Job prospects should be excellent for people who complete formal training programs.

Employment change. Employment of small engine mechanics is expected to grow 12 percent between 2006 and 2016, about as fast as the average for all occupations. An increase in the population of retired people is expected to increase the number of people who have leisure time and income to spend on recreational equipment such as motorcycles and motorboats. Moreover, the increase in the population of coastal and lake regions should add to the popularity of motorboats, and continued motorcycle use among 18- to 24-year-olds will contribute to rising motorcycle sales. The need for mechanics to maintain and repair motorcycles and motorboats is expected to increase with sales.

Outdoor equipment mechanics will not experience the same level of growth. Although the construction of new single-family houses will result in an increase in the sale of lawn and garden machinery and the need for mechanics to repair it, growth will be strongly tempered by a trend toward smaller lawns and the contracting out of maintenance to landscaping firms that often repair their own equipment. Small engine mechanics' growth also will be tempered by the tendency of many consumers to replace relatively inexpensive items rather than have them repaired.

Job prospects. Job prospects should be excellent for people who complete formal training programs. Employers prefer mechanics who have knowledge of both 2- and 4-stroke engines and other emissions-reducing technology as the government increases regulation of the emissions produced by small engines. Many of the job openings for small engine mechanics will result from the need to replace the many experienced small engine mechanics who are expected to transfer to other occupations, retire, or stop working for other reasons.

Work tends to be more available in summer months.

Earnings

Median wage-and-salary earnings of motorcycle mechanics were $14.45 an hour in May 2006, as compared to $17.65 for all installation, maintenance, and repair occupations. The middle 50 percent earned between $11.31 and $18.41. The lowest 10 percent earned less than $8.96, and the highest 10 percent earned more than $23.31. Median hourly earnings in other motor vehicle dealers, the industry employing the largest number of motorcycle mechanics, were $14.42.

Median wage-and-salary earnings of motorboat mechanics were $15.96 an hour in May 2006. The middle 50 percent earned between $12.66 and $20.01. The lowest 10 percent earned less than $9.94, and the highest 10 percent earned more than $24.40. Median hourly earnings in other motor vehicle dealers, the industry employing the largest number of motorboat mechanics, were $15.68.

Median wage-and-salary earnings of outdoor power equipment and other small engine mechanics were $12.94 an hour in May 2006. The middle 50 percent earned between $10.36 and $16.05. The lowest 10 percent earned less than $8.31, and the highest 10 percent earned more than $19.31. Median hourly earnings in lawn and garden equipment and supplies stores, the industry employing the largest number of outdoor power equipment and other small engine mechanics, were $12.74.

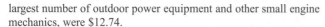

Small engine mechanics in small shops usually receive few benefits, but those employed in larger shops often receive paid vacations, sick leave, and health insurance. Some employers also pay for work-related training, provide uniforms, and help mechanics purchase new tools.

Related Occupations

Mechanics and repairers who work on durable equipment other than small engines include automotive service technicians and mechanics, diesel service technicians and mechanics, heavy vehicle and mobile equipment service technicians and mechanics, and home appliance repairers.

Sources of Additional Information

To learn about work opportunities, contact local motorcycle, motorboat, and lawn and garden equipment dealers, boatyards, and marinas. Local offices of the state employment service also may have information about employment and training opportunities.

Social Scientists, Other

(O*NET 19-3041.00, 19-3091.00, 19-3091.01, 19-3091.02, 19-3092.00, 19-3093.00, 19-3094.00, and 19-3099.99)

Significant Points

- About 41 percent of these workers are employed by governments, mostly by the federal government.
- The educational attainment of social scientists is among the highest of all occupations, with most positions requiring a master's or Ph.D. degree.
- Overall employment is projected to grow about as fast as the average for all occupations, but varies by specialty.
- Job seekers may face competition, and those with higher educational attainment will have the best prospects.

Nature of the Work

The major social science occupations covered in this statement are anthropologists, archaeologists, geographers, historians, political scientists, and sociologists. (Economists, psychologists, and urban and regional planners are covered elsewhere in this book.)

Social scientists study all aspects of society—from past events and achievements to human behavior and relationships among groups. Their research provides insights into the different ways individuals, groups, and institutions make decisions, exercise power, and respond to change. Through their studies and analyses, social scientists suggest solutions to social, business, personal, governmental, and environmental problems. In fact, many work as policy analysts for government or private organizations.

Research is a major activity of many social scientists, who use a variety of methods to assemble facts and construct theories. Applied research usually is designed to produce information that will enable people to make better decisions or manage their affairs more effectively. Social scientists often begin by collecting existing information. Collecting information takes many forms, including conducting interviews and questionnaires to gather demographic and opinion data, living and working among the population being studied, performing other field investigations, and experimenting with human or animal subjects in a laboratory. Social scientists also look at data in detail, such as studying the data they've collected, reanalyzing already existing data, analyzing historical records and documents, and interpreting maps and the effect of location on culture and other aspects of society. Following are several major types of social scientists. Specialists in one field may find that their research overlaps work being conducted in another discipline.

Anthropologists study the origin and the physical, social, and cultural development and behavior of humans. They may examine the way of life, archaeological remains, language, or physical characteristics of people in various parts of the world. Some compare the customs, values, and social patterns of different cultures. Anthropologists usually concentrate in sociocultural anthropology, linguistics, biophysical, or physical anthropology. Sociocultural anthropologists study the customs, cultures, and social lives of groups in settings that range from unindustrialized societies to modern urban centers. Linguistic anthropologists investigate the role of, and changes to, language over time in various cultures. Biophysical anthropologists research the evolution of the human body, look for the earliest evidences of human life, and analyze how culture and biology influence one another. Physical anthropologists examine human remains found at archaeological sites in order to understand population demographics and factors, such as nutrition and disease, which affected these populations. *Archaeologists* examine and recover material evidence including the ruins of buildings, tools, pottery, and other objects remaining from past human cultures in order to determine the history, customs, and living habits of earlier civilizations. With continued technological advances making it increasingly possible to detect the presence of underground anomalies without digging archaeologists will be able to better target excavation sites. Another technological advancement is the use of geographic information systems (GIS) for tasks such as analyzing how environmental factors near a site may have affected the development of a society. Most anthropologists and archaeologists specialize in a particular region of the world.

Political scientists study the origin, development, and operation of political systems and public policy. They conduct research on a wide range of subjects, such as relations between the United States and other countries, the institutions and political life of nations, the politics of small towns or major metropolises, and the decisions of the U.S. Supreme Court. Studying topics such as public opinion, political decision making, ideology, and public policy, they analyze the structure and operation of governments, as well as various political entities. Depending on the topic, a political scientist might conduct a public-opinion survey, analyze election results or public documents, or interview public officials.

Sociologists study society and social behavior by examining the groups, cultures, organizations, and social institutions people form. They also study the activities in which people participate, including social, religious, political, economic, and business organizations. They study the behavior of, and interaction among, groups, organizations, institutions, and nations and how they react to phenomena such as the spread of technology, health epidemics, crime, and social movements. They also trace the origin and growth of these groups and interactions. Sociologists analyze how social influences affect different individuals. They also are concerned with the ways organizations and institutions affect the daily lives of individuals and groups. To analyze social patterns, sociologists design research projects that use a variety of methods, including historical analysis, comparative analysis, and quantitative and qualitative techniques. The results of sociological research aid educators, lawmakers, administrators, and others who are interested in resolving social problems and formulating public policy. Most sociologists work in one or more specialties, such as social organization, stratification, and mobility; racial and ethnic relations; education; the family; social psychology; urban, rural, political, and comparative sociology; gender relations; demography; gerontology; criminology; and sociological practice.

Geographers analyze distributions of physical and cultural phenomena on local, regional, continental, and global scales. Economic geographers study the distribution of resources and economic activities. Political geographers are concerned with the relationship of geography to political phenomena, and cultural geographers study the geography of cultural phenomena. Physical geographers examine variations in climate, vegetation, soil, and landforms and their implications for human activity. Urban and transportation geographers study cities and metropolitan areas. Regional geographers study the physical, economic, political, and cultural characteristics of regions ranging in size from a congressional district to entire continents. Medical geographers investigate health care delivery systems, epidemiology (the study of the causes and control of epidemics), and the effect of the environment on health. Most geographers use GIS technology to assist with their work. For example, they may use GIS to create computerized maps that can track information such as population growth, traffic patterns, environmental hazards, natural resources, and weather patterns, after which they use the information to advise governments on the development of houses, roads, or landfills. Many of the people who study geography and work with GIS technology are classified in other occupations, such as surveyors, cartographers, photogrammetrists, and survey technicians (who develop maps and other location-based information), urban and regional planners (who help to decide on and evaluate the locations of building and roads and other aspects of physical society), and geoscientists (who study earthquakes and other physical aspects of the Earth). (These occupations are described elsewhere in this book.)

Historians research, analyze, and interpret the past. They use many sources of information in their research, including government and institutional records, newspapers and other periodicals, photographs, interviews, films, and unpublished manuscripts such as personal diaries and letters. Historians usually specialize in a country or region, a particular period, or a particular field, such as social, intellectual, cultural, political, or diplomatic history. Other historians help study and preserve archival materials, artifacts, and historic buildings and sites.

Work environment. Most social scientists have regular hours. Generally working behind a desk, either alone or in collaboration with other social scientists, they read and write research articles or reports. Many experience the pressures of writing and publishing, as well as those associated with deadlines and tight schedules. Sometimes they must work overtime, for which they usually are not compensated. Social scientists often work as an integral part of a research team. Travel may be necessary to collect information or attend meetings. Social scientists on foreign assignment must adjust to unfamiliar cultures, climates, and languages.

Some social scientists do fieldwork. For example, anthropologists, archaeologists, and geographers may travel to remote areas, live among the people they study, learn their languages, and stay for long periods at the site of their investigations. They may work under rugged conditions, and their work may involve strenuous physical exertion.

Social scientists employed by colleges and universities usually have flexible work schedules, often dividing their time among teaching, research, writing, consulting, and administrative responsibilities. Those who teach in these settings are classified as postsecondary teachers.

Training, Other Qualifications, and Advancement

The educational attainment of social scientists is among the highest of all occupations, with most positions requiring a master's or Ph.D. degree.

Education and training. Graduates with master's degrees in applied specialties usually are qualified for positions outside of colleges and universities, although requirements vary by field. A Ph.D. degree may be required for higher-level positions. Bachelor's degree holders have limited opportunities and do not qualify for most of the occupations discussed above. A bachelor's degree does, however, provide a suitable background for many different kinds of entry-level jobs in related occupations, such as research assistant, writer, management trainee, or market analyst.

Training in statistics and mathematics is essential for many social scientists Geographers, political scientists, and those in other fields increasingly use mathematical and quantitative research methods. The ability to use computers for research purposes is mandatory in most disciplines. Social scientists also must keep up-to date on the latest technological advances that affect their discipline and research. For example, most geographers use GIS technology extensively, and GIS is also becoming more commonly used by archaeologists, sociologists, and other workers.

Many social science students also benefit from internships or field experience. Numerous local museums, historical societies, government agencies, non-profit and other organizations offer internships or volunteer research opportunities. Archaeological field schools instruct future anthropologists, archaeologists, and historians in how to excavate, record, and interpret historical sites.

Other qualifications. Social scientists need excellent written and oral communication skills to report research findings and to collaborate on research. Successful social scientists also need intellectual curiosity and creativity because they constantly seek new information about people, things, and ideas. The ability to think logically and methodically is also essential to analyze complicated issues, such as the relative merits of various forms of government. Objectivity, an open mind, and systematic work habits are important in all kinds of social science research. Perseverance, too, is often necessary, as when an anthropologist spends years studying artifacts from an ancient civilization before making a final analysis and interpretation.

Advancement. Some social scientists advance to top-level research and administrative positions. Advancement often depends on the number and quality of reports that social scientists publish or their ability to design studies.

Many social scientists choose to teach in their field, often while pursuing their own research. These workers are usually classified as postsecondary teachers. The minimum requirement for most positions in colleges and universities is a Ph.D. degree. Graduates with a master's degree in a social science may qualify for teaching positions in community colleges. Social science graduates with sufficient education courses can qualify for teaching positions in secondary and elementary schools.

Employment

Social scientists held about 18,000 jobs in 2006. Many worked as researchers, administrators, and counselors for a wide range of employers. About 41 percent worked for federal, state, and local governments, mostly for the federal government. Other employers included scientific research and development services; management, scientific, and technical consulting services; business, professional, labor, political, and similar organizations; and architectural, engineering, and related firms.

Many individuals with training in a social science discipline teach in colleges and universities and in secondary and elementary schools. The proportion of social scientists who teach varies by specialty. For example, graduates in history are more likely to teach than are graduates in most other social science fields.

The following tabulation shows employment, by social science specialty.

Anthropologists and archeologists	5,500
Political scientists	4,700
Sociologists	3,700
Historians	3,400
Geographers	1,100

Job Outlook

Overall employment is projected to grow about as fast as average, but varies by detailed occupation. Job seekers may face competition, and those with higher educational attainment will have the best prospects.

Employment change. Overall employment of social scientists is expected to grow 10 percent from 2006 to 2016, about as fast as the average for all occupations. However, projected growth rates vary by specialty. Anthropologists and archaeologists, sociologists, and historians are projected to grow about as fast as average. Employment of geographers and political scientists is projected to grow more slowly than average, reflecting the relatively few opportunities outside of the federal government. Employment is projected to decline slowly in the federal government, a key employer of social scientists.

The following tabulation shows projected percent change in employment, by social science specialty.

Anthropologists and archeologists	15%
Sociologists	10
Historians	8
Geographers	6
Political scientists	5

Anthropologists and archaeologists will experience the majority of their job growth in the management, scientific, and technical consulting services industry. Anthropologists who work as consultants apply anthropological knowledge and methods to problems ranging from economic development issues to forensics. As construction projects increase, more archaeologists also will be needed to monitor the work, ensuring that historical sites and artifacts are preserved.

Political scientists, sociologists, and historians will mainly find jobs in policy or research. Demand for political science research is growing because of increasing interest about politics and foreign affairs, including social and environmental policy issues and immigration. Political scientists will use their knowledge of political institutions to further the interests of nonprofit, political lobbying, and social organizations. Likewise, the incorporation of sociology into research in other fields will continue to increase the need for sociologists. They may find work conducting policy research for consulting firms and nonprofit organizations, and their knowledge of society and social behavior may be used by a variety of companies in product development, marketing, and advertising. Historians may find opportunities with historic preservation societies or working as a consultant as public interest in preserving and restoring historical sites increases.

Geographers will work advising government, real estate developers, utilities, and telecommunications firms on where to build new roads, buildings, power plants, and cable lines. Geographers also will advise on environmental matters, such as where to build a landfill or preserve wetland habitats. Geographers with a background in GIS will find numerous job opportunities applying GIS technology in nontraditional areas, such as emergency assistance, where GIS can track locations of ambulances, police, and fire rescue units and their proximity to the emergency. Workers in these jobs may not necessarily be called "geographers," but instead may be referred to by a different title, such as "GIS analyst" or "GIS specialist."

Job prospects. In addition to opportunities from employment growth, some job openings for social scientists will come from the need to replace those who retire, enter teaching or other occupations, or leave their social science occupation for other reasons.

People seeking social science positions may face competition for jobs, and those with higher educational attainment will have the best prospects. Many jobs in policy, research, or marketing for which social scientists qualify are not advertised exclusively as social scientist positions. Because of the wide range of skills and knowledge possessed by these social scientists, many compete for jobs with other workers, such as market and survey researchers, psychologists, engineers, urban and regional planners, and statisticians.

Some people with social science degrees will find opportunities as university faculty rather than as applied social scientists. Although there will be keen competition for tenured positions, the number of faculty expected to retire over the decade and the increasing number of part-time or short-term faculty positions will lead to better opportunities in colleges and universities than in the past. The growing importance and popularity of social science subjects in secondary schools also is strengthening the demand for social science teachers at that level.

Earnings

In May 2006, anthropologists and archaeologists had median annual wage-and-salary earnings of $49,930; geographers, $62,990; historians, $48,520; political scientists, $90,140; and sociologists, $60,290.

Projections data from the National Employment Matrix

Occupational Title	SOC Code	Employment, 2006	Projected employment, 2016	Change, 2006-2016	
				Number	Percent
Social scientists, other	—	54,000	58,000	3,500	6
Sociologists	19-3041	3,700	4,100	400	10
Anthropologists and archeologists	19-3091	5,500	6,400	800	15
Geographers	19-3092	1,100	1,200	100	6
Historians	19-3093	3,400	3,700	300	8
Political scientists	19-3094	4,700	4,900	300	5

NOTE: Data in this table are rounded.

In the federal government, social scientists with a bachelor's degree and no experience often started at a yearly salary of $28,862 or $35,572 in 2007, depending on their college records. Those with a master's degree could start at $43,731, and those with a Ph.D. degree could begin at $52,912, while some individuals with experience and an advanced degree could start at $63,417. Beginning salaries were higher in selected areas of the country where the prevailing local pay level was higher.

Related Occupations

The duties and training of these social scientists are similar to other social scientists, including economists, market and survey researchers, psychologists, and urban and regional planners. Many social scientists conduct surveys, study social problems, teach, and work in museums, performing tasks similar to those of statisticians; counselors; social workers; teachers—postsecondary; teachers—preschool, kindergarten, elementary, middle, and secondary; and archivists, curators, and museum technicians.

Political scientists often research the function of government, including the legal system, as do lawyers; paralegals and legal assistants; and judges, magistrates, and other judicial workers. Many political scientists analyze and report on current events, as do news analysts, reporters, and correspondents.

Geographers often study the Earth's environment and natural resources, as do conservation scientists and foresters, atmospheric scientists, and environmental scientists and hydrologists. Geographers also use GIS computer technology to make maps. Other occupations with similar duties include surveyors, cartographers, photogrammetrists, and surveying technicians; computer systems analysts; and computer scientists and database administrators.

Sources of Additional Information

For information about careers in anthropology, contact

- American Anthropological Association, 2200 Wilson Blvd., Suite 600, Arlington, VA 22201. Internet: http://www.aaanet.org

For information about careers in archaeology, contact

- Archaeological Institute of America, 656 Beacon St., 6th Floor, Boston, MA 02215. Internet: http://www.archaeological.org
- Society for American Archaeology, 900 2nd St. NE, Suite 12, Washington, DC 20002. Internet: http://www.saa.org

For information about careers in geography, contact

- Association of American Geographers, 1710 16th St. NW, Washington, DC 20009. Internet: http://www.aag.org

Also see "Geography jobs," online at http://www.bls.gov/opub/ooq/2005/spring/art01.pdf and in the spring 2005 issue of the *Occupational Outlook Quarterly.*

Information on careers for historians is available from

- American Historical Association, 400 A St. SE, Washington, DC 20003. Internet: http://www.historians.org

For information about careers in political science, contact

- American Political Science Association, 1527 New Hampshire Ave. NW, Washington, DC 20036. Internet: http://www.apsanet.org
- National Association of Schools of Public Affairs and Administration, 1029 Vermont Ave. NW, Suite 1100, Washington, DC 20005. Internet: http://www.naspaa.org

Information about careers in sociology is available from

- American Sociological Association, 1307 New York Ave. NW, Suite 700, Washington, DC 20005. Internet: http://www.asanet.org

For information about careers in policy analysis, an important task for some social scientists, see "Policy analysts: Shaping society through research and problem-solving," online at http://www.bls.gov/opub/ooq/2007/spring/art03.pdf and in the spring 2007 issue of the *Occupational Outlook Quarterly.*

Speech-Language Pathologists

(O*NET 29-1127.00)

Significant Points

- About half worked in educational services; most others were employed by health care and social assistance facilities.
- A master's degree in speech-language pathology is the standard credential required for licensing in most states.
- Excellent job opportunities are expected.

Nature of the Work

Speech-language pathologists, sometimes called *speech therapists*, assess, diagnose, treat, and help to prevent disorders related to speech, language, cognitive-communication, voice, swallowing, and fluency.

Speech-language pathologists work with people who cannot produce speech sounds or cannot produce them clearly; those with speech rhythm and fluency problems, such as stuttering; people with voice disorders, such as inappropriate pitch or harsh voice; those with problems understanding and producing language; those who wish to improve their communication skills by modifying an accent; and those with cognitive communication impairments, such as attention, memory, and problem solving disorders. They also work with people who have swallowing difficulties.

Speech, language, and swallowing difficulties can result from a variety of causes including stroke, brain injury or deterioration, developmental delays or disorders, learning disabilities, cerebral palsy, cleft palate, voice pathology, mental retardation, hearing loss, or emotional problems. Problems can be congenital, developmental, or acquired. Speech-language pathologists use special instruments and qualitative and quantitative assessment methods, including standardized tests, to analyze and diagnose the nature and extent of impairments.

Speech-language pathologists develop an individualized plan of care, tailored to each patient's needs. For individuals with little or no speech capability, speech-language pathologists may select augmentative or alternative communication methods, including automated devices and sign language, and teach their use. They teach patients how to make sounds, improve their voices, or increase their oral or written language skills to communicate more effectively. They also teach individuals how to strengthen muscles or use compensatory strategies to swallow without choking or inhaling food or liquid. Speech-language pathologists help patients develop, or recover, reliable communication and swallowing skills so patients can fulfill their educational, vocational, and social roles.

Speech-language pathologists keep records on the initial evaluation, progress, and discharge of clients. This helps pinpoint problems, tracks client progress, and justifies the cost of treatment when applying for reimbursement. They counsel individuals and their families concerning communication disorders and how to cope with the stress and misunderstanding that often accompany them. They also work with family members to recognize and change behavior patterns that impede communication and treatment and show them communication-enhancing techniques to use at home.

Most speech-language pathologists provide direct clinical services to individuals with communication or swallowing disorders. In medical facilities, they may perform their job in conjunction with physicians, social workers, psychologists, and other therapists. Speech-language pathologists in schools collaborate with teachers, special educators, interpreters, other school personnel, and parents to develop and implement individual or group programs, provide counseling, and support classroom activities.

Some speech-language pathologists conduct research on how people communicate. Others design and develop equipment or techniques for diagnosing and treating speech problems.

Work environment. Speech-language pathologists usually work at a desk or table in clean comfortable surroundings. In medical settings, they may work at the patient's bedside and assist in positioning the patient. In schools, they may work with students in an office or classroom. Some work in the client's home.

Although the work is not physically demanding, it requires attention to detail and intense concentration. The emotional needs of clients and their families may be demanding. Most full-time speech-language pathologists work 40 hours per week. Those who work on a contract basis may spend a substantial amount of time traveling between facilities.

Training, Other Qualifications, and Advancement

A master's degree is the most common level of education among speech-language pathologists. Licensure or certification requirements also exist, but vary by state.

Education and training. Most speech-language pathologist jobs require a master's degree. In 2007, more than 230 colleges and universities offered graduate programs in speech-language pathology accredited by the Council on Academic Accreditation in Audiology and Speech-Language Pathology. While graduation from an accredited program is not always required to become a speech-language pathologist, it may be helpful in obtaining a license or may be required to obtain a license in some states.

Speech-language pathology courses cover anatomy, physiology, and the development of the areas of the body involved in speech, language, and swallowing; the nature of disorders; principles of acoustics; and psychological aspects of communication. Graduate students also learn to evaluate and treat speech, language, and swallowing disorders and receive supervised clinical training in communication disorders.

Licensure and certification. In 2007, 47 states regulated speech-language pathologists through licensure or registration. A passing score on the national examination on speech-language pathology, offered through the Praxis Series of the Educational Testing Service, is required. Other usual requirements include 300 to 375 hours of supervised clinical experience and nine months of postgraduate professional clinical experience. Forty-one states have continuing education requirements for licensure renewal. Medicaid, Medicare, and private health insurers generally require a practitioner to be licensed to qualify for reimbursement.

Only 12 states require this same license to practice in the public schools. The other states issue a teaching license or certificate that typically requires a master's degree from an approved college or university. Some states will grant a provisional teaching license or certificate to applicants with a bachelor's degree, but a master's degree must be earned within three to five years. A few states grant a full teacher's certificate or license to bachelor's degree applicants.

In some states, the Certificate of Clinical Competence in Speech-Language Pathology (CCC-SLP) offered by the American Speech-Language-Hearing Association meets some or all of the requirements for licensure. To earn a CCC, a person must have a graduate degree from an accredited university, 400 hours of supervised clinical experience, complete a 36-week postgraduate clinical fellowship, and pass the Praxis Series examination in speech-language pathology administered by the Educational Testing Service. Contact your state's Licensing Board for details on your state's requirements.

Other qualifications. Speech-language pathologists should be able to effectively communicate diagnostic test results, diagnoses, and proposed treatment in a manner easily understood by their patients and their families. They must be able to approach problems objectively and be supportive. Because a patient's progress may be slow, patience, compassion, and good listening skills are necessary.

Advancement. As speech-language pathologists gain clinical experience and engage in continuing professional education, many develop expertise with certain populations, such as preschoolers and adolescents, or disorders, such as aphasia and learning disabilities. Some may obtain board recognition in a specialty area, such as child language, fluency, or feeding and swallowing. Experienced clinicians may become mentors or supervisors of other therapists or be promoted to administrative positions.

Projections data from the National Employment Matrix

Occupational Title	SOC Code	Employment, 2006	Projected employment, 2016	Change, 2006-2016	
				Number	Percent
Speech-language pathologists	29-1127	110,000	121,000	12,000	11

NOTE: Data in this table are rounded.

Employment

Speech-language pathologists held about 110,000 jobs in 2006. About half were employed in educational services, primarily in preschools and elementary and secondary schools. Others were employed in hospitals; offices of other health practitioners, including speech-language pathologists; nursing care facilities; home health care services; individual and family services; outpatient care centers; and child day care centers.

A few speech-language pathologists are self-employed in private practice. They contract to provide services in schools, offices of physicians, hospitals, or nursing care facilities, or work as consultants to industry.

Job Outlook

Average employment growth is projected. Job opportunities are expected to be excellent.

Employment change. Employment of speech-language pathologists is expected to grow 11 percent from 2006 to 2016, about as fast as the average for all occupations. As the members of the baby boom generation continue to age, the possibility of neurological disorders and associated speech, language, and swallowing impairments increases. Medical advances also are improving the survival rate of premature infants and trauma and stroke victims, who then need assessment and sometimes treatment.

Employment in educational services will increase with the growth in elementary and secondary school enrollments, including enrollment of special education students. Federal law guarantees special education and related services to all eligible children with disabilities. Greater awareness of the importance of early identification and diagnosis of speech and language disorders in young children will also increase employment.

In health care facilities, restrictions on reimbursement for therapy services may limit the growth of speech-language pathologist jobs in the near term. However, the long-run demand for therapists should continue to rise as growth in the number of individuals with disabilities or limited function spurs demand for therapy services.

The number of speech-language pathologists in private practice will rise because of the increasing use of contract services by hospitals, schools, and nursing care facilities.

Job prospects. The combination of growth in the occupation and an expected increase in retirements over the coming years should create excellent job opportunities for speech-language pathologists. Opportunities should be particularly favorable for those with the ability to speak a second language, such as Spanish. Job prospects also are expected to be especially favorable for those who are willing to relocate, particularly to areas experiencing difficulty in attracting and hiring speech-language pathologists.

Earnings

Median annual earnings of wage-and-salary speech-language pathologists were $57,710 in May 2006. The middle 50 percent earned between $46,360 and $72,410. The lowest 10 percent earned less than $37,970, and the highest 10 percent earned more than $90,400. Median annual earnings in the industries employing the largest numbers of speech-language pathologists were

Nursing care facilities $70,180
Offices of other health practitioners 63,240
General medical and surgical hospitals 61,970
Elementary and secondary schools 53,110

Some employers may reimburse speech-language pathologists for their required continuing education credits.

Related Occupations

Speech-language pathologists specialize in the prevention, diagnosis, and treatment of speech and language problems. Workers in related occupations include audiologists, occupational therapists, optometrists, physical therapists, psychologists, and recreational therapists. Speech-language pathologists in school systems often work closely with special education teachers in assisting students with disabilities.

Sources of Additional Information

State licensing boards can provide information on licensure requirements. State departments of education can supply information on certification requirements for those who wish to work in public schools.

For information on careers in speech-language pathology, a description of the CCC-SLP credential, and a listing of accredited graduate programs in speech-language pathology, contact

- American Speech-Language-Hearing Association, 10801 Rockville Pike, Rockville, MD 20852. Internet: http://www.asha.org

Stationary Engineers and Boiler Operators

(O*NET 51-8021.00, 51-8021.01, and 51-8021.02)

Significant Points

- Workers usually acquire their skills through a formal apprenticeship program or through on-the-job training supplemented by courses at a trade or technical school.
- Most workers need to be licensed, but licensing requirements vary across the nation.
- Employment is projected to grow slowly, and applicants may face competition for jobs.

- Opportunities will be best for workers with training in computerized controls and instrumentation.

Nature of the Work

Most large office buildings, malls, warehouses, and other commercial facilities have extensive heating, ventilation, and air-conditioning systems that keep them comfortable all year long. Industrial plants often have additional facilities to provide electrical power, steam, or other services. Stationary engineers and boiler operators control and maintain these systems, which include boilers, air-conditioning and refrigeration equipment, diesel engines, turbines, generators, pumps, condensers, and compressors. The equipment that stationary engineers and boiler operators control is similar to equipment operated by locomotive or marine engineers, except that it is used to generate heat or electricity, rather than to move a train or ship.

Stationary engineers and boiler operators start up, regulate, repair, and shut down equipment. They ensure that the equipment operates safely, economically, and within established limits by monitoring meters, gauges, and computerized controls. Stationary engineers and boiler operators control equipment manually in many older buildings and, if necessary, make adjustments. They watch and listen to machinery and routinely check safety devices, identifying and correcting any trouble that develops.

In newer buildings, stationary engineers typically use computers to operate the mechanical, electrical, and fire safety systems. They monitor, adjust, and diagnose these systems from a central location, using a computer linked into the buildings' communications network.

Routine maintenance is a regular part of the work of stationary engineers and boiler operators. Engineers use hand and power tools to perform maintenance and repairs ranging from a complete overhaul to replacing defective valves, gaskets, or bearings. They lubricate moving parts, replace filters, and remove soot and corrosion that can reduce the boiler's operating efficiency. They also test the water in the boiler and add chemicals to prevent corrosion and harmful deposits. In most facilities, stationary engineers are responsible for the maintenance and balancing of air systems, as well as hydronic systems that heat or cool buildings by circulating fluid (such as water or water vapor) in a closed system of pipes. They may check the air quality of the ventilation system and make adjustments to keep the operation of the boiler within mandated guidelines. Servicing, troubleshooting, repairing, and monitoring modern systems all require the use of sophisticated electrical and electronic test equipment. Additionally, many stationary engineers perform other maintenance duties, such as carpentry, plumbing, locksmithing, and electrical repairs.

Stationary engineers and boiler operators keep a record of relevant events and facts concerning the operation and maintenance of the equipment. When working with steam boilers, for example, stationary engineers and boiler operators observe, control, and record steam pressure, temperature, water level, chemistry, power output, fuel consumption, and emissions from the boiler. They also note the date and nature of all maintenance and repairs.

In a large building or industrial plant, a senior stationary engineer may be in charge of all mechanical systems in the building and may supervise a team of assistant stationary engineers, turbine operators, boiler tenders, and air-conditioning and refrigeration operators and mechanics. In a small building or industrial plant, there may be only one stationary engineer.

Work environment. Engine rooms, power plants, boiler rooms, mechanical rooms, and electrical rooms are usually clean and well lighted. Even under the most favorable conditions, however, some stationary engineers and boiler operators are exposed to high temperatures, dust, dirt, and high noise levels from the equipment. Maintenance duties also may require contact with oil, grease, or smoke. Workers spend much of the time on their feet. They also may have to crawl inside boilers and work in crouching or kneeling positions to inspect, clean, or repair equipment.

Stationary engineers and boiler operators work around hazardous machinery, such as low- and high-pressure boilers and electrical equipment. They must follow procedures to guard against burns, electric shock, and noise, danger from moving parts, and exposure to hazardous materials, such as asbestos or toxic chemicals.

Stationary engineers and boiler operators generally have steady, year-round employment. The average work week is 40 hours. In facilities that operate around the clock, engineers and operators usually work one of three daily 8-hour shifts on a rotating basis. Weekend and holiday work often is required.

Training, Other Qualifications, and Advancement

Many stationary engineers and boiler operators begin their careers in mechanic or helper positions and are trained on-the-job by more experienced engineers. Others begin by entering formal apprenticeships or training programs. After completing the required training, workers can become licensed, which allows them to work on boilers of a certain size without supervision.

Education and training. Most employers prefer to hire persons with at least a high school diploma or the equivalent for stationary engineers and boiler operator jobs. Workers primarily acquire their skills on the job and usually start as boiler tenders or as helpers to more experienced workers. This practical experience may be supplemented by postsecondary vocational training in subjects such as computerized controls and instrumentation. Other workers complete formal apprenticeship programs. Becoming an engineer or operator without completing a formal apprenticeship program usually requires many years of work experience.

The International Union of Operating Engineers sponsors apprenticeship programs and is the principal union for stationary engineers and boiler operators. In selecting apprentices, most local labor-management apprenticeship committees prefer applicants with a basic understanding of mathematics, science, computers, mechanical drawing, machine shop practice, and chemistry. An apprenticeship usually lasts four years and includes 8,000 hours of on-the-job training. In addition, apprentices receive 600 hours of classroom instruction in subjects such as boiler design and operation, elementary physics, pneumatics, refrigeration, air-conditioning, electricity, and electronics.

Continuing education—such as vocational school or college courses—is becoming increasingly important for stationary engineers and boiler operators, in part because of the growing complexity of the equipment with which engineers and operators now work. In 2006, roughly half of all stationary engineers between the ages of 25 and 44 had at least some college coursework.

Projections data from the National Employment Matrix

Occupational Title	SOC Code	Employment, 2006	Projected employment, 2016	Change, 2006-16	
				Number	Percent
Stationary engineers and boiler operators	51-8021	45,000	47,000	1,600	3

NOTE: Data in this table are rounded.

Most large and some small employers encourage and pay for skill-improvement training for their employees. These employers often realize major cost savings due to greater efficiency of their workers; improved maintenance, reliability, and effective lifespan of equipment; and a better safety record. Well-trained workers manage energy better, which can also greatly reduce an employer's energy costs. Training is almost always provided when new equipment is introduced or when regulations concerning some aspect of the workers' duties change.

Licensure. Most states and cities have licensing requirements for stationary engineers and boiler operators. Applicants for licensure usually must be at least 18 years of age, reside for a specified period in the state or locality in which they wish to work, meet experience requirements, and pass a written examination. A stationary engineer or boiler operator who moves from one state or city to another may have to pass an examination for a new license due to regional differences in licensing requirements.

There are several classes of stationary engineer licenses. Each class specifies the type and size of equipment the engineer is permitted to operate without supervision. A licensed first-class stationary engineer is qualified to run a large facility, supervise others, and operate equipment of all types and capacities. An applicant for this license may be required to have a high school education, have completed an apprenticeship or lengthy on-the-job training, and have several years of experience working with a lower class license. Licenses below first class limit the types or capacities of equipment the engineer may operate without supervision.

Other qualifications. In addition to training, stationary engineers and boiler operators need mechanical aptitude and manual dexterity. Being in good physical condition is also important.

Advancement. Stationary engineers and boiler operators advance by being placed in charge of larger, more powerful, or more varied equipment. Generally, engineers advance to these jobs as they obtain higher class licenses. Some stationary engineers and boiler operators advance to become boiler inspectors, chief plant engineers, building and plant superintendents, or building managers. A few obtain jobs as examining engineers or technical instructors.

Because most stationary engineering staffs are relatively small, workers may find it difficult to advance, especially within a company. Most high-level positions are held by experienced workers with seniority. Workers wishing to move up to these positions must often change employers or wait for older workers to retire before they can advance.

Employment

Stationary engineers and boiler operators held about 45,000 jobs in 2006. They worked throughout the country, generally in the more heavily populated areas in which large industrial and commercial establishments are located. Jobs were dispersed throughout a variety of industries. The majority of jobs were in state and local government, manufacturing, and hospitals.

Job Outlook

Employment in this occupation is expected to grow more slowly than the average through 2016. Applicants may face competition for jobs. Employment opportunities will be best for those with apprenticeship training and experience using computerized systems.

Employment change. Employment of stationary engineers and boiler operators is expected to grow by 3 percent between 2006 and 2016, which is more slowly than the average for all occupations. Continuing commercial and industrial development will increase the amount of equipment to be operated and maintained. However, automated systems and computerized controls are making newly installed equipment more efficient, thus reducing the number of jobs needed for its operation.

Job prospects. People interested in working as stationary engineers and boiler operators should expect to face competition for these relatively high-paying positions. Slow job growth coupled with the tendency of experienced workers to stay in a job for decades should continue to make openings scarce. While many workers will reach retirement age within the next decade, the number of workers who need to be replaced will be small relative to other occupations.

Earnings

Median annual earnings of stationary engineers and boiler operators were $46,040 in May 2006. The middle 50 percent earned between $36,490 and $57,380. The lowest 10 percent earned less than $28,370, and the highest 10 percent earned more than $68,690.

Related Occupations

Workers who monitor and operate stationary machinery include chemical plant and system operators; gas plant operators; petroleum pump system operators, refinery operators, and gaugers; power plant operators, distributors, and dispatchers; and water and liquid waste treatment plant and system operators. Other workers who maintain the equipment and machinery in a building or plant are industrial machinery mechanics and maintenance workers, and millwrights.

Sources of Additional Information

Information about apprenticeships, vocational training, and work opportunities is available from state employment service offices, locals of the International Union of Operating Engineers, vocational schools, and state and local licensing agencies. Apprenticeship information is also available from the U.S. Department of Labor's toll-free helpline: 1 (877) 282-5627.

Specific questions about this occupation should be addressed to

- International Union of Operating Engineers, 1125 17th St. NW, Washington, DC 20036. Internet: http://www.iuoe.org
- National Association of Power Engineers, Inc., 1 Springfield St., Chicopee, MA 01013. Internet: http://www.powerengineers.com

- Building Owners and Managers Institute International, 1521 Ritchie Hwy., Arnold, MD 21012. Internet: http://www.bomi-edu.org

STEM Statisticians

(O*NET 15-2041.00)

Significant Points

- About 30 percent of statisticians work for federal, state, and local governments; other employers include scientific research and development services and finance and insurance firms.
- A master's degree in statistics or mathematics is the minimum educational requirement for most jobs as a statistician.
- Employment of statisticians is projected to grow about as fast as average.
- Individuals with a degree in statistics should have opportunities in a variety of fields.

Nature of the Work

Statistics is the scientific application of mathematical principles to the collection, analysis, and presentation of numerical data. Statisticians apply their mathematical and statistical knowledge to the design of surveys and experiments; the collection, processing, and analysis of data; and the interpretation of the experiment and survey results. Opinion polls, statements of accuracy on scales and other measuring devises, and information about average earnings in an occupation are all usually the work of statisticians.

Statisticians may apply their knowledge of statistical methods to a variety of subject areas, such as biology, economics, engineering, medicine, public health, psychology, marketing, education, and sports. Many economic, social, political, and military decisions cannot be made without statistical techniques, such as the design of experiments to gain federal approval of a newly manufactured drug. Statistics might be needed to show whether the seemingly good results of a drug were likely because of the drug rather than just the effect of random variation in patient outcomes.

One technique that is especially useful to statisticians is sampling—obtaining information about a population of people or group of things by surveying a small portion of the total. For example, to determine the size of the audience for particular programs, television-rating services survey only a few thousand families, rather than all viewers. Statisticians decide where and how to gather the data, determine the type and size of the sample group, and develop the survey questionnaire or reporting form. They also prepare instructions for workers who will collect and tabulate the data. Finally, statisticians analyze, interpret, and summarize the data using computer software.

In business and industry, statisticians play an important role in quality control and in product development and improvement. In an automobile company, for example, statisticians might design experiments to determine the failure time of engines exposed to extreme weather conditions by running individual engines until failure and breakdown. Working for a pharmaceutical company, statisticians might develop and evaluate the results of clinical trials to determine the safety and effectiveness of new medications. At a computer software firm, statisticians might help construct new statistical software packages to analyze data more accurately and efficiently. In addition to product development and testing, some statisticians also are involved in deciding what products to manufacture, how much to charge for them, and to whom the products should be marketed. Statisticians also may manage assets and liabilities, determining the risks and returns of certain investments.

Statisticians also are employed by nearly every government agency. Some government statisticians develop surveys that measure population growth, consumer prices, or unemployment. Other statisticians work for scientific, environmental, and agricultural agencies and may help figure out the average level of pesticides in drinking water, the number of endangered species living in a particular area, or the number of people afflicted with a particular disease. Statisticians also are employed in national defense agencies, determining the accuracy of new weapons and the likely effectiveness of defense strategies.

Because statistical specialists are employed in so many work areas, specialists who use statistics often have different professional designations. For example, a person using statistical methods to analyze economic data may have the title econometrician, while statisticians in public health and medicine may hold titles such as biostatistician or biometrician.

Work environment. Statisticians generally work regular hours in an office environment. Sometimes, they may work more hours to meet deadlines.

Some statisticians travel to provide advice on research projects, supervise and set up surveys, or gather statistical data. While advanced communications devices such as e-mail and teleconferencing are making it easier for statisticians to work with clients in different areas, there still are situations that require the statistician to be present, such as during meetings or while gathering data.

Training, Other Qualifications, and Advancement

A master's degree in statistics or mathematics is the minimum educational requirement, but research and academic jobs generally require a Ph.D., federal government jobs require at least a bachelor's degree.

Education and training. A master's degree in statistics or mathematics usually is the minimum educational requirement for most statistician jobs. Research and academic positions usually require a Ph.D. in statistics. Beginning positions in industrial research often require a master's degree combined with several years of experience.

Jobs with the federal government require at least a bachelor's degree. The training required for employment as an entry-level statistician in the federal government is a bachelor's degree, including at least 15 semester hours of statistics or a combination of 15 hours of mathematics and statistics, if at least six semester hours are in statistics. Qualifying as a mathematical statistician in the federal government requires 24 semester hours of mathematics and statistics, with a minimum of six semester hours in statistics and 12 semester hours in an area of advanced mathematics, such as calculus, differential equations, or vector analysis.

In 2007, more than 200 universities offered a degree program in statistics, biostatistics, or mathematics. Many other schools also offered graduate-level courses in applied statistics for students majoring in biology, business, economics, education, engineering,

Projections data from the National Employment Matrix

Occupational Title	SOC Code	Employment, 2006	Projected employment, 2016	Change, 2006-2016	
				Number	Percent
Statisticians	15-2041	22,000	24,000	1,900	9

NOTE: Data in this table are rounded.

psychology, and other fields. Acceptance into graduate statistics programs does not require an undergraduate degree in statistics, although good training in mathematics is essential.

Many schools also offered degrees in mathematics, operations research, and other fields that include a sufficient number of courses in statistics to qualify graduates for some entry-level positions with the federal government. Required subjects for statistics majors include differential and integral calculus, statistical methods, mathematical modeling, and probability theory. Additional recommended courses for undergraduates include linear algebra, design and analysis of experiments, applied multivariate analysis, and mathematical statistics.

Because computers are used extensively for statistical applications, a strong background in computer science is highly recommended. For positions involving quality and productivity improvement, training in engineering or physical science is useful. A background in biological, chemical, or health science is important for positions involving the preparation and testing of pharmaceutical or agricultural products. Courses in economics and business administration are helpful for many jobs in market research, business analysis, and forecasting.

Advancements in technology have made a great impact on statistics. Statistical modeling continues to become quicker and easier because of increased computational power and new analytical methods or software. Continuing education is important for statisticians; they need to stay abreast emerging technologies to perform well.

Other qualifications. Good communications skills are important for prospective statisticians in industry, who often need to explain technical matters to persons without statistical expertise. An understanding of business and the economy also is valuable for those who plan to work in private industry.

Advancement. Beginning statisticians generally are supervised by an experienced statistician. With experience, they may advance to positions with more technical responsibility and, in some cases, supervisory duties. Opportunities for promotion are greater for people with advanced degrees. Master's and Ph.D. degree holders usually enjoy independence in their work and may engage in research; develop statistical methods; or, after a number of years of experience in a particular area, become statistical consultants.

Employment

Statisticians held about 22,000 jobs in 2006. About 20 percent of these jobs were in the federal government, where statisticians were concentrated in the Departments of Commerce, Agriculture, and Health and Human Services. Another 10 percent were found in state and local governments, including state colleges and universities. Most of the remaining jobs were in private industry, especially in scientific research and development services, insurance carriers, and pharmaceutical and medicine manufacturing.

Job Outlook

Average employment growth is projected. Individuals with a degree in statistics should have opportunities in a variety of fields.

Employment change. Employment of statisticians is projected to grow 9 percent from 2006 to 2016, about as fast as the average for all occupations. The demand for individuals with a background is statistics is expected to grow, although some jobs will be in occupations with titles other than "statistician."

The use of statistics is widespread and growing. Statistical models aid in decision making in both private industry and government. There will always be a demand for the skills statistical modeling provides. Technological advances are expected to spur demand for statisticians. Ever faster computer processing allows statisticians to analyze greater amounts of data much more quickly, and to gather and sort through large amounts of data that would not have been analyzed in the past. As these processes continue to become more efficient and less expensive, an increasing number of employers will want to employ statisticians to take advantage of the new information available.

Biostatisticians should experience employment growth, primarily because of the booming pharmaceuticals business. As pharmaceutical companies develop new treatments and medical technologies, biostatisticians will be needed to do research and clinical trials.

Job prospects. Individuals with a degree in statistics should have opportunities in a variety of fields. For example, many jobs involve the analysis and interpretation of data from economics, biological science, psychology, computer software engineering, education, and other disciplines. Additional job openings will become available as statisticians transfer to other occupations, retire, or leave the workforce for other reasons.

Among graduates with a master's degree in statistics, those with a strong background in an allied field, such as finance, biology, engineering, or computer science, should have the best prospects of finding jobs related to their field of study.

Those who meet state certification requirements may become high school statistics teachers, for example.

Earnings

Median annual wage-and-salary earnings of statisticians were \$65,720 in May 2006. The middle 50 percent earned between \$48,480 and \$87,850. The lowest 10 percent earned less than \$37,010, while the highest 10 percent earned more than \$108,630.

The average annual salary for statisticians in the federal government was \$85,690 in 2007, while mathematical statisticians averaged \$96,121.

Some employers offer tuition reimbursement.

Related Occupations

People in diverse occupations work with statistics. Among these are actuaries; mathematicians; operations research analysts; computer scientists and database administrators; computer systems analysts; computer programmers; computer software engineers; engineers; economists, market and survey researchers, and other social scientists; and financial analysts and personal financial advisors. Some statisticians also work as secondary school teachers or postsecondary teachers.

Sources of Additional Information

For information about career opportunities in statistics, contact

- American Statistical Association, 1429 Duke St., Alexandria, VA 22314. Internet: http://www.amstat.org

For more information on doctoral-level careers and training in mathematics, a field closely related to statistics, contact

- American Mathematical Society, 201 Charles St., Providence, RI 02904. Internet: http://www.ams.org

Information on obtaining positions as statisticians with the federal government is available from the Office of Personnel Management through USAJOBS, the federal government's official employment information system. This resource for locating and applying for job opportunities can be accessed through the Internet at http://www.usajobs.opm.gov or through an interactive voice response telephone system at (703) 724-1850 or TDD (978) 461-8404. These numbers are not toll free, and charges may result. For advice on how to find and apply for federal jobs, see the *Occupational Outlook Quarterly* article "How to get a job in the Federal Government," online at http://www.bls.gov/opub/ooq/2004/summer/art01.pdf.

Surgical Technologists

(O*NET 29-2055.00)

Significant Points

- Employment is expected to grow much faster than average.
- Job opportunities will be best for technologists who are certified.
- Training programs last 9 to 24 months and lead to a certificate, diploma, or associate degree.
- Hospitals will continue to be the primary employer, although much faster employment growth is expected in other health care industries.

Nature of the Work

Surgical technologists, also called scrubs and surgical or operating room technicians, assist in surgical operations under the supervision of surgeons, registered nurses, or other surgical personnel. Surgical technologists are members of operating room teams, which most commonly include surgeons, anesthesiologists, and circulating nurses.

Before an operation, surgical technologists help prepare the operating room by setting up surgical instruments and equipment, sterile drapes, and sterile solutions. They assemble both sterile and nonsterile equipment, as well as check and adjust it to ensure it is working properly. Technologists also get patients ready for surgery by washing, shaving, and disinfecting incision sites. They transport patients to the operating room, help position them on the operating table, and cover them with sterile surgical drapes. Technologists also observe patients' vital signs, check charts, and help the surgical team put on sterile gowns and gloves.

During surgery, technologists pass instruments and other sterile supplies to surgeons and surgeon assistants. They may hold retractors, cut sutures, and help count sponges, needles, supplies, and instruments. Surgical technologists help prepare, care for, and dispose of specimens taken for laboratory analysis and help apply dressings. Some operate sterilizers, lights, or suction machines, and help operate diagnostic equipment.

After an operation, surgical technologists may help transfer patients to the recovery room and clean and restock the operating room.

Certified surgical technologists with additional specialized education or training also may act in the role of the surgical first assistant or circulator. The surgical first assistant, as defined by the American College of Surgeons (ACS), provides aid in exposure, hemostasis (controlling blood flow and stopping or preventing hemorrhage), and other technical functions under the surgeon's direction that help the surgeon carry out a safe operation. A circulating technologist is the "unsterile" member of the surgical team who interviews the patient before surgery; prepares the patient; helps with anesthesia; obtains and opens packages for the "sterile" people to remove the sterile contents during the procedure; keeps a written account of the surgical procedure; and answers the surgeon's questions about the patient during the surgery.

Work environment. Surgical technologists work in clean, well-lighted, cool environments. They must stand for long periods and remain alert during operations. At times, they may be exposed to communicable diseases and unpleasant sights, odors, and materials.

Most surgical technologists work a regular 40-hour week, although they may be on call or work nights, weekends, and holidays on a rotating basis.

Training, Other Qualifications, and Advancement

Training programs last nine to 24 months and lead to a certificate, diploma, or associate degree. Professional certification can help in getting jobs and promotions.

Education and training. Surgical technologists receive their training in formal programs offered by community and junior colleges, vocational schools, universities, hospitals, and the military. In 2006, the Commission on Accreditation of Allied Health Education Programs (CAAHEP) recognized more than 400 accredited training programs. Programs last from nine to 24 months and lead to a certificate, diploma, or associate degree. High school graduation normally is required for admission. Recommended high school courses include health, biology, chemistry, and mathematics.

Programs provide classroom education and supervised clinical experience. Students take courses in anatomy, physiology, microbiology, pharmacology, professional ethics, and medical terminology. Other topics covered include the care and safety of patients during surgery, sterile techniques, and surgical procedures. Students also learn to sterilize instruments; prevent and control infection; and handle special drugs, solutions, supplies, and equipment.

Certification and other qualifications. Most employers prefer to hire certified technologists. Technologists may obtain voluntary professional certification from the Liaison Council on Certification for

Projections data from the National Employment Matrix

Occupational Title	SOC Code	Employment, 2006	Projected employment, 2016	Change, 2006-2016	
				Number	Percent
Surgical technologists	29-2055	86,000	107,000	21,000	24

NOTE: Data in this table are rounded.

the Surgical Technologist by graduating from a CAAHEP-accredited program and passing a national certification examination. They may then use the Certified Surgical Technologist (CST) designation. Continuing education or reexamination is required to maintain certification, which must be renewed every four years.

Certification also may be obtained from the National Center for Competency Testing (NCCT). To qualify to take the exam, candidates follow one of three paths: complete an accredited training program; undergo a two-year hospital on-the-job training program; or acquire seven years of experience working in the field. After passing the exam, individuals may use the designation Tech in Surgery-Certified, TS-C (NCCT). This certification must be renewed every five years through either continuing education or reexamination.

Surgical technologists need manual dexterity to handle instruments quickly. They also must be conscientious, orderly, and emotionally stable to handle the demands of the operating room environment. Technologists must respond quickly and must be familiar with operating procedures in order to have instruments ready for surgeons without having to be told. They are expected to keep abreast of new developments in the field.

Advancement. Technologists advance by specializing in a particular area of surgery, such as neurosurgery or open heart surgery. They also may work as circulating technologists. With additional training, some technologists advance to first assistant. Some surgical technologists manage central supply departments in hospitals, or take positions with insurance companies, sterile supply services, and operating equipment firms.

Employment

Surgical technologists held about 86,000 jobs in 2006. About 70 percent of jobs for surgical technologists were in hospitals, mainly in operating and delivery rooms. Other jobs were in offices of physicians or dentists who perform outpatient surgery and in outpatient care centers, including ambulatory surgical centers. A few technologists, known as private scrubs, are employed directly by surgeons who have special surgical teams, like those for liver transplants.

Job Outlook

Employment of surgical technologists is expected to grow much faster than the average for all occupations. Job opportunities will be best for technologists who are certified.

Employment change. Employment of surgical technologists is expected to grow 24 percent between 2006 and 2016, much faster than the average for all occupations, as the volume of surgeries increases. The number of surgical procedures is expected to rise as the population grows and ages. Older people, including the baby boom generation, who generally require more surgical procedures, will account for a larger portion of the general population. In addition, technological advances, such as fiber optics and laser technology, will permit an increasing number of new surgical procedures to be performed and also will allow surgical technologists to assist with a greater number of procedures.

Hospitals will continue to be the primary employer of surgical technologists, although much faster employment growth is expected in offices of physicians and in outpatient care centers, including ambulatory surgical centers.

Job prospects. Job opportunities will be best for technologists who are certified.

Earnings

Median annual earnings of wage-and-salary surgical technologists were $36,080 in May 2006. The middle 50 percent earned between $30,300 and $43,560. The lowest 10 percent earned less than $25,490, and the highest 10 percent earned more than $51,140. Median annual earnings in the industries employing the largest numbers of surgical technologists were

Offices of physicians	$37,300
Outpatient care centers	37,280
General medical and surgical hospitals	35,840
Offices of dentists	34,160

Benefits provided by most employers include paid vacation and sick leave, health, medical, vision, dental insurance and life insurance, and retirement program. A few employers also provide tuition reimbursement and child care benefits.

Related Occupations

Other health occupations requiring approximately 1 year of training after high school include dental assistants, licensed practical and licensed vocational nurses, clinical laboratory technologists and technicians, and medical assistants.

Sources of Additional Information

For additional information on a career as a surgical technologist and a list of CAAHEP-accredited programs, contact

- Association of Surgical Technologists, 6 West Dry Creek Circle, Suite 200, Littleton, CO 80120. Internet: http://www.ast.org

For information on becoming a Certified Surgical Technologist, contact

- Liaison Council on Certification for the Surgical Technologist, 6 West Dry Creek Circle, Suite 100, Littleton, CO 80120. Internet: http://www.lcc-st.org

For information on becoming a Tech in Surgery-Certified, contact

- National Center for Competency Testing, 7007 College Blvd., Suite 705, Overland Park, KS 66211.

Surveyors, Cartographers, Photogrammetrists, and Surveying and Mapping Technicians

(O*NET 17-1021.00, 17-1022.00, 17-3031.00, 17-3031.01, and 17-3031.02)

Significant Points

- About 7 out of 10 jobs are in architectural, engineering, and related services.
- Opportunities will be best for surveyors, cartographers, and photogrammetrists who have a bachelor's degree and strong technical skills.
- Overall employment of surveyors, cartographers, photogrammetrists, and surveying technicians is expected to grow much faster than the average for all occupations through the year 2016.

Nature of the Work

Surveyors, cartographers, and photogrammetrists are responsible for measuring and mapping the Earth's surface. *Surveyors* establish official land, airspace, and water boundaries. They write descriptions of land for deeds, leases, and other legal documents; define airspace for airports; and take measurements of construction and mineral sites. Other surveyors provide data about the shape, contour, location, elevation, or dimension of land or land features. *Cartographers and photogrammetrists* collect, analyze, interpret, and map geographic information from surveys and from data and photographs collected using airplanes and satellites. *Surveying and mapping technicians* assist these professionals by collecting data in the field, making calculations, and helping with computer-aided drafting. Collectively, these occupations play key roles in the field of geospatial information.

Surveyors measure distances, directions, and angles between points and elevations of points, lines, and contours on, above, and below the Earth's surface. In the field, they select known survey reference points and determine the precise location of important features in the survey area using specialized equipment. Surveyors also research legal records, look for evidence of previous boundaries, and analyze data to determine the location of boundary lines. They are sometimes called to provide expert testimony in court about their work. Surveyors also record their results, verify the accuracy of data, and prepare plots, maps, and reports.

Some surveyors perform specialized functions closer to those of cartographers and photogrammetrists than to those of traditional surveyors. For example, *geodetic surveyors* use high-accuracy techniques, including satellite observations, to measure large areas of the earth's surface. *Geophysical prospecting surveyors* mark sites for subsurface exploration, usually to look for petroleum. *Marine or hydrographic surveyors* survey harbors, rivers, and other bodies of water to determine shorelines, the topography of the bottom, water depth, and other features.

Surveyors use the Global Positioning System (GPS) to locate reference points with a high degree of precision. To use this system, a surveyor places a satellite signal receiver—a small instrument mounted on a tripod—on a desired point, and another receiver on a point for which the geographic position is known. The receiver simultaneously collects information from several satellites to establish a precise position. The receiver also can be placed in a vehicle for tracing out road systems. Because receivers now come in different sizes and shapes, and because the cost of receivers has fallen, much more surveying work can be done with GPS. Surveyors then interpret and check the results produced by the new technology.

Field measurements are often taken by a survey party that gathers the information needed by the surveyor. A typical survey party consists of a party chief and one or more surveying technicians and helpers. The party chief, who may be either a surveyor or a senior surveying technician, leads day-to-day work activities. Surveying technicians assist the party chief by adjusting and operating surveying instruments, such as the total station, which measures and records angles and distances simultaneously. Surveying technicians or assistants position and hold the vertical rods, or targets, that the operator sights on to measure angles, distances, or elevations. They may hold measuring tapes if electronic distance-measuring equipment is not used. Surveying technicians compile notes, make sketches, and enter the data obtained from surveying instruments into computers either in the field or at the office. Survey parties also may include laborers or helpers who perform less-skilled duties, such as clearing brush from sight lines, driving stakes, or carrying equipment.

Photogrammetrists and cartographers measure, map, and chart the Earth's surface. Their work involves everything from performing geographical research and compiling data to producing maps. They collect, analyze, and interpret both spatial data—such as latitude, longitude, elevation, and distance—and nonspatial data—for example, population density, land-use patterns, annual precipitation levels, and demographic characteristics. Their maps may give both physical and social characteristics of the land. They prepare maps in either digital or graphic form, using information provided by geodetic surveys and remote sensing systems including aerial cameras, satellites, and LIDAR.

LIDAR—light-imaging detection and ranging—uses lasers attached to planes and other equipment to digitally map the topography of the Earth. It is often more accurate than traditional surveying methods and also can be used to collect other forms of data, such as the location and density of forests. Data developed by LIDAR can be used by surveyors, cartographers, and photogrammetrists to provide spatial information to specialists in geology, seismology, forestry, and construction, and other fields.

Geographic Information Systems (GIS) have become an integral tool for surveyors, cartographers and photogrammetrists, and surveying and mapping technicians. Workers use GIS to assemble, integrate, analyze, and display data about location in a digital format. They also use GIS to compile information from a variety of sources. GIS typically are used to make maps which combine information useful for environmental studies, geology, engineering, planning, business marketing, and other disciplines. As more of these systems are developed, many mapping specialists are being called *geographic information specialists*.

Work environment. Surveyors and surveying technicians usually work an 8-hour day, 5 days a week and may spend a lot of time

outdoors. Sometimes, they work longer hours during the summer, when weather and light conditions are most suitable for fieldwork. Construction-related work may be limited during times of inclement weather.

Surveyors and technicians engage in active, sometimes strenuous, work. They often stand for long periods, walk considerable distances, and climb hills with heavy packs of instruments and other equipment. They also can be exposed to all types of weather. Traveling is sometimes part of the job, and land surveyors and technicians may commute long distances, stay away from home overnight, or temporarily relocate near a survey site. Surveyors also work indoors while planning surveys, searching court records for deed information, analyzing data, and preparing reports and maps.

Cartographers and photogrammetrists spend most of their time in offices using computers. However, certain jobs may require extensive field work to verify results and acquire data.

Training, Other Qualifications, and Advancement

Most surveyors, cartographers, and photogrammetrists have a bachelor's degree in surveying or a related field. Every state requires that surveyors be licensed.

Education and training. In the past, many people with little formal training started as members of survey crews and worked their way up to become licensed surveyors, but this has become increasingly difficult to do. Now, most surveyors need a bachelor's degree. A number of universities offer bachelor's degree programs in surveying, and many community colleges, technical institutes, and vocational schools offer one-, two-, and three-year programs in surveying or surveying technology.

Cartographers and photogrammetrists usually have a bachelor's degree in cartography, geography, surveying, engineering, forestry, computer science, or a physical science, although a few enter these positions after working as technicians. With the development of GIS, cartographers and photogrammetrists need more education and stronger technical skills—including more experience with computers—than in the past.

Most cartographic and photogrammetric technicians also have specialized postsecondary education. High school students interested in surveying and cartography should take courses in algebra, geometry, trigonometry, drafting, mechanical drawing, and computer science.

Licensure. All 50 states and all U.S. territories license surveyors. For licensure, most state licensing boards require that individuals pass a written examination given by the National Council of Examiners for Engineering and Surveying (NCEES). Most states also require surveyors to pass a written examination prepared by the state licensing board.

Licensing happens in stages. After passing a first exam, the Fundamentals of Surveying, most candidates work under the supervision of an experienced surveyor for four years and then for licensure take a second exam, the Principles and Practice of Surveyors.

Specific requirements for training and education vary among the states. An increasing number of states require a bachelor's degree in surveying or in a closely related field, such as civil engineering or forestry, regardless of the number of years of experience. Some states require the degree to be from a school accredited by the Accreditation Board for Engineering and Technology. Many states also have a continuing education requirement.

Additionally a number of states require cartographers and photogrammetrists to be licensed as surveyors, and some states have specific licenses for photogrammetrists.

Other qualifications. Surveyors, cartographers, and photogrammetrists should be able to visualize objects, distances, sizes, and abstract forms. They must work with precision and accuracy because mistakes can be costly.

Members of a survey party must be in good physical condition because they work outdoors and often carry equipment over difficult terrain. They need good eyesight, coordination, and hearing to communicate verbally and using hand signals. Surveying is a cooperative operation, so good interpersonal skills and the ability to work as part of a team is important. Good office skills also are essential because surveyors must be able to research old deeds and other legal papers and prepare reports that document their work.

Certification and advancement. High school graduates with no formal training in surveying usually start as apprentices. Beginners with postsecondary school training in surveying usually can start as technicians or assistants. With on-the-job experience and formal training in surveying—either in an institutional program or from a correspondence school—workers may advance to senior survey technician, then to party chief. Depending on state licensing requirements, in some cases they may advance to licensed surveyor.

The National Society of Professional Surveyors, a member organization of the American Congress on Surveying and Mapping, has a voluntary certification program for surveying technicians. Technicians are certified at four levels requiring progressive amounts of experience and the passing of written examinations. Although not required for state licensure, many employers require certification for promotion to positions with greater responsibilities.

The American Society for Photogrammetry and Remote Sensing has voluntary certification programs for technicians and professionals in photogrammetry, remote sensing, and GIS. To qualify for these professional distinctions, individuals must meet work experience and training standards and pass a written examination. The professional recognition these certifications can help workers gain promotions.

Employment

Surveyors, cartographers, photogrammetrists, and surveying technicians held about 148,000 jobs in 2006. Employment was distributed by occupational specialty as follows:

Surveying and mapping technicians	76,000
Surveyors	60,000
Cartographers and photogrammetrists	12,000

The architectural, engineering, and related services industry—including firms that provided surveying and mapping services to other industries on a contract basis—provided 7 out of 10 jobs for these workers. Federal, state, and local governmental agencies provided about 14 percent of these jobs. Major federal government employers are the U.S. Geological Survey (USGS), the Bureau of Land Management (BLM), the National Geodetic Survey, the National Geospatial Intelligence Agency, and the Army Corps of Engineers. Most surveyors in state and local government work for highway departments or urban planning and redevelopment agencies. Construction, mining and utility companies also employ surveyors, cartographers, photogrammetrists, and surveying technicians.

Projections data from the National Employment Matrix

Occupational Title	SOC Code	Employment, 2006	Projected employment, 2016	Change, 2006-2016 Number	Percent
Surveyors, cartographers, photogrammetrists, and surveying technicians	—	148,000	179,000	31,000	21
Cartographers and photogrammetrists	17-1021	12,000	15,000	2,500	20
Surveyors	17-1022	60,000	74,000	14,000	24
Surveying and mapping technicians	17-3031	76,000	90,000	15,000	19

NOTE: Data in this table are rounded.

Job Outlook

Surveyors, cartographers, photogrammetrists, and surveying and mapping technicians should have favorable job prospects. These occupations should experience much faster than average employment growth.

Employment change. Overall employment of surveyors, cartographers, photogrammetrists, and surveying and mapping technicians is expected to increase by 21 percent from 2006 to 2016, which is much faster than the average for all occupations. Increasing demand for fast, accurate, and complete geographic information will be the main source of growth for these occupations.

An increasing number of firms are interested in geographic information and its applications. For example, GIS can be used to create maps and information used in emergency planning, security, marketing, urban planning, natural resource exploration, construction, and other applications. Also, the increased popularity of online mapping systems has created a higher demand for and awareness of geographic information among consumers.

Job prospects. In addition to openings from growth, job openings will continue to arise from the need to replace workers who transfer to other occupations or who leave the labor force altogether. Many of the workers in these occupations are approaching retirement age.

Opportunities for surveyors, cartographers, and photogrammetrists should remain concentrated in engineering, surveying, mapping, building inspection, and drafting services firms. However, employment may fluctuate from year to year with construction activity or with mapping needs for land and resource management.

Opportunities should be stronger for professional surveyors than for surveying and mapping technicians. Advancements in technology, such as total stations and GPS, have made surveying parties smaller than they once were. Additionally, cartographers, photogrammetrists, and technicians who produce more basic GIS data may face competition for jobs from offshore firms and contractors.

As technologies become more complex, opportunities will be best for surveyors, cartographers, and photogrammetrists who have a bachelor's degree and strong technical skills. Increasing demand for geographic data, as opposed to traditional surveying services, will mean better opportunities for cartographers and photogrammetrists who are involved in the development and use of geographic and land information systems.

Earnings

Median annual earnings of cartographers and photogrammetrists were $48,240 in May 2006. The middle 50 percent earned between $37,480 and $65,240. The lowest 10 percent earned less than $30,910 and the highest 10 percent earned more than $80,520.

Median annual earnings of surveyors were $48,290 in May 2006. The middle 50 percent earned between $35,720 and $63,990. The lowest 10 percent earned less than $26,690 and the highest 10 percent earned more than $79,910. Median annual earnings of surveyors employed in architectural, engineering, and related services were $47,570 in May 2006.

Median annual earnings of surveying and mapping technicians were $32,340 in May 2006. The middle 50 percent earned between $25,070 and $42,230. The lowest 10 percent earned less than $20,020, and the highest 10 percent earned more than $53,310. Median annual earnings of surveying and mapping technicians employed in architectural, engineering, and related services were $30,670 in May 2006, while those employed by local governments had median annual earnings of $37,550.

Related Occupations

Surveying is related to the work of civil engineers, architects, and landscape architects because an accurate survey is the first step in land development and construction projects. Cartographic and geodetic surveying are related to the work of environmental scientists and geoscientists, who study the earth's internal composition, surface, and atmosphere. Cartography also is related to the work of geographers and urban and regional planners, who study and decide how the earth's surface is being and may be used.

Sources of Additional Information

For career information on surveyors, cartographers, photogrammetrists, and surveying technicians, contact

- American Congress on Surveying and Mapping, Suite 403, 6 Montgomery Village Ave., Gaithersburg, MD 20879. Internet: http://www.acsm.net

Information about career opportunities, licensure requirements, and the surveying technician certification program is available from

- National Society of Professional Surveyors, Suite 403, 6 Montgomery Village Ave., Gaithersburg, MD 20879.

For information on a career as a geodetic surveyor, contact

- American Association of Geodetic Surveying (AAGS), Suite 403, 6 Montgomery Village Ave., Gaithersburg, MD 20879.

For career information on photogrammetrists, photogrammetric technicians, remote sensing scientists and image-based cartographers or geographic information system specialists, contact

- ASPRS: Imaging and Geospatial Information Society, 5410 Grosvenor Lane., Suite 210, Bethesda, MD 20814-2160. Internet: http://www.asprs.org

General information on careers in photogrammetry, mapping, and surveying is available from

- MAPPS: Management Association for Private Photogrammetric Surveyors, 1760 Reston Parkway, Suite 515, Reston, VA 20190. Internet: http://www.mapps.org

Information on about careers in remote sensing, photogrammetry, surveying, GIS, and other geography-related disciplines also is available from the Spring 2005 *Occupational Outlook Quarterly* article, "Geography Jobs", available online at http://www.bls.gov/opub/ooq/2005/spring/art01.pdf

STEM Teachers—Postsecondary

(O*NET 25-1011.00, 25-1021.00, 25-1022.00, 25-1031.00, 25-1032.00, 25-1041.00, 25-1042.00, 25-1043.00, 25-1051.00, 25-1052.00, 25-1053.00, 25-1054.00, 25-1061.00, 25-1062.00, 25-1063.00, 25-1064.00, 25-1065.00, 25-1066.00, 25-1067.00, 25-1069.99, 25-1071.00, 25-1072.00, 25-1081.00, 25-1082.00, 25-1111.00, 25-1112.00, 25-1113.00, 25-1121.00, 25-1122.00, 25-1123.00, 25-1124.00, 25-1125.00, 25-1126.00, 25-1191.00, 25-1192.00, 25-1193.00, 25-1194.00, and 25-1199.99)

Significant Points

- Educational qualifications range from expertise in a particular field to a Ph.D., depending on the subject taught and the type of educational institution.
- Job opportunities are expected to be very good, but many new openings will be for part-time or non-tenure-track positions.
- Prospects will be better and earnings higher in rapidly growing fields that offer many nonacademic career options.

Nature of the Work

Postsecondary teachers instruct students in a wide variety of academic and vocational subjects beyond the high school level. Most of theses students are working toward a degree, but many others are studying for a certificate or certification to improve their knowledge or career skills. Postsecondary teachers include college and university faculty, postsecondary career and technical education teachers, and graduate teaching assistants. Teaching in any venue involves forming a lesson plan, presenting material to students, responding to students learning needs, and evaluating student progress. In addition to instruction, postsecondary teachers, particularly those at 4-year colleges and universities, also perform a significant amount of research in the subject they teach. They must also keep up with new developments in their field and may consult with government, business, nonprofit, and community organizations.

College and university faculty make up the majority of postsecondary teachers. Faculty usually are organized into departments or divisions, based on academic subject or field. They typically teach several different related courses in their subject—algebra, calculus, and statistics, for example. They may instruct undergraduate or graduate students, or both. College and university faculty may give lectures to several hundred students in large halls, lead small seminars, or supervise students in laboratories. They prepare lectures, exercises, and laboratory experiments; grade exams and papers; and advise and work with students individually. In universities, they also supervise graduate students' teaching and research. College faculty work with an increasingly varied student population made up of growing shares of part-time, older, and culturally and racially diverse students.

Faculty keep up with developments in their field by reading current literature, talking with colleagues, and participating in professional conferences. They also are encouraged to do their own research to expand knowledge in their field by performing experiments; collecting and analyzing data; or examining original documents, literature, and other source material. They publish their findings in scholarly journals, books, and electronic media.

Most postsecondary teachers extensively use computer technology, including the Internet, e-mail, and software programs. They may use computers in the classroom as teaching aids and may post course content, class notes, class schedules, and other information on the Internet. The use of e-mail, chat rooms, and other techniques has greatly improved communications between students and teachers and among students.

Some instructors use the Internet to teach courses to students at remote sites. These so-called "distance learning" courses are an increasingly popular option for students who work while attending school. Faculty who teach these courses must be able to adapt existing courses to make them successful online or design a new course that takes advantage of the format.

Most full-time faculty members serve on academic or administrative committees that deal with the policies of their institution, departmental matters, academic issues, curricula, budgets, equipment purchases, and hiring. Some work with student and community organizations. Department chairpersons are faculty members who usually teach some courses but have heavier administrative responsibilities.

The proportion of time spent on research, teaching, administrative, and other duties varies by individual circumstance and type of institution. Faculty members at universities normally spend a significant part of their time doing research; those in 4-year colleges, somewhat less; and those in 2-year colleges, relatively little. The teaching load, however, often is heavier in 2-year colleges and somewhat lighter at 4-year institutions. At all types of institutions, full professors—those that have reached the highest level in their field—usually spend a larger portion of their time conducting research than do assistant professors, instructors, and lecturers.

In addition to traditional 2- and 4-year institutions, an increasing number of postsecondary educators work in alternative schools or in programs aimed at providing career-related education for working adults. Courses are usually offered online or on nights and weekends. Instructors at these programs generally work part time and are only responsible for teaching, with little to no administrative and research responsibilities.

Postsecondary vocational education teachers, also known as *postsecondary career and technical education teachers*, provide instruction for occupations that require specialized training but not usually a 4-year degree. They may teach classes in welding, dental hygienics, x-ray technician techniques, auto mechanics, or cosmetology, for example. Classes often are taught in an industrial or laboratory setting where students are provided hands-on experience. For example, welding instructors show students various welding techniques and essential safety practices, watch them use tools and equipment, and have them repeat procedures until they meet the specific standards required by the trade. Increasingly, career and technical education teachers are integrating academic and vocational curriculums so that students obtain a variety of skills that can be applied on the job. In addition, career and technical education teachers at community colleges and career and technical schools also often play a key role in students' transition from school to work by helping to establish internship programs for students and by facilitating contact between students and prospective employers.

Graduate teaching assistants, often referred to as *graduate TAs*, assist faculty, department chairs, or other professional staff at colleges and universities by performing teaching or teaching-related duties. In addition to their work responsibilities, assistants have their own school commitments, as they are also students who are working towards earning a graduate degree, such as a Ph.D. Some teaching assistants have full responsibility for teaching a course—usually one that is introductory—which can include preparation of lectures and exams, and assigning final grades to students. Others help faculty members, which may include doing a variety of tasks such as grading papers, monitoring exams, holding office hours or help-sessions for students, conducting laboratory sessions, or administering quizzes to the class. Teaching assistants generally meet initially with the faculty member whom they are going to assist to determine exactly what is expected of them, as each faculty member may have his or her own needs. For example, some faculty members prefer assistants to sit in on classes, but others assign them other tasks to do during class time. Graduate teaching assistants may work one-on-one with a faculty member or, for large classes, they may be one of several assistants.

Work environment. Many postsecondary teachers find the environment intellectually stimulating and rewarding because they are surrounded by others who enjoy their subject. The ability to share their expertise with others is also appealing to many.

Most postsecondary teachers have flexible schedules. They must be present for classes, usually 12 to 16 hours per week, and for faculty and committee meetings. Most establish regular office hours for student consultations, usually 3 to 6 hours per week. Otherwise, teachers are free to decide when and where they will work, and how much time to devote to course preparation, grading, study, research, graduate student supervision, and other activities.

Classes are typically scheduled during weekdays, although some occur at night or during the weekend. This is particularly true for teachers at 2-year community colleges or institutions with large enrollments of older students who have full-time jobs or family responsibilities. Most colleges and universities require teachers to work 9 months of the year, which allows them time during the summer and school holidays to teach additional courses, do research, travel, or pursue nonacademic interests.

About 30 percent of college and university faculty worked part time in 2006. Some part-timers, known as "adjunct faculty," have primary jobs outside of academia—in government, private industry, or nonprofit research—and teach "on the side." Others may have multiple part-time teaching positions at different institutions. Most graduate teaching assistants work part time while working on their graduate studies. The number of hours that they work may vary, depending on their assignments.

University faculty may experience a conflict between their responsibilities to teach students and the pressure to do research and publish their findings. This may be a particular problem for young faculty seeking advancement in 4-year research universities. Also, recent cutbacks in support workers and the hiring of more part-time faculty have put a greater administrative burden on full-time faculty. Requirements to teach online classes also have added greatly to the workloads of postsecondary teachers. Many find that developing the courses to put online is very time-consuming, especially when learning how to operate the technology and answering large amounts of e-mail.

Graduate TAs usually have flexibility in their work schedules like college and university faculty, but they also must spend a considerable amount of time pursuing their own academic coursework and studies. Work may be stressful, particularly when assistants are given full responsibility for teaching a class. However, these types of positions allow graduate students the opportunity to gain valuable teaching experience, which is especially helpful for those who seek to become college faculty members after completing their degree.

Training, Other Qualifications, and Advancement

The education and training required of postsecondary teachers varies widely, depending on the subject taught and educational institution employing them. Educational requirements for teachers are generally highest at research universities, where a Ph.D. is the most commonly held degree; at career and technical institutes, experience and expertise in a related occupation is the principal qualification.

Education and training. Four-year colleges and universities usually require candidates for full-time, tenure-track positions, to hold a doctoral degree. However, they may hire master's degree holders or doctoral candidates for certain disciplines, such as the arts, or for part-time and temporary jobs.

Doctoral programs take an average of six years of full-time study beyond the bachelor's degree; this includes time spent completing a master's degree and a dissertation. Some programs, such as those in the humanities, may take longer to complete; others, such as those in engineering, usually are shorter. Candidates specialize in a subfield of a discipline, for example, organic chemistry, counseling psychology, or European history, and also take courses covering the entire discipline. Programs typically include 20 or more increasingly specialized courses and seminars plus comprehensive examinations on all major areas of the field. Candidates also must complete a dissertation—a written report on original research in the candidate's major field of study. The dissertation sets forth an original hypothesis or proposes a model and tests it. Students in the natural sciences and engineering usually do laboratory work; in the humanities, they study original documents and other published material. The dissertation is done under the guidance of one or more faculty advisors and usually takes one or two years of full-time work.

In two-year colleges, master's degree holders fill most full-time teaching positions. However, in certain fields where there may be more applicants than available jobs, institutions can be more selective in their hiring practices. In these fields, master's degree holders may be passed over in favor of candidates holding Ph.Ds. Many two-year institutions increasingly prefer job applicants to have some teaching experience or experience with distance learning. Preference also may be given to those holding dual master's degrees, especially at smaller institutions, because they can teach more subjects.

Training requirements for postsecondary career and technical education teachers vary by state and subject. In general, career and technical education teachers need a bachelor's or graduate degree, plus at least three years of work experience in their field. In some fields, a license or certificate that demonstrates one's qualifications may be all that is required. These teachers may need to update their skills through continuing education to maintain certification. They must also maintain ongoing dialogue with businesses to determine the skills most needed in the current workplace.

Other qualifications. Postsecondary teachers should communicate and relate well with students, enjoy working with them, and be able to motivate them. They should have inquiring and analytical minds, and a strong desire to pursue and disseminate knowledge. Additionally, they must be self-motivated and able to work in an environment in which they receive little direct supervision.

Obtaining a position as a graduate teaching assistant is a good way to gain college teaching experience. To qualify, candidates must be enrolled in a graduate school program. In addition, some colleges and universities require teaching assistants to attend classes or take some training prior to being given responsibility for a course.

Although graduate teaching assistants usually work at the institution and in the department where they are earning their degree, teaching or internship positions for graduate students at institutions that do not grant a graduate degree have become more common in recent years. For example, a program called Preparing Future Faculty, administered by the Association of American Colleges and Universities and the Council of Graduate Schools, has led to the creation of many programs that are now independent. These programs offer graduate students at research universities the opportunity to work as teaching assistants at other types of institutions, such as liberal arts or community colleges. Working with a mentor, the graduate students teach classes and learn how to improve their teaching techniques. They may attend faculty and committee meetings, develop a curriculum, and learn how to balance the teaching, research, and administrative roles that faculty play. These programs provide valuable learning opportunities for graduate students interested in teaching at the postsecondary level, and also help to make these students aware of the differences among the various types of institutions at which they may someday work.

Some degree holders, particularly those who studied in the natural sciences, spend additional years after earning their graduate degree on postdoctoral research and study before taking a faculty position. Some Ph.D.s are able to extend postdoctoral appointments, or take new ones, if they are unable to find a faculty job. Most of these appointments offer a nominal salary.

Advancement. For faculty, a major goal in the traditional academic career is attaining tenure. The process of attaining tenure can take approximately seven years with faculty moving up the ranks in tenure-track positions as they meet specific criteria. The ranks are instructor, assistant professor, associate professor, and professor. Colleges and universities usually hire new tenure-track faculty as instructors or assistant professors under term contracts. At the end of the period, their record of teaching, research, and overall contribution to the institution is reviewed and tenure may be granted if the review is favorable. Those denied tenure usually must leave the institution. Tenured professors cannot be fired without just cause and due process. Tenure protects the faculty's academic freedom—the ability to teach and conduct research without fear of being fired for advocating controversial or unpopular ideas. It also gives both faculty and institutions the stability needed for effective research and teaching, and provides financial security for faculty. Some institutions have adopted post-tenure review policies to encourage ongoing evaluation of tenured faculty.

The number of tenure-track positions is declining as institutions seek flexibility in dealing with financial matters and changing student interests. Institutions rely more heavily on limited term contracts and part-time, or adjunct, faculty, thus shrinking the total pool of tenured faculty. Limited-term contracts—typically two- to five years, may be terminated or extended when they expire but generally do not lead to the granting of tenure. In addition, some institutions have limited the percentage of faculty who can be tenured.

For tenured postsecondary teachers, further advancement involves a move into administrative and managerial positions, such as departmental chairperson, dean, and president. At four-year institutions, such advancement requires a doctoral degree. At two-year colleges, a doctorate is helpful but not usually required, except for advancement to some top administrative positions.

Employment

Postsecondary teachers held nearly 1.7 million jobs in 2006. Most were employed in 4-year colleges and universities and in 2-year community colleges. Other postsecondary teachers are employed by schools and institutes that specialize in training people in a specific field, such as technology centers or culinary schools, or work for businesses that provide professional development courses to employees of companies. Some career and technical education teachers work for state and local governments and job training facilities. The following tabulation shows postsecondary teaching jobs in specialties having 20,000 or more jobs in 2006:

Health specialties teachers	145,000
Graduate teaching assistants	144,000
Vocational education teachers	119,000
Art, drama, and music teachers	88,000
Business teachers	82,000
English language and literature teachers	72,000
Education teachers	67,000
Biological science teachers	65,000
Mathematical science teachers	54,000
Nursing instructors and teachers	46,000
Computer science teachers	44,000
Engineering teachers	40,000
Psychology teachers	37,000
Foreign language and literature teachers	30,000
Communications teachers	29,000
History teachers	26,000
Philosophy and religion teachers	25,000
Chemistry teachers	24,000
Recreation and fitness studies teachers	20,000

Job Outlook

Employment of postsecondary teachers is expected to grow much faster than average as student enrollments continue to increase. However, a significant proportion of these new jobs will be part-time and non-tenure-track positions. Retirements of current postsecondary teachers should create numerous openings for all types of postsecondary teachers, so job opportunities are generally expected to be very good, although they will vary by the subject taught and the type of educational institution.

Employment change. Postsecondary teachers are expected to grow by 23 percent between 2006 and 2016, much faster than the

Projections data from the National Employment Matrix

Occupational Title	SOC Code	Employment, 2006	Projected employment, 2016	Change, 2006-2016	
				Number	Percent
Postsecondary teachers	25-1000	1,672,000	2,054,000	382,000	23

NOTE: Data in this table are rounded.

average for all occupations. Because of the size of this occupation and its much faster than average growth rate, postsecondary teachers will account for 382,000 new jobs, which is among the largest number of new jobs for an occupation. Projected growth in the occupation will be primarily due to increases in college and university enrollment over the next decade. This enrollment growth stems mainly from the expected increase in the population of 18- to 24-year-olds, who constitute the majority of students at postsecondary institutions, and from the increasing number of high school graduates who choose to attend these institutions. Adults returning to college to enhance their career prospects or to update their skills also will continue to create new opportunities for postsecondary teachers, particularly at community colleges and for-profit institutions that cater to working adults. However, many postsecondary educational institutions receive a significant portion of their funding from state and local governments, so expansion of public higher education will be limited by state and local budgets.

Job prospects. A significant number of openings in this occupation will be created by growth in enrollments and the need to replace the large numbers of postsecondary teachers who are likely to retire over the next decade. Many postsecondary teachers were hired in the late 1960s and the 1970s to teach members of the baby boom generation, and they are expected to retire in growing numbers in the years ahead. As a result, Ph.D. recipients seeking jobs as postsecondary teachers will experience favorable job prospects over the next decade.

Although competition will remain tight for tenure-track positions at 4-year colleges and universities, there will be available a considerable number of part-time or renewable, term appointments at these institutions and at community colleges. Opportunities for master's degree holders are also expected to be favorable because there will be considerable growth at community colleges, career education programs, and other institutions that employ them.

Opportunities for graduate teaching assistants are expected to be very good, reflecting expectations of higher undergraduate enrollments coupled with more modest increases in graduate student enrollment. Constituting almost 9 percent of all postsecondary teachers, graduate teaching assistants play an integral role in the postsecondary education system, and they are expected to continue to do so in the future.

Opportunities will also be excellent for postsecondary vocational teachers due to an increased emphasis on career and technical education at the postsecondary level. Job growth, combined with a large number of expected retirements, will result in many job openings for these workers. Prospects will be best for instructors in specialties that pay well outside of the teaching field, such as the construction trades and manufacturing technology.

One of the main reasons why students attend postsecondary institutions is to prepare themselves for careers, so the best job prospects for postsecondary teachers are likely to be in rapidly growing fields that offer many nonacademic career options. These will include fields such as business, nursing and other health specialties, and biological sciences. Community colleges and other institutions offering career and technical education have been among the most rapidly growing, and these institutions are expected to offer some of the best opportunities for postsecondary teachers.

Earnings

Median annual earnings of all postsecondary teachers in 2006 were $56,120. The middle 50 percent earned between $39,610 and $80,390. The lowest 10 percent earned less than $27,590, and the highest 10 percent earned more than $113,450.

Earnings for college faculty vary according to rank and type of institution, geographic area, and field. According to a 2006-07 survey by the American Association of University Professors, salaries for full-time faculty averaged $73,207. By rank, the average was $98,974 for professors, $69,911 for associate professors, $58,662 for assistant professors, $42,609 for instructors, and $48,289 for lecturers. Faculty in 4-year institutions earn higher salaries, on average, than do those in 2-year schools. In 2006-07, faculty salaries averaged $84,249 in private independent institutions, $71,362 in public institutions, and $66,118 in religiously affiliated private colleges and universities. In fields with high-paying nonacademic alternatives—medicine, law, engineering, and business, among others—earnings exceed these averages. In others fields, such as the humanities and education, earnings are lower. Earnings for postsecondary career and technical education teachers vary widely by subject, academic credentials, experience, and region of the country.

Many faculty members have significant earnings in addition to their base salary from consulting, teaching additional courses, research, writing for publication, or other employment. In addition, many college and university faculty enjoy unique benefits, including access to campus facilities, tuition waivers for dependents, housing and travel allowances, and paid leave for sabbaticals. Part-time faculty and instructors usually have fewer benefits than full-time faculty.

Related Occupations

Postsecondary teaching requires the ability to communicate ideas well, motivate students, and be creative. Workers in other occupations that require these skills are preschool, kindergarten, elementary, middle, and secondary school teachers; education administrators; librarians; counselors; writers and editors; public relations specialists; and management analysts. Faculty research activities often are similar to those of life, physical, and social scientists, as well as to those of managers and administrators in industry, government, and nonprofit research organizations.

Sources of Additional Information

Professional societies related to a field of study often provide information on academic and nonacademic employment opportunities. Names and addresses of many of these societies appear in statements elsewhere in this book.

Special publications on higher education, such as *The Chronicle of Higher Education*, list specific employment opportunities for faculty. These publications are available in libraries.

For information on the Preparing Future Faculty program, contact

- Council of Graduate Schools, One Dupont Circle, NW, Suite 430, Washington, DC 20036-1173. Internet: http://www.preparing-faculty.org

For information on postsecondary career and technical education teaching positions, contact state departments of career and technical education. General information on adult and career and technical education is available from

- Association for Career and Technical Education, 1410 King St., Alexandria, VA 22314. Internet: http://www.acteonline.org

Television, Video, and Motion Picture Camera Operators and Editors

(O*NET 27-4031.00 and 27-4032.00)

Significant Points

- Workers acquire their skills through on-the-job or formal postsecondary training.
- Keen competition for jobs is expected due to the large number of people who wish to enter the broadcasting and motion picture industries, where many camera operators and editors are employed.
- Those with the most experience and the most advanced computer skills will have the best job opportunities.

Nature of the Work

Television, video, and motion picture camera operators produce images that tell a story, inform or entertain an audience, or record an event. *Film and video editors* edit soundtracks, film, and video for the motion picture, cable, and broadcast television industries. Some camera operators do their own editing.

Camera operators use television, video, or motion picture cameras to shoot a wide range of material, including television series, studio programs, news and sporting events, music videos, motion pictures, documentaries, and training sessions. This material is constructed from many different shots by film and video editors. With the increase in digital technology, much of the editing work is now done on a computer. Many camera operators and editors are employed by independent television stations; local affiliate stations of television networks; large cable and television networks; or smaller, independent production companies.

Making commercial-quality movies and video programs requires technical expertise and creativity. Producing successful images requires choosing and presenting interesting material, selecting appropriate equipment, and applying a good eye and a steady hand to ensure smooth, natural movement of the camera.

Some camera operators film or videotape private ceremonies and special events, such as weddings and conference program sessions. Those who record these images on videotape are often called *videographers*. *Studio camera operators* work in a broadcast studio and usually videotape their subjects from a fixed position. *News camera operators*, also called *electronic news gathering (ENG) operators*, work as part of a reporting team, following newsworthy events as they unfold. To capture live events, they must anticipate the action and act quickly. ENG operators sometimes edit raw footage on the spot for relay to a television affiliate for broadcast.

Camera operators employed in the entertainment field use motion picture cameras to film movies, television programs, and commercials. Those who film motion pictures also are known as *cinematographers*. Some specialize in filming cartoons or special effects. Cinematographers may be an integral part of the action, using cameras in any of several different mounts. For example, the camera can be stationary and shoot whatever passes in front of the lens, or it can be mounted on a track, with the camera operator responsible for shooting the scene from different angles or directions. Wider use of digital cameras has enhanced the number of angles and the clarity that a camera operator can provide. Other camera operators sit on cranes and follow the action while crane operators move them into position. *Steadicam operators* mount a harness and carry the camera on their shoulders to provide a clear picture while they move about the action. Camera operators who work in the entertainment field often meet with directors, actors, editors, and camera assistants to discuss ways of filming, editing, and improving scenes.

Work environment. ENG operators and those who cover major events, such as conventions or sporting events, frequently travel locally and stay overnight or travel to distant places for longer periods. Camera operators filming television programs or motion pictures may travel to film on location.

Some camera operators—especially ENG operators covering accidents, natural disasters, civil unrest, or military conflicts—work in uncomfortable or even dangerous surroundings. Many camera operators must wait long hours in all kinds of weather for an event to take place and must stand or walk for long periods while carrying heavy equipment. ENG operators often work under strict deadlines.

Hours of work and working schedules for camera operators and editors vary considerably. Those employed by television and cable networks and advertising agencies usually work a 5-day, 40-hour week; however, they may work longer hours to meet production schedules. ENG operators often work long, irregular hours and must be available to work on short notice. Camera operators and editors working in motion picture production also may work long, irregular hours.

Training, Other Qualifications, and Advancement

Television, video, and motion picture camera operators and editors usually acquire their skills through formal postsecondary training at vocational schools, colleges, universities, or photographic institutes. A bachelor's degree may be required for some positions, particularly those for film and video editors. Employers usually seek applicants with a good eye, imagination, and creativity, as well as a good technical understanding of how the camera operates.

Education and training. Many universities, community and junior colleges, vocational-technical institutes, and private trade and technical schools offer courses in camera operation and videography. Basic courses cover equipment, processes, and techniques. It is increasingly important for camera operators to have a good understanding of computer technology. Bachelor's degree programs, especially those including business courses, provide a well-rounded education. Film schools also may provide training on the artistic or aesthetic aspects of filmmaking.

Individuals interested in camera operations should subscribe to videographic newsletters and magazines, join audio-video clubs, and seek summer or part-time employment in cable and television networks, motion picture studios, or camera and video stores.

To enter the occupation, many camera operators first become production assistants to learn how film and video production works. In entry-level jobs they learn to set up lights, cameras, and other equipment. They also may receive routine assignments requiring adjustments to their cameras or decisions on what subject matter to capture. Camera operators in the film and television industries usually are hired for a project on the basis of recommendations from individuals such as producers, directors of photography, and camera assistants from previous projects or through interviews with the producer. ENG and studio camera operators who work for television affiliates usually start in small markets to gain experience.

Other qualifications. Camera operators need good eyesight, artistic ability, and hand-eye coordination. They should be patient, accurate, and detail oriented. Camera operators also should have good communication skills and, if needed, the ability to hold a camera by hand for extended periods.

Camera operators, who run their own businesses or do freelance work, need business skills as well as talent. These individuals must know how to submit bids, write contracts, get permission to shoot on locations that normally are not open to the public, obtain releases to use film or tape of people, price their services, secure copyright protection for their work, and keep financial records.

Advancement. With experience, operators may advance to more demanding assignments or to positions with larger or network television stations. Advancement for ENG operators may mean moving to larger media markets. Other camera operators and editors may become directors of photography for movie studios, advertising agencies, or television programs. Some teach at technical schools, film schools, or universities.

Employment

Television, video, and motion picture camera operators and editors held about 47,000 jobs in 2006. About 27,000 were camera operators and film and video editors held about 21,000 jobs.

Many are employed by independent television stations, local affiliate stations of television networks or broadcast groups, large cable and television networks, or smaller independent production companies. About 17 percent of camera operators and film editors were self-employed. Some self-employed camera operators contracted with television networks, documentary or independent filmmakers, advertising agencies, or trade show or convention sponsors to work on individual projects for a set fee, often at a daily rate.

Most of the salaried camera operators and editors were employed by television broadcasting stations or motion picture studios. More than half of the salaried film and video editors worked for motion picture studios. Most camera operators and editors worked in large metropolitan areas.

Job Outlook

Keen competition for jobs is expected due to the large number of people who wish to enter the broadcasting and motion picture industries, where many camera operators and editors are employed. Those with the most experience and the most advanced computer skills will have the best job opportunities. Employment is expected to grow about as fast as the average.

Employment change. Employment of camera operators and editors is expected to grow 12 percent over the 2006–2016 decade, which is about as fast as the average for all occupations through 2016. Rapid expansion of the entertainment market, especially motion picture production and distribution, will spur growth of camera operators. In addition, computer and Internet services will provide new outlets for interactive productions. Camera operators will be needed to film made-for-Internet broadcasts, such as live music videos, digital movies, sports features, and general information or entertainment programming. These images can be delivered directly into the home either on compact discs or as streaming video over the Internet. Growth will be tempered, however, by the increased offshore production of motion pictures. Job growth in television broadcasting will be tempered by the use of automated cameras under the control of a single person working either on the studio floor or in a director's booth.

Job prospects. Television, video, and motion picture camera operators and editors can expect keen competition for job openings because of the large number of people who wish to enter the broadcasting and motion picture industries, where many of these workers are employed. The number of individuals interested in positions as videographers and movie camera operators usually is much greater than the number of openings. Those who succeed in landing a salaried job or attracting enough work to earn a living by freelancing are likely to be the most creative and highly motivated people, able to adapt to rapidly changing technologies and adept at operating a business. The change to digital cameras has increased the importance of strong computer skills. Those with the most experience and the most advanced computer skills will have the best job opportunities.

Earnings

Median annual earnings for television, video, and motion picture camera operators were $40,060 in May 2006. The middle 50 percent earned between $26,930 and $59,440. The lowest 10 percent earned less than $18,810, and the highest 10 percent earned more than $84,500. Median annual earnings were $44,010 in the motion

Projections data from the National Employment Matrix

Occupational Title	SOC Code	Employment, 2006	Projected employment, 2016	Change, 2006-2016	
				Number	Percent
Television, video, and motion picture camera operators and editors	27-4030	47,000	53,000	5,700	12
Camera operators, television, video, and motion picture	27-4031	27,000	30,000	3,100	12
Film and video editors	27-4032	21,000	23,000	2,600	13

NOTE: Data in this table are rounded.

picture and video industries and $32,200 in radio and television broadcasting.

Median annual earnings for film and video editors were $46,670 in May 2006. The middle 50 percent earned between $30,610 and $74,650. The lowest 10 percent earned less than $22,710, and the highest 10 percent earned more than $110,720. Median annual earnings were $53,580 in the motion picture and video industries, which employed the largest numbers of film and video editors.

Many camera operators who work in film or video are freelancers, whose earnings tend to fluctuate each year. Because most freelance camera operators purchase their own equipment, they incur considerable expense acquiring and maintaining cameras and accessories. Some camera operators belong to unions, including the International Alliance of Theatrical Stage Employees, and the National Association of Broadcast Employees and Technicians.

Related Occupations

Related arts and media occupations include artists and related workers, broadcast and sound engineering technicians and radio operators, graphic designers, and photographers.

Sources of Additional Information

For information about careers as a camera operator, contact

- International Cinematographer's Guild, 80 Eighth Ave., 14th Floor, New York, NY 10011.
- National Association of Broadcast Employees and Technicians, 501 Third St. NW, 6th floor, Washington, DC 20001. Internet: http://www.nabetcwa.org

Information about career and employment opportunities for camera operators and film and video editors also is available from local offices of state employment service agencies, local offices of the relevant trade unions, and local television and film production companies that employ these workers.

Tool and Die Makers

(O*NET 51-4111.00)

Significant Points

- Most tool and die makers need 4 or 5 years of classroom instruction and on-the-job training to become fully qualified.
- Employment is projected to decline because of strong foreign competition and advancements in automation.
- Despite the decline in employment, excellent job opportunities are expected.

Nature of the Work

Tool and die makers are among the most highly skilled workers in manufacturing. These workers produce and repair tools, dies, and special guiding and holding devices that enable machines to manufacture a variety of products we use daily—from clothing and furniture to heavy equipment and parts for aircraft.

Toolmakers craft precision tools and machines that are used to cut, shape, and form metal and other materials. They also produce jigs and fixtures—devices that hold metal while it is bored, stamped, or drilled—and gauges and other measuring devices. Die makers construct metal forms, called dies, that are used to shape metal in stamping and forging operations. They also make metal molds for diecasting and for molding plastics, ceramics, and composite materials. Some tool and die makers craft prototypes of parts, and then, working with engineers and designers, determine how best to manufacture the part. In addition to developing, designing, and producing new tools and dies, these workers also may repair worn or damaged tools, dies, gauges, jigs, and fixtures.

To perform these functions, tool and die makers employ many types of machine tools and precision measuring instruments. They also must be familiar with the machining properties, such as hardness and heat tolerance, of a wide variety of common metals, alloys, plastics, ceramics, and other composite materials. Tool and die makers are knowledgeable in machining operations, mathematics, and blueprint reading. In fact, tool and die makers often are considered highly specialized machinists. The main difference between tool and die makers and machinists is that machinists normally make a single part during the production process, while tool and die makers make many parts and assemble and adjust machines used in the production process. (See the section on machinists elsewhere in this book.)

While many tools and dies are designed by engineers or tool designers, tool and die makers are also trained to design tools and often do. They may travel to a customer's plant to observe the operation and suggest ways in which a new tool could improve the manufacturing process.

Once a tool or die is designed, tool and die makers, working from blueprints, plan the sequence of operations necessary to manufacture the tool or die. They measure and mark the pieces of metal that will be cut to form parts of the final product. At this point, tool and die makers cut, drill, or bore the part as required, checking to ensure that the final product meets specifications. Finally, these workers assemble the parts and perform finishing jobs such as filing, grinding, and polishing surfaces. While manual machining has declined, it is still used for unique or low-quantity parts that are often required in building tools and dies.

Tool and die makers use computer-aided design (CAD) to develop products and parts. Specifications entered into computer programs can be used to electronically develop blueprints for the required tools and dies. Numerical tool and process control programmers use computer-aided design or computer-aided manufacturing (CAD/CAM) programs to convert electronic drawings into CAM-based computer programs that contain instructions for a sequence of cutting tool operations. (See the section on computer control programmers and operators elsewhere in this book.) Once these programs are developed, computer numerically controlled (CNC) machines follow the set of instructions contained in the program to produce the part. Computer-controlled machine tool operators or machinists normally operate CNC machines, but tool and die makers are trained in both operating CNC machines and writing CNC programs, and they may perform either task. CNC programs are stored electronically for future use, saving time and increasing worker productivity.

After machining the parts, tool and die makers carefully check the accuracy of the parts using many tools, including coordinate measuring machines, which use sensor arms and software to compare the dimensions of the part to electronic blueprints. Next, they assemble the different parts into a functioning machine. They file, grind, shim, and adjust the different parts to properly fit them together. Finally,

tool and die makers set up a test run using the tools or dies they have made to make sure that the manufactured parts meet specifications. If problems occur, they compensate by adjusting the tools or dies.

Work environment. Tool and die makers usually work in toolrooms that are normally quieter than typical manufacturing production floors because there are fewer machines running at once. Toolrooms also are generally kept clean and cool to minimize heat-related expansion of metal workpieces. To minimize the exposure of workers to moving parts, machines have guards and shields. Most computer-controlled machines are totally enclosed, minimizing workers' exposure to noise, dust, and the lubricants used to cool workpieces during machining. Tool and die makers also must follow safety rules and wear protective equipment, such as safety glasses to shield against bits of flying metal, earplugs to protect against noise, and gloves and masks to reduce exposure to hazardous lubricants and cleaners. These workers also need stamina because they often spend much of the day on their feet and may do moderately heavy lifting. Companies employing tool and die makers have traditionally operated only one shift per day. Overtime and weekend work are common, especially during peak production periods.

Training, Other Qualifications, and Advancement

It usually takes four or five years of classroom and paid on-the-job training to become a fully trained tool and die maker. Good math, problem-solving, and computer skills are important requirements for these workers.

Education and training. Most tool and die makers learn their trade through four or five years of education and training in formal apprenticeships or in other postsecondary programs offered at local community colleges or technical schools. These programs often include a mix of classroom instruction and paid hands-on experience. According to most employers, apprenticeship programs are the best way to learn all aspects of tool and die making. Most apprentices must have a high school diploma, GED, or equivalent, and high school mathematics and shop classes make it easier to get into an apprenticeship program.

Traditional apprenticeships usually require that the apprentice complete a specific number of work and classroom hours to complete the program, which typically takes four or five years. Some companies and state apprenticeship programs, however, are now shifting from time-based programs to competency-based programs. Under competency-based programs, apprentices can move ahead more quickly by passing a series of exams and demonstrating competency in a particular job skill.

While formal apprenticeship programs may be the best way to learn the job, many tool and die makers receive most of their formal classroom training from community and technical colleges while working for a company that often supports the employee's training goals and provides the needed on-the-job training less formally. These trainees often begin as machine operators and gradually take on more difficult assignments. Many machinists become tool and die makers.

During their training, tool and die maker trainees learn to operate milling machines, lathes, grinders, laser and water cutting machines, wire electrical discharge machines, and other machine tools. They also learn to use handtools for fitting and assembling gauges and other mechanical and metal-forming equipment. In addition, they study metalworking processes, such as heat treating and plating. Classroom training usually consists of tool designing, tool programming, blueprint reading, and, if needed, mathematics courses, including algebra, geometry, trigonometry, and basic statistics. Tool and die makers must have good computer skills to work with CAD/CAM technology, CNC machine tools, and computerized measuring machines.

Even after completing a formal training program, tool and die makers still need years of experience to become highly skilled. Most specialize in making certain types of tools, molds, or dies.

Certification and other qualifications. State apprenticeship boards certify tool and die makers as journey workers after they have completed a licensed program. While a state certification is not necessary to work as a tool and die maker, it gives workers more flexibility in employment and is required by some employers. Apprentices usually must be at least 18 years old, in addition to having a high school education and high school mathematics classes.

Because tools and dies must meet strict specifications—precision to one ten-thousandth of an inch is common—the work of tool and die makers requires skill with precision measuring devices and a high degree of patience and attention to detail. Good eyesight is essential. People entering this occupation also should be mechanically inclined, able to work and solve problems independently, have strong mathematical skills, and be capable of doing work that requires concentration and physical effort. Tool and die makers who visit customers' plants need good interpersonal and sales skills.

Employers generally look for someone with a strong educational background as an indication that the person can more easily adapt to change, which is a constant in this occupation. As automation continues to change the way tools and dies are made, workers regularly need to update their skills to learn how to operate new equipment. Also, as materials such as alloys, ceramics, polymers, and plastics are increasingly used, tool and die makers need to learn new machining techniques to deal with the new materials.

Advancement. There are several ways for skilled workers to advance. Some move into supervisory and administrative positions in their firms or they may start their own shop. Others may take computer courses and become computer-controlled machine tool programmers. With a college degree, a tool and die maker can go into engineering or tool design.

Employment

Tool and die makers held about 101,000 jobs in 2006. Most worked in industries that manufacture metalworking machinery, transportation equipment such as motor vehicle parts, fabricated metal products, and plastics products. Although they are found throughout the country, jobs are most plentiful in the Midwest and the Northeast, where many of metalworking companies are located.

Job Outlook

Employment of tool and die makers is projected to decline rapidly. However, excellent job opportunities are expected as many employers report difficulty finding qualified applicants.

Employment change. Employment of tool and die makers is projected to decline rapidly by 10 percent over the 2006–2016 decade because of strong foreign competition in manufacturing and advances in automation, including CNC machine tools and computer-aided design, that should improve worker productivity. On the other hand, tool and die makers play a key role in building and

Projections data from the National Employment Matrix

Occupational Title	SOC Code	Employment, 2006	Projected employment, 2016	Change, 2006-16	
				Number	Percent
Tool and die makers	51-4111	101,000	91,000	-9,700	-10

NOTE: Data in this table are rounded.

maintaining advanced automated manufacturing equipment, which makes them less susceptible to lay-offs than other less-skilled production workers. As firms invest in new equipment, modify production techniques, and implement product design changes more rapidly, they will continue to rely heavily on skilled tool and die makers for retooling.

Job prospects. Despite declining employment, excellent job opportunities are expected. Employers in certain parts of the country report difficulty attracting skilled workers and apprenticeship candidates with the necessary abilities to replace retiring workers and fill other openings. The number of workers receiving training in this occupation is expected to continue to be fewer than the number of openings created each year by tool and die makers who retire or transfer to other occupations. A major factor limiting the number of people entering the occupation is that many young people who have the educational and personal qualifications necessary to learn tool and die making usually prefer to attend college or do not wish to enter production occupations.

Earnings

Median hourly wage-and-salary earnings of tool and die makers were $21.29 in May 2006. The middle 50 percent earned between $17.29 and $26.77. The lowest 10 percent had earnings of less than $13.85, while the top 10 percent earned more than $32.41. Median hourly wage-and-salary earnings in the manufacturing industries employing the largest numbers of tool and die makers were as follows:

Motor vehicle parts manufacturing	$26.45
Plastics product manufacturing	20.79
Forging and stamping	20.24
Metalworking machinery manufacturing	20.08
Machine shops; turned product; and screw, nut, and bolt manufacturing	19.41

The pay of apprentices is tied to their skill level. As they gain more skills and reach specific levels of performance and experience, their pay increases.

Related Occupations

The occupations most closely related to the work of tool and die makers are other machining occupations. These include machinists; computer control programmers and operators; and machine setters, operators, and tenders—metal and plastic. Another occupation that requires precision and skill in working with metal is welding, soldering, and brazing workers.

Like tool and die makers, assemblers and fabricators assemble and repair complex machinery. Millwrights and industrial machinery mechanics also repair and assemble manufacturing equipment. When measuring parts, tool and die makers use some of the same tools and equipment that inspectors, testers, sorters, samplers, and weighers use in their jobs.

Sources of Additional Information

For career information and to have inquiries on training and employment referred to member companies, contact

- Precision Machine Products Association, 6700 West Snowville Rd., Brecksville, OH 44141. Internet: http://www.pmpa.org

For lists of schools and employers with tool and die apprenticeship and training programs, contact

- National Tooling and Machining Association, 9300 Livingston Rd., Ft. Washington, MD 20744. Internet: http://www.ntma.org

For information on careers, education and training, earnings, and apprenticeship opportunities in metalworking, contact

- Precision Metalforming Association Educational Foundation, 6363 Oak Tree Blvd., Independence, OH 44131. Internet: http://www.pmaef.org
- The National Institute for Metalworking Skills, 10565 Fairfax Boulevard, Suite 203, Fairfax, VA 22030. Internet: http://www.nims-skills.org

Information on the registered apprenticeship system with links to state apprenticeship programs can be found on the U.S. Department of Labor's Web site: http://www.doleta.gov/atels_bat. Apprenticeship information is also available from the U.S. Department of Labor's toll free helpline: (877) 872-5627.

Urban and Regional Planners

(O*NET 19-3051.00)

Significant Points

- Local governments employ about 68 percent of urban and regional planners.
- Most new jobs will be in affluent, rapidly growing communities.
- Job prospects will be best for those with a master's degree and strong computer skills; bachelor's degree holders may find positions, but advancement opportunities are limited.

Nature of the Work

Urban and regional planners develop long- and short-term plans for the use of land and the growth and revitalization of urban, suburban, and rural communities and the region in which they are located. They help local officials alleviate social, economic, and environmental problems by recommending locations for roads, schools, and other infrastructure and suggesting zoning regulations for private property. This work includes forecasting the future needs of the population. Because local governments employ the majority of urban and regional planners, they often are referred to as community or city planners.

Planners promote the best use of a community's land and resources for residential, commercial, institutional, and recreational purposes.

They address environmental, economic, and social health issues of a community as it grows and changes. They may formulate plans relating to the construction of new school buildings, public housing, or other kinds of infrastructure. Planners also may help to make decisions about developing resources and protecting ecologically sensitive regions. Some planners are involved in environmental issues including pollution control, wetland preservation, forest conservation, and the location of new landfills. Planners also may help to draft legislation on environmental, social, and economic issues, such as planning a new park, sheltering the homeless, or making the region more attractive to businesses.

Before preparing plans for community development, planners study and report on the current use of land for residential, business, and community purposes. Their reports include information on the location and capacity of streets, highways, airports, water and sewer lines, schools, libraries, and cultural and recreational sites. They also provide data on the types of industries in the community, the characteristics of the population, and employment and economic trends. Using this information, along with input from citizens, planners try to optimize land use for buildings and other public facilities. Planners prepare reports showing how their programs can be carried out and what they will cost.

Planners examine proposed community facilities, such as schools, to be sure that these facilities will meet the needs of a growing or changing population. They keep abreast of economic and legal issues involved in zoning codes, building codes, and environmental regulations and ensure that builders and developers follow these codes and regulations. Planners also deal with land-use issues created by population movements. For example, as suburban growth and economic development create more jobs outside cities, the need for public transportation that gets workers to those jobs increases. In response, planners develop and model possible transportation systems and explain them to planning boards and the general public.

Planners use computers to record and analyze information and to prepare reports and recommendations for government executives and others. Computer databases, spreadsheets, and analytical techniques are used to project program costs and forecast future trends in employment, housing, transportation, or population. Computerized geographic information systems (GIS) enable planners to map land areas, to overlay maps with geographic variables such as population density, and to combine or manipulate geographic information to produce alternative plans for land use or development.

Urban and regional planners often confer with land developers, civic leaders, and public officials and may function as mediators in community disputes, presenting alternatives that are acceptable to opposing parties. Planners may prepare material for community relations programs, speak at civic meetings, and appear before legislative committees and elected officials to explain and defend their proposals.

Most urban and regional planners focus on one or more areas of specialization. Among the most common are community development and redevelopment and land-use or code enforcement. While planners may specialize in areas such as transportation planning or urban design, they are also required to keep the bigger picture in mind, and do what's best for the community as a whole.

Work environment. Urban and regional planners often travel to inspect the features of land under consideration for development or regulation. Some local government planners involved in site development inspections spend most of their time in the field. Although most planners have a scheduled 40-hour work week, they frequently attend evening or weekend meetings or public hearings with citizens' groups. Planners may experience the pressure of deadlines and tight work schedules, as well as political pressure generated by interest groups affected by proposals related to urban development and land use.

Training, Other Qualifications, and Advancement

A master's degree from an accredited planning program provides the best training for a wide range of planning positions. Experience and acquiring and maintaining certification lead to the best opportunities for advancement.

Education and training. Most entry-level jobs in federal, state, and local governments require a master's degree from an accredited program in urban or regional planning or a related field, such as urban design or geography. Students are admitted to master's degree programs in planning with a wide range of undergraduate backgrounds; a bachelor's degree in economics, geography, political science, or environmental design is especially good preparation. A few schools offer a bachelor's degree in urban planning, and graduates from these programs qualify for some entry-level positions, but their advancement opportunities are often limited unless they acquire an advanced degree.

In 2007, 66 colleges and universities offered an accredited master's degree program, and 15 offered an accredited bachelor's degree program, in planning. Accreditation for these programs is from the Planning Accreditation Board, which consists of representatives of the American Institute of Certified Planners, the American Planning Association, and the Association of Collegiate Schools of Planning. Most graduate programs in planning require at least two years of study.

Most college and university planning departments offer specialization in areas such as community development and redevelopment, land-use or code enforcement, transportation planning, environmental and natural resources planning, urban design, and economic planning and development.

Highly recommended also are courses in related disciplines, such as architecture, law, earth sciences, demography, economics, finance, health administration, and management, in addition to courses in planning. Because familiarity with computer models and statistical techniques is important, courses in statistics, computer science, and geographic information systems also are recommended or required.

Graduate students spend considerable time in studios, workshops, and laboratory courses, learning to analyze and solve planning problems. They often are required to work in a planning office part time or during the summer. Local government planning offices frequently offer students internships, providing experience that proves invaluable in obtaining a full-time planning position after graduation.

Licensure. As of 2007, New Jersey was the only state that required planners to be licensed, although Michigan required registration to use the title "community planner." Licensure in New Jersey is based on two examinations—one testing generalized knowledge of planning and another testing knowledge of New Jersey planning laws. Registration as a community planner in Michigan is based on professional experience and national and state examinations.

Projections data from the National Employment Matrix

Occupational Title	SOC Code	Employment, 2006	Projected employment, 2016	Change, 2006-2016	
				Number	Percent
Urban and regional planners	19-3051	34,000	39,000	4,900	15

NOTE: Data in this table are rounded.

Other qualifications. Planners must be able to think in terms of spatial relationships and visualize the effects of their plans and designs. They should be flexible and be able to reconcile different viewpoints and make constructive policy recommendations. The ability to communicate effectively, both orally and in writing, is necessary for anyone interested in this field.

Certification and advancement. The American Institute of Certified Planners, a professional institute within the American Planning Association, grants certification to individuals who have the appropriate combination of education and professional experience and pass an examination. Professional development activities are required to maintain certification. Certification may be helpful for promotion.

After a few years of experience, planners may advance to assignments requiring a high degree of independent judgment, such as designing the physical layout of a large development or recommending policy and budget options. Some public sector planners are promoted to community planning director and spend a great deal of time meeting with officials, speaking to civic groups, and supervising a staff. Further advancement occurs through a transfer to a larger jurisdiction with more complex problems and greater responsibilities or into related occupations, such as director of community or economic development.

Employment

Urban and regional planners held about 34,000 jobs in 2006. About 68 percent were employed by local governments. Companies involved with architectural, engineering, and related services, as well as management, scientific, and technical consulting services, employ an increasing proportion of planners in the private sector. Others are employed in state government agencies dealing with housing, transportation, or environmental protection, and a small number work for the federal government.

Job Outlook

Average employment growth is projected for urban and regional planners. Most new jobs will be in affluent, rapidly expanding communities. Job prospects will be best for those with a master's degree and strong computer skills.

Employment change. Employment of urban and regional planners is expected to grow 15 percent from 2006 to 2016, faster than the average for all occupations. Employment growth will be driven by the need for state and local governments to provide public services such as regulation of commercial development, the environment, transportation, housing, and land use and development for an expanding population. Nongovernmental initiatives dealing with historic preservation and redevelopment will also create employment growth.

Most new jobs for urban and regional planners will be in local government, as planners will be needed to address an array of problems associated with population growth, especially in affluent, rapidly expanding communities. For example, new housing developments require roads, sewer systems, fire stations, schools, libraries, and recreation facilities that must be planned for within budgetary constraints.

The fastest job growth for urban and regional planners will occur in the private sector, primarily in the professional, scientific, and technical services industries. For example, planners may be employed by firms to help design security measures for a building that are effective but also subtle and able to blend in with the surrounding area. However, because the private sector employs only 21 percent of urban and regional planners, not as many new jobs will be created in the private sector as in government.

Job prospects. In addition to those from employment growth, job openings will arise from the need to replace experienced planners who transfer to other occupations, retire, or leave the labor force for other reasons. Graduates with a master's degree from an accredited program should have better job opportunities than those with only a bachelor's degree. Also, computers and software—especially GIS software—are increasingly being used in planning, and those with strong computer skills and GIS experience will have an advantage in the job market.

Earnings

Median annual wage-and-salary earnings of urban and regional planners were $56,630 in May 2006. The middle 50 percent earned between $44,480 and $71,390. The lowest 10 percent earned less than $35,610, and the highest 10 percent earned more than $86,880. Median annual earnings in the industries employing the largest numbers of urban and regional planners in May 2006 were

Engineering services	$63,840
Architectural, engineering, and related services	62,890
Architectural services	61,700
State government	57,490
Local government	54,550

Related Occupations

Urban and regional planners develop plans for the growth of urban, suburban, and rural communities. Others whose work is similar include architects; civil engineers; environmental engineers; landscape architects: geographers; property, real estate, and community association managers; surveyors, cartographers, photogrammetrists, and surveying technicians; and market and survey researchers.

Sources of Additional Information

Information on careers, salaries, and certification in urban and regional planning is available from

- American Planning Association, 1776 Massachusetts Ave. NW, Washington, DC 20036. Internet: http://www.planning.org

Information on accredited urban and regional planning programs is available from

- Association of Collegiate Schools of Planning, 6311 Mallard Trace, Tallahassee, FL 32312. Internet: http://www.acsp.org

For addition information on urban and regional planning and on related occupations, see "Geography jobs" in the Spring 2005 *Occupational Outlook Quarterly*. The article is online at http://www.bls.gov/opub/ooq/2005/spring/art01.pdf.

Veterinarians

(O*NET 29-1131.00)

Significant Points

- Veterinarians should have an affinity for animals and the ability to get along with their owners.
- Graduation from an accredited college of veterinary medicine and a state license are required.
- Competition for admission to veterinary school is keen; however, graduates should have excellent job opportunities.
- About 3 out of 4 veterinarians work in private practice.

Nature of the Work

Veterinarians care for the health of pets, livestock, and animals in zoos, racetracks, and laboratories. Some veterinarians use their skills to protect humans against diseases carried by animals and conduct clinical research on human and animal health problems. Others work in basic research, broadening our knowledge of animals and medical science, and in applied research, developing new ways to use knowledge.

Most veterinarians diagnose animal health problems; vaccinate against diseases, such as distemper and rabies; medicate animals suffering from infections or illnesses; treat and dress wounds; set fractures; perform surgery; and advise owners about animal feeding, behavior, and breeding.

According to the American Medical Veterinary Association, more than 70 percent of veterinarians who work in private medical practices predominately, or exclusively, treat small animals. Small-animal practitioners usually care for companion animals, such as dogs and cats, but also treat birds, reptiles, rabbits, ferrets, and other animals that can be kept as pets. About one-fourth of all veterinarians work in mixed animal practices, where they see pigs, goats, cattle, sheep, and some wild animals in addition to companion animals.

A small number of private-practice veterinarians work exclusively with large animals, mostly horses or cattle; some also care for various kinds of food animals. These veterinarians usually drive to farms or ranches to provide veterinary services for herds or individual animals. Much of this work involves preventive care to maintain the health of the animals. These veterinarians test for and vaccinate against diseases and consult with farm or ranch owners and managers regarding animal production, feeding, and housing issues. They also treat and dress wounds, set fractures, and perform surgery, including cesarean sections on birthing animals. Other veterinarians care for zoo, aquarium, or laboratory animals. Veterinarians of all types euthanize animals when necessary.

Veterinarians who treat animals use medical equipment such as stethoscopes, surgical instruments, and diagnostic equipment, including radiographic and ultrasound equipment. Veterinarians working in research use a full range of sophisticated laboratory equipment.

Veterinarians contribute to human as well as animal health. A number of veterinarians work with physicians and scientists as they research ways to prevent and treat various human health problems. For example, veterinarians contributed greatly in conquering malaria and yellow fever, solved the mystery of botulism, produced an anticoagulant used to treat some people with heart disease, and defined and developed surgical techniques for humans, such as hip and knee joint replacements and limb and organ transplants. Today, some determine the effects of drug therapies, antibiotics, or new surgical techniques by testing them on animals.

Some veterinarians are involved in food safety and inspection. Veterinarians who are livestock inspectors, for example, check animals for transmissible diseases, such as E. coli, advise owners on the treatment of their animals, and may quarantine animals. Veterinarians who are meat, poultry, or egg product inspectors examine slaughtering and processing plants, check live animals and carcasses for disease, and enforce government regulations regarding food purity and sanitation. More veterinarians are finding opportunities in food security as they ensure that the nation has abundant and safe food supplies. Veterinarians involved in food security often work along the nation's borders as animal and plant health inspectors, where they examine imports and exports of animal products to prevent disease here and in foreign countries. Many of these workers are employed by the Department of Homeland Security or the Department of Agriculture's Animal and Plant Health Inspection Service division.

Work environment. Veterinarians in private or clinical practice often work long hours in a noisy indoor environment. Sometimes they have to deal with emotional or demanding pet owners. When working with animals that are frightened or in pain, veterinarians risk being bitten, kicked, or scratched.

Veterinarians in large-animal practice spend time driving between their office and farms or ranches. They work outdoors in all kinds of weather and may have to treat animals or perform surgery, under unsanitary conditions.

Veterinarians working in nonclinical areas, such as public health and research, have working conditions similar to those of other professionals in those lines of work. These veterinarians enjoy clean, well-lit offices or laboratories and spend much of their time dealing with people rather than animals.

Veterinarians often work long hours. Those in group practices may take turns being on call for evening, night, or weekend work; solo practitioners may work extended and weekend hours, responding to emergencies or squeezing in unexpected appointments.

Training, Other Qualifications, and Advancement

Veterinarians must obtain a Doctor of Veterinary Medicine degree and a state license. There is keen competition for admission to veterinary school.

Education and training. Prospective veterinarians must graduate with a Doctor of Veterinary Medicine (D.V.M. or V.M.D.)

degree from a four-year program at an accredited college of veterinary medicine. There are 28 colleges in 26 states that meet accreditation standards set by the Council on Education of the American Veterinary Medical Association (AVMA).

The prerequisites for admission to veterinary programs vary. Many programs do not require a bachelor's degree for entrance, but all require a significant number of credit hours—ranging from 45 to 90 semester hours—at the undergraduate level. However, most of the students admitted have completed an undergraduate program and earned a bachelor's degree. Applicants without a degree face a difficult task gaining admittance.

Preveterinary courses should emphasize the sciences. Veterinary medical colleges typically require applicants to have taken classes in organic and inorganic chemistry, physics, biochemistry, general biology, animal biology, animal nutrition, genetics, vertebrate embryology, cellular biology, microbiology, zoology, and systemic physiology. Some programs require calculus; some require only statistics, college algebra and trigonometry, or pre-calculus. Most veterinary medical colleges also require some courses in English or literature, other humanities, and the social sciences. Increasingly, courses in general business management and career development have become a standard part of the curriculum to teach new graduates how to effectively run a practice.

In addition to satisfying preveterinary course requirements, applicants must submit test scores from the Graduate Record Examination (GRE), the Veterinary College Admission Test (VCAT), or the Medical College Admission Test (MCAT), depending on the preference of the college to which they are applying. Currently, 22 schools require the GRE, 4 require the VCAT, and 2 accept the MCAT.

There is keen competition for admission to veterinary school. The number of accredited veterinary colleges has remained largely the same since 1983, but the number of applicants has risen significantly. Only about one in three applicants was accepted in 2005.

New graduates with a Doctor of Veterinary Medicine degree may begin to practice veterinary medicine once they receive their license, but many new graduates choose to enter a one-year internship. Interns receive a small salary but often find that their internship experience leads to better paying opportunities later, relative to those of other veterinarians. Veterinarians who then seek board certification also must complete a three- to four-year residency program that provides intensive training in one of the 20 AVMA-recognized veterinary specialties including internal medicine, oncology, pathology, dentistry, nutrition, radiology, surgery, dermatology, anesthesiology, neurology, cardiology, ophthalmology, preventive medicine, and exotic small-animal medicine.

Licensure. All states and the District of Columbia require that veterinarians be licensed before they can practice. The only exemptions are for veterinarians working for some federal agencies and some state governments. Licensing is controlled by the states and is not strictly uniform, although all states require the successful completion of the D.V.M. degree—or equivalent education—and a passing grade on a national board examination, the North American Veterinary Licensing Exam. This eight-hour examination consists of 360 multiple-choice questions covering all aspects of veterinary medicine as well as visual materials designed to test diagnostic skills.

The Educational Commission for Foreign Veterinary Graduates grants certification to individuals trained outside the United States who demonstrate that they meet specified requirements for English language and clinical proficiency. This certification fulfills the educational requirement for licensure in all states.

Most states also require candidates to pass a state jurisprudence examination covering state laws and regulations. Some states do additional testing on clinical competency as well. There are few reciprocal agreements between states, veterinarians who wish to practice in a different state usually must first pass that state's examinations.

Other qualifications. When deciding whom to admit, some veterinary medical colleges place heavy consideration on a candidate's veterinary and animal experience. Formal experience, such as work with veterinarians or scientists in clinics, agribusiness, research, or some area of health science, is particularly advantageous. Less formal experience, such as working with animals on a farm or ranch or at a stable or animal shelter, also can be helpful. Students must demonstrate ambition and an eagerness to work with animals.

Prospective veterinarians must have good manual dexterity. They should have an affinity for animals and the ability to get along with their owners, especially pet owners, who usually have strong bonds with their pets. Veterinarians who intend to go into private practice should possess excellent communication and business skills, because they will need to manage their practice and employees successfully and to promote, market, and sell their services.

Advancement. Most veterinarians begin as employees in established group practices. Despite the substantial financial investment in equipment, office space, and staff, many veterinarians with experience eventually set up their own practice or purchase an established one.

Newly trained veterinarians can become U.S. Government meat and poultry inspectors, disease-control workers, animal welfare and safety workers, epidemiologists, research assistants, or commissioned officers in the U.S. Public Health Service or various branches of the U.S. Armed Forces. A state license may be required.

Nearly all states have continuing education requirements for licensed veterinarians. Requirements differ by state and may involve attending a class or otherwise demonstrating knowledge of recent medical and veterinary advances.

Employment

Veterinarians held about 62,000 jobs in 2006. According to the American Veterinary Medical Association, about 3 out of 4 veterinarians were employed in a solo or group practice. Most others were salaried employees of another veterinary practice. Data from the U.S. Bureau of Labor Statistics show that the federal government employed about 1,400 civilian veterinarians, chiefly in the U.S. Departments of Agriculture, Health and Human Services, and, increasingly, Homeland Security. Other employers of veterinarians are state and local governments, colleges of veterinary medicine, medical schools, research laboratories, animal food companies, and pharmaceutical companies. A few veterinarians work for zoos, but most veterinarians caring for zoo animals are private practitioners who contract with the zoos to provide services, usually on a part-time basis.

In addition, many veterinarians hold veterinary faculty positions in colleges and universities and are classified as teachers. (See the statement on teachers—postsecondary elsewhere in this book.)

Projections data from the National Employment Matrix

Occupational Title	SOC Code	Employment, 2006	Projected employment, 2016	Change, 2006-2016	
				Number	Percent
Veterinarians	29-1131	62,000	84,000	22,000	35

NOTE: Data in this table are rounded.

Job Outlook

Employment is expected to increase much faster than average. Excellent job opportunities are expected.

Employment change. Employment of veterinarians is expected to increase 35 percent over the 2006–2016 decade, much faster than the average for all occupations. Veterinarians usually practice in animal hospitals or clinics and care primarily for companion animals. Recent trends indicate particularly strong interest in cats as pets. Faster growth of the cat population is expected to increase the demand for feline medicine and veterinary services, while demand for veterinary care for dogs should continue to grow at a more modest pace.

Many pet owners are relatively affluent and consider their pets a member of the family. These owners are becoming more aware of the availability of advanced care and are more willing to pay for intensive veterinary care than owners in the past. Furthermore, the number of pet owners purchasing pet insurance is rising, increasing the likelihood that considerable money will be spent on veterinary care.

More pet owners also will take advantage of nontraditional veterinary services, such as cancer treatment and preventive dental care. Modern veterinary services have caught up to human medicine; certain procedures, such as hip replacement, kidney transplants, and blood transfusions, which were once only available for humans, are now available for animals.

Continued support for public health and food and animal safety, national disease control programs, and biomedical research on human health problems will contribute to the demand for veterinarians, although the number of positions in these areas is limited. Homeland security also may provide opportunities for veterinarians involved in efforts to maintain abundant food supplies and minimize animal diseases in the U.S. and in foreign countries.

Job prospects. Excellent job opportunities are expected because there are only 28 accredited schools of veterinary medicine in the United States, resulting in a limited number of graduates—about 2,700—each year. However, applicants face keen competition for admission to veterinary school.

New graduates continue to be attracted to companion-animal medicine because they prefer to deal with pets and to live and work near heavily populated areas, where most pet owners live. Employment opportunities are good in cities and suburbs, but even better in rural areas because fewer veterinarians compete to work there.

Beginning veterinarians may take positions requiring evening or weekend work to accommodate the extended hours of operation that many practices are offering. Some veterinarians take salaried positions in retail stores offering veterinary services. Self-employed veterinarians usually have to work hard and long to build a sufficient client base.

The number of jobs for large-animal veterinarians is likely to grow more slowly than jobs for companion-animal veterinarians. Nevertheless, job prospects should be better for veterinarians who specialize in farm animals because of lower earnings in the farm-animal specialty and because many veterinarians do not want to work in rural or isolated areas.

Veterinarians with training in food safety and security, animal health and welfare, and public health and epidemiology should have the best opportunities for a career in the federal government.

Earnings

Median annual earnings of veterinarians were $71,990 in May 2006. The middle 50 percent earned between $56,450 and $94,880. The lowest 10 percent earned less than $43,530, and the highest 10 percent earned more than $133,150.

The average annual salary for veterinarians in the federal government was $84,335 in 2007.

According to a survey by the American Veterinary Medical Association, average starting salaries of veterinary medical college graduates in 2006 varied by type of practice as follows:

Large animals, exclusively $61,029
Small animals, predominantly 57,117
Small animals, exclusively..................................56,241
Private clinical practice 55,031
Large animals, predominantly 53,397
Mixed animals...52,254
Equine (horses)...40,130

Related Occupations

Veterinarians prevent, diagnose, and treat diseases, disorders, and injuries in animals. Those who do similar work for humans include chiropractors, dentists, optometrists, physicians and surgeons, and podiatrists. Veterinarians have extensive training in physical and life sciences, and some do scientific and medical research, as do biological scientists and medical scientists.

Animal care and service workers and veterinary technologists and technicians also work extensively with animals. Like veterinarians, they must have patience and feel comfortable with animals. However, the level of training required for these occupations is substantially less than that needed by veterinarians.

Sources of Additional Information

For additional information on careers in veterinary medicine, a list of U.S. schools and colleges of veterinary medicine, and accreditation policies, send a letter-size, self-addressed, stamped envelope to

- American Veterinary Medical Association, 1931 N. Meacham Rd., Suite 100, Schaumburg, IL 60173. Internet: http://www.avma.org

For information on veterinary education, contact

- Association of American Veterinary Medical Colleges, 1101 Vermont Ave. NW, Suite 301, Washington, DC 20005. Internet: http://www.aavmc.org

For information on scholarships, grants, and loans, contact the financial aid officer at the veterinary schools to which you wish to apply.

For information on veterinarians working in zoos, see the *Occupational Outlook Quarterly* article "Wild jobs with wildlife," online at http://www.bls.gov/opub/ooq/2001/spring/art01.pdf.

Information on obtaining a veterinary position with the federal government is available from the Office of Personnel Management through USAJOBS, the federal government's official employment information system. This resource for locating and applying for job opportunities can be accessed through the Internet at http://www.usajobs.opm.gov or through an interactive voice response telephone system at (703) 724-1850 or TDD (978) 461-8404. These numbers are not toll free, and charges may result. For advice on how to find and apply for federal jobs, see the *Occupational Outlook Quarterly* article "How to get a job in the Federal Government," online at http://www.bls.gov/opub/ooq/2004/summer/art01.pdf.

Veterinary Technologists and Technicians

(O*NET 29-2056.00)

Significant Points

- Animal lovers get satisfaction from this occupation, but aspects of the work can be unpleasant, physically and emotionally demanding, and sometimes dangerous.
- Entrants generally complete a 2-year or 4-year veterinary technology program and must pass a state examination.
- Employment is expected to grow much faster than average.
- Overall job opportunities should be excellent; however, keen competition is expected for jobs in zoos and aquariums.

Nature of the Work

Owners of pets and other animals today expect state-of-the-art veterinary care. To provide this service, Veterinarians use the skills of veterinary technologists and technicians, who perform many of the same duties for a veterinarian that a nurse would for a physician, including routine laboratory and clinical procedures. Although specific job duties vary by employer, there often is little difference between the tasks carried out by technicians and by technologists, despite some differences in formal education and training. As a result, most workers in this occupation are called technicians.

Veterinary technologists and technicians typically conduct clinical work in a private practice under the supervision of a licensed veterinarian. They often perform various medical tests and treat and diagnose medical conditions and diseases in animals. For example, they may perform laboratory tests such as urinalysis and blood counts, assist with dental prophylaxis, prepare tissue samples, take blood samples, or assist Veterinarians in a variety of tests and analyses in which they often use various items of medical equipment, such as test tubes and diagnostic equipment. While most of these duties are performed in a laboratory setting, many are not. For example, some veterinary technicians obtain and record patients' case histories, expose and develop x rays and radiographs, and provide specialized nursing care. In addition, experienced veterinary technicians may discuss a pet's condition with its owners and train new clinic personnel. Veterinary technologists and technicians assisting small-animal practitioners usually care for companion animals, such as cats and dogs, but can perform a variety of duties with mice, rats, sheep, pigs, cattle, monkeys, birds, fish, and frogs. Very few veterinary technologists work in mixed animal practices where they care for both small companion animals and larger, nondomestic animals.

Besides working in private clinics and animal hospitals, veterinary technologists and technicians may work in research facilities, where they administer medications orally or topically, prepare samples for laboratory examinations, and record information on an animal's genealogy, diet, weight, medications, food intake, and clinical signs of pain and distress. Some may sterilize laboratory and surgical equipment and provide routine postoperative care. At research facilities, veterinary technologists typically work under the guidance of Veterinarians or physicians. Some veterinary technologists vaccinate newly admitted animals and occasionally may have to euthanize seriously ill, severely injured, or unwanted animals.

While the goal of most veterinary technologists and technicians is to promote animal health, some contribute to human health as well. Veterinary technologists occasionally assist Veterinarians in implementing research projects as they work with other scientists in medical-related fields such as gene therapy and cloning. Some find opportunities in biomedical research, wildlife medicine, the military, livestock management, or pharmaceutical sales.

Work environment. People who love animals get satisfaction from working with and helping them. However, some of the work may be unpleasant, physically and emotionally demanding, and sometimes dangerous. At times, veterinary technicians must clean cages and lift, hold, or restrain animals, risking exposure to bites or scratches. These workers must take precautions when treating animals with germicides or insecticides. The work setting can be noisy.

Veterinary technologists and technicians who witness abused animals or who euthanize unwanted, aged, or hopelessly injured animals may experience emotional stress. Those working for humane societies and animal shelters often deal with the public, some of whom might react with hostility to any implication that the owners are neglecting or abusing their pets. Such workers must maintain a calm and professional demeanor while they enforce the laws regarding animal care.

In some animal hospitals, research facilities, and animal shelters, a veterinary technician is on duty 24 hours a day, which means that some may work night shifts. Most full-time veterinary technologists and technicians work about 40 hours a week, although some work 50 or more hours a week.

Training, Other Qualifications, and Advancement

There are primarily two levels of education and training for entry to this occupation: a two-year program for veterinary technicians and a four-year program for veterinary technologists.

Education and training. Most entry-level veterinary technicians have a two-year associate degree from an American Veterinary Medical Association (AVMA)-accredited community college program in veterinary technology in which courses are taught in clinical and laboratory settings using live animals. About 16 colleges offer veterinary technology programs that are longer and that culminate in a four-year bachelor's degree in veterinary technology. These four-year colleges, in addition to some vocational schools, also offer two-year programs in laboratory animal science. Several schools offer distance learning.

In 2006, 131 veterinary technology programs in 44 states were accredited by the American Veterinary Medical Association (AVMA). Graduation from an AVMA-accredited veterinary technology program allows students to take the credentialing exam in any state in the country.

Persons interested in careers as veterinary technologists and technicians should take as many high school science, biology, and math courses as possible. Science courses taken beyond high school, in an associate or bachelor's degree program, should emphasize practical skills in a clinical or laboratory setting.

Technologists and technicians usually begin work as trainees in routine positions under the direct supervision of a veterinarian. Entry-level workers whose training or educational background encompasses extensive hands-on experience with a variety of laboratory equipment, including diagnostic and medical equipment, usually require a shorter period of on-the-job training.

Licensure and certification. Each state regulates veterinary technicians and technologists differently; however, all states require them to pass a credentialing exam following coursework. Passing the state exam assures the public that the technician or technologist has sufficient knowledge to work in a veterinary clinic or hospital. Candidates are tested for competency through an examination that includes oral, written, and practical portions and that is regulated by the state Board of Veterinary Examiners or the appropriate state agency. Depending on the state, candidates may become registered, licensed, or certified. Most states, however, use the National Veterinary Technician (NVT) exam. Prospects usually can have their passing scores transferred from one state to another, so long as both states use the same exam.

Employers recommend American Association for Laboratory Animal Science (AALAS) certification for those seeking employment in a research facility. AALAS offers certification for three levels of technician competence, with a focus on three principal areas—animal husbandry, facility management, and animal health and welfare. Those who wish to become certified must satisfy a combination of education and experience requirements prior to taking the AALAS examination. Work experience must be directly related to the maintenance, health, and well-being of laboratory animals and must be gained in a laboratory animal facility as defined by AALAS. Candidates who meet the necessary criteria can begin pursuing the desired certification on the basis of their qualifications. The lowest level of certification is Assistant Laboratory Animal Technician (ALAT), the second level is Laboratory Animal Technician (LAT), and the highest level of certification is Laboratory Animal Technologist (LATG). The AALAS examination consists of multiple-choice questions and is longer and more difficult for higher levels of certification, ranging from two hours and 120 multiple choice questions for the ALAT to three hours and 180 multiple choice questions for the LATG.

Other qualifications. As veterinary technologists and technicians often deal with pet owners, communication skills are very important. In addition, technologists and technicians should be able to work well with others, because teamwork with Veterinarians is common. Organizational ability and the ability to pay attention to detail also are important.

Advancement. As they gain experience, technologists and technicians take on more responsibility and carry out more assignments under only general veterinary supervision. Some eventually may become supervisors.

Employment

Veterinary technologists and technicians held about 71,000 jobs in 2006. About 91 percent worked in veterinary services. The remainder worked in boarding kennels, animal shelters, stables, grooming salons, zoos, state and private educational institutions, and local, state, and federal agencies.

Job Outlook

Excellent job opportunities will stem from the need to replace veterinary technologists and technicians who leave the occupation and from the limited output of qualified veterinary technicians from 2-year programs, which are not expected to meet the demand over the 2006–2016 period. Employment is expected to grow much faster than average.

Employment change. Employment of veterinary technologists and technicians is expected to grow 41 percent over the 2006–2016 projection period, which is much faster than the average for all occupations. Pet owners are becoming more affluent and more willing to pay for advanced veterinary care because many of them consider their pet to be part of the family. This growing affluence and view of pets will continue to increase the demand for veterinary care. The vast majority of veterinary technicians work at private clinical practice under Veterinarians. As the number of Veterinarians grows to meet the demand for veterinary care, so will the number of veterinary technicians needed to assist them.

The number of pet owners who take advantage of veterinary services for their pets—currently about 6 in 10—is expected to grow over the projection period, increasing employment opportunities. The availability of advanced veterinary services, such as preventive dental care and surgical procedures, also will provide opportunities for workers specializing in those areas as they will be needed to assist licensed Veterinarians. The rapidly growing number of cats kept as companion pets is expected to boost the demand for feline medicine and services. Further demand for these workers will stem from the desire to replace veterinary assistants with more highly skilled technicians and technologists in animal clinics and hospitals, shelters, boarding kennels, and humane societies.

Projections data from the National Employment Matrix

Occupational Title	SOC Code	Employment, 2006	Projected employment, 2016	Change, 2006-2016	
				Number	Percent
Veterinary technologists and technicians	29-2056	71,000	100,000	29,000	41

NOTE: Data in this table are rounded.

Biomedical facilities, diagnostic laboratories, wildlife facilities, humane societies, animal control facilities, drug or food manufacturing companies, and food safety inspection facilities will provide additional jobs for veterinary technologists and technicians. However, keen competition is expected for veterinary technologist and technician jobs in zoos and aquariums, due to expected slow growth in facility capacity, low turnover among workers, the limited number of positions, and the fact that the work in zoos and aquariums attracts many candidates.

Job prospects. Excellent job opportunities are expected because of the relatively few veterinary technology graduates each year. The number of 2-year programs has recently grown to 131, but due to small class sizes, fewer than 3,000 graduates are anticipated each year, which is not expected to meet demand. Additionally, many veterinary technicians remain in the field for only 7-8 years, so the need to replace workers who leave the occupation each year also will produce many job opportunities.

Employment of veterinary technicians and technologists is relatively stable during periods of economic recession. Layoffs are less likely to occur among veterinary technologists and technicians than in some other occupations because animals will continue to require medical care.

Earnings

Median hourly earnings of veterinary technologists and technicians were $12.88 in May 2006. The middle 50 percent earned between $10.44 and $15.77. The bottom 10 percent earned less than $8.79, and the top 10 percent earned more than $18.68.

Related Occupations

Others who work extensively with animals include animal care and service workers, and veterinary assistants and laboratory animal caretakers. Like veterinary technologists and technicians, they must have patience and feel comfortable with animals. However, the level of training required for these occupations is less than that needed by veterinary technologists and technicians. Veterinarians, who need much more formal education, also work extensively with animals, preventing, diagnosing, and treating their diseases, disorders, and injuries.

Sources of Additional Information

For information on certification as a laboratory animal technician or technologist, contact

- American Association for Laboratory Animal Science, 9190 Crestwyn Hills Dr., Memphis, TN 38125. Internet: http://www.aalas.org

For information on careers in veterinary medicine and a listing of AVMA-accredited veterinary technology programs, contact

- American Veterinary Medical Association, 1931 N. Meacham Rd., Suite 100, Schaumburg, IL 60173-4360. Internet: http://www.avma.org

Water and Liquid Waste Treatment Plant and System Operators

(O*NET 51-8031.00)

Significant Points

- Employment is concentrated in local government and private water, sewage, and other systems utilities.
- Because of a large number of upcoming retirements and the difficulty of filling these positions, job opportunities will be excellent.
- Completion of an associate degree or a 1-year certificate program increases an applicant's chances for employment and promotion.

Nature of the Work

Clean water is essential for everyday life. *Water treatment plant and system operators* treat water so that it is safe to drink. *Liquid waste treatment plant and system operators*, also known as wastewater treatment plant and system operators, remove harmful pollutants from domestic and industrial liquid waste so that it is safe to return to the environment.

Water is pumped from wells, rivers, streams, and reservoirs to water treatment plants, where it is treated and distributed to customers. Wastewater travels through customers' sewer pipes to wastewater treatment plants, where it is treated and either returned to streams, rivers, and oceans or reused for irrigation and landscaping. Operators in both types of plants control equipment and processes that remove or destroy harmful materials, chemicals, and microorganisms from the water. Operators also control pumps, valves, and other equipment that moves the water or wastewater through the various treatment processes, after which they dispose of the removed waste materials.

Operators read, interpret, and adjust meters and gauges to make sure that plant equipment and processes are working properly. Operators control chemical-feeding devices, take samples of the water or wastewater, perform chemical and biological laboratory analyses, and adjust the amounts of chemicals, such as chlorine, in the water. They employ a variety of instruments to sample and measure water quality, and they use common hand and power tools to make repairs to valves, pumps, and other equipment.

Water and wastewater treatment plant and system operators increasingly rely on computers to help monitor equipment, store the results of sampling, make process-control decisions, schedule and record maintenance activities, and produce reports. In some modern plants, operators also use computers to monitor automated systems and determine how to address problems.

Occasionally, operators must work during emergencies. A heavy rainstorm, for example, may cause large amounts of wastewater to flow into sewers, exceeding a plant's treatment capacity. Emergencies also can be caused by conditions inside a plant, such as chlorine gas leaks or oxygen deficiencies. To handle these conditions, operators are trained to make an emergency management response and use special safety equipment and procedures to protect public health and the facility. During these periods, operators may work under extreme pressure to correct problems as quickly as possible. Because working conditions may be dangerous, operators must be extremely cautious.

The specific duties of plant operators depend on the type and size of the plant. In smaller plants, one operator may control all of the machinery, perform tests, keep records, handle complaints, and perform repairs and maintenance. Operators in this type of plant may have to be on-call 24 hours a day in case of an emergency. In medium-sized plants, operators monitor the plant throughout the night by working in shifts. In large plants, operators may be more specialized and monitor only one process. They might work with chemists, engineers, laboratory technicians, mechanics, helpers, supervisors, and a superintendent.

Water quality standards are largely set by two major federal environmental statutes: the Safe Drinking Water Act, which specifies standards for drinking water, and the Clean Water Act, which regulates the discharge of pollutants. Industrial facilities that send their wastes to municipal treatment plants must meet certain minimum standards to ensure that the wastes have been adequately pretreated and will not damage municipal treatment facilities. Municipal water treatment plants also must meet stringent standards for drinking water. The list of contaminants regulated by these statutes has grown over time. As a result, plant operators must be familiar with the guidelines established by federal regulations and how they affect their plant. In addition, operators must be aware of any guidelines imposed by the state or locality in which the plant operates.

Work environment. Water and wastewater treatment plant and system operators work both indoors and outdoors and may be exposed to noise from machinery and to unpleasant odors. Operators' work is physically demanding and often is performed in unclean locations; they must pay close attention to safety procedures because of the presence of hazardous conditions, such as slippery walkways, dangerous gases, and malfunctioning equipment.

Plants operate 24 hours a day, 7 days a week. In small plants, operators may work during the day and be on-call in the evening, nights and weekends. Medium and large plants that require constant monitoring may employ workers in three 8-hour shifts. Because larger plants require constant monitoring, weekend and holiday work is generally required. Operators may be required to work overtime.

Training, Other Qualifications, and Advancement

Employers usually hire high school graduates who are trained on-the-job, and later become licensed. Education after high school improves job prospects.

Education and training. A high school diploma usually is required for an individual to become a water or wastewater treatment plant operator. The completion of an associate degree or a one-year certificate program in water quality and wastewater treatment technology increases an applicant's chances for employment and promotion because plants are becoming more complex. The majority of such programs are offered by trade associations, and can be found throughout the country. These programs provide a good general knowledge of water and wastewater treatment processes, as well as basic preparation for becoming an operator. In some cases, a degree or certificate program can be substituted for experience, allowing a worker to become licensed at a higher level more quickly.

Trainees usually start as attendants or operators-in-training and learn their skills on the job under the direction of an experienced operator. They learn by observing and doing routine tasks such as recording meter readings, taking samples of wastewater and sludge, and performing simple maintenance and repair work on pumps, electric motors, valves, and other plant equipment. Larger treatment plants generally combine this on-the-job training with formal classroom or self-paced study programs.

Most state drinking water and water pollution control agencies offer courses to improve operators' skills and knowledge. The courses cover principles of treatment processes and process control, laboratory procedures, maintenance, management skills, collection systems, safety, chlorination, sedimentation, biological treatment, sludge treatment and disposal, and flow measurements. Some operators take correspondence courses on subjects related to water and wastewater treatment, and some employers pay part of the tuition for related college courses in science or engineering.

Licensure. The Safe Drinking Water Act Amendments of 1996, enforced by the U.S. Environmental Protection Agency, specify national minimum standards for certification of public water system operators. Operators must pass an examination certifying that they are capable of overseeing water treatment operations. Mandatory certification is implemented at the state level, and licensing requirements and standards vary widely depending on the state. There are generally three to four different levels of certification, depending on the operator's experience and training. Higher levels qualify the operator to oversee a wider variety of treatment processes. Although relocation may mean having to become certified in a new jurisdiction, many states accept other states' certifications.

Other qualifications. Water and wastewater treatment plant operators need mechanical aptitude and the ability to solve problems intuitively. They should also be competent in basic mathematics, chemistry, and biology. They must have the ability to apply data to formulas that determine treatment requirements, flow levels, and concentration levels. Some basic familiarity with computers also is necessary, as operators generally use them to record data. Some plants also use computer-controlled equipment and instrumentation.

Certification and advancement. In addition to mandatory certifications required by law, operators can earn voluntary certifications that demonstrate their skills and knowledge. The Association of Boards of Certification offers several levels and types of certification to people who pass exams and have sufficient education and experience.

As operators are promoted, they become responsible for more complex treatment processes. Some operators are promoted to plant supervisor or superintendent; others advance by transferring to a larger facility. Postsecondary training in water and wastewater treatment, coupled with increasingly responsible experience as an operator, may be sufficient to qualify a worker to become superintendent of a small plant, where a superintendent also serves as an operator. However, educational requirements are rising as larger, more complex treatment plants are built to meet new drinking water and water pollution control standards. With each promotion, the operator must have greater knowledge of federal, state, and local regulations. Superintendents of large plants generally need an engineering or science degree.

A few operators get jobs as technicians with state drinking water or water pollution control agencies. In that capacity, they monitor and

Projections data from the National Employment Matrix

Occupational Title	SOC Code	Employment, 2006	Projected employment, 2016	Change, 2006-16 Number	Change, 2006-16 Percent
Water and liquid waste treatment plant and system operators	51-8031	111,000	126,000	15,000	14

NOTE: Data in this table are rounded.

provide technical assistance to plants throughout the state. Vocational-technical school or community college training generally is preferred for technician jobs. Experienced operators may transfer to related jobs with industrial liquid waste treatment plants, water or liquid waste treatment equipment and chemical companies, engineering consulting firms, or vocational-technical schools.

Employment

Water and wastewater treatment plant and system operators held about 111,000 jobs in 2006. Almost 4 in 5 operators worked for local governments. Others worked primarily for private water, sewage, and other systems utilities and for private waste treatment and disposal and waste management services companies. Private firms are increasingly providing operation and management services to local governments on a contract basis.

Water and wastewater treatment plant and system operators were employed throughout the country, but most jobs were in larger towns and cities. Although nearly all operators worked full time, those in small towns may work only part time at the treatment plant, with the remainder of their time spent handling other municipal duties.

Job Outlook

Water and wastewater treatment plant and system operators jobs are expected to grow faster than the average for all occupations. Job opportunities should be excellent for qualified workers.

Employment change. Employment of water and wastewater treatment plant and system operators is expected to grow by 14 percent between 2006 and 2016, which is faster than the average for all occupations. An increasing population and the growth of the economy are expected to boost demand for water and wastewater treatment services. As new plants are constructed to meet this demand, new water and wastewater treatment plant and system operator new jobs will arise.

Local governments are the largest employers of water and wastewater treatment plant and system operators. Employment in privately owned facilities will grow faster, as federal certification requirements have increased utilities' reliance on private firms specializing in the operation and management of water and wastewater treatment facilities.

Job prospects. Job opportunities should be excellent because the retirement of the baby boomer generation will require that many operators with years of experience be replaced. Further, the number of applicants for these jobs is normally low, due primarily to the physically demanding and unappealing nature of some of the work. Opportunities should be best for persons with mechanical aptitude and problem solving skills.

Earnings

Median annual earnings of water and wastewater treatment plant and system operators were $36,070 in May 2006. The middle 50 percent earned between $28,120 and $45,190. The lowest 10 percent earned less than $21,860, and the highest 10 percent earned more than $55,120. Median annual earnings of water and liquid waste treatment plant and systems operators in May 2006 were $36,200 in local government and $34,180 in water, sewage, and other systems.

In addition to their annual salaries, water and wastewater treatment plant and system operators usually receive benefits that may include health and life insurance, a retirement plan, and educational reimbursement for job-related courses.

Related Occupations

Other workers whose main activity consists of operating a system of machinery to process or produce materials include chemical plant and system operators; gas plant operators; petroleum pump system operators, refinery operators, and gaugers; power plant operators, distributors, and dispatchers; and stationary engineers and boiler operators.

Sources of Additional Information

For information on employment opportunities, contact state or local water pollution control agencies, state water and liquid waste operator associations, state environmental training centers, or local offices of the state employment service.

For information on certification, contact

- Association of Boards of Certification, 208 Fifth St., Ames, IA 50010-6259. Internet: http://www.abccert.org

For educational information related to a career as a water or liquid waste treatment plant and system operator, contact

- American Water Works Association, 6666 West Quincy Ave., Denver, CO 80235. Internet: http://www.awwa.org
- National Rural Water Association, 2915 S. 13th St., Duncan, OK 73533. Internet: http://www.nrwa.org
- Water Environment Federation, 601 Wythe St., Alexandria, VA 22314-1994. Internet: http://www.wef.org

Part III

QUICK JOB SEARCH

Seven Steps to Getting a Good Job in Less Time

The Complete Text of a Results-Oriented Minibook by Michael Farr

Millions of job seekers have found better jobs faster using the techniques in the *Quick Job Search.* So can you! The *Quick Job Search* covers the essential steps proven to cut job search time in half and is used widely by job search programs throughout North America. Topics include how to identify your key skills, define your ideal job, write a great resume quickly, use the most effective job search methods, get more interviews, and much more.

If you completed "Using the Job-Match Grid to Choose a Career" earlier in this book, the activities in this section will complement those efforts by helping you to define other skills you possess, focus your resume, and get a job quickly.

While it is a section in this book, the *Quick Job Search* is available from JIST Publishing as a separate booklet.

Quick Job Search Is Short, But It May Be All You Need

While *Quick Job Search* is short, it covers the basics on how to explore career options and conduct an effective job search. While these topics can seem complex, I have found some simple truths about looking for a job:

- If you are going to work, you might as well look for what you really want to do and are good at.
- If you are looking for a job, you might as well use techniques that will reduce the time it takes to find one—and that help you get a better job than you might otherwise.

That's what I emphasize in *Quick Job Search.*

Trust Me—Do the Worksheets. I know you will resist completing the worksheets. But trust me. They are worth your time. Doing them will give you a better sense of what you are good at, what you want to do, and how to go about getting it. You will also most likely get more interviews and present yourself better. Is this worth giving up a night of TV? Yes, I think so.

Once you finish this minibook and its activities, you will have spent more time planning your career than most people do. And you will know more than the average job seeker about finding a job.

Why Such a Short Book? I've taught job seeking skills for many years, and I've written longer and more detailed books than this one. Yet I have often been asked to tell someone, in a few minutes or hours, the most important things they should do in their career planning or job search. Instructors and counselors also ask the same question because they have only a short time to spend with folks they're trying to help. I've given this a lot of thought, and the seven topics in this book are the ones I think are most important to know.

This minibook is short enough to scan in a morning and conduct a more effective job search that afternoon. Granted, doing all the activities would take more time, but they will prepare you far better than scanning the book. Of course, you can learn more about all the topics it covers, but this minibook, *Quick Job Search,* may be all you need.

You can't just read about getting a job. The best way to get a job is to go out and get interviews! And the best way to get interviews is to make a job out of getting a job.

After many years of experience, I have identified just seven basic things you need to do that make a big difference in your job search. Each will be covered and expanded on in this minibook.

1. Identify your key skills.
2. Define your ideal job.
3. Learn the two most effective job search methods.
4. Create a superior resume and a portfolio.
5. Organize your time to get two interviews a day.
6. Dramatically improve your interviewing skills.
7. Follow up on all leads.

So, without further delay, let's get started!

STEP 1: Identify Your Key Skills and Develop a "Skills Language" to Describe Yourself

One survey of employers found that about 90 percent of the people they interviewed might have the required job skills, but they could not describe those skills and thereby prove that they could do the job they sought. They could not answer the basic question "Why should I hire you?"

Knowing and describing your skills are essential to doing well in interviews. This same knowledge is important to help you decide what type of job you will enjoy and do well. For these reasons, I consider identifying your skills a necessary part of a successful career plan or job search.

The Three Types of Skills

Most people think of their skills as job-related skills, such as using a computer. But we all have other types of skills that are important for success on a job—and that are important to employers. The following triangle arranges skills in three groups, and I think that this is a very useful way to consider skills.

Let's look at these three types of skills—self-management, transferable, and job-related—and identify those that are most important to you.

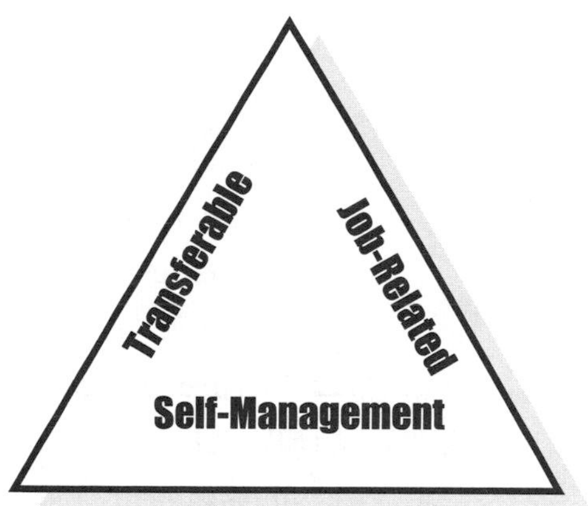

We all have thousands of skills. Consider the many skills required to do even a simple thing like ride a bike or bake a cake. But, of all the skills you have, employers want to know those key skills you have for the job they need done. You must clearly identify these key skills and then emphasize them in interviews.

Self-Management Skills

To begin identifying your skills, answer the question in the box that follows.

Your Good Worker Traits

Write down three things about yourself that you think make you a good worker. Think about what an employer might like about you or the way you work.

1. ______________________________
2. ______________________________
3. ______________________________

You just wrote down the most important things for an employer to know about you! They describe your basic personality and your ability to adapt to new environments. They are some of the most important skills to emphasize in interviews, yet most job seekers don't realize their importance—and don't mention them.

Review the Self-Management Skills Checklist that follows and put a check mark beside any skills you have. The key self-management skills listed first cover abilities that employers find particularly important. If one or more of the key self-management skills apply to you, mentioning them in interviews can help you greatly.

Self-Management Skills Checklist

Following are the key self-management skills that employers value highly. Place a check by those you already have.

- ❑ Have good attendance
- ❑ Get work done on time
- ❑ Am honest
- ❑ Get along with supervisor
- ❑ Arrive on time
- ❑ Get along with co-workers
- ❑ Follow instructions
- ❑ Am hard working/productive

(continued)

(continued)

Place a check by other self-management skills you have.

- ❑ Ambitious
- ❑ Mature
- ❑ Assertive
- ❑ Methodical
- ❑ Capable
- ❑ Modest
- ❑ Cheerful
- ❑ Motivated
- ❑ Competent
- ❑ Natural
- ❑ Conscientious
- ❑ Open-minded
- ❑ Creative
- ❑ Optimistic
- ❑ Culturally tolerant
- ❑ Original
- ❑ Decisive
- ❑ Patient
- ❑ Dependable
- ❑ Persistent
- ❑ Discreet
- ❑ Physically strong
- ❑ Eager
- ❑ Practical
- ❑ Efficient
- ❑ Problem-solving
- ❑ Energetic
- ❑ Proud of work
- ❑ Enthusiastic
- ❑ Quick to learn
- ❑ Expressive
- ❑ Reliable
- ❑ Flexible
- ❑ Resourceful
- ❑ Formal
- ❑ Responsible
- ❑ Friendly
- ❑ Results-oriented
- ❑ Good-natured
- ❑ Self-confident
- ❑ Helpful
- ❑ Sincere
- ❑ Humble
- ❑ Spontaneous
- ❑ Humorous
- ❑ Steady
- ❑ Imaginative
- ❑ Tactful
- ❑ Independent
- ❑ Team player
- ❑ Industrious
- ❑ Tenacious
- ❑ Informal
- ❑ Thrifty
- ❑ Intelligent
- ❑ Trustworthy
- ❑ Intuitive
- ❑ Versatile
- ❑ Loyal
- ❑ Well-organized

List the other self-management skills you have that have not been mentioned but you think are important to include.

____

____

____

After you finish checking the list, circle the five skills you feel are most important and write them in the box that follows.

Your Top Five Self-Management Skills

1. ______________________________
2. ______________________________
3. ______________________________

4. ____

5. ____

When thinking about their skills, some people find it helpful to complete the Essential Job Search Data Worksheet that starts on page 340. It organizes skills and accomplishments from previous jobs and other life experiences. Take a look at it and decide whether to complete it now or later.

Transferable Skills

We all have skills that can transfer from one job or career to another. For example, the ability to organize events could be used in a variety of jobs and may be essential for success in certain occupations. Your mission is to find a job that requires the skills you have and enjoy using.

It's not bragging if it's true. Using your new skills language may be uncomfortable at first, but employers need to learn about your skills. So practice saying positive things about the skills you have for the job. If you don't, who will?

Transferable Skills Checklist

Following are the key transferable skills that employers value highly. Place a check by those you already have. You may have used them in a previous job or in some nonwork setting.

- ❑ Managing money/budgets
- ❑ Speaking in public
- ❑ Managing people
- ❑ Organizing/managing projects
- ❑ Meeting deadlines
- ❑ Using computers
- ❑ Meeting the public
- ❑ Writing well
- ❑ Negotiating

Place a check by the skills you have for working with data.

- ❑ Analyzing data
- ❑ Counting/taking inventory
- ❑ Auditing/checking for accuracy
- ❑ Investigating
- ❑ Budgeting
- ❑ Keeping financial records
- ❑ Calculating/computing
- ❑ Observing/inspecting
- ❑ Classifying data
- ❑ Paying attention to details
- ❑ Comparing/evaluating
- ❑ Researching/locating information
- ❑ Compiling/recording facts
- ❑ Synthesizing

Place a check by the skills you have for working with people.

- ❑ Administering
- ❑ Counseling people
- ❑ Being diplomatic
- ❑ Demonstrating
- ❑ Being kind
- ❑ Having insight
- ❑ Being outgoing
- ❑ Helping others
- ❑ Being patient
- ❑ Instructing others
- ❑ Being pleasant
- ❑ Interviewing people

(continued)

(continued)

- ❑ Being sensitive
- ❑ Listening
- ❑ Being sociable
- ❑ Persuading
- ❑ Being tactful
- ❑ Supervising
- ❑ Being tough
- ❑ Tolerating
- ❑ Caring for others
- ❑ Trusting
- ❑ Coaching
- ❑ Understanding
- ❑ Confronting others

Place a check by your skills in working with words and ideas.

- ❑ Being articulate
- ❑ Creating new ideas
- ❑ Being ingenious
- ❑ Designing
- ❑ Being inventive
- ❑ Editing
- ❑ Being logical
- ❑ Remembering information
- ❑ Communicating verbally
- ❑ Speaking publicly
- ❑ Corresponding with others
- ❑ Writing clearly

Place a check by the leadership skills you have.

- ❑ Being competitive
- ❑ Mediating problems
- ❑ Delegating
- ❑ Motivating people
- ❑ Directing others
- ❑ Motivating yourself
- ❑ Getting results
- ❑ Negotiating agreements
- ❑ Having self-confidence
- ❑ Planning events
- ❑ Influencing others
- ❑ Running meetings
- ❑ Making decisions
- ❑ Solving problems
- ❑ Making explanations
- ❑ Taking risks

Place a check by your creative or artistic skills.

- ❑ Appreciating music
- ❑ Expressing yourself
- ❑ Being artistic
- ❑ Performing/acting
- ❑ Dancing
- ❑ Playing instruments
- ❑ Drawing
- ❑ Presenting artistic ideas

Place a check by your skills for working with things.

- ❑ Assembling things
- ❑ Driving or operating vehicles
- ❑ Building things
- ❑ Operating tools/machines
- ❑ Constructing or repairing things

Add the other transferable skills you have that have not been mentioned but you think are important to include.

____

____

____

When you are finished, circle the five transferable skills you feel are most important for you to use in your next job and list them below.

YOUR TOP FIVE TRANSFERABLE SKILLS

1. ____________________
2. ____________________
3. ____________________
4. ____________________
5. ____________________

Job-Related Skills

Job content or job-related skills are those you need to do a particular occupation. A carpenter, for example, needs to know how to use various tools. Before you select job-related skills to emphasize, you must first have a clear idea of the jobs you want. So let's put off developing your job-related skills list until you have defined the job you want—the topic that is covered next.

STEP 2: Define Your Ideal Job

Too many people look for a job without clearly knowing what they are looking for. Before you go out seeking a job, I suggest that you first define exactly what you want—not *just a job* but *the job.*

Most people think that a job objective is the same as a job title, but it isn't. You need to consider other elements of what makes a job satisfying for you. Then, later, you can decide what that job is called and what industry it might be in. You can compromise on what you consider your ideal job later if you need to.

EIGHT FACTORS TO CONSIDER IN DEFINING YOUR IDEAL JOB

As you try to define your ideal job, consider the following eight important questions. When you know what you want, your task then becomes finding a position that is as close to your ideal job as possible.

1. **What skills do you want to use?** From the skills lists in Step 1, select the top five skills that you enjoy using and most want to use in your next job.

   a.____________________

   b.____________________

   c.____________________

   d.____________________

   e.____________________

(continued)

(continued)

2. **What type of special knowledge do you have?** Perhaps you know how to fix radios, keep accounting records, or cook food. Write down the things you know from schooling, training, hobbies, family experiences, and other sources. One or more of these knowledge areas could make you a very special applicant in the right setting.______________________________

3. **With what types of people do you prefer to work?** Do you like to work with competitive people, or do you prefer hardworking folks, creative personalities, relaxed people, or some other types?__________

4. **What type of work environment do you prefer?** Do you want to work inside, outside, in a quiet place, in a busy place, or in a clean or messy place; or do you want to have a window with a nice view? List the types of environments you prefer.______________________________

5. **Where do you want your next job to be located—in what city or region?** If you are open to living and working anywhere, what would your ideal community be like? Near a bus line? Close to a childcare center?______________________________

6. **What benefits or income do you hope to have in your next job?** Many people will take less money or fewer benefits if they like a job in other ways—or if they need a job quickly to survive. Think about the minimum you would take as well as what you would eventually like to earn. Your next job will probably pay somewhere in between.______________________________

7. **How much and what types of responsibility are you willing to accept?** Usually, the more money you want to make, the more responsibility you must accept. Do you want to work by yourself, be part of a group, or be in charge? If you want to be in charge, how many people are you willing to supervise?

8. **What values are important or have meaning to you?** Do you have important values you would prefer to include in considering the work you do? For example, some people want to work to help others, clean up the environment, build structures, make machines work, gain power or prestige, or care for animals or plants. Think about what is important to you and how you might include this in your next job.____

____

____

____

Is It Possible to Find Your Ideal Job?

Can you find a job that meets all the criteria you just defined? Perhaps. Some people do. The harder you look, the more likely you are to find it. But you will likely need to compromise, so it is useful to know what is *most* important to include in your next job. Go back over your responses to the eight factors and mark a few of those that you would most like to have or include in your ideal job.

Factors I Want in My Ideal Job

Write a brief description of your ideal job. Don't worry about a job title, or whether you have the experience, or other practical matters yet.____

____

____

____

How Can You Explore Specific Job Titles and Industries?

You might find your ideal job in an occupation you haven't considered yet. And, even if you are sure of the occupation you want, it may be in an industry that is unfamiliar to you. This combination of occupation and industry forms the basis for your job search, and you should consider a variety of options.

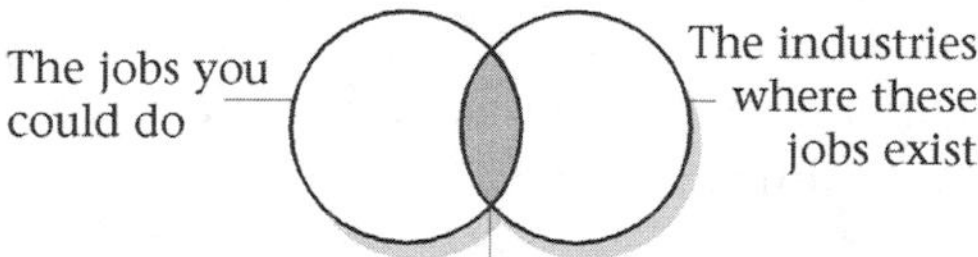

Your ideal job exists in the overlap of those jobs that interest you most *and* in those industries that best meet your needs and interests!

There are thousands of job titles, and many jobs are highly specialized, employing just a few people. While one of these more specialized jobs may be just what you want, most work falls within more general job titles that employ large numbers of people.

Review the Top Jobs in the Workforce

The list of job titles that follows was based on a list developed by the U.S. Department of Labor. It contains 270 major jobs that employ about 90 percent of the U.S. workforce.

The job titles are organized within 16 major groupings called interest areas, presented in bold type. These groupings will help you quickly identify fields most likely to interest you. Job titles are presented in regular type within these groupings.

Begin with the interest areas that appeal to you most, and underline any job title that interests you. (Don't worry for now about whether you have the experience or credentials to do these jobs.) Then quickly review the remaining interest areas, underlining any job titles there that interest you. Note that some job titles are listed more than once because they fit into more than one interest area. When you have gone through all 16 interest areas, go back and circle the 5 to 10 job titles that interest you most. These are the ones you will want to research in more detail.

1. **Agriculture and Natural Resources:** Agricultural and Food Scientists; Agricultural Workers; Biological Scientists; Conservation Scientists and Foresters; Engineers; Farmers, Ranchers, and Agricultural Managers; Fishers and Fishing Vessel Operators; Forest, Conservation, and Logging Workers; Grounds Maintenance Workers; Material Moving Occupations; Pest Control Workers; Purchasing Managers, Buyers, and Purchasing Agents; Science Technicians.
2. **Architecture and Construction:** Architects, except Landscape and Naval; Boilermakers; Brickmasons, Blockmasons, and Stonemasons; Carpenters; Carpet, Floor, and Tile Installers and Finishers; Cement Masons, Concrete Finishers, Segmental Pavers, and Terrazzo Workers; Construction and Building Inspectors; Construction Equipment Operators; Construction Laborers; Construction Managers; Drafters; Drywall Installers, Ceiling Tile Installers, and Tapers; Electrical and Electronics Installers and Repairers; Electricians; Elevator Installers and Repairers; Glaziers; Hazardous Materials Removal Workers; Heating, Air-Conditioning, and Refrigeration Mechanics and Installers; Insulation Workers; Landscape Architects; Line Installers and Repairers; Maintenance and Repair Workers, General; Material Moving Occupations; Painters and Paperhangers; Pipelayers, Plumbers, Pipefitters, and Steamfitters; Plasterers and Stucco Masons; Roofers; Sheet Metal Workers; Structural and Reinforcing Iron and Metal Workers; Surveyors, Cartographers, Photogrammetrists, and Surveying and Mapping Technicians.
3. **Arts and Communication:** Actors, Producers, and Directors; Advertising, Marketing, Promotions, Public Relations, and Sales Managers; Air Traffic Controllers; Announcers; Artists and Related Workers; Barbers, Cosmetologists, and Other Personal Appearance Workers; Broadcast and Sound Engineering Technicians and Radio Operators; Commercial and Industrial Designers; Dancers and Choreographers; Dispatchers; Fashion Designers; Floral Designers; Graphic Designers; Interior Designers; Interpreters and Translators; Musicians, Singers, and Related Workers; News Analysts, Reporters, and Correspondents; Photographers; Public Relations Specialists; Television, Video, and Motion Picture Camera Operators and Editors; Writers and Editors.
4. **Business and Administration:** Accountants and Auditors; Administrative Services Managers; Billing and Posting Clerks and Machine Operators; Bookkeeping, Accounting, and Auditing Clerks; Brokerage Clerks; Budget Analysts; Communications Equipment Operators; Data Entry and Information Processing Workers; Engineering Technicians; File Clerks; Gaming Cage Workers; Human Resources Assistants, except Payroll and Timekeeping; Human Resources, Training, and Labor Relations Managers and

Specialists; Management Analysts; Meeting and Convention Planners; Meter Readers, Utilities; Office and Administrative Support Worker Supervisors and Managers; Office Clerks, General; Operations Research Analysts; Payroll and Timekeeping Clerks; Postal Service Workers; Procurement Clerks; Production, Planning, and Expediting Clerks; Secretaries and Administrative Assistants; Shipping, Receiving, and Traffic Clerks; Stock Clerks and Order Fillers; Top Executives; Weighers, Measurers, Checkers, and Samplers, Recordkeeping.

5. **Education and Training:** Archivists, Curators, and Museum Technicians; Counselors; Education Administrators; Fitness Workers; Health Educators; Instructional Coordinators; Librarians; Library Assistants, Clerical; Library Technicians; Teacher Assistants; Teachers—Adult Literacy and Remedial Education; Teachers—Postsecondary; Teachers—Preschool, Kindergarten, Elementary, Middle, and Secondary; Teachers—Self-Enrichment Education; Teachers—Special Education.
6. **Finance and Insurance:** Advertising Sales Agents; Appraisers and Assessors of Real Estate; Bill and Account Collectors; Claims Adjusters, Appraisers, Examiners, and Investigators; Cost Estimators; Credit Authorizers, Checkers, and Clerks; Financial Analysts and Personal Financial Advisors; Financial Managers; Insurance Sales Agents; Insurance Underwriters; Interviewers; Loan Officers; Market and Survey Researchers; Securities, Commodities, and Financial Services Sales Agents; Tellers.
7. **Government and Public Administration:** Agricultural Workers; Court Reporters; Fire Fighting Occupations; Inspectors, Testers, Sorters, Samplers, and Weighers; Occupational Health and Safety Specialists and Technicians; Police and Detectives; Science Technicians; Tax Examiners, Collectors, and Revenue Agents; Top Executives; Urban and Regional Planners.
8. **Health Science:** Agricultural Workers; Animal Care and Service Workers; Athletic Trainers; Audiologists; Cardiovascular Technologists and Technicians; Chiropractors; Clinical Laboratory Technologists and Technicians; Dental Assistants; Dental Hygienists; Dentists; Diagnostic Medical Sonographers; Dietitians and Nutritionists; Licensed Practical and Licensed Vocational Nurses; Massage Therapists; Medical and Health Services Managers; Medical Assistants; Medical Records and Health Information Technicians; Medical Transcriptionists; Nuclear Medicine Technologists; Nursing, Psychiatric, and Home Health Aides; Occupational Therapist Assistants and Aides; Occupational Therapists; Opticians, Dispensing; Optometrists; Pharmacists; Pharmacy Aides; Pharmacy Technicians; Physical Therapist Assistants and Aides; Physical Therapists; Physician Assistants; Physicians and Surgeons; Podiatrists; Radiation Therapists; Radiologic Technologists and Technicians; Recreational Therapists; Registered Nurses; Respiratory Therapists; Science Technicians; Speech-Language Pathologists; Surgical Technologists; Veterinarians; Veterinary Technologists and Technicians.
9. **Hospitality, Tourism, and Recreation:** Athletes, Coaches, Umpires, and Related Workers; Barbers, Cosmetologists, and Other Personal Appearance Workers; Building Cleaning Workers; Chefs, Cooks, and Food Preparation Workers; Flight Attendants; Food and Beverage Serving and Related Workers; Food Processing Occupations; Food Service Managers; Gaming Services Occupations; Hotel, Motel, and Resort Desk Clerks; Lodging Managers; Recreation Workers; Reservation and Transportation Ticket Agents and Travel Clerks; Travel Agents.
10. **Human Service:** Child Care Workers; Counselors; Interviewers; Personal and Home Care Aides; Probation Officers and Correctional Treatment Specialists; Psychologists; Social and Human Service Assistants; Social Workers.

(continued)

(continued)

11. **Information Technology:** Coin, Vending, and Amusement Machine Servicers and Repairers; Computer and Information Systems Managers; Computer Operators; Computer Programmers; Computer Scientists and Database Administrators; Computer Software Engineers; Computer Support Specialists and Systems Administrators; Computer Systems Analysts; Computer, Automated Teller, and Office Machine Repairers.
12. **Law and Public Safety:** Correctional Officers; Emergency Medical Technicians and Paramedics; Fire Fighting Occupations; Job Opportunities in the Armed Forces; Judges, Magistrates, and Other Judicial Workers; Lawyers; Paralegals and Legal Assistants; Police and Detectives; Private Detectives and Investigators; Science Technicians; Security Guards and Gaming Surveillance Officers.
13. **Manufacturing:** Agricultural Workers; Aircraft and Avionics Equipment Mechanics and Service Technicians; Assemblers and Fabricators; Automotive Body and Related Repairers; Automotive Service Technicians and Mechanics; Bookbinders and Bindery Workers; Computer Control Programmers and Operators; Desktop Publishers; Diesel Service Technicians and Mechanics; Electrical and Electronics Installers and Repairers; Electronic Home Entertainment Equipment Installers and Repairers; Food Processing Occupations; Heavy Vehicle and Mobile Equipment Service Technicians and Mechanics; Home Appliance Repairers; Industrial Machinery Mechanics and Maintenance Workers; Industrial Production Managers; Inspectors, Testers, Sorters, Samplers, and Weighers; Jewelers and Precious Stone and Metal Workers; Machine Setters, Operators, and Tenders—Metal and Plastic; Machinists; Material Moving Occupations; Medical, Dental, and Ophthalmic Laboratory Technicians; Millwrights; Painting and Coating Workers, except Construction and Maintenance; Photographic Process Workers and Processing Machine Operators; Power Plant Operators, Distributors, and Dispatchers; Precision Instrument and Equipment Repairers; Prepress Technicians and Workers; Printing Machine Operators; Radio and Telecommunications Equipment Installers and Repairers; Semiconductor Processors; Small Engine Mechanics; Stationary Engineers and Boiler Operators; Textile, Apparel, and Furnishings Occupations; Tool and Die Makers; Water and Liquid Waste Treatment Plant and System Operators; Water Transportation Occupations; Welding, Soldering, and Brazing Workers; Woodworkers.
14. **Retail and Wholesale Sales and Service:** Advertising, Marketing, Promotions, Public Relations, and Sales Managers; Cashiers; Counter and Rental Clerks; Customer Service Representatives; Demonstrators, Product Promoters, and Models; Funeral Directors; Order Clerks; Property, Real Estate, and Community Association Managers; Purchasing Managers, Buyers, and Purchasing Agents; Real Estate Brokers and Sales Agents; Receptionists and Information Clerks; Retail Salespersons; Sales Engineers; Sales Representatives, Wholesale and Manufacturing; Sales Worker Supervisors.
15. **Scientific Research, Engineering, and Mathematics:** Actuaries; Atmospheric Scientists; Biological Scientists; Chemists and Materials Scientists; Drafters; Economists; Engineering and Natural Sciences Managers; Engineering Technicians; Engineers; Environmental Scientists and Hydrologists; Geoscientists; Mathematicians; Medical Scientists; Photographers; Physicists and Astronomers; Psychologists; Science Technicians; Social Scientists, Other; Statisticians; Surveyors, Cartographers, Photogrammetrists, and Surveying and Mapping Technicians.
16. **Transportation, Distribution, and Logistics:** Aircraft Pilots and Flight Engineers; Bus Drivers; Cargo and Freight Agents; Couriers and Messengers; Material Moving Occupations; Postal Service Workers; Rail Transportation Occupations; Taxi Drivers and Chauffeurs; Truck Drivers and Driver/Sales Workers; Water Transportation Occupations.

You can find thorough descriptions for the job titles in the preceding list in the Occupational Outlook Handbook, *written by the U.S. Department of Labor. Its descriptions include information on earnings, training and education needed to hold specific jobs, work environment, advancement opportunities, projected growth, and sources for additional information. Most libraries have this book.*

You also can find descriptions of these jobs on the Internet. Go to www.bls.gov/oco/.

The New Guide for Occupational Exploration, *Fourth Edition, also provides more information on the interest areas used in this list. This book is published by JIST Works and describes about 1,000 major jobs, arranged within groupings of related jobs.*

Finally, "A Short List of Additional Resources" at the end of this minibook gives you resources for more job information.

Consider Major Industries

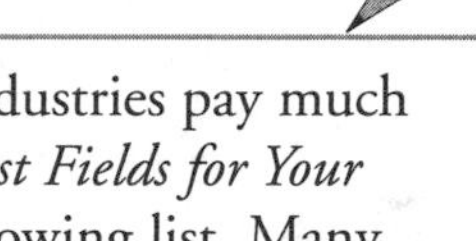

What industry you work in is often as important as the career field. For example, some industries pay much better than others, and others may simply be more interesting to you. A book titled *40 Best Fields for Your Career* contains very helpful reviews for each of the major industries mentioned in the following list. Many libraries and bookstores carry this book, as well as the U.S. Department of Labor's *Career Guide to Industries.*

Underline industries that interest you, and then learn more about the opportunities they present. Jobs in most careers are available in a variety of industries, so consider what industries fit you best and focus your job search in these.

Agriculture and natural resources: Agriculture, forestry, and fishing; mining; oil and gas extraction.

Manufacturing, construction, and utilities: Aerospace product and parts manufacturing; chemical manufacturing, except drugs; computer and electronic product manufacturing; construction; food manufacturing; machinery manufacturing; motor vehicle and parts manufacturing; pharmaceutical and medicine manufacturing; printing; steel manufacturing; textile, textile products, and apparel manufacturing; utilities.

Trade: Automobile dealers, clothing, accessories, and general merchandise stores; grocery stores; wholesale trade.

Transportation: Air transportation; truck transportation and warehousing.

Information: Broadcasting; Internet service providers, Web search portals, and data processing services; motion picture and video industries; publishing, except software; software publishing; telecommunications.

Financial activities: Banking; insurance; securities, commodities, and other investments.

Professional and business services: Advertising and public relations; computer systems design and related services; employment services; management, scientific, and technical consulting services; scientific research and development services.

Education, health care, and social services: Child daycare services; educational services; health care; social assistance, except child care.

(continued)

(continued)

Leisure and hospitality: Art, entertainment, and recreation; food services and drinking places; hotels and other accommodations.

Government and advocacy, grantmaking, and civic organizations: Advocacy, grantmaking, and civic organizations; federal government; state and local government, except education and health care.

The Top Jobs and Industries That Interest You

Go back over the lists of job titles and industries. For numbers 1 and 2 below, list the jobs that interest you most. Then select the industries that interest you most, and list them below in number 3. These are the jobs and industries you should research most carefully. Your ideal job is likely to be found in some combination of these jobs and industries, or in more specialized but related jobs and industries.

1. The five job titles that interest you most
   a.________________________________
   b.________________________________
   c.________________________________
   d.________________________________
   e.________________________________

2. The five next most interesting job titles
   a.________________________________
   b.________________________________
   c.________________________________
   d.________________________________
   e.________________________________

3. The industries that interest you most
   a.________________________________
   b.________________________________
   c.________________________________
   d.________________________________
   e.________________________________

Is Self-Employment or Starting a Business an Option?

More than one in 10 workers are self-employed or own their own businesses. If these options interest you, consider them as well. Talk to people in similar roles to gather information and look for books and Web sites that provide information on options that are similar to those that interest you. A book titled *Best Jobs for the 21st*

Century (JIST Works) includes lists and descriptions of jobs with high percentages of self-employed. Also, the Small Business Administration's Web site at www.sba.gov is a good source of basic information on related topics.

Self-Employment Areas of Interest

In the following space, write your current interest in self-employment or starting a business in an area related to your general job objective.

____

____

____

Can You Identify Your Job-Related Skills Now That You've Defined Your Ideal Job?

Earlier, I suggested that you should first define the job you want and then identify key job-related skills you have that support your ability to do that job. These are the job-related skills to emphasize in interviews.

So, now that you have determined your ideal job, you can pinpoint the job-related skills it requires. If you haven't done so, complete the Essential Job Search Data Worksheet starting on page 340. Completing it will give you specific skills and accomplishments to highlight.

Yes, completing that worksheet requires time, but doing so will help you clearly define key skills to emphasize in interviews—when what you say matters so much. People who complete that worksheet will do better in their interviews than those who don't. After you complete the Essential Job Search Data Worksheet, you are ready to list your top five job-related skills.

Quip

It's a hassle, but... Completing the Essential Job Search Data Worksheet that starts on page 340 will help you define what you are good at—and remember examples of when you did things well. This information will help you define your ideal job and will be of great value in interviews. Look at the worksheet now, and promise to do it later today.

Your Top Five Job-Related Skills

List the top five job-related skills you think are most important. Include the job-related skills you have that you would most like to use in your next job.

1. ______________________________
2. ______________________________
3. ______________________________
4. ______________________________
5. ______________________________

STEP 3: Use the Most Effective Methods to Find a Job in Less Time

Employer surveys have found that most employers don't advertise their job openings. They most often hire people they already know, people who find out about the jobs through word of mouth, or people who happen to be in the right place at the right time. Although luck plays a part in finding job openings, you can use the tips in this step to increase your luck.

Most job seekers don't know how ineffective some traditional job-hunting techniques tend to be. For example, the chart below shows that fewer than 15 percent of all job seekers get jobs from the newspaper want ads, most of which also appear online. Other traditional techniques include using public and private employment agencies, filling out paper and electronic applications, and mailing or e-mailing unsolicited resumes.

How people find jobs.

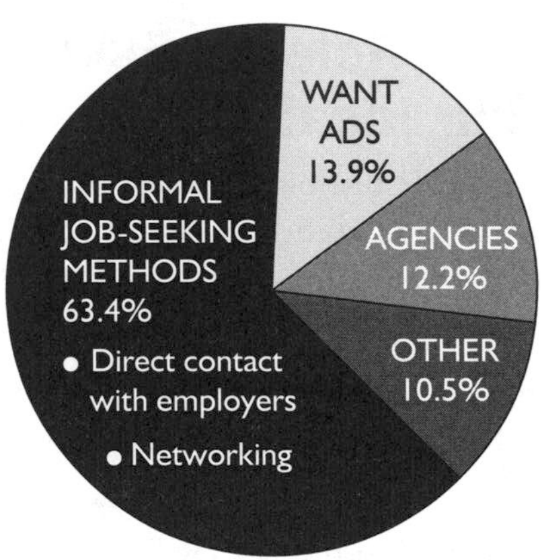

This step covers a number of job search methods. Most of the material is presented as information, with a few interactive activities. While each topic is short and reasonably interesting, taking a break now and then will help you absorb it all.

Informal, nontraditional job-seeking methods have a much larger success rate. These methods are active rather than passive and include making direct contact with employers and networking.

Your job search objective. Almost everyone finds a job eventually, so your objective should be to find a good job in less time. The job search methods I emphasize in this minibook will help you do just that.

Get the Most Out of Less Effective Job Search Methods

The truth is that every job search method works for someone. But experience and research show that some methods are more effective than others are. Your task in the job search is to spend more of your time using more effective methods—and increase the effectiveness of all the methods you use.

So let's start by looking at some traditional job search methods and how you can increase their effectiveness. Only about one-third of all job seekers get their jobs using one of these methods, but you should still consider using them to some extent in your search. Later in the step, you'll read about the most effective methods, the ones you should devote the most time to in your search.

Newspaper and Internet Help Wanted Ads

Most jobs are never advertised, and fewer than 15 percent of all people get their jobs through the want ads. Everyone who reads the paper knows about these openings, so competition is fierce for the few advertised jobs.

The Internet also lists many job openings. But, as happens with newspaper ads, enormous numbers of people view these postings. Many job seekers make direct contact with employers via a company's Web site. Some people do get jobs through the bigger sites, so go ahead and apply. Just be sure to spend most of your time using more effective methods.

Filling Out Applications

Most employers require job seekers to complete an application form or an application online. Applications are designed to collect negative information, and employers use applications to screen people out. If, for example, your training or work history is not the best, you will often never get an interview, even if you can do the job.

Completing applications is a more effective approach for young and entry-level job seekers. The reason is that there is a shortage of workers for the relatively low-paying jobs typically sought by less-experienced job seekers. As a result, when trying to fill those positions, employers are more willing to accept a lack of experience or fewer job skills. Even so, you will get better results by filling out the application, if asked to do so, and then requesting an interview with the person in charge.

When you complete an application, make it neat and error-free, and do not include anything that could get you screened out. If necessary, leave a problem section blank. You can always explain situations in an interview.

Employment Agencies

There are three types of employment agencies. One is operated by the government and is free. The others, private employment agencies and temp agencies, are run as for-profit businesses and charge a fee to either you or an employer. Following are the advantages and disadvantages to using each.

The government employment service and One-Stop centers. Each state and province has a network of local offices to pay unemployment compensation, provide job leads, and offer other services—at no charge to you or to employers. The service's name varies by region. It may be called Job Service, Department of Labor, Unemployment Office, Workforce Development, or another name. Most of these offices are also online, and some require their users to sign up with a login and password to search for job leads and use other services on the Internet.

The Employment and Training Administration Web site at www.doleta.gov gives you information on the programs provided by the government employment service, plus links to other useful sites.

Visit your local office early in your job search. Find out whether you qualify for unemployment compensation and learn more about its services. Look into it—the price is right.

Private employment agencies. Private employment agencies are businesses that charge a fee either to you or to the employer who hires you. Fees can be from less than one month's pay to 15 percent or more of your annual salary. You will often see these agencies' ads in the help wanted section of the newspaper. Most have Web sites.

Be careful about using fee-based employment agencies. Recent research indicates that more people use and benefit from fee-based agencies than in the past. However, relatively few people who register with private agencies get a job through them.

If you use a private employment agency, ask for interviews with the employers who agree to pay the agency's fee. Do not sign an exclusive agreement or be pressured into accepting a job. Also, continue to actively look for your own leads. You can find these agencies in the phone book's yellow pages, and many state- or province-government Web sites offer lists of the private employment agencies in their states.

Temporary agencies. Temporary agencies offer jobs that last from several days to many months. They charge the employer an hourly fee, and then pay you a bit less and keep the difference. You pay no direct fee to the agency. Many private employment agencies now provide temporary jobs as well.

Temp agencies have grown rapidly for good reason. They provide employers with short-term help, and employers often use them to find people they might want to hire later. If the employers are dissatisfied, they can just ask the agency for different temp workers.

Temp agencies can help you survive between jobs and get experience in different work settings. Temp jobs provide a very good option while you look for long-term work, and you might get a job offer while working in a temp job. Holding a temporary job might even lead to a regular job with the same or a similar employer.

School and Other Employment Services

Only a small percentage of job seekers use school and other special employment services, probably because few job seekers have the service available to them. If you are a student or graduate, find out about any employment services at your school. Some schools provide free career counseling, resume-writing help, referrals to job openings, career interest tests, reference materials, Web sites listing job openings, and other services. Special career programs work with veterans, people with disabilities, welfare recipients, union members, professional groups, and many others. So check out these services and consider using them.

Mailing Versus Posting Resumes on the Internet

Many job search experts used to suggest that sending out lots of resumes was a great technique. That advice probably helped sell their resume books, but mailing resumes to people you do not know was never an effective approach. It very rarely works. A recent survey of 1,500 successful job seekers showed that only 2 percent found their positions through sending an unsolicited resume. The same is true for the Internet.

Although mailing your resume to strangers doesn't make much sense, posting it on the Internet might because

- It doesn't take much time.
- Many employers have the potential of finding your resume.
- You can post your resume on niche sites that attract only employers in your field.
- Your Internet resume is easily updated, allowing you to post your current accomplishments.
- You can easily link your resume to projects and Web sites that highlight your accomplishments.

Job searching on the Internet has its limitations, just like other methods. I'll cover resumes in more detail later and provide tips on using the Internet throughout this minibook.

Use the Two Job Search Methods That Work Best

The fact is that most jobs are not advertised, so how do *you* find them? The same way that about two-thirds of all job seekers do: networking with people you know (which I call making warm contacts) and directly contacting employers (which I call making cold contacts). Both of these methods are based on the job search rule you should know above all:

The Most Important Job Search Rule: Don't wait until the job opens before contacting the employer!

Employers fill most jobs with people they meet before a job is formally open. The trick is to meet people who can hire you before a job is formally available. Instead of asking whether the employer has any jobs open, I suggest that you say, *"I realize you may not have any openings now, but I would still like to talk to you about the possibility of future openings."*

Most Effective Job Search Method 1: Develop a Network of Contacts in Five Easy Stages

Studies find that 40 percent of all people located their jobs through a lead provided by a friend, a relative, or an acquaintance. That makes the people you know your number one source of job leads—more effective than all the traditional methods combined! Developing and using your contacts is called *networking,* and here's how it works:

Most jobs are never advertised because employers don't need to advertise or don't want to. Employers trust people referred to them by someone they know far more than they trust strangers. And most jobs are filled by referrals and people that the employer knows, eliminating the need to advertise. So, your job search must involve more than looking at ads.

1. **Make lists of people you know.** Make a thorough list of anyone you are friendly with. Then make a separate list of all your relatives. These two lists alone often add up to 25 to 100 people or more. Next, think of other groups of people that you have something in common with, such as former co-workers or classmates, members of your social or sports groups, members of your professional association, former employers, neighbors, and other groups. You might not know many of these people personally or well, but most will help you if you ask them. An easy way to find networking contacts is to join an online networking site such as LinkedIn (www.linkedin.com).
2. **Contact each person in your list in a systematic way.** Obviously, some people will be more helpful than others, but any one of them might help you find a job lead.
3. **Present yourself well.** Begin with your friends and relatives. Call and tell them you are looking for a job and need their help. Be as clear as possible about the type of employment you want and the skills and qualifications you have. Look at the sample JIST Card and phone script later in this step for good presentation ideas.
4. **Ask your contacts for leads.** It is possible that your contacts will know of a job opening that interests you. If so, get the details and get right on it! More likely, however, they will not, so you should ask each person the Three Magic Networking Questions.

The Three Magic Networking Questions

- **Do you know of any openings for a person with my skills?**

  If the answer is "No" (which it usually is), then ask...
- **Do you know of someone else who might know of such an opening? If your contact does, get that name and ask for another one.**

  If he or she doesn't, ask...

(continued)

(continued)

- **Do you know of anyone who might know of someone else who might know of a job opening?**

  Another good way to ask this is "Do you know someone who knows lots of people?" *If all else fails, this will usually get you a name.*

5. **Contact these referrals and ask them the same questions.** From each person you contact, try to get two names of other people you might contact. Doing this consistently can extend your network of acquaintances by hundreds of people. Eventually, one of these people will hire you or refer you to someone who will!

If you are persistent in following these five steps, networking might be the only job search method you need. It works.

Dialing for dollars. The phone can get you more interviews per hour than any other job search tool. But it won't work unless you use it actively.

The yellow pages in print and online provide the most complete, up-to-date listing of potential job search targets you can get. It organizes them into categories that are very useful for job seekers. Just find a category that interests you, call each listing, and then contact employers listed there. All it takes is a 30-second phone call. Ask to speak with the hiring authority.

Most Effective Job Search Method 2: Contact Employers Directly

It takes more courage, but making direct contact with employers is a very effective job search technique. I call these cold contacts because people you don't know in advance will need to warm up to your inquiries. Two basic techniques for making cold contacts follow.

Use the yellow pages to find potential employers. Begin by looking at the index in the front of your phone book's yellow pages. For each entry, ask yourself, *"Would an organization of this kind need a person with my skills?"* If you answer *"Yes,"* then that organization or business type is a possible target. You can also rate "Yes" entries based on your interest, writing a "1" next to those that seem very interesting, a "2" next to those that you are not sure of, and a "3" next to those that aren't interesting at all.

Next, select a type of organization that got a "Yes" response and turn to that section of the yellow pages. Call each organization listed there and ask to speak to the person who is most likely to hire or supervise you—typically the manager of the business or a department head—not the personnel or human resources manager. A sample telephone script is included later in this section to give you ideas about what to say.

You can easily adapt this approach for use on the Internet by using sites such as www.yellowpages.com to get contacts anywhere in the world, or you can find phone and e-mail contacts on an employer's own Web site.

Drop in without an appointment. Another effective cold contact method is to just walk into a business or organization that interests you and ask to speak to the person in charge. Although dropping in is particularly effective in small businesses, it also works surprisingly well in larger ones. Remember to ask for an interview even if there are no openings now. If your timing is inconvenient, ask for a better time to come back for an interview.

Most Jobs Are with Small Employers

Businesses and organizations with fewer than 250 employees employ about 72 percent of all U.S. workers. Small organizations are also the source for around 75 percent of the new jobs created each year. They are simply too important to overlook in your job search! Many of them don't have personnel departments, which makes direct contacts even easier and more effective.

Create a Powerful Job Search Tool—the JIST Card®

Look at the sample cards that follow—they are JIST Cards, and they get results. Computer printed or even neatly written on a 3-by-5–inch card, JIST Cards include the essential information employers want to know.

A JIST Card Is a Mini Resume

JIST Cards have been used by thousands of job search programs and millions of people. Employers like their direct and timesaving format, and they have been proven as an effective tool to get job leads. Attach one to your resume. Give them to friends, relatives, and other contacts and ask them to pass them along to others who might know of an opening. Enclose them in thank-you notes after interviews. Leave one with employers as a business card. However you get them in circulation, you may be surprised at how well they work.

You can easily create JIST Cards on a computer and print them on card stock you can buy at any office supply store. Or have a few hundred printed cheaply by a local quick print shop. While they are often done as 3-by-5 cards, they can be printed in any size or format.

Sandy Nolan

Position: General Office/Clerical

Cell phone: (512) 232-9213

Email: snolan@aol.com

More than two years of work experience plus one year of training in office practices. Type 55 wpm, trained in word processing, post general ledger, have good interpersonal skills, and get along with most people. Can meet deadlines and handle pressure well.

Willing to work any hours.

Organized, honest, reliable, and hardworking.

Richard Straightarrow

Home: (602) 253-9678
Message: (602) 257-6643
E-mail: RSS@email.cmm

Objective: Electronics installation, maintenance, and sales

Four years of work experience plus a two-year A.S. degree in Electronics Engineering Technology. Managed a $360,000/year business while going to school full time, with grades in the top 25%. Familiar with all major electronic diagnostic and repair equipment. Hands-on experience with medical, consumer, communication, and industrial electronics equipment and applications. Good problem-solving and communication skills. Customer service oriented.

Willing to do what it takes to get the job done.

Self-motivated, dependable, learn quickly.

A JIST Card Can Lead to an Effective Phone Script

The phone is an essential job search tool that can get you more interviews per hour than any other job search tool. But the technique won't work unless you use it actively throughout your search. After you have created your JIST Card, you can use it as the basis for a phone script to make warm or cold calls. Revise your JIST Card content so that it sounds natural when spoken, and then edit it until you can read it out loud in about 30 seconds. The sample phone script that follows is based on the content of a JIST Card. Use it to help you modify your own JIST Card into a phone script.

Overcome phone phobia! Making cold calls takes guts, but most people can get one or more interviews an hour using cold calls. Start by calling people you know and people they refer you to. Then try calls to businesses that don't sound very interesting. As you get better, call more desirable targets.

"Hello. My name is Pam Nykanen. I am interested in a position in hotel management. I have four years' experience in sales, catering, and accounting with a 300-room hotel. I also have an associate degree in hotel management, plus one year of experience with the Brady Culinary Institute. During my employment, I helped double revenues from meetings and conferences and increased bar revenues by 46 percent. I have good problem-solving skills and am good with people. I am also well-organized, hard working, and detail-oriented. When may I come in for an interview?"

With your script in hand, make some practice calls to warm or cold contacts. If making cold calls, contact the person most likely to supervise you. Then present your script just as you practiced it—without stopping.

Although the sample script assumes that you are calling someone you don't know, you can change it to address warm contacts and referrals. Making cold calls takes courage but works very well for many who are willing to do it.

Use the Internet in Your Job Search

The Internet has limitations as a job search tool. While many have used it to get job leads, it has not worked well for far more. Too many assume they can simply add their resume to resume databases, and employers will line up to hire them. Just like the older approach of sending out lots of resumes, good things sometimes happen, but not often.

I recommend two points that apply to all job search methods, including using the Internet:

- It is unwise to rely on just one or two methods in conducting your job search.
- It is essential that you use an active rather than a passive approach in your job search.

Use More Than One Job Search Method

I encourage you to use the Internet in your job search, but I suggest that you use it along with other techniques. Use the same sorts of job search techniques online as you do offline, including contacting employers directly and building up a network of personal contacts that can help you with your search.

Tips to Increase Your Effectiveness in Internet Job Searches

The following tips can increase the effectiveness of using the Internet in your job search:

- **Be as specific as possible in the job you seek.** This is important in using any job search method, and it's even more important in using the Internet in your job search. The Internet is enormous, so it is essential to be as focused as possible in your search. Narrow your job title or titles to be as specific as possible. Limit your search to specific industries or areas of specialization. Locate and use specialized job banks in your area of interest.

- **Have reasonable expectations.** Success on the Internet is more likely if you understand its limitations and strengths. For example, employers trying to find someone with skills in high demand, such as nurses, are more likely to use the Internet to recruit job candidates.
- **Limit your geographic options.** If you don't want to move or would move only to certain areas, state this preference on your resume and restrict your search to those areas. Many Internet sites allow you to view or search for only those jobs that meet your location criteria.
- **Create an electronic resume.** With few exceptions, resumes submitted on the Internet end up as simple text files with no graphic elements. Employers search databases of many resumes for those that include key words or meet other searchable criteria. So create a simple text resume for Internet use and include words that are likely to be used by employers searching for someone with your abilities. (See Step 4 for more on creating an electronic resume.)
- **Get your resume into the major resume databases.** Most Internet employment sites let you add your resume for free and then charge employers to advertise openings or to search for candidates. Although adding your resume to these databases is not likely to result in job offers, doing so allows you to use your stored resume to easily apply for positions that are posted at these sites. These easy-to-use sites often provide all sorts of useful information for job seekers.
- **Make direct contacts.** Visit the Web sites of organizations that interest you and learn more about them. Many post openings, allow you to apply online, offer information on benefits and work environment, or even provide access to staff who can answer your questions. Even if they don't, you can always search the site or e-mail a request for the name of the person in charge of the work that interests you and then communicate with that person directly.
- **Network.** You can network online, too, finding names and e-mail addresses of potential employer contacts or of other people who might know someone with job openings. Look at and participate in interest groups, professional association sites, alumni sites, chat rooms, e-mail discussion lists, and employer sites—these are just some of the many creative ways to network and interact with people via the Internet.

Check Out Career-Specific Sites First

Thousands of Internet sites provide lists of job openings and information on careers or education. Many have links to other sites that they recommend. Service providers such as Yahoo! (www.yahoo.com) and the Microsoft Network (www.msn.com) have partnered with sites such as Careerbuilder.com to include career information and job listings plus links to other sites. Also check out www.jist.com. Three additional career-related sites are Riley Guide at www.rileyguide.com, Monster at www.monster.com, and Indeed, a job aggregator, at www.indeed.com.

STEP 4: Write a Simple Resume Now and a Better One Later

Sending out or e-mailing resumes and waiting for responses is not an effective job-seeking technique. But, many employers *will* ask you for a resume, and it can be a useful tool in your job search. I suggest that you begin with a simple resume you can complete quickly. I've seen too many people spend weeks working on a resume when they could have been out getting interviews instead. If you want a better resume, you can work on it on weekends and evenings. So let's begin with the basics.

Tips for Creating a Superior Resume

The following tips make sense for any resume format:

- **Write it yourself.** It's okay to look at other resumes for ideas, but write yours yourself. Doing so will force you to organize your thoughts and background.
- **Make it error-free.** One spelling or grammar error will create a negative impressionist (see what I mean?). Get someone else to review your final draft for any errors. Then review it again because these rascals have a way of slipping in.
- **Make it look good.** Poor copy quality, cheap paper, bad type quality, or anything else that creates a poor appearance will turn off employers to even the best resume content. Get professional help with design and printing if necessary. Many professional resume writers and even print shops offer writing and desktop design services if you need help.
- **Be brief, be relevant.** Many good resumes fit on one page, and few justify more than two. Include only the most important points. Use short sentences and action words. If it doesn't relate to and support the job objective, cut it!
- **Be honest.** Don't overstate your qualifications. If you end up getting a job you can't handle, who does it help? And a lie can result in your being fired later.
- **Be positive.** Emphasize your accomplishments and results. A resume is no place to be too humble or to display your faults.
- **Be specific.** Instead of saying, "I am good with people," say, "I supervised four people in the warehouse and increased productivity by 30 percent." Use numbers whenever possible, such as the number of people served, percentage of sales increase, or amount of dollars saved.

You should also know that everyone feels that he or she is a resume expert. Whatever you do, someone will tell you that it's wrong. Remember that a resume is simply a job search tool.

You should never delay or slow down your job search because your resume is not good enough. The best approach is to create a simple and acceptable resume as quickly as possible and then use it. As time permits, create a better one if you feel you must.

Writing Chronological Resumes

Most resumes use a chronological format where the most recent experience is listed first, followed by each previous job. This arrangement works fine for someone with work experience in several similar jobs, but not as well for those with limited experience or for career changers.

Look at the two resumes for Judith Jones that follow. Both use the chronological approach.

The first resume would work fine for most job search needs. It could be completed in about an hour.

Notice that the second one includes some improvements. The first resume is good, but most employers would like the additional positive information in the improved resume.

Avoid the resume pile. Resume experts often suggest that a dynamite resume will jump out of the pile. This is old-fashioned advice. It assumes that you are applying to large organizations and for advertised jobs. Today most jobs are with small employers and are not advertised. To avoid joining that stack of resumes in the first place, look for job openings that others overlook.

Basic Chronological Resume Example

Judith J. Jones

115 South Hawthorne Avenue
Chicago, Illinois 66204
tel: (312) 653-9217
email: jj@earthlink.com

JOB OBJECTIVE

A position in the office management, accounting, or administrative assistant area that enables me to grow professionally.

EDUCATION AND TRAINING

Acme Business College, Lincoln, IL
Graduate of a one-year business program.

John Adams High School, South Bend, IN
Diploma, business education.

U.S. Army
Financial procedures, accounting functions.

Other: Continuing-education classes and workshops in business communication, spreadsheet and database applications, scheduling systems, and customer relations.

EXPERIENCE

2006–present—Claims Processor, Blue Spear Insurance Co., Wilmette, IL. Process customer medical claims, develop management reports based on created spreadsheets and develop management reports based on those forms, exceed productivity goals.

2005–2006—Returned to school to upgrade business and computer skills. Completed courses in advanced accounting, spreadsheet and database programs, office management, human relations, and new office techniques.

2002–2005—E4, U.S. Army. Assigned to various stations as a specialist in finance operations. Promoted prior to honorable discharge.

2001–2002—Sandy's Boutique, Wilmette, IL. Responsible for counter sales, display design, cash register, and other tasks.

1999–2001—Held part-time and summer jobs throughout high school.

STRENGTHS AND SKILLS

Reliable, hardworking, and good with people. General ledger, accounts payable, and accounts receivable. Proficient in Microsoft Word, WordPerfect, Excel, and Outlook.

I give some tips you can use when you write your simple chronological resume. Use this resume as your guide.

Improved Chronological Resume Example

Judith J. Jones

115 South Hawthorne Avenue
Chicago, IL 66204

jj@earthlink.com
(312) 653-9217 (cell)

JOB OBJECTIVE

A position requiring excellent business management expertise in an office environment. Position should require a variety of skills, including office management, word processing, and spreadsheet and database application use.

EDUCATION AND TRAINING

Acme Business College, Lincoln, IL
Completed one-year program in **Professional Office Management.** Achieved GPA in top 30% of class. Courses included word processing, accounting theory and systems, advanced spreadsheet and database applications, graphics design, time management, and supervision.

John Adams High School, South Bend, IN
Graduated with emphasis on **business courses.** Earned excellent grades in all business topics and won top award for word-processing speed and accuracy.

Other: Continuing-education programs at own expense, including business communications, customer relations, computer applications, and sales techniques.

EXPERIENCE

2006–present—**Claims Processor, Blue Spear Insurance Company,** Wilmette, IL. Process 50 complex medical insurance claims per day, almost 20% above department average. Created a spreadsheet report process that decreased department labor costs by more than $30,000 a year. Received two merit raises for performance.

2005–2006—**Returned to business school to gain advanced office skills.**

2002–2005—**Finance Specialist (E4), U.S. Army.** Systematically processed more than 200 invoices per day from commercial vendors. Trained and supervised eight employees. Devised internal system allowing 15% increase in invoices processed with a decrease in personnel. Managed department with a budget equivalent of more than $350,000 a year. Honorable discharge.

2001–2002—**Sales Associate promoted to Assistant Manager, Sandy's Boutique,** Wilmette, IL. Made direct sales and supervised four employees. Managed daily cash balances and deposits, made purchasing and inventory decisions, and handled all management functions during owner's absence. Sales increased 26% and profits doubled during tenure.

1999–2001—**Held various part-time and summer jobs through high school while maintaining GPA 3.0/4.0.** Earned enough to pay all personal expenses, including car insurance. Learned to deal with customers, meet deadlines, work hard, and handle multiple priorities.

STRENGTHS AND SKILLS

Reliable, with strong work ethic. Excellent interpersonal, written, and oral communication and math skills. Accept supervision well, effectively supervise others, and work well as a team member. General ledger, accounts payable, and accounts receivable expertise. Proficient in Microsoft Word, Excel, PowerPoint, and Outlook; WordPerfect.

Tips for Writing a Simple Chronological Resume

Follow these tips as you write a basic chronological resume:

- **Name.** Use your formal name (not a nickname).
- **Address and contact information.** Avoid abbreviations in your address and include your ZIP code. If you may move, use a friend's address or include a forwarding address. Most employers will not write to you, so provide reliable phone numbers and other contact options. Always include your area code in your phone number because you never know where your resume might travel. Make sure that you have an answering machine or voice mail, and record a professional-sounding message. Include alternative ways to reach you, such as a cell phone and e-mail address.
- **Job objective.** You should almost always have one, even if it is general. Notice how Judith Jones keeps her options open with her broad job objective in her basic resume on page 325. Writing "secretary" or "clerical" might limit her from being considered for other jobs.
- **Education and training.** Include any training or education you've had that supports your job objective. If you did not finish a formal degree or program, list what you did complete and emphasize accomplishments. If your experience is not strong, add details here such as related courses and extracurricular activities. In the two examples, Judith Jones puts her business schooling in both the education and experience sections. Doing this fills a job gap and allows her to present her training as equal to work experience.
- **Previous experience.** Include the basics such as employer name, job title, dates employed, and responsibilities–but emphasize specific skills, results, accomplishments, superior performance, and so on.
- **Personal data.** Do not include irrelevant details such as height, weight, and marital status or a photo. Current laws do not allow an employer to base hiring decisions on these points. Providing this information can cause some employers to toss your resume. You can include information about hobbies or leisure activities in a special section that directly supports your job objective.
- **References.** Make sure that each reference will make nice comments about you and ask each to write a letter of recommendation that you can give to employers. You do not need to list your references on your resume. List them on a separate page and give it to employers who ask. If your references are particularly good, however, you can mention this somewhere–the last section is often a good place.

When you have a simple, errorless, and eye-pleasing resume, get on with your job search. There is no reason to delay! If you want to create a better resume in your spare time (evenings or weekends), use the name and contact information you currently have and improve the other sections of the resume.

Tips for an Improved Chronological Resume

Use these tips to improve your simple resume:

- **Job objective.** A poorly written job objective can limit the jobs an employer might consider you for. Think of the skills you have and the types of jobs you want to do; describe them in general terms. Instead of using a narrow job title such as "restaurant manager," you might write "manage a small to mid-sized business."
- **Education and training.** New graduates should emphasize their recent training and education more than those with a few years of related work experience would. A more detailed education and training section might include specific courses you took, and activities or accomplishments that support your job objective or reinforce your key skills. Include other details that reflect how hard you work, such as working your way through school or handling family responsibilities.
- **Skills and accomplishments.** Include those that support your ability to do well in the job you seek now. Even small details count. Maybe your attendance was perfect, you met a tight deadline, or you did the work of others during vacations. Be specific and include numbers–even if you have to estimate them. Judith's improved chronological resume example features more accomplishments and skills. Notice the impact of the numbers to reinforce results.
- **Job titles.** Past job titles may not accurately reflect what you did. For example, your job title may have been "cashier," but you also opened the store, trained new staff, and covered for the boss on vacations. Perhaps "head cashier and assistant manager" would be more accurate. Check with your previous employer if you are not sure.

(continued)

(continued)

- **Promotions.** If you were promoted or got good evaluations, say so—"cashier, promoted to assistant manager," for example. You can list a promotion to a more responsible job as a separate job if doing so results in a stronger resume.
- **Gaps in employment and other problem areas.** Employee turnover is expensive, so few employers want to hire people who won't stay or who won't work out. Gaps in employment, jobs held for short periods, or a lack of direction in the jobs you've held are all concerns for employers. So consider your situation and try to give an explanation of a problem area. Here are a few examples:

  2007—Continued my education at...

  2007—Traveled extensively throughout...

  2006 to present—Self-employed as barn painter and...

  2006—Took year off to have first child

  Use entire years to avoid displaying employment gaps you can't explain easily. If you had a few months of unemployment at the beginning of 2007 and then began a job in mid-2007, for example, you can list the job as "2007 to present."

Writing Skills and Combination Resumes

Quip

Skip the negatives. Remember that a resume can get you screened out, but it is up to you to get the interview and the job. Cut out anything negative in your resume!

The skills resume emphasizes your most important skills, supported by specific examples of how you have used them. This type of resume allows you to use any part of your life history to support your ability to do the job you want.

While skills resumes can be very effective, creating them requires more work. And some employers don't like them because they can hide a job seeker's faults (such as job gaps, lack of formal education, or little related work experience) better than can a chronological resume. Still, a skills resume may make sense for you.

Look over the sample resumes that follow for ideas. Notice that one resume includes elements of a skills *and* a chronological resume. This so-called combination resume makes sense if your previous job history or education and training are positive.

More Resume Examples

Quip

A resume is not the most effective tool for getting interviews. A better approach is to make direct contact with those who hire or supervise people with your skills and ask them for an interview, even if no openings exist now. Then send a resume.

Find resume layout and presentation ideas in the four samples that follow.

The chronological resume sample on page 329 focuses on accomplishments through the use of numbers. While Jon's resume does not say so, it is obvious that he works hard and that he gets results.

The skills resume on page 330 is for a recent high school graduate whose only work experience was at a school office!

The combination resume on page 331 emphasizes Grant's relevant education and transferable skills because he has little work experience in the field.

The electronic resume on page 332 is appropriate for scanning or e-mail submission. It has a plain format that is easily read by scanners. It also has lots of key words that increase its chances of being selected when an employer searches a database.

Use the information from your completed Essential Job Search Data Worksheet to write your resume.

The Chronological Resume to Emphasize Results

This simple chronological resume has few but carefully chosen words. It has an effective summary at the beginning, and every word supports his job objective.

Jon Feder

2140 Beach Road
Pompano Beach, Florida 20000

Phone: (222) 333-4444
E-mail: jfeder@com.com

Objective: Management position in a major hotel

He emphasizes results!

Summary of Experience: Three years of experience in sales, catering banquet services, and guest relations in a 75-room hotel. Doubled sales revenues from conferences and meetings. Increased dining room and bar revenues by 40%. Won prestigious national and local awards for increased productivity and services.

Experience:

Beachcomber Hotel, Pompano Beach, Florida
Assistant Manager
20XX to Present

- Oversee a staff of 24, including dining room and bar, housekeeping, and public relations operations.
- Introduced new menus and increased dining room revenues by 40%. Awarded *Saveur* magazine's prestigious first place Hotel Cuisine award as a result of my selection of chefs.
- Attracted 58% more bar patrons by implementing Friday night Jazz at the Beach.

Notice his use of numbers to increase the impact of the statements.

Beachcombers' Suites, Hollywood Beach, Florida
Sales and Public Relations
20XX to 20XX

- Doubled venues per month from weddings, conferences, and meetings.
- Chosen Chamber of Commerce Newcomer of the Year 20XX for the increase in business within the community.

Bullets here and above improve readability and emphasize key points.

Education: Associate Degree in Hotel Management from Sullivan Technical Institute
Certificate in Travel Management from Phoenix University

While Jon had only a few years of related work experience, he used this resume to help him land a very responsible job in a large resort hotel.

The Skills Resume for Those with Limited Work Experience

In this skills resume, each skill directly supports the job objective of this recent high school graduate with very limited work experience.

Catalina A. Garcia
2340 N. Delaware Street · Denver, Colorado 81613
Home: (413) 643-2173 (Leave Message)
Cell phone: (413) 345-2189
E-mail: cagarcia@net.net

Position Desired
Office assistant in a fast-paced business

Support for her key skills comes from her activities: school, clubs, and volunteer work.

Note her key skills.

Skills and Abilities

Communications	Excellent written and verbal presentation skills. Use proper grammar and have a good speaking voice.
Interpersonal	Able to get along well with all types of people. Accept supervision. Received positive evaluation from previous supervisors.
Flexible	Willing to try new things and am interested in improving efficiency on assigned tasks.
Attention to Detail	Maintained confidential student records accurately and efficiently. Uploaded 500 student records in one day without errors.
Hard Working	Worked 30 hours per week throughout high school and maintained above-average grades.
Student Contact	Cordially dealt with as many as 150 students a day in Dean's office.
Dependable	Never absent or tardy in four years.
Awards	English Department Student of the Year, April 20XX 20XX Outstanding Student Newspaper, Newspaper Association of America

Notice the emphasis on adaptive skills.

She makes good use of numbers.

This statement is very strong.

Education
Denver North High School. Took advanced English and communication classes. Member of student newspaper staff and FCCLA for four years. Graduated in top 30% of class.

Other
Girls' basketball team for four years. This taught me discipline, teamwork, how to follow instructions, and hard work. I am ambitious, outgoing, reliable, and willing to work.

Catalina's resume makes it clear that she is talented and hard working.

The Combination Resume

Grant just finished computer programming school and has no work experience in the field. After listing the topics covered in the course, he summarized his employment experience, specifying that he earned promotions quickly. This would be attractive to any employer.

Grant Thomas

717 Carlin Court • Mendelein, IL 60000 • (555) 555-3333
E-mail: gthomas@com.com

Profile

- Outstanding student and tutor
- Winner of international computer software design competition three years
- Capable of being self-directed and independent, but also a team player
- Effective communicator, both orally and written
- Creative problem solver

Education and Training

M.S. in Software Engineering, Massachusetts Institute of Technology, Cambridge, MA
B.S. in Computer Engineering, California State University, Fullerton, CA
A rigorous education that focuses on topics such as

He includes important information that specifies topics he studied.

- Structure and interpretation of computer programs
- Circuits and electronics
- Signals and systems
- Computation structures
- Microelectronic devices and circuits
- Computer system engineering
- Computer language engineering
- Mathematics for computer science
- Analog electronics laboratory
- Digital systems laboratory

The work experiences support the job objective.

Highlights of Experience and Abilities

- Develop, create, and modify general computer applications software.
- Analyze user needs and develop software solutions.
- Confer with system analysts, computer programmers, and others.
- Modify existing software to correct errors.
- Coordinate software system installation and monitor equipment functioning to ensure specifications are met.
- Supervise work of programmers and technicians.
- Train customers and employees to use new and modified software.

Employment History

Software Specialist, First Rate Computers, Mendelein, IL 20XX – Present

- Technician and Customer and Employee Trainer throughout high school
- Promoted to software specialist and worked as a full-time telecommuting employee while completing the B.S. and M.S. degrees

References available on request

The Electronic Resume

William Brown
409 S. Maish Road
Phoenix, AZ 50000

Because this electronic format is to be scanned or e-mailed, it has no bold, bullets, or italics.

Phone message: (300) 444-5567

E-mail: wbrown@email.com

The many key words ensure that the employers' computer searches will select this resume.

OBJECTIVE

Store management career track in car audio store

==

SUMMARY OF SKILLS

Strategic planning, time management, team building, leadership, problem solving, quality customer service, conflict resolution, increasing productivity, confident, outgoing, high performing, aggressive sales

==

EXPERIENCE

Note the results statements and numbers used below.

Total of three years in sales

* SHIFT SUPERVISOR, Tech World, Audio Department, Phoenix, AZ, April 20XX to present: Promoted to Shift Supervisor of nine salespeople in three months. Responsible for strategic planning, time management, team building, leadership, problem solving, quality customer service, conflict resolution, and increasing productivity. Highest-selling team for three years.

* AUDIO SALESPERSON, Tech World, Audio Department, Phoenix, AZ, January 20XX to April 20XX: Arranged display, organized stockroom, sales to customers, and tracked inventory. Highest-selling staff member for three months.

==

EDUCATION AND TRAINING

Phoenix High School, top 40% of class

Additional training: Team Building, Franklin Time Management seminar, Team Building seminar

==

OTHER

* Installed audio systems in 10 cars: family, friends, and my own.

* Member of United States Autosound Association (USAA)

Use a Career Portfolio to Support Your Resume

Your resume is impressive, but there is another way that you can show prospective employers evidence of who you are and what you can do—a career portfolio.

What Is a Career Portfolio?

Unlike a resume, a career portfolio is a collection of documents that can include a variety of items. Here are some items you may want to place in your portfolio:

- Resume
- School transcripts
- Summary of skills
- Credentials, such as diplomas and certificates of recognition
- Reference letters from school officials and instructors, former employers, or co-workers
- List of accomplishments: Describe hobbies and interests that are not directly related to your job objective and are not included on your resume.
- Examples of your work: Depending on your situation, you can include samples of your art, photographs of a project, audiotapes, videotapes, images of Web pages you developed, and other media that can provide examples of your work.

Place each item on a separate page when you assemble your career portfolio.

Create a Digital Portfolio

A digital portfolio, also known as an electronic portfolio, contains all the information from your career portfolio in an electronic format. This material is then copied onto a CD-ROM or published on a Web site. With a digital portfolio, you can present your skills to a greater number of people than you can your paper career portfolio.

YOUR CAREER PORTFOLIO

On the following lines, list the items you want to include in your career portfolio. Think specifically of those items that show your skills, education, and personal accomplishments.

STEP 5: Redefine What Counts as an Interview, and Then Get Two a Day

The average job seeker gets about five interviews a month—fewer than two a week. Yet many job seekers use the methods in this *Quick Job Search* to get two interviews a day. Getting two interviews a day equals 10 a week and 40 a month. That's 800 percent more interviews than the average job seeker gets. Who do you think will get a job offer quicker?

However, getting two interviews a day is nearly impossible unless you redefine what counts as an interview. If you define an interview in a different way, getting two a day is quite possible.

The New Definition of an Interview: Any face-to-face contact with someone who has the authority to hire or supervise a person with your skills—even if no opening exists at the time you talk with him or her.

If you use this new definition, it becomes *much* easier to get interviews. You can now interview with all sorts of potential employers, not just those who have job openings now. While most other job seekers look for advertised or actual openings, you can get interviews before a job opens up or before it is advertised and widely known. You will be considered for jobs that may soon be created but that others will not know about. And, of course, you can also interview for existing openings just as everyone else does.

Spending as much time as possible on your job search and setting a job search schedule are important parts of this step.

Make Your Search a Full-Time Job

Job seekers average fewer than 15 hours a week looking for work. On average, unemployment lasts three or more months, with some people out of work far longer (for example, older workers and higher earners). My many years of experience researching job seeking indicate that the more time you spend on your job search each week, the less time you will likely remain unemployed.

Of course, using the more effective job search methods presented in this minibook also helps. Many job search programs that teach job seekers my basic approach of using more effective methods and spending more time looking have proven that these seekers often find a job in half the average time. More importantly, many job seekers also find better jobs using these methods.

So, if you are unemployed and looking for a full-time job, you should plan to look on a full-time basis. It just makes sense to do so, although many do not, or they start out well but quickly get discouraged. Most job seekers simply don't have a structured plan—they have no idea what they are going to do next Thursday. The plan that follows will show you how to structure your job search like a job.

Decide How Much Time You Will Spend Looking for Work Each Week and Day

First and most importantly, decide how many hours you are willing to spend each week on your job search. You should spend a minimum of 25 hours a week on hard-core job search activities with no goofing around. The following worksheet walks you through a simple but effective process to set a job search schedule for each week.

PLAN YOUR JOB SEARCH WEEK

1. How many hours are you willing to spend each week looking for a job? ______________________
2. Which days of the week will you spend looking for a job? ______________________
3. How many hours will you look each day? ______________________
4. At what times will you begin and end your job search on each of these days? ______________________

____

Create a Specific Daily Job Search Schedule

Having a specific daily schedule is essential because most job seekers find it hard to stay productive each day. The sample daily schedule that follows is the result of years of research into what schedule gets the best results. I tested many schedules in job search programs I ran, and this particular schedule worked best.

Consider using a schedule like this sample daily schedule. Why? Because it works.

A Sample Daily Schedule That Works

Time	*Activity*
7–8 a.m.	Get up, shower, dress, eat breakfast
8–8:15 a.m.	Organize work space, review schedule for today's interviews and promised follow-ups, check e-mail, update schedule as needed
8:15–9 a.m.	Review old leads for follow-up needed today; develop new leads from want ads, yellow pages, the Internet, warm contact lists, and other sources; complete daily contact list
9–10 a.m.	Make phone calls and set up interviews
10–10:15 a.m.	Take a break
10:15–11 a.m.	Make more phone calls, set up more interviews
11 a.m.–Noon	Send follow-up notes and do other office activities as needed
Noon–1 p.m.	Lunch break, relax
1–3 p.m.	Go on interviews, make cold contacts in the field
Evening	Read job search books, make calls to warm contacts not reachable during the day, work on a better resume, spend time with friends and family, exercise, relax

If you are not accustomed to using a daily schedule book or electronic planner, promise yourself to get a good one tomorrow. Choose one that allows for each day's plan on an hourly basis, plus daily to-do lists. Record your daily schedule in advance, and then add interviews as they come. Get used to carrying your planner with you and use it!

You can find a variety of computer programs or pocket-sized electronic schedulers to help organize your job search. If you don't use electronic tools, a simple schedule book and other paper systems will work just fine.

STEP 6: Dramatically Improve Your Interviewing Skills

Interviews are where the job search action is. You have to get them; then you have to do well in them. According to surveys of employers, most job seekers do not effectively present the skills they have to do the job. Even worse, most job seekers can't answer one or more problem questions.

This lack of performance in interviews is one reason why employers will often hire a job seeker who does well in the interview over someone with better credentials. The good news is that you can do simple things to dramatically improve your interviewing skills. This section will emphasize interviewing tips and techniques that make the most difference.

Your First Impression May Be the Only One You Make

Some research suggests that if the interviewer forms a negative impression in the first five minutes of an interview, your chances of getting a job offer approach zero. I know from experience that many job seekers can create a lasting negative impression within seconds.

Tips for Interviewing

Because a positive first impression is so important, I share these suggestions to help you get off to a good start:

- **Make a good impression before you arrive.** Your resume, e-mails, applications, and other written correspondence create an impression before the interview, so make them professional and error-free.
- **Do some homework on the organization before you go.** You can often get information on a business and on industry trends from the Internet or a library.
- **Dress and groom the same way the interviewer is likely to be dressed—but cleaner!** Employer surveys find that almost half of all people's dress or grooming creates an initial negative impression. So this is a big problem. If necessary, get advice on your interviewing outfits from someone who dresses well. Pay close attention to your grooming, too—little things do count.
- **Be early.** Leave in plenty of time to be a few minutes early to an interview.
- **Be friendly and respectful with the receptionist.** Doing otherwise will often get back to the interviewer and result in a quick rejection.
- **Follow the interviewer's lead in the first few minutes.** It's often informal small talk but very important for that person to see how you interact. This is a good time to make a positive comment on the organization or even something you see in the office.
- **Understand that a traditional interview is not a friendly exchange.** In a traditional interview situation, there is a job opening, and you will be one of several applicants for it. In this setting, the employer's task is to eliminate all applicants but one. The interviewer's questions are designed to elicit information that can be used to screen you out. And your objective is to avoid getting screened out. It's hardly an open and honest interaction, is it?

  Setting up interviews before an opening exists eliminates the stress of a traditional interview. In pre-interviews, employers are not trying to screen you out, and you are not trying to keep them from finding out stuff about you. Having said that, knowing how to answer questions that might be asked in a traditional interview is good preparation for any interview you face.
- **Be prepared to answer the tough interview questions.** Your answers to a few key problem questions may determine whether you get a job offer. There are simply too many possible interview questions to cover one by one. Instead, 10 basic questions cover variations of most other interview questions. So, if you can learn to answer the Top 10 Problem Interview Questions well, you will know how to answer most others.
- **Be prepared for the most important interview question of all.** "Why should I hire you?" is the most important question of all to answer well. Do you have a convincing argument why someone should hire you over someone else? If you don't, you probably won't get that job you really want. So think carefully about why someone should hire you and practice your response. Then make sure you communicate this in the interview, even if the interviewer never asks the question in a clear way.

Top 10 Problem Interview Questions

1. **Why should I hire you?**
2. **Why don't you tell me about yourself?**
3. **What are your major strengths?**
4. **What are your major weaknesses?**
5. **What sort of pay do you expect to receive?**
6. **How does your previous experience relate to the jobs we have here?**
7. **What are your plans for the future?**
8. **What will your former employer (or references) say about you?**
9. **Why are you looking for this type of position, and why here?**
10. **Why don't you tell me about your personal situation?**

Follow the Three-Step Process for Answering Interview Questions

I've developed a three-step process for answering interview questions. I know this might seem too simple, but the three-step process is easy to remember and can help you create a good answer to most interview questions. The technique has worked for thousands of people, so consider trying it.

1. **Understand what is really being asked.**

   Most questions are designed to find out about your self-management skills and personality, but interviewers are rarely this blunt. The employer's *real* question is often one or more of the following:

   - Can I depend on you?
   - Are you easy to get along with?
   - Are you a good worker?
   - Do you have the experience and training to do the job if we hire you?
   - Are you likely to stay on the job for a reasonable period of time and be productive?

   Ultimately, if you don't convince the employer that you will stay and be a good worker, it won't matter if you have the best credentials—he or she won't hire you.

2. **Answer the question briefly in a nondamaging way.** Present the facts of your particular work experience as advantages, not disadvantages. Many interview questions encourage you to provide negative information. One classic question I included in my list of Top 10 Problem Interview Questions was "What are your major weaknesses?" This is obviously a trick question, and many people are just not prepared for it.

   A good response is to mention something that is not very damaging, such as *"I have been told that I am a perfectionist, sometimes not delegating as effectively as I might."*

   But your answer is not complete until you continue with the next step.

3. **Answer the real question by presenting your related skills.** Base your answer on the key skills you have that support the job, and give examples to support these skills. For example, an employer might say to a recent graduate, *"We were looking for someone with more experience in this field. Why should we consider you?"* Here is one possible answer:

"I'm sure there are people who have more experience, but I do have more than six years of work experience, including three years of advanced training and hands-on experience using the latest methods and techniques. Because my training is recent, I am open to new ideas and am used to working hard and learning quickly."

In the previous example (about your need to delegate), a good skills statement might be

"I've been working on this problem and have learned to let my staff do more, making sure that they have good training and supervision. I've found that their performance improves, and it frees me up to do other things."

Whatever your situation, learn to answer questions that present you well. It's essential to communicate your skills during an interview, and the three-step process can help you answer problem questions and dramatically improve your responses. It works!

How to Earn a Thousand Dollars a Minute

What do you do when the employer asks, "How much money would it take to get you to join our company?"

Tips on Negotiating Pay

Remember these few essential tips when it comes time to negotiate your pay:

- **The Number 1 Salary Negotiation Rule: The person who names a specific amount first loses.**
- **The only time to negotiate is after you have been offered the job.** Employers want to know how much you want to be paid so that they can eliminate you from consideration. They figure if you want too much, you won't be happy with their job and won't stay. And if you will take too little, they may think you don't have enough experience. So never discuss your salary expectations until an employer offers you the job.
- **If pressed, speak in terms of wide pay ranges.** If you are pushed to reveal your pay expectations early in an interview, ask the interviewer what the normal pay range is for this job. Interviewers will often tell you, and you can say that you would consider offers in this range.

  If you are forced to be more specific, speak in terms of a wide pay range. If you figure that the company will likely pay from $25,000 to $29,000 a year, for example, say that you would consider "any fair offer in the mid- to upper-twenties." This statement covers the employer's range and goes a bit higher. If all else fails, tell the interviewer that you would consider any reasonable offer.

  For this tip to work, you must know in advance what the job is likely to pay. You can get this information by asking people who do similar work, or from a variety of books and Internet sources of career information.
- **If you want the job, you should say so.** This is no time to be playing games.
- **Don't say "no" too quickly.** Never, ever turn down a job offer during an interview! Instead, thank the interviewer for the offer and ask to consider the offer overnight. You can turn it down tomorrow, saying how much you appreciate the offer and asking to be considered for other jobs that pay better or whatever. And it is okay to ask for additional pay or other concessions. But if you simply can't accept the offer, say why and ask the interviewer to keep you in mind for future opportunities. You just never know.

STEP 7: Follow Up on All Job Leads

It's a fact: People who follow up with potential employers and with others in their network get jobs more quickly than those who do not.

Rules for Effective Follow-Up

Here are four rules to guide you in your job search:

- **Send a thank-you note or e-mail to every person who helps you in your job search.**
- **Send the note within 24 hours after speaking with the person.**
- **Enclose JIST Cards with thank-you notes and all other correspondence.**
- **Develop a system to keep following up with good contacts.**

Thank-You Notes Make a Difference

Although thank-you notes can be e-mailed, most people appreciate and are more impressed by a mailed note. Here are some tips about mailed thank-you notes that you can easily adapt to e-mail use:

- You can handwrite or type thank-you notes on quality paper and matching envelopes.
- Keep the notes simple, neat, and error-free.
- Make sure to include a few copies of your JIST Card in the envelope.

Here is an example of a simple thank-you note.

April 5, XXXX

Mr. Kijek,

Thanks so much for your willingness to see me next Wednesday at 9 a.m. I know that I am one of many who are interested in working with your organization. I appreciate the opportunity to meet you and learn more about the position.

I've enclosed a JIST Card that presents the basics of my skills for this job and will bring my resume to the interview. Please call me if you have any questions at all.

Sincerely,

Bruce Vernon

Use Job Lead Cards to Follow Up

If you use contact management software, use it to schedule follow-up activities. But the simple paper system I describe here can work very well or can be adapted for setting up your contact management software.

- Use a simple 3-by-5–inch card to record essential information about each person in your network.
- Buy a 3-by-5–inch card file box and tabs for each day of the month.
- File the cards under the date you want to contact the person.
- Follow through by contacting the person on that date.

Quip

The JibberJobber Web site (www.jibberjobber.com) provides online tools for tracking your contacts.

I've found that staying in touch with a good contact every other week can pay off big. Here's a sample card to give you ideas about creating your own.

ORGANIZATION: Mutual Health Insurance

CONTACT PERSON: Anna Tomey PHONE: 317-355-0216

SOURCE OF LEAD: Aunt Ruth

NOTES: 4/10 Called. Anna on vacation. Call back 4/15. 4/15 Interview set 4/20 at 1:30. 4/20 Anna showed me around. They use the same computers we used in school! (Friendly people.) Sent thank-you note and JIST Card, call back 5/1. 5/1 Second interview 5/8 at 9 a.m.!

In Closing

This is a short book, but it may be all you need to get a better job in less time. I hope this will be true for you, and I wish you well in your search. Remember this: You won't get a job offer because someone knocks on your door and offers one. Job seeking does involve luck, but you are more likely to have good luck if you are out getting interviews.

I'll close this minibook with a few final tips:

- **Approach your job search as if it were a job itself.** Create and stick to a daily schedule, and spend at least 25 hours a week looking.
- **Follow up on each lead you generate and ask each contact for referrals.**
- **Set out each day to schedule at least two interviews.** Remember the new definition of an interview—an interview includes talking to potential employers who don't have an opening now.
- **Send out lots of thank-you notes and JIST Cards.**
- **When you want the job, tell the employer that you want it and why you should be hired over everyone else.**

Don't get discouraged. There are lots of jobs out there, and someone needs an employee with your skills—your job is to find that someone.

I wish you luck in your job search and in your life.

Essential Job Search Data Worksheet

Take some time to complete this worksheet carefully. It will help you write your resume and answer interview questions. You can also photocopy it and take it with you to help complete applications and as a reference throughout your job search. Use an erasable pen or pencil to allow for corrections. Whenever possible, emphasize skills and accomplishments that support your ability to do the job you want. Use extra sheets as needed.

Your name____________________

Date completed____

Job objective____

Key Accomplishments

List three accomplishments that best prove your ability to do the kind of job you want.

1. ____
2. ____
3. ____

Education and Training

Name of high school(s) and specific years attended____________________

Subjects related to job objective____________________________

Related extracurricular activities/hobbies/leisure activities________________

Accomplishments/things you did well__________________________

Specific things you can do as a result_________________________

Schools you attended after high school, specific years attended, and degrees/certificates earned________

Courses related to job objective____________________________

Related extracurricular activities/hobbies/leisure activities________________

Accomplishments/things you did well__________________________

Specific things you can do as a result_________________________

Other Training

Include formal or informal learning, workshops, military training, skills you learned on the job or from hobbies—anything that will help support your job objective. Include specific dates, certificates earned, or other details as needed.____________________________

(continued)

(continued)

Work and Volunteer History

List your most recent job first, followed by each previous job. Military experience, unpaid or volunteer work, and work in a family business should be included here, too. If needed, use additional sheets to cover *all* significant paid or unpaid work experiences. Emphasize details that will help support your new job objective. Include numbers to support what you did: the number of people served over one or more years, number of transactions processed, percentage of sales increased, total inventory value you were responsible for, payroll of the staff you supervised, total budget responsible for, and so on. Emphasize results you achieved, using numbers to support them whenever possible. Mentioning these things on your resume and in an interview will help you get the job you want.

Job 1

Dates employed__________

Name of organization__________

Supervisor's name and job title__________

Address__________

Phone number/e-mail address/Web site__________

What did you accomplish and do well?__________

Things you learned; skills you developed or used__________

Raises, promotions, positive evaluations, awards__________

Computer software, hardware, and other equipment you used__________

Other details that might support your job objective__________

Job 2

Dates employed__________

Name of organization__________

Supervisor's name and job title__________

Address__________

Phone number/e-mail address/Web site__________

What did you accomplish and do well?__________

Things you learned; skills you developed or used__________

Raises, promotions, positive evaluations, awards ________________

Computer software, hardware, and other equipment you used ________________

Other details that might support your job objective ________________

Job 3

Dates employed ________________

Name of organization ________________

Supervisor's name and job title ________________

Address ________________

Phone number/e-mail address/Web site ________________

What did you accomplish and do well? ________________

Things you learned; skills you developed or used ________________

Raises, promotions, positive evaluations, awards ________________

Computer software, hardware, and other equipment you used ________________

Other details that might support your job objective ________________

References

Think of people who know your work well and will be positive about your work and character. Past supervisors are best. Contact them and tell them what type of job you want and your qualifications, and ask what they will say about you if contacted by a potential employer. Some employers will not provide references by phone, so ask them for a letter of reference in advance. If a past employer may say negative things, negotiate what he or she will say or get written references from others you worked with there.

Reference name ________________

Position or title ________________

Relationship to you ________________

Contact information (complete address, phone number, e-mail address) ________________

(continued)

(continued)

Reference name ______________________________

Position or title ______________________________

Relationship to you ______________________________

Contact information (complete address, phone number, e-mail address) ______________________________

____

Reference name ______________________________

Position or title ______________________________

Relationship to you ______________________________

Contact information (complete address, phone number, e-mail address) ______________________________

____

A Short List of Additional Resources

Thousands of books and countless Internet sites provide information on career subjects. Space limitations do not permit me to describe the many good resources available, so I list here some of the most useful ones. Because this is my list, I've included books I've written or that JIST publishes. You should be able to find these and many other resources at libraries, bookstores, and Web bookselling sites.

Resume and Cover Letter Books

My books. *The Quick Resume & Cover Letter Book* is one of the top-selling resume books at various large bookstore chains. It is very simple to follow, is inexpensive, has good design, and has good sample resumes written by professional resume writers. For more in-depth but still quick help, check out my two books in the *Help in a Hurry* series: *Same-Day Resume* (with advice on creating a simple resume in an hour and a better one later) and *15-Minute Cover Letter,* co-authored with Louise Kursmark (offering sample cover letters and tips for writing them fast and effectively).

Other books published by JIST. The following titles include many sample resumes written by professional resume writers, as well as good advice: *Amazing Resumes* by Jim Bright and Joanne Earl; *Cover Letter Magic* by Wendy S. Enelow and Louise M. Kursmark; the entire *Expert Resumes* series by Enelow and Kursmark; *Federal Resume Guidebook* by Kathryn Kraemer Troutman; *Gallery of Best Resumes, Gallery of Best Cover Letters,* and other books by David F. Noble; and *Résumé Magic* by Susan Britton Whitcomb.

Job Search and Interviewing Books

My books. In addition to the books mentioned above, check out *Next-Day Job Interview* (quick tips for preparing for a job interview at the last minute). *The Very Quick Job Search* is a thorough book with detailed advice and a "quick" section of key tips you can finish in a few hours. *Getting the Job You Really Want* includes many activities and good career decision-making and job search advice.

Other books published by JIST. Titles include *Inside Secrets of Finding a Teaching Job* by Warner, Bryan, and Warner; *Insider's Guide to Finding a Job* by Wendy S. Enelow and Shelly Goldman; *Job Search Handbook for People with Disabilities* by Daniel J. Ryan; *Job Search Magic* and *Interview Magic* by Susan Britton Whitcomb; *Ultimate Job Search* by Richard H. Beatty; and *Over-40 Job Search Guide* by Gail Geary.

Books with Information on Jobs

The primary reference books. The *Occupational Outlook Handbook* is the source of job titles listed in this book. Published by the U.S. Department of Labor and updated every other year, the *OOH* covers about 90 percent of the workforce. The *O*NET Dictionary of Occupational Titles* book has descriptions for almost 1,000 jobs based on the O*NET (Occupational Information Network) database developed by the Department of Labor. The *Enhanced Occupational Outlook Handbook* includes the *OOH* descriptions plus more than 7,000 additional descriptions of related jobs from the O*NET and other sources. The *New Guide for Occupational Exploration* allows you to explore major jobs based on your interests.

Other books published by JIST. Here are a few good books that include job descriptions and helpful details on career options: *Overnight Career Choice, Best Jobs for the 21st Century, 50 Best Jobs for Your Personality, 200 Best Jobs for College Graduates, 300 Best Jobs Without a Four-Year Degree, Salary Facts Handbook,* and *Health-Care CareerVision.*

Internet Resources

There are too many Web sites to list, but here are a few places you can start. A book by Anne Wolfinger titled *Best Career and Education Web Sites* gives unbiased reviews of the most helpful sites and ideas on how to use them. *Job Seeker's Online Goldmine,* by Janet Wall, lists the extensive free online job search tools from government and other sources. This book's job descriptions also include Internet addresses for related organizations. Be aware that some Web sites provide poor advice, so ask your librarian, instructor, or counselor for suggestions on those best for your needs.

Other Resources

Libraries. Most libraries have the books mentioned here, as well as many other resources. Most provide Internet access so that you can research online information. Ask the librarian for help finding what you need.

People. People who hold the jobs that interest you are one of the best career information sources. Ask them what they like and don't like about their work, how they got started, and the education or training needed. Most people are helpful and will give advice you can't get any other way.

Career Counseling. A good vocational counselor can help you explore career options. Take advantage of this service if it is available to you! Also consider a career-planning course or program, which will encourage you to be more thorough in your thinking.

Sample Resumes for Some of the Top Computer and Technical Careers

If you read the previous information, you know that I believe you should not depend on a resume alone in your job search. Even so, you will most likely need one, and you should have a good one.

Unlike some career authors, I do not preach that there is only one right way to do a resume. I encourage you to be an individual and to do what you think will work well for you. But I also know that some resumes are clearly better than others. The following pages contain some resumes that you can use as examples when preparing your own resume.

Each resume was written by a professional resume writer who is a member of one or more professional associations. These writers are highly qualified and hold various credentials. Most will provide help (for a fee) and welcome your contacting them (although this is not a personal endorsement).

The resumes appear in books published by JIST Works, including the following:

- *Gallery of Best Resumes* by David F. Noble
- *Gallery of Best Resumes for People Without a Four-Year Degree* by David F. Noble

Contact Information for Resume Contributors

The following professional resume writers contributed resumes to this section. Their names are listed in alphabetical order. Each entry indicates which resume that person contributed.

Ann Baehr
Best Resumes of New York
East Islip, NY 11730
Phone: (631) 314-6871
E-mail: resumesbest@earthlink.net
Web site: www.ebestresumes.com or www.nyresumewriter.com
Member: CMI, NRWA, PARW/CC
Certification: CPRW
Resume on page 357

Beverly Baskin and Mitchell I. Baskin
Baskin Business & Career Services
6 Alberta Dr.
Marlboro, NJ 07746
Also at Iselin, NJ; Princeton, NJ; and Freehold, NJ
Toll-free: (800) 300-4079
Fax: (732) 536-0076
E-mail: bev@bbcscounseling.com
Web site: www.baskincareer.com
Member: NRWA, NCDA, NECA, MACCA, AMHCA, NJCA
Certification: Ed.S., MA, MS, LPC, MCC, CPRW, CCHMC, NCCC, PE, NAJST
Resume on pages 355–356

Janet L. Beckstrom
Word Crafter
1717 Montclair Ave.
Flint, MI 48503
Toll-free: (800) 351-9818
Fax: (810) 232-9257
E-mail: wordcrafter@voyager.net
Member: CMI, PARW/CC
Certification: CPRW
Resume on pages 358–359

Carolyn S. Braden
Braden Resume Solutions
108 La Plaza Drive
Hendersonville, TN 37075
Phone: (615) 822-3317
Fax: (615) 826-9611
E-mail: bradenresume@comcast.net
Member: CMI, PARW/CC
Certification: CPRW
Resume on pages 347–348

Daniel J. Dorotik, Jr.
100PercentResumes
5401 68th St.
Lubbock, TX 79424
Phone: (806) 783-9900
Fax: (806) 993-3757
E-mail: dan@100percentresumes.com
Web site: www.100percentresumes.com
Member: NEWA, PARW/CC
Certification: NCRW
Resume on page 352

MJ Feld
Careers by Choice, Inc.
205 E Main St., Ste. 2-4
Huntington, NY 11743
Phone: (631) 673-5432
Fax: (631) 673-5824
E-mail: mj@careersbychoice.com
Web site: www.careersbychoice.com
Member: PARW/CC
Certification: MS, CPRW
Resume on Page 360

Peter Hill
Distinctive Resumes
Honolulu, HI
Phone: (808) 306-3920
E-mail: distinctiveresumes@yahoo.com
Web site: www.peterhill.biz
Member: CMI, NRWA, PARW/CC
Certification: CPRW
Resume on pages 349–350

Pat Kendall
Advanced Resume Concepts
Tigard, OR 97224
Phone: (503) 639-6098
Toll-free: (800) 591-9143
Fax: (503) 213-6022
E-mail: pat@reslady.com
Web site: www.reslady.com
Member: NRWA
Certification: NCRW, JCTC
Resume on pages 353–354

Vivian VanLier
Advantage Resume & Career Services
6701 Murietta Ave.
Valley Glen, CA 91405
Phone: (818) 994-6655
Fax: (818) 994-6620
E-mail: vvanlier@aol.com
Web site: www.CuttingEdgeResumes.com
Member: CMI, NRWA, PARW/CC
Certifications: CPRW, JCTC, CEIP, CCMC
Resume on page 351

Aircraft and Avionics Equipment Mechanics and Service Technicians

THOMAS A. NABORS 476 Murray Lane • Goodlettsville, TN 00000 • Home (555) 000-0000

AIRCRAFT MAINTENANCE & TECHNOLOGY

FAA-LICENSED A&P MECHANIC with more than 18 years of experience in the maintenance, repair, troubleshooting, and inspection of civilian and military aircraft. Familiar with all Federal Aviation Regulations (FARs). Qualified by experience, education, and training to assume new leadership and supervisory challenges. Expertise includes the following:

Civilian Aircraft:	Saab 340 (A, B, B+ models) – Saab 2000 – British Aerospace Bae-146 100/200 and JS 3100/3200 – Canadair CRJ – Embraer 120/135/145 – ATR-42/72 – DeHavilland Dash-8 – Shorts 360
Military Aircraft:	B-52 (G, H models) – C-130
Airframe Structures:	Sheet Metal – Composite – Painting
Systems:	Electrical Hydraulic – Landing Gear – Instrument – Flight Controls – Pneumatic – Heating/Pressurization – Fuel – Oxygen – Fire Extinguishing
Powerplant:	Turbine Engine – Fuel-Metering Systems – Ignition Systems – Propeller and Governing Systems

PROFESSIONAL EXPERIENCE

READYSTEP AIRTECH (a full-service, FAA Class 4 certified repair station)—Nashville, TN.................1997–Present

Lead Aircraft Maintenance Technician (2001–Present)
- Promoted to manage and schedule work assignments of four Technicians and supervise training and performance. Make certain that Technicians use correct technical data.
- Ensure that planes are inspected according to schedule and are ready by delivery date. Order parts for various aircraft models.
- Follow FARs and airlines' procedures on standard maintenance and custom-requested items.

Aircraft Inspector (2000–2001)
- Evaluated the quality of maintenance and repair work performed by Technicians. Inspected and followed up on completed work and advised supervisor of any problem areas.

Aircraft Maintenance Technician (1997–2000)
- Performed maintenance, troubleshooting, and repair of aircraft systems.

U.S. AIR FORCE—Stationed at various AFBs throughout the country 1986–1997

Advanced through a series of increasingly responsible assignments based on knowledge of aircraft maintenance and repair, technical abilities, and overall performance. Received numerous medals for meritorious service and outstanding achievement throughout military career, including Commendation Medal, Achievement Medal, Outstanding Unit Award, and National Defense Service Medal. Served four years in support of Operation Desert Shield/Desert Storm. Held Secret Security Clearance.

Aircraft Maintenance Supervisor / Crew Chief—Ellsworth AFB, SD (1992–1997)
- Achieved impeccable quality assurance and safety records and was cited for superior after-flight inspections.

Continued . . .

(continued)

(continued)

Thomas A. Nabors

Page 2

PROFESSIONAL EXPERIENCE (continued)

Aircraft Maintenance Supervisor—Wurtsmith AFB, MI (1991–1992)

- Selected for special maintenance position servicing B-52 aircraft for first-strike "real-world" missions in the Persian Gulf during Desert Storm. Inspected and troubleshot all types of problems under time-critical schedules. Twelve planes launched and 17 recovered in 48 hours; 24 ready aircraft launched in only five days.

Aircraft Maintenance Assistant Crew Chief—Fairchild AFB, WA (1987–1991)

- Trained and mentored mechanics servicing B-52H airplanes.
- Member of a team that achieved unprecedented aircraft sortie rates and systems reliability; received consistent 100% pass rates on safety practice evaluations.

Aircraft Maintenance Team Technician—Fairchild AFB, WA (1986–1987)

- Completed on-the-job training program ahead of peers with a final "closed book" test score of 90% in all areas (significantly above unit average).

EDUCATION & PROFESSIONAL DEVELOPMENT

FAA Airframe & Powerplant License, 1994
License #000000000

Aircraft Maintenance Technology
Community College of the Air Force—Maxwell AFB, AL
Successfully completed 110 hours toward A.A.S. degree.

Supervisory Training:
Management & Human Resources Development / Total Quality Concepts, 1993
Introduction to Supervision & Training Management Courses, 1989

Technical Training:
Fam Classes in Saab 340 and ATR 72
Canadair CRJ Training
Weight and Balance & Hazardous Materials Handling Training, 1994
B-52H Engine Operations Certification Training
Aircraft Maintenance (B-52G/H) Crew Chief & Follow-On Training Courses
Aircraft Maintenance Career Development Course (with Honors), 1987
Aircraft Maintenance Technical Training School (160 hours), 1987

Computer Skills:
Sperry Remote Computer Terminal for Maintenance Data Collection
Microsoft Office (Word), Windows 3.1/95/98/Me/2000/XP
Internet navigation and research, e-mail, faxing, scanning

ADDITIONAL INFORMATION

Member of Tennessee Air National Guard (1998–Present)
Maintain and repair C-130H aircraft.

Willing to travel worldwide. Hold current U.S. passport.

Computer and Information Systems Managers

DAVID KENT
5555 Kalanianaole Hwy. • Honolulu, Hawaii 00000
808-555-5555 • dkent@islandemail.com

COMPUTER AND INFORMATION SYSTEMS MANAGER
Administrative Intranets/Public Web Sites/Software Engineering

7+ years of Web planning, development, and administration experience. Thorough knowledge and effective execution of state-of-the-art Internet and intranet systems technology. Proven communication and presentation skills. Easily introduce technical information to project participants and to the public. Project management expertise spans single and multi-institutional organizations, and academia.

- Information and Reporting Systems
- Real-Time Database Management Systems
- IT/Web-Based Media Support
- Scientific Document/Media Support
- Science Communication
- Web/Database Servers
- Project Quality Control
- Content Development

Specializing in the development and implementation of automated and paperless systems for data collection; procedures reporting; information submission, storage, and retrieval; and formal report and Web content production.

RELEVANT EXPERIENCE

RESEARCH CORPORATION OF THE UNIVERSITY OF HAWAII, Honolulu, 1998–Present

Computer and Information Systems Manager (1/2000–Present)
Marine Bioproducts Engineering Center (MarBEC)

Supervise Information and Reporting System (IRS) software development team of up to 8 (2 faculty and 6 students). Establish IRS content management and administrative procedures. Provide comprehensive annual report preparation support, including research updates and timely production and delivery. Plan and meet marketing, IT, and AV requirements of MarBEC-sponsored meetings and symposiums.

- Designed and developed proprietary IRS software, securing $500,000 in additional funding. Anticipated time savings of 40%–60% in annual report content preparation, 80%–90% in research-related Web content publishing. Has potential to save NSF $2.2 million of ERC annual expenditures if fully deployed.
- Completed special project: Culture Collection (CC) database management system resulting in real-time online availability of CC content.
- Delivered Beta version of Annual report Volume II reporting system 8 weeks ahead of schedule. Delivered full system version 1.01 on schedule and within budget.
- Presented several successful Web development and software engineering multimedia seminars: PowerPoint site visit presentations; ERC annual meeting IRS demonstrations; IRS demo to University Information and Computing Sciences (ICS) Department.
- Assisted with planning and production of Fourth Asia-Pacific Marine Biotechnology Conference (produced proceedings and coordinated AV requirements) and Microalgae Production for the Aquaculture Industry Workshop (produced workshop video).

Database/Web Development Specialist (7/1999–1/2000)
MarBEC

Coordinated planning, development, and implementation of Relational Database Management System (RDMS), including time frame for deliverables. Maintained and estimated budgets for subcontracted work and personal assistant. Created Internet and intranet content/applications in support of internal and external activities. Trained users at multiple sites. Developed related standards, policies, and procedures.

(continued)

(continued)

DAVID KENT—COMPUTER AND INFORMATION SYSTEMS MANAGER
Page 2

Computer Specialist III (6/1998–6/1999)
NOAA National Marine Fisheries Service (NMFS) Honolulu Laboratory

Coordinated NMFS Honolulu Laboratory, PIAO, WPCFIN, and Coast Watch Web sites to comply with NOAA standards. Collaborated to develop and implement standards for these and other sub-webs. Established and chaired laboratory's Web committee. Established laboratory's Web presence. Identified, obtained, and published Web site material.

- Designed and developed intranet and Internet Web sites in 6 months, 10 weeks ahead of schedule. Conceptualized and built from scratch NOAA R/V *Townsend Cromwell* student connection outreach Web site.

CHESAPEAKE BAY RESEARCH CONSORTIUM, Annapolis, Maryland, 1995–1998

Environmental Management Fellow
EPA Chesapeake Bay Program (CBP) Office

Worked closely and in coordination with CBP management committee members and other federal, state, and university staff to provide means of publishing and maintaining CBP Web site material.

- Established notable Web presence through coding, designing, and administering intranet and Internet World Wide Web sites. Co-authored CBP *Web Document Guidance.*

TECHNICAL EXPERTISE

HARDWARE: Intel-Based Systems • Macintosh • UNIX • Digital Imaging Devices • Telecommunications • Local Area Networks

SOFTWARE: Operating Systems • HTML • Database/Spreadsheet • Microsoft Project 2000 • Graphics Packages • File Manipulations • E-mail Editors • GIS • FTP • Word Processors • Directory Manipulations • Multimedia Digital Imaging

PROGRAMMING AND CODING PROFICIENCIES/FAMILIARITIES: HTML Editors • XHTML • CSS • JavaScript • Dynamic HTML • SQL • CGI Scripting • Visual Basic • DOM • COM • ColdFusion Markup Language • DTDs • XML • XSL • XSLT

ADDITIONAL TRAINING

Troubleshooting and Maintaining the Macintosh • XML Certification • Web Process and Project Management • Web Site Development and Design • Brochure, Catalog Ad, Newsletter, and Report Design • Graphics and Animation Creation • Data and Information Presentation • Windows-Based Environment Programming

EDUCATION

Bachelor of Science—Oceanography (Mathematics Emphasis), 1992
Humboldt State University, Arcata, California

Computer Programmers

JOHN STRONG

555 South Lynn Road
Pasadena, California 55555

(626) 555-5555
jstrong@email.com

APPLICATIONS PROGRAMMER—VISUAL BASIC

- Technical training plus more than 2 years of experience in program design, development, documentation, implementation and debugging.
- Able to understand and interpret needs of end user to design quality software. Consistent attention to detail with an ability to analyze and interpret the implications of decisions to minimize bugs and create user-friendly programs. Skilled in troubleshooting and problem solving.
- Quick learner who enjoys challenges and possesses a high level of energy and motivation. Dedicated to seeing projects through to completion.
- Experienced collaborating with clients and team members. Ability to convey technical information at all levels.

Computer Applications: *Visual Basic... ADO... SQL... Crystal Reports... Windows... Word... Excel... Access... Outlook... FoxPro... Citrix... PC Anywhere... HTML (basic knowledge)... Internet*

PROFESSIONAL EXPERIENCE

Application Programmer • 2001 to Present
APPLICATION LEADERS, INC., Pasadena, CA
Write programs in Visual Basic for company providing software solutions to manufacturing industry.
Representative Projects:

- Created, debugged and perfected entry screens for new release of company's main product.
- Produced reports providing critical information on gross profit, inventory transactions/projections, sales forecasts and purchase requirements.
- Wrote program to read EDI documents and generate sales-related reports.
- Collaborated on development of program that enables manufacturer to directly transfer orders to banks for approval using FTP.
- Developed customized programs to meet customer needs.

EDUCATION

PASADENA CITY COLLEGE, Pasadena, CA
Associate of Arts, Social Science May 2003
Honors: Deans List, Honors for Superior Achievement in Economics Award

COMPUTER LEARNING CENTER, Los Angeles, CA
Certificate in Client/Server Programming 2001
Relevant Course Work: Visual Basic, Integrating a Visual Basic Front-End with a SQL Server Back-End, Access, C, C++, Oracle, Client/Server Architecture
Honors: Awarded National Vocational Technical Honors Society Membership

UCLA EXTENSION, Los Angeles, CA, 2002
ActiveX Component Development with Visual Basic 6

Computer Software Engineers

RICHARD LEVINSON
0000 Preston Avenue ◆ Houston, TX 77000 ◆ (281) 000-0000 ◆ myname@aol.com

Career Target: Software Programmer / Software Engineer

PROFILE

Talented software programmer with BBA degree, strong educational background in programming, and experience using cutting-edge development tools. Articulate and professional communication skills, including formal presentations and technical documentation. Productive in both team-based and self-managed projects; dedicated to maintaining up-to-date industry knowledge and IT skills.

Knowledge & Skill Areas:

- Software Development Lifecycle
- Object-Oriented Programming
- Problem Analysis & Resolution
- Web Site Design & Development
- Requirements Gathering & Analysis
- Technical & End User Documentation
- Software Testing & Troubleshooting
- Project Teamwork & Communications

TECHNICAL SUMMARY

Languages:	Java, C, C++, JSP, ASP, Rational, HTML, SQL, Unified Process
Operating Systems:	Linux, Windows XP/2000/9x
Object-Oriented Design:	UML, Design Patterns

EDUCATION

TEXAS UNIVERSITY, Houston, TX
Bachelor of Business Administration in Computer Science, 2002

- Earned place on President's List for 3 semesters (4.0 GPA)
- Member, Golden Key National Honor Society & Honors Fraternity
- Selected for listing in *Who's Who Among Students in American Universities and Colleges*

Relevant Coursework:

- Software Engineering
- Project Management
- Database Design
- Systems Engineering
- Differential Equations
- Classical / Modern Physics
- Calculus I, II, III
- Logic Circuits
- Systems Analysis

Project Highlights:

- **Software Engineering**—Served as Design Team Leader and member of Programming group for semester-long project involving development of software for actual implementation within Texas University Recreation Center. Determined requirements, created "look and feel" for user interface, and maintained explicit written documentation.
- **Systems Engineering**—Teamed with group of 4 in conceptualizing and designing client-server application to interconnect POS and inventory systems for retail outlet, delivering class presentation that highlighted specifications and projected $2 million in cost savings.

COMMUNITY COLLEGE, Houston, Texas

- 3.96 GPA / Concentration in Computer Science coursework

EXPERIENCE

DATAFRAME CONCEPTS, L.L.C., Houston, TX 2000–Present
Software Developer

- Worked with small team of developers to brainstorm and implement ideas for shipping/receiving software representing leading-edge concept within transportation industry.
- Planned and initiated redesign of existing standalone application, utilizing object-oriented design/programming and Java in creating thin-client GUI for new distributed system.
- Collaborated with marketing director in strategies to further business growth, including Web site enhancement that drove 65% increase in visitor interest for product offering.

** References and additional information will gladly be provided upon request.*

Computer Support Specialists and Systems Administrators

FRANKLIN JOHNSON, MCSE

55555 55th Avenue ▪ Cell (555) 555-3925
Tigard, Oregon 97224 ▪ Home (555) 555-2953
www.careerfolio.com/mcse ▪ fjohnson@careerfolio.com

NETWORK ADMINISTRATION / IS MANAGEMENT

Professional Profile

Service-driven IT professional with 13 years of experience in network administration, system maintenance, technical troubleshooting, team building, and infrastructure planning. Reputation for creative problem solving and effectiveness in resource management and cost control. Broad experience with diverse enterprise and network systems and remote administration.

- **Dedicated Team Leader:** Skilled in building motivated teams and supervising engineering and support staff in complex business and technical environments. Solid experience in coaching, staff training, goal setting, and performance evaluation.
- **Strategic Technology Planner:** Successful at developing long-range plans and managing application integration / data networking projects across multiple platforms. Current knowledge of emerging technologies such as VPN, wireless, office automation, data communications, and SAN.
- **Seasoned Project Manager:** Organized and detail-oriented. Able to work under tight deadline pressure and consistently meet deadlines and quality goals. Accustomed to managing multiple projects and priorities in fast-paced, high-performance environments.

Certifications

MCSE—Windows NT4

MCSE—Windows 2003

Experience

ABCO SYSTEMS—Salem, Oregon

Advanced Systems Administrator / Team Lead (7/05–Present)

- Coordinate the delivery of server engineering support and supervise the design of server solutions for multiple departments. Oversee and maintain 847 servers.
- Use Microsoft Virtual Server and VM Ware ESX Server to design test environments and consolidate servers.
- Acquired extensive experience with SAN storage solutions, external storage arrays, data center operations, RAID configurations, firewall / security implementation projects, and small wireless LAN support.

Network Operations Supervisor (3/01–7/05)

- Managed and developed a team of 23 network engineers.
- Supervised the maintenance of 70+ Windows NT and Novell servers supporting a user base of 1,900 in Oregon, Washington, Alaska, Hawaii, California, Utah, Arizona, and Colorado.
- Maintained a SAN (80 servers) and related hardware. Installed and configured Novell 3.x / 4.x, Windows NT4, and Windows 2000 servers and clients.
- Updated network systems.

—CONTINUED—

(continued)

(continued)

FRANKLIN JOHNSON, MCSE

PAGE TWO

Experience *(continued)*

ADVO COMPUTER CORPORATION—Houston, Texas

Software Test Developer (Contract, 5/99–2/01)

- Developed test procedures for a line of laptop computers to ensure compatibility with multiple operating systems and hardware.
- Operating systems: Windows 95, Windows XP, Windows Server 2000, OS/2. Network operating systems: Novell 6.x, Microsoft Peer-to-Peer, Banyan VINES

AMERICAN DIGITAL SOLUTIONS—Irvine, California

Computer Technician / Technical Support Team (1/98–4/99)

- Provided technical support for end users (in-house, over the telephone, and online).
- Supported American Digital's line of hard disk drives; Windows, Windows NT, OS/2, Novell NetWare, and UNIX.

COMPUTER SOLUTIONS—Santa Ana, California

Computer Consultant (Contract, 12/95–1/98)

- Analyzed needs of small- to medium-sized firms to ensure optimum cost efficiency and productive use of applications and data processing, networking, and data communication systems.
- Developed custom configurations and installed IBM and Macintosh systems, standalone PCs, local-area Novell Networks, computer bulletin board systems (BBS), and Internet solutions.
- Provided onsite training and user support.

REQUIM CORPORATION—Irvine, California

Production Lead, Injection Molding (2/93–11/95)

- Oversaw department operations and capacity planning functions.
- Established production goals, prepared budget, and ensured that all quality, yield, and production standards were met.
- Supervised, scheduled, trained, and evaluated a 27-person injection molding crew.

Education

IRVINE COMMUNITY COLLEGE—Portland, Oregon

B.S. Mathematics (1993)

PROFESSIONAL DEVELOPMENT

- AC Nielsen Burke Institute: Tools and Techniques of Data Analysis
- AC Nielsen Burke Institute: Translating Data into Actionable Information
- Institute for International Research: Choice-Based Modeling Essentials
- Team Building: Improving Decision-Making Effectiveness
- Total Quality Management: Implementing, Leading, and Managing the Continuous Improvement Process
- Deming: Quality, Productivity, and Competitive Position
- Dale Carnegie: Effective Speaking and Human Relations
- Covey: Leadership Workshop / Seven Habits of Highly Effective People
- McNellis: Team Dynamics and Problem Solving

Engineering and Natural Sciences Managers

Martin G. Morrison III, P.E., L.S.

234 Laurel Court • Freehold, NJ 07728 • 732.555.5555 (H & F)

PROJECT MANAGER / ENGINEERING

Professional Engineer ~ Professional Planner ~ Professional Land Surveyor

Competencies Include

- Engineering Management
- Inspection Bonding
- Municipal/Township Engineering
- Budget Management
- Storm Water Management
- Planning/Zoning Board Reviews
- Sanitary Sewer Design
- Site Development
- Staff Training/Motivation/Development
- Project Management

Profile

Results-oriented Professional Engineer and Manager...known for technical resourcefulness and creativity...interact with governmental agencies, privately owned businesses, and individuals.

Professional Experience

MARCO ENGINEERING AND LAND SURVEYING, *New York, NY (2000–Present)*
Vice President

Management and supervision of field survey crews and office personnel. Performed analysis of field work; prepared field schedules, topographical mapping, and right-of-way appropriation maps. Clients included the New York State Department of Transportation, the New York State Throughway Authority, the Metro-North Commuter Railroad, and the New York City Department of Design and Construction.

- Survey Project Manager for the LIRR East Side Access Project to Grand Central Station. This project employed a unique method of construction. Managed the scheduling, quality, and coordination of rail and topographic surveys with the Tunnel and Systems consultant.
- Managed the design survey for a noise barrier on the Grand Central Parkway, completing the project on time and within budget.
- Project Manager for the utility survey of the JFK Air Train Project for the Port Authority of NY/NJ. This project integrated light rail service between JFK Airport and New York City.
- Supervised the MTA-NYC Transit system project for a topographic, utility, and property survey of 12 subway stations in preparation for ADA improvements.
- Directed the site surveys for the New York State Department of Transportation on the following projects:
  - Completed the Hutchinson River Parkway safety improvements project on time and within budget. Prepared an Abstract Request Map for property acquisition for a pedestrian bridge, and a survey for ground photo controls using GPS, 3-D with GPS, and Einstein Loop.
  - The FDR Drive main roadways and service roads including a hydrographic survey of the East River for bulkhead treatment.
  - The rebuilding and rehabilitation of 3 bridges on I-95, requiring bridge structure surveys and roadway cross-sections.
  - The re-signing of the Henry Hudson Parkway from 72nd Street to Westchester County. Directed the topographic survey, the photogram metric survey, the ground survey, and the survey control report.
  - Supervised mapping of the Cross Bronx Expressway Right-of-Way, preparation of Abstract Request Maps for property acquisition, and a Right-of-Way report.
  - Successfully completed the survey of 3 bridges as part of the Van Wyck Expressway widening project.
- Project Manager for the New York City Department of Environmental Protection's Westchester Creek CSO Detention Site Preparation Survey, which was completed on time and within budget. Directed preparation of the site survey, the title search, and setting of the property corners.

(continued)

(continued)

Page Two MARTIN G. MORRISON III, P.E., L.S.

Professional Experience *(Continued)*

CORMAN ENGINEERING, HIGHTSTOWN, NJ (1997–2000)
Project Manager
- As consultant to Marlboro Township, supervised inspections, bonded item compliance, bond reduction, billing, and recommendation for bond release.
- Managed the site-development surveys for a variety of projects in order to obtain final approvals from the Planning Board, Department of Environmental Protection, and other applicable agencies. Projects included an Assisted Living facility, a franchise restaurant, and a townhouse community.
- Responsible for the surveying and engineering of Sewer and Water Extensions, Stream Encroachment, Soil Conservation Service, Soil Erosion, and Sediment Control.

L & F ASSOCIATES, MIDDLETOWN, NJ (1995–1996)
Principal Engineer

Consulting Engineering assignment as Assistant Township Engineer for Holmdel Township.
- Supervised the administration and inspection of active bonded projects of 16 subdivisions and 21 site plans.
- Prepared estimates to determine quantities for bonded projects.
- Reviewed plans for Planning Board compliance.
- Provided day-to-day response to residential complaints and inquiries.

As the in-house Bonding Specialist, represented L & F at various Planning and Zoning Boards throughout New Jersey for plan review and meeting participation.

LOMAN, CARMICHAEL, GIFFORD & KASE, BRICK, NJ (1986–1994)
Associate, Project Manager

Managed the site-development engineering and surveys for several types of projects. Obtained approvals from local Planning and Zoning Boards, as well as other government agencies.
- Provided a unique roadway and log design for the Knob Hill Development, Howell Township, NJ, consisting of 24 homes. The road, lot grading, and detention area were constructed without affecting a wetland area in the middle of the site.
- Supervised engineering, surveying, and final approvals for the Shore Oaks Golf Course Development in Howell Township, NJ. The 450-acre site included 170 single-family homes and an 18-hole golf course. The project required a zoning change and offsite utility extensions for sewer, water, gas, and electric.
- Completed the site plan and survey for a 50,000-square-foot commercial warehouse, which involved wetlands delineation, stream encroachment applications, and sanitary sewer extensions to the site.

HAMMOND, FREEHOLD, NJ (1982–1986)
Corporate Engineer
- Responsible for the coordination and design of all corporate land-development projects.
- Managed the activities of in-house personnel, and supervised the coordination of outside contractors.
- Designed and directed the planning of water and sewer extensions, pumping stations, production wells, and water towers of the Adelphia Water & Sewer companies.

BOROUGH OF FREEHOLD, FREEHOLD, NJ (1975–1982)
Assistant Engineer
- Prepared plans and specifications for all contract work.
- Inspected and supervised all construction, maintenance, and repair work on streets, curbs, sidewalks, and drainage systems.
- In charge of maintaining the municipal tax maps and all surveying required for construction, reconstruction, and modifications to borough streets.

Education and Certifications

BS ~ Civil Engineering, *NEW JERSEY INSTITUTE OF TECHNOLOGY*, Newark, NJ
Licensed Professional Engineer—NJ, NY, PA, and CT
Licensed Professional Land Surveyor—NJ and NY
Licensed Professional Planner—NJ

Medical, Dental, and Ophthalmic Laboratory Technicians

LORI GREEN

55 Southern Bend Way
Brentwood, New York 22222
(555) 555-0000 • labtech@health.com

LABORATORY TECHNICIAN

PROFESSIONAL EXPERIENCE

Laboratory Technician — **1986–present**
Briarcliff Medical Center, The Islips, New York — **Evening Shift**

▶ ***Profile***

- ♦ 20+ years of comprehensive in-service training and experience managing multifaceted laboratory functions; A.A.S., Medical Laboratory Technology.
- ♦ Broadly cross-trained in areas that include, but are not limited to, hematology, phlebotomy and blood-bank procedures interfacing directly with professional staff and patients in ER, ICU, OR and Recovery.
- ♦ Perform and interpret laboratory tests, demonstrating a keen ability to identify and correct discrepancies; record and communicate test results.
- ♦ Recognized for ability to organize, prioritize, coordinate and perform tasks concurrently during periods of limited staffing and supervision.
- ♦ Ensure quality control of laboratory procedures, staff communication, equipment functionality, and OSHA/FDA compliance.
- ♦ Render in-house and off-site phlebotomy services utilizing exceptional organizational, time-management and interpersonal skills.
- ♦ Effectively train personnel in all areas of laboratory procedures; coordinate staff schedules; maintain timely and accurate computerized data entry.

▶ ***Diagnostic Testing***

- – Hematology
- – Phlebotomy
- – Blood Bank
- – Bone Marrow Slides
- – Urinalysis
- – Coagulation
- – Chemistry
- – Serology

▶ ***In-service Training***
15 years, ongoing

- – CPR
- – Vital Signs
- – Venipuncture
- – Specimen Handling
- – Infection Control
- – Fire and Safety
- – Information Systems
- – OSHA/FDA

▶ ***Equipment***

- – Beckman CX3, CX7
- – TDX
- – IMX
- – Hemo-Cell-Dyne 1600
- – Coulter S+4
- – Coulter T-660

Secretary, Computer Department, Storage Warehouse — **1978–1986**
Space Savers, The Islips, New York

- ♦ Provided secretarial support in areas of typing and customer service.
- ♦ Operated and maintained functionality of IBM and Hitachi mainframes to ensure accurate and timely processing of sensitive government information.
- ♦ Organized, labeled and supervised the release of tape inventory.

EDUCATION

Bachelor of Science, Medical Laboratory Technology, 1987
Stony Brook University, Stony Brook, New York

Occupational Therapists

Rebecca T. Ferguson, OTR/L
2418 Magnolia Street
Atlanta, GA 30344

fergie@isp.com
Residence: 404-555-5822
Cellular: 319-555-8492

Professional Highlights

- ❖ Highly skilled Registered Occupational Therapist whose record speaks for itself. Extensive clinical experience complemented by additional experience educating students, health-care providers, patients and the general public.
- ❖ Intimately involved in start-up of innovative hospital-based rehab program that has increased elective surgeries and improved patient outcomes.
- ❖ Maintain competency in all treatment modalities, including ultrasound, phonopherisis, electric stimulation and various massage techniques.
- ❖ Passionate about providing the best possible patient care leading to independence.
- ❖ Challenge-driven . . . dynamic . . . creative . . . mature work ethic.

Employment History

FIRST CHOICE • Atlanta, Georgia 2005–Present

Director of Rehab

- Manage all aspects of contractual department within a 79-bed skilled nursing facility providing short- and long-term care, primarily to geriatric patients. Tripled case load within months of hire.
- Hire, train, schedule and manage staff. Develop and monitor budgets and financial performance.
- Collaborate with medical staff to identify patients' RUG levels. Also provide direct patient care.
- Act as liaison with facility's administrator.

MERCY HOSPITAL • Iowa City, Iowa 2000–2005

Staff Occupational Therapist

Inpatient, Transitional and Acute Care

- Provided OT treatment for full case load of patients. Participated in treatment and discharge planning as well as patient assessment. Communicated with patients and their families. Conducted patient teaching and facilitated understanding of the rehab process.
- Performed occupational therapy in outpatient and pediatric units as needed.

Joint Care Team (JCT)

- Represented OT during development and launch of Joint Care, a wellness-based and patient-directed recovery program for elective surgery of the knees and hips focusing on preoperative education, personalized pain management and advanced therapy techniques.
- Collaborated with other members of the JCT to present orientation/education class for patients. Met with patients individually to assess home setting and make equipment recommendations.
- Followed up with patients within two days of surgery to evaluate status and design OT treatment plan. Assisted with delivering OT services to patients individually and in groups.

Professional Service

- *Up Team (UT)*—Incorporated uplifting strategies into daily activities that impacted patients and staff. Encouraged communication between disciplines, leading to greater independence for patients. Cultivated positive attitudes that resulted in more positive outcomes.
- *Health & Safety*—As Rehabilitation representative, responded to patient codes facility-wide. Prepared Rehab department for JCAHO and CARF accreditation visits. Conducted drills and quarterly inspections. Generated reports for the facility's Health & Safety commissioner.
- *Functional Independence Measures (FIM)*—Educated new rehab employees and other disciplines on assessment process to maximize consistency of scores between evaluators.
- *Chart Audit*—Reviewed 30 randomly selected charts for adherence to JCAHO guidelines.

- continued -

Rebecca T. Ferguson 404-555-5822

Employment History

MERCY HOSPITAL • Iowa City, Iowa

Staff Occupational Therapist (continued)

Professional Service

- *Team Conference Committee*—Championed the introduction of this multidisciplinary team that rounded three times per week and saw every patient at least once per week. The open-forum concept facilitated communication between health-care providers, patients and their families.
- *Rehab Recognition Awards*—Cochaired committee responsible for evaluating nominations and recognizing outstanding performance of staff members.
- *Spinal Cord Injury*—Mentored into involvement with program and subsequently became the facility's informal "spinal cord expert." Completed ongoing self-study to improve clinical knowledge. Participated in planning and strategy meetings.
- *CARE Club*—Conceived concept and introduced activities to boost morale and build camaraderie among employees in Rehabilitation department.

EASTERN IOWA COMMUNITY COLLEGE • Cedar Rapids, Iowa 2001–2005

Instructor (part-time)

- Taught classes and delivered guest lectures in ACOTE-certified OTA program.

SELECT CARE HOME HEALTH CARE • Coralville, Iowa 2004–2005
HEARTHSIDE • Hills, Iowa & 1999–2000

Home Health Therapist

BAY MEDICAL CENTER • Bay City, Michigan 1998–1999

Staff Occupational Therapist

Education

COE COLLEGE • Davenport, Iowa

Bachelor of Occupational Therapy 1997

Certifications

- ❖ Occupational Therapist-Registered—National Board for Certification in Occupational Therapy
- ❖ Licensed Occupational Therapist—State of Georgia
- ❖ Registered Occupational Therapist—State of Iowa
- ❖ Licensed Occupational Therapist—State of Michigan
- ❖ Level 1 Reiki Certificate—The International Center for Reiki Training

Community Service

- ❖ *Iowa Adaptive Golf*—Helped disabled people of all ages participate in the sport of golf. Delivered programs that provided golf professionals with knowledge, strategies and tools to teach the disabled. Provided clinics for disabled golfers.
- ❖ *Safe Kids Coalition of Southeast Iowa*—Instructed new parents and family members in the correct usage of infant car seats. Certified by National Highway Safety and Transportation Department.
- ❖ *Eastern Iowa Community College Advisory Board*—Participated in student recruitment and strategic planning for OT program.
- ❖ *Arthritis on the Golf Course*—As guest speaker, delivered presentation to symposium sponsored by the Arthritis Foundation of Iowa.

Registered Nurses

Sara Applebaum, RN

55 Prince Avenue, Northport, New York 11768 ▪ *residence* (555) 555-5555 ▪ *cellular* (555) 555-5555

Career Interest: School Nursing

Offering a gentle disposition combined with strong diagnostic skills.
Physical Assessments—Safety & Public Health—Healthcare Documentation

NURSING EXPERIENCE

Registered Nurse, January 2005–Present. Syosset Community Hospital, Syosset, NY

- In a 40-bed medical-surgical unit, care for patients with a variety of medical conditions, including pre- and postoperative status.
- Conduct physical assessments, including evaluation of heart and lung functioning.
- Provide complete wound care and manage medicine administration through all modalities: oral, central line, intravenous, intramuscular, subcutaneous, and peg-tube routes.
- Attend to psychiatric patients temporarily placed on the unit. Assess cognitive/psychological states and implement detoxification protocols.
- Instruct family members on proper adjunctive support, including preventive care and medicine administration.
- Maintain accurate patient records in accordance with HIPAA regulations.
- Collaborate with physicians to assist in treatment plans.

Registered Nurse *(per diem),* April 2005–Present. Maria Regina Infirmary, Brentwood, NY

- Through physical and mental assessments, provide healthcare support to the residents of this convent.
- Evaluate environment for safety and comfort issues. Suggest and implement strategies for accident prevention.
- Handle medical crises with accountability for determining the proper course of action. Evaluate injuries and other medical issues and contact physicians or coordinate transfers to hospitals as warranted.
- Document all interventions and noteworthy events.

Nurse-in-Training Fieldwork, 2002–2004. St. John's Hospital, Huntington Hospital, Northport Veterans' Psychiatric Hospital, Syosset Community Hospital, and Nassau Community College Health Clinic.

- Participated in comprehensive clinical rotations, including the pediatrics unit at Syosset Community Hospital. Under supervision, evaluated children with the following conditions: asthma, dehydration, pre- and postop tonsillectomy, appendicitis, and hernia. Administered medicines PO and IM.

ADDITIONAL EXPERIENCE

Funeral Director, 1991–2001. Sunset Funeral Chapels, Deer Park, NY

- Coordinated all funeral plans for grieving families.
- Provided compassionate support, interacting with family members in an empathic, caring way.
- Conceptualized and completed several initiatives, including a reorganization of the office files and a child-friendly area within the chapel.

EDUCATION & TRAINING

Associate in Applied Science, Nursing (2004). Nassau County Community College, Garden City, NY

Associate in Applied Science (1990). SUNY Farmingdale, Farmingdale, NY

Certificate in Cardiopulmonary Resuscitation, *current*

Part IV

Important Trends in Jobs and Industries

In putting this section together, my objective was to give you a quick review of major labor market trends. To accomplish this, I included three excellent articles that originally appeared in U.S. Department of Labor publications.

The first article is "Tomorrow's Jobs." It provides a superb—and short—review of the major trends that will affect your career in the years to come. Read it for ideas on selecting a career path for the long term.

The second article is "Employment Trends in Major Industries." While you may not have thought much about it, the industry you work in is just as important as your occupational choice. This great article will help you learn about major trends affecting various industries.

The third article, "STEM Occupations: High-Tech Jobs for a High-Tech Economy," tells you about STEM occupations and their earnings, educational requirements, and job prospects. It can also help you find out how to prepare for a STEM career and where to find more information.

Tomorrow's Jobs

Making informed career decisions requires reliable information about opportunities in the future. Opportunities result from the relationships between the population, the labor force, and the demand for goods and services.

Population ultimately limits the size of the labor force—individuals working or looking for work—which limits the goods and services that can be produced. Demand for various goods and services is largely responsible for employment in the industries providing them. Employment opportunities, in turn, result from demand for skills needed within specific industries. Opportunities for medical assistants and other healthcare occupations, for example, have surged in response to rapid growth in demand for health services.

Examining the past and present and projecting changes in these relationships are the foundation of the Occupational Outlook Program. This chapter presents highlights of the Bureau of Labor Statistics' projections of the labor force and occupational and industry employment that can help guide your career plans.

Population

Population trends affect employment opportunities in a number of ways. Changes in population influence the demand for goods and services. For example, a growing and aging population has increased the demand for health services. Equally important, population changes produce corresponding changes in the size and demographic composition of the labor force.

The U.S. civilian noninstitutional population is expected to increase by 21.8 million over the 2006–2016 period (Chart 1). The 2006–2016 rate of growth is slower than the growth rate over the 1986–1996 and 1996–2006 periods—9 percent, 11 percent, and 13 percent, respectively. Continued growth, however, will mean more consumers of goods and services, spurring demand for workers in a wide range of occupations and industries. The effects of population growth on various occupations will differ. The differences are partially accounted for by the age distribution of the future population.

Chart 1. **Numeric change in the population and labor force, 1986–1996, 1996–2006, and projected 2006–2016**

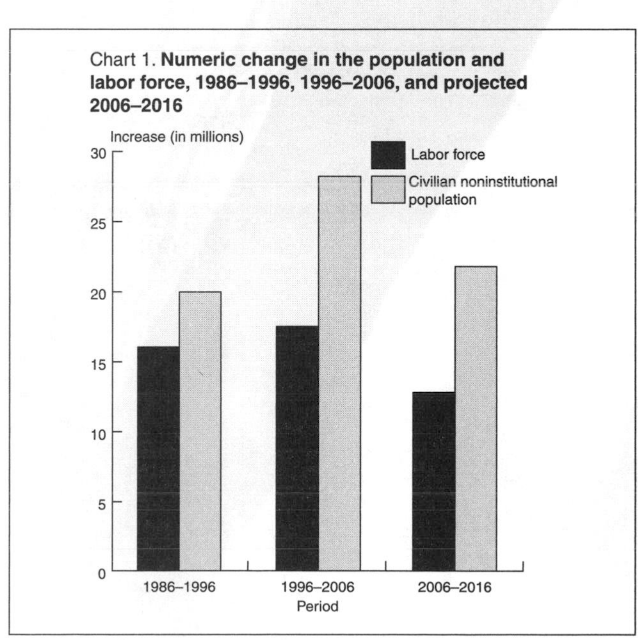

As the baby boomers continue to age, the 55-to-64 age group will increase by 30.3 percent or 9.5 million persons, more than any other group. The 35-to-44 age group will decrease by 5.5 percent, reflecting a slowed birth rate following the baby boom generation, while the youth population, aged 16 to 24, will decline 1.1 percent over the 2006–2016 period.

Minorities and immigrants will constitute a larger share of the U.S. population in 2016. The numbers of Asians and people of Hispanic origin are projected to continue to grow much faster than other racial and ethnic groups.

Labor Force

Population is the single most important factor in determining the size and composition of the labor force—people either working or looking for work. The civilian labor force is projected to increase by 12.8 million, or 8.5 percent, to 164.2 million over the 2006–2016 period.

The U.S. workforce will become more diverse by 2016. White, non-Hispanic persons will continue to make up a decreasing share of the labor force, falling from 69.1 percent in 2006 to 64.6 percent in 2016 (Chart 2). However, despite relatively slow growth, white non-Hispanics will remain the overwhelming majority of the labor force. Hispanics are projected to be the fastest-growing ethnic group, growing by 29.9 percent. By 2016, Hispanics will continue to constitute an increasing proportion of the labor force, growing from 13.7 percent to 16.4 percent. Asians are projected to account for an increasing share of the labor force by 2016, growing from 4.4 to 5.3 percent. Blacks will also increase their share of the labor force, growing from 11.4 percent to 12.3 percent.

The numbers of men and women in the labor force will grow, but the number of women will grow at a slightly faster rate than the number of men. The male labor force is projected to grow by 8.0 percent from 2006 to 2016, compared with 8.9 percent for women, down from 12.7 and 13.4 percent, respectively, from 1996 to 2006. As a result, men's share of the labor force is expected to decrease from 53.7 to 53.4 percent, while women's share is expected to increase from 46.3 to 46.6 percent.

Chart 2. **Percentage of labor force by race and ethnic origin, 2006 and projected 2016**

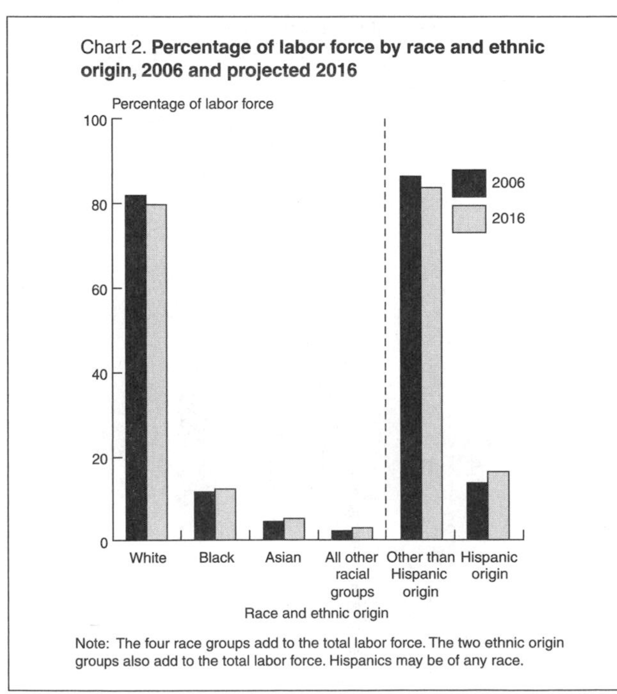

Note: The four race groups add to the total labor force. The two ethnic origin groups also add to the total labor force. Hispanics may be of any race.

Chart 3. **Percentage of labor force by age group, 2006 and projected 2016**

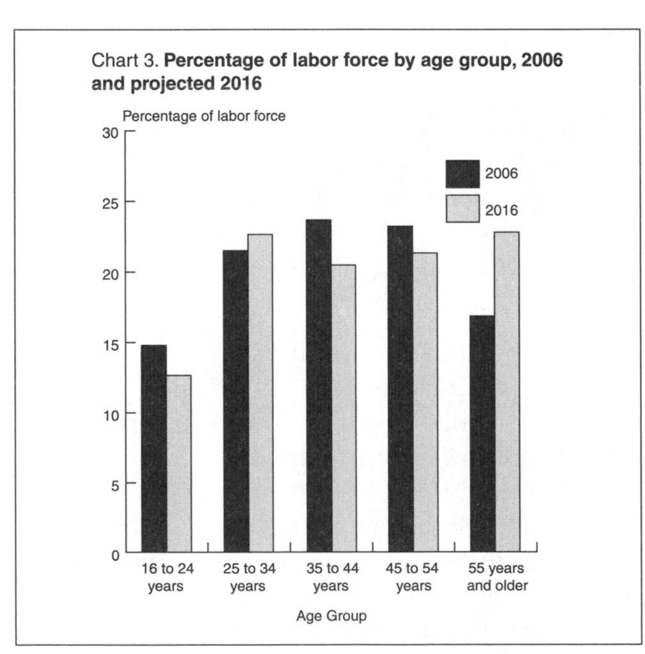

The youth labor force, aged 16 to 24, is expected to decrease its share of the labor force to 12.7 percent by 2016. The primary working age group, between 25 and 54 years old, is projected to decline from 68.4 percent of the labor force in 2006 to 64.6 percent by 2016. Workers 55 and older, on the other hand, are projected to leap from 16.8 percent to 22.7 percent of the labor force between 2006 and 2016 (Chart 3). The aging of the baby boom generation will cause not only an increase in the percentage of workers in the oldest age category, but a decrease in the percentage of younger workers.

Employment

Total employment is expected to increase from 150.6 million in 2006 to 166.2 million in 2016, or by 10 percent. The 15.6 million jobs that will be added by 2016 will not be evenly distributed across major industrial and occupational groups. Changes in consumer demand, technology, and many other factors will contribute to the continually changing employment structure in the U.S. economy.

The following two sections examine projected employment change from industrial and occupational perspectives. The industrial profile is discussed in terms of primary wage and salary employment. Primary employment excludes secondary jobs for those who hold multiple jobs. The exception is employment in agriculture, which includes self-employed and unpaid family workers in addition to wage and salary workers.

The occupational profile is viewed in terms of total employment—including primary and secondary jobs for wage and salary, self-employed, and unpaid family workers. Of the roughly 150 million jobs in the U.S. economy in 2006, wage and salary workers accounted for 138.3 million, self-employed workers accounted for 12.2 million, and unpaid family workers accounted for about 130,000. Secondary employment accounted for 1.8 million jobs. Self-employed workers held nearly 9 out of 10 secondary jobs and wage and salary workers held most of the remainder.

Industry

Service-providing industries. The long-term shift from goods-producing to service-providing employment is expected to continue. Service-providing industries are expected to account for approximately 15.7 million new wage and salary jobs generated over the 2006–2016 period (Chart 4), while goods-producing industries will see overall job loss.

Education and health services. This industry supersector is projected to grow by 18.8 percent and add more jobs, nearly 5.5 million, than any other industry supersector. More than 3 out of every 10 new jobs created in the U.S. economy will be in either the healthcare and social assistance or public and private educational services sectors.

Health care and social assistance—including public and private hospitals, nursing and residential care facilities, and individual and family services—will grow by 25.4 percent and add 4 million new jobs. Employment growth will be driven by increasing demand for health care and social assistance because of an aging population and longer life expectancies. Also, as more women enter the labor force, demand for childcare services is expected to grow.

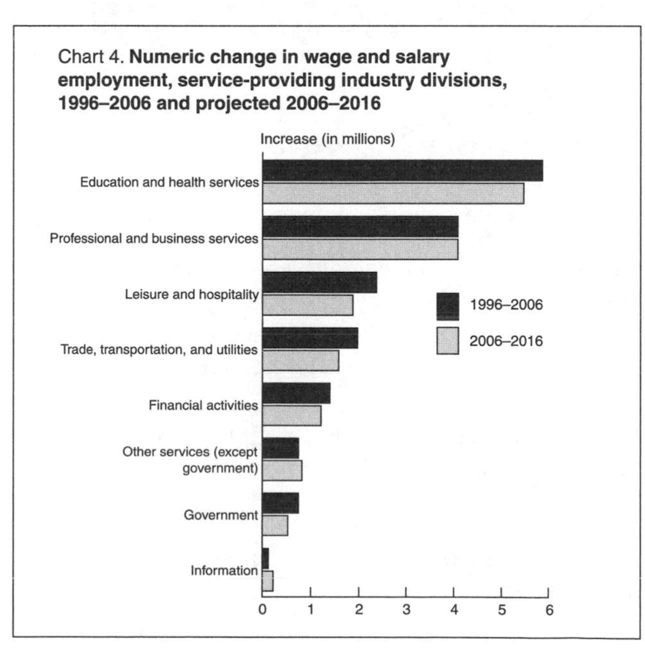

Public and private educational services will grow by 10.7 percent and add 1.4 million new jobs through 2016. Rising student enrollments at all levels of education will create demand for educational services.

Professional and business services. This industry supersector, which includes some of the fastest-growing industries in the U.S. economy, will grow by 23.3 percent and add 4.1 million new jobs.

Employment in administrative and support and waste management and remediation services will grow by 20.3 percent and add 1.7 million new jobs to the economy by 2016. The largest industry growth in this sector will be enjoyed by employment services, which will be responsible for 692,000 new jobs, or more than 40 percent of all new jobs in administrative and support and waste management and remediation services. Employment services ranks second among industries with the most new employment opportunities in the nation and is expected to have a growth rate that is faster than the average for all industries. This will be due to the need for seasonal and temporary workers and for highly specialized human resources services.

Employment in professional, scientific, and technical services will grow by 28.8 percent and add 2.1 million new jobs by 2016. Employment in computer systems design and related services will grow by 38.3 percent and add nearly one-fourth of all new jobs in professional, scientific, and technical services. Employment growth will be driven by the increasing reliance of businesses on information technology and the continuing importance of maintaining system and network security. Management, scientific, and technical consulting services also will grow at a staggering 78 percent and account for another third of growth in this supersector. Demand for these services will be spurred by the increased use of new technology and computer software and the growing complexity of business.

Management of companies and enterprises will grow by 14.9 percent and add 270,000 new jobs.

Information. Employment in the information supersector is expected to increase by 6.9 percent, adding 212,000 jobs by 2016. Information contains some of the fast-growing computer-related industries such as software publishing, Internet publishing and broadcasting, and wireless telecommunication carriers. Employment in these industries is expected to grow by 32 percent, 44.1 percent, and 40.9 percent, respectively. The information supersector also includes motion picture production; broadcasting; and newspaper, periodical, book, and directory publishing. Increased demand for telecommunications services, cable service, high-speed Internet connections, and software will fuel job growth among these industries.

Leisure and hospitality. Overall employment will grow by 14.3 percent. Arts, entertainment, and recreation will grow by 30.9 percent and add 595,000 new jobs by 2016. Most of these new job openings, 79 percent, will be in the amusement, gambling, and recreation sector. Job growth will stem from public participation in arts, entertainment, and recreation activities, reflecting increasing incomes, leisure time, and awareness of the health benefits of physical fitness.

Accommodation and food services is expected to grow by 11.4 percent and add 1.3 million new jobs through 2016. Job growth will be concentrated in food services and drinking places, reflecting increases in population, dual-income families, and the convenience of many new food establishments.

Trade, transportation, and utilities. Overall employment in this industry supersector will grow by 6 percent between 2006 and 2016. Transportation and warehousing is expected to increase by 496,000 jobs, or by 11.1 percent, through 2016. Truck transportation will grow by 11 percent, adding 158,000 new jobs, while rail transportation is projected to decline. The warehousing and storage sector is projected to grow rapidly at 23.5 percent, adding 150,000 jobs. Demand for truck transportation and warehousing services will expand as many manufacturers concentrate on their core competencies and contract out their product transportation and storage functions.

Employment in retail trade is expected to increase by 4.5 percent. Despite slower-than-average growth, this industry will add almost 700,000 new jobs over the 2006–2016 period, growing from 15.3 million employees to 16 million. While consumers will continue to demand more goods, consolidation among grocery stores and department stores will temper growth. Wholesale trade is expected to increase by 7.3 percent, growing from 5.9 million to 6.3 million jobs.

Employment in utilities is projected to decrease by 5.7 percent through 2016. Despite increased output, employment in electric power generation, transmission, and distribution and natural gas distribution is expected to decline through 2016 because of improved technology that increases worker productivity. However, employment in water, sewage, and other systems is expected to increase 18.7 percent by 2016. Jobs are not easily eliminated by technological gains in this industry because water treatment and waste disposal are very labor-intensive activities.

Financial activities. Employment is projected to grow 14.4 percent over the 2006–2016 period. Real estate and rental and leasing is expected to grow by 18 percent and add 392,000 jobs by 2016. Growth will be due, in part, to increased demand for housing as the population grows. The fastest-growing industry in the real estate and rental and leasing services sector will be activities related to real estate, such as property management and real estate appraisal, which will grow by 29 percent—remnants of the housing boom that pervaded much of the first half of the decade.

Finance and insurance are expected to add 815,000 jobs, an increase of 13.2 percent, by 2016. Employment in securities, commodity contracts, and other financial investments and related activities is expected to grow 46 percent by 2016, reflecting the increased number of baby boomers in their peak savings years, the growth of tax-favorable retirement plans, and the globalization of the securities markets. Employment in credit intermediation and related services, including banks, will grow by 8.2 percent and add almost one-third of all new jobs within finance and insurance. Insurance carriers and related activities are expected to grow by 7.4 percent and add 172,000 new jobs by 2016. The number of jobs within agencies, brokerages, and other insurance-related activities is expected to grow about 15.4 percent. Growth will stem from the needs of an increasing population and new insurance products on the market.

Government. Between 2006 and 2016, government employment, not including employment in public education and hospitals, is expected to increase by 4.8 percent, from 10.8 million to 11.3 million jobs. Growth in government employment will be fueled by an increased demand for pubic safety, but dampened by budgetary constraints and outsourcing of government jobs to the private sector. State and local governments, excluding education and hospitals, are expected to grow by 7.7 percent as a result of the continued shift of responsibilities from the federal government to state and local governments. Federal government employment, including the Postal Service, is expected to decrease by 3.8 percent.

Other services (except government and private households). Employment will grow by 14.9 percent. About 2 out of every 5 new jobs in this supersector will be in religious organizations, which are expected to grow by 18.9 percent. Automotive repair and maintenance (as opposed to mechanical/electrical and body repair and maintenance) will be the fastest-growing industry at 40.7 percent, reflecting demand for quick maintenance services for the increasing number of automobiles on the nation's roads. Also included among other services are business, professional, labor, political, and similar organizations, which are expected to increase by 13.6 percent and add 68,000 new jobs. This industry includes homeowner, tenant, and property owner associations.

Goods-producing industries. Employment in the goods-producing industries has been relatively stagnant since the early 1980s. Overall, this sector is expected to decline 3.3 percent over the 2006–2016 period. Although employment is expected to decline overall, projected growth among goods-producing industries varies considerably (Chart 5).

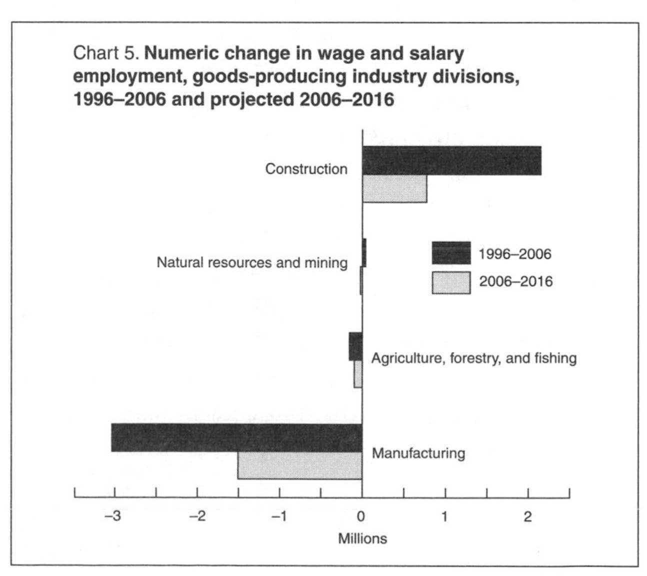

Construction. Employment in construction is expected to increase by 10.2 percent, from 7.7 million to 8.5 million. Demand for commercial construction and an increase in road, bridge, and tunnel construction will account for the bulk of job growth in this supersector.

Manufacturing. While overall employment in this supersector will decline by 10.6 percent or 1.5 million jobs, employment in a few detailed manufacturing industries will increase. For example, employment in pharmaceutical and medicine manufacturing is expected to grow by 23.8 percent and add 69,000 new jobs by 2016. However, productivity gains, job automation, and international competition will adversely affect employment in most manufacturing industries. Employment in household appliance manufacturing is expected to decline by 25.8 percent and lose 21,000 jobs over the decade. Similarly, employment in machinery manufacturing, apparel manufacturing, and computer and electronic product manufacturing will decline by 146,000, 129,000, and 157,000 jobs, respectively.

Agriculture, forestry, fishing, and hunting. Overall employment in agriculture, forestry, fishing, and hunting is expected to decrease by 2.8 percent. Employment is expected to continue to decline due to rising costs of production, increasing consolidation, and more imports of food and lumber. The only industry within this supersector expected to grow is support activities for agriculture and forestry, which includes farm labor contractors and farm management services. This industry is expected to grow by 10.5 percent and add 12,000 new jobs. Crop production will see the largest job loss, with 98,000 fewer jobs in 2016 than in 2006.

Mining. Employment in mining is expected to decrease 1.6 percent, or by some 10,000 jobs, by 2016. Employment in support activities for mining will be responsible for most of the employment decline in this industry, seeing a loss of 17,000 jobs. Other mining industries, such as coal mining and metal ore mining, are expected to see little or no change or a small increase in employment. Employment stagnation in these industries is attributable mainly to technology gains that boost worker productivity and strict environmental regulations.

Occupation

Expansion of service-providing industries is expected to continue, creating demand for many occupations. However, projected job growth varies among major occupational groups (Chart 6).

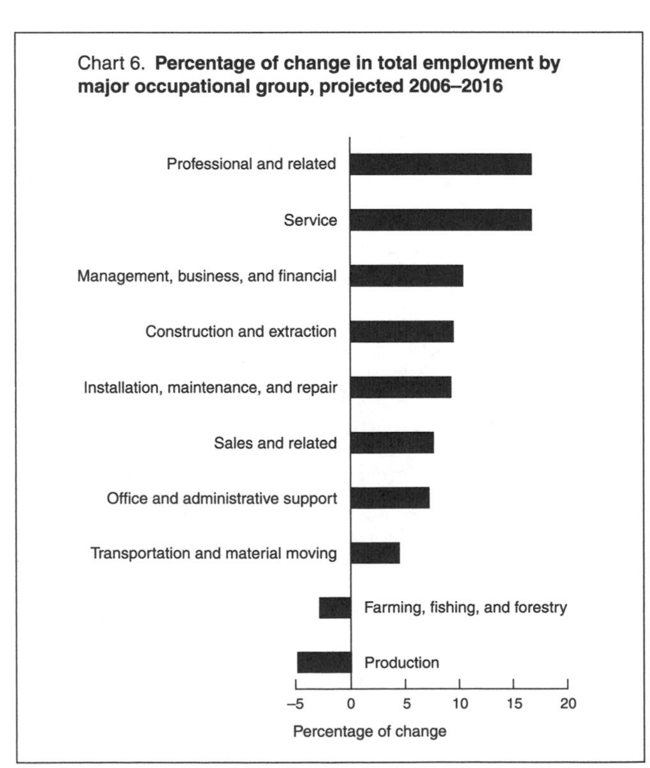

Professional and related occupations. These occupations include a wide variety of skilled professions. Professional and related occupations will be one of the two fastest-growing major occupational groups and will add the most new jobs. Over the 2006–2016 period, a 16.7 percent increase in the number of professional and related jobs is projected, which translates into nearly 5 million new jobs. Professional and related workers perform a wide variety of duties and are employed throughout private industry and government. Almost three-quarters of the job growth will come from three groups of professional occupations—computer and mathematical occupations; healthcare practitioners and technical occupations; and education, training, and library occupations—which together will add 3.5 million jobs.

Service occupations. Duties of service workers range from fighting fires to cooking meals. Employment in service occupations is projected to increase by 4.8 million, or 16.7 percent, the second-largest numerical gain and tied with professional and related occupations for the fastest rate of growth among the major occupational groups. Food preparation and serving related occupations are expected to add the most jobs among the service occupations, 1.4 million, by 2016. However, healthcare support occupations and personal care and service occupations are expected to grow the fastest, at 26.8 percent and 22 percent, respectively. Combined, these two occupational groups will account for 2.1 million new jobs.

Management, business, and financial occupations. Workers in management, business, and financial occupations plan and direct the activities of business, government, and other organizations. Their employment is expected to increase by 1.6 million, or 10.4 percent, by 2016. Among management occupations, the numbers of social and community service managers and gaming managers will grow the fastest, by 24.7 percent and 24.4 percent, respectively. Construction managers will add the most new jobs—77,000—by 2016. Farmers and ranchers are the only workers whose numbers are expected to see a large decline, losing 90,000 jobs. Among business and financial occupations, accountants and auditors and all other business operation specialists will add the most jobs, 444,000 combined. Financial analysts and personal financial advisors will be the fastest-growing occupations in this group, with growth rates of 33.8 percent and 41 percent, respectively.

Construction and extraction occupations. Construction and extraction workers build new residential and commercial buildings and also work in mines, quarries, and oil and gas fields. Employment of these workers is expected to grow 9.5 percent, adding 785,000 new jobs. Construction trades and related workers will account for nearly 4 out of 5 of these new jobs, or 622,000, by 2016. Minor declines in extraction occupations will reflect overall employment stagnation in the mining and oil and gas extraction industries.

Installation, maintenance, and repair occupations. Workers in installation, maintenance, and repair occupations install new equipment and maintain and repair older equipment. These occupations will add 550,000 jobs by 2016, growing by 9.3 percent. Automotive service technicians and mechanics and general maintenance and repair workers will account for close to half of all new installation, maintenance, and repair jobs. The fastest growth rate will be among locksmiths and safe repairers, an occupation that is expected to grow 22.1 percent over the 2006–2016 period.

Transportation and material moving occupations. Transportation and material moving workers transport people and materials by land, sea, or air. Employment of these workers should increase by 4.5 percent, accounting for 462,000 new jobs by 2016. Among transportation occupations, motor vehicle operators will add the most jobs, 368,000. Material moving occupations will decline slightly, 0.5 percent, losing 25,000 jobs.

Sales and related occupations. Sales and related workers solicit goods and services to businesses and consumers. Sales and related occupations are expected to add 1.2 million new jobs by 2016, growing by 7.6 percent. Retail salespersons will contribute the most to this growth by adding 557,000 new jobs.

Office and administrative support occupations. Office and administrative support workers perform the day-to-day activities of the office, such as preparing and filing documents, dealing with the public, and distributing information. Employment in these occupations is expected to grow by 7.2 percent, adding 1.7 million new jobs by 2016. Customer service representatives will add the most new jobs, 545,000, while stock clerks and order fillers are expected to see the largest employment decline among all occupations, losing 131,000 jobs.

Farming, fishing, and forestry occupations. Farming, fishing, and forestry workers cultivate plants, breed and raise livestock, and catch animals. These occupations will decline 2.8 percent and lose 29,000 jobs by 2016. Agricultural workers, including farmworkers and laborers, will account for nearly three out of four lost jobs in this group. The number of fishing and hunting workers is expected to decline by 16.2 percent, while the number of forest, conservation, and logging workers is expected to decline by 1.4 percent.

Production occupations. Production workers are employed mainly in manufacturing, where they assemble goods and operate plants. Production occupations are expected to decline by 4.9 percent, losing 528,000 jobs by 2016. Some jobs will be created in production occupations, mostly in food processing and woodworking. Metal workers and plastic workers; assemblers and fabricators; textile, apparel, and furnishings occupations; and other production workers will account for most of the job loss among production occupations.

Among all occupations in the economy, healthcare occupations are expected to make up 7 of the 20 fastest-growing occupations, the largest proportion of any occupational group (Chart 7). These seven healthcare occupations, in addition to exhibiting high growth rates, will add nearly 750,000 new jobs between 2006 and 2016. Other occupational groups that have more than one occupation in the 20 fastest-growing occupations are computer occupations, personal care and service occupations, community and social services occupations, and business and financial operations occupations. High growth rates among occupations in the top 20 fastest-growing occupations reflect projected rapid growth in the healthcare and social assistance industries and the professional, scientific, and technical services industries.

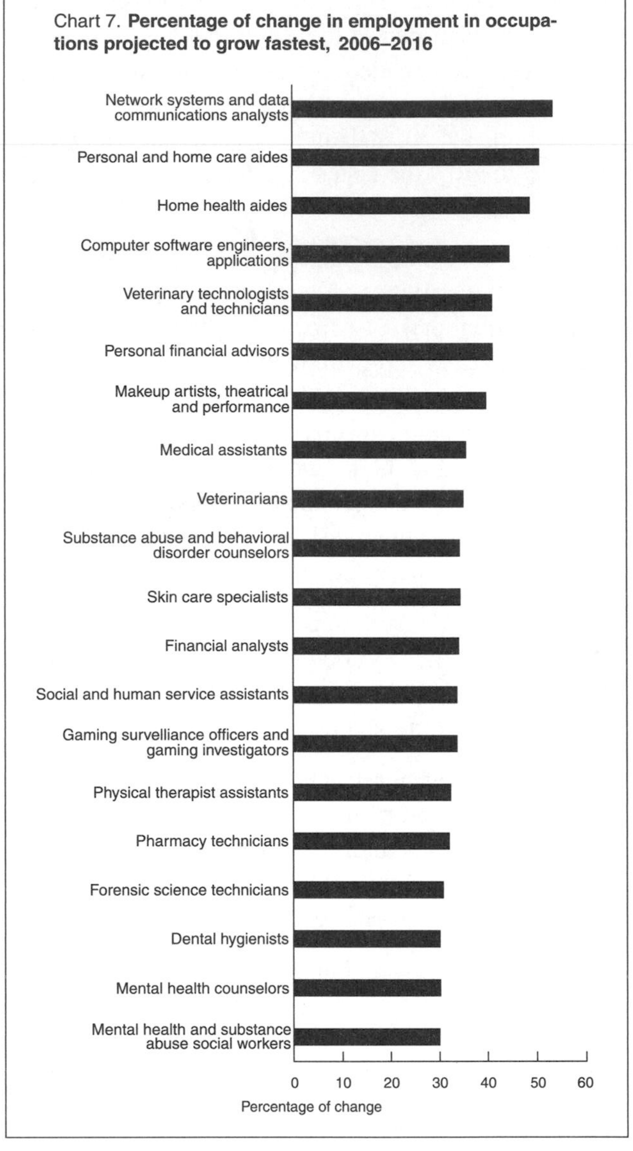

The 20 occupations listed in Chart 8 will account for more than one-third of all new jobs, 6.6 million combined, over the 2006–2016 period. The occupations with the largest numerical increases cover a wider range of occupational categories than do those occupations with the fastest growth rates. Health occupations will account for some of these increases in employment, as will occupations in education, sales, and food service. Occupations in office and administrative services will grow by 1.7 million jobs, one-fourth of the job growth among the 20 occupations with the largest job growth. Many of the occupations listed below are very large and will create more new jobs than will those with high growth rates. Only 3 out of the 20 fastest-growing occupations—home health aides, personal and home care aides, and computer software application engineers—also are projected to be among the 20 occupations with the largest numerical increases in employment.

Declining occupational employment stems from declining industry employment, technological advances, changes in business practices, and other factors. For example, installation of self-checkouts and other forms of automation will increase productivity and are expected to contribute to a decline of 118,000 cashiers over the 2006–2016 period (Chart 9). Fourteen of the 20 occupations with the largest numerical decreases are either production occupations or office and administrative support occupations, which are affected by increasing plant and factory automation and the implementation of office technology that reduces the need for these workers. The difference between the office and administrative occupations that are expected to experience the largest declines and those that are expected to see the largest increases is the extent to which job functions can be easily automated or performed by other workers. For instance, the duties of executive secretaries and administrative assistants involve a great deal of personal interaction that cannot be automated, while the duties of file clerks—adding, locating, and removing business records—can be automated or performed by other workers.

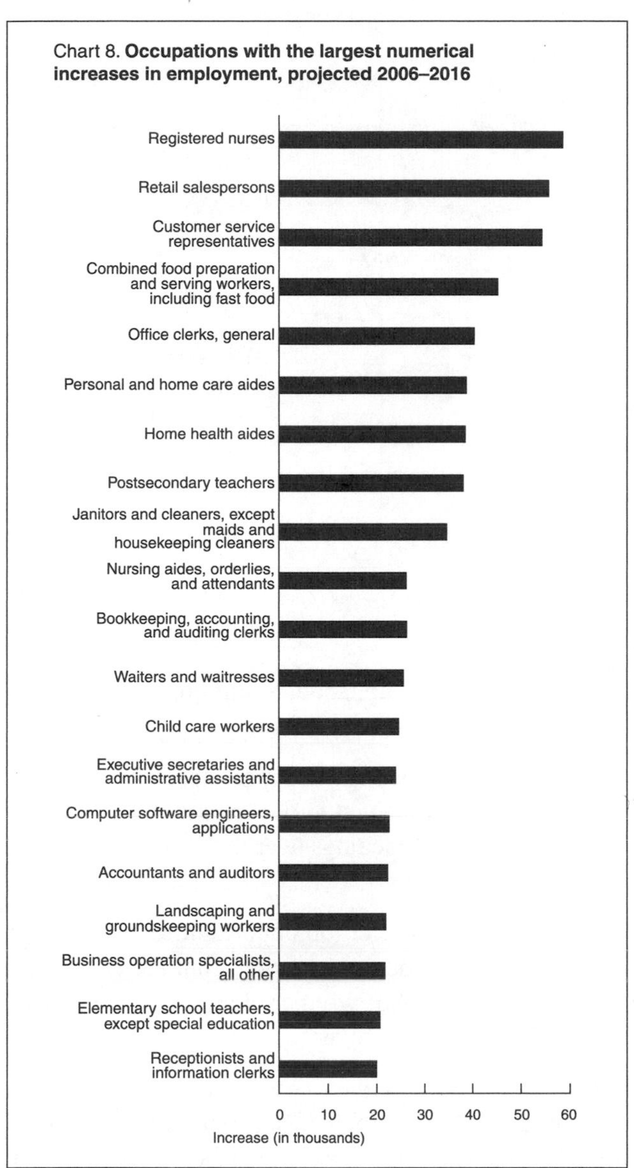

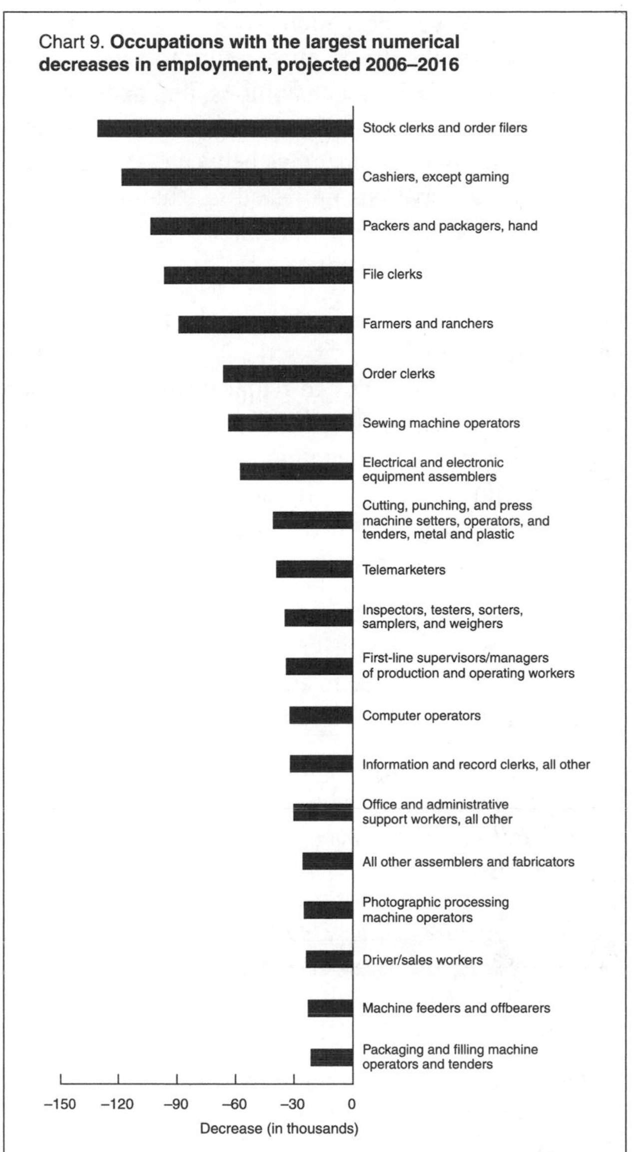

Education and Training

For 12 of the 20 fastest-growing occupations, an associate degree or higher is the most significant level of postsecondary education or training. On-the-job training is the most significant level of postsecondary education or training for another 6 of the 20 fastest-growing occupations. In contrast, on-the-job training is the most significant level of postsecondary education or training for 12 of the 20 occupations with the largest numerical increases, while 6 of these 20 occupations have an associate degree or higher as the most significant level of postsecondary education or training. On-the-job training is the most significant level of postsecondary education or training for 19 of the 20 occupations with the largest numerical decreases.

Total Job Openings

Job openings stem from both employment growth and replacement needs (Chart 10). Replacement needs arise as workers leave occupations. Some transfer to other occupations while others retire, return to school, or quit to assume household responsibilities. Replacement needs are projected to account for 68 percent of the approximately 50 million job openings between 2006 and 2016. Thus, even occupations projected to experience slower-than-average growth or to decline in employment still may offer many job openings.

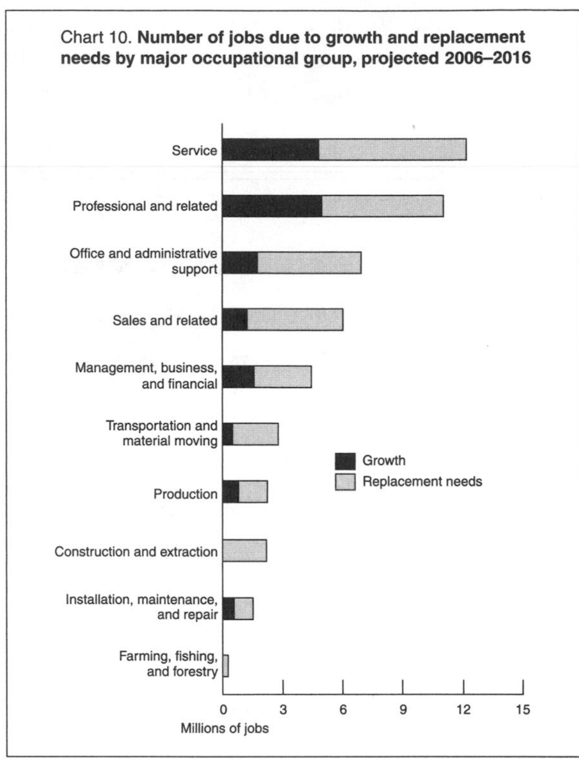

Service occupations are projected to have the largest number of total job openings, 12.2 million, and 60 percent of those will be due to replacement needs. A large number of replacements will be necessary as young workers leave food preparation and service occupations. Replacement needs generally are greatest in the largest occupations and in those with relatively low pay or limited training requirements.

Professional and related occupations are projected to be one of the two fastest-growing major occupational groups and are expected to add more jobs than any other major occupational group, about 5 million, by 2016. However, the majority of job openings are expected to come from more than 6 million replacements.

Office automation will significantly affect many individual office and administrative support occupations. While these occupations are projected to grow about as fast as average, some are projected to decline rapidly. Office and administrative support occupations are projected to create 6.9 million total job openings over the 2006–2016 period, ranking third behind service occupations and professional and related occupations.

Farming, fishing, and forestry occupations and production occupations should offer job opportunities despite overall declines in employment. These occupations will lose 29,000 and 528,000 jobs, respectively, but are expected to provide more than 2.4 million total job openings. Job openings among these groups will be solely due to the replacement needs of a workforce that is exhibiting high levels of retirement and job turnover.

Editor's Note: "Tomorrow's Jobs," with minor changes, came from the *Occupational Outlook Handbook* and was written by the U.S. Department of Labor staff. Much of this section uses 2006 data, the most recent available at press time. By the time it is carefully collected and analyzed, data used by the U.S. Department of Labor is typically several years old. Because market trends tend to be gradual, this delay does not affect the material's usefulness.

Employment Trends in Major Industries

The U.S. economy can be broken down into numerous industries, each with its own set of characteristics. The Department of Labor has identified 45 industries that account for three-quarters of all workers. This section provides an overview of these industries and the economy as a whole.

Nature of the Industry

Industries are defined by the processes they use to produce goods and services. Workers in the United States produce and provide a wide variety of products and services and, as a result, the types of industries in the U.S. economy range widely—from agriculture, forestry, and fishing to aerospace manufacturing. Each industry has a unique combination of occupations, production techniques, inputs and outputs, and business characteristics. Understanding the nature of industries that interest you is important because it is this unique combination that determines working conditions, educational requirements, and the job outlook.

Industries consist of many different places of work, called establishments. Establishments are physical locations in which people work, such as the branch office of a bank, a gasoline service station, a school, a department store, or a plant that manufactures machinery. Establishments range from large factories and corporate office complexes employing thousands of workers to small community stores, restaurants, professional offices, and service businesses employing only a few workers. Establishments should not be confused with companies or corporations, which are legal entities. Thus, a company or corporation may have a single establishment or more than one establishment. Establishments that use the same or similar processes to produce goods or services are organized together into industries. Industries are, in turn, organized together into industry groups such as Information and Trade. These are further organized into industry subsectors and then ultimately into industry sectors. For the purposes of labor market analysis, the Bureau of Labor Statistics organizes industry sectors into industry supersectors. A company or corporation could own establishments classified in more than one industry, industry sector, or even industry supersector.

Each industry subsector is made up of a number of industry groups, which are, as mentioned, determined by differences in production processes. An easily recognized example of these distinctions is in the food manufacturing subsector, which is made up of industry groups that produce meat products, preserved fruits and vegetables, bakery items, and dairy products, among others. Each of these industry groups requires workers with varying skills and employs unique production techniques. Another example of these distinctions is found in utilities, which employs workers in establishments that provide electricity, natural gas, and water.

There were almost 8.8 million private business establishments in the United States in 2006. Business establishments in the United States are predominantly small; 60.4 percent of all establishments employed fewer than 5 workers in

March 2006. However, the medium-sized to large establishments employ a greater proportion of all workers. For example, establishments that employed 50 or more workers accounted for only 4.7 percent of all establishments, yet employed 56.5 percent of all workers. The large establishments—those with more than 500 workers—accounted for only 0.2 percent of all establishments, but employed 17.1 percent of all workers. Table 1 presents the percent distribution of employment according to establishment size.

The average size of these establishments varies widely across industries. Most establishments in the construction, wholesale trade, retail trade, finance and insurance, real estate and rental and leasing, and professional, scientific, and technical services industries are small, averaging fewer than 20 employees per establishment. However, wide differences within industries can exist. Hospitals, for example, employ an average of 542.7 workers, while physicians' offices employ an average of 10.3. Similarly, although there is an average of 14.7 employees per establishment for all of retail trade, department stores employ an average of 130.3 people but jewelry stores employ an average of only 5.9.

Establishment size can play a role in the characteristics of each job. Large establishments generally offer workers greater occupational mobility and advancement potential, whereas small establishments may provide their employees with broader experience by requiring them to assume a wider range of responsibilities. Also, small establishments are distributed throughout the nation—every locality has a few small businesses. Large establishments, in contrast, employ more workers and are less common, but they play a much more prominent role in the economies of the areas in which they are located.

Table 1. Percent distribution of establishments and employment in all private industries by establishment size, March 2006

Establishment size (number of workers)	Percent of Establishments	Percent of Employment
Total	100.0	100.0
1 to 4	60.4	6.8
5 to 9	16.5	8.3
10 to 19	10.9	11.2
20 to 49	7.6	17.3
50 to 99	2.6	13.4
100 to 249	1.5	16.6
250 to 499	0.4	9.4
500 to 999	0.1	6.7
1,000 or more	0.1	10.4

Working Conditions

Just as the goods and services produced in each industry are different, working conditions vary significantly among industries. In some industries, the work setting is quiet, temperature-controlled, and virtually hazard-free, while other industries are characterized by noisy, uncomfortable, and sometimes dangerous work environments. Some industries require long workweeks and shift work, but standard 40-hour workweeks are common in many other industries. In still other industries, a lot of the jobs can be seasonal, requiring long hours during busy periods and abbreviated schedules during slower months. Production processes, establishment size, and the physical location of work usually determine these varying conditions.

One of the most telling indicators of working conditions is an industry's injury and illness rate. Overexertion, being struck by an object, and falls on the same level, are among the most common incidents causing work-related injury or illness. In 2006, approximately 4.1 million nonfatal injuries and illnesses were reported throughout private industry. Among major industry divisions, manufacturing had the highest rate of injury and illness—6.0 cases for every 100 full time workers—while financial activities had the lowest rate—1.5 cases. About 5,703 work-related fatalities were reported in 2006; the most common events resulting in fatal injuries were transportation incidents, contact with objects and equipment, assaults and violent acts, and falls.

Work schedules are another important reflection of working conditions, and the operational requirements of each industry lead to large differences in hours worked and in part-time versus full-time status. In food services and drinking places, for example, fully 36.5 percent of employees worked part time in 2006 compared with only 2.0 percent in motor vehicles and motor vehicle equipment manufacturing. Table 2 presents industries having relatively high and low percentages of part-time workers.

Table 2. Part-time workers as a percent of total employment, selected industries, 2006

Industry	Percent part-time
All industries	15.4
Many part-time workers	
Food services and drinking places	36.5
Grocery stores	31.9
Clothing, accessories, and general merchandise stores	36.4
Arts, entertainment, and recreation	27.2
Child day care services	26.1
Motion picture and video industries	23.6
Social assistance, except child day care	23.6
Few part-time workers	
Mining	2.6
Computer and electronic product manufacturing	2.4
Pharmaceutical and medicine manufacturing	2.4
Steel manufacturing	2.1
Motor vehicle and parts manufacturing	2.0
Utilities	1.8
Aerospace product and parts manufacturing	1.8

The low proportion of part-time workers in some manufacturing industries often reflects the continuous nature of the production processes that makes it difficult to adapt the volume of production to short-term fluctuations in product demand. Once these processes are begun, it is costly to halt them; machinery must be tended and materials must be moved continuously. For example, the chemical manufacturing industry produces many different chemical products through controlled chemical reactions. These processes require chemical operators to monitor and adjust the flow of materials into and out of the line of production. Because production may continue 24 hours a day, 7 days a week under the watchful eyes of chemical operators who work in shifts, full-time workers are more likely to be employed. Retail trade and service industries, on the other hand, have seasonal cycles marked by various events that affect the hours worked, such as school openings or important holidays. During busy times of the year, longer hours are common, whereas slack periods lead to cutbacks in work hours and shorter workweeks. Jobs in these industries are generally appealing to students and others who desire flexible, part-time schedules.

Employment

The total number of jobs in the United States in 2006 was 150.6 million. This included 12.2 million self-employed workers, 130,000 unpaid workers in family businesses, and 138.3 million wage and salary jobs—including primary and secondary job holders. The total number of jobs is projected to increase to 166.2 million by 2016, and wage and salary jobs are projected to account for almost 153.3 million of them.

As shown in table 3, wage and salary jobs are the vast majority of all jobs, but they are not evenly divided among the various industries. Education, health, and social services had the largest number of jobs in 2006 with almost 29.1 million. The trade supersector was the second largest, with about 21.2 million jobs, followed by professional and business services with 17.6 million jobs in 2006. Manufacturing accounted for roughly 14.2 million jobs in the United States in 2006. Among the industries covered in the *Career Guide*, wage and salary employment ranged from only 154,300 in steel manufacturing to more than 13.6 million in health care. The three largest industries—education services, health care, and food services and drinking places—together accounted for 38.5 million jobs, more than one-quarter of the nation's wage and salary employment.

Table 3. Wage and salary employment in industries covered in the *Career Guide,* 2006 and projected change, 2006–2016 (Employment in thousands)

	2006		2016		2006–2016	
Industry	Employment	Percent distribution	Employment	Percent distribution	Percent change	Employment change
All industries	138,310	100.0	153,262	100.0	10.8	14,951
Natural resources, construction, and utilities	10,076	7.3	10,710	7.0	6.3	634
Agriculture, forestry, and fishing	1,220	0.9	1,114	0.7	-8.6	-105
Construction	7,689	5.6	8,470	5.5	10.2	781
Mining	619	0.4	609	0.4	-1.6	-10
Utilities	548	0.4	518	0.3	-5.7	-31
Manufacturing	14,197	10.3	12,695	8.3	-10.6	-1,503
Aerospace product and parts manufacturing	472	0.3	497	0.3	5.4	25
Chemical manufacturing, except drugs	576	0.4	486	0.3	-15.7	-90
Computer and electronic product manufacturing	1,316	1.0	1,159	0.8	-12.0	-157
Food manufacturing	1,484	1.1	1,489	1.0	0.3	5
Machinery manufacturing	1,192	0.9	1,045	0.7	-12.3	-146
Motor vehicle and parts manufacturing	1,070	0.8	918	0.6	-14.3	-153
Pharmaceutical and medicine manufacturing	292	0.2	362	0.2	23.7	69
Printing	636	0.5	497	0.3	-21.8	-138
Steel manufacturing	154	0.1	116	0.1	-25.1	-39
Textile, textile product, and apparel manufacturing	595	0.4	385	0.3	-35.4	-211
Trade	21,217	15.3	22,332	14.6	5.3	1,115
Automobile dealers	1,247	0.9	1,388	0.9	11.3	141
Clothing, accessory, and general merchandise stores	4,352	3.1	4,676	3.1	7.5	324
Grocery stores	2,463	1.8	2,479	1.6	0.7	16
Wholesale trade	5,898	4.3	6,326	4.1	7.3	428
Transportation and warehousing	4,466	3.2	4,962	3.2	11.1	496
Air transportation	486	0.4	522	0.3	7.3	35
Truck transportation and warehousing	2,074	1.5	2,381	1.6	14.8	307

Industry	2006 Employment	2006 Percent distribution	2016 Employment	2016 Percent distribution	2006–2016 Percent change	2006–2016 Employment change
Information	3,055	2.2	3,267	2.1	6.9	212
Broadcasting	331	0.2	362	0.2	9.3	31
Motion picture and video industries	357	0.3	396	0.3	10.9	39
Publishing, except software	660	0.5	611	0.4	-7.5	-49
Software publishers	243	0.2	321	0.2	32.0	78
Telecommunications	973	0.7	1,022	0.7	5.0	48
Internet services providers, web search portals, and data processing services	383	0.3	437	0.3	14.0	54
Financial activities	8,363	6.0	9,570	6.2	14.4	1,207
Banking	1,825	1.3	1,898	1.2	4.0	74
Insurance	2,316	1.7	2,488	1.6	7.4	172
Securities, commodities, and other investments	816	0.6	1,192	0.8	46.1	376
Professional and business services	17,552	12.7	21,644	14.1	23.3	4,092
Advertising and public relations services	458	0.3	520	0.3	13.6	62
Computer systems design and related services	1,278	0.9	1,768	1.2	38.3	489
Employment services	3,657	2.6	4,348	2.8	18.9	692
Management, scientific, and technical consulting services	921	0.7	1,639	1.1	77.9	718
Scientific research and development services	593	0.4	649	0.4	9.4	56
Education, health, and social services	29,082	21.0	34,543	22.5	18.8	5,461
Child day care services	807	0.6	1,078	0.7	33.7	272
Educational services	13,152	9.5	14,564	9.5	10.7	1,412
Health services	13,621	9.8	16,576	10.8	21.7	2,954
Social assistance, except child day care	1,502	1.1	2,326	1.5	54.8	823
Leisure and hospitality	13,143	9.5	15,016	9.8	14.2	1,873
Arts, entertainment, and recreation	1,927	1.4	2,522	1.6	30.9	595
Food services and drinking places	9,383	6.8	10,407	6.8	10.9	1,024
Hotels and other accommodations	1,833	1.3	2,088	1.4	13.9	254
Government and advocacy, grantmaking, and civic organizations	11,210	8.1	11,895	7.8	6.1	685
Advocacy, grantmaking, and civic organizations	1,234	0.9	1,392	0.9	12.8	158
Federal Government	1,958	1.4	1,868	1.2	-4.6	-90
State and local government, except education and health	8,018	5.8	8,634	5.6	7.7	617

NOTE: May not add to totals due to omission of industries not covered.

Although workers of all ages are employed in each industry, certain industries tend to possess workers of distinct age groups. For the previously mentioned reasons, retail trade employs a relatively high proportion of younger workers to fill part-time and temporary positions. The manufacturing sector, on the other hand, has a relatively high median age because many jobs in the sector require a number of years to learn and perfect specialized skills that do not easily transfer to other industries. Also, manufacturing employment has been declining, providing fewer opportunities for younger workers to get jobs. As a result, more than one-fourth of the workers in retail trade were 24 years of age or younger in 2006, compared with only 8.1 percent of workers in manufacturing. Table 4 contrasts the age distribution of workers in all industries with the distributions in five very different industries.

Table 4. Percent distribution of wage and salary workers by age group, selected industries, 2006

	Age group			
Industry	**16 to 24**	**25 to 44**	**45 to 64**	**65 and older**
All industries	14	45	37	4
Computer systems design and related services	5	63	30	2
Educational services	9	42	45	4
Food services and drinking places	43	38	17	2
Telecommunications	8	53	37	2
Utilities	4	42	54	1

Employment in some industries is concentrated in one region of the country. Such industries often are located near a source of raw or unfinished materials upon which the industry relies. For example, oil and gas extraction jobs are concentrated in Texas, Louisiana, and Oklahoma; many textile mills and products manufacturing jobs are found in North Carolina, South Carolina, and Georgia; and a significant proportion of motor vehicle manufacturing jobs are located in Michigan and Ohio. On the other hand, some industries—such as grocery stores and educational services—have jobs distributed throughout the nation, reflecting the general population density.

Occupations in the Industry

The occupations found in each industry depend on the types of services provided or goods produced. For example, because construction companies require skilled trades workers to build and renovate buildings, these companies employ large numbers of carpenters, electricians, plumbers, painters, and sheet metal workers. Other occupations common to construction include construction equipment operators and mechanics, installers, and repairers. Retail trade, on the other hand, displays and sells manufactured goods to consumers. As a result, retail trade employs numerous retail salespersons and other workers, including more than three-fourths of all cashiers. Table 5 shows the industry sectors and the occupational groups that predominate in each.

Table 5. Industry sectors and their largest occupational group, 2006

Industry sector	**Largest occupational group**	**Percent of industry wage and salary jobs**
Agriculture, forestry, fishing, and hunting	Farming, fishing, and forestry occupations	58.3
Mining	Construction and extraction occupations	37.8
Construction	Construction and extraction occupations	66.8
Manufacturing	Production occupations	52.5
Wholesale trade	Sales and related occupations	26.3
Retail trade	Sales and related occupations	54.1
Transportation and warehousing	Transportation and material moving occupations	59.8
Utilities	Installation, maintenance, and repair occupations	27.1
Information	Professional and related occupations	33.3
Finance and insurance	Office and administrative support occupations	49.8
Real estate and rental and leasing	Sales and related occupations	24.5
Professional, scientific, and technical services	Professional and related occupations	45.0

Industry sector	Largest occupational group	Percent of industry wage and salary jobs
Management of companies and enterprises	Management, business, and financial occupations	33.1
Administrative and support and waste management and remediation services	Service occupations	31.4
Educational services, public and private	Professional and related occupations	67.4
Health care and social assistance	Professional and related occupations	43.3
Arts, entertainment, and recreation	Service occupations	58.8
Accommodation and food services	Service occupations	86.6
Government	Service occupations	25.0

The occupational distribution clearly is influenced by the structure of its industries, yet there are many occupations, such as general managers or secretaries, that are found in all industries. In fact, some of the largest occupations in the U.S. economy are dispersed across many industries. For example, the group of professional and related occupations is among the largest in the nation while also experiencing the fastest growth rate. (See table 6.) Other large occupational groups include service occupations; office and administrative support occupations; sales and related occupations; and management, business, and financial occupations.

Table 6. Total employment and projected change by broad occupational group, 2006–2016 (Employment in thousands)

Occupational group	Employment, 2006	Percent change, 2006–2016
Total, all occupations	150,620	10.4
Professional and related occupations	29,819	16.7
Service occupations	28,950	16.7
Office and administrative support occupations	24,344	7.2
Sales and related occupations	15,985	7.6
Management, business, and financial occupations	15,397	10.4
Production occupations	10,675	-4.9
Transportation and material moving occupations	10,233	4.5
Construction and extraction occupations	8,295	9.5
Installation, maintenance, and repair occupations	5,883	9.3
Farming, fishing, and forestry occupations	1,039	-2.8

Training and Advancement

Workers prepare for employment in many ways, but the most fundamental form of job training in the United States is a high school education. Better than 88 percent of the nation's workforce possessed a high school diploma or its equivalent in 2006. However, many occupations require more training, so growing numbers of workers pursue additional training or education after high school. In 2006, 28.7 percent of the nation's workforce reported having completed some college or an associate degree as their highest level of education, while an additional 30.2 percent continued in their studies and attained a bachelor's or higher degree. In addition to these types of formal education, other sources of qualifying training include formal company-provided training, apprenticeships, informal on-the-job training, correspondence courses, Armed Forces vocational training, and non–work-related training.

The unique combination of training required to succeed in each industry is determined largely by the industry's production process and the mix of occupations it requires. For example, manufacturing employs many machine operators who generally need little formal education after high school, but sometimes complete considerable on-the-job training. In contrast, educational services employs many types of teachers, most of whom require a bachelor's or higher degree. Training requirements by industry sector are shown in table 7.

Table 7. Percent distribution of workers by highest grade completed or degree received, by industry sector, 2006

Industy sector	High school diploma or less	Some college or associate degree	Bachelor's or higher degree
All industries	41.1	28.7	30.2
Agriculture, forestry, fishing, and hunting	62.3	22.0	15.8
Mining	58.8	24.9	16.3
Construction	64.5	24.2	11.3
Manufacturing	50.7	25.6	23.6
Wholesale trade	43.0	29.3	27.8
Retail trade	50.8	32.1	17.1
Transportation and warehousing	52.3	32.1	15.7
Utilities	39.3	34.4	26.3
Information	25.6	31.6	42.8
Finance and insurance	22.7	31.0	46.3
Real estate and rental and leasing	33.6	32.5	33.9
Professional, scientific, and technical services	13.4	24.6	61.9
Administrative and support and waste management services	53.9	28.3	17.9
Educational services	17.3	19.2	63.5
Health care and social assistance	29.8	34.6	35.5
Arts, entertainment, and recreation	39.5	32.1	28.3
Accommodation and food services	61.3	27.8	10.9

Persons with no more than a high school diploma accounted for about 64.5 percent of all workers in construction; 62.3 percent in agriculture, forestry, fishing, and hunting; 61.3 percent in accommodation and food services; 58.8 percent in mining; 53.9 percent in administrative and support and waste management services; and 52.3 in transportation and warehousing. On the other hand, those who had acquired a bachelor's or higher degree accounted for 63.6 percent of all workers in private educational services; 61.9 percent in professional, scientific, and technical services; 46.3 percent in finance and insurance; and 42.8 percent in information.

Education and training also are important factors in the variety of advancement paths found in different industries. Each industry has some unique advancement paths, but workers who complete additional on-the-job training or education generally help their chances of being promoted. In much of the manufacturing sector, for example, production workers who receive training in management and computer skills increase their likelihood of being promoted to supervisory positions. Other factors that impact advancement and that may figure prominently in industries include the size of the establishments, institutionalized career tracks, and the mix of occupations. As a result, persons who seek jobs in particular industries should be aware of how these advancement paths and other factors may later shape their careers.

Earnings

Like other characteristics, earnings differ by industry, the result of a highly complicated process that reflects a number of factors. For example, earnings may vary due to the nature of occupations in the industry, average hours worked, geographical location, workers' average age, educational requirements, profits, and the degree of union representation of the workforce. In general, wages are highest in metropolitan areas to compensate for the higher cost of living. Also, as would be expected, industries that employ a large proportion of unskilled minimum-wage or part-time workers tend to have lower earnings.

The difference in earnings between software publishers and the food services and drinking places industries illustrates how various characteristics of industries can result in great differences in earnings. In software publishers, earnings of all wage and salary workers averaged $1,444 a week in 2006, while in food services and drinking places, earnings of all wage and salary workers averaged only $215 weekly. The difference is large primarily because software publishing establishments employ more highly skilled, full-time workers, while food services and drinking places employ many lower skilled workers on a part-time basis. In addition, most workers in software publishing are paid an annual salary, while many workers in food services and drinking places are paid an hourly wage, but many are able to supplement their low hourly wage rate with money they receive as tips. Table 8 highlights the industries with the highest and lowest average weekly earnings.

Table 8. Average weekly earnings of production or nonsupervisory workers on private nonfarm payrolls, selected industries, 2006

Industry	Earnings
All industries	$568
Industries with high earnings	
Software publishers	1,444
Computer systems design and related services	1,265
Scientific research and development services	1,136
Utilities	1,136
Aerospace product and parts manufacturing	1,153
Securities, commodities, and other investments	1,055
Industries with low earnings	
Employment services	453
Grocery stores	328
Arts, entertainment, and recreation	332
Hotels and other accommodations	353
Child day care services	316
Food services and drinking places	215

Employee benefits, once a minor addition to wages and salaries, continue to grow in diversity and cost. In addition to traditional benefits—paid vacations, life and health insurance, and pensions—many employers now offer various benefits to accommodate the needs of a changing labor force. Such benefits sometimes include childcare, employee assistance programs that provide counseling for personal problems, and wellness programs that encourage exercise, stress management, and self-improvement. Benefits vary among occupational groups, full- and part-time workers, public and private sector workers, regions, unionized and nonunionized workers, and small and large establishments. Data indicate that full-time workers and those in medium-sized and large establishments—those with 100 or more workers—usually receive better benefits than do part-time workers and those in smaller establishments.

Union representation of the workforce varies widely by industry, and it also may play a role in determining earnings and benefits. In 2006, about 13.2 percent of workers throughout the nation were union members or covered by union contracts. As table 9 demonstrates, union affiliation of workers varies widely by industry. 51.6 percent of the workers in air transportation were union members, the highest rate of all the industries, followed by 37.6 percent in educational services, and 34.4 percent in public administration. Industries with the lowest unionization rate include computer systems design and related services, 1.7 percent; food services and drinking places, 1.5 percent; and Internet service providers, web search portals, and data processing services and software publishing, both with virtually no union workers.

Table 9. Union members and other workers covered by union contracts as a percent of total employment, selected industries, 2006

Industry	Percent union members or covered by union contract
All industries	13.2
Industries with high unionization rates	
Air transportation	51.6
Educational services	37.6
Public administration	34.4
Utilities	31.9
Industries with low unionization rates	
Computer systems design and related services	1.7
Food services and drinking places	1.5
Internet service providers, web search portals, and data processing services	0.0
Software publishing	0.0

Outlook

Total wage and salary employment in the United States is projected to increase by about 10.8 percent over the 2006–2016 period. Employment growth, however, is only one source of job openings. The total number of openings in any industry also depends on the industry's current employment level and its need to replace workers who leave their jobs. Throughout the economy, replacement needs will create more job openings than will employment growth. Employment size is a major determinant of job openings—larger industries generally have larger numbers of workers who must be replaced and provide more openings. The occupational composition of an industry is another factor. Industries with high concentrations of professional, technical, and other jobs that require more formal education—occupations in which workers tend to leave their jobs less frequently—generally have fewer openings resulting from replacement needs. On the other hand, more replacement openings generally occur in industries with high concentrations of service, laborer, and other jobs that require little formal education and have lower wages because workers in these jobs are more likely to leave their occupations.

Employment growth is determined largely by changes in the demand for the goods and services provided by an industry, worker productivity, and foreign competition. Each industry is affected by a different set of variables that determines the number and composition of jobs that will be available. Even within an industry, employment may grow at different rates in different occupations. For example, changes in technology, production methods, and business practices in an industry might eliminate some jobs, while creating others. Some industries may be growing rapidly overall, yet opportunities for workers in occupations within those industries could be stagnant or even declining because they are adversely affected by technological change. Similarly, employment of some occupations may be declining in the economy as a whole, yet may be increasing in a rapidly growing industry.

As shown earlier in table 3, employment growth rates over the next decade will vary widely among industries. Natural resources, construction, and utilities are primarily expected to grow due to growth in construction, offsetting job declines in agriculture, mining, and utilities. Growth in construction employment will stem from new factory construction as existing facilities are modernized; from new school construction, reflecting growth in the school-age population; and from infrastructure improvements, such as road and bridge construction. Employment in agriculture, forestry, and fishing should continue to decrease with consolidation of farm land, increasing worker productivity, and depletion of wild fish stocks. Employment in mining is expected to decline due to the use of new laborsaving technology and with the continued reliance on foreign sources of energy.

Employment in manufacturing is expected to decline overall with some growth in selected manufacturing industries. Employment declines are expected in chemical manufacturing, except drugs; computer and electronic product manufacturing; machinery manufacturing; motor vehicle and parts manufacturing; printing; steel manufacturing; and textile, textile product, and apparel manufacturing. Textile, textile product, and apparel manufacturing is projected to lose about 211,000 jobs over the 2006–2016 period—more than any other manufacturing industry—due primarily to increasing imports replacing domestic products.

Employment gains are expected in some manufacturing industries. Small employment gains in food manufacturing are expected, as a growing and ever more diverse population increases the demand for manufactured food products. Employment growth in pharmaceutical and medicine manufacturing is expected as sales of pharmaceuticals increase with growth in the population, particularly among the elderly, and with the introduction of new medicines to the market. Both food and pharmaceutical and medicine manufacturing also have growing export markets. Aerospace product and parts manufacturing is expected to have modest employment increases as well.

Growth in overall employment will result primarily from growth in service-providing industries over the 2006–2016 period, almost all of which are expected to have increasing employment. Job growth is expected to be led by health care and educational services, with large numbers of new jobs also in food services and drinking places; social assistance, except child day care; management, scientific, and technical consulting services; employment services, state and local government, except education and health care; arts entertainment, and recreation; computer systems design and related services; and wholesale trade. When combined, these sectors will account for nearly two-thirds of all new wage and salary jobs across the nation. Employment growth is expected in many other service-providing industries, but they will result in far fewer numbers of new jobs.

Health care will account for the most new wage and salary jobs, almost 3.0 million over the 2006–2016 period. Population growth, advances in medical technologies that increase the number of treatable diseases, and a growing share of the population in older age groups will drive employment growth. General medical and surgical hospitals, public and private—the largest health care industry group—is expected to account for about 691,000 of these new jobs.

Educational services is expected to grow by 10.7 percent over the 2006–2016 period, adding about 1.4 million new jobs. A growing emphasis on improving education and making it available to more children and young adults will be the primary factors contributing to employment growth. Employment growth is expected at all levels of education, particularly at the postsecondary level, as children of the baby boomers continue to reach college age, and as more adults pursue continuing education to enhance or update their skills.

Employment in the nation's fastest growing industry—management, scientific, and technical consulting services—is expected to increase by almost 78 percent, adding another 718,000 jobs over the 2006–2016 period. Projected job growth can be attributed primarily to economic growth and to the continuing complexity of business. A growing number of businesses means increased demand for advice in all areas of business operations and planning.

The food services and drinking places industry is expected to add more than 1.0 million new jobs over the 2006–2016 projection period. Increases in population, dual-income families, and dining sophistication will contribute to job growth. In addition, the increasing diversity of the population will contribute to job growth in food services and drinking places that offer a wider variety of ethnic foods and drinks.

Almost 617,000 new jobs are expected to arise in state and local government, except education and health care, growth of almost 8 percent over the 2006–2016 period. Job growth will result primarily from growth in the population and its demand for public services. Additional job growth will result as state and local governments continue to receive greater responsibility from the federal government for administering federally funded programs.

Wholesale trade is expected to add more than 428,000 new jobs over the coming decade, reflecting growth both in trade and in the overall economy. Most new jobs will be for sales representatives at the wholesale and manufacturing levels. However, industry consolidation and the growth of electronic commerce using the Internet are expected to limit job growth to 7.3 percent over the 2006–2016 period, less than the 10.8 percent projected for all industries.

Continual changes in the economy have far-reaching and complex effects on employment in industries. Job seekers should be aware of these changes, keeping alert for developments that can affect job opportunities in industries and the variety of occupations that are found in each industry.

Editor's Note: The preceding article was adapted from the Career Guide to Industries*, a publication of the U.S. Department of Labor. A book titled* 40 Best Fields for Your Career *(JIST Publishing) includes information from the* Career Guide to Industries *plus useful "best fields" lists and other helpful insights.*

STEM Occupations: High-Tech Jobs for a High-Tech Economy

Faster aircraft, bolder video games, better medicines—technology moves forward every day. And tech-savvy workers make those advances happen. Without the work of scientists, technicians, engineers, mathematicians, and other skilled workers, most new products and discoveries would never be developed.

The need for technical work continues to grow. Technical occupations are often defined as those related to science, technology, engineering, and mathematics (STEM). Workers in STEM occupations use science and math to solve problems. Educational requirements for STEM occupations range from a high school diploma and on-the-job training to a Ph.D. But all require the ability to think logically.

There are several ways to identify and count STEM occupations. Some researchers, for example, count social scientists and science managers; others include any occupation that uses science and technology. Adopting a more focused definition, this article describes the occupations that most clearly concentrate on STEM.

On the pages that follow, you'll find information about STEM occupations, earnings, educational requirements, and job prospects. There are also suggestions on how to prepare for a STEM career and where to find more information.

STEM Jobs

There are many kinds of work within STEM's divisions of science, technology, engineering, and mathematics.

Science

When you think of science workers, you might picture a chemist in a white lab coat running experiments—and you'd be right. But science goes beyond the laboratory. Scientists are also involved in teamwork, communication, and data analysis. And although many scientists spend time in laboratories, they work in offices, too. Some work outdoors, as when wildlife biologists observe animals in their habitats or geoscientists measure movements in the Earth's crust.

Scientists design experiments to find out how things work. They conduct or oversee those experiments, analyze the results, and explain what the results mean. They use scientific methods to learn about the world. In 2005, according to the U.S. Bureau of Labor Statistics (BLS), 13 percent of STEM jobs as defined here were in natural science occupations. (See chart 1.)

Natural science occupations fall into three broad groups: life scientists, physical scientists, and natural science technicians.

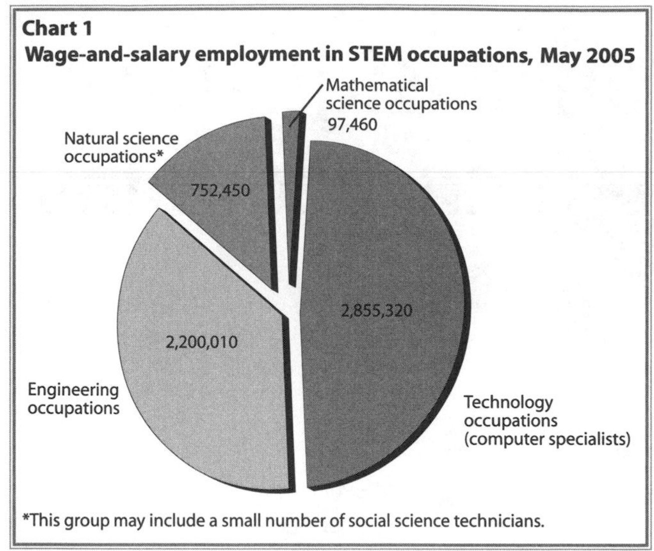

Life scientists. Life scientists study living systems, from organisms to ecosystems. Agricultural and food scientists, for example, study the production and distribution of food. They work to increase food quantity, quality, and safety.

Biological scientists study animals, plants, and bacteria. They also analyze metabolic processes and other life elements.

Conservation scientists and foresters manage natural resources to maximize their long-term economic, recreational, and conservation value; for example, they might decide when and how to plant trees or chop them down. And medical scientists look for both causes of and treatments for human diseases.

Physical scientists. Physical scientists study the parts of nature that are not alive. They might ponder the motion of distant suns or the bonds between nuclear particles. Atmospheric scientists, for example, monitor weather conditions to understand trends and to forecast atmospheric changes.

Chemists and materials scientists conduct research to create new chemicals and other materials for use in many products.

Environmental scientists and hydrologists investigate environmental hazards and pollutants and the circulation of underground and surface waters. Geoscientists study the composition and structure of the earth, often in search of available supplies of natural resources.

Physicists and astronomers explore the fundamental laws governing matter and energy in the universe, mathematically modeling the forces of nature.

Natural science technicians. These technicians assist scientists in conducting experiments and analyzing the results. They might prepare experimental apparatus, collect samples or readings, and summarize the results.

Biological technicians generally work as laboratory assistants engaged in biological and medical research. Chemical technicians in research and development also work as laboratory assistants, and those involved in manufacturing typically monitor industrial processes.

Technology

This category could include any occupation that requires technical skill, but it usually refers to information technology or computer-related occupations. Workers in these occupations use logic, mathematics, and computer science to make computers function.

Some technology workers create new software, design computer systems, and develop databases. Others focus on helping people use computers and on keeping computers running well.

Designing and developing. Many computer workers find ways to make computers more useful. Computer software engineers, for example, create new computer programs or systems. They develop an overall plan for how the program works. They design algorithms that tell the computer how to complete tasks. And they figure out how to make software work faster.

Computer programmers often help software engineers implement their plans. They write code to tell the computer to do specific tasks.

Computer systems analysts help organizations to use computers effectively. They choose computer hardware and software that meet an organization's needs and oversee its computer-related policies and plans.

Computer research scientists study advanced computer technology. Database analysts design methods of organizing and storing data for quick retrieval.

Helping users. Other information technology workers focus on helping people with computer problems and on keeping computers running smoothly. These workers, called computer support specialists or systems administrators, provide administrative and technical assistance to computer users.

Engineering

Almost every product, from cars to carrots, is the result of engineering. Engineers use science to solve practical problems. They design, develop, and test new products, such as computers, machines, and chemical fertilizers; they also design, develop, and maintain systems, including assembly lines and electric power grids. Drafters, engineering, and mapping technicians help in those efforts.

Specialties. Most engineers specialize. Agricultural engineers, for example, design farming equipment, irrigation systems, and food processing systems. Biomedical engineers develop medical devices and instruments. Civil engineers, the largest specialty, design bridges, dams, and other public works projects; some plan highways and solve traffic problems.

Electrical and electronics engineers design consumer electronics, electrical robotics, and other electrical equipment. Mechanical engineers design, manufacture, and test tools and other mechanical devices.

Among the other engineering specialties are aerospace, chemical, environmental, and petroleum.

Drafters and technicians. Drafters, engineering, and mapping technicians assist in the development of new products. Drafters use computers to make detailed technical drawings of products or construction projects. They sometimes suggest what type of components to use in a product or structure.

Engineering technicians build models, do calculations, and perform other engineering tasks. Mapping technicians aid surveyors, cartographers, and photogrammetrists in measuring and mapping the earth's surface.

Mathematics

Many occupations use mathematics. But some occupations focus on mathematics almost exclusively.

Actuaries, for example, analyze statistical information to determine the risk of uncertain future events, such as hurricanes or automobile collisions. They use these calculations to decide what kinds of insurance a company should offer and how much that insurance should cost.

Mathematicians develop new mathematical theories and tools to solve problems. Some devise or decipher encryption methods to protect confidential information.

Operations research analysts use math to model complex logistical chains to determine the most efficient way to move materials or meet other management objectives.

Statisticians collect, analyze, and interpret data. Some write surveys.

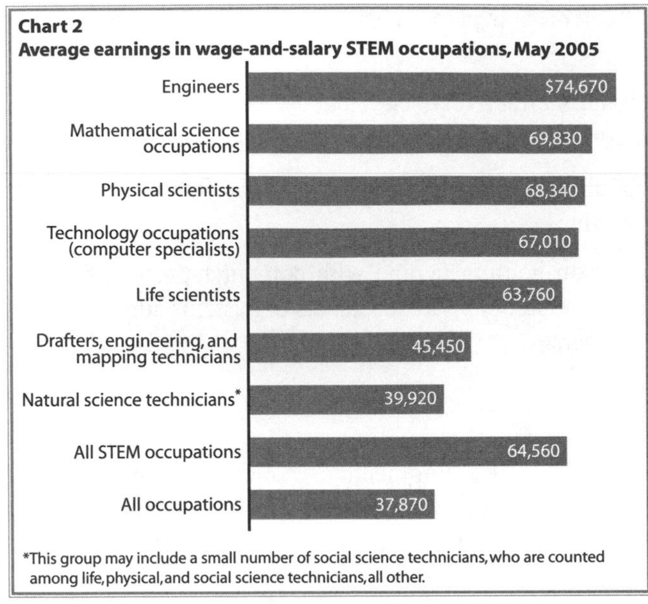

Earnings

As a group, STEM workers earned about 70 percent more than the national average in 2005, according to BLS. Every major group of STEM occupations enjoys overall median earnings that are above the national average. (See chart 2.) Higher than average earnings are often an indicator of strong demand for workers.

Like occupations in other disciplines, STEM occupations that require more education usually pay more than those that need less.

For example, biochemists and biophysicists, who often have a Ph.D., had median earnings of $71,000 in 2005; biological technicians, who often have an associate degree or less education, earned a median of $34,270.

Earnings vary by subject matter for the highest paid occupations within each STEM group. The highest earning scientists were astronomers, with median earnings of $104,670. Among technicians, nuclear technicians had the highest median earnings, at $61,120. The highest earning engineering specialty was petroleum engineering, with median earnings of $93,000. And actuaries, with median earnings of $81,640, made more than other mathematical specialists did.

In addition, starting salaries are higher for STEM workers than for workers in many other disciplines. According to a fall 2006 survey by the National Association of Colleges and Employers, students with a bachelor's degree in engineering had the highest starting salary offers, on average, compared with students who have bachelor's degrees in other subjects. (See table 1.)

Table 1
Average starting salary offers for college graduates by bachelor's degree category, 2005–2006

Degree field	Average salary offer
Engineering	$51,313
Computer science	50,744
Engineering technology	48,514
Information sciences and systems	47,182
Construction science/management	45,516
Management information systems/business data processing	45,391
Nursing	45,347
Geological and related sciences	45,091
Accounting	44,928
Logistics/materials management	44,810
Mathematics, including statistics	44,672

Source: Fall 2006 Salary Survey, National Association of Colleges and Employers

Learning STEM

Success in STEM requires both technical and nontechnical skills and attributes. Curiosity, the ability to think logically, and creative problem-solving are highly valuable. Communication skills and teamwork are helpful, too.

All STEM workers need a firm grasp of mathematics; science knowledge is also important for many of the occupations. Preparation should begin in high school, with coursework and extracurricular activities focusing on honing problem-solving skills. After high school, STEM career requirements are more specific to the occupations.

High school preparation

Students interested in a STEM career should get started in high school by taking as much math and science as they can. Even those who struggle in these subjects during school can succeed on the job; with perseverance, many people who may have had difficulty with early math or science classes can later thrive in a STEM career.

There are many ways to build skills in math and science. Teachers may be available to give students extra help or to provide information about tutoring. School counselors might also have advice.

Associations sometimes provide educational assistance over the Internet. To learn more, see the sources of information at the end of this article.

Students might also be able to take courses at two- and four-year colleges during the summer. The more math and science students learn in high school, the easier it is to tackle advanced subjects later.

To further sharpen skills and explore career options, students might consider joining a math, science, engineering, or computer club at school. Starting a club at schools that don't already have one might not be difficult; ask a teacher or counselor for help. Club members often take field trips to science museums, go to math and science competitions, and help each other study.

Students can also participate in summer camps that are related to math, science, and computers. Campers take part in games and challenges and learn what it's like to have a STEM career. Depending on the type of camp, students might design and create their own computer programs or secret codes. Or they might build robots, motors, or architectural models.

Preparation after high school

As noted previously, the knowledge and abilities needed differ for specific STEM occupations. Education, certification, and experience are of varied importance. Changes in the number of degrees granted in STEM fields show how educational requirements are shifting and how the demand for these workers is increasing.

Specific requirements. Many scientists have a bachelor's degree; often, these scientists work as research assistants or in applied sciences. But for those who focus on research, a doctorate and, possibly, years of postdoctoral training are usually the minimum requirements.

Science technicians often need an associate degree or experience in building and using scientific equipment, in helping with data collection and analysis, or in other technical tasks. Some of these workers have a bachelor's degree.

Computer-related jobs usually require a degree, certification, or both. A bachelor's degree is the usual requirement for software engineers, systems analysts, and database administrators, but a master's degree is becoming more common for workers doing higher level development. Computer support workers and network analysts often have an associate degree, certifications, or both. Computer scientists, like other scientists, often have a Ph.D.

Engineers need at least a bachelor's degree, and a master's degree is becoming common. Engineering technicians and drafters often have an associate degree or experience in building models, helping with calculations, or doing other tasks.

Mathematical occupations usually require a master's or doctoral degree. A notable exception is actuaries, who usually need at least a bachelor's degree and a passing score on an actuarial exam.

Degree trends. The number of bachelor's degrees awarded in STEM subjects has been increasing in the past few years after several years of slight decline, according to the U.S. Department of Education. (See chart 3.) But the number of degrees in computer and information science has grown dramatically, reflecting increases both in the number of computer jobs available and in employers' preference for workers who have formal education in computer sciences.

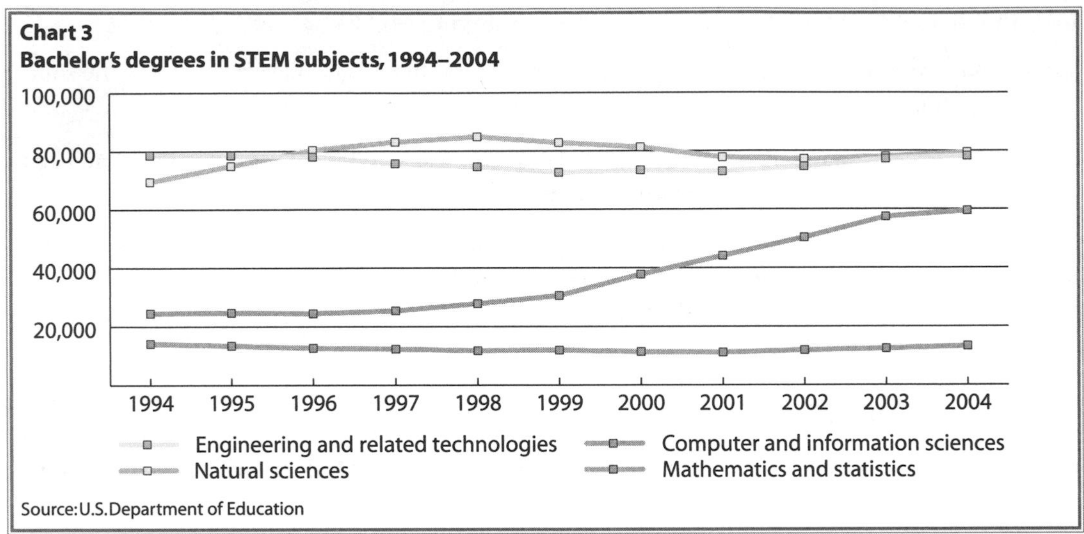

Increases in degree awards for some STEM subjects are also apparent at the associate and master's degree levels. For example, the number of associate degrees awarded in computer fields more than tripled in a decade, growing from about 12,600 degrees in 1994 to about 41,800 in 2004.

In that same decade, the number of master's degrees granted in engineering declined before increasing from more than 30,000 in 1994 to more than 35,000 in 2004. Because more engineers are taking on managerial responsibilities, more schools are offering master's degree programs that focus on the application of engineering principles to industry rather than on basic research. These programs include coursework in finance, project management, and other areas of business. They may increase workers' chances for advancement.

Job Prospects

STEM workers hold jobs in every state. But six states—California, Texas, New York, Florida, Virginia, and Illinois—accounted for 40 percent of these jobs in 2005.

Growing demand for technological advances means more jobs for STEM workers. BLS projects job growth for STEM occupations as a whole between 2004 and 2014.

Nearly all the major STEM groups are expected to have about the same rate of growth as the national average. The exception is computer specialist occupations, which are expected to grow much faster than the average. (See table 2.)

Projected job growth varies widely by specific occupation, from a 55-percent projected growth for network systems and data communications analysts to about a 2-percent decline for mining and geological engineers.

More STEM workers also will be needed to replace those who are leaving these occupations. Many highly skilled workers will retire, change careers, or move to management positions over the next decade. Between 2004 and 2014, employers are expected to hire about 2.5 million STEM workers who are entering their occupation for the first time.

Table 2
Employment growth and job openings in STEM occupations, projected 2004–14

Occupational group	Employment		2004-14 change		Job openings due to growth and net replacement, 2004-14
	2004	2014	Numeric	Percent	
Science occupations, natural*	**806,330**	**931,027**	**124,697**	**15%**	**315,000**
Life scientists	231,723	279,890	48,166	21	103,000
Physical scientists	250,417	280,913	30,496	12	94,000
Natural science technicians	324,190	370,224	46,034	14	118,000
Technology occupations (computer specialists)	**3,045,836**	**4,002,547**	**956,711**	**31**	**1,350,000**
Engineering occupations	**2,299,778**	**2,576,906**	**277,128**	**12**	**798,000**
Engineers	1,448,871	1,643,500	194,629	13	507,000
Drafters, engineering, and mapping technicians	850,906	933,406	82,500	10	291,000
Mathematical science occupations	**106,965**	**117,297**	**10,332**	**10**	**39,000**
STEM occupations, total	**6,258,909**	**7,627,777**	**1,368,867**	**22**	**2,503,000**

* This group may include a small number of social science technicians, who are counted among life, physical, and social science technicians, all other.

For More Information

Although this article describes STEM occupations generally, there are important distinctions among the occupations. Detailed information about these occupations is in the *Occupational Outlook Handbook.* The *Handbook* is available in many libraries and career counseling offices and is online at www.bls.gov/oco.

Detailed earnings and employment information is also available from the BLS Occupational Employment Statistics survey. The information is online at www.bls.gov/oes. Specific projections of job growth in occupations and industries are available from the BLS Office of Occupational Statistics and Employment Projections. This information is also available online at www.bls.gov/emp.

To receive BLS information by phone or in another format, call (202) 691-5200.

More information about careers in STEM occupations is available from professional associations. In addition to the associations listed below, the *Handbook* lists some associations for each occupation it describes.

To learn about engineering careers and activities, contact

- American Design Drafting Association, 105 E. Main St., Newbern, TN 38059. Phone: (731) 627-0802. Internet: www.adda.org
- American Society for Engineering Education 1818 N St. NW, Suite 600, Washington, DC 20036. Phone: (202) 331-3500. Internet: www.asee.org
- Junior Engineering Technical Society 1420 King St., Suite 405, Alexandria, VA 22314. Phone: (703) 548-5387. Internet: www.jets.org

To learn more about mathematics careers or for help learning math, contact

- American Mathematical Society, 201 Charles St., Providence, RI 02904. Toll-free phone: (800) 321-4267. Internet: www.ams.org/employment
- Mathematical Association of America, 1529 18th St. NW, Washington, DC 20036. Toll-free phone: (800) 741-9415. Internet: www.maa.org
- Society for Industrial and Applied Mathematics 3600 University City Science Center Philadelphia, PA 19104. Phone: (215) 382-9800. Internet: www.siam.org/students

For more information about the STEM workforce, contact

- Commission on Professionals in Science and Technology 1200 New York Ave. NW, Suite 113, Washington, DC 20005. Phone: 202-326-7080. Internet: www.cpst.org

To learn more about summer camps, tutoring, and other special STEM programs, check with school counselors, school district offices, and professional associations.

From the* Occupational Outlook Quarterly *by the U.S. Department of Labor. Written by Nicholas Terrell, an economist in the Office of Occupational Statistics and Employment Projections, BLS.

Index

L–M

N–O

P

Q–R

S

T

U–Z